1812

1812

THE NAVY'S WAR

GEORGE C. DAUGHAN

BASIC BOOKS

A Member of the Perseus Books Group

New York

Books published by Basic Books are available at special discounts for bulk purchases in the
United States by corporations, institutions, and other organizations. For more information,
please contact the Special Markets Department at the Perseus Books Group, 2300 Chestnut
Street, Suite 200, Philadelphia, PA 19103, or call (800) 810-4145, ext. 5000, or e-mail
special.markets@perseusbooks.com.

Designed by Pauline Brown
Typeset in 10.5 pt Minion Pro by the Perseus Books Group

Library of Congress Cataloging-in-Publication Data

Daughan, George C.
  1812 : the navy's war / George C. Daughan.
    p. cm.
  Includes bibliographical references and index.
  ISBN 978-0-465-02046-1 (hc : alk. paper)—ISBN: 978-0-465-02808-5 (e-book)
  1. United States—History—War of 1812—Naval operations. 2. United States. Navy—
History—War of 1812. I. Title.
  E360.D25 2011
  973.5'2—dc23

                                                                    2011020923

10 9 8 7 6 5 4 3 2 1

For Mary, Mark, Alex, Tyler, and Kay with love

*"If our first struggle was that of our infancy, this last was that of our youth;
and the issue of both, wisely improved, may long postpone if not forever
prevent a necessity for exerting the strength of our manhood."*

— JAMES MADISON

CONTENTS

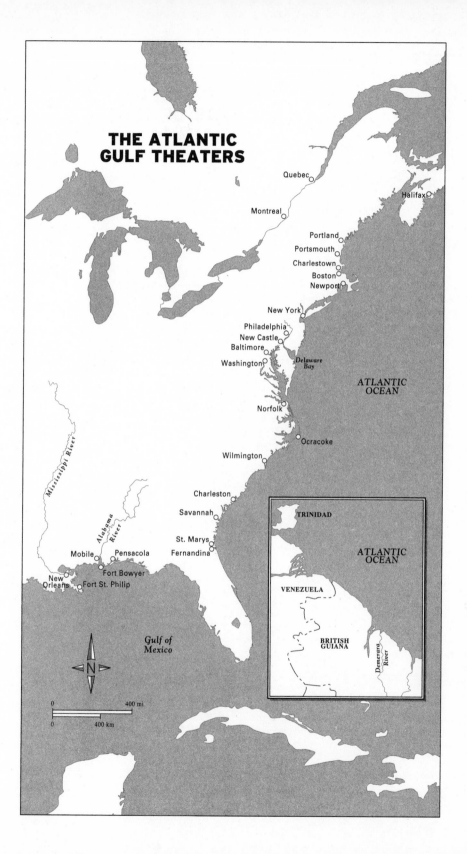

THE ATLANTIC
GULF THEATERS

Quebec

Halifax

Montreal

Portland
Portsmouth
Charlestown
Boston
Newport

New York
Philadelphia
New Castle
Baltimore
Washington

*Delaware
Bay*

ATLANTIC
OCEAN

Norfolk

Ocracoke

Wilmington

Mississippi River

Charleston

Savannah

Alabama River

St. Marys
Fernandina

Mobile   Pensacola
          Fort Bowyer
New
Orleans   Fort St. Philip

TRINIDAD

ATLANTIC
OCEAN

VENEZUELA

BRITISH
GUIANA

Demerara River

*Gulf of
Mexico*

N

0   400 mi.

0   400 km

THE NORTHERN THEATRE OF WAR 1812-1814

Lake Superior

St. Joseph Island

Mackinac Island

Lake Michigan

Georgian Bay

Lake Huron

Nottawasaga Bay

Penetanguishene

Lake Simcoe

UPPER

York

Burlington Bay

Stoney Creek

Ft. George

Grand River

Niagra River

Ft. Erie

MICHIGAN TERRITORY

St. Clair River

Thames River

Moraviantown

Long Point

Detroit

Detroit River

Amherstburg (Fort Malden)

Lake Erie

Presque Isle

Put-In Bay

OHIO

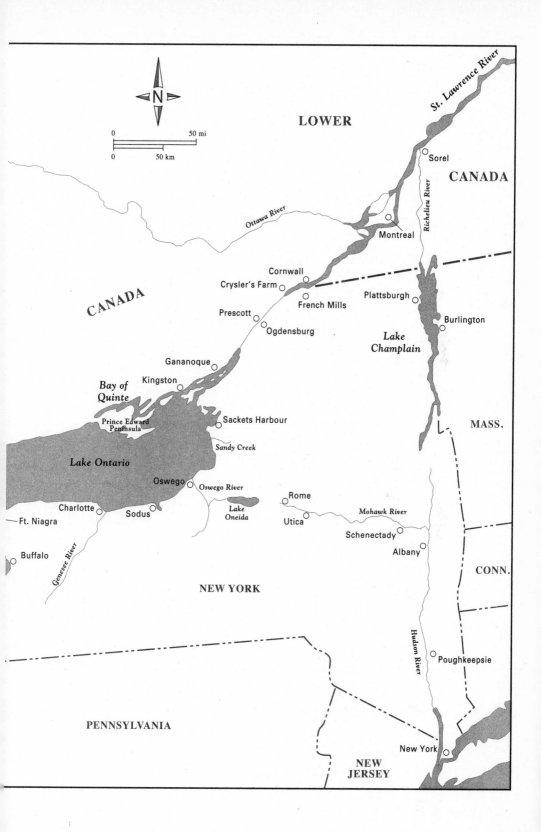

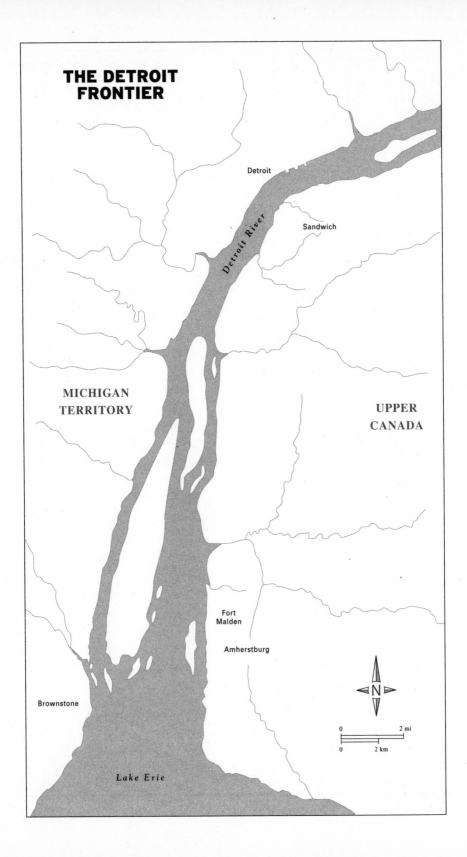

THE DETROIT
FRONTIER

Detroit

Sandwich

Detroit River

MICHIGAN
TERRITORY

UPPER
CANADA

Fort
Malden

Amherstburg

N

Brownstone

0   2 mi

0   2 km

Lake Erie

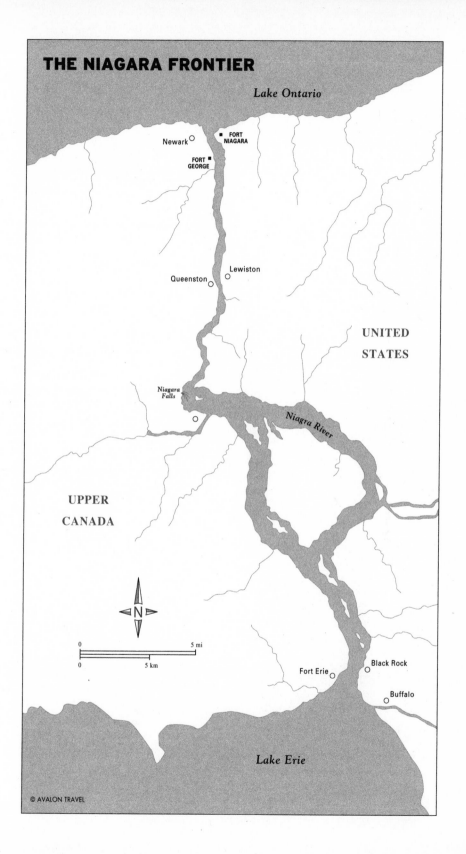

THE NIAGARA FRONTIER

Lake Ontario

Newark

FORT
NIAGARA

FORT
GEORGE

Queenston   Lewiston

UNITED
STATES

Niagara
Falls

Niagra River

UPPER

CANADA

N

0   5 mi
0   5 km

Fort Erie   Black Rock

Buffalo

Lake Erie

© AVALON TRAVEL

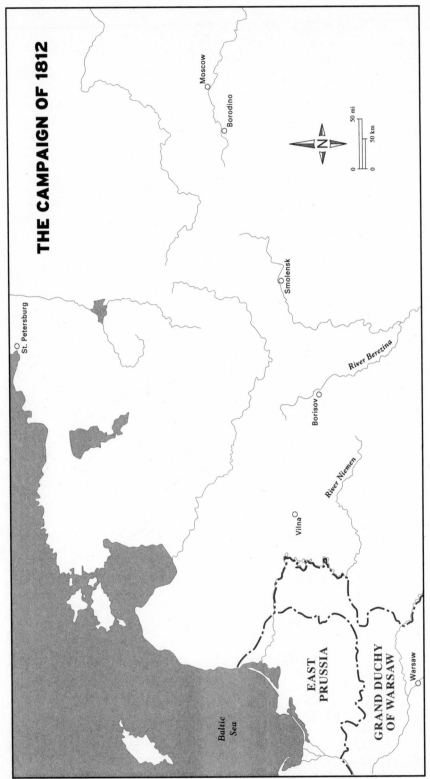

THE CAMPAIGN OF 1812

Moscow

Borodino

N

50 mi

50 km

St. Petersburg

Smolensk

River Berezina

Borisov

River Niemen

Vilna

Baltic
Sea

EAST
PRUSSIA

GRAND DUCHY
OF WARSAW

Warsaw

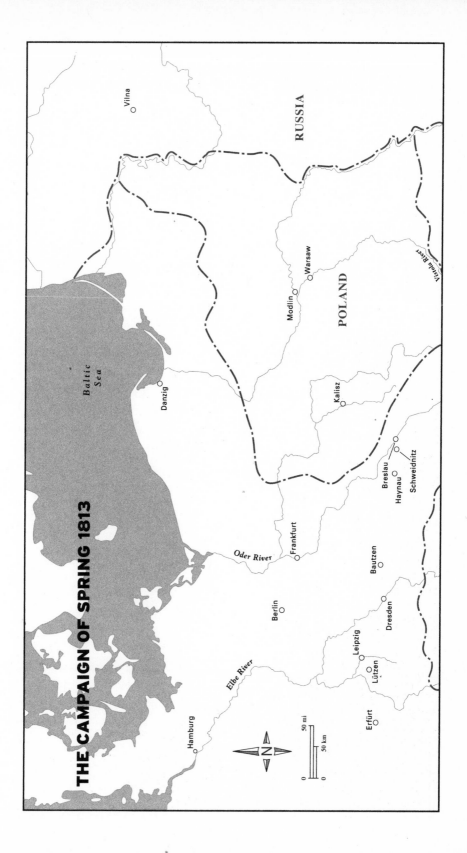

THE CAMPAIGN OF SPRING 1813

Baltic
Sea

RUSSIA

POLAND

Vistula River

Vilna

Warsaw

Modlin

Kalisz

Danzig

Breslau
Haynau
Schweidnitz

Frankfurt

Oder River

Bautzen

Berlin

Dresden

Leipzig

Lützen

Elbe River

Erfürt

Hamburg

50 mi

50 km

0

0

N

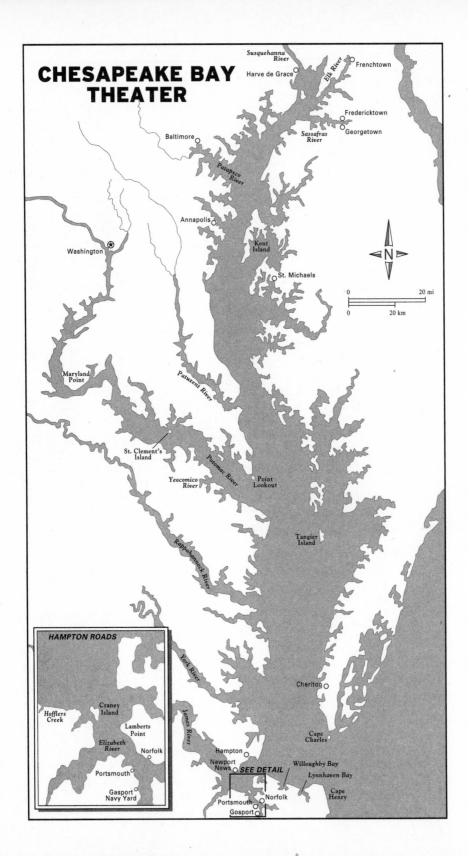

CHESAPEAKE BAY THEATER

Susquehanna River
Harve de Grace
Elk River
Frenchtown
Fredericktown
Georgetown
Sassafras River
Baltimore
Patapsco River
Annapolis
Kent Island
Washington
St. Michaels

0   20 mi
0   20 km

Maryland Point
Patuxent River
St. Clement's Island
Potomac River
Yeocomico River
Point Lookout
Tangier Island
Rappahannock River

HAMPTON ROADS

Hofflers Creek
Craney Island
Lamberts Point
Elizabeth River
Norfolk
Portsmouth
Gasport Navy Yard

York River
Cheriton
Cape Charles
James River
Hampton
Newport News
SEE DETAIL
Willoughby Bay
Lynnhaven Bay
Cape Henry
Portsmouth
Gosport
Norfolk

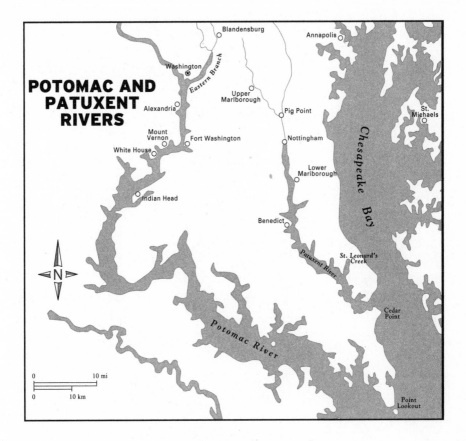

POTOMAC AND
PATUXENT
RIVERS

Blandensburg
Annapolis
Washington
Eastern Branch
Upper
Marlborough
St.
Michaels
Alexandria
Pig Point
Mount
Vernon
Fort Washington
Nottingham
White House
Lower
Marlborough
Indian Head
Benedict
Chesapeake Bay
St. Leonard's
Creek
Patuxent River
Cedar
Point
Potomac River
N
0   10 mi
0   10 km
Point
Lookout

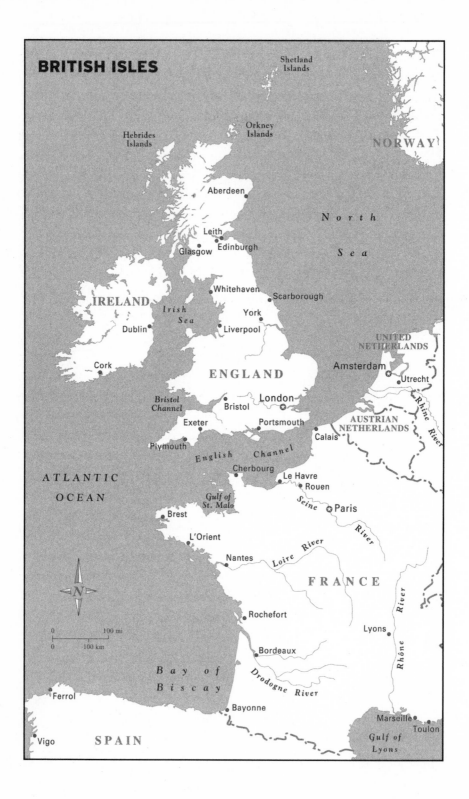

BRITISH ISLES

Shetland
Islands

Orkney
Islands

Hebrides
Islands

NORWAY

Aberdeen

North

Sea

Leith
Glasgow Edinburgh

IRELAND

Irish
Sea

Whitehaven

Scarborough

Dublin

York

Liverpool

UNITED
NETHERLANDS

Cork

ENGLAND

Amsterdam

Utrecht

Bristol
Channel

Bristol

London

Rhine River

Exeter

Portsmouth

AUSTRIAN
NETHERLANDS

Plymouth

Calais

English Channel

ATLANTIC

Cherbourg

OCEAN

Gulf of
St. Malo

Le Havre
Rouen

Seine

Paris

Brest

River

L'Orient

Loire River

Nantes

FRANCE

Rhône River

Rochefort

Lyons

Bordeaux

Rhône River

Bay of

Biscay

Drodogne River

Ferrol

Bayonne

Marseille

Toulon

Vigo

SPAIN

Gulf of
Lyons

0   100 mi
0   100 km

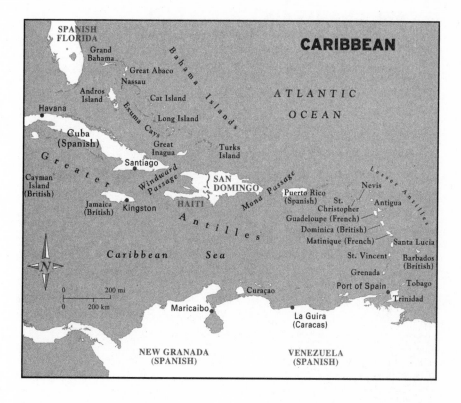

SPANISH
FLORIDA

Grand
Bahama

Great Abaco
Nassau

Andros
Island

Cat Island

Bahama Islands

CARIBBEAN

ATLANTIC

OCEAN

Havana

Exuma Cays

Long Island

Cuba
(Spanish)

Great
Inagua

Turks
Island

Greater

Santiago

Lesser Antilles

Cayman
Island
(British)

Windward Passage

SAN
DOMINGO

Mona Passage

Nevis

Jamaica
(British)

Kingston

HAITI

Puerto Rico
(Spanish)

St.
Christopher

Antigua

Guadeloupe (French)

Antilles

Dominica (British)

Matinique (French)

Santa Lucia

Caribbean   Sea

St. Vincent

Barbados
(British)

Grenada

0   200 mi

0   200 km

Curaçao

Port of Spain

Tobago

Maricaibo

La Guira
(Caracas)

Trinidad

NEW GRANADA
(SPANISH)

VENEZUELA
(SPANISH)

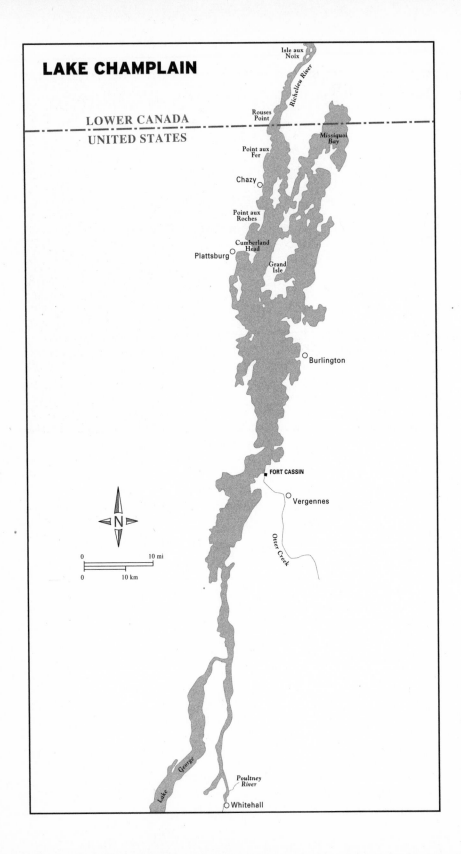

LAKE CHAMPLAIN

Isle aux
Noix

Richelieu River

LOWER CANADA

UNITED STATES

Rouses
Point

Missiquoi
Bay

Point aux
Fer

Chazy

Point aux
Roches

Cumberland
Head

Plattsburg

Grand
Isle

Burlington

FORT CASSIN

Vergennes

Otter Creek

N

| 0 | 10 mi |

| 0 | 10 km |

Lake George

Poultney
River

Whitehall

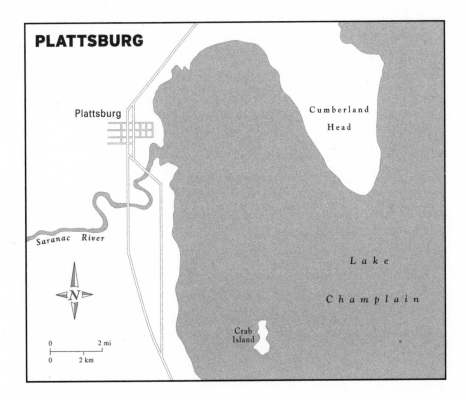

PLATTSBURG

Plattsburg

Cumberland
Head

Saranac River

N

L a k e

C h a m p l a i n

Crab
Island

0   2 mi

0   2 km

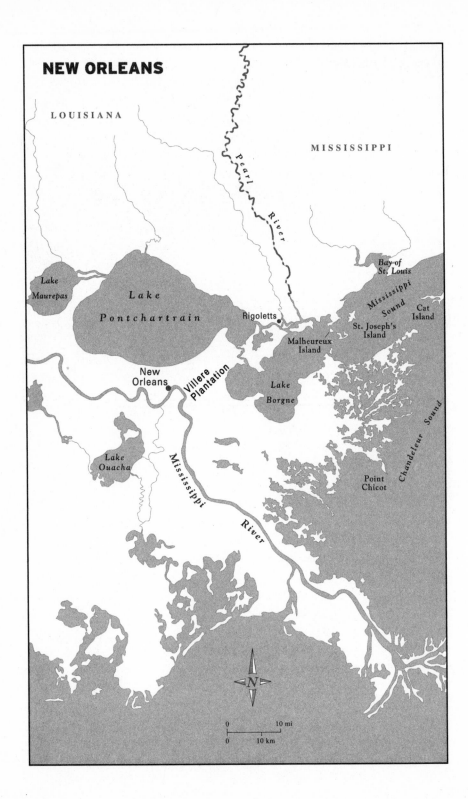

NEW ORLEANS

LOUISIANA

MISSISSIPPI

Pearl River

Lake Maurepas

Lake Pontchartrain

Rigoletts

Bay of St. Louis

Mississippi Sound

St. Joseph's Island

Cat Island

Malheureux Island

New Orleans

Villere Plantation

Lake Borgne

Lake Ouacha

Mississippi River

Chandeleur Sound

Point Chicot

N

| 0 | | 10 mi |
| 0 | | 10 km |

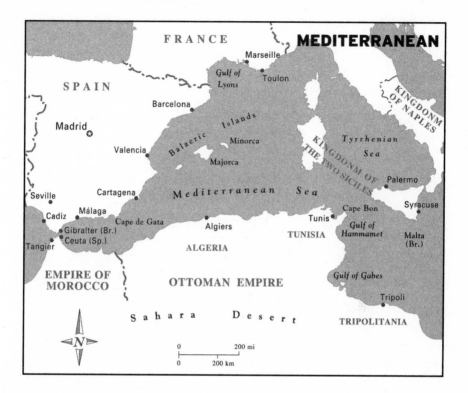

MEDITERRANEAN

FRANCE

Marseille

Gulf of Lyons

Toulon

SPAIN

Barcelona

Balearic Islands

Minorca

KINGDONM OF NAPLES

Tyrrhenian Sea

KINGDONM OF THE TWO SICILIES

Madrid

Valencia

Majorca

Palermo

Seville

Cartagena

Mediterranean Sea

Syracuse

Cadiz

Málaga

Cape de Gata

Algiers

Cape Bon

Tunis

Gulf of Hammamet

Malta (Br.)

Gibralter (Br.)

Ceuta (Sp.)

TUNISIA

Tangier

ALGERIA

EMPIRE OF MOROCCO

OTTOMAN EMPIRE

Gulf of Gabes

Tripoli

S a h a r a   D e s e r t

TRIPOLITANIA

◁N▷

| 0 | | 200 mi |
| 0 | | 200 km |

The Sails of a Square-Rigged Ship

1. Flying jib
2. Jib
3. Fore topmast staysail
4. Fore staysail
5. Foresail, or course
6. Fore topsail
7. Fore topgallant
8. Mainstaysail
9. Maintopmast staysail
10. Middle staysail
11. Main topgallant staysail
12. Mainsail, or course
13. Maintopsail
14. Main topgallant
15. Mizzen staysail
16. Mizzen topmast staysail
17. Mizzen topgallant staysail
18. Mizzen sail
19. Mizzen topsail
20. Mizzen topgallant
21. Spanker

INTRODUCTION

"SAIL HO!" CRIED a lookout from the main masthead of the USS *President*. It was six o'clock in the morning on June 23, 1812, and the 44-gun heavy frigate was sailing in latitude 39°26' north, and longitude 71°10' west, one hundred miles southwest of Nantucket Shoals. Commodore John Rodgers stepped quickly on deck and took a well-used bronze telescope from a binnacle drawer. The sails of a large ship came immediately into view. Before long it was plain the stranger was a frigate sailing alone. Rodgers could hardly believe his good luck. She could only be British, probably out of Halifax or Bermuda, and she was standing toward him.

At nearly the same moment, the officer of the watch aboard His Majesty's 36-gun frigate *Belvidera* informed Captain Richard Byron that a lookout had caught sight of the upper sails of five ships in the southwest. Byron had orders from Admiral Sawyer, commander of the British North American Station at Halifax, to intercept the French privateer *Marengo*, expected to sortie from New London, Connecticut. He was not expecting to run into an American squadron, much less a hostile one, for the news had not yet reached him that the United States had declared war on June 18. There had been rumors and speculation in Halifax before he left, certainly, but nothing more. The British government, worried about Napoleon's growing strength in Europe, was determined to avoid a conflict. The Admiralty had directed commanders in American waters to "take special care" to avoid clashes with the U. S. Navy and to exercise "all possible forbearance towards the citizens of the United States."

Uncertain whether the five sails were British or American, Byron stood toward them. When he was within six miles, he made the private signal but received no reply. Instead, Commodore Rodgers hoisted flags ordering a general chase. He was leading a powerful squadron comprised of nearly all of the navy's serviceable warships. This included his own 44-gun *President*; the 44-gun *United States*, under Captain Stephen Decatur, the navy's most famous officer; the 36-gun *Congress*, under Captain John Smith; the 18-gun sloop of war *Hornet*, under Master Commandant James Lawrence; and the 16-gun brig *Argus*, under Master Commandant Arthur Sinclair. The *President*, being the fastest ship, took the lead close-hauled on the larboard tack, while Decatur trailed behind in the slower *United States*.

Seeing how aggressively the Americans (their identity no longer in doubt) were approaching, and how outnumbered he was, Byron tacked from his pursuers and made all sail to the northeast with the wind on his larboard beam. At 8:30 he edged away a point and set topgallant studding sails. The slower ships in the American squadron lagged behind, but the *President* gradually drew closer to the *Belvidera*, and at eleven o'clock Rodgers ordered the ship cleared for action.

A marine drummer beat the familiar call to quarters, as the crew raced to battle stations alow and aloft. By now the breeze had hauled around to the westward and was lighter. Rodgers positioned himself at the starboard bow chaser on the forecastle with two midshipmen acting as messengers.

Despite his very best efforts, Byron was unable to get away. The *President* kept creeping closer. At 11:30—still confused as to what was happening—Byron hoisted British colors in answer to the *President* and her lagging companions, which were already flying American standards.

At 4:20—more than eight hours after first sighting her—the *President* at last pulled to within gunshot range of the *Belvidera*. The wind was from the westsouthwest and diminishing. Still unclear as to the intentions of the nearest ship, and seeing the odds stacked mightily against him, Byron did not want to initiate a fight. But his only chance of escaping was to shoot first and smash enough of the *President*'s spars and rigging to slow her down. He decided to run out his stern guns—two thirty-two-pound carronades and two eighteen-pound long guns—and be ready for anything. Not wanting to shoot accidentally, however, he ordered his lieutenants to have the gunners prick the cartridges but not prime the guns. He would wait and see what the Americans intended to do.

Byron did not have to wait long. Rodgers pulled to within point-blank range—less than half a mile—on the *Belvidera*'s weather quarter and, seeing Byron's stern guns out and taking aim, fired two starboard bow chasers, one from the main deck and the other above it on the forecastle, where Rodgers was standing. He aimed and fired the gun on the forecastle himself, directing it at the *Belvidera*'s rigging. It was the first shot of the war. In no time, three balls from the well-trained American gun crews had hit their mark and did considerable damage. One of them struck the *Belvidera*'s rudder coat and careened into the gunroom. Another smashed the muzzle of a larboard chase gun.

Byron was from an old navy family known for its bad luck, and fortune seemed once more to have deserted them. With the rest of the American squadron straining to get closer, and the *President*'s deadly bow chasers firing in convincing fashion, his chances of escaping appeared dim.

This unprovoked attack could only be explained by the Americans having declared war, Byron decided, and so he ordered his four stern guns to return fire, which they did with considerable effect.

The two ships now blasted away at each other for several minutes. Suddenly, the chase gun on the *President*'s main deck (underneath where Rodgers was standing) exploded, hurling the commodore high enough into the air that his leg cracked as he landed. The bursting gun, in turn, ignited the passing box that served it with powder, causing an explosion that shattered the main and forecastle decks around it. Midshipman John Taylor was killed and thirteen others wounded, including the gun captain and a nineteen-year-old midshipman named Matthew Calbraith Perry, who had been standing next to Rodgers.

With the other starboard chase gun on the *President*'s forecastle put out of commission for a time, Byron won a temporary reprieve. Halifax was to leeward, and if Byron lightened his load enough, the *Belvidera* had a slim chance of escaping. But Rodgers was not about to let this prize slip away, and he refused to go below to have his leg treated. Ignoring the excruciating pain, he continued to direct the battle from the quarterdeck.

The *President*'s starboard chase guns might be useless, but her main deck guns were ready to fire with single shots, and so Rodgers decided to end the whole business with dispatch. Ordering the helm put to starboard, he fired a full broadside aimed at Byron's spars and rigging to slow her down. Some of these balls damaged the *Belvidera*, but not appreciably. And the time consumed by turning to fire a broadside only allowed Byron to increase his lead.

The erratic wind was so light now that all the ships were moving in slow motion. Byron continued to pull away, however, even as he continued firing his stern guns. Rodgers countered "by altering [his] course a half point to port and wetting [his] sails to gain a more effective position" on Byron's starboard quarter, but all he managed to do was lose more ground. A similar attempt to position the *President* on Byron's larboard quarter brought no better result, so Rodgers simply steered directly for the *Belvidera* and blazed away with his serviceable bow chasers, aiming at her spars and rigging, trying to get close enough to turn and fire a conclusive broadside.

Watching the *President* yaw and launch broadsides puzzled Byron. Rodgers had the faster ship; he had no reason to lose ground by yawing, when he could have run up to the *Belvidera*, blazed away with his heavy guns, and forced a surrender. "I acknowledge I was much surprised at [the *President*'s] yawing repeatedly and giving starboard and larboard broadsides," Byron would later write, "when it was fully in his power to have run up alongside the *Belvidera*."

At five o'clock—with the *Belvidera*'s stern guns continuing to tear at the *President*'s sails and rigging—Rodgers finally pulled to within point-blank range. But once again, instead of running up alongside his prey, he attempted to end the fight by ordering the helm put to starboard. The *President* turned and let loose yet another broadside from the main deck guns, which did more harm but did not appreciably slow the *Belvidera* down.

Byron's fore topsail yard was shot through, causing him some difficulty, but the wind was light and the sea smooth, and he lost little ground. Rodgers continued the chase, while Byron's stern guns kept up their deadly fire until 6:30, when Rodgers, in view of the damage done to his spars, rigging, and main yard, by now hanging by the lifts and braces alone, gave the order to luff across *Belvidera*'s stern and fire two more broadsides. Again they were ineffective.

At one point, noticing something odd in the movement of the *President*'s head sails, Byron thought perhaps she had lost control of her helm, and he suddenly yawed to fire a broadside. When he saw Rodgers's fast reaction, however, he quickly reversed himself and resumed his flight. To increase speed he threw overboard several boats (a barge, yawl, gig, and jolly boat); a number of anchors (one bower, one stream anchor, and two sheet anchors); and fourteen tons of water. Gradually the *Belvidera* crept away from her pursuers, who were weighed down with the heavy provisions required for an extended cruise.

By 6:45 Byron was out of range of the *President*'s bow chasers, and with a heavy heart Rodgers recognized that, in spite of his having superior power and speed, he had lost the chase. "I now perceive with more mortification than words can express," he wrote in his journal, "that there was little or no chance left of getting within gunshot of the enemy again." Nonetheless, he vainly continued the chase with all the sail he could muster until 11:30, by which time the *Belvidera* was miles ahead, and Rodgers gave up, signaling the rest of the squadron to do likewise.

The *President* had three men killed and nineteen wounded, sixteen of them from the bursting of the chase gun. The *Belvidera* had two killed and twenty-two wounded.

Decatur was unhappy. Watching the *Belvidera*'s sails disappear over the horizon was painful. Had the chase been conducted properly, he believed, she surely would have surrendered. "We have lost the *Belvidera*; [she] . . . ought to have been ours," he wrote to his fiscal agent, Littleton Tazewell.

Figure Intro.1: *Escape of the* Belvidera, *June 23, 1812* (courtesy of U.S. Naval Academy Museum).

The *Belvidera* sailed on to Halifax, capturing three surprised American merchantmen along the way, none of whose captains had any idea war had been declared—the *Fortune*, out of Newburyport, Massachusetts; the *Malcolm*, from Portland, Maine; and the *Pickering*, of Gloucester, Massachusetts. When Byron dropped anchor in Halifax Harbor on June 27, however, Admiral Sawyer unexpectedly released the three prizes. He had yet to be officially notified that war had broken out, and so far as he was concerned, his orders were to placate the Americans. The *Times* of London later declared that Sawyer had acted "in furtherance of that spirit of amity and conciliation so repeatedly displayed" by the British government. This characterization of His Majesty's policies toward America would have brought a sardonic grin to President Madison's face, for they had, from his point of view, been just the opposite.

The clash between the *President* and the *Belvidera* was the opening battle in what Americans came to view as their second war of independence. Like all wars, once begun it took on a life of its own, lasting far longer than expected, producing one unpleasant surprise after another, stirring the most hateful passions, precipitating heinous crimes, and sacrificing enough young fighters on land and at sea to touch the hardest heart.

CHAPTER ONE

Road to War

For President Madison there was a certain inevitability about the War of 1812. Ever since his initiation into national politics during the latter stages of the Revolutionary War, he had found British policies toward their former colonies to be marked—except for brief periods—by enmity and condescension.

The roots of Britain's hostility, of course, dated to well before the Revolution, when George III—who dominated the cabinet and Parliament—refused to acknowledge that his subjects in America had the same rights as those in Britain (with the exception of Irish Catholics, who had no rights). The refusal of American patriots to submit to unequal status eventually led to armed conflict at Lexington and Concord, and then, over a year later, to a Declaration of Independence. The obdurate king had fought back—hard—to make the American traitors submit and return to the empire. The lengthy war that followed gradually wore down the colonial rebels. Only the timely intervention of France—seeking revenge for her defeat in the Seven Years War—prevented George III from restoring America to his kingdom. Great-power rivalry thus gave the colonists their first taste of independence.

The Treaty of Paris, which ended the war in September 1783, hardly reconciled the king or his people to colonial liberty. Bitter about their humiliating defeat, the British watched with satisfaction as the thirteen states floundered without a central government under the Articles of Confederation. Many in London expected the American experiment in republican government to fail. Prime Minister William Pitt the Younger, who took office in December 1783 at age twenty-four, refused to send an ambassador to the United States or withdraw from the forts along the northern frontier with Canada, as required by the Treaty of Paris. And he vigorously enforced the navigation acts, which, among other things, excluded American ships from trading with British colonies in the West Indies. Thomas Jefferson, the American ambassador to France at the time, wrote that Britain was "the only nation on earth who wishes us ill from the bottom of her soul."

Nor did Britain's sour attitude diminish when the Constitution was approved in 1788 or when George Washington became president in 1789—the year the French Revolution began. Most Americans welcomed the changes taking place in France, believing that the French revolutionaries represented the future and Britain the past. But skeptics admired British constancy far more than French experimentation, and early in Washington's first term two incipient political parties began developing unexpectedly, one of them, forming around Alexander Hamilton, the Treasury secretary, was pro-British, while the other, gathering around Thomas Jefferson, the secretary of state, and James Madison, the leader of the House of Representatives, was decidedly pro-French.

Hamilton admired in particular Britain's mixed constitution, which supported a hierarchical, supposedly paternalistic government featuring a strong but limited monarch, as well as a hereditary aristocracy with enough political power to check both the king and society's lower elements. More impressive yet was its House of Commons, elected by a small number of wealthy voters and thus representing the opinion of the country's well-to-do in a reasonable fashion. Such structural elitism Hamilton considered indispensable to Britain's liberty and well-being. Similarly he felt that a moneyed, well-educated, and morally upright business class in America would provide the necessary leadership for its new republican government, protecting it against the irrational impulses of the untutored masses.

The British economic system, too, appealed to Hamilton. In spite of her defeat in the American war, Great Britain remained an economic colossus, the world's dominant nation. The sources of her strength were manifold: she led the world in technological innovation, which sustained a growing manufacturing base that made her the leader of the Industrial Revolution; she had a strong central government that encouraged economic development and protected the free flow of ideas; her manufacturers and traders were preeminent in the world's commerce, well supported by strong merchant banking houses. Britain's commercial fleet was the largest in the world, supported by a naval infrastructure of huge proportions, and her navy surpassed all rivals, particularly after Pitt revitalized it during the 1780s.

It seemed self-evident to Hamilton that friendship with Britain should be the cornerstone of America's foreign policy. Ninety percent of the republic's trade, after all, was with the British Isles. American merchants were most comfortable dealing in the same language with British counterparts they had been doing business with for years before the Revolution. And London banking houses, like Baring Brothers, were willing, as they had been in the past, to extend essential credit, which could not be said of Dutch and French bankers, whom American traders had burned too often. The business relationship between America and Britain was not about to change, as far as Hamilton was concerned, and it dictated close ties to London.

As Treasury secretary responsible for developing plans to put America's fiscal house in order, Hamilton was ever mindful that customs revenue derived from British imports was critical to the financial health of the fledgling republic. The country was in dreadful financial condition when he came into office. He believed that the United States could never develop solid fiscal underpinnings without a close relationship with the British. It might not even survive.

Jefferson, unlike Hamilton, maintained a profound distrust of Britain, along with a great love for France. When the French Revolution began halfway through his final year as American ambassador in Paris, he cultivated its leaders and helped write the famous Declaration of the Rights of Man, inspired by his own Declaration of Independence. The prospect of France becoming the world's second great republic alongside the United States thrilled him. He believed deeply that people in every country would thrive if only they could rid themselves of the artificial burdens of useless kings and aristocrats.

Jefferson had a powerful ally in James Madison, a devoted friend and fellow Virginian eight years his junior. Jefferson's vast learning, supple mind, and gift for writing appealed to Madison, while his ability to remain a slave-owning despot, even as he passionately advocated for human rights, provided necessary balm for Madison's sometimes troubled conscience.

When he became leader of the House of Representatives during Washington's first term, Madison was widely recognized as the father of the Constitution. He had been instrumental in persuading Washington to chair the Constitutional Convention, and he was a leader during its proceedings in the summer of 1787. Afterward, his brilliant advocacy was critical to getting the Constitution ratified by the state conventions. He was coauthor of the *Federalist Papers*, and he led the fight against Patrick Henry and the anti-Federalists at the Virginia ratifying convention in the summer of 1788. Following ratification, Madison won a battle against James Monroe—his close friend—to win a seat in Congress, despite strong opposition from Patrick Henry and his cohorts. Once in office, Madison became the leader in the House of Representatives and a confidant of Washington, working closely with the president to establish the new government.

Washington was as impressed with Madison's intellectual capacity as Jefferson was. Madison had been educated at Princeton, which was unusual for a wealthy Virginian; most promising young men in Madison's part of the country went to the College of William and Mary, as Jefferson had. Perhaps his intelligence and erudition were all the more noticeable for the qualities he lacked. Madison was physically unimposing. Slightly balding, with large ears, he was barely five feet six inches tall and weighed only one hundred and forty pounds. His slight frame held a stout heart, however, and although he spoke softly in a low voice, his well-considered speeches reflected tenaciously held beliefs and commanded respect.

Before traveling to New York for the opening of the new government in the spring of 1789, Madison—a bachelor—stayed for a week at Mount Vernon, where he and Washington had long conversations about how to turn the stirring words of the Constitution into a workable republican government. They knew what they were up against; the world had never seen a republic succeed over such a wide expanse of territory.

As Washington's first term progressed, he was dismayed to find Madison and Jefferson on one side of a political divide and Hamilton on the other, with the chasm between them growing. The differences between what became known as the Federalist and Republican parties emerged as early as 1790, when Madison and Jefferson opposed Hamilton's far-reaching fiscal reforms. What Hamilton saw as necessary to establish the public credit of the new republic and create the financial underpinnings necessary for the Constitution to succeed, Madison and Jefferson saw as programs that strengthened the federal government far beyond the intent of the Constitution and opened the way for the tyrannical abuse of power, thereby undermining, not securing, the Constitution. They accused Hamilton of trying to impose the British system on America. Jefferson called him a "Monocrat."

Much of Madison and Jefferson's opposition had to do with the culture in which they were raised; to these two tidewater aristocrats Hamilton's proposals to establish public credit (by refinancing the country's foreign, national, and state debts; creating a national bank; and raising internal taxes) favored financiers, speculators, northerner merchants, ship owners, and manufacturers over the landed gentry and ordinary farmers of the South. Hamilton's programs, the Virginians felt, would create an aristocracy of wealth divorced from, and indeed at odds with, agriculture. They had no desire to increase the power of urban-based traders, bankers, manufacturers, and speculators over farmers. The strength of independent tillers of the soil, they believed, was the best guarantee of the sort of republic envisioned in the Constitution. Public policy ought to support agriculture, in their view; it was the bedrock of the American economy and the indispensable foundation of republican government. "Those who labor in the earth," Jefferson wrote, "are the chosen people of God if ever he had a chosen people, whose breasts he has made his peculiar deposit for substantial and genuine virtue." Needless to say, Jefferson's idyllic, self-righteous vision was restricted to white farmers and of greatest benefit to large landholders.

PRESIDENT WASHINGTON WAS deeply concerned that these two competing political creeds, growing shriller and more tendentious, might threaten the unity of the republic. Factions in general were pernicious, he felt, and these two, under the circumstances, all the more so. With one party favoring Britain and the other France, he worried that competing political passions could draw the United States into the great European war then under way between revolutionary France and reactionary Europe.

Convinced that if the United States allowed herself to be drawn into the European maelstrom, the republic would be destroyed, Washington issued his famous proclamation of neutrality on April 22, 1793. Keeping out of the Wars of the French Revolution proved far more difficult than simply making a proclamation, however. By the time Washington issued his call for neutrality, extreme elements had taken over the French Revolution and had already begun to make aggressive efforts to involve the United States in their war against monarchical Europe. At the same time, William Pitt, who was still the British prime minister, confiscated hundreds of American merchantmen and impressed American seamen, showing no respect whatever for the United States—treating her as if she were still a colony.

With most Americans still pro-French and outraged at British aggression on the high seas, Washington found himself being dragged into a war against Britain, a conflict he knew would be suicidal. Hamilton and other prominent Federalists urged him to try a last-minute negotiation with Pitt in order to avoid war, and Washington accepted their advice. In a last-ditch effort to preserve neutrality, he sent Chief Justice John Jay as a special envoy to London. Washington also urged Congress to begin building a navy. The United States was essentially defenseless; she had had no naval force since the Revolution. Initially Washington asked for only six frigates, though he wanted more, but given the temper of Congress, six were all he felt he could obtain.

The president's request met with strong opposition from Republicans, led by Madison and Jefferson. These six frigates, Madison maintained, would inevitably lead to a naval force that would be not only useless but prohibitively expensive. A navy consisting of only six frigates, after all, would be quickly dispatched by the huge British fleet. Even if more ships were added, they could not succeed in any contest with the Royal Navy. All that an American navy would do, he argued, was add to the public debt or create a crushing tax burden. He urged using economic coercion against Britain.

In the end Congress voted to build six frigates, but with severe restrictions, and the navy Washington wanted, although begun during his tenure, would not materialize until the Adams administration. Fortunately for Washington, by the time he sent Chief Justice Jay to London, the war against France was going so poorly for Britain that Pitt decided to reach an accommodation with the United States. The prime minister's change of policy resulted in the Jay Treaty, which was signed in London on November 19, 1794. The British foreign secretary, Lord Grenville, said that he hoped the agreement would promote "lasting friendship between our two countries."

As part of the Jay Treaty, Pitt agreed to withdraw from the forts along the Canadian border, to extend commercial reciprocity, and to grant trade privileges in India. The rest of the treaty, however, decidedly favored the British, reflecting the fact that the United States was defenseless. Jay agreed to prohibit French warships or privateers from using American ports or selling prizes there, while British ships would be allowed to seize enemy goods from neutral (American) ships. And he accepted Britain's Rule of 1756, which, in effect, prohibited American vessels from transporting French goods from their colonies in the West Indies to Europe. In addition, American trade with Britain's colonies in the West Indies, although opened, was severely restricted. No mention was made of British impressment practices, which continued apace.

Washington was disappointed with the treaty, which he considered one-sided. But he reluctantly accepted it because it kept the United States out of a war for which she was entirely unprepared. Madison, Jefferson, and their Republican followers bitterly opposed the treaty, considering it to be humiliating and, worse, a de facto alliance with Britain against France. The fight over the treaty was so fierce it destroyed whatever remained of the personal relationship between Washington and Madison.

If the treaty angered American Republicans, it outraged the French. The latest regime in Paris, the conservative Directory, promptly authorized wholesale attacks on American commerce, a decision that led to a quasi-war between the two countries during the presidency of John Adams. Like Washington, Adams sought neutrality, and through deft diplomacy, supported by the building of a strong navy of fifty-four ships, he managed to avoid having to declare war on France. Among the ships he deployed were the original six frigates: the 44-gun super frigates *Constitution*, *United States*, and *President* and the 36-gun *Congress*, *Constellation*, and *Chesapeake*.

Adams saw no possibility that France would even think about invading the American mainland, so he relied on the navy almost exclusively to support his diplomacy and to fight the Quasi-War. Congress approved his request to separate the navy from the army and establish an independent navy department, whereupon he appointed Benjamin Stoddert as the first secretary of the navy. Stoddert proved to be the most effective of Adams's cabinet members and one of the finest secretaries of the navy in the nation's history. Under him, a cadre of officers—John Rodgers, Stephen Decatur Jr., David Porter, Oliver Hazard Perry, Isaac Hull, Thomas Macdonough, James Lawrence, Charles Morris, and many others—received their first training aboard warships under battle conditions. These men would form the core of professionals who made the tiny American navy a potent force during the War of 1812.

The most celebrated hero of the Quasi-War, Captain Thomas Truxtun, skipper of the USS *Constellation*, was especially influential in training the new officers, paying special attention to their education aboard his ship. Through his example during combat and the books he wrote, Truxtun had a significant impact on the entire officer corps. Retired Vice Admiral George Emery would call Truxtun the "first mentor of the Federal Navy."

The new navy was expensive, and President Adams insisted on imposing taxes to finance it, a decision for which he would pay a heavy political price. The Republicans, led by Jefferson, who was now vice president, fought Adams every step of the way, vigorously opposing the Quasi-War, the new navy, and the new taxes alike. Madison, who by this point had left the House of Representatives and returned to Virginia, lent his support to the opposition.

By the time Adams stood for reelection in 1800, the tax increases had cooled whatever enthusiasm remained in the country for the Quasi-War and contributed to his defeat. The Federalist Party, which Adams had never actively associated himself with, had by this time become less potent. Its divisions, elitism, and emphasis on a strong central government, a big navy, and high taxes lessened its appeal. Federalists continued to believe that government should be entrusted to wealthy individuals with high moral standards and significant education who would exercise authority over a public that was often misguided and sometimes dangerous. Federalist leaders like Alexander Hamilton and Gouverneur Morris of New York and George Cabot, Fisher Ames, and Harrison Gray Otis of Massachusetts associated democracy with the uncontrolled mobs and Jacobin massacres of the French Revolution.

Republicans, on the other hand, represented the agrarian interests of the South and West, as well as those in the northeast and the middle Atlantic states. They were angry about tax increases, which would only be used, they felt, to support an enlarged central government. They viewed Federalists as representing moneyed urban interests seeking to impose a plutocracy on agricultural America. The Republicans put their faith in farmers, the vast majority of the population. Jefferson was their leader, and in 1800 they elected him president, albeit by a narrow margin.

When Jefferson took the oath of office on March 4, 1801, the Wars of the French Revolution, which began in 1792, were continuing, and it was his avowed policy to remain neutral. To that extent, he was following the policy of his predecessors. Staying out of the ongoing conflict, however, was even more difficult for Jefferson than it had been for Washington and Adams. They had not had to contend with Napoleon Bonaparte.

Having seized power on November 9, 1799, Napoleon immediately showed an outsized appetite for expanding the French Empire. Federalists like Hamilton had long predicted that the French Revolution, by carrying democracy too far, would end in dictatorship. Jeffersonian Republicans, on the other hand, still clinging to the belief that British imperialism was a greater danger to the United States than that of France, were shocked and saddened by the turn of events.

When Jefferson took office in March 1801, he had no idea that the first of Napoleon's grand projects was reestablishing the vast French Empire in North America. To achieve this, the French dictator had to crush the armies of the Second Coalition in Europe, which he did with stunning victories over the Austrians at Marengo on June 14, 1800, and again, under French general Moreau, at Hohenlinden, twenty miles east of Munich, on December 3 of the same year.

Napoleon also had to neutralize the Royal Navy. This proved unexpectedly easy. Pitt had resigned in 1801 because of differences with King George III over

Catholic Emancipation, which the prime minister advocated and the king did not. The new ministry of Henry Addington, seeking a respite from the war with France, agreed to peace in the fall of 1801 and then signed the Treaty of Amiens on March 25, 1802, ending hostilities between the two countries.

By the time Napoleon reached an accord with Britain, he had already secretly acquired Louisiana from a hapless Spain and was preparing a large army to secure Haiti, which he planned to use as a base from which to occupy New Orleans. Once on the North American mainland, he could easily absorb Spanish Florida and even attack the United States.

As early as the summer of 1801, Jefferson and his new secretary of state, Madison, became aware of Napoleon's lust for the Floridas and Louisiana. In spite of this direct threat to the United States, they were demobilizing, drastically cutting back President Adams's navy and placing reliance for an army almost entirely on unproven state militias. As a substitute for military force, Jefferson tried using diplomacy against Bonaparte, threatening him with an Anglo-American alliance. This would have come as a surprise to Prime Minister Addington, who never contemplated such a thing. A strong American navy would have spoken far more loudly to Napoleon than empty threats about a British alliance, but Republicans had always opposed building a fleet.

Luckily for Jefferson, Bonaparte's troops never made it beyond Haiti. Haitian rebels, who refused to be reenslaved (which Napoleon announced he would do), as well as disease crushed the French expeditionary force and, with it, Bonaparte's grandiose scheme for North America. He then completely reversed himself—a characteristic trait—changing course without consulting anyone and selling all of Louisiana to a bedazzled Jefferson, turning potential disaster for the president into his crowning achievement. Most Americans applauded the miracle-working Jefferson for his wondrous feat, accomplished at so little cost. No mention was made of the actual reasons—Haiti's former slaves fighting for their freedom and blind luck—Jefferson was able to acquire Louisiana. Although the Republicans were enthralled, the Federalists were not; they maintained that buying Louisiana was unconstitutional. Federalists expected the vast new territory to further dilute their political power while providing a huge area for the extension of slavery, which northern Federalists steadfastly opposed.

Jefferson further enhanced his electoral appeal during his first term by doing away with the noxious internal taxes imposed by his predecessors. To do so, he drastically reduced the size of the navy, which was the largest item in the budget. He could not do away with the service entirely, however. Tripoli had declared war on the United States in 1801, plunging the nation into an unwelcome conflict with the Barbary pirate state that demanded the use of a limited navy. Still, he kept the service small, which allowed for significant tax reduction.

The tiny navy that Jefferson deployed against Tripoli was officered by the same men who had trained during the Quasi-War with France. They acquired further indispensable experience fighting the Barbary pirates. Another hero in the tradition of Thomas Truxtun, Captain Edward Preble of Portland, Maine, emerged to motivate and inspire them. He and Truxtun would be the most powerful influences on the exceptional officers who went on to lead the navy during the War of 1812.

BY THE TIME Jefferson stood for reelection in 1804, internal taxes had been eliminated. And while the country's defenses had been hollowed out, Jefferson could boast that tax collectors no longer bothered the people. Voters were extremely grateful, reelecting him overwhelmingly to a second term. The Federalist Party, which had opposed both the Louisiana Purchase and Jefferson's dismantling of the navy, was handed a devastating defeat.

Jefferson's luck did not hold in his second term, however. The Napoleonic menace came back with a vengeance. On May 17, 1803, immediately after his Haitian fiasco, Bonaparte terminated the Treaty of Amiens and turned to his next great project: conquering Britain. For him, the key to unlimited world power was crushing the British and their all-powerful navy. By the summer of 1805 he had collected a massive army of 100,000 men and seven hundred barges around Boulogne on the French coast. Once he was across the narrow English Channel, nothing could stop him from occupying London. He waited anxiously for Admiral Villeneuve's French fleet to appear and protect his advance across the water.

Napoleon's army at Boulogne was the greatest menace to Britain since William the Conqueror. To counter it, Pitt, who had been out of office since February 4, 1801, was asked to resume leadership of the cabinet on May 10, 1804. Eight days later, Bonaparte, having destroyed all his rivals, including General Moreau, made himself emperor of France. To fight him, Pitt organized another alliance with Russia, Austria, and Sweden, known as the Third Coalition, and large Austrian and Russian armies were soon on the march, threatening France from the east.

Napoleon grew increasingly apprehensive, waiting at Boulogne for his ships to arrive, and on August 26—even before he knew that Villeneuve was never coming to the English Channel, having instead put into Cadiz—he left a small force of 30,000 to guard the French coast, wheeled around abruptly, and drove east beyond the Rhine to attack the Third Coalition's armies.

Napoleon wanted to fight them individually (*en detail*), and the Coalition cooperated. He caught a large Austrian army at Ulm on October 20, 1805, and crushed it. Then, on December 2, 1805, he defeated a combined Russian-Austrian army at Austerlitz, knocking Austria out of the war. The following year he dealt with Prussia, whose king, Frederick William, had belatedly joined the Coalition. Napoleon defeated the Prussian armies at Jena and Auerstadt in 1806. The final showdown with the Russians came during the winter of 1807 at Eylau and Friedland; Napoleon won decisively. He then held a famous conference with Czar Alexander at Tilsit on July 7, 1807. The victorious French dictator redrew the map of Europe, supposedly with the czar's connivance, but no one was deceived: Bonaparte was master of Europe, and Britain stood alone.

Immediately after Tilsit, Napoleon invaded Portugal and then Spain, despite the objections of his foreign minister, Talleyrand. Never enthusiastic about Bonaparte's expansion beyond France's traditional borders, Talleyrand had nonetheless continued to serve him. The invasion of Portugal and Spain in 1807 and 1808 was too much, however, and Talleyrand resigned. Before doing so, he urged the emperor to consolidate his gains, which were already immense. Napoleon ridiculed him. He was intent on ruling not just Portugal and Spain but their vast American empires as well—including all of South and Central America, large portions of the West Indies, and huge parcels of North America.

To Napoleon's surprise, Portugal, Spain, and their American colonies refused to knuckle under, precipitating the Peninsula War, which dragged on year after year with no end in sight, tying down 250,000 French troops on the Iberian Peninsula. The British came to the aid of the guerrilla resistance in Spain and Portugal, deploying the army that eventually achieved fame under the Duke of Wellington.

EVEN AS NAPOLEON was making himself master of continental Europe, Admiral Horatio Nelson demonstrated at the Battle of Trafalgar on October 21, 1805, that Britain remained dominant on the world's oceans. Although Nelson died a heroic death during the fighting, he managed to destroy or capture most of Admiral Villeneuve's Franco-Spanish fleet in what would be regarded as the most consequential naval battle of the age. In the months after Trafalgar, the British moved aggressively to thwart Napoleon's efforts to revive his fleet, first by capturing the entire Danish navy and moving it to England, and then by inducing a beleaguered Portugal to move her fleet to Britain. By the time of Tilsit, Bonaparte was no longer a factor on the high seas.

CHAPTER TWO

~~~~~~~~~~~~~~~

Free Trade
and Sailors' Rights

U NABLE TO DEFEAT Britain at sea or to cross the English Channel with his army, Napoleon turned to economic warfare against the hated British. On November 21, 1806, he issued the Berlin Decree, in which he announced a block-ade of the entire British Isles and forbade any British goods from being imported into Europe. The blockade was mere rhetoric; Napoleon had no means of en-forcing it. But sealing continental ports was something he could put into effect. He did not implement his decree right away, however, and the British did not respond immediately.

Back on January 23, 1806, Prime Minister Pitt had died suddenly of exhaus-tion, shocking the British, who had looked to him for leadership since 1783 and had never felt the need for him quite as much as they did now in the face of the Napoleonic menace. For a brief thirteen-month period in 1806 and 1807, a Whig Ministry of All the Talents replaced Pitt. Lord Grenville, who had negotiated the Jay Treaty, became prime minister, while Charles James Fox took over the Foreign Office. They offered some hope of a reconciliation with the United States. Pitt, growing more reactionary over the years, had become increasingly hard on Amer-ica. The new government now tried a different approach, hoping by easing rela-tions with the United States to ensure her neutrality. Jefferson dispatched special envoy William Pinkney to joined Ambassador James Monroe in London to ne-gotiate an agreement on trade and impressment. Monroe and Pinkney reached

13

agreement with Grenville and Fox on a new treaty that covered trade but not impressment. Grenville simply could not overcome objections from the Admiralty on this point. He did agree, however, to issue guidelines for naval officers to make certain they impressed only British citizens on American ships, which, under the circumstances, Monroe and Pinkney found satisfactory.

A rapprochement between London and Washington appeared to be in the making, but Jefferson turned down the deal because of the impressment issue. For months he had been annoyed by the antics of British warships along the American coast—*Cambria*, *Driver*, and *Leander* in particular, which stationed themselves boldly off Sandy Hook, stopping ships and impressing men indiscriminately. The *Leander* even killed an innocent seaman on April 25, 1806, causing a great furor in New York. Jefferson, in no mood to accept an informal arrangement on impressment, refused to submit the Monroe-Pinkney Treaty to the Senate.

Unfortunately, Fox died in September 1806, and the Ministry of All the Talents was replaced in March 1807 by another anti-American Tory cabinet, led by the Duke of Portland, a mere figurehead. The dominant members of the ministry were Spencer Perceval and George Canning, reactionaries with a deep contempt for the United States and its republican government. Pitt's policies toward America would appear liberal when compared to those of Perceval and Canning.

IN THE FALL of 1807, roughly a year after issuing the Berlin Decree, Napoleon began enforcing it. Perceval, Britain's chancellor of the exchequer, responded with far-reaching Orders in Council designed to control neutral trade with Europe. The most egregious of the Orders was issued on November 11, 1807, requiring all neutral shipping to pass through a British port, obtain a license, and pay a duty before proceeding to any port in Napoleonic Europe, making all neutral goods more expensive than Britain's own. Any vessel not complying was subject to seizure. Napoleon answered a month later with the Milan Decree, which stipulated that any vessel obtaining a British license or paying duty to Britain was subject to confiscation.

The economic warfare between Britain and Napoleonic Europe was not quite what it seemed, however. The two enemies continued to trade with each other through an elaborate, cynically conceived system of licenses. Thus, while Britain was attempting to control and profit from neutral trade, she was herself engaged in a brisk business with Europe through the licenses, supplying Napoleon's needs while denying the United States, the largest neutral carrier, the right to trade independently.

As the Napoleonic War dragged on, the British ministry grew more reactionary, and its enmity toward America deepened. The animus Jefferson and Madison felt toward Britain naturally grew in equal measure. Again and again, their belief that the British had never reconciled themselves to American independence was confirmed. These British policies, it seemed to Madison, could only be directed at "strangling the maritime power of the United States in its cradle." The Orders in Council were a bald attempt by Britain to monopolize world trade, "to make the English navigation and markets the medium through which alone the different parts of the world should exchange their superfluities and supply their wants." Madison was even more incensed by the Royal Navy's increasingly energetic impressment of American seamen. Surely there was no better demonstration of Britain's open contempt for the United States.

The reaction of Federalists to the economic warfare in Europe and to impressment was dramatically different from that of the Republicans. Federalists, believing that Napoleon presented a real danger to the United States, wanted Jefferson to put the country squarely on the side of England in her fight with France. If Britain fell, it would be only a matter of time before the French dictator turned on the United States just as he had before, when he attempted to put a large army into New Orleans. The British, in that sense, were fighting America's fight. "The most intelligent and respectable men in the country," Federalist leader Harrison Gray Otis wrote, ". . . tremble for the prosperity and fate of Britain, and consider her justly as the bulwark of the liberties of this country and mankind."

Federalists, of course, were not happy about the Orders in Council, nor about impressment, but they were willing to tolerate them as wartime necessities. After all, once Napoleon was defeated, the need for them would disappear. And many Federalists felt that Madison had grossly exaggerated the impressment problem, pointing out that far more British seamen were serving on American merchantmen than Americans serving in the Royal Navy. "The general business of impressing American seamen was . . . not worth mooting about," Federalist senator John Rutledge Jr. of South Carolina wrote, "where Great Britain has in her service one of our sailors we have twenty of hers on board our merchantmen." "This whole controversy respecting sailors," Harrison Gray Otis wrote, "was practically to us not worth mooting, we have always had ten to their one." Napoleon had been harder on American commerce than Britain had been, Federalists maintained, seizing ships at a faster rate than the Royal Navy.

IT WAS PRECISELY this reflexive sympathy for Britain on the part of the Federalists, Republicans felt, that had encouraged London's intransigence over the years. By viewing America through the eyes of Jefferson's and Madison's Federalist critics, the British became convinced that a divided country would never stand up to them. To do nothing in the face of the Orders and impressment, Republicans believed, would be to sacrifice the independence and honor of the United States, thereby bringing the entire republican experiment into disrepute, if not failure.

At only one point during Jefferson's presidency were the Federalists and Republicans briefly united, and that was after the *Chesapeake-Leopard* affair. On June 22, 1807, fifteen miles southeast of Virginia's Cape Henry, the 50-gun British warship *Leopard*, under Captain Salusbury Pryce Humphreys, hailed the American 36-gun frigate *Chesapeake*, under Captain James Barron. When Barron hove to, Humphreys sent over a lieutenant with a message demanding that the *Chesapeake*'s crew be mustered and searched for British deserters. As surprised as he was outraged, Barron denied there were any deserters aboard his ship and refused to muster the crew. The British lieutenant returned to the *Leopard* empty-handed.

Humphreys was not about to be put off, however; he was operating under strict orders from Vice Admiral Sir George Berkeley, commander of the North American Station and a rabid anti-American Tory. Within minutes of the lieutenant's return to the *Leopard*, even as Barron belatedly prepared the *Chesapeake* for battle, Humphreys fired three broadsides into her without warning, killing three and wounding eighteen. Barron quickly struck his colors. The British lieutenant then returned and seized four of Barron's crew, claiming they were deserters. There were probably other British deserters aboard, but the lieutenant failed to identify them. One of the men taken, Jenkin Ratford, was indeed a British deserter, but the other three were Americans. Ratford was given a quick court-martial and then hanged from the yardarm of a warship in Halifax harbor on August 31, 1807. The three Americans were sentenced to receive five hundred lashes, but that was remitted, and they wound up in jail, where one of them died. The other two remained incarcerated until returned to the deck of the *Chesapeake* in Boston five years later.

The incident caused a reaction in the United States so furious that Jefferson could have asked for a declaration of war and had the whole country united behind him, including the Federalists. He decided to avoid a war, however, for the same reason Washington had: the country was unprepared and essentially defenseless. The fact that America's defenseless state was due to Jefferson's own policies was an irony that would not have been lost on either Hamilton or Adams, but the fact remained that declaring war was out of the question. Instead Jefferson looked for another, more peaceful, way to change British policies.

NOTHING RANKLED AMERICANS more than the issue of impressment, but it also touched British sensitivities deeply. The Admiralty and the Perceval ministry felt that impressment was essential to the Royal Navy and thus to British security. Calling the practice into question was, in their view, tantamount to asking the country to abandon the main weapon in her life-and-death struggle with Napoleon.

At the root of the problem, however, was something the Admiralty would never admit—namely, the unnecessarily brutal conditions aboard His Majesty's warships. So horrendous was the working environment that British tars deserted in droves, creating a manpower shortage in the Royal Navy that the Admiralty could only solve by continually impressing more men. Britain's leaders—not just the Admiralty—steadfastly refused to recognize the true source of their problem. On the rare occasions in Parliament when any mention was made of the deplorable state of the crews, the Admiralty was quick to deny the obvious. No less a figure than Thomas Cochrane, a storied British sea captain, whom the novelist Patrick O'Brian would use as a model for the character of Jack Aubrey, brought up the taboo subject in the House of Commons. When Cochrane deplored "the decayed and heartless state of the crews," John W. Croker, first secretary of the Admiralty, challenged him, calling his charges "grossly exaggerated, . . . an absolute misrepresentation, . . . [and] a scandalous libel on the Navy." The House cheered as Croker's rebuttal progressed. Members simply did not want to hear the truth, not even from such an unimpeachable source as Cochrane.

Britain's ruling class preferred the comfortable illusion that the thousands of deserters were happy tars lured away from their ships by the Americans. They could not bring themselves to think about, much less reform, the bestial conditions aboard their warships. Such indifference was all the more remarkable when one considers that warships functioned far better when working conditions were improved even slightly. No military need required the brutal treatment of sailors; wartime necessity did not mandate that trained men be treated as animals.

Tradition governed life aboard a British man-of-war, as well as the personalities of the captain and his officers. It was not uncommon for upper-class officers to be contemptuous of their crewmen, nearly all of whom were lower-class and illiterate. Discipline was harsh and often arbitrary on every warship. Being a ruthless disciplinarian never impeded an officer's advancement. If a pressed man had a brutal, flogging skipper, his life became an intolerable hell. His only recourse was to desert.

Service in the Royal Navy was, after all, indeterminate. Once dragged aboard, an impressed man was trapped until the war—which by 1807 had already gone on for fifteen years—was over. Given the innumerable hazards on men-of-war, and the bestial punishment code, he would be lucky if he made it out alive. Impressment was thus akin to a death sentence.

Ships became prisons. Shore leave was never granted to men whom officers suspected might desert, even in the most remote locations. It was not uncommon for pressed men to spend years aboard ship without ever once being allowed on dry land. There were instances when men were so desperate to escape they deserted to forbidding, uninhabited islands. An American naval prisoner-of-war, Benjamin Waterhouse, wrote while in Dartmoor prison, "an American in England pines to get home, while an Englishman and an Irishman longs to become an American citizen."

Bad food was universal and made worse by contractors who had a habit of cheating the Royal Navy. Furthermore, the quantity of food aboard ship was always reduced by the custom of allowing the purser to keep some of it for his own profit. Food was measured aboard in pounds, but the purser's pound amounted to fourteen ounces, rather than sixteen. He took the extra two ounces for himself and shorted the men in their meals.

Alcohol was liberally dispensed each day aboard every ship to dull the pain: a half pint of hard liquor mixed with water was given out at noon, followed by a pint of wine at four o'clock. The alcohol did not need to be consumed on the spot, or even that day. Saved and accumulated, it became a sort of currency aboard all warships. Every scheme was used to obtain it, particularly when the ship was in port. A man could get whatever he needed whenever he could pay the price. Drunkenness, predictably, was a continuing problem, and dealt with severely, usually by a liberal dose of the fearsome cat-o'-nine-tails. Four dozen lashes— enough to kill some men—was a common sentence for being in one's cups.

The cat was the preferred tool for effecting discipline. A single blow would knock a man down. To give him a dozen or more—the usual dose—his wrists had to be tied securely to a hard-as-iron oak grating, which in turn kept his body from giving, making the blows all the more terrible. Reactions to whipping varied greatly from man to man. Some would die from a few lashes; others could withstand far more. Regardless, the severity of the punishment was frightening, and no man witnessing it ever forgot it.

The first stroke from the cat broke open the flesh, causing bleeding and bruising. After two, pain in the lungs, as well as the back, was severe. As the beating progressed, blood from biting one's tongue nearly off was common, as was the face turning a deep reddish brown. The back soon became a bloody mess, turning black; one seaman described a lacerated back as "inhuman [resembling] roasted meat burnt . . . before a scorching fire." In 1806 the Admiralty removed the injunction against sentencing to more than a dozen lashes without a court-martial because captains never observed it. After 1806 they were free to order whatever they pleased, and they did.

Samuel Leech, a British seaman, gave this account of the practices of Captain John S. Carden, skipper of the British frigate H.M.S. *Macedonian*. Carden was an experienced officer with a good record, not judged particularly cruel by his peers or, indeed, by later historians. "A midshipman named Gale, a most rascally, unprincipled fellow, found his pocket handkerchief in possession of one of the crew. He charged the man with stealing it. It was in vain that the poor wretch asserted that he found it under his hammock." A court-martial sentenced Gale to receive three hundred lashes through the fleet and one year's imprisonment. "Fifty were laid on alongside of the *Macedonian*, in conformity with a common practice of inflicting the most strokes at the first ship, in order that the gory back of the criminal may strike terror into the crews of the other ships. This poor tortured man bore two hundred and twenty, and was pronounced by the attending surgeon unfit to receive the rest." Miraculously, the man survived, but when he recovered his health, Captain Carden ordered him to receive the remaining eighty lashes.

"No plea of necessity can be successfully urged in behalf of whipping men," Leech wrote. "Punishment leads to revenge; revenge to punishment. What is intended to cure, only aggravates the disease; the evil enlarges under the remedy; voluntary subordination ceases; gloom overspreads the crew; fear fills the breasts of the officers; the ship becomes a miniature of the house of fiends. While, on the other hand, mild regulations, enforced without an appeal to brute force, are easily carried into operation."

Abysmal pay added to a tar's disillusionment. One of the chief complaints of the mutineers at Spithead in 1797 was that seamen in the Royal Navy had not received a raise in one hundred and fifty years, and conditions had not improved much since. In theory ordinary seamen received a bounty of four pounds when they originally signed on, plus eighteen pounds a year, but they received none of this until their ship returned to England and the crew had been paid off. The Admiralty argued that if a sailor had money, he would be tempted to desert.

Seamen were deserting anyway, of course, but the Admiralty did not want to give them an added incentive. On long voyages men often had to go to the purser to purchase items such as clothing at grossly inflated prices. "Hence, what with poor articles, high charges and false charges," Leech argued, "the purser almost always had a claim that made Jack's actual receipts for two or three years service, woefully small." Pay in the Royal Navy was always lower than in the British merchant service and much lower than in the American navy or aboard American merchantmen.

If a man were lucky enough to stay alive, he could be returning home at last, looking forward to being on shore, having money, obtaining fresh food, and a decent night's sleep, yet meet with one more cruel trick. Instead of being allowed ashore he could be herded onto another warship standing out to sea, without ever setting foot on land, even though he might have already served years at sea. Worse, men wounded in action were routinely dismissed from the service, sent home with their wounds not yet healed, and their pay summarily cut off. "Here was encouragement for seamen to fight for their king and country!" wrote a bitter impressed man. "A coolie in India was better off!"

To save themselves from a cruel imprisonment and early death, British tars deserted by the thousands, many to American ships. The Admiralty estimated the number serving in American vessels during the Napoleonic wars to be between 15,000 and 20,000. In a Royal Navy that employed 145,000 men, that was a significant figure. Yet had the Admiralty only improved life for the lower deck, men would not have deserted in the numbers they did, and there would have been no need to stop American vessels to search for them. A few modest changes would have gone a long way to ensure the required number of men: an increase in enlistment bonuses and wages; disbursement on a regular basis, rather than at long intervals; a set time of enlistment; a more humane punishment code; a modicum of respect for seamen; more and better food, including fresh vegetables when available; better medical treatment; a definite leave policy; pensions for the permanently injured; and a more equitable distribution of prize money. It could reasonably be supposed that patriotic men would have joined the Royal Navy when the country was fighting for its life against its traditional enemy, France.

IF THERE WAS no need for Britain to impress and brutalize her own subjects, there was certainly no need to impress citizens of the United States, particularly when the number of Americans involved was so small. No one has an exact figure, but it is generally agreed that the number of Americans impressed into the British navy from the start of the Wars of the French Revolution in 1793 until 1812 was probably less than 6,000, although some scholars have it as high as 9,000.

Rather than addressing its manpower shortage by improving conditions for seamen, however, the Admiralty adopted a severe punishment code, including death, for any man caught leaving his ship without permission, particularly one found aboard an American warship. "We must on no account shrink from the duty of putting to death every British subject caught fighting against his country," the *Times* lectured, never once mentioning that conditions aboard the ships themselves might be to blame and could be easily corrected. Instead, they continually asserted that British seamen left their ships because the Americans had seduced them.

Neither terror nor impressment solved the Admiralty's manning problems, however. In desperation, their lordships tried a variety of expedients, such as offering five pounds for any able seaman under fifty who signed up, three pounds for anyone who informed the press of where they could lay hands on an able seaman, and a guinea for a landsman who volunteered. The Admiralty swept the prisons and even took impoverished orphans. Youngsters who were orphaned and found themselves taken in by parishes were often sent to merchant ships when they were twelve or thirteen (and sometimes younger). After training, they would be taken into the Royal Navy, which then became their life. The Admiralty employed any device, fair or foul, to man its ships, save the most obvious one: improving the lives of those who served. The Royal Navy had done so spectacularly well against all competitors that changing methods of recruitment seemed ludicrous to an Admiralty steeped in tradition, particularly when change was demanded by America, a nation that seemed to annoy the British more than any other.

THE PASSIONS IMPRESSMENT unleashed on both sides were not easily tamed. The British saw themselves in mortal danger from a French enemy who ought to have been America's foe as well, while, even as Napoleon threatened to extinguish the very liberties Americans insisted were the foundation of their society, the United States was acting as if she had no stake in the outcome of the struggle in Europe. The Royal Navy, as far as the British were concerned, was the only force preventing Napoleon from realizing his dream of a North American empire, uniting Louisiana with Canada. And to think he would stop there was naïve: Bonaparte would never rest until he had destroyed the republican regime in America; it was a living rebuke to everything he stood for.

The British, then, fighting what they saw as America's fight, found it strange indeed that the sympathies of Jefferson and Madison remained with a dictator openly hostile to their professed ideals. Even more galling, America's insistence on the right of neutrals to trade freely with both belligerents looked as if short-term profits were more important than European liberty. Surely America's moral sense had been deadened by gross materialism, as Yankee merchants sought to profit from Europe's misery.

Deserters from the Royal Navy, the British believed, were necessary for the American merchant fleet to carry on its burgeoning wartime trade, which in turn supported the revenues of an American government financed largely by customs duties. By insisting on carrying on their international commerce, then, regardless of the consequences, Americans were endangering British liberty—and ultimately their own—for the sake of money. Even worse, the British felt that the real reason Jefferson and Madison wanted to do away with impressment was to destroy Britain's maritime power, regardless of the consequences.

Given this attitude, it is not surprising that Britain refused to alter an official policy hallowed by three centuries of practice in order to appease American demands. The Royal Navy had trebled in size since the war with France began in January 1793, and the Admiralty needed every seaman it could lay its hands on. Volunteers alone were not enough. For every citizen of the United States in the Royal Navy, their lordships estimated, there were ten Englishmen in American ships, private and public. The ministry wanted them back—or at least hanged as a deterrent.

The United States, for her part, could not suffer ships flying her flag to be boarded and seamen impressed and still call herself an independent country. Allowing such an outrage to continue would be to submit to colonial status again. In the eyes of Jefferson and Madison, accepting impressment was unthinkable. Britain had no right whatever, they insisted, to seize anyone from a vessel flying the American flag, no matter what the pretext.

In America a seaman could obtain citizenship by being naturalized after a period of five years, no matter where he'd been born, whereas Britian now maintained, as most countries did at the time, that if you were born a British subject, you remained one for life. The British conveniently overlooking their own laws, dating back to Queen Anne and George II, which stipulated that any foreigner who served two years in a British warship or merchantman automatically became a naturalized British subject without the need for an oath or any other requirement.

Regardless of these old laws, Great Britain, faced with the Napoleonic menace, was not about to change her ways, and Americans, with vivid memories of how hard they had fought for independence, were not about to accept them.

CHAPTER THREE

Jefferson's Embargo
and the Slide Toward War

A T THE END of 1807 Jefferson decided to counter Britain's Orders in Council and its practice of impressment, as well as Napoleon's decrees, by instituting a wide-ranging embargo. Jefferson believed that Britain and her West Indian colonies were so dependent on American trade, particularly in raw materials, that London would be forced to withdraw her Orders in Council and to put a stop to impressment in a matter of weeks. He hoped that, faced with an Anglo-American entente, Napoleon would follow suit. Jefferson liked to think of the embargo as a form of "peaceful coercion," an alternative to either war or submission, and he had the enthusiastic support of Madison, who also believed that the embargo was the only way to avoid having to choose between a costly war or abject surrender to colonial status.

In December 1807, Congress passed the Embargo Act by a wide margin. The legislation prohibited all exports to any foreign port and required a bond for coastal traders. Foreign ships could still bring goods to American ports, but they had to return in ballast. Albert Gallatin, the Treasury secretary whose job it would be to enforce the act, did not like it, but he dutifully took on the nearly impossible task of implementing it.

Jefferson's hope was that by sacrificing America's trade for a short period the embargo would save the nation's ships and men from British and French depredations. Meanwhile, to defend the coasts, he dramatically increased the navy's fleet of gunboats—small craft ranging in size from forty-five to seventy feet and carrying one to two heavy guns. By the end of 1807 the Republican Congress had authorized construction of 278 of these boats, though by the time the War of 1812 broke out, just 165 were available.

Jefferson viewed this fleet of gunboats as defensive in nature and far less expensive than building frigates or ships of the line. He thought the navy's larger ships contributed almost nothing to the nation's defense. In a war with Britain, he assumed the Royal Navy would quickly seize them. Gunboats, on the other hand, could "withdraw from the reach of the enemy," he argued, and be "formidable . . . in shoally waters." Not a single officer in the navy agreed with him, however. None thought the gunboats could protect the coasts. They viewed Jefferson's mosquito fleet with scorn, and when war came, the gunboats proved nearly useless.

————

FOR NEW ENGLAND Federalists, the embargo was the last straw. Shutting off the region's seagoing commerce would wreak havoc on its economy. And so the Federalist Party, moribund since Jefferson's stunning reelection in 1804, came back to life, invigorated by opposition to the embargo. Flouting of the law was widespread. Jefferson, surprised by this level of resistance, grew more tenacious in his attempts at enforcement. He should not have been shocked that so many Americans despised the embargo, however. Despite widespread evasion, exports plunged from over one hundred million in 1807 to just twenty two million the following year.

Even more maddening, while the law proved exceptionally hard on the United States, it appeared to have little effect on Britain or France. Foreign Secretary Canning ridiculed it. But this was just a pretense. The British were indeed hampered by their inability to import American raw materials, and the embargo played a role in causing Britain's depression in 1809–10. Nevertheless, London and Paris ignored the embargo and steadfastly refused to change their maritime policies, forcing Jefferson to keep the increasingly unpopular law in force far longer than he anticipated. Week after week the economy declined, and increasingly strident calls for relief came from across the country, particularly from New England. By the winter of 1809 a civil war was brewing over the domestic distress caused by the stoppage of trade. "The evils which are menaced by the continuance of this policy," the Massachusetts legislature informed Congress, ". . . must soon become intolerable, and endanger our domestic peace, and the union of these states." Finally, on March 1, 1809, just three days before Jefferson

left office, Congress repealed the hated embargo. The president, with great reluctance, signed the bill, bequeathing to his successor the problem of what to do
about British and French provocations.

It was not a legacy President Madison coveted. Despite his strong support
for the unpopular embargo, he had been elected handily in 1808 with 122 electoral
votes to 47. He was furious with the New England Federalists for doing everything
they could to thwart a policy he believed could have achieved American goals
without war or submission. Like Jefferson, Madison was convinced that if the
country had persevered with the embargo just a while longer, the British would
have relented. That may have been true, but politically the embargo was dead.

On March 15, 1809, immediately after Madison took office, Congress replaced the embargo with the Non-Intercourse Act, which permitted trade with
all nations except Britain and France. The legislation unintentionally favored the
British. Despite the law, goods flowed freely to Britain through a number of channels, while the Royal Navy enforced the blockade of Napoleonic Europe.

The British, of course, did not feel favored by the new law, and their ambassador in Washington, David Erskine (the only British ambassador who genuinely
liked America), sought ways to prevent Anglo-American relations from deteriorating further. He approached Madison in April 1809 for talks about easing
tensions between the two countries. The president was receptive, and in a short
six weeks he and Erskine negotiated an agreement whereby Britain would revoke
the Orders in Council if the United States would end non-intercourse against
Great Britain. Both Erskine and Madison felt they had achieved a genuine breakthrough. In the end, however, Canning rejected the agreement, recalling Erskine
and replacing him with a hard-line, anti-American Tory, Francis J. Jackson, who
went out of his way to sour relations between the two countries. Federalists, particularly in Massachusetts, supported Jackson against their own government,
which only encouraged Perceval and Canning, to suppose that with the United
States so hopelessly divided, Madison could never act effectively against them.
With the end of the Embargo Act, American ships reappeared on the high seas,
and the British again went right after them, exacerbating relations between the
two countries. Perceval and Canning were showing no restraint whatever.

On May 1, 1810, in order to revive the revenue stream flowing to the cash-
starved Treasury, Congress replaced the Non-Intercourse Act with Macon's Bill
#2, which restored trade with the entire world, including Britain and France.
Moreover, the bill stipulated that if either Britain or France ceased interfering
with neutral trade, the United States would stop trading with the other nation.
This provision moved Napoleon to notify the United States that he was removing

his Berlin and Milan decrees, although, in truth, he had no intention of doing so. Madison, choosing to believe him, asked Britain to rescind the Orders in Council, or be faced with the prospect of having trade with America cut off. London was quick to point out that Napoleon had not actually done what he said and so refused.

On February 11, 1811, Madison, having given Perceval three months' warning, imposed nonimportation against Great Britain, and as 1811 progressed, relations between the two governments further deteriorated. The Royal Navy appeared again off New York, stopping and seizing American ships, and aggressively impressing American seamen. Particularly noxious were the frigates *Guerriere* and *Melampus*.

On May 1 the *Guerriere* stopped the brig *Spitfire* and impressed an innocent Maine man serving as apprentice to the master. New York City was in an uproar over the incident, and the secretary of the navy ordered Captain John Rodgers, then at Annapolis, to rush to New York in the *President* and "vindicate the injured honor of our navy and revive the drooping spirits of the nation." On May 16, 1811, while he was on his way to New York, Rodgers spotted a British warship forty-five miles northeast of Cape Henry. Thinking she might be the *Guerriere*, he went after her. The stranger fled, but Rodgers caught up with her at eight-thirty that evening, when visibility was poor. Confusion ensued as both ships started shooting before they knew who the other was.

The stranger turned out to be the 20-gun British sloop of war *Little Belt*, a two-decked, formerly Danish warship. She was much smaller than the *President*, and Rodgers forced her to strike her colors in a few minutes. After the brief fight, the captain of the badly banged-up *Little Belt*, Arthur Bingham, refused all help from Rodgers and struggled back to Halifax, while Rodgers sailed the *President* to New York, where he received a hero's welcome. Such was the state of British-American relations that the president was quick to publicly congratulate Rodgers.

AS 1811 PROGRESSED, Madison, in utter frustration, was coming to the conclusion that war with Britain was unavoidable. He would not give up on trying to get the British to change their policies, but it looked increasingly unlikely they would do so. During the summer he conferred at length with Jefferson and Secretary of State James Monroe at Monticello and decided that only an actual declaration of war would move Perceval to the negotiating table. "We have been so long dealing in small ways of embargoes, non-intercourse, and non-importation, with menaces of war, &c.," explained Monroe, "that the British Government has not believed us. We must actually get to war before the intention to make it will be credited either here or abroad." In a similar vein, the president wrote that, "Perceval [and his colleagues] . . . prefer war with us to a repeal of their Orders in Council. We have nothing left therefore, but to make ready for it."

On November 4, 1811, Madison urged Congress to strengthen the nation's defenses, which for the last eleven years under Republican rule had been allowed to deteriorate. He asked Congress to authorize an additional 10,000 men for the regular army, which would have brought it up to 20,000. Congress responded on January 11, 1812, by increasing bounties for an enlistment of five years from $12 to $16, plus three months pay and 160 acres of land, and it approved an increase in the regular army of 25,000—in other words, 15,000 more troops than the 10,000 Madison asked for. The legislation thus authorized a regular force of up to 35,000.

Republican malcontents like Senator William Giles of Virginia, eager to chastise the president for being too soft on Britain and too lax about keeping up the nation's defenses, promoted the larger number. Giles, paradoxically, had been a strong supporter and, indeed, an intimate of President Jefferson, and he had worked hard for the election of Madison, but his antipathy toward Treasury Secretary Gallatin estranged him from the president, and he became a bitter opponent.

Madison felt that he would have great difficulty bringing the existing regular army up to full strength and then raising 10,000 more men. Enlisting 25,000 seemed impossible. Nonetheless, his supporters in the House approved the higher number, 94 to 34. Speaker Henry Clay declared that a larger army was indispensable to America's "commerce, character, [and] a nation's best treasure, honor!"

Considering its size and prosperity, the United States could have easily supported a regular force of 100,000, but Madison never wanted a large standing army, nor would Republicans in Congress have approved one, since they considered it a threat to the Constitution. Like Jefferson and most other Republicans, Madison intended to rely on state militias—citizen soldiers who could be organized, equipped, and trained ahead of time and then called upon when needed. Militiamen would serve only for brief periods before returning to their civilian pursuits, making it impossible for an American Caesar or Napoleon to misuse them.

In April, with war increasingly likely, Congress authorized the president to call up to 100,000 state militiamen for six months of federal service. The militiamen were an unknown quantity, however. It was not at all certain they could fight or would be willing to march beyond the country's borders. Thirty days later, Congress authorized Madison to call up 50,000 volunteers in addition to the militiamen and the regulars. Volunteers were neither militiamen nor regulars but something in between. They were men who served for brief periods of a few months and then went home. Regular army personnel signed on for five years. No one was confident that volunteers in sufficient numbers would respond to the president's call. Indeed, it was unlikely they would. By June recruitment had produced no more than 5,000 additional men for the regular army, bringing it near 12,000, out of the authorized total of 35,000. The War Department was so disorganized it could not even give Congress exact figures on their present manpower.

The legislation also authorized the appointment of two major generals and five brigadier generals. The president, if he saw fit, could make one major general senior to the others and thus the leader of the army. Back on January 27, Madison had appointed the former secretary of war under Jefferson, sixty-two-year-old Henry Dearborn, as the senior major general, and he was given command of the entire northern army based outside Albany, New York. Dearborn's advanced age did not seem to bother the president. A distinguished veteran of the Revolutionary War and a physician, Dearborn had been in the thick of the fighting from Bunker Hill to Valley Forge and Yorktown, rising to colonel and later, at the close of the war, serving on Washington's staff as deputy quartermaster general. No one had seen more combat than Henry Dearborn, and no one was better acquainted with the suffering of the patriot army. After the war he had become a successful congressman and then, for eight years, Jefferson's secretary of war. During that time he had formed a close personal relationship with Secretary of State Madison.

For his second major general, Madison appointed sixty-two-year-old Thomas Pinckney of South Carolina, to whom he gave command of the southern army. Pinckney had had a long, distinguished career as a soldier during the Revolution, as a diplomat afterward, and as a politician, but his capacity to lead an army at this stage in his life was limited. Congressman Nathaniel Macon of North Carolina, reflecting the views of many Southerners, observed that he "was not more at a loss to account for any proceeding than the nomination of Pinckney to be major-general." Macon assumed Pinckney's appointment was the work of Navy Secretary Paul Hamilton, who, he said, "is about as fit for his place as the Indian Prophet would be for Emperor of Europe."

Macon's slur against Paul Hamilton was a gross exaggeration. It's true that Hamilton had been appointed in 1809 strictly for political reasons; he was a landsman, after all, with no obvious qualifications to lead the Navy Department. Madison appointed him first and foremost to achieve geographical balance in his cabinet. Still, Secretary Hamilton had fought with distinction in the Revolutionary War in South Carolina under guerilla leaders like Francis Marion, and in 1804, after many years as a successful planter and local politician, he became governor of South Carolina. A strong patriot, Hamilton did his best to strengthen the navy with little help from the chief executive or the Republican Congress. Unfortunately, having little understanding of naval strategy, he was unable to give sound advice to the president on how to use the country's limited naval resources. His appointment can only be seen as one more indication of the little regard Madison had for the navy.

ON NOVEMBER 4, 1811, Madison requested Congress to increase the navy. It was not that the president had suddenly become enamored of the fleet; rather, he wanted to send a message to London. On January 17 Langdon Cheves, chairman of the House Naval Committee, asked his colleagues to approve building twelve 74-gun ships-of-the-line and twenty frigates. That touched off an acrimonious debate that ended on January 27, with the House voting 62–59 to defeat a drastically reduced bill to add ten frigates to the navy. Instead of expanding the navy, Congress appropriated $600,000 to acquire timber over a three-year period. The message was the exact opposite of the one Madison wanted to send. Perceval could only view the bill's defeat as another sign that the United States lacked the will to fight.

The arguments against expanding the navy had been heard inside and outside of Congress for many years, and they had not changed. A larger navy, its opponents said, would endanger liberty, plunge the country into unnecessary wars, and become an enormous burden on taxpayers. Congressman Adam Seybert of Philadelphia, the well-known scientist, warned that an expanded navy would not return to its small state after the war but would become a permanent force at great expense and "a powerful engine in the hands of an ambitious Executive." Attempting to make the United States into a naval power, Seybert predicted, would likely destroy the Constitution. "We cannot contend with Great Britain on the ocean," he said, "but we can undermine our form of government by trying to do so."

The lack of Republican support did not prevent the navy from being ready when Congress declared war, however. Its leaders were veterans of two conflicts—the Quasi-War with France, from 1798 to 1800, and the war with Tripoli, from 1801 to 1805. They were eager to test their mettle against the British. Although the warships they commanded were old and few in number, these men were anxious to prove they were the finest afloat. Composed entirely of volunteers, their crews included no shortage of experienced fighters. And all of them received far better treatment than their British counterparts, making their ships—other things being equal—more potent. In spite of the young navy's excellence and fighting spirit, however, its small size would remain an enormous handicap.

CHAPTER FOUR

Madison's Strategy

A S THE UNITED STATES approached war in the winter and spring of 1812, President Madison had a clear strategy for winning: while Napoleon was launching his widely anticipated invasion of Russia in the summer of 1812, the United States would invade lightly defended Canada. Bonaparte's success in Russia and America's in Canada, Madison expected, would bring Perceval to the negotiating table. The president's strategy did not include a major role for the navy. He assumed, as he always had, that in the early stages of the war the Royal Navy would make quick work of the tiny American fleet. Instead of relying on the navy, Madison intended to unleash hundreds of privateers and bring pressure on British commerce, as privateers had done so successfully during the War of Independence. They would be America's navy.

Madison's confidence in Napoleon was widely shared in the United States and in Europe, particularly Britain. Long before the president urged Congress to declare war on June 1, it was common knowledge that the French dictator intended to invade Russia in 1812 as soon as the weather permitted. "If war should not commence soon," wrote John Quincy Adams, the American ambassador in St. Petersburg, on October 11, 1811, "there is . . . nobody who thinks it possible it should be postponed longer than until next summer." Napoleon was at the apogee of his power. The stupendous French forces gathering along the Russian frontier during the winter and spring of 1812 could not be hidden, and they looked invincible. By June 1812 his Grand Army had grown to an astonishing 600,000 plus, the largest in history. Czar Alexander could summon less than half that number, and perhaps only a third. The belief that Russia would be on her knees in a matter of weeks was all but universal.

War between Napoleon and Alexander had appeared certain since at least December 31, 1810. On that date the czar issued a ukase (decree) that opened trade with Britain while imposing high tariffs on the French, thus breaking Napoleon's continental trading system and ending Russia's alliance with France. Knowing full well how violent Napoleon's reaction would be, Alexander prepared for war. Few observers expected him to be able to withstand Bonaparte, but Alexander was determined to resist to the last. In the winter of 1811–12, General Mikhail Kutuzov defeated Russia's old nemesis the Turks, ending for the moment their interminable conflict, which had flared up again in 1811. Kutuzov's force could then combine with other elements of the Russian army and concentrate on the French and their allies. In April 1812 the czar further improved his position by making an alliance with Sweden, eliminating the possibility of Bernadotte's army attacking St. Petersburg while Napoleon was invading Russia's heartland.

In May, even as Bonaparte's hordes were gathering along the Russian border, he demonstrated to the world his dominion over Europe by throwing a lavish ball for himself in Dresden, the capital of Saxony. The proud princes and monarchs of Europe, including those of Prussia and Austria, were required to attend and pay homage to their new master at his grand soiree. When the reluctant guests were assembled in the lavish ballroom of the King of Saxony, the crowd suddenly grew silent, and then a loud voice announced, "the emperor!" After a pause, Napoleon, dressed in his green uniform, made a dramatic, solitary entrance. His message was clear enough; he was not just the Emperor of France. He was *The Emperor*—certainly of Europe, but after that, who knew? In June 1812 it was hard to imagine what country, or what coalition, could curb his unlimited ambition. Once he subdued Russia and pacified Spain, Britain would stand alone. Could she survive the tidal wave that was sure to follow? It seemed unlikely.

The emperor had convinced nearly everyone that he was unbeatable, and Madison, it would seem, believed he was—at least for the moment. To be sure, Napoleon had 250,000 troops stuck in Spain for four years, unable to defeat the guerrillas and their British allies. Of course, it was Joseph Bonaparte leading the French army there, not his brother. It was widely assumed that once Napoleon turned his full attention to the Iberian Peninsula, he would prevail. Eventually the French dictator would overreach, Madison thought, and that would be the end of him. But for now he was supreme and a useful lever against the British.

In the wake of the grand May ball, Napoleon traveled to the front and took personal command of the Grand Army, his confidence—like that of his generals—

absolute. Ignoring the yearning of all Europeans, including his own people, for an end to the mass killing that had been going on for twenty years, he was determined to bring Russia to heel. Once he had done so, his dominance of the European mainland would be complete. Britain would then be in danger of seeing the French dictator, in the not too distant future, strutting in London.

It appeared likely that after subduing Russia, Bonaparte would force the small British army out of Spain and Portugal, while simultaneously building a fleet large enough to challenge the Royal Navy in preparation for an invasion of the British mainland. Of course, there were other possibilities. After throwing Wellington out of the Iberian Peninsula, the emperor might eject Britain from Gibraltar, sweep across North Africa into Egypt, and from there push east with the compliance of his new Russian ally and conquer India, which he had long dreamed of doing. Sooner or later, though, he would invade Britain; there could be no doubt about it. Madison was sure that, faced with this reality, the intractable Perceval would at last seek a rapprochement with the United States.

To bring added pressure on the prime minister, Madison planned to invade Canada in the summer of 1812. Once in possession of even part of Canada, he would have a powerful bargaining tool, particularly when a French victory in Russia would threaten British security as never before. In addition, American privateers would be attacking British commerce and disrupting the supply line moving troops, equipment, money, and food to Wellington's army in Portugal and Spain. The president even hoped that faced with the prospect of having to fight both France and the United States, the stubborn prime minister might come to terms without the need for actual combat.

EMBARRASSED BY HIS dependence on as noxious a dictator as Napoleon, and stung by Federalist accusations that he was a French puppet, Madison consistently denied that he timed his call for war to coincide with Bonaparte's plunge into Russia. The president was always careful to distance himself in public from the French dictator, insisting that no matter what critics claimed, he was not allied with Napoleon nor dependent on him in any way and never would be. "Our government will not under any circumstances that may occur, form a political connection with France," Madison wrote in Washington's semiofficial *National Intelligencer*. "It is not desirable to enter the lists with the two great belligerents at once; but if England acts with wisdom, and France perseveres in her career of injustice and folly, we should not be surprised to see the attitude of the United States change toward these powers."

Indifferent to Madison's warnings, Napoleon attacked American commerce—to the limited extent he could, given the strength of the Royal Navy—throughout 1812. The armada of Yankee merchantmen supplying food to British forces in Spain annoyed the emperor. The ports of Lisbon and Cadiz, it seemed, were always crowded with American vessels, protected by British licenses that permitted them to ship food to Wellington's army. French privateer attacks on these licensed merchantmen embarrassed and frustrated the president, but he continued to focus his anger on Britain, while condemning Bonaparte and denying any dependence on him.

Secretary of State Monroe underscored the distance the administration was keeping from Bonaparte in public by writing anti-French editorials in the *National Intelligencer*, which Madison sent to Joel Barlow, the harried American ambassador in Paris, telling him, "in the event of a pacification with Great Britain, the full tide of indignation with which the public mind here is boiling will be directed against France, if not obviated by a due reparation of her wrongs. War will be called for by the nation almost *una voce*."

Many years later, in 1827, Madison continued to insist that the American declaration of war and Napoleon's invasion happening at the same time were a "fortuitous" coincidence. "The moment chosen for the war," he said, "would, therefore, have been well chosen with a reference to the French expedition against Russia; and although not so chosen, the coincidence between the war and the expedition promised at the time to be as it was fortuitous."

"Had the French emperor not been broken down," Madison wrote in the same letter, "as he was to a degree at variance with all probability and which no human sagacity could anticipate, can it be doubted that Great Britain would have been constrained by her own situation and the demands of her allies to listen to our reasonable terms of reconciliation?"

No matter how much Madison protested, however, the fact remained that without Bonaparte, his war strategy was incomprehensible. The normal instruments a president used to fight a war, namely, an army and a navy, were not available to him. The pigmy American navy could not contend with Britain's mighty fleet, and the U. S. Army was in even worse shape than the navy. Led by a group of elderly generals, the army had not engaged in combat (except against Native Americans) since the end of the Revolution. Legislation in April 1808—hastily passed in response to the *Chesapeake-Leopard* affair—had authorized an increase in the regular force from 3,000 to 10,000, but its actual size fluctuated between 5,000 and 7,000. Low pay and miserly enlistment bonuses, coupled with America's deep political divisions, made recruitment excruciatingly difficult.

In June 1812 the army had men scattered in twenty-three locations around the nation's periphery. The tiny War Department was not organized to fight a major European power, and fifty-nine-year-old Dr. William Eustis, the secretary of war, was incapable of leading it. Eustis's experience of war was as a surgeon many years earlier. He had never commanded a fighting unit. A former medical student of Dr. Joseph Warren—the legendary patriot leader killed during the Battle of Bunker Hill—Eustis had bravely tended the wounded during that famous fight, placing his own life in danger, and for the rest of the war he served as a doctor in the Continental Army. Eventually he went into politics and became a powerful Republican ally of Jefferson and Madison. As good a man as Eustis was, however, he was utterly unqualified to lead the War Department.

By the same token, even a person of greater ability would have had enormous problems managing the department, raising an army in a country where the vast majority of men did not want to serve, or invading Canada when the congressmen who urged doing so did not dare raise taxes to fund it. Congress's refusal to increase taxes was an accurate barometer of public support for the war.

Even if the public were behind the war, the secretary had a staff of only eight clerks, and they had to handle Indian affairs and pensions as well as army business. Furthermore, Eustis did not have a quartermaster branch until the end of March 1812. Until then, that critical function was performed in the Treasury Department. From uniforms to food to artillery, the army suffered from organizational chaos. Only in the matter of muskets and gunpowder did the troops have adequate supplies. A vibrant small arms industry supplied the muskets, and gunpowder was plentiful.

Despite the well-known deficiencies of the army and navy, Madison could not let pass the singular opportunity presented by Napoleon's invasion of Russia. The time to act was now, he thought; to wait would be to lose his best chance of moving Spencer Perceval to change his American policy. The president had been threatening war for so long that he feared if he delayed any longer he would lose all credibility.

Lack of preparedness was not a reason to avoid war, Madison insisted. He thought that real preparations would begin only when war was actually declared. "It had become impossible to avoid or even delay war," he wrote, "at a moment when we were not prepared for it and when it was certain that effective preparations would not take place whilst the question of war was undecided." The president hoped the declaration would bring the country together and set in motion a real push to arm. He did not envision a long war. The sudden, unexpected declaration of one, he thought, might be enough to change Perceval's mind and bring peace before Christmas.

EVEN WITH THE army in the disorganized, embryonic state it was, Madison assumed—as did most Republicans, including Jefferson—that Canada was there for the taking. With a diverse population of less than half a million scattered over a wide expanse of territory and tenuously ruled by a not-very-popular British minority, the colony appeared exceptionally vulnerable. In the spring of 1812, forcing Britain out of Canada looked particularly easy. The British were tied down in Portugal, Spain, Sicily, Ireland, India, and the West Indies, and they now had to contend with an apparent Napoleonic victory in Russia. Only a token army of perhaps 7,000 of His Majesty's regulars was stationed in the Canadian provinces, and they were dispersed from Halifax to Quebec to Montreal, and farther west at Kingston, York, Detroit, and Lake Huron. Provincial troops supplemented the regulars, but their capacity and commitment were suspect. It had become an article of faith among Madison's supporters that, if attacked, Canada would fall like a ripe apple. Jefferson famously declared, "The acquisition of Canada this year [1812], as far as the neighborhood of Quebec, will be a mere matter of marching, and will give us experience for the attack of Halifax the next, and the final expulsion of England from the American continent." Jefferson told Revolutionary War hero General Thaddeus Kosciusko, "The partisans of England here [the Federalists] have endeavored much to goad us into the folly of choosing the ocean instead of the land. . . . That would be to meet their strength with our own weakness, instead of their weakness with our strength."

Chasing the British out of North America had long been a cherished dream of both Madison and Jefferson. Although they repeatedly denied being anti-British, their anger, in fact, ran deep. They had no love for Napoleon, but they believed the danger he presented was far less than that posed by Britain. The French dictator would eventually go too far, they felt; his ambition far exceeded his capacity, and, in any event, his system would die with him, whereas the British impulse to control the oceans and expand their empire had been exhibited for centuries through the reigns of many monarchs. Imperialism was inherent in the country's nature, they believed, and therefore a greater danger.

Conquering Canada would deprive hostile Indian nations of critical support from the British and cut off the supply of natural resources Britain required for her economy and defense. As Napoleon spread his dominion over Europe and shut down trade with Britain, the raw materials needed to sustain the Royal Navy came increasingly from Canada, making this vast territory, once considered of limited use to the fleet, critically important.

Madison planned to make a sudden thrust across the Canadian border as soon as Congress declared war, capitalizing on the eagerness of people in the western states of Kentucky, Ohio, and Tennessee and the territories of Indiana, Michigan, and Illinois to drive the British out of Canada. Along the entire American frontier, people were convinced that British agents operating out of Canada were inciting the Indian nations and supplying them with weapons. Feeling intensified when the charismatic chief Tecumseh and his brother Tenskwatawa (known as the Prophet) emerged as leaders of a movement to unite the tribes, north and south, and make them strong enough to secure their territory and their way of life. Tecumseh, who was part Shawnee and part Creek, adamantly opposed selling more Indian lands to the United States; he urged the tribes to remain true to their traditions and reject American attempts to turn them into docile farmers.

Tecumseh's power grew appreciably on September 30, 1809, when William Henry Harrison, governor of the Indiana Territory, concluded the lopsided Treaty of Fort Wayne with the Potawatomis, Miamis, Eel Rivers, Delawares, Lenape, Weas, and Kickapoos, dispossessing the tribes of over three million acres for an equivalent of $5,250. This was but one in a series of unequal treaties that Harrison had concluded with the Indians. Since becoming governor of the newly formed Indiana Territory in 1800, he had carried out President Jefferson's policy of turning as many Indians as possible into farmers. Jefferson wanted those who resisted to be driven west beyond the Mississippi. His policy left no room for Native Americans to remain on the land and pursue their traditional way of life.

The American government's tactics outraged Tecumseh. His movement, which had been strengthening since 1810, grew even stronger when the Treaty of Fort Wayne became fully understood. The contest between Tecumseh, the Prophet, and Harrison eventually led to the Battle of Tippecanoe on November 7, 1811, which was portrayed as a victory for Governor Harrison but led Tecumseh and his growing number of followers to draw ever closer to the British.

Governor Harrison was a great hero among settlers along the frontier, where people mindlessly placed all the blame for sour relations with the tribes on the British. In the western states and territories frontiersmen were convinced that, deprived of British aid, the Indians could easily be driven beyond the Mississippi, allowing Americans to appropriate their lands. A tidal wave of farmers and speculators awaited their opportunity.

Annexing Canada also had support in other areas of the country, although to a far lesser degree than in the South and West. Congressman John Adams Harper of Deerfield (Manchester), New Hampshire, for instance, believed that, "The Author of Nature marked our limits in the south by the south of Mexico, and on the north by the regions of eternal frosts."

Henry Clay, the new Speaker of the House in the 12th Congress, spoke for the westerners and southerners when he called for troops to drive Britain out of Canada. Clay was only thirty-four years old, and he was a new congressman, but he was nonetheless chosen Speaker. He provided the House of Representatives with more energy and direction than it had had since the days of Madison and Albert Gallatin in the 1790s. "We must take the continent from [the British]," he told the House. "I wish never to see a peace until we do."

Clay's enthusiasm was strengthened by the knowledge that perhaps 60 percent of Upper Canada's population of 90,000 were recent immigrants from the United States in search of cheap land and no taxes. Britain formed Upper Canada in 1791 by dividing the old province of Quebec into Upper Canada in the west and Lower Canada to the east. Upper Canada ran from Montreal west along the St. Lawrence River, around the northern shores of Lake Ontario, Lake Erie, Lake Huron, and Lake Superior. The British attracted new immigrants to the sparsely populated province by offering them free land and no taxes. Henry Clay believed that the thousands of former American farmers who had emigrated to Upper Canada probably had no loyalty to the small coterie of upper-class British loyalists who ruled them or to the distant king in London.

A small group of talented young congressmen between the ages of twenty-nine and thirty-six—dubbed by Madison's enemy, Congressman John Randolph of Virginia, as "War Hawks"—supported Clay. There were only about twelve War Hawks, but under Clay's skilled leadership they dominated the House in the 12th Congress, which ran from March 1811 to March 1813, and they had a strong influence on the president.

Four of the War Hawks were from South Carolina—John C. Calhoun, William Lowndes, David R. Williams, and Langdon Cheves, the chairman of the Naval Committee. Two were from Kentucky, Richard M. Johnson and Joseph Desha, and another was from Tennessee, Felix Grundy. George M. Troup was from Georgia, Peter B. Porter from western New York, and John A. Harper from New Hampshire. Speaker Clay, his wife, Lucretia, and their six children lived in the same Washington boardinghouse—known as the "war mess"—with Cheves, Lowndes, Calhoun, and Grundy. On occasion, Secretary of State Monroe was a dinner guest.

Madison never acknowledged publicly that his aim was to annex Canada. The president insisted the invasion was for the purpose of obtaining a bargaining tool, not for conquest. On June 13, 1812, Monroe explained, "In case of war it might be necessary to invade Canada; not as an object of the war, but as a means to bring it to a satisfactory conclusion." Few took him seriously. He admitted himself that it would be "difficult to relinquish territory which had been conquered."

Absorbing Canada was an old ambition of American patriots, going back to the earliest days of the Revolution. Once the United States had overrun Canada, it was inconceivable that Madison would give it back. The political backlash along the frontier would be fearsome. The president's strongest allies in the South and the West would have strenuously objected.

Southerners, including the president, had more on their minds than just Canada. On June 26, only days after Congress declared war, the House, with Madison's approval, passed a resolution allowing the president to occupy East Florida and the rest of West Florida. Madison had already occupied the portion of West Florida between the Mississippi and Pearl Rivers in 1810. He wanted to prevent the British from obtaining East Florida from their dependent ally Spain and also to realize an old dream of the South. On July 3, however, the Senate unexpectedly killed the measure by a vote of 16 to 14. Federalists voted against it as a bloc, and they were joined by Republicans Bradley of Vermont, Howell of Rhode Island, Leib of Pennsylvania, Giles of Virginia, and Samuel Smith of Maryland.

ALTHOUGH CANADA AND Napoleon were the most important elements of Madison's grand strategy, he thought privateers and letters of marque would give America a potent sea force. He expected dozens and then hundreds of privateers to put out from American ports, as they had during the Revolution. And he foresaw American merchantmen routinely applying for letters of marque, arming themselves, and looking to increase profits by capturing whatever unlucky British merchantman crossed their paths.

Madison expected little or nothing from the official navy. To be sure, trying to divine how the United States could fight the mighty British fleet was next to impossible. After years of neglect under two Republican administrations, America's navy—in a prosperous, seafaring country of nearly eight million—consisted of only twenty men-of-war, seven of which—the *Chesapeake, Constellation, New York, Adams, Essex, John Adams,* and *Boston* (all frigates and all built prior to Jefferson taking office in 1801)—were laid up for repairs. Some thought the *Boston* and the *New York* were so rotten they were beyond fixing. The Royal Navy, on the other hand, had 1,000 warships—at least 600 of which were continually at sea, while the rest were undergoing repairs or in various stages of completion.

Of course, most of Britain's fleet was occupied blockading Napoleonic Europe and servicing distant parts of the empire. The Admiralty's North American Station at Halifax had only one 64-gun ship-of-the-line, five frigates of between 32 and 38 guns, eleven sloops of war between 16 and 20 guns, and six smaller armed schooners and brigs. Even so, the Halifax squadron was stronger than anything the American navy could assemble. And Halifax was augmented by a small force at St. John's, Newfoundland, and larger fleets at Antigua in the Leeward Islands and at Port Royal, Jamaica.

The huge disparity of forces had long since led Madison to conclude the American fleet would be either blockaded, captured, or destroyed early in the war and be of no real help in securing victory. He could not say so publicly, of course, not even to his intimates—except perhaps for Jefferson and Albert Gallatin, the secretary of the Treasury—but the conclusion was inescapable.

Nonetheless, Madison still needed to concoct some plan for the navy, and when he held discussions with his advisors in the winter and spring of 1812, he toyed with the idea of keeping all the ships secure in their home ports, acting as defensive batteries and not venturing out to sea at all. At the time, the navy was spread thinly, from Portland in the Maine District of Massachusetts to New Orleans, with major bases at Portsmouth, New Hampshire; Boston; New York; Philadelphia; Washington; and Norfolk.

Hamilton and Gallatin were in favor of keeping the ships in port, but Madison was unsure. He had heard a version of the same strategy from Jefferson, who proposed gathering the fleet in a single place, presumably New York, keeping it safe, and not having it put to sea except on important occasions. In fact, Gallatin and Jefferson thought privateering should be the only naval weapon employed on the high seas. Instead of wasting scarce dollars on the navy, they urged spending it on the army for the invasion of Canada.

Concerned about the president's frame of mind, Charles Goldsborough, chief clerk of the navy, alerted two prominent captains who were in Washington at the time, William Bainbridge and Charles Stewart, and they protested loudly to both Hamilton and Madison. The two distraught officers explained the negative consequences of confining the fleet to port: British marauders would have the sea to themselves, they argued, with dire consequences for American trade and defense. They saw no reason to allow Britain such a luxury. When properly deployed, they maintained, the American navy could have an impact out of all proportion to its size. If the Admiralty had to contend with enemy frigates and sloops of war operating singly or in pairs over the vast ocean, it would be forced to employ a substantial fleet to convoy merchantmen, blockade ports, and hunt down America's elusive warships. Furthermore, Bainbridge and Stewart insisted, the individual ships in the U.S. fleet were better than their counterparts in the Royal Navy, and the American officer corps welcomed the chance to prove it.

While skeptical of Bainbridge and Stewart's claims, Madison paid some attention to their advice and rejected the recommendation of Gallatin and Hamilton. But he still did not commit himself to an alternate strategy. He remained uncertain. The only thing he was sure about was that the pipsqueak navy would not matter.

CHAPTER FIVE

The United States Declares War

MADISON APPROACHED HIS call for a declaration of war with great reluctance, so much so that some historians later claimed the War Hawks forced him into it. This view, however, overlooks the president's inner strength. He had a backbone that could withstand any political pressure. His desire for peace was the result not of a weak character but rather of deeply held convictions. Over the years, as leader in the House of Representatives, as secretary of state, and finally as president, he had worked hard to reconcile America's differences with Britain over free trade and impressment. And he continued to do so in the winter and spring of 1812. He tried to convince Prime Minister Perceval that American complaints about the Orders in Council and impressment could no longer be ignored, that the United States preferred war to dishonor.

But Perceval ignored the president's warnings. Had Congress passed the proposed naval expansion bill in January, or approved internal taxes to pay for a military buildup, or if New England Federalists had not been so relentless in their attacks on Madison, perhaps Perceval might have been more attentive. But no matter what the president said or did, the prime minister clung to his conviction that the Orders in Council and impressment were necessary for survival, even though they might lead to war with the United States. Perceval preferred that the Americans not declare war, of course, but he would not alter his policies to prevent it. And he did not believe for an instant that either Madison or Congress had the stomach for a fight. He thought that in the end the United States would swallow whatever indignities he heaped on her, because internal divisions and a miniscule army and navy would keep her leadership restrained. On May 30, only two days before Madison called for a declaration of war, the British ambassador in Washington reaffirmed to Secretary of State Monroe that the cabinet would not repeal the Orders.

It did not help matters that the British ambassador was thirty-two-year-old Sir John Augustus Foster, an upper-class Tory snob, with a pronounced dislike for the republic and an inability to understand its people or their politics. Foster was singularly unable to grasp Madison's determination to fight rather than submit to Perceval's indignities. The ambassador kept reporting to London what Perceval wanted to hear—that the president had no intention of asking for a declaration of war and the divided Congress had no intention of passing one. The pathetic state of America's armed forces was so notorious, and so often commented on in Congress and the press, that right up until war was actually declared, Foster believed that when the president or congressional leaders threatened war, they were bluffing. The ambassador was encouraged in his views by British sympathizers in the Federalist Party like Congressman Josiah Quincy of Massachusetts, the Federalist leader in the House of Representatives, who met with Foster regularly and confirmed that the president and the Republican Congress were not really contemplating war. It was not until May 1812 that Foster, responding to what he was hearing generally in Washington, began warning London of the possibility that Madison might be serious. But by then it was too late.

On the first of June the president delivered an impassioned appeal to Congress, urging a declaration of war against Great Britain for threatening "the United States as an independent and neutral nation." In listing America's grievances, Madison pointed first to impressment. "American citizens," he wrote, "under the safeguard of public law and of their national flag, have been torn from their country and everything dear to them; have been dragged on board ships of war of a foreign nation and exposed, under the severest of their discipline, to be exiled to the most distant and deadly climes, to risk their lives in the battles of their oppressors, and to be melancholy instruments of taking away those of their brethren."

The president then condemned "British cruisers [for] . . . violating the rights and peace of our coasts. They hover over and harass our entering and departing commerce," he wrote. "To the most insulting pretensions they have added the most lawless proceedings in our very harbors, and have wantonly spilt American blood within the sanctuary of our territorial jurisdiction." He further charged the British with "plundering our commerce in every sea." And he accused them of instituting a "sweeping system of blockades, under the name of orders in council . . . [which have established a] monopoly . . . for her own commerce and navigation." Lastly, he abhorred British encouragement of the Indian nations to war against America on her extensive frontiers. He said that the warfare spared "neither age nor sex and [was] . . . distinguished by features peculiarly shocking to humanity."

The House of Representatives immediately took up the president's appeal. In presenting the war measure to his colleagues, Congressman John C. Calhoun declared, "The United States must support their character and station among nations of the earth, or submit to the most shameful degradation." On June 4 the House approved the declaration of war 79 to 49. The Senate voted on June 17 and narrowly passed the measure 19 to 13. Madison signed the bill the following day. All thirty-nine Federalists voted against going to war; the Republicans in both houses voted 98 to 23 in favor.

Opposition was more of a party matter than a sectional one. To be sure, Federalist strength was centered in New England, but Federalists existed throughout the country, including in Virginia, South Carolina, and Maryland. Only in New England, however, did the party control state governments, as well as finance, shipping, and manufacturing. Republicans were spread across the country as well—even in New England. No area of the United States was completely under the control of either party. While the West and the South generally favored the war and the Northeast opposed it, the surest guide to one's position was his political party.

In addition to Federalist opposition, members of the president's own party, like Congressman John Randolph of Roanoke Virginia, spokesman for the Old Republicans or the so-called Quids faction of the Republican Party, also opposed the war. In May, as war approached, the eccentric Randolph appeared on the House floor in hunting garb, complete with boots and spurs, a whip, and a favorite hound. He shouted in his high-pitched voice, "Go to war without money, without men, without a navy! Go to war when we have not the courage, while your lips utter war, to lay war taxes! When your whole courage is exhibited in passing resolutions."

Randolph insisted that war would endanger the South's way of life. Citing old fears slaveholders had of war loosening "habits of subordination," he predicted uprisings that would destroy the easy life plantation masters and their families enjoyed. Randolph declared that as bad as Britain was, Napoleon was much worse. He said that if the French navy dominated the oceans instead of the British, Napoleon would make life hell for the United States. Why, Randolph asked, would Americans associate themselves with a tyrant who was worse than Attila the Hun?

The declaration of war exacerbated the country's already deep political divisions. Federalists were outraged that the president and his party were committing the country to a de facto alliance with Napoleonic France. They viewed Britain as America's natural ally. On June 26, eight days after Madison signed the declaration, Federalist governor Caleb Strong of Massachusetts issued a proclamation famously calling for a public fast on July 23 to protest the war resolution "against the nation from which we are descended and which for many generations has been the bulwark of the religion we profess." Governor Strong wanted, among other things, to allow the vehemently antiwar Massachusetts clergy to rail against Madison's war from their pulpits. The lower house of the Massachusetts legislature urged citizens to "let the sound of your disapprobation of this war be loud and deep." Josiah Quincy told his constituents that the war was "an event awful, unexpected, hostile to your interests, menacing to your liberties, and revolting to your feelings."

A sickening incident in Baltimore demonstrated the degree to which political differences were tearing the country apart. Four days after the war declaration, on June 22, a Republican mob attacked Alexander C. Hanson's Federalist newspaper, the *Federal Republican*. Readers could depend on Hanson to bitterly oppose Madison no matter what he did, but when the disgruntled publisher heard war had been declared, he was apoplectic. His June 19 issue was so vehement in its denunciation of the president that the next day a Republican mob broke into his newspaper, smashed the printing presses, and destroyed the building, shutting down the paper—they thought for good.

The fiery Hanson was not so easily silenced, however. With help from his partner, Jacob Wagner, he removed to Georgetown and in five days put out a paper again, distributing it in Baltimore as well as Georgetown and Washington. That was not good enough, though; Hanson was determined to go back to Baltimore and set up his operation again. He asked Revolutionary War heroes General Henry (Light-Horse Harry) Lee and General James Lingan to find a suitable fortresslike edifice in Baltimore where he could set up a new press. He also elicited help from a number of Federalist friends who wanted to defy the Republican mob. In a remarkably short time, Hanson began publishing out of a well-fortified brick building in Baltimore. His first newspaper hit the streets on July 27, and, predictably, he defied the Republican goons by lambasting the president.

That night, a menacing crowd gathered outside Hanson's building. Inside, two dozen armed supporters waited nervously, and when the mob pressed forward toward them, they fired into the crowd, killing Dr. Thadeus Gale, one of the mob leaders, and wounding several others. In a fury, the Republicans left the scene and procured an artillery piece, whereupon Baltimore's authorities intervened and persuaded Hanson and his men, including the venerable Lee and Lingan, to move to the protection of the city's jail. Not to be deterred, a vicious gang of Republicans broke into the jail after the guards had retired for the evening. The frenzied mob attacked the defenseless prisoners, killing General Lingan, bludgeoning Lee (who remained crippled for life) and Hanson, while maiming nine others.

Federalist newspapers throughout the country, but especially in New England, expressed horror. They denounced the Republican massacre, likening it to deadly Jacobin rampages in France. Federalists accused Madison of condoning the violence and predicted he would soon attempt to suppress opinion throughout the country.

Just the opposite was the case, however. The mob's violence upset the president and most other Republicans, and it no doubt influenced them to be more tolerant of Federalist dissent. Madison had nothing but contempt for the Baltimore miscreants. He had no intention of suppressing political opinion, as the Federalists tried to do when they passed the sedition law during the Quasi-War with France. Madison was determined to allow all opinions to have free rein—even in wartime. Hanson's *Federal Republican* remained in circulation throughout the war, viciously criticizing Madison with impunity.

IRONICALLY, AFTER MADISON finally decided to go to war, the British government unexpectedly changed. On May 11, a man named Bellingham, for reasons wholly imaginary and personal to him, put a bullet through Perceval's heart as he entered Parliament, killing him instantly. The prime minister was on his way to attend a meeting of a parliamentary committee to urge continued support for the Orders in Council, which had become increasingly unpopular with a growing number of members.

Confusion followed as the British tried to form a new government. The prince regent, who had assumed the duties of monarch from his father George III, who was mentally ill, had trouble finding a leader who was willing and able to fashion a new government. Time passed. Finally, the veteran Lord Liverpool, secretary of state for war and the colonies, a member of the House of Lords, and a loyal Perceval supporter, took on the assignment and on June 8 announced the formation of a new cabinet.

Liverpool believed his tenure as prime minister would be brief, but he was to serve in that stressful post for the next fifteen years. His longevity can be accounted for by his extensive experience in high office before becoming prime minister and for his consistent pragmatism. His political strength derived from an ability to get along with his colleagues and a willingness to adjust his policies to the changing views of Parliament and the country.

When Liverpool took office, war with the United States was becoming more likely, and he moved to head it off. Avoiding a war with America was the one matter that the cabinet and Parliament were agreed on. Liverpool and his colleagues had a high appreciation of the mortal danger Napoleon presented, and they were hearing loud cries to reopen the huge American market from distressed merchants, manufacturers, and workmen. On June 16 Foreign Minister Castlereagh (Liverpool's leader in the House of Commons) told members that the ministry intended to suspended the Orders in Council, and on June 23 it did.

At last, a British government appeared willing to do what Madison and Jefferson had long hoped—ease its maritime restrictions on the United States. But it was too late; the news did not reach Washington in time. Had it, Madison's hand might have been stayed. But by the time he learned of the repeal, he had already made the decision for war, and the British had said nothing about impressment, which Madison considered an even greater affront than the Orders in Council.

The president insisted that he had done everything possible to honorably avoid a rupture with Britain. "Arguments and expostulations had been exhausted," he wrote, and "a positive declaration had been received [from Perceval] that the wrongs provoking [the declaration of war] would not be discontinued." For Madison, war "could no longer be delayed without breaking down the spirit of the nation, destroying all confidence in itself and in its political institutions . . . [and losing all hope of regaining] our lost rank and respect among independent powers." If Americans did not fight for their rights on the high seas now, Madison argued, they were "not independent people, but colonists and vassals."

On the day Congress declared war, Ambassador Foster was chagrined by an event he had long predicted would never happen. He was so rattled he failed to inform the governor-general of Canada, Sir George Prevost, that war had been declared and Canada was threatened with an invasion. (That vital piece of intelligence would have to come from the alert agent for the British North American Company in New York.) Knowing his government did not want a war, Foster hurried to the White House and asked the president for a suspension of hostilities until he could obtain London's reaction to the declaration. But Madison turned him down.

Unaware the Orders in Council had already been repealed, the ambassador then asked if repealing them and beginning negotiations on impressment would be enough to change the president's mind. Again, Madison said no. He did not want to forfeit the advantage of immediate military action before the British were ready, when he had no idea if London would change its policies. What's more, the president's Canadian invasion depended on a prompt attack.

The following evening Foster attended Dolley Madison's weekly levee at the White House—as was his habit—and found her and the president shaking hands with guests, congratulating each another on the declaration of war. Foster later claimed that the president was "white as a sheet," but the *New York Evening Post*, which opposed the war, reported that he was "all life and spirits." Actually, Madison was deadly serious, neither elated nor afraid. He felt the enormous burden he had taken on, and he was willing to bear it. Foster was understandably bitter that he had misled his government about the president's willingness to fight, thus playing a not insignificant part in bring the war about.

A few days later, on June 23, a more realistic basis for a suspension of hostilities appeared when the *National Intelligencer* reported Perceval's assassination. Believing this presaged dramatic changes in policy, Foster hurried back to the White House and again asked for an armistice until a new cabinet could make its views known. He thought it likely the next ministry would repair relations with the United States.

Madison again rejected the idea, however, and Foster was furious. "As our councils appeared likely to become weaker," he wrote, "the American cabinet felt stronger, and had a disposition to bully. They now insisted on the impressment question as the main point at issue and declared that a modification, or even a repeal of the Orders in Council would not suffice without a final settlement of the questions of impressment and blockade; and, as the Congress were separating, the Government declared they had no power during recess to do more than listen to our proposals."

Although Madison would not agree to an immediate armistice, he did arrange for the American chargé d'affaires in London, Jonathan Russell, to remain there, and for British legation secretary Anthony Baker to stay in Washington and keep a channel open for negotiations after Ambassador Foster returned home. Madison also agreed to let British packet boats pass freely under a flag of truce. When he made these decisions, he was confident about the pressure of events moving the new British government. Negotiations with the Liverpool ministry were made more difficult, however, by the fact that the experienced American ambassador to Britain, William Pinkney, had left London back in April 1811, and Madison had not replaced him. Pinkney departed because he felt Perceval would never change his hard-line policies toward the United States.

When Foster sailed back to London, he carried with him a ciphered dispatch for Chargé Russell, containing Madison's terms for ending hostilities. "To render the justice of the war on our part the more conspicuous," the president explained later, "the reluctance to commence it was followed by the earliest and strongest manifest disposition to arrest its progress. The sword was scarcely out of the scabbard, before the enemy was apprised of the reasonable terms on which it would have been resheathed."

The president's terms were: Repeal the Orders in Council; end illegal, or paper, blockades; provide indemnities for spoliations; cease impressment; and dismiss impressed Americans from the Royal Navy. Russell delivered Madison's message to Castlereagh on August 24.

Russell did not need to point out to Castlereagh the obvious: If Britain did not act now to conciliate the United States, the president would be forced into ever closer relations with France. Russell had no way to divine Napoleon's thinking, of course. No one did, not even his closest advisors. He kept his own counsel and could change his mind with disturbing rapidity. It was safe to say, however, that Bonaparte was pleased to have Britain and America at each other's throats. But at the same time, he was unhappy that American food shipments to Wellington's army in Spain were continuing under British licenses. Madison refused to end them for fear of political repercussions in Pennsylvania and other states, where farmers and shipowners were reaping handsome profits from the trade. It was an election year, after all, and Pennsylvania was critical to the president's reelection. At Madison's urging, Congress had enacted a ninety-day embargo on April 4 prohibiting shipments to Britain of all kinds, but an exception was made for grain going to Wellington.

MEANWHILE, WITH THE Napoleonic danger looming ever larger, Lord Liverpool also hoped to have a quick end to a conflict that had begun, in his view, by mistake. On July 22, the British 10-gun brig *Bloodhound* arrived at Annapolis with official word that the Orders in Council had been withdrawn, and on August 5 Chargé Baker went to the White House and presented the news to Madison, telling him that the Orders were suspended as of August 1. Baker also informed the president that Admiral Sawyer at Halifax was anxious to work out the details of an armistice, as was Governor-General Prevost and the lieutenant governor of Nova Scotia, Sir John Sherbrooke. Madison's reaction was that he had sent his terms to Russell, and they would have to be accepted before he would consider an armistice. The president did not want the war effort weakened by premature talk of peace, when the British had not actually agreed to his conditions.

Madison was right to be cautious, for when Foreign Secretary Castlereagh saw the president's proposals, he rejected them out of hand. He wrote to Russell on August 29 that His Majesty's government could not, under any circumstances, "consent to suspend the exercise of a right [impressment] upon which the naval strength of the Empire mainly depends." Castlereagh believed, with good cause, that if he accepted Madison's terms, he would be thrown out of office, as would the entire ministry. And those who replaced them would not accept American terms either.

Anticipating this response, Russell offered "to give assurance that a law shall be passed (to be reciprocal) to prohibit the employment of British seamen in the public or commercial service of the United States." Monroe had authorized Russell to offer the British, by an act of Congress, a prohibition on the employment of British seamen in the public or private marine of the United States. And Madison wrote an editorial in the *National Intelligencer* offering to "prevent the employment of British seamen in American vessels if Britain would stop making impressments from them."

But Castlereagh would not be moved. British seamen could easily obtain American papers (bogus or real) by purchase or theft, making it impossible to determine who were British subjects. Castlereagh considered impressment so vital to British interests that only a guarantee that the Royal Navy could retrieve British seamen from American ships would suffice. This could only be accomplished, in his view, by the Royal Navy searching the vessels. He emphasized that no British government could rely on the United States, no matter what legislation was passed, to retrieve her deserters. Few in Britain disagreed with him. The *Times* wrote that giving up the impressment of British subjects on American ships is to "demand of us the sacrifice of our very existence." Castlereagh was willing to admit that in practice overly zealous British officers had committed abuses, and he was willing to talk about putting a rein on them but not about the necessity of stopping and searching American ships for deserters.

Castlereagh's rejection of Madison's terms made it clear that impressment was at the heart of the dispute between the two governments. It would remain so throughout the war. Madison pointed out later that Castlereagh's attitude left him no alternative but to fight. "Still more precise advances were repeated," the president wrote, "and have been received in a spirit forbidding every reliance not placed on the military resources of the nation."

At the same time that he was trying to negotiate a quick settlement with the British, Madison was taking a tougher line with Napoleon, threatening that if the United States reached a settlement with Britain, she would turn on France for the depredations Bonaparte had committed over many years and was continuing. The French dictator was unimpressed. Ambassador Joel Barlow did his best to convey the president's messages to the emperor and, in fact, later died trying to do so, but Barlow failed to make an impression.

No matter how badly Napoleon treated the United States, however, Madison was determined to uphold the country's honor by fighting Britain. He knew he could not fight both the British and the French at the same time; he chose the one he considered the more serious threat.

CHAPTER SIX

∽∽∽∽∽∽∽

Blue-Water Victories

WHEN COMMODORE JOHN Rodgers spotted H.M.S. *Belvidera* on June 23 and began the first naval action of the war, he was operating far beyond the orders given to him by Secretary of the Navy Paul Hamilton, who had instructed Rodgers to remain close to New York with his squadron and await further orders. Even though war had been declared five days earlier, the president still had not decided how to employ his miniscule fleet.

During the first three weeks of June, Rodgers, expecting war to be declared, had waited in New York for specific orders. But none came. As the days passed, he grew more anxious, fearing a superior British fleet might sail down from Halifax, Nova Scotia, and trap his squadron in New York. The commodore had the *President* and her crew set to weigh the moment he received new orders from Washington. What he received instead was a letter from Secretary Hamilton warning that hostilities were likely (which Rodgers already knew) and urging, "For God's sake get ready and let us strike a good blow."

Rodgers didn't need prodding; he had his men and ship well prepared. What he lacked was specific orders tied to an overall strategy. Being told to "strike a good blow" was not a substitute. Madison had known for months that hostilities were likely. Early in the year, he had held discussions with his advisors on how to deploy the fleet, but as war approached, he still had not settled on a strategy. Instead, he ordered what few warships were ready for sea to assemble in New York under Rodgers's command and await further instructions. Rodgers was still waiting for them when, on Saturday, June 20, Revolutionary War hero Brigadier

General Joseph Bloomfield, commander of the army in New York, told him that war had been declared. Early the next morning, a signal gun sounded from the *President*, alerting all officers and men to repair on board. Before long, the entire crew mustered on the big frigate's weather deck. "Now lads," the stern-faced Rodgers told them, "we have got something to do that will shake the rust from our jackets. War is declared! We shall have another dash at our old enemies. It is the very thing you have long wanted. The rascals have been bullying us these ten years, and I am glad the time is come at last when we can have satisfaction. If there are any among you who are unwilling to risk your lives with me, say so, and you shall be paid off and discharged. I'll have no skulkers on board my ship, by God!"

Their patriotic instincts aroused, the crew greeted Rodgers's words with spontaneous cheers. Every man declared his willingness to remain aboard and fight. As on all American warships, the crew was made up of a variety of men. Many were foreigners—often British citizens from Ireland. Some of the foreigners were naturalized Americans, but most were not. Those who had served in the British navy, whether they hailed from Ireland, Scotland, Wales, or England, were happy to be in the far more benign American service, even though they risked hanging if they were caught. The majority of Rodgers's crew, however, were Americans, including a number of free African Americans.

Even though Rodgers could be a choleric taskmaster, his officers and crew respected him as an experienced leader who could bring them glory and prize money. Before joining the navy in 1798 during the Quasi-War with France, Rodgers had been in the merchant marine for eleven years, learning his trade and rising to become a captain, sailing out of Baltimore. President Adams appointed him to be second officer aboard the famed frigate *Constellation,* under Captain Thomas Truxtun. Rodgers was twenty-four years old and soon became the first lieutenant, playing a major role in the *Constellation*'s victory over the French frigate *L'Insurgent*, the most famous battle of the Quasi-War. He absorbed invaluable lessons from Truxtun in how to manage a warship. Rodgers was already a tough disciplinarian, but Truxtun, who was also a stern skipper, showed Rodgers how to avoid becoming a martinet. Truxtun believed that physical punishment should be used sparingly aboard an American man-of-war. Having to whip a man demonstrated the absence of leadership. Rodgers rarely administered a beating aboard the *President.*

After the Quasi-War with France, Rodgers played a leading role in the war against Tripoli. In June 1805 he brought an end to the conflict by threatening an all-out attack on the capital of Tripoli with a large American fleet. And two months later, Rodgers used his fleet to force a settlement on the ruler of Tunis. After the war Rodgers suffered through the navy's lean years during Jefferson's second term and Madison's early presidency, remaining committed to the service and its high standards.

HEARTENED BY THE crew's enthusiasm for getting to sea, Rodgers weighed anchor at 10 A.M. on June 21 and saluted New York. The 16-gun sloop of war *Hornet*, under Master Commandant James Lawrence, pulled her hook at the same time and saluted the city as well. The two ships then dropped down the Upper Bay with a fair wind, passed through the Narrows to the Lower Bay and then to Sandy Hook, arriving early in the afternoon. Waiting for them were three additional warships that had come up from Norfolk under thirty-three-year-old Commodore Stephen Decatur.

Secretary Hamilton had ordered Decatur to take what ships were available at the Norfolk naval base and join Rodgers in New York, but for what purpose the secretary did not say. Decatur could muster only his flagship, the 44-gun *United States*; the 36-gun *Congress*, under John Smith; and the 16-gun brig *Argus*, under Lieutenant Arthur Sinclair. At the same time, Hamilton had ordered Captain Isaac Hull, skipper of the *Constitution*—then refitting at the Washington Navy Yard—to join Rodgers as soon as possible and Captain David Porter, commander of the 32-gun *Essex*—undergoing repairs at the New York Navy Yard in Brooklyn—to join Rodgers when his ship was ready.

Decatur had been anchored at Sandy Hook for two days, waiting impatiently for Rodgers. He wasn't happy that Madison had decided to assemble all of the navy's serviceable men-of-war in one place, risking entrapment or destruction by the Halifax squadron. Decatur had written to Hamilton on June 8 suggesting that instead of concentrating the navy's few ships in one area, he should send them "out with as large a supply of provisions as they can carry, distant from our coast and singly, or no more than two frigates in company, without giving them any specific instructions as to place of cruising, but to rely on the enterprise of the officers. . . . If war takes place, it will . . . be of greatest importance to the country that we should receive our instruction and be sent out before the declaration shall be known to the enemy—it would no doubt draw from our coast in search of us, the greater part of their cruisers."

Despite this advice, the president remained undecided about what to do with the navy, and his confusion was heightened by the fact that Rodgers was giving him markedly different counsel from Decatur's. Rodgers thought the fleet should be kept together, not sent out singly. He envisioned his squadron attacking large convoys and scattered warships before the British knew a war was on. He thought that having a potent American fleet offshore would force the British to keep their Halifax squadron together, away from the coast, looking for the American fleet. This would allow the huge number of American merchantmen then at sea to return home safely. The Royal Navy did not have enough ships at their North American base to go after Rodgers's squadron and at the same time blockade the coast.

The American navy's principal target ought to be British commerce, Rodgers argued. He urged attacking the great merchant fleets sailing between the West Indies and England and those near the coasts of Britain itself, "menacing them in the very teeth, and effecting the destruction of their commerce in a manner the most perplexing to their government, and in a way the least expected by the nation generally, including those belonging to the Navy: the self styled Lords of the Ocean!!" Rodgers assured Hamilton that Britain's home islands were poorly defended, that her huge fleets were deployed far from her shores.

At three o'clock on the afternoon of the twenty-first, while he was waiting off Sandy Hook, Rodgers received another message from Secretary Hamilton dated June 18: "I apprize you that war has been this day declared. . . . For the present it is desirable that with the force under your command you remain in such position as to enable you most conveniently to receive further, more extensive, and more particular orders, which will be conveyed to you through New York. But, as it is understood that there are one or more British cruisers on the coast in the vicinity of Sandy Hook, you are at your discretion free to strike them, returning immediately after into port. . . . Extend these orders to Commodore Decatur."

The title of commodore was not a permanent rank in the navy; it was an honorary title assigned to the commander of a squadron. Rodgers was senior to Decatur and would be in command of the five- to seven-ship squadron assembling at New York. At age forty Rodgers was the navy's second ranking officer. Fifty-seven-year-old Revolutionary War veteran Commodore Alexander Murray, commandant of the Philadelphia Navy Yard, was senior to him, but Murray was nearly deaf and considered too old for sea duty, which made Rogers the fleet's senior officer in command.

Rodgers would have preferred more specific orders long before now, but he could not wait for them. His first priority was simply getting to sea, where he'd be safe from a blockade and where his location would be unknown. This would affect the calculations of Vice Admiral Herbert Sawyer, the British commander at Halifax—once he knew a war was on. Rodgers hoped Sawyer would not find out for a while and might have his men-of-war scattered, allowing the American squadron to pick them off in detail (one at a time). "We may be able to cripple and reduce their force," Rodgers explained to Secretary Hamilton, ". . . to such an extent as to place our own upon a footing until their loss can be supplied by a reinforcement from England."

WITHIN TEN MINUTES of receiving Hamilton's latest message, Rodgers hoisted the signal to weigh anchor, and shortly thereafter the potent American squadron glided past the lighthouse on Sandy Hook and stood out into the Atlantic. If Rodgers remained at sea for any length of time, he would be acting contrary to Hamilton's instructions. Nonetheless, he ignored his orders and set a course to intercept a huge Jamaica convoy of perhaps one hundred and ten merchantmen that regularly sailed during June and July from the Caribbean to England. Rodgers and Decatur agreed to split prize money evenly—a common practice.

The Jamaica convoy's general route was well-known. Using the Gulf Stream and the prevailing southwesterly winds, the convoy would work up the Atlantic coast until it caught the westerlies north of Bermuda and use them to power it to England. The convoy would have escorts, of course. Since Parliament passed the Convoy Act in 1798, all British merchantmen were required to sail in protected convoys. But that didn't faze Rodgers: His squadron would normally be much stronger than the men-of-war guarding the Jamaica convoy. If all went well, his fleet would capture or sink the escorting warships and then destroy or take much of the convoy as prizes. It would be the rousing start to the conflict that the administration hoped for but scarcely expected. And it would create a row in London; Parliament would want to know why the government had not anticipated war breaking out and positioned a squadron off New York to blockade Rodgers. At a minimum, disrupting the convoy would embarrass the Liverpool ministry.

WHILE RODGERS WAS putting out from New York, Secretary of the Treasury Gallatin wrote a hasty note to the president expressing concern that a significant percentage of the American merchant fleet—whose captains had no way of knowing war had been declared—were at sea and would be vulnerable to British attacks, particularly when they approached their home ports. Back on April 4, when Madison and Congress passed the ninety-day embargo on all shipments to Britain in order to pressure London, large numbers of American merchantmen put to sea before the law went into effect. Gallatin worried about the effect on the U.S. Treasury if it were deprived of the customs duties from these ships. He expected that "arrivals from foreign ports will for the coming four weeks average from one to one-and-a-half million dollars a week." He considered it of the first importance that Madison direct the navy "to protect these and our coasting vessels, whilst the British have still an inferior force on our coasts. . . . I think orders to that effect, ordering them to cruise accordingly, ought to have been sent yesterday, and that, at all events, not one day longer ought to be lost. I will wait on you tomorrow at one o'clock."

Gallatin had little difficulty convincing Madison, and on the following day, June 22, Hamilton wrote to Rodgers, ordering him to consider the returning American merchant fleet his first priority. To protect it, Rodgers was to take the *President, Essex, John Adams, Hornet,* and *Nautilus* on patrol from the Chesapeake Capes eastward, while Decatur patrolled from New York southward with the *United States,* the *Congress,* and the *Argus.* Hamilton expected the two squadrons to overlap somewhat, creating the possibility they might at times act in concert.

The orders appeared to be a compromise between Rodgers's idea of a unified fleet and Decatur's preference for a dispersed one, but they were actually based on Gallatin's concerns and issued with little thought, since the president had no overall strategy. Fortunately, Rodgers did not receive Hamilton's instructions for many weeks—after he returned from his cruise. If carried out, they would have left both squadrons so weak they would have been easy targets for the Halifax fleet. Neither Gallatin nor the president nor Hamilton, it would seem, considered that possibility.

AFTER HIS FRUSTRATING encounter with the *Belvidera* on June 23, Rodgers— with his broken leg in splints—continued hunting for the rich Jamaica convoy, repairing the *President* as he went. He had a good idea of where his prey was. Hours before running into the *Belvidera,* he had spoken with the American brig *Indian Chief* out of Madeira bound for New York. Her master reported that four days earlier he spotted a huge convoy—over a hundred ships, he thought— eastbound in latitude 36° north and longitude 67° west (just north of Bermuda). A frigate and a brig were escorting them.

Rodgers had no doubt that the ships the *Indian Chief* saw were the merchantmen he was after. The huge convoy had sailed from Negril Bay, Jamaica, on May 20 and passed the eastern tip of Cuba on June 4, guarded by the 36-gun frigate H.M.S. *Thalia* (Captain James Vashon) and the 18-gun sloop of war *Reindeer* (Captain Manners)—easy pickings for Rodgers. He estimated the convoy was only three hundred miles away.

ON JULY 3, while Rodgers was on the hunt, Captain David Porter put out to sea from New York in the restored *Essex*. The commandant of the New York Navy Yard in Brooklyn, Captain Isaac Chauncey, had brought the old frigate up to a high state of readiness, careening her, cleaning and repairing the copper bottom, caulking her inside and out, putting on a false keel, and replacing all the masts. Although she had been launched thirteen long years ago in Salem, Massachusetts, during the Quasi-War with France, she was ready for combat, and so was her skipper.

As he passed Sandy Hook and drove into the Atlantic, Captain Porter was in high spirits. No British squadron was about, and the day before, he had received his promotion to captain—after an inordinately long wait, he thought. His orders, dated June 24, directed him to join Rodgers's squadron, but it was nowhere in sight, and Porter was glad of it. He'd rather be on his own, free to conduct the hunt as he saw fit, without being under Rodgers's thumb, having to share laurels and prize money.

If Porter failed to find Rodgers, his orders directed him to patrol between Bermuda and Newfoundland's Grand Banks. Eight days out from Sandy Hook, on July 11, the *Essex* was in latitude 33° north and longitude 66° west—northeast of the Bermudas—when at two o'clock in the morning a lookout glimpsed the vague outlines of eight ships in the distance, running northward. Porter was out of bed and on deck in a hurry. He grabbed a telescope, and with the moon providing some hazy light, he counted seven troop transports, with a frigate as an escort. The vessels were spread apart in loose formation typical of convoys in which ships sailed at different speeds.

Porter decided to attack the rearmost vessel and cut her out in hopes of provoking a fight with the frigate. As the *Essex* closed in, the armed transport *Samuel & Sarah*—carrying 197 soldiers—did not attempt to escape. Porter had the weather gauge, and when he fired a single shot across her bow, she hauled down her colors. Her skipper assumed his escorting frigate, the 32-gun *Minerva* (Captain Richard Hawkins), would quickly engage the enemy.

By then it was 4 A.M., and, as expected, the *Minerva* broke away from the convoy and steered toward the *Essex*. Within a short time, however, she inexplicably came about and returned to the middle of the troop transports. Porter was puzzled. He was eager for a fight; the two frigates appeared evenly matched. He could not understand why Hawkins did not accept his challenge. Instead, the *Minerva* drew the remaining armed transports around her, so they could act in consort, and sailed on, daring Porter to approach.

Captain Hawkins's orders were to transport the First Regiment of Royal Scots infantrymen from Barbados to Quebec and reinforce the small Canadian army. He probably judged it more important to accomplish his mission than to take on the *Essex*, although he must have wanted to. Except in extraordinary circumstances, no British captain would avoid fighting an American of equal strength. Doing so would earn him a court-martial and severe punishment.

With the odds now heavily against him, Porter decided it would be suicide to fight the entire convoy and settled for just taking the *Samuel & Sarah*. The number of men she had on board presented a problem, however. Porter did not want to be encumbered by so many prisoners. After throwing her armament overboard, he released the transport and all the soldiers on parole with a ransom bond of $14,000 and continued his cruise.

WHILE RODGERS AND Porter were off hunting in the mid-Atlantic, Commodore Philip B. V. Broke's Halifax squadron arrived off Sandy Hook on July 14, only to discover that Rodgers's fleet was gone and the *Essex* nowhere in sight. Broke's task force was formidable; it consisted of his flagship, the 38-gun frigate *Shannon*, the 64-gun battleship *Africa* (Captain John Bastard), the 38-gun *Guerriere* (Captain James R. Dacres), the 32-gun *Aeolus* (Captain Lord James Townsend), and the 36-gun *Belvidera*—fully recovered from her run-in with Rodgers and still under Captain Richard Byron.

Two days later, Broke happened on the 12-gun American brig *Nautilus*, under Lieutenant William Crane, who had sailed out of New York on July 15, passing Sandy Hook at 6 P.M. with a fresh, squally wind out of the northeast. At 4 the following morning Crane was seventy-five miles off Sandy Hook when he spied Broke's squadron two points off his weather beam. He immediately wore ship, "turned out the reefs and made all sail the vessel would bear."

Crane was carrying yet more orders from Secretary Hamilton to Rodgers dated July 10. They read: "There will be a strong British force on our coast in a few days—be upon your guard—we are anxious for your safe return into port." This was a far cry from Hamilton's bombastic "strike a good blow" of a month earlier, when war had not actually been declared. When the declaration was made official on June 18, he toned down his aggressive talk and became more cautious. The new orders were apparently meant to keep the American fleet safe in New York and not have it out patrolling. Hamilton's lack of consistency was for the most part caused by Madison's continued indecision about naval strategy.

As soon as Broke spotted the *Nautilus*, he bore up and made all sail in chase, displaying American colors. A heavy swell from the north slowed the *Nautilus* and gave the bigger ships an edge. When Broke closed in, he made recognition signals that Crane did not understand. At the same time, Crane hoisted his own private signal and ensign, which Broke did not answer. Not that Crane expected him to; it had been clear from the beginning that this was a British squadron.

Crane was forced to take in sail to preserve spars, while Broke continued to gain. "Every maneuver in trimming ship was tried," Crane reported, "but this not having the desired effect I ordered the anchors cut from the bows." Nothing helped. "At nine o'clock the wind became lighter, and the brig labored excessively in the swell."

With Broke closing in, Crane threw overboard part of his water, the lee guns, and a portion of his round shot. Instantly, the *Nautilus* was relieved and bore her sail with greater ease. But Broke continued to close. By 11 the *Shannon* had pulled within cannon shot, and for some unknown reason, Broke hoisted French colors but held his fire. Seeing no need to destroy the *Nautilus*, he kept pressing forward. At midnight he was within musket shot.

Knowing he could not escape, Crane destroyed his signal books and the dispatches for Rodgers. He then consulted his principal officers and decided to surrender. Crane took in the studding sails and light sails, trained the weather guns aft, and put the helm alee. Broke responded by putting the *Shannon*'s helm up, hoisting a broad pendant and British colors, and ranging up under the *Nautilus*'s lee quarter to accept Crane's surrender.

In short order, the *Shannon*'s boats rowed over to take possession of the *Nautilus*. They returned later with Lieutenant Crane, who had a strained chat with his captor. Broke then put the officers and crew of the *Nautilus* in the battleship *Africa*, except for Crane, whom he sent back to the *Nautilus* as a lone prisoner with a British prize crew. The *Nautilus* was the first British capture of the war, and for the time being, Broke made her part of his squadron.

WHILE BROKE WAS corralling the *Nautilus*, Captain Isaac Hull was at sea in the newly refurbished *Constitution*, sailing from Chesapeake Bay to New York with orders to join Rodgers and Decatur. Hull departed the Chesapeake Capes on Sunday morning, July 12, with a fine southwesterly breeze, expecting to be off

Figure 6.1: Samuel L. Waldo, *Commodore Isaac Hull, USN (1773-1843)* (courtesy of U.S. Naval Academy Museum).

Sandy Hook within five days. His latest orders showed that the president and Secretary Hamilton were still confused about strategy. Rodgers had already left New York, which Hamilton had had time to learn, and he also knew a powerful British squadron was sailing down from Halifax to the New York area. Nonetheless, Hamilton ordered Hull to sail directly into the jaws of Broke's fleet and certain disaster. "If . . . you fall in with an enemy vessel," Hamilton wrote, "you will be guided in your proceedings by your own judgment, bearing in mind, however, that you are not voluntarily to encounter a force superior to your own. On your arrival at New York, you will report yourself to Commodore Rodgers. If he should not be in port, you will remain there till further orders."

This was the *Constitution*'s first cruise since April 5, when Hull had put into the Washington Navy Yard for extensive repairs. Of the navy's six major shipyards, where men-of-war were built, fitted out, and repaired, the Washington yard was generally considered the best and Portsmouth, New Hampshire, the worst. The others—New York, Boston, Philadelphia, and Norfolk—were rated in between. Hull considered New York better because it was supervised by Captain Isaac Chauncey. By putting into the Washington Navy Yard, however, he wasn't sacrificing anything. The superintendent, Commodore Thomas Tingey, had been in charge since the yard's inception in January 1800, and he had established a solid record.

Hull had been skipper of the *Constitution* for two years, having taken command from John Rodgers on July 17, 1810. She was in poor condition then, not having had an extensive overhaul since 1803. Rodgers was leaving her because he wanted another ship, and, asserting his seniority, he had taken command of the *President*, which he considered the navy's finest.

Luckily, Nathaniel "Jumping Billy" Haraden, who had been the *Constitution's* master during the war with Tripoli, was at the Washington yard in April, and he worked with Hull and his officers seven days a week to get the aged ship into fighting condition. Much work needed to be done; her copper was in bad shape, and so were her upper works. She needed a complete suit of sails and new running rigging. Her hull and decks needed caulking, the ballast washed, and the hold cleaned out. By the time war was declared, however, the big frigate was ready for action.

The *Constitution's* refurbishment exposed yet more ways in which the United States was unprepared for combat. Repairing and provisioning her had drawn down supplies and armament at the yard to a point where it could not serve the urgent needs of other warships and yards. Tingey was getting urgent requests from naval stations at Gosport, Wilmington, and Charleston for supplies, but he didn't have them.

Although the *Constitution* was now in excellent shape, Hull needed to add to the crew. Enlistments in the American navy were typically for two years, which meant that able seamen left the ship at regular intervals. In wartime this presented a big problem. A majority of Hull's crew had signed on when he took command from Rodgers in 1810. Many of them had departed at the end of their tour and now had to be replaced.

Hull even had trouble holding on to his talented first lieutenant, Charles Morris. When the *Constitution* put into Washington in April, Morris tried to obtain a command of his own, since that was the surest path to rapid promotion. He had already had a distinguished career. During Decatur's famous attack and burning of the captured *Philadelphia* during the war with Tripoli, Midshipman Morris was the first man to board the unlucky frigate. Secretary Hamilton recognized Morris's ability and was sympathetic, but in the end he ordered him back to the *Constitution*. Needless to say, Hull was happy to see him return.

On June 18 Hull sailed over to Annapolis to recruit crew members. Because of its proximity to Baltimore, where the war was popular, he thought recruitment would be easier than in thinly populated Washington. The *Constitution* departed

Annapolis on July 5 with a full complement of four hundred forty men. Many of the newcomers had signed on in a fit of patriotic fervor. Not a few of them were green, however, and in need of training. Hull wrote to Hamilton, "The crew, you will readily conceive, must yet be unacquainted with a ship of war, as many of them have but lately joined us and never were in an armed ship before. We are doing all that we can to make them acquainted with [their] duty, and in a few days, we shall have nothing to fear from any single deck ship."

In spite of having thirty men sick from dysentery and the various maladies prevalent during the bay's unhealthy summers, Hull worked the crew hard. As he made his way up Chesapeake Bay, practice at the guns and the sails went on every day. By the time he passed the Chesapeake Capes and pushed out to sea, Hull was conducting gunnery practice twice a day and felt the crew was rounding into shape.

Five days after Hull entered the Atlantic, on July 17, a lookout at the main masthead spied four strange sails to the northward and in shore of the *Constitution*. They were definitely men-of-war. The wind was light, and thinking they were part of Rodgers's squadron, Hull threw on all sail and steered toward them.

Around the same time, a lookout aboard H.M.S. *Shannon* saw a strange sail to the south and east standing to the northeast. He hollered down to the quarter-deck, where Broke soon had his telescope focused on the big ship in the distance. The *Shannon* was twelve miles east of Egg Harbor on the New Jersey coast. Broke had no doubt this was an American, and he gave the signal for a general chase. It was two o'clock in the afternoon. Broke's squadron, in addition to the *Shannon*, included the 64-gun *Africa* and her tender, the 36-gun *Belvidera*, the 32-gun *Aeolus*, and the recently captured *Nautilus* with Lieutenant Crane still on board.

At four o'clock, one of Hull's lookouts discovered another ship bearing northeast, standing for the *Constitution* with all her sail billowing. Hull thought she might be an American as well. For the next several hours the stranger sailed closer, but by sundown she was still too far away for her or the *Constitution* to distinguish recognition signals. The other four warships could only be seen from their tops.

Hull decided to steer toward the single ship and approach near enough to make the night signal. At ten o'clock he hoisted signal lights and kept them aloft for almost an hour, but got no answer. He now felt certain this ship, as well as the four inshore, were British, and he "hauled off to the southward and eastward" to escape. The ship he had been chasing raced after him, making signals to the others as she went.

At daylight, two frigates from the inshore group had pulled closer to the *Constitution*—one of them to within five or six miles, while the other four ships were ten or twelve miles astern. All were in vigorous pursuit with a fine breeze filling their sails. In the area where the *Constitution* was, however, the wind had died. The ship "would not steer," Hull recorded, "but fell round off with her head" toward her pursuers. In desperation, Hull ordered boats hoisted out and sent ahead to tow the ship's head round and get on some speed. By now three enemy frigates were five miles away, but they, too, had lost their wind and had their boats out towing.

With the enemy ships continuing to close, Hull ordered the men to quarters. He then ran "two of the guns on the gun deck . . . out at the cabin window for stern guns, and hoisted one of the twenty-four pounders off the gun deck, and ran that, with a forecastle gun, an eighteen pounder, out" the taffrail, where carpenters had cut away spaces. At seven o'clock Hull fired one stern gun at the nearest ship, but the ball splashed harmlessly into the water.

By eight o'clock four enemy ships were nearly within gunshot range and coming up methodically. The breeze was insignificant. Hull's situation looked desperate. "It . . . appeared we must be taken," he wrote. But, no matter the odds, he would not surrender. He intended to fire as many broadsides as he could and go down fighting. Before resorting to this grim measure, however, he accepted Charles Morris's suggestion that they try using kedge anchors. That required warping the ship ahead by carrying out kedge anchors in the ship's boats, dropping them, and warping the ship up to them. The ship was in only twenty-four fathoms of water—shallow enough. He ordered his men to gather three hundred to four hundred feet of rope and sent two big anchors out.

The kedging allowed the *Constitution* to gradually pull ahead, but the British saw what Hull was doing, and they began using kedge anchors themselves. The ships farthest behind sent their boats to tow and warp those nearest the *Constitution*. Soon they were again getting closer to Hull. At nine o'clock the nearest ship, the *Belvidera*, began firing her bow guns. Hull replied with the stern chasers from his cabin and the quarterdeck. The *Belvidera*'s balls fell short, but Hull thought a couple of his hit home because he could not see them strike the water. Soon, H.M.S. *Guerriere* (the single ship Hull's lookout had spotted before) pulled close enough to unload a broadside, but her balls all fell short. She quickly ceased firing and resumed the chase.

For the next three hours all hands on the *Constitution* were at the backbreaking task of warping the ship ahead with the heavy kedge anchors. To lighten and trim the ship, Hull pumped 2,300 gallons of drinking water—out of a total of almost 40,000—overboard, and with the help of a light air he gained a bit on his hounds.

The British redoubled their efforts. At two o'clock in the afternoon all the boats from the battleship *Africa* and some from the frigates were sent to tow the *Shannon*. But as luck would have it, a providential breeze sprang up that enabled Hull to maintain his lead. The light wind stayed with the *Constitution* until eleven o'clock that night, and with her boats towing, she was able to keep ahead of the *Shannon*. Shortly after eleven, the *Constitution* caught a strengthening southerly wind that brought her abreast of her boats, which she hoisted up without losing any speed. Her pursuers were still near, but she was holding her own. To keep up, the *Shannon* abandoned her boats as the wind took her.

The ships sailed through the second night of their engagement with Hull maintaining his lead by employing every device he could think of. A portion of the log read: "At midnight moderate breeze and pleasant, took in the royal studding sails. . . . At 1 A.M. set the sky sails [they had just been installed at the Washington Navy Yard]. At [1:30] got a pull of the weather brace and set the lower [studding] sail. At 3 A.M. set the main topmast studding sail. At [4:15] hauled up to SE by S." And so it went, as Hull, the great maestro, employed every instrument at his command.

At daylight on the nineteenth, six enemy ships were still visible. Hull now had to tack to the east, and in doing so, he passed close to the 32-gun *Aeolus*. The *Constitution* braced for a broadside, but the British frigate held her fire. Perhaps she feared becalming, "as the wind was light," Hull speculated. In any event, after the *Constitution* passed, the *Aeolus* tacked and commenced her pursuit again.

At 9 A.M. an innocent American merchantman happened on the scene. The British ships instantly hoisted American colors to decoy her toward them. Hull responded by hoisting British colors. The merchantman's skipper correctly assessed the situation, hauled his wind, and raced away.

As the day progressed, the wind increased, and the *Constitution* gained on her pursuers, lengthening her lead to as much as eight miles, but Broke kept after her—all through the day and night.

At daylight on the twentieth, only three pursuers were visible from the *Constitution*'s main masthead, the nearest being twelve miles astern. Hull set all hands to work wetting the sails, from the royals down, "with the engine and fire buckets, and we soon found that we left the enemy very fast," Hull reported.

Commodore Broke recognized that even his lead ships were falling behind at an increasing rate, and at 8:15 he conceded the superior seamanship of the American and gave up the chase.

When Hull saw Broke hauling his wind and heading off to the north, he was enormously proud of his crew. They might have been green, but in a grueling, fifty-seven-hour chase, they had outsailed every one of Broke's ships. It was an amazing display of seamanship, stamina, collaborative effort, and, indeed, patriotism. And especially so when one considers that Commodore Broke was among the best in the business. The *Constitution*'s crew had beaten Britain's finest.

Having won this singular race in spectacular fashion, Hull now decided to make for Boston instead of New York, where his orders had directed him to go. He assumed Broke would be steering toward Sandy Hook to begin a blockade of New York, and he certainly did not want to run into him again.

After Hull's incredible escape, the legend of his sailing prowess grew, and a story began circulating that during the Quasi-War with France, First Lieutenant Hull, then aboard the *Constitution*, had demonstrated that he was among the foremost sailing masters of his day. Britain and America had been quasi-allies against France at the time, and the *Constitution*'s skipper, Commodore Silas Talbot, had become engaged in a friendly race with the captain of the British frigate H.M.S. *Santa Margaretta*. The competition ran from sunup to sunset, with Hull serving as the *Constitution*'s sailing master. Long after the incident, James Fenimore Cooper wrote, "the manner in which the *Constitution* beat her companion out of the wind was not the least striking feature of this trial, and it must in great degree be subscribed to Hull, whose dexterity in handling a craft under her canvas was remarkable . . . he was perhaps one of the most skilful seamen of his time." Needless to say, the *Constitution* won the race.

Inevitably, details were exaggerated: Hull was actually second lieutenant, not first, and this story was told to Cooper many years later by some surviving officers of the *Constitution*, including Hull. Even so, Hull's prowess as a sailor was unquestionable. He might well have been the finest seaman in the American navy and perhaps in the world. In any event, Hull's fledgling crew now had an esprit de corps that would have been the envy of any British captain.

WHILE HULL WAS eluding Broke, David Porter continued his cruise in the *Essex*. Two days after encountering the troop convoy, he captured the brig *Lamprey*, carrying rum from Jamaica to Halifax via Bermuda. He put a prize crew aboard and sent her into Baltimore to be condemned. Then, between July 26 and August 9, he took six more prizes. Two of them, the *Hero* and the *Mary*, he burned, as they were of little value; another, the *Nancy*, he ransomed for $14,000; and two others, the *Leander* and the *King George*, he sent into port as prizes.

On August 9 Porter seized his last prize, the brig *Brothers*. She had only recently been captured by Revolutionary War hero Joshua Barney in the privateer schooner *Rossie*. After seizing the *Brothers*, Barney had placed sixty-two prisoners aboard her—including men from five other vessels he had taken. Barney had then sent the *Brothers* on to St. John's, Newfoundland, as a cartel vessel (a ship carrying only a signal gun whose sole purpose was to effect a prisoner exchange). Porter now added twenty-five prisoners of his own and sent all of them in the *Brothers* to St. John's, under the charge of midshipman Stephen Decatur McKnight (Commodore Decatur's nephew).

When McKnight arrived at St. John's, the admiral in command, Sir John T. Duckworth, was none too happy. In making the *Brothers* a cartel vessel, Porter was attempting to affect an unorthodox prisoner exchange, which Duckworth protested in letters sent to Porter and to Secretary Hamilton. The admiral pointed out that by giving the *Brothers* a flag of truce and a proposal for an exchange of prisoners, she was insulated from possible recapture, while the *Essex*, without a diminished crew, could continue her rampage unencumbered.

As it turned out, the prisoners seized the *Brothers* from McKnight and put into another port on the island, but allowed McKnight to travel to St. John's. When he met Admiral Duckworth, all he could do was hand him a list of names but no actual British prisoners. Nonetheless, Duckworth magnanimously acknowledged receipt of the British seamen and sent McKnight to Vice Admiral Sawyer, in Halifax, with a request that Sawyer see that McKnight got home, which Sawyer did. McKnight was saved from a dreadful incarceration aboard a prison ship in Halifax harbor. When he reached the United States, he rejoined the *Essex*.

Four days after sending the *Brothers* to St. John's, Porter was on the quarterdeck at 9:30 A.M. when lookouts shouted down to him that a merchantman was in sight to windward. He extended his telescope and had a good look at her. She appeared to be an English West Indiaman. But the more he examined her, the more suspicious he got. "Every means had been used to give her that appearance," he wrote. Suspecting she was really a warship in disguise, he quietly sent the crew to battle stations, while "concealing every appearance of preparation." He kept the gun deck ports closed, the topgallant masts housed, and the sails set and trimmed in the careless manner of a merchantman. Since the *Essex* was small and lightly sparred, when her gun ports were closed, she looked—from a distance—more like a merchant vessel than a warship.

Porter was right about the stranger's identity. The ship rushing toward him was the 18-gun British sloop of war *Alert*, under Thomas L. P. Laugharne. Either Laugharne was taken in by the *Essex*'s disguise, or in the finest British tradition—going back to Sir Francis Drake—he was defying the odds and continuing his mad dash toward the much larger frigate, bent on evening the odds by surprising her and hitting her hard before she knew what was up.

Porter held his fire and let Laugharne approach. By 11:30 the *Alert* was within short pistol shot, preparing to rake the *Essex*, when Porter suddenly ran up American colors and wore short around. While he did, the *Alert* unloaded a full broadside, which, Porter said, "did us no more injury than the cheers that accompanied it."

The *Essex*'s larboard guns then exploded, carronades firing in unison, their heavy metal smashing into the *Alert* from point-blank range. Stunned by the broadside, Laugharne tried to escape, but Porter was on him, ranging up close on the sloop's starboard quarter. As he came up, Porter hoisted a flag bearing the motto, "FREE TRADE AND SAILORS RIGHTS." Another broadside or two at this distance would have been devastating, and so, with five men wounded, two guns disabled, the ship badly cut up and sinking, and his crew having deserted their stations and run below, Laugharne, according to Porter, "avoided the dreadful consequences that our broadside would in a few moments have produced by prudentially striking his colors."

The entire action took eight minutes. Porter passed off the victory as a "trifling skirmish." The only injury the *Essex* sustained was "having her cabin windows broken by the concussion of her own guns." There was nothing trifling about the incident, however. It was the first time in the war that a British warship had struck her colors to an American. Both London and Washington had assumed the entire U. S. Navy would be crushed at the outset of the conflict, but Porter and his comrades were proving otherwise.

The triumphant *Essex* now headed home for a refit and to deal with the prisoners she had acquired. Eighty-six were from the *Alert*, raising the total number on board to a dangerous three hundred. Two days into the trip, in the middle of the night, eleven-year-old Midshipman David Farragut was lying half awake in his hammock—with other reefers, as midshipmen were then called, in the crowded steerage below the main deck—when out of a sleepy eye he glimpsed one of the prisoners standing beside him, gripping a pistol. The man was looking straight ahead into the darkness and not down at the hammock. Farragut froze and closed his eyes. A moment later, he slowly opened them. The man had disappeared. Without making a sound, Farragut rolled out of his hammock. Not seeing any more prisoners, he made his way through the darkened ship, slipped into the captain's cabin, and awakened Porter, who, grasping the situation immediately, leapt to his feet and rushed on deck, shouting, "FIRE! FIRE!"

In a flash, the *Essex* men were out of their hammocks and rushing to their stations, as word was shouted around about the real crisis aboard. Part of Porter's training was periodically sounding a fire alarm at night. Confused and frightened by the commotion, the prisoners meekly surrendered. Young Farragut was an instant hero.

The adventurous first cruise of the *Essex* was not over yet. On the way home to the Delaware River, Porter fell in with three powerful British warships off Georges Bank, northeast of Cape Cod. One was a brig-of-war in chase of an American merchantman. The other two were farther away and much bigger, probably frigates. Porter went after the brig, but the wind was light, and the brig had sweeps (long oars), which allowed her to escape.

After the *Essex* displayed American colors, the bigger warships sped after her. "At 4 P.M. they had gained our wake," Porter reported. He kept on every sail, however, and managed to stay just beyond cannon range until dark, whereupon he hove about and steered straight for the largest pursuer, intending to either sneak past him or "fire a broadside into him and lay him on board. . . . The crew, in high spirits, . . . gave three cheers when the plan was proposed to them." At 7:20 Porter hove about and stood southeast by south until 8:30, "when we bore away southwest without seeing anything more of them."

Porter was unhappy he had not engaged one of the frigates and puzzled because a pistol aboard the *Essex* was accidentally fired at the time he calculated she was near the biggest enemy ship. He did make good his escape, however, and sailed for the Delaware River and home.

WHILE PORTER WAS making the most of his cruise, Commodore Rodgers and his squadron continued to search for the elusive Jamaica convoy. Thick fog plagued Rodgers, however. "At least 6 days out of 7 [were] so . . . obscure," he wrote, that every vessel farther than four or five miles away was invisible. At times "the fog was so thick . . . it prevented us seeing each other, even at a cable's length" (two hundred yards). On June 29 Rodgers spoke an American schooner from Teneriffe. The master said he had passed the convoy two days before, one hundred and fifty miles to the northeast. Rodgers set all sail in that direction, and on July 1 he saw garbage strewn over the water, "quantities of cocoa nut shells, orange peels &c &c," indicating "the convoy was not too far distant, and we pursued it with zeal."

During the next three days Rodgers captured two enemy ships, the brigs *Tionella* and the *Dutchess of Portland,* and burned them, but the convoy was nowhere in sight. On July 9, he captured the 10-gun privateer, *Dolphin*, north of the Azores, and sent her into Philadelphia under a prize master. On the same day, the *Hornet* captured a British privateer in latitude 45° 30' north, and longitude 23° west. Her master reported seeing the convoy the evening before. Rodgers continued the chase, sailing east toward the English Channel. On July 13 his squadron was a day's sail from the chops of the Channel when he abruptly changed course and stood south toward Madeira. He had decided to cut short the cruise and head back to Boston. Scurvy had broken out aboard the *United States* and the *Congress.* They had a troubling number of cases—perhaps as many as eighty—between them. No scurvy appeared aboard the *President*, however.

Rodgers was off Madeira on the twenty-first, and on the twenty-fourth, northwest of the Canaries, he captured the 16-gun letter of marque *John*, which he sent to the United States as a prize. He sailed next to the Azores, and from there to Newfoundland's Grand Banks and then to Cape Sable, before setting a course for Boston, sorely disappointed at the lack of action. Returning to New York would have been too risky; Boston was much less likely to be blockaded. On the way, Rodgers captured four more vessels. For the entire voyage, however, he took only nine stray British merchantmen and privateers, and recaptured an American vessel—little enough, given his efforts and the high hopes he had originally entertained for the squadron.

CHAPTER SEVEN

The *Constitution* and the *Guerriere*

AFTER HE OUTRACED Commodore Broke and shaped a course for Boston, Captain Hull worried that Broke might have split up his squadron and ordered some of his ships to blockade the port. Actually, after leaving the *Constitution*, Broke had gone after Rodgers with his entire squadron, trying to intercept him before he reached the Jamaica convoy. In doing so, Broke left American ports open for dozens of returning merchantmen, which is precisely what Rodgers had hoped he would do.

What was happening to Rodgers was not on Hull's mind, however. As he made his way to Boston, he was far more concerned with Secretary Hamilton. Hull expected to receive new orders, and he feared the cautious secretary might direct him to remain in port. Hull hoped to be in and out of Boston in three days, before any new orders arrived. On the way to Boston, however, Hull spoke to the *Diana*, a merchant vessel bound for Baltimore, and he gave her captain a message for Secretary Hamilton requesting new orders. Proceeding without them could cause Hull considerable trouble. He wanted to at least appear ready to receive them.

The *Constitution* reached Boston on July 26. No British cruisers were around, but a large number of vessels from Europe and the West Indies were working their way in and out of the busy port. Uncooperative winds forced Hull to tow the *Constitution* into port. The town was not expecting her. Reports from New York newspapers claimed that Broke had taken her prisoner. But there she was, and Boston, her home port, was ecstatic. Even though Boston's Federalists hated Madison and his war, and were excoriating the president in their newspapers, they gave Hull a hero's welcome.

As soon as he got the chance, Hull sent a letter to Hamilton, telling him that if new orders did not arrive, he planned to sail eastward and join Rodgers's squadron, although it's hard to believe he didn't prefer being on his own. He immediately began replenishing the *Constitution*, particularly the water he had pumped overboard. When he left Chesapeake Bay two weeks before, he expected to be sailing to New York and had taken on board only eight weeks' worth of supplies. He had already consumed over a third of them. While he worked, the dreaded new orders from Hamilton were on the way, directing him to turn over command of the *Constitution* to his senior, Captain William Bainbridge, and return to Washington, where he was to take command of the smaller frigate *Constellation*. A bit later, after Hamilton found out about Hull's inspiring escape from Broke, he changed these instructions and directed Hull to "remain at Boston until further orders"—just what Hull did not want to hear. Hamilton and the president still had no confidence in the fleet and no plan for it, other than confining it to port.

While the new orders were still in transit, Hull completed work on the *Constitution*, and when the wind had hauled far to the westward during the wee hours of Sunday morning, August 2, Hull unmoored and fetched out of the harbor. At seven o'clock he was hove to beyond Boston Light, waiting for a boat he had dispatched to check the post office one last time. When the boat returned with no news from Hamilton, a relieved Hull sped out to sea.

At first, he sailed northeast along the Maine coast to the Bay of Fundy. Finding no enemy ships, he turned east and steered for Cape Sable Island at the southern tip of Nova Scotia, intending to patrol between there and Halifax. Four uneventful days later, Hull decided to stand toward Newfoundland. He was under full sail when he passed Sable Island, and he then hauled in to take up a station off the Gulf of St. Lawrence near Cape Race at the southeastern tip of Newfoundland, hoping to intercept ships bound for Quebec or Halifax.

On August 10 and 11, Hull captured two small, empty British vessels, and after taking their crews aboard the *Constitution*, he burned them. Four days later, as dawn approached on the fifteenth, lookouts saw five sail dead ahead, looking like a convoy. Hull put on a full press of sail in pursuit. By sunrise it was clear that one was a small warship (the 18-gun British sloop of war *Avenger* with a crew of 121). At six o'clock the *Avenger* discovered the *Constitution* and immediately cast off a prize she had in tow and burned her, before making all sail to

Figure 7.1: Michele Felice Cornè, Constitution *and* Guerriere, *19 August 1812* (courtesy of U.S. Naval Academy Museum).

windward and fleeing. Being more weatherly than the *Constitution*, that is, able to sail closer to the wind with little leeway, she made good her escape. While she did, Hull chased down another vessel in the vicinity, which turned out to be a British prize of the privateer *Dolphin* out of Salem, Massachusetts. The *Dolphin* was nowhere in sight; she had abandoned her prize and raced away when she saw the *Avenger*.

That same day Hull gave chase to another brig the *Constitution*'s lookouts had spotted, and when he caught up with her, he discovered she was an American prize of the *Avenger*, with a British prize master and a small British crew aboard. From the master Hull learned he had narrowly missed sailing into Broke's squadron, which was at the western edge of the Grand Banks looking for Commodore Rodgers, trying to intercept him before he caught the Jamaica convoy. Hull decided to put some distance between himself and Broke and turned south toward Bermuda.

On the eighteenth at 9:30 at night, lookouts saw a brig close by, and Hull gave chase, catching up with her at 11. She turned out to be the 14-gun American privateer *Decatur* out of Newburyport, Massachusetts, with a crew of 108, under Captain William Nicholls. In trying to escape from the big unknown frigate,

Nicholls had thrown overboard twelve precious guns. He had taken nine prizes during a short cruise, demonstrating that Madison's privateers were already swarming around British shipping lanes. In these waters, the privateers were usually from Federalist Massachusetts. Even though most of the merchants in places like Newburyport and Salem opposed the war, they were not averse to making money from it.

When Nicholls came aboard the *Constitution*, he told Hull he had seen a large warship nearby standing southward. Hull was excited; he immediately turned south, hoping to fall in with her. At 2 P.M. the following day, August 19, Hull's lookouts spied a sail in the distance to leeward. The *Constitution* was moving south southwest in latitude 41° 42' and longitude 55° 48'. With an accommodating wind from the northwest, Hull put on all sail and sped toward the stranger. She did not appear to be running away. By three o'clock Hull could see she was a large ship on the starboard tack, close by the wind under easy sail. By 3:30 it was plain she was just what he had hoped, a British frigate. His heart must have been racing, for there is no doubt he recognized her as the *Guerriere*, one of the frigates that chased him during his race with Broke's squadron.

Fifteen minutes later, the British ship backed her main topsail and lay by on the starboard tack, inviting a duel with the bigger *Constitution*. The *Guerriere's* skipper, twenty-eight-year-old Captain James Dacres, had been detached from Broke's squadron and was making his way to Halifax for a refit. He could not have been happier to see the *Constitution*. Even at his young age, he was an accomplished fighter with a distinguished record. He was from an old navy clan—his father and uncle were both admirals—and he proudly carried on the family's tradition. Although his ship was smaller than the *Constitution*, she was one of the finest frigates in the British fleet. Dacres expected to make quick work of the American. He was so confident he magnanimously allowed ten impressed Americans aboard to go below when they insisted they would not fight against their countrymen. The British had grown accustomed to victory, even when the odds were against them. A difference in size between the two frigates, even a significant one, made no difference to the proud lions of the Royal Navy. Defeat at the hands of an American crew was inconceivable. The officers and men of the *Guerriere*, like all their countrymen, had nothing but contempt for the American navy.

The *Constitution* had a complement of 456 men and was rated at forty-four guns but mounted fifty-six, including thirty twenty-four-pound long guns on the main deck, twenty-four thirty-two-pound carronades on the spar deck, and two long eighteen-pounders at the bow. (Carronades were small, lightweight cannon with wide, short barrels that had a limited effective range of less than five hundred yards but fired large-caliber projectiles.) The *Guerriere*—undermanned as most British warships—had a crew of only 272, not counting the Americans aboard. She was rated at thirty-eight guns and carried forty-nine. On her main deck thirty eighteen-pound long guns were mounted, and on her spar deck she had sixteen thirty-two-pound carronades, two long twelves, and a twelve-pound howitzer. The *Constitution*'s broadside in weight of metal was a potent 762 pounds, while the *Guerriere*'s was a bit more than 550. The quality of the officers and crews of both ships, which in the end would make the difference, could not be so easily measured.

Hull cleared for action around three o'clock, ordering light sails taken in and royal yards struck down, two reefs taken in the topsails, and the foresail and mainsail hauled up. While a marine drummer beat the call to quarters, and all hands raced to their battle stations, Hull steered straight for the enemy, some three miles away now. As the big ship plowed ahead, the crew gave three cheers, even though everyone knew a gruesome, bloody brawl was only minutes away. Hull later claimed there were no anxious faces. He said the men made it clear to him they wanted to lay the *Constitution* close alongside the enemy and blaze away. That may or may not have been the case, but there was no doubt Hull himself was fixed on a toe-to-toe slugfest, and by the look of things, so was the British captain.

"Hull was now all animation," Moses Smith reported. "With great energy and calmness . . . he passed around among the officers and men, [saying] . . . 'now do your duty. Your officers cannot have entire command over you now. Each man must do all in his power for his country.'"

As Hull bore up, Dacres hoisted an ensign at the mizzen gaff, another in the mizzen shrouds, and jacks at the foretopgallant and mizzen topgallant mastheads. At 5:05 the *Constitution* continued to run down on the enemy, and as she did, the *Guerriere* fired a broadside, but the balls fell short. A sea was running, and her gunners might not have adjusted sufficiently for the roll of the ship. Dacres then wore and gave the *Constitution* a broadside with his larboard guns. Only two balls struck, however, and they bounced harmlessly off the *Constitution*'s thick hide, earning her the immortal sobriquet "Old Ironsides." Hull moved closer and hoisted American colors at the mizzen peak, the foretopgallant, and the mizzen topgallant mastheads, and he made one ready for hoisting at the main masthead. All the while, Dacres had been maneuvering to gain the weather gauge, but finding he could not, he bore up to bring the wind on his quarter and ran under topsails and jib, firing at the *Constitution* as he went.

Hull responded by setting his main topgallant and closing on the *Guerriere's* larboard quarter. Once there, the *Constitution* passed to the *Guerriere's* beam, the distance between them narrowing from two hundred yards to a half pistol shot (ten yards). It was six o'clock. Hull had fired only a few shots as he approached, but now he let loose a barrage of crushing broadsides, his double-shotted twenty-four-pounders spewing out deadly round and grapeshot. They were far more devastating than the *Guerriere's* eighteens, and they staggered the smaller ship. Dacres fired back as fast as he could. But in fifteen minutes the *Guerriere's* mizzenmast went by the board, and her main yard was in the slings, while her hull and sails had taken a tremendous beating.

Dacres was in trouble. His mizzenmast had fallen over the starboard quarter, but its still uncut standing rigging held it fast to the ship, making her impossible to maneuver, and she swung up into the wind. Meanwhile, Hull put the *Constitution* hard to port, crossed the enemy's bows, and raked her. He then wore ship and came back across her bows again, delivering another crushing broadside with his portside guns. The two raking broadsides created havoc on the *Guerriere's* forecastle, and ripped into her sails and fore rigging. At the same time, she had use of only a few of her bow guns. Meanwhile, Hull's sharpshooters in the tops rained musket balls down on the *Guerriere's* deck.

Dacres tried putting his ship hard to port, but her helm would not answer, and her bowsprit and jib-boom swept over the *Constitution's* quarterdeck, becoming entangled in the lee mizzen rigging, causing the *Guerriere* to fall astern of the *Constitution*. The ships were now tenuously hitched together. Lieutenant Charles Morris leaped up on the taffrail to see if Dacres was forming a boarding party. He was. Boarding was his only chance now. Although the American crew far outnumbered his own, he might get lucky. In any event, he was determined to fight it out hand-to-hand.

When Morris saw Dacres preparing to board, he shouted to Hull, and the captain ordered his own boarders to assemble. Trumpets were now sounding on both ships, calling the boarding parties. While waiting for his men to gather, Morris began wrapping the main brace over the *Guerriere's* bowsprit to better fasten the ships together. Suddenly, a musket ball, fired by one of the *Guerriere's* marines assembling to board, struck him in the body, and threw him back on deck, stunned. Lieutenant William Bush of the marines was standing nearby, and another ball hit him, killing him instantly. Sailing Master John Aylwin was grazed on the shoulder by another. Despite his injury, Morris somehow stood up and remained in the fight.

The ships now separated unexpectedly, making boarding impossible. Hull resumed pummeling the enemy from a short distance for several minutes, when the *Guerriere*'s foremast and mainmast suddenly went over the side, taking with them the jib boom and every spar except the bowsprit. She was now completely disabled, rolling helplessly in the trough of the sea, taking in water from open gun ports and shot holes in her hull.

Seeing that his ship was doomed, and probably sinking, Dacres called his officers, and they agreed that further resistance would be a needless waste of lives. Dacres fired a gun to leeward, indicating he had struck his colors. He could not actually haul them down because they had all gone over the side with the masts.

Hull, in the meantime, had ordered his sails filled and hauled off to repair damages to the braces and other rigging before returning to the fray; all the while he watched to see if Dacres had surrendered. It was impossible to find out; no enemy flags were visible. Hull heard the single cannon blast, but that could have been a stray gun going off. He needed to confirm if Dacres had actually given up. He hoisted out a boat and sent Third Lieutenant Read and Midshipman Gilliam over to the *Guerriere* under a flag of truce to determine if Dacres had surrendered, and if he had, to inquire if he needed assistance. Hull thought the *Guerriere* was sinking.

In twenty minutes Read returned with Captain Dacres, who confirmed the surrender and offered his sword to Hull. Without hesitating, Hull refused to take it from so gallant a foe and invited Dacres to his cabin. Having been badly wounded in the back by one of the *Constitution*'s sharpshooters, Dacres moved with great difficulty. Although he was grateful for Hull's solicitude, he was shocked when he later discovered (or thought he did) that "a large portion" of the ship's company were British seamen. There was no way he could prove they were, of course.

Before conferring with the defeated captain, Hull ordered all boats out to ferry prisoners, especially the wounded, over to the *Constitution* and get them and their baggage off the stricken ship before it sank. The butcher's bill for the *Guerriere* was grim. Fifteen tars were dead and sixty-three wounded. An additional twenty-four were missing, presumed killed when the masts went by the board. Hull's men and boats were at the depressing business of transferring the British crew all night and into the next day. The moans and cries of the injured men were heartrending.

Dacres later said, "I feel it my duty to state that the conduct of Captain Hull and his officers to our men has been that of a brave enemy, the greatest care being taken to prevent our men losing the smallest trifle, and the greatest attention being paid to the wounded who through the attention and skill of Mr. [John] Irvine, surgeon, I hope will do well." Irvine was the *Guerriere*'s doctor. Dacres didn't mention Amos Evans, the *Constitution*'s surgeon who tended the wounded as well. Most of them were British; the *Constitution* had only seven killed and seven wounded, one of them being Lieutenant Morris, who, in spite of his life-threatening injury, had remained on deck during the entire battle. When the firing ceased, he suddenly felt the full effects of his wound and went below to the cockpit to have it treated. He shortly became feverish. Doctor Evans feared for Morris's life, but the patient continued breathing. If Morris survived, Evans thought it would be weeks before he recovered.

At daylight, it was clear the *Guerriere* could not be salvaged and taken triumphantly into Boston, which Hull badly wanted to do. He ordered the rest of the prisoners removed as quickly as possible so that he could burn her. By three o'clock in the afternoon all the British tars were safely aboard the *Constitution*, and Hull told Read to set the *Guerriere* on fire. The lieutenant spread gunpowder in her storerooms, with long trails leading to the ship's side, and lit them. Flames soon engulfed the entire ship, and her guns started popping off one at a time. Then, suddenly, without warning, she blew up. Hundreds of jagged pieces of wood spewed into the air and then drifted slowly down to the water trailing smoke and fire, a spectacular, chilling sight.

In his report to Secretary Hamilton, Hull explained that the main action had taken only thirty minutes. During that time the *Guerriere* was reduced to a floating log, while the *Constitution* was practically unscathed. He also reported that at the height of the action, Lieutenant Charles Morris, although badly wounded, remained on deck in the thick of the fight. Hull credited Morris with being a key to victory, and he still feared for his life. Hull also credited the rest of his brave crew, including the African American sailors—"niggers," he mindlessly called them. "They stripped to the waist and fought like devils," he wrote, "seeming to be utterly insensible to danger and to be possessed with a determination to outfight the white sailors."

The ship's company was integrated, although not free of racial prejudice, as Hull's remarks made clear. It was common for American warships to have 15 to 20 percent of their crews African American—free and slave. Hull appeared surprised that his black seamen performed as well as they did under fire—the supreme test.

Hull now made his way to Boston with over three hundred prisoners. Ten uneventful days later, he rounded Cape Cod and beat up toward the city against a stiff southwest wind. It took all night to reach Little Brewster Island and Boston

Lighthouse, where he anchored on Sunday morning, August 29. The crew spent the day sprucing up the ship for what they expected to be a rousing welcome in the city. The following morning, however, they were jolted when lookouts spied five warships—four frigates and a brig—racing toward them.

Hull was enjoying his first complete night's sleep in a long time, and he reluctantly rolled out of bed to prepare a run into the harbor and the protection of its forts. At eight o'clock, however, he trained his telescope on the approaching fleet and was relieved to see American flags hoisted. Commodore Rodgers's *President* was in the lead. He was returning from his unsuccessful chase after the Jamaica convoy.

Rodgers had spotted the *Constitution* at daylight, but being too far away to identify her, he cleared for action, hoping she was a British frigate. Midshipman Matthew Calbraith Perry recorded in his journal, "At daylight discovered a frigate lying in Nantasket Roads, cleared ship for action and stood for her. At 7:00 she proved the frigate *Constitution* from a cruise, having captured the British frigate *Guerriere*."

The *Constitution* led a parade of nearly the entire American fleet into town. The reception was tremendous. The Washington artillery fired one salute after another, while people gathered on the wharves, the rooftops, and the ships in the harbor to cheer and applaud.

Rodgers knew the ovation was for the *Constitution*. He appeared to have accomplished little on his lengthy cruise. And making matters worse, he had been forced to return prematurely because of scurvy. It was inexcusable to have a mission aborted because of widespread scurvy. Although the cause of the disease had not been identified, and would not be until the twentieth century, measures to prevent it were well-known. The *President* managed to complete the voyage without suffering a single case; the *United States* and the *Congress* should have been able to do the same. Six men had died on the two frigates, and thirty-three had to be taken to the hospital. Forty-one others had symptoms but did not need hospitalization.

At first glance, Rodgers's cruise paled in comparison to Hull's. Rodgers failed to capture the *Belvidera* when she was within his grasp, and he could not find the Jamaica convoy. The nine vessels he did capture were insignificant compared to the *Guerriere*. Nonetheless, Rodgers did perform a signal service, which the general public may not have appreciated, but President Madison and secretaries Hamilton and Gallatin certainly did.

Rodgers explained to Hamilton, "Even if I did not succeed in destroying the convoy, . . . leaving the coast in the manner we did would tend to distract the enemy, oblige him to concentrate a considerable portion of his most active force and at the same time prevent his single cruisers from laying before any of our principal ports from their not knowing to which port or what moment we might return; and it is now acknowledged even by the enemies of the administration that this disposition has been attended with infinite benefit to our returning commerce."

Indeed it was. By diverting Broke's squadron, Rodgers allowed hundreds of American merchant vessels to reach their home ports safely. A remarkable 250 got into Boston, and 266 more put into New York, Baltimore, and Philadelphia. It was plain to Madison and Gallatin that Rodgers had prevented a disaster. In his annual message to Congress the president noted with satisfaction that the merchant fleet had reached home safely "having been much favored in it by a squadron of our frigates under the command of Commodore Rodgers." The fact that Rodgers did it by disobeying orders wasn't mentioned.

The British paid scant attention to Rodgers's achievement, but when news of the *Constitution*'s victory reached London during the first week of October, it caused at first disbelief and then widespread alarm. The *Times* wrote that the loss "spread a degree of gloom through the town, which it was painful to observe." The paper declared that far more than a single ship was lost. The invaluable reputation of the Royal Navy was undermined with incalculable consequences. In fact, the *Times* said that it knew "not any calamity of twenty times its amount that might have been attended with more serious consequences to the worsted party." George Canning told Parliament the defeat of the *Guerriere* threatened "the sacred spell of the invincibility" of the Royal Navy.

When the British had more time to think about it, they rationalized the defeat by pointing out that the *Constitution* was more of a line-of-battle ship than a frigate. They maintained that the *Guerriere* would have been justified in refusing combat with an obviously superior foe. Captain Dacres had a different excuse. At his court-martial he testified that the *Guerriere*'s weak condition before going into battle caused the defeat. Her mizzen mast went by the board early in the battle, he claimed, because it was in need of repair, and her mainmast fell from decay, not enemy fire. The court completely exonerated him.

Reaction in the United States was one of surprise and then widespread acclaim. Even disgruntled Federalists in New England applauded. For years they had supported a strong navy against determined opposition from Republicans, who took it as an article of faith that American warships could never succeed under any circumstances against the Royal Navy. Captain Hull's triumph proved they were wrong, and Federalists delighted in saying, "We told you so." And Madi-

son, who over many years—going back to Washington's presidency—had consistently fought against building a respectable navy, grappled on to Hull's victory
like a lifeline, basking in the public acclaim, using it to offset his sagging popularity
and to give his reelection campaign a much needed boost. He never imagined
that the navy would be an important political asset.

CHAPTER EIGHT

Ripe Apples and Bitter Fruit:
The Canadian Invasion

WHILE THE BLUE-WATER fleet was performing brilliantly, Madison's Canadian campaign was experiencing one difficulty after another. The president's notion that America could prepare quickly for war after it had been declared turned out to be a pipe dream. A new army did not instantly materialize, nor did volunteers sign up in significant numbers, nor did the untrained militiamen, who were called suddenly to arms, perform as seasoned veterans. Jefferson's ripe apple began looking more like a prickly pear.

Key players in Madison's invasion appeared unacquainted with his strategy and their roles. On July 16, nearly a month after the president signed the declaration of war, Army Lieutenant Porter Hanks, commander of strategically important Fort Michilimackinac on Mackinac Island, had not been favored with any new orders from the War Department. He had not even received notice that war had been declared.

He knew something was up, however. For the past two weeks an unusual number of warriors—Sioux, Chippewa, Winnebago, Menominee, Ottawa, and others—had paddled canoes passed his fort. He naturally wondered why. He assumed they were traveling to St. Joseph Island, forty miles away on the Canadian side of the border, where a tiny force of British regulars occupied decrepit Fort St. Joseph. The warriors' dress and weaponry indicated they were not traveling for a peaceful powwow. Clearly something was going on, but he didn't know what it was.

Hanks was naturally concerned about the defense of Mackinac Island, located at the western end of Lake Huron. It guarded the entrance to the Straits of Mackinac, connecting Lake Huron with Lake Michigan, a key point in the fur trade and in communications with the western Indian nations. The British prized the fur trade, as did the Native Americans, but of much greater importance now was whose side the tribes of the Northwest would fight on. The defense of Upper Canada, and indeed all of Canada, depended on whether the Indians would stand with the British or remain neutral.

What Hanks needed more than anything else was a pair of armed schooners to protect his island from a seaborne attack. He did not have the soldiers or weapons to defend Mackinac against an amphibious assault. A warship or two patrolling the surrounding waters would have secured Fort Michilimackinac. Hank's superior, Brigadier General William Hull, had requested naval support from Washington long ago but was ignored. An administration that did not even think to tell Hanks a war was on could not be expected to provide naval support, nor could it furnish the soldiers and armament he required.

Hanks could not count on any friendly Indians to support him, as the British could. After the recent Battle of Tippecanoe (November 7, 1811) and the cruel treatment the tribes received generally from Americans, the Indians were not going to side with the United States. The most Madison could hope for was their neutrality. To be sure, the British had treated the Indians badly as well, and the memory of their double dealing created a good deal of caution on the part of the tribes, but Britain's treatment was not to be compared with America's. In fact, the angry relations Native Americans had with the United States did not have any parallel in Canada. Thanks to the wise policies of colonial administrators like General Frederick Haldimand, relations with the tribes were relatively peaceful in Canada compared with the constant turmoil in the United States. The British needed the Indians to defend Canada, and they were careful in their treatment of them. They were not trying to change their way of life, nor were they gobbling up their lands, as the Americans were.

As war approached, Madison's policy was to placate the tribes. He did not want to be fighting them and the British at the same time. Some of the larger, more powerful nations like the Miami and the Delaware were open to an accommodation, but there was unrest among younger warriors in all the tribes, and they looked to Tecumseh and his brother the Prophet for leadership.

Brigadier General William Hull, the governor and Indian agent for the vast Michigan Territory, was aware of Tecumseh's importance and attempted to entice him into remaining neutral, but the zealous chief would have none of it. The

British, as much as Tecumseh distrusted them, were his only hope. He saw clearly what would happen to the Miami, Shawnee, Kickapoo, Potawatomi, Delaware, Wyandot (the remnants of the mighty Huron, destroyed in the French and Indian War), and the other tribes should America prevail. Only by uniting and allying themselves with the British, Tecumseh believed, could the tribes hope to protect themselves against the tidal wave of American settlers sure to push them off their ancient lands and destroy their way of life should the United States prevail.

But Tecumseh did not want to start a fight with the Americans prematurely; he waited for war to be declared. This accorded perfectly with British policy, which was to make an alliance with the Indian nations but restrain them from attacking the United States, initiating a war London did not want. The British needed the Indians only if America attacked Canada. Tecumseh had no illusions about Britain; he understood the limits of her support. The British were primarily interested in keeping Canada, not in advancing Indian goals. If they had to sacrifice their Indian allies in order to secure Canada, they would. The British were all Tecumseh had, however, and he intended to use them to the extent he could.

Despite their preference for Britain, the Indians did not want to be caught on the losing side. They hoped the British, as devious and unreliable as they were, would win, but they would not fight alongside them if they thought they were going to lose. The principal British leaders in Canada, General Isaac Brock in Upper Canada and his superior at Quebec, Governor-General Sir George Prevost, appreciated the importance of an Indian alliance and the need to win the confidence of the tribes by projecting a powerful image. If the Indians were confident of a British victory, they could more than make up for the lack of regulars. Capturing Fort Michilimackinac would demonstrate the relative strength of the British and American forces in the Northwest and be of enormous value in defending Canada.

In the spring of 1812 Madison told the Indian agents and territorial governors to conciliate the tribes and keep them neutral but, at the same time, to warn them of severe consequences if they sided with the British. He even had William Henry Harrison invite the Prophet and Tecumseh to Washington for a talk. Tecumseh was open to the idea, but the meeting never took place.

Madison's threats were hard to take seriously when only a few tiny forts defended the entire frontier. Little defense existed west of the Maumee River that flowed northeast 175 miles from Fort Wayne, to Toledo at the western end of Lake Erie, or west of the Wabash River, which flowed southwest 475 miles from Fort Recovery, Ohio, through Indiana to the Ohio River. Only small contingents of soldiers—from fifty to one hundred and twenty—were stationed at Detroit,

Fort Wayne, Fort Harrison (Terra Haute), Fort Dearborn (Chicago), and Fort Michilimackinac. Lieutenant Hanks had only sixty-one men.

Unaware war had broken out, and unacquainted with the president's war plans, Hanks was on his own. In fact, he had not received any messages from the War Department since the fall of 1811. It was not that the president and secretary of war did not understand the importance of Native American warriors to the British, or of Fort Michilimackinac; they certainly did, but with everything else needing attention and the War Department thinly staffed, many essential details were overlooked.

Unfortunately for Hanks, the British commander at Fort St. Joseph, Captain Charles Roberts, was an experienced fighter, and he did know a war was on. Furthermore, he had orders from the energetic General Brock to conduct a surprise attack on Fort Michilimackinac. Roberts's force of forty-four regulars was pathetically weak, but with reinforcements from the Indians—perhaps three hundred—and from French-Canadian voyageurs (fur trappers), he had an excellent chance of overpowering Hanks.

The attack Hanks feared came suddenly on July 17. Roberts struck with a mixed force of regulars, fur trappers, and Indians, numbering in the hundreds. The enterprising Roberts had command of the water and landed on Mackinac with no opposition. Earlier, he had seized John Jacob Astor's eighty-six-ton brig *Caledonia* that Astor used in the fur trading he conducted on both sides of the border. Roberts simply appropriated it; Astor, a staunch supporter of Madison, had no choice in the matter. With the *Caledonia* Roberts was able to transport two brass six-pounders, as well as all the ordinance he needed for the assault.

Continuing to meet no resistance after he landed, Roberts quickly surrounded Fort Michilimackinac and warned Hanks that if he fired a single gun, the tribesmen would massacre everyone at the fort and the adjacent village. It was a believable threat.

Surprised, greatly outnumbered, and fearing what the Native Americans would do to his men and the civilians in the fort and on the island, Hanks surrendered.

Along with Hanks and his men, Roberts captured four small, privately owned schooners. He put Hanks and his soldiers on parole and used two of the schooners, *Salina* and *Mary*, to transport them to Fort Detroit. Hanks was grateful to be keeping his scalp, but he was not looking forward to landing at Detroit, where General Hull was sure to initiate court-martial proceedings. Since Hanks had surrendered without a fight, he would face charges of cowardice.

Captain Roberts's seizure of Fort Michilimackinac meant that hundreds, and perhaps thousands, of warriors, energized by the American defeat, would be added to British ranks in Canada. General Hull at Fort Detroit would now have to worry about warriors from the western tribes descending on him, coordinating an attack with their British ally, taking Detroit, and not only destroying Madison's plans for a quick thrust into Upper Canada but seizing the whole of Michigan Territory as well. Instead of America annexing Upper Canada, the British would be acquiring the huge, sparsely populated northwestern part of the United States.

UNAWARE OF THE disaster at Fort Michilimackinac, General Hull was busy preparing to carry out his twin directives of defending Detroit and invading Upper Canada. Of course, the invasion would have to wait until war was declared. He did not receive word of it until July 2; the British, who were just across the Detroit River at Fort Malden in Amherstburg, Canada, knew on June 30.

General Hull (Captain Isaac Hull's uncle) was a distinguished veteran of the Revolutionary War, whom Jefferson had appointed governor and Indian agent for the Michigan Territory in 1805. Madison made him a brigadier general on April 8, 1812. Hull preferred appointment as secretary of war, but Madison had no intention of offering him that post and prevailed upon him to take the army command, promising he could continue as governor of Michigan.

Discussions about invading Upper Canada from Detroit had been going on in Washington since the spring of 1812, and Hull participated in them. On March 6, he wrote to Secretary of War Eustis, explaining the need to reinforce the small fort at Detroit and gain control of Lake Erie, then in possession of the small Canadian Provincial Marine. Hull was in favor of attacking Upper Canada from Detroit, but he pointed out that success depended on mounting a simultaneous attack in the Niagara area, creating a diversion that would force the British to divide their forces. Hull did not think Madison should concentrate his army and attack Montreal alone, leaving the Northwest to fend for itself.

Hull needed all the help he could get. He faced a formidable foe in forty-two-year-old Brigadier General Isaac Brock, the lieutenant governor of Upper Canada. A fearless professional soldier with a keen desire to distinguish himself on the battlefield, Brock was charismatic, aggressive to the point of recklessness, always at the head of his troops, willing to bear any hardship, beloved by his men—a soldier's soldier. He was also an imperialist with a marked devotion to the British Empire and a disdain for republican government.

Brock's superior was Governor-General Sir George Prevost, who was well acquainted with Canadian-American affairs, having served as lieutenant governor of Nova Scotia from 1808 to 1811. His headquarters were at Quebec, where he kept most of his sparse army of 7,000 to protect the fortress and the city against an American attack. He had been appointed as much for his diplomatic skills as for his fighting ability. Nationalism had begun to stir among French-Canadians in the 1790s, creating a headache for London, which Prevost was expected to handle. He spoke French and was particularly effective in enlisting French Canadians to defend Canada against the United States. Far more cautious than Brock, Prevost was focused exclusively on defending Canada. He gave no thought to invading the United States and kept the forceful, often rash Brock on a short leash. As long as Britain was tied down fighting Napoleon, Prevost expected to be on the defensive and vulnerable.

Brock's headquarters were at the tiny capital of Upper Canada at York (now Toronto) on Lake Ontario—a long way from Amherstburg and the surrounding settlements on the Detroit River. Brock was determined to defend the province, but he had only 1,200 regular British troops, which was a formidable small force but miniscule compared to what the United States could potentially put in the field. The size of the United States would have intimidated a lesser man, but adverse odds never fazed the romantic Brock. He did have to face certain realities, however. If the Americans attacked Amherstburg and the Niagara River towns simultaneously, which is what General Hull proposed and Madison promised, Brock would not know whether to commit his few troops to Detroit or to the Niagara area, or to divide them. No matter what he did, he had little prospect of success, unless he had the support of a large number of Native Americans. Relying on the Indians made Brock uncomfortable; he knew he needed them, but he had little respect for their military capacity.

General Hull insisted that without Indian support, "the British cannot hold Upper Canada." He foolishly suggested to Madison in the spring of 1812 that if enough reinforcements were sent to Detroit, the Indians would be intimidated, which in turn might cause the British to abandon weakly defended Upper Canada altogether. Their small lake fleet might then fall into American hands, giving the United States control of Lake Erie without having to build a fleet. The idea that Brock would just give up or that the United States did not have to build a fleet on Lake Erie was pure fantasy, although pleasing to the president, who did not want to spend time constructing warships when his grand strategy demanded action now.

But action required soldiers, and Madison did not have these any more than he had warships. Hull told the president that he required 4,000 troops to defend his headquarters at Detroit and invade Upper Canada. At the time, Hull had only

120 regulars at Detroit. Madison offered him 400 more, supplemented by militiamen from the adjacent states of Ohio and Kentucky. This arrangement seemed fine to the president. For him, the salient features of the British position in Canada were political weakness, a miniscule army, and an impossibly long supply line. Madison fancied that pro-American sentiment in Upper Canada was so strong that General Hull would probably have an easy time convincing her people to join the United States.

Generals Brock and Prevost worried about the same pro-American sentiment. As late as July 21, 1812, Brock wrote, "My situation is most critical, not from anything the enemy can do, but from the disposition of the people—the population, believe me—is essentially bad—a full belief possesses them all that the Province must inevitably succumb—this prepossession is fatal to every exertion."

Given this political reality, Madison thought a relatively small force could overrun Upper Canada. Invading from Fort Detroit was only one part of his grand plan, however. While Hull struck from Detroit, three more thrusts into Canada were to take place: one in the Niagara region at the western end of Lake Ontario, another against Kingston at the eastern end of Lake Ontario, and, the most important, against Montreal via Lake Champlain. Once Montreal was in American hands, Madison planned to assault Quebec and eventually overrun all of Canada. If he did not reach Quebec in the fall of 1812, he planned to attack in the spring of 1813.

The president was aware that dividing America's small army to invade a vast country at four widely separated points made no strategic sense. Concentrating his forces and striking directly at Montreal was a far better strategy. Once in control of Montreal, the army could choke off provisions flowing west to Upper Canada by way of the St. Lawrence River and the Great Lakes. Supply lines stretched all the way back to England; Canada produced almost nothing of her own, except raw materials. Everything else came from the mother country or from the United States. Cut off from the eastern provinces, Upper Canada would soon fall without the need for an invasion.

Quebec remained the most important target in Canada, but given the size of the American army and the political disposition of New England, Madison thought it made more sense to attack Montreal first. Instead of doing this, however, the president, for political reasons, decided to divide his forces and attack Detroit and the Niagara area first in order to take advantage, as he told Jefferson, "of the unanimity and ardor of Kentucky and Ohio." He also believed that concentrating on Montreal alone would risk "sacrificing the Western and Northwestern frontier, threatened with an inundation of savages under the influence of the British establishment near Detroit."

Madison appeared unaware of how important naval supremacy on lakes Erie, Ontario, and Champlain was to his Canadian project. In June 1812 the British had control of all three lakes, albeit with weak provincial forces. The only American warships on the Great Lakes were the 6-gun *Adams*—an old army transport built in 1800 but still serviceable—at Detroit and the 18-gun brig *Oneida* at Oswego on Lake Ontario, under Lieutenant Melancthon Woolsley. The *Oneida* had been stationed there originally to enforce Jefferson's embargo.

The Canadian Provincial Marine, on the other hand, had the 16-gun *Queen Charlotte*, the 12-gun *Hunter*, and the 12-gun *Lady Prevost* on Lake Erie, and the 22-gun *Royal George*, the 18-gun *Earl of Moira*, the 14-gun armed schooner *Duke of Gloucester*, and the recently launched 18-gun *Prince Regent* on Lake Ontario. With command of both lakes the British could use their fleet of 190 bateaux (flat-bottomed river craft from twenty-four feet to forty feet in length and tapered at both ends) to ferry men and supplies between Montreal and Amherstburg.

"The decided superiority I have obtained on the Lakes in consequence of the precautionary measures adopted the last winter," Prevost wrote to Henry Bathurst, the secretary of state for war and the colonies, "has permitted me to move without interruption . . . both troops and supplies of every description toward Amherstburg, while those for General Hull, having several hundred miles of wilderness to pass before they can reach Detroit, are exposed to be harassed and destroyed by the Indians."

SECRETARY EUSTIS LOOKED to Ohio's governor, Return J. Meigs, to supply significant numbers of militiamen to supplement the 400 regulars the administration was sending to Hull. Meigs was able to call up 1,800, but this was only half what Hull said he needed. The prospect of invading Canada and ending British support for the Indian nations was very popular in Ohio, but finding men to fight was still difficult.

Hull was compelled to organize his army at Urbana, Ohio, and hack a road for two hundred miles through dense forests, creeks, and swamps to Detroit. He began putting together his men at Dayton and then marched them to Urbana, where he picked up the rest of his army, and proceeded north to the rapids of the Maumee River, cutting through the wilderness terrain with enormous difficulty.

When Hull reached the Maumee, his army consisted of 1,800 inexperienced, unruly Ohio militiamen, augmented by 400 regular army troops. Three colonels,

Duncan McArthur, James Finlay, and Lewis Cass, led the militia. They were in competition with each other and had no respect for the aged Hull.

From the rapids of the Maumee, Hull moved slowly toward Detroit. On June 26, when he was about halfway there, he received a letter from Eustis, dated June 18, ordering him to move quickly to Detroit and await further instructions. Incredibly, the secretary made no mention of the declaration of war. Hull was lulled into thinking he had nothing to fear from the British strongpoint at Amherstburg on the Canadian side of the Detroit River. Since he was beyond the rapids of the Maumee, he chartered the *Cuyahoga Packet* and put his papers, heavy baggage, and sick troops aboard for a quick passage down the Maumee to Lake Erie and then to Detroit. As the unsuspecting packet attempted to pass by the town of Amherstburg, the Provincial Marine's 12-gun brig *Hunter* easily captured it. Lieutenant Colonel Thomas Bligh St. George, the commander at Fort Malden in Amherstburg, now had full details of Hull's plans and his state of readiness. St. George passed the information on to General Brock, who relayed it to General Prevost in Quebec.

Hull arrived at Detroit on July 5, concerned about his shrinking supplies. The population of the town and fort was 1,200, and he judged the food supply there would last only a few weeks. He sent an urgent message to Governor Meigs for provisions, and Meigs responded handsomely, organizing a huge supply train of pack horses loaded with flour and other essential goods, along with a small herd of cattle and ninety-five guards. Getting them to Detroit, however, was no easy matter. They had to trudge two hundred difficult miles through the same forest and swamps that Hull had, and then travel overland, avoiding the western shore of Lake Erie, where the cruisers of the Provincial Marine patrolled. If that were not difficult enough, the pack train would be subject to Indian attack along the entire route, particularly when it neared Lake Erie and Fort Malden.

On July 9, four days after arriving at Detroit, Hull received instructions from Eustis to invade Canada. Given the precarious state of his army and supplies, he warned Washington not to be too sanguine about what he could accomplish. Nonetheless, in obedience to his orders, he crossed the Detroit River into Canada on July 12, and easily took the small village of Sandwich (now Windsor), lying directly across the river from Detroit and sixteen miles north of Fort Malden.

The Canadian militiamen at Sandwich fled without a fight, much to the annoyance of General Brock. Sandwich's few inhabitants welcomed the Americans, which Hull took as an indication that most of the citizens of Upper Canada would cross over to his side. Flush from his first victory, he issued a proclamation promising the people, "You will be emancipated from tyranny and oppression and restored to the dignified station of free men."

Dozens of deserters appeared at his camp every day, giving him the feeling that Fort Malden would fall easily. He was further buoyed by the expectation that General Dearborn had already launched an attack in the Niagara area, diverting some, if not all, of Brock's available forces there, making a reinforcement of Malden unlikely.

Meanwhile, the British commander at Malden, Lieutenant Colonel St. George, was making his own preparations to resist the American invasion. He formed a defense line on the southern bank of the Canard River seven miles north of the fort and requested reinforcements. His force of three hundred regulars, four hundred fifty militiamen, and four hundred of Tecumseh's warriors would not be enough to withstand Hull's army.

The 6-gun army brig *Adams* added to Hull's force. He had men working on her for some time in a yard above Detroit, and while he was away, the work was completed. She was launched on July 4 and brought at night to the Detroit waterfront for arming under the guns of the fort.

Despite having an overwhelming advantage, Hull did not attack Fort Malden immediately. He inexplicably wasted days preparing two twenty-four pounders and three howitzers, while raiding the countryside for supplies, enraging the farmers he took them from. The delay puzzled his men and made them restless. They feared the old man did not have the stomach for a fight.

Hull was still preparing when, on July 26, the captured American schooners *Salina* and *Mary* appeared suddenly at Detroit, carrying Lieutenant Hanks and his party of soldiers and citizens from Fort Michilimackinac. Hull was aghast. "The surrender opened the Northern hive of Indians," he wrote to Secretary Eustis, "and they were swarming down in every direction."

Instead of immediately moving on Malden before it could be reinforced, Hull continued to wait at Sandwich, frustrating his officers, who wanted to attack right away. Morale in the ranks deteriorated as day after day of inaction followed. General Brock, meanwhile, was trying hard to take advantage of Hull's lethargy by raising five hundred militiamen to strengthen Fort Malden.

Hull continued to vacillate. He sent a detachment of two hundred men under Major Thomas Van Horne to find the supply train Governor Meigs had sent from Chillicothe (Ohio's capital) under militia Captain Henry Brush. Overcoming near impossible terrain, Brush had reached the rapids of the Maumee on August 5, but he did not dare go farther because he would have to pass too close to Fort Malden and the British warships on Lake Erie.

Tecumseh was keeping a close eye on Hull, and he convinced the Wyandot—who were heavily influenced by the easy British victory at Michilimackinac—to join him in a surprise attack on Van Horne's column. Tecumseh struck on August 5 at the village of Brownstone, about twenty miles south of Detroit. Taken completely by surprise, the Americans were scared out of their wits, and they ran wildly.

Even before Hull received word of the Brownstone debacle, he called a council of war to discuss the possibility of retreating. After a stormy session with officers who had lost all confidence in him, he reluctantly agreed to attack Fort Malden in three days. When he received word of the disaster at Brownstone, however, he changed his mind again. He was further rattled when two days later he heard that Brock had succeeded in sending reinforcements to Malden under Colonel Henry Proctor, who assumed command of the fort. The British position at Amherstburg was further strengthened by Wyandot and other Indians, whom the Provincial Marine ferried across Lake Erie. Even more disconcerting was intelligence that arrived on August 6, reporting that the diversion Hull was expecting General Dearborn to initiate in the Niagara area had not yet taken place.

Hull would have been shocked had he known what Major General Dearborn was actually doing. Instead of creating a diversion, he was at his headquarters in Greenbush outside Albany on August 9, discussing an armistice with Sir George Prevost's representative, Colonel Edward Baynes, the British adjutant general in Canada. Baynes explained to Dearborn that Lord Liverpool had repealed the Orders in Council in June and was seeking a temporary armistice to give the American government time to respond.

Even though he had known since the spring that Madison expected simultaneous attacks along the Canadian border at Detroit, Niagara, Kingston, and Montreal, and Secretary Eustis had issued orders again on August 1 to begin the offensive at once, Dearborn decided to accept the armistice. It did not seem to matter that by doing so he was leaving General Hull in the lurch. Since Dearborn was not in the least ready to invade anyway (partly because of his own lack of initiative), he viewed the armistice as a godsend. It would give him time to prepare, something he should have been doing for weeks.

Ignoring instructions from Secretary Eustis was a habit of General Dearborn's. He had been secretary of war for eight years under Jefferson, and he had trouble accepting Eustis as his superior. Earlier, when he was supposed to be at his headquarters assembling the army of invasion, he was in New England, and remained there until late July, discussing coastal defense and the calling up and use of militia with the antiwar Federalist governors of Massachusetts,

Connecticut, and Rhode Island. Eustis wrote to him saying that the president wanted him at Albany, but Dearborn remained in Massachusetts.

As part of the armistice, Dearborn agreed to put whatever invasion plans he had on hold and act only on the defensive until Washington could respond to London's peace initiative. To say the least, he was acting far beyond his authority. He knew, of course, that no invasion was going to take place anyway, whether he agreed to an armistice or not. The U. S. Army was utterly unprepared for an invasion. Dearborn was simply adjusting Madison's dreams to reality. He wrote to Secretary Eustis, "I consider the agreement as favorable . . . for we could not act offensively except at Detroit for some time, and there will probably [be no] effect on General Hull or his movements."

His claim that his actions would have no effect on Hull was astonishing. Dearborn was acting as if Hull's command was somehow independent of his own, despite the fact that the president had clearly placed Dearborn in charge of the entire northern front. The armistice technically did not even apply to Hull. Dearborn did send a message to Hull informing him of the armistice, but it never reached him.

Not only did Dearborn disregard Hull, but he gave no thought to how the armistice would influence General Brock's calculations. Brock had already set out for Fort Malden with reinforcements, but when he later heard of the armistice, he considered it a great boon. It would allow him time to complete his business at Detroit and return to the Niagara area and direct the defense there.

Dearborn's letter to Eustis announcing the armistice arrived in Washington on August 13. Madison was flabbergasted and rejected it out of hand. Not only did it emasculate his whole war strategy, but he had already turned down the idea of an armistice when Ambassador Foster and Chargé Baker had proposed it in Washington earlier. Furthermore, Madison did not want to hear that his grand scheme to drive into Canada was, to say the least, unrealistic. Eustis, reflecting the president's exasperation, fired back to Dearborn, "you will inform Sir George Prevost [that the armistice is terminated, and then] you will proceed with the utmost vigor in your operations."

To protect himself, Dearborn had already written to his friend Madison, blaming Eustis for the mix-up. He told the president—inaccurately—that he had no orders or directions relating to Upper Canada, "which I had considered as not attached to my command, until my last arrival at this place." He insisted that he had been "detained at Boston *by direction*." He then went on to assert that, "If I had been directed to take measures for acting offensively on Niagara and Kingston, with authority such as I now posses, for calling out the militia, we might have been prepared to act on those points as early as General Hull commenced his operations at Detroit; but unfortunately no explicit orders had been received by me in relation to Upper Canada until it was too late even to make an effectual diversion in favor of General Hull."

Despite his unwillingness to take responsibility for the inaction at Niagara and Kingston, the politically savvy Dearborn could see that the president was unwilling to accept the realities on the ground. Wanting to back off from an escalating confrontation, Dearborn sent Washington a feel-good message to relieve Madison's anxiety for the moment. "If the troops are immediately pushed on from the southward," he wrote to Eustis, "I think we may calculate on being able to possess ourselves of Montreal and Upper Canada before the winter sets in."

Given the state of the American army and the lack of naval supremacy on the lakes, this assessment was laughable. Nonetheless, the president and Eustis were receptive—as Dearborn knew they would be—to the notion that with the forces in hand, Hull and Dearborn, could still "secure Upper Canada" before the year was over.

The reality was far different. At Sandwich General Hull was growing more pessimistic by the hour. He thought his position had markedly deteriorated, and he was reconsidering his decision to attack Fort Malden. He feared that large numbers of western Indians were descending on his rear, and he believed that Fort Malden itself had been reinforced to the point where it was now equal in strength to his own force. Furthermore, the British had control of the Detroit River, and Captain Brush was stuck miles away at the Maumee with Governor Meig's supply train. In view of all this, Hull decided to retreat back to Fort Detroit. He even considered going all the way to the Maumee and making a juncture with Brush, but Ohio colonel Lewis Cass, furious at Hull's lack of aggressiveness, warned him that if he retreated to the rapids of the Maumee, all the Ohio militiamen would go home.

On the night of August 8, under cover of darkness, Hull surprised Colonel Proctor and the Provincial Marine and moved his army across the Detroit River to the safety of Fort Detroit without incident. The next day, Hull dispatched a substantial part of his effective force, six hundred men, including two hundred regulars with cavalry and artillery under Lieutenant Colonel James Miller, to escort Brush's supply train to Detroit and reestablish the fort's link with Ohio. Fourteen miles south of Detroit, however, at the Indian village of Maguaga, a mixed force of two hundred fifty British regulars, militiamen, and Tecumseh's Indians attacked Miller. After a vicious fight, Miller drove them back across the river to Amherstburg, but his men were so beaten up he returned to Detroit without making contact with Captain Brush, who by now had reached as far north as the River Raison, forty miles south of Detroit.

Meanwhile, General Brock, knowing nothing of the armistice worked out between Dearborn and Prevost, made the critical decision to ignore the threat from the Niagara area for the moment and concentrate on Hull. He also decided to take command at Fort Malden personally. Aided immeasurably by control of Lake Erie, he left Long Point on August 8 with three hundred additional troops and traveled by boat to Amherstburg, arriving five days later on the night of August 13.

The very same day, Colonel Proctor's men began preparing a battery at Sandwich to bombard Detroit. As they did, the Ohio militia colonels and many of their men had grown so tired of Hull's wavering they were seriously considering mutiny. Colonel Miller refused to go along with them, however, and since he was the ranking regular army officer, they backed off.

At the same time, Hull was growing increasingly despondent, worrying about what would happen to the women and children of Detroit if he were defeated. He envisioned thousands of angry tribesmen eviscerating them. While he brooded, General Brock held a strategy meeting the morning after he arrived at Fort Malden. Tecumseh, who now had 1,000 warriors at the fort, attended. He was delighted when Brock proposed crossing the river and attacking Fort Detroit right away.

Meanwhile, on August 14, Hull, knowing of the discontent bordering on mutiny in his ranks, sent the two chief malcontents, Colonels Lewis Cass and Duncan McArthur, away with four hundred men to bring the supply train on the River Raison forward to Detroit by a more circuitous route. After seeing the Ohio militiamen off, Hull got word of General Brock's arrival at Fort Malden with reinforcements, and on the fifteenth he hurriedly sent orders to Cass and McArthur to return.

Directly across the river at Sandwich, Brock was preparing a full-scale attack. On August 15 he sent a note to Fort Detroit, demanding Hull's surrender. "It is far from my inclination to join in a war of extermination," he wrote, "but you must be aware that the numerous body of Indians who have attached themselves to my troops, will be beyond my control the moment the contest commences."

Brock's demand seemed an outlandish, arrogant ploy, even to his own officers. Colonel Proctor thought the note was preposterous. Hull rejected Brock's demand, but he continued to be nervous and depressed about what he viewed as his worsening situation.

Immediately after Hull's refusal to surrender, the Provincial Marine's *Queen Charlotte* and *Hunter* moved upriver directly before Fort Detroit and, in concert with the batteries at Sandwich, opened fire. Hull replied with thirty-three pieces of iron and brass ordinance, and an inconclusive artillery duel commenced. One of the British cannonballs struck Lieutenant Porter Hanks, who was awaiting his court-martial, and cut him in two.

While the bombardment distracted Hull, Tecumseh and six hundred warriors silently crossed the river at night, followed in the wee hours of the morning by Brock with seven hundred fifty regulars. They brought five field pieces with them. Brock had no orders from Prevost to invade the United States, but he thought the situation demanded it. He soon discovered that the American colonels Cass and McArthur were in his rear with a substantial body of men and could possibly be returning to the fort. Brock decided to attack before the Ohioans reached the battlefield. He faced a substantial roadblock, however. Hull had placed two twenty-four pounders on the road, where the British troops had to pass. Brock's guns were six- and three-pounders. His men would have been cut to pieces. All the while, cannonballs from Sandwich on the other side of the river kept falling into the fort.

Refusing to back off, Brock exhibited a white flag and sent another message to Hull demanding that he surrender and save the fort and town from a bloody massacre. Brock's officers were astonished at his audacity. They did not expect to succeed against the fort's artillery, especially if Cass and McArthur were in their rear—although, as it turned out, they actually were not. (After leaving the fort, the disgruntled Ohio colonels ignored Hull's order to return, and deliberately stayed away.)

By this time Hull was more deeply depressed than ever about his position. He believed he was greatly outnumbered, that thousands of Indians were coming from the west, and that Tecumseh's force was three times the size it was. Brock's demand did not seem outlandish to him at all. Fearing the entire fort and town would be butchered, he did not delay long before surrendering without a fight. The British officers and Hull's own troops were astonished.

Brock's unexpected triumph produced a windfall for him. Hull forfeited not only the soldiers at Fort Detroit but the troops under Cass and McArthur and even those under Captain Henry Brush at the River Raisin—2,200 regulars and militiamen. In addition, Hull surrendered 33 pieces of artillery, 2,500 muskets, 5,000 pounds of gunpowder, and all the fort's other supplies, as well as the 6-gun brig *Adams*, tied up at Detroit's waterfront. The British later rename her *Detroit* in honor of their victory.

Adding to Hull's disaster, on August 15 a large force of Potawatomi massacred the American soldiers and civilians evacuating Fort Dearborn (Chicago). Afraid of just such an attack, Hull had ordered the evacuation, but it came much too late. The fort was burned, ending the last vestige of American authority west of the Maumee River. A few days later, similar Indian attacks were repulsed at Fort Harrison on the Wabash and at Fort Madison on the upper Mississippi. The battle at Fort Harrison went on for ten difficult days, from September 4 to 14. Captain Zachary Taylor was commander of the tiny American garrison, and he emerged as a hero. Hull's evacuation order had prevented Fort Dearborn from mounting a similar defense.

Immediately after taking Detroit, General Brock annexed all of Michigan Territory in the name of George III. It was the biggest loss of territory in American history. Tecumseh's dream of expelling the Americans from Indian lands north of the Ohio now came closer to reality.

ON AUGUST 28 President Madison and his wife were on the road, traveling to Montpelier, their plantation in Orange, Virginia, unaware of the momentous events at Detroit. The president was seriously ill with a recurring stomach ailment and in need of a long rest. Dolley feared for his life. As they approached the village of Dumfries, where they planned to stay for the night, an express rider galloped up unexpectedly and handed Madison an urgent message from Secretary Eustis, informing him of Hull's surrender. The president was dumbfounded. His entire war plan and his political future were suddenly in peril. In spite of his health, he returned to Washington the following morning.

Not surprisingly, as they were engaged in a tight reelection fight against De-Witt Clinton of New York, the president and his closest political allies thought the first order of business was to deflect blame away from the commander in chief and place it entirely on General Hull. Madison felt that accepting any responsibility for what happened at Detroit would be politically disastrous. Jefferson reflected the administration's approach when he wrote, "The treachery of Hull, like that of Arnold, cannot be a matter of blame to our government." Monroe called Hull "weak, indecisive, and pusillanimous." Colonel Lewis Cass wrote a scathing report of Hull's surrender, which Madison had printed in the *National Intelligencer*.

Much later, long after the election, the discredited Hull, who had returned on parole from captivity in Canada, received a court-martial that lasted from January 3 to March 26, 1814. The presiding judge was the president's close friend

Henry Dearborn. With two-thirds of the members concurring, the court convicted Hull of cowardice and neglect of duty and sentenced him to be shot, but the general's age and outstanding service during the Revolutionary War moved the court to recommend clemency to the president. On April 25 Madison solemnly pardoned Hull and cashiered him from the service. The culpability of the president, Secretary Eustis, and General Dearborn in the Canadian fiasco of 1812 was covered up.

Assigning exclusive blame to Hull, however, did not mitigate the dislike of the war that now spread over the entire country. Enthusiasm for invading Canada had never been strong, except in a few states, and it now sank to a new low, making recruitment for the army even more difficult. Madison's ability to lead the war inevitably came into question. Had it not been for the wildly popular victory of the *Constitution* over the *Guerriere*, happening at the same time, Hull's defeat probably would have cost the president reelection.

Naturally, Brock's wholly unexpected victory delighted the British. The news reached London the first week of October—before reports of the *Guerriere's* defeat. The *Times* wrote that General Hull's surrender "was a glorious occurrence." But when news of the *Constitution's* success arrived only hours later, the *Times* could scarcely believe it. "The disaster . . . is one of that nature, with which England is but little familiar," the editors lamented. "We would gladly give up all the laurels of Detroit, to have it still to say, that no British frigate ever struck to an American."

The debacle at Detroit and the loss of Michigan Territory did not mean Madison was giving up his plan to invade Canada. He was more determined than ever to carry it out. Once fixed on a design, particularly one as important as the Canadian invasion, he stuck with it. This mild-mannered man, who had never seen military service, was a stubborn fighter. He viewed General Hull's surrender as merely an unfortunate episode. In the middle of September he found another general to recover Detroit and resume the invasion. Secretary of State Monroe had volunteered for the job, but pressured by Henry Clay and the War Hawks, Madison appointed another Virginian, thirty-nine-year-old William Henry Harrison. Harrison was enormously popular in Kentucky, where the president hoped to raise a large contingent of militiamen.

Harrison was on the move quickly, trying to prevent a further deterioration of the American position in the Northwest. He dispatched an initial force of 900 from Piqua, Ohio, to relieve Fort Wayne in northeastern Indiana, which was under Indian and British attack. He then followed with 2,000 reinforcements. They drove the Indian besiegers away with no trouble.

Matters were proceeding so well in the fall that Harrison began thinking about a quick strike on Detroit. In preparation for it, he sent men to burn and butcher the inhabitants of as many hostile Indian villages as possible, but his raiders found that most of the inhabitants had already evacuated to the protection of Fort Malden.

Harrison then began running into the same difficulties that had bedeviled Hull—atrocious weather, lack of supplies, difficult terrain, and, above all, British control of Lake Erie, which permitted them to transport men and supplies with relative ease. Moving soldiers and equipment overland through thick forests and extensive swamps was next to impossible. Harrison soon became less confident about the Canadian invasion. Detroit and Fort Malden remained his objectives, but it was now obvious that capturing them would be far more difficult than the president had hoped.

CHAPTER NINE

~~~~~~~~

Canadian
Disasters Accumulate

E VEN BEFORE APPOINTING General Harrison, the president—finally realizing how important naval supremacy was to his Canadian invasion—began a crash program to dominate lakes Ontario, Erie, and Champlain. On August 31, fifteen days after Hull's surrender, Secretary Hamilton wrote to the talented navy veteran, forty-year-old Captain Isaac Chauncey, at the New York Navy Yard, "The President . . . has determined to obtain command of the Lakes Ontario and Erie with the least possible delay, and the execution of this highly important object is committed to you." Hamilton also wrote to naval hero Lieutenant Thomas Macdonough, giving him command of the moribund program on Lake Champlain.

Captain Chauncey had been in the navy since September 1798 and had served continuously through the Quasi-War with France and the war with Tripoli. During the Quasi-War he superintended construction of the 44-gun *President*, which Captain Thomas Truxtun pronounced "the finest frigate that ever floated on the waters of this globe." Before joining the service, Chauncey had sailed and traded around the world as skipper of merchant vessels owned by John Jacob Astor. Except for a brief period when he sailed to China for Astor, Chauncey remained in the navy after the war with Tripoli, being promoted to captain in 1806. During his naval career he had not attained the notoriety of other officers like Decatur, Rodgers, or Preble, but his peers respected him as a brave, competent skipper, a solid administrator, and a wizard at the building and refitting of warships.

Lieutenant Macdonough was also an experienced seaman and known for his fighting ability. He began his naval career during the later stages of the Quasi-War with France. His father had been a hero during the Revolutionary War, and his brother James was a wounded hero of the Quasi-War. Macdonough was intelligent, studious, thoughtful, but also, like his mentor, Stephen Decatur, a fearless warrior. It was during the conflict with Tripoli, while Macdonough was serving under Decatur as a midshipman, that he showed his audacious fighting qualities. He was part of Decatur's crew aboard the tiny ketch *Intrepid* on February 2, 1804, when they slipped into the well-guarded harbor of Tripoli, boarded the captured American frigate *Philadelphia* through trickery, and, after a brief, fierce fight, drove the Tripolitans off the ship and burned her. Decatur, Macdonough, and their crew then jumped back into the *Intrepid* and escaped, as the *Philadelphia* became a giant ball of flame and the Tripolitans fired at them from their extensive shore batteries and warships. As the Americans inched their way out of the harbor, balls flew over their boat, but only one came near them. Miraculously, no one aboard the *Intrepid* was hit.

Some months later, on August 3, 1804, Macdonough was again with Decatur in gunboat number four when Commodore Preble sent six gunboats as part of a small squadron to attack Tripoli's nineteen gunboats and galleys and assorted other craft in Tripoli harbor. Both Decatur and Macdonough distinguished themselves in the fierce hand-to-hand fights that followed. Preble organized more attacks in the month that followed, but he was ultimately unsuccessful. His countrymen, however, appreciated his gallantry and the heroic efforts of his men. Macdonough was recognized by Preble, Decatur, and the entire officer corps as one of their finest officers, and that opinion had not changed by the time he was put in charge at Lake Champlain.

IT WAS OBVIOUS from the correspondence that passed during the next few days in August that although the administration was on fire to get its new project moving, Madison and his advisors knew next to nothing about the lakes. Fortunately, Daniel Dobbins appeared in Washington at the time to enlighten them. He was a master lake mariner and shipwright, intimately acquainted with lakes Ontario and Erie. He knew where vessels suitable for conversion to warships might be obtained, and the best harbors to use. He also had a good idea of British naval strength on the lakes.

The president would need all the help he could get. When Chauncey received his orders, it was already September, and Madison wanted to achieve naval dominance before winter set in. It was a daunting assignment, but Chauncey was happy to have it. He did not want to be stuck in the New York Navy Yard and miss his chance for the glory other officers were acquiring. Isaac Hull's great victory had set the ambitions of the whole officer corps on fire.

The only suitable place for a naval facility on Lake Ontario was Sackets Harbor at its eastern extremity. Other possible sites farther west, such as Mexico Bay, the mouth of the Oswego River, Sodus Bay, Irondequoit Bay at the mouth of the Genesee River, or the mouth of the Niagara River, were not suitable for one reason or another. Fortunately for Chauncey, thirty-year-old Lieutenant Melancthon T. Woolsey had already established a small naval base at Sackets Harbor, and he had a potent brig, the *Oneida*, with eighteen twenty-four-pound carronades ready to go. More importantly, he had a trained crew that could fight. No comparable base existed on Lake Erie, however. Secretary Hamilton directed Chauncey to organize one at Buffalo, but after Daniel Dobbins had a chance to enlighten the secretary, he ordered Chauncey to set up a base at Presque Isle (Erie), Pennsylvania, where the harbor was spacious and deep.

While Madison was rushing to catch up on the lakes, the British were building more warships at Kingston to strengthen their hold on Lake Ontario. Kingston was only thirty-five miles from Sackets Harbor. The British were also building warships at York.

Chauncey was in an arms race, and he didn't lose any time getting to work. With remarkable speed, he stripped the New York Navy Yard of equipment, tools, skilled workmen, and every article of war, including cannon, carriages, shot, power, and small arms, shipping them to Sackets Harbor. He also took officers, sailors, and marines off the frigate *John Adams* and the gunboats in his command and sent them to Sackets as well.

Incredibly bad roads forced Chauncey to transport everything via a tortuous, time-consuming water route, made more difficult because Robert Fulton's steamboats were unavailable. Chauncey had to rely on sail alone. His supply vessels worked their way laboriously from New York up the Hudson and then the Mohawk, where varying depths of water made the going treacherous. From there, they navigated over Wood Creek and then a portage to Oneida Lake, across the lake and down the Oneida River, which brought them to Oswego on Lake Ontario. Finally, they had to sail almost fifty treacherous miles north, hugging the coast until they reached Sackets Harbor. Along this final leg of their journey, they were subject to British attacks out of Kingston.

On September 7 Chauncey dispatched his able subordinate Lieutenant Jesse D. Elliott to construct the base on Lake Erie, purchase three merchantmen for conversion to warships, and begin building two three-hundred-ton warships. Seven days later, Elliott arrived at Buffalo and decided, in spite of Dobbins's advice, that Black Rock—just north of Buffalo on the Niagara River—was a better place for a base, even a temporary one, than Presque Isle.

Elliott set to work immediately, buying three merchant vessels and converting them to armed schooners. While he was doing so, two British warships appeared nearby and anchored across the Niagara River at Fort Erie. They were the *Detroit*—formerly the *Adams* that General Brock had just seized at Detroit—and the brig *Caledonia*, taken from Jacob Astor for the attack on Fort Michilimackinac.

On September 22, while Elliott was contemplating how he might capture the two British ships, ninety men arrived in camp. Chauncey had sent them from New York. Elliot decided to put them to work right away. As luck would have it, a brigade of American regulars was in Buffalo at the time, under Brigadier General Alexander Smyth—part of the army that was supposed to have invaded Canada weeks before. With help from General Smyth and a new arrival, Lieutenant Colonel Winfield Scott, Elliott set out at one o'clock in the morning on October 8 in two large boats from Buffalo Creek with a mixed force of a hundred men— fifty to a boat—to "cut out [the] two British vessels under the guns of Fort Erie."

Elliott's boats pulled silently across the Niagara River, and within minutes they were alongside the enemy unobserved. Taken by surprise, the watches aboard the ships surrendered after a short, sharp fight in which two Americans were killed outright and four mortally wounded.

Once in control of the ships, Elliott sheeted home the topsails and made for the opposite shore. The wind was light and the current running at a brisk four miles an hour. The *Caledonia*, under Sailing Master George Watts, struggled across the river to Black Rock, where Watts beached her near a protective battery. Elliott was aboard the larger brig *Detroit*, but the breeze wasn't strong enough to take her into safe water. Instead, the current carried her down past the batteries at Fort Erie. Alerted by all the commotion, British gunners sprayed the *Detroit* with round, grape, and canister shot as she sailed by. Elliott continued drifting downriver, firing back at Fort Erie until he was beyond the reach of her guns. He landed on the American side at Squaw Island and went ashore with his officers and prisoners. As soon as he arrived, he asked Lieutenant Colonel Scott to protect the *Detroit* with his artillery. Scott began firing on a party of forty British soldiers sent in three boats to retrieve the abandoned brig. In a short time, nearly every British soldier was dead, and the brig badly shot up. The few British soldiers who were still alive retreated, but the *Detroit* could not be salvaged.

Despite the loss of the *Detroit*, Elliott did manage to capture the *Caledonia*, and he took sixty prisoners. He also salvaged four twelve-pounders, a large quantity of shot, and two hundred muskets, depriving General Brock of two scarce vessels and an important supply of munitions at a critical moment in the subsequent battle of Queenston.

WHILE CHAUNCEY WAS straining every nerve to gain naval supremacy on Lake Ontario, preparations for crossing the Niagara River and invading Canada were moving at a glacial pace. Dearborn's dithering had allowed General Brock to rush from Detroit to the Niagara area and take personal command of all the troops in the area. On August 17, only one day after Hull's surrender, Brock set sail from Amherstburg. Fighting contrary winds the entire way, he arrived at Fort Erie on August 23. His haste was unnecessary. The disorganized American army was not in the least ready to cross the Niagara. Its leader, New York militia general Stephen Van Rensselaer, had only just arrived in Lewiston to take command.

The Niagara region is a thirty-six-mile-wide neck of land separating Lake Ontario from Lake Erie. The Niagara River, the boundary between the United States and Canada, flows through it northward for thirty-one miles from Lake Erie to Lake Ontario. Fort Erie was located at the southern end of the river on the Canadian side, directly across the river from Buffalo, a small town of around five hundred. Fort George was at the northern end of the river on the Canadian side. Opposed to it on the American side was old Fort Niagara, built originally by the French in 1729. General Dearborn was headquartered outside Albany, a distant three hundred miles away.

When Major General Van Rensselaer rode into Lewiston on the twenty-third of August, he found that only four hundred regulars and a few hundred unreliable militiamen were scattered along the river. Before doing anything else, he consolidated them at Lewiston, six miles north of Niagara Falls. He was appalled at their condition. The army's inadequate supply system left the men improperly clothed, many without shoes, no tents, less than ten rounds of ammunition per man, and all with pay in arrears. Van Rensselaer's position was so weak he feared Brock would attack him, rather than the other way around. Dearborn feared the same thing.

Their fears were justified. Even though Brock had no more than 2,000 men guarding the Niagara area and only 300 at Queenston (directly across the river from Van Rensselaer's headquarters at Lewiston), he seriously considered crossing the river and disrupting Van Rensselaer's invasion plans, as he had done so effectively against Hull. Brock thought that waiting for the American army to get stronger was a strategic mistake. In his view, remaining on the defensive would bring disaster to Upper Canada. But at the moment he had no choice. The armistice prevented him from taking immediate action, and he had orders from Governor-General Prevost not to invade New York.

Brock was fortunate in his opponent, General Van Rensselaer, an earnest man and a patriot but with no military experience. The head of the vastly wealthy Van Rensselaer family from the Albany area, he was a formidable Federalist politician and a likely candidate for governor, but he was not a soldier. Why Republican governor Daniel Tompkins appointed him was a mystery. If Van Rensselaer successfully invaded Canada, his chances of becoming governor, or even president, would be greatly enhanced. Van Rensselaer wasn't going anywhere soon, however. He believed that Brock had 3,000 soldiers at Queenston, rather than 300. His intelligence was as bad as General Hull's had been.

Van Rensselaer received word of Dearborn's armistice on August 18, even before he reached Lewiston, and a few days later he was informed of Hull's surrender. The defeat stunned him, but at the same time, he was relieved that the armistice would allow him time to assemble more men, guns, equipment, and supplies. Without them, an invasion was inconceivable.

The armistice began officially on August 20. But six days later, when Dearborn received orders from Washington to get on with the invasion, he notified Governor-General Prevost that the armistice would end in four days. This did not matter to Van Rensselaer, who felt he could not begin his attack until many weeks later.

In the meantime, Dearborn, for once, worked hard sending troops to the front. Governor Tompkins gave him indispensable aid. Thanks for the most part to the energetic Tompkins, men and equipment began pouring into Lewiston and Buffalo. As they did, Van Rensselaer worried that Brock might attack him before he was ready. And Brock might well have, but Prevost kept him on a tight leash, continuing to forbid any further invasion of American territory. By the middle of October, Van Rensselaer had assembled 2,400 regulars and 4,000 militiamen, mostly from New York but some from Pennsylvania. Even though half of the militiamen were untrained, Van Rensselaer now had more than enough fighters to overpower Brock, who by then had 1,200 regulars, 810 Canadian militiamen, and 300 or 400 Native American warriors.

While Van Rensselaer was building his army, Brigadier General Alexander Smyth, the adjutant general of the U. S. Army, appeared at Dearborn's camp and asked for a command at the front. Dearborn obliged, sending him to Buffalo with a brigade. He made it clear to Smyth, however, that Van Rensselaer was in overall command.

Smyth arrived at Buffalo on September 29 and soon became convinced that the main action in the Niagara region would be above the falls, and for that reason he insisted on remaining at Buffalo. Van Rensselaer, however, planned to attack Brock below the falls at Fort George and Queenston. Refusing to subordinate himself to a state militia officer, Smyth stubbornly maintained his independence and stayed at Buffalo with his brigade of regulars, cooperating only when it suited him. He even failed to attend Van Rensselaer's councils of war.

Neither Dearborn nor Van Rensselaer forced Smyth to cooperate. Having never held a command before, Van Rensselaer was unsure of himself. An experienced, confident officer would have quickly put Smyth in his place. Dearborn—far away in Albany—acted as if he were unaware of Smyth's gross insubordination. He also ignored the fact that New York militia general Amos Hall and quartermaster Peter B. Porter were remaining in Buffalo and not giving Van Rensselaer their full cooperation either.

Even with all his difficulties, Van Rensselaer had an overwhelming advantage in numbers, and Dearborn, not understanding what the delay was, ordered him to get on with the invasion. Dearborn still hoped to make simultaneous attacks at Detroit, Queenston, and Montreal before winter set in.

Van Rensselaer's troops were just as unhappy with his lack of initiative as Dearborn was. With winter getting closer, their morale was sinking fast. Van Rensselaer reported that "the partial success of Lieutenant Elliott at Black Rock began to excite a strong disposition on the part of the troops to act," threatening that "they would go home" otherwise.

Continuing to be overly cautious, Van Rensselaer decided to attack only Queenston for the moment, not Fort George. He planned to make his crossing under the cover of darkness on October 13. What would happen if he succeeded was unclear. Dearborn had no general plan to exploit a victory; he apparently just wanted to establish a foothold on Canadian soil before winter arrived.

Crossing the river at any time, but particularly at night, would be dangerous. In the Queenston-Lewiston area, the Niagara was two hundred fifty yards wide and had a fast, four-mile-an-hour current with swirling eddies. Astonishingly, Van Rensselaer had only thirteen bateaux assembled for the crossing. Dozens existed on the American side, but he was able to muster only thirteen. If all the boats made it across, they could bring over only three hundred men at a time.

The invasion began as planned on the cold clear night of October 13. Thirteen bateaux began embarking from Lewiston at 3:30 in the morning with roughly twenty-five men in each boat. They were all regulars. Confusion at the embarkation point forced the assembled militiamen to wait for the second wave. An experienced officer, state militia lieutenant colonel Solomon Van Rensselaer, the general's cousin and chief advisor, went in the first wave. Unlike his cousin, Solomon was a strong, competent leader. Lieutenant Colonel John Christie led the regulars, along with Captain John Wool.

As expected, the passage was difficult. The current caught three of the bateaux and carried them swirling downstream, where they landed with great difficulty on the American side. The men were lucky not to have drowned. Christie was in one of the lost boats, and Wool had to take over for him.

With British sentries firing on them from the top of a forty-foot-high bank, the other ten bateaux crossed the river. When they reached the Canadian side, they quickly debarked on the beach, sent the boats back, and raced for cover. Once the Americans had all landed, the sentries retired. Lieutenant Colonel Van Rensselaer and Captain Wool led the men as they crawled up the treacherous bank and marched toward Queenston Heights, the commanding hill that overlooked the village and the British encampment. On the opposite shore a few American cannon fired tentatively to support the landing. It was so dark the gunners did not know where to fire without hitting their own troops. They soon had to stop and wait for daylight.

The gunfire alerted the British camp, and redcoats hurriedly assembled. Captain James Dennis, their commander, directed an attack on the American column, and a fierce firefight developed. Solomon Van Rensselaer was shot several times and badly wounded. Although injured himself, Captain Wool assumed command. Savage fighting continued, and under Wool's leadership, the Americans drove off the British, who retreated back to Queenston Village. Wool then moved Van Rensselaer and the rest of their men back down to the beach to regroup.

When alerted to the American attack, General Brock was at Fort George. He called for his horse and galloped seven difficult miles in the dark to Queenston, arriving at daybreak. The first thing he did was climb to the battery on Queenston Heights and survey the battlefield. He left a short time later, narrowly avoiding capture, for just after he departed, the enterprising Wool, taking an unguarded path up the back of the hillside, appeared suddenly on the hilltop with two hundred and forty men. The British artillerymen working the battery panicked and ran.

Not wanting to concede the strategic heights and the cannon on it, Brock hastily organized fifty men at the base of the hill and counterattacked, leading the charge himself. He had no idea how many enemy fighters were above. At six feet three inches tall, in full uniform, brandishing a sword, he was an easy target. One of Wool's sharpshooters stepped forward, leveled his musket, and shot Brock in the chest. George Jervis, a lad of fifteen, was fighting at General Brock's side and saw him slump to the ground, put a hand on his chest, and expire without saying a word. The shock of his death caused the attack to collapse, and the British retreated.

Captain Wool, with blood still oozing from his wound, now commanded the heights. If reinforcements arrived in time, victory was assured. And reinforcements did come, swelling Wool's force to four hundred men, but he needed far more to hold his position. He did manage to beat back a determined counterattack by Lieutenant Colonel John Macdonell and Captain John Williams later that morning. Williams was wounded and Macdonell killed. Afterward, Captain Dennis, who was now the senior British officer, ordered a retreat to the village, and then evacuated it, intending to regroup and attack the heights again when reinforcements arrived. If General Van Rensselaer could ferry more troops over the now undefended river, he could easily secure Queenston and win a great victory.

Meanwhile, Major General Roger Hale Sheaffe was at Fort George directing a bombardment of Fort Niagara and the village of Niagara when he learned of Brock's death. Sheaffe had already received an urgent request for reinforcements, and he was soon on the road to Queenston with eight hundred men, supplemented by an Indian contingent under John Norton, a protégé of Joseph Brant, the fiercely anti-American Iroquois leader who died in 1807. John Brant, Joseph's son, was with Norton. Sheaffe was a much different character from the beloved, charismatic Brock. A heartless martinet from a Boston Tory family, he was a successful, although far from brilliant, soldier.

When Sheaffe arrived at Queenston, he assembled a counterattack aimed at the heights. By then, Lieutenant Colonel Winfield Scott had crossed the river and had taken command at the heights, replacing Brigadier General William Wadsworth of the New York militia and Lieutenant Colonel John Christie, who had recrossed the river and sent the wounded Wool back to Lewiston for care. The Americans now had over 925 men in Queenston. But a third of them were stuck at the riverbank, huddled down, not taking part in the action, leaving Scott with fewer than 600 fighting men. And his numbers were dwindling. Some men died fighting off John Norton's Iroquois snipers, and others, frightened by the Indians, deserted.

Meanwhile, all was confusion on the American side of the river, where the hapless Van Rensselaer was trying desperately to move more men across the river and into the fight. If he had succeeded, Scott would have had overwhelming numbers, and Sheaffe would have been forced to retreat. Sheaffe's Indian allies would likely have melted back into the woods and gone home. But Van Rensselaer was unable to persuade more militiamen to cross. While he was trying, the British were cannonading the embarkation points, making getting into the bateaux so dangerous that finding rowers was difficult. The New York militiamen claimed they could not be forced to invade another country. Undoubtedly frightened by the Iroquois, they were willing to leave their comrades—many of whom were militiamen like themselves—stranded.

Communications with General Smyth in Buffalo remained poor. Smyth tried to send men to help Van Rensselaer earlier, but bad weather had driven them back, and now he was unaware that his regulars were sorely needed at Queenston. They could have made the difference. They would not have refused to cross. But deprived of Smyth's men, Van Rensselaer became convinced he had run out of options, and he sent word to Scott that he could expect no reinforcements. Van Rensselaer, as he had throughout the battle, stayed on the New York side of the river away from the fighting. He had crossed only once and remained briefly; otherwise he kept away, uncertain how to proceed. His severely wounded cousin Solomon was not available to advise him, and he appeared lost.

In the meantime, the British force under Sheaffe was swelling to over 1,000, not including Norton's men, while Scott's contingent on the heights had dwindled to fewer than 400. Sheaffe attacked and pushed Scott down to the riverbank, where he was trapped. By four o'clock Scott was forced to give up. He had a hard time getting to Sheaffe to surrender, however. The Indians wanted no compromise; they were intent on a massacre. When Scott, at great personal risk, finally reached Sheaffe, his surrender was accepted, saving himself and his men from a merciless scalping. To Sheaffe's amazement, he rounded up 958 prisoners, many of them men who had crossed the river but had remained hidden under the cover of the high riverbank. Ninety Americans were killed during the day and a hundred wounded. The British suffered fourteen killed, eighty-four wounded, and fifteen missing.

In his report to Dearborn, General Van Rensselaer wrote, "the victory was really won, but lost for want of a small reinforcement; one-third of the idle men might have saved all." Sheaffe sent the American regulars, including Scott, to prison in Quebec and paroled the militiamen to their homes.

On October 16, Van Rensselaer resigned, and Dearborn, who was quick to put all the blame for the disaster on Van Rensselaer, replaced him with Smyth, who had plans to attack Fort Erie and plant the American standard on Canadian soil before winter. Dearborn hoped to attack Montreal at the same time. While Smyth was preparing his invasion, Dearborn organized a campaign against Montreal. He had over 6,000 men, the largest army on either side of the border. Brigadier General Joseph Bloomfield was at Plattsburg in command of the troops, but he was ill, and Dearborn decided to lead the attack himself with 3,000 regulars and nearly 4,000 militiamen.

On November 19, Dearborn marched twenty-five miles from Plattsburg to the Canadian border, but when his militiamen refused to go any farther, he retreated back to winter quarters at Plattsburg on November 23, completing a humiliating, farcical, four-day campaign. In his report to Secretary Eustis, Dearborn bemoaned the lack of more regular troops and offered to resign.

Smyth, meanwhile, was preparing a river crossing and assault on Fort Erie. While he was getting ready, so were the British, who were well informed about his activities. They were aided by Smyth himself, who made no effort to conceal what he was doing, perhaps thinking that if he made enough noise the Canadian militiamen would lose heart and surrender without the need for heavy fighting. Whatever his motives, he made pretentious, widely publicized statements condemning Van Rensselaer's strategy and ability while trumpeting the zeal and prowess of his own army. He also announced his intention to invade, and he even gave details of his plans.

If Smyth hoped the Canadians would lose heart, he was mistaken. The Canadian militia and British regulars were buoyed by their victory at Queenston, and they awaited Smyth with increasing confidence and numbers. The defeatist talk that Brock worried about earlier had disappeared from Upper Canada.

While Smyth was threatening Fort Erie, the British began bombarding Fort Niagara again from Fort George. General Sheaffe hoped to divert American attention from Fort Erie by threatening to follow up his victory at Queenston by capturing Fort Niagara. Cannonading commenced at five o'clock on the morning of November 21 and lasted until sunset.

Under Lieutenant Colonel George McFeeley, the garrison at Fort Niagara responded in kind, and they gave as good as they got. A Mrs. Doyle, wife of a private captured at Queenston, fired a six-pounder from the old mess house, pouring out red hot shot for as long as she had ammunition. McFeeley said she "showed fortitude equal to the *maid of Orleans*." The Americans fought so well that Sheaffe gave up any thought of attacking.

At the other end of the Niagara, on November 28, General Smyth began his attack on Fort Erie at three o'clock in the morning. Two advance parties, totaling two hundred men, under Lieutenant Colonel Charles Boerstler and Captain William King, rowed silently across the river in ten boats. Smyth had enlisted the help of navy lieutenant Samuel Angus, who was temporarily in charge at Black Rock while Lieutenant Elliott was at the other end of Lake Ontario helping Chauncey. Angus supplied seventy seamen to row Smyth's troops.

The British were well prepared. They fired on the boats as they crossed and attacked the men when they landed. Nonetheless, Boerstler and King fought their way inland and managed to spike a number of guns, but they were hopelessly outnumbered. British lieutenant colonel Cecil Bisshop counterattacked and forced them back to their boats under fire. The Americans brought what wounded they could with them, but many were captured before they reached the boats.

On the other side of the river, Smyth began embarking the main force at dawn, but in spite of his earlier bombast, only 1,200 regulars were ready. Both he and Dearborn thought at least 3,000 were required for success, but the militiamen would not cross over, and many of Smyth's regulars were in poor health. In view of this, Smyth called off the attack. He tried once more on the first of December, but he could only assemble 1,500 men, and they were not physically ready to fight either. Again, Smyth canceled the invasion. By this time his men had lost all faith in him. Many wanted to kill him. Winfield Scott in his *Memoirs* wrote that Smyth "showed no talent for command and made himself ridiculous on the Niagara frontier."

Having lost the confidence of the troops and his superiors, and having become something of a laughingstock, Smyth requested leave, which Dearborn quickly granted. Smyth returned to Washington, where a much annoyed president had him dropped from the army's rolls.

With the Niagara region now in the grip of winter, military activity came to an end until spring. From time to time both sides expressed fears that the other might initiate surprise attacks, but nothing materialized.

GENERAL WILLIAM HENRY Harrison was also running into severe difficulties trying to recapture Detroit and invade Upper Canada. In September, October, and November, he concentrated on building an army that could retake Detroit. But just provisioning the troops was impossible. On October 25 from his headquarters at Piqua, Ohio, he complained that his men were "without blankets, and much the greater part of them totally destitute of every article of winter clothing."

Harrison recognized that attempting to recapture Detroit would invite another disaster if he did not also take Fort Malden. He thought that when the ground froze, he might be able to attack Malden over the ice. So despite the lateness of the season, he kept organizing for a campaign, absorbing an enormous amount of the War Department's resources. Harrison's army of perhaps 4,000 was strung out over two hundred miles of hazardous terrain from the Maumee River in the west to the Sandusky River in the east. He divided his force into three columns. The left, consisting of 1,300 Kentucky militiamen and regulars, was headquartered in Fort Defiance at the juncture of the Maumee and Auglaize rivers under sixty-one-year-old Brigadier General James Winchester, an old Revolutionary War veteran. Harrison commanded the rest of the army himself. He hoped to converge the columns at the rapids of the Maumee, but the terrain and weather stymied him. Trying to march men and equipment through swamps during the autumn rains in that part of Ohio was incredibly difficult. Time passed, and delay followed delay. When January 1813 arrived, Harrison was still far from mounting an attack on either Detroit or Fort Malden.

General Winchester, meanwhile, was itching to do something, and on January 17, when Americans from Frenchtown on the River Raison requested help destroying a small British occupying force that General Henry Proctor had sent from Fort Malden, he decided to escape the boredom of the fort and rescue the town. Acting on flimsy intelligence, Winchester dispatched half his men, about six hundred fifty, to Frenchtown, where they met a small but tenacious British force and, after a violent fight, defeated them and captured the town. Winchester soon followed with two hundred fifty more men, and Harrison marched to Fort Defiance to support him.

With good intelligence of Winchester's movements, General Proctor led a force of regulars and Potawatomi from Fort Malden across the frozen Detroit River to Frenchtown, surprised Winchester, and easily defeated him. Unaccountably, no American patrols were out watching for the British. Proctor returned to Fort Malden with five hundred prisoners, including Winchester, leaving behind forty American wounded, whom the Potawatomi mercilessly scalped. The story of this massacre grew in the telling, and "Remember the Raison" became a rallying cry in the South and West throughout the war.

After Winchester's defeat at Frenchtown, Harrison, who had reached Fort Defiance, took 2,000 men to the rapids of the Maumee, where he constructed a stronghold called Fort Meigs. To all intents and purposes, the land campaign was over for the season. It had been a complete failure. Harrison escaped blame, however; criticism focused on Winchester.

UNLIKE HIS ARMY colleagues, Commodore Chauncey was having great success. On October 6, 1812, he arrived at Sackets Harbor, where Lieutenant Melancthon Woolsey welcomed him. Woolsey had been the senior officer in command on the Great Lakes, and Chauncey superseded him, but Woolsey would remain as Chauncey's deputy and skipper of the 16-gun *Oneida*. Woolsey was an under-appreciated veteran who had served in the navy since the Quasi-War with France. His roots went back to the Revolutionary War, when his father fought in the Continental Army. Although Chauncey took over command, Woolsey showed no animosity and did everything he could to support him.

The *Oneida* was a small ship—eighty-five feet on the upper deck—but potent. She carried eighteen thirty-two-pound carronades, and under Woolsey her crew was the best by far on the Great Lakes. The renowned New York City shipbuilder Henry Eckford, an old friend of Chauncey's who would play a major role in the building of the American fleet on Lake Ontario, had built the *Oneida* at Oswego in 1808. She helped enforce Jefferson's embargo. Nineteen-year-old Midshipman James Fenimore Cooper served on board her for a time under Woolsey. When Chauncey saw the *Oneida* for the first time, he judged her to be a fine ship. To supplement her, Woolsey had purchased five schooners for conversion to warships. In addition, he had a ship on the stocks, the *Madison*, designed to mount twenty-four thirty-two-pound carronades. He hoped to have her ready in six weeks.

The Canadian Provincial Marine had already built the 24-gun vessel *Royal George* at Kingston. She was meant to be larger and stronger than the *Oneida*. But the Provincial Marine was engaged almost exclusively in transportation and did not have crews trained for naval warfare, which gave Woolsey's *Oneida* a distinct edge.

Before Chauncey arrived at Sackets Harbor, a British force had appeared un-expectedly off shore on July 19, 1812, intent on capturing the *Oneida*. The British ships were the *Royal George, Earl of Moira, Duke of Gloucester, Seneca*, and *Simcoe*, a squadron that sounded far more powerful than it was because the crews lacked training. The *Oneida* alone would have given them trouble in a fight. The British demanded the surrender of the *Oneida* and the *Lord Nelson*, a Canadian merchant schooner Woolsey had captured on June 5. Woolsey answered with a single, long thirty-two-pounder he had mounted on a battery to defend the port. After a two-hour exchange from long range, the British vessels withdrew.

By a Herculean effort, Chauncey and Woolsey had a fleet up and running during the first week of November. With it, Chauncey was ready to challenge the British for control of Lake Ontario. Winter had already begun, but he was planning an expedition against Kingston. Ned Myers, one of Chauncey's young seamen, pointed out that this was "rather a latish month for active service on those waters."

The same month that Chauncey's fleet became ready on Lake Ontario, an event occurred that underscored his growing strength. On November 2, while he was in the midst of planning his attack, he set out in the *Oneida* to find a British vessel reported to be keeping an eye on Sackets Harbor. He stood for Kingston to cut her off, but the night was exceptionally dark and rainy with squalls. At daylight, when the haze cleared, he discovered that he was off Kingston, where he saw the main British lake fleet—the 26-gun *Royal George* and the armed schooners *Duke of Gloucester* (14 guns) and *Prince Regent* (18 guns)—lying at anchor about five miles away. Thinking they would be after him, Chauncey wore ship to the southward and cleared for action. But strangely, the British squadron remained immobile, appearing to take no notice of Chauncey. He could not understand what was going on.

Hard as it was for Chauncey to comprehend, Master and Commander Hugh Earl, the British commanding officer, decided to forgo a fight, judging perhaps that his crews were not ready to get into a brawl with the *Oneida*. Whatever the reason, Chauncey, more than a little puzzled, returned to Sackets Harbor and continued preparing for an attack on Kingston and on Earl's squadron, even though it was early winter and the weather was severe.

On November 7, Chauncey sailed from Sackets Harbor to strike the British fleet. His squadron consisted of his flagship *Oneida* and six schooners—all converted merchantmen. His task force was strong, mounting in total forty guns of different calibers and four hundred thirty men, including marines. It was a bold move. Ned Myers, later made famous by James Fenimore Cooper in the book *Ned Myers; Or, Life Before the Mast*, was aboard the *Oneida*. Lieutenant Elliott, who had left Black Rock and joined Chauncey for the occasion, was skipper of the schooner *Conquest*.

An untimely gale kept Chauncey away from Kingston that day. It blew through the night, and in the morning, when the wind abated, Chauncey discovered the *Royal George* and gave chase. He kept her barely in sight through a long day but lost her during the night. The following morning, the ninth, he saw her again and chased her into Kingston Harbor, where she anchored under the guns of Kingston's strong battery. Undaunted, Chauncey closed and exchanged fire with the ship and the batteries for an hour and forty-five minutes. The wind was blowing Chauncey's ships directly toward the batteries, however, and he decided to haul off and resume the fight the next day. In the morning gale force winds were again blowing, forcing Chauncey to reluctantly beat out in a narrow channel under a heavy press of sail to the open lake and return to Sackets Harbor.

Although he failed to attack Earl's squadron successfully, Chauncey now had command of Lake Ontario and could transport troops and supplies to any part of it while preventing the British from doing the same. It was a significant achievement. Chauncey had cut the vital route moving critical supplies from the St. Lawrence to the Niagara region and west. If he could maintain superiority, Upper Canada would fall easily into American hands. Whether the Madison administration could exploit Chauncey's remarkable victory, however, was uncertain.

After returning to Sackets Harbor, Chauncey kept his shipwrights busy converting three more schooners and completing the 24-gun *Madison*. On November 26, master shipwright Eckford had her in the water, floating and ready to receive masts, spars, and guns. Chauncey wrote to Secretary Hamilton that it had only been "nine weeks since the timber that she is composed of was growing in the forest." Much finishing work remained, but seeing her in the water at her winter mooring at this early date boosted everyone's spirits.

Both sides now hunkered down for the long winter, but they remained on guard against a possible surprise strike over the frozen lake. Chauncey prepared defenses, but no attack occurred. While he was doing it, he planned an attack of his own over the ice, but the severity of the weather prevented him from executing it.

WHILE CHAUNCEY WAS extending control over Lake Ontario, Lieutenant Macdonough was busy on Lake Champlain. Both sides recognized how vital the lake was. An attack on Montreal or Quebec was impossible without the ability to move men and supplies over its waters. The lake formed the boundary between the northwestern part of Vermont and the northeastern portion of New York, flowing north into Canada for a brief period, before emptying into the Richelieu River. Ten miles of strong rapids blocked the entrance to the Richelieu, prohibiting ships from moving directly between the two bodies of water. Beyond the rapids, the Richelieu flowed north for ninety-six miles, emptying into the St. Lawrence River northeast of Montreal. Invaders since the days of Samuel de Champlain in the early seventeenth century had used the lake and related waterways as a highway to move armies and supplies either north or south.

Lieutenant Macdonough arrived at White Hall at the southern end of the lake on October 13. Even though Montreal was the most important objective of the president's campaign against Canada, Secretary Hamilton did not send Macdonough orders to move to the lake until September 28, and he did not receive them until the first week of October. He was in Portland, Maine, when the orders arrived, and like Chauncey, he was delighted to be getting into the fight rather than sitting on the sidelines minding gunboats.

Lieutenant Sidney Smith, who had been in command on Lake Champlain and would now be Macdonough's second, was there to greet him when he arrived. Smith had mixed feelings about being superseded by Macdonough and would not give him the wholehearted support that Chauncey was getting from Woolsey at Sackets Harbor.

Smith's meager force was at Vergennes, Vermont, and consisted of two undermanned sloops, the *Growler* and the *Eagle*, both of which needed work, and two decrepit gunboats. One of them was partially sunk in the water, and the seams in both were so open one could put a hand through them.

Like Chauncey, Macdonough was in an arms race. At the northern end of the lake, in a well-protected harbor on the Isle aux Noix, the British were working on vessels that would give them naval supremacy on Lake Champlain. To win the shipbuilding race, Macdonough needed at least a hundred more seamen, additional officers, and supplies of every kind.

In addition to his other problems, Macdonough had problems coordinating with Chauncey and with General Dearborn. Sailors of the type Macdonough needed were not available on Lake Champlain, and he naturally looked to Chauncey for help, but little was forthcoming. Chauncey needed men as much as Macdonough did. Also, Macdonough had difficulty working with the army at Plattsburg and Albany. In preparing for his abortive attack on Montreal, General Dearborn had commandeered the six best schooners on the lake without consulting Macdonough.

With the failure of Dearborn's Montreal campaign, naval activity on the lake stopped for the winter. On December 12, 1812, Macdonough wrote to Hamilton that his vessels were in a secure harbor and that he was "getting everything in readiness for the spring." He reported that the British had two gunboats at their Isle aux Noix base and three sloops, and they were working on a large schooner, designed to carry twelve or fourteen guns.

By then, Macdonough had a squadron of his own, consisting of the *President*, mounting two long twelve-pounders and six heavy army shell guns; the *Growler*, with two twelve-pounders, four six-pounders, and one long eighteen-pounder on a circle; the *Eagle* with six six-pounders and one eighteen in a circle; and two gunboats, carrying one long twelve-pounder each. In addition, he had three sloops for troop transports. Macdonough judged that his fleet was potentially superior to the British, but he was still woefully short of men.

CHAPTER TEN

More Blue-Water Victories

WHILE INAUGURATING A crash program on the lakes, Madison was also providing a new strategy for his blue-water fleet. During the first week of September, he decided to deploy the navy's ships in three small squadrons, rather than grouping them together, as Commodore Rodgers recommended. Influenced by the success of Isaac Hull and David Porter operating on their own, the president returned to Decatur's idea of cruising singly or in small groups, leaving the details of where the ships went to the enterprise of their commanders.

On September 9, Secretary Hamilton ordered the fleet split into three squadrons led by Rodgers, Decatur, and Bainbridge. In order of seniority, each commodore was to select one heavy frigate, one light frigate, and a brig. In addition to his flagship *President*, Rodgers chose the *Congress*, under Captain John Smith, and the *Wasp*, under Master Commandant Jacob Jones. Decatur kept the *United States* and picked the *Chesapeake*, under Captain Samuel Evans, and the *Argus*, under Arthur Sinclair. Bainbridge was left with the *Constitution*, the *Essex*, under Captain Porter, and the *Hornet*, under Master Commandant James Lawrence, an arrangement Bainbridge found more than satisfactory. The *Constitution* had proven herself a superb ship, and he regarded Porter and Lawrence as brilliant fighters.

Madison gave the three commodores broad discretion in carrying out their assignments. Hamilton told them to "pursue that course which . . . may . . . appear the most expedient to afford protection to our trade and to annoy the enemy; returning to port as speedily as circumstances will permit, consistent with the great objects in view and writing to the Department by all proper opportunities." Needless to say, Rodgers, Decatur, and Bainbridge were happy to be charting their own courses.

When Hamilton issued the new orders, nearly the entire fleet was in Boston. The *President*, the *United States*, the *Constitution*, the *Congress*, the *Argus*, and the *Hornet* were there. The *Chesapeake* was as well, but she was undergoing extensive repairs and would not be ready to sail until the middle of December. Decatur would have to leave without her. The 18-gun sloop-of-war *Wasp* was in the Delaware River, as was David Porter's *Essex*. The *Constellation* and the *Adams* were in Washington. The 16-gun *Syren* was at New Orleans, and both the 14-gun *Vixen* and the 10-gun *Viper* were at Charleston.

In order to deceive the British, Rogers suggested to Hamilton that his squadron and Decatur's leave Boston together and separate afterward. Rodgers thought the British might be fooled into thinking they were dealing with a large squadron, rather than single ships. The British might then keep their cruisers together in a large squadron or two, taking their ships away from blockading major ports to pursue a phantom fleet.

MADISON'S FRESH APPROACH to the navy roughly coincided with the appointment of a new British commander at Halifax. On August 12 the Admiralty announced it was replacing Vice Admiral Herbert Sawyer with a shrewd diplomat in naval garb, Admiral Sir John Borlase Warren, a senior admiral with experience dating back to before the Revolution. At fifty-nine, Warren had served at all levels of the Royal Navy, including ordinary seaman. And he had seen plenty of combat, though he was known more as an administrator and a diplomat than a fighter. At one time he was Britain's ambassador to Russia.

Before leaving for his new post, Warren traveled from his home in Nottingham to London for extensive talks with the First Lord of the Admiralty, Viscount Melville. During the conversations Melville made it clear that Lord Liverpool wanted Warren to initiate an immediate armistice so that serious negotiations to end the war could start. But if that failed, he was to vigorously prosecute the war. To help him, the Admiralty was enlarging his command to include not only the old North American Station but the Leeward Islands Station and the Jamaica Station as well. Warren's authority would then extend over all of the West Indies, the entire American coastline from Maine to Louisiana, the Great Lakes, and Lake Champlain.

Warren reached Halifax on September 27, and by that time the fight with America had markedly changed. The war "seems to assume a new as well as more active and inveterate aspect than before," he wrote to the Admiralty after only eight days on the job. Indeed it had, and the Madison administration was adamant about continuing the war until Britain renounced impressment. So Warren had a real fight on his hands, and the Americans were performing far better on the ocean than anyone had expected. Their privateers were swarming in the West Indies and in the approaches to the St. Lawrence River. They were even appearing around the British Isles and the important trade routes. But of much greater importance, the despised American navy had won two single-ship duels, baffling and enraging London.

Before doing anything else, Warren sought an armistice. On September 30 he wrote to Secretary of State Monroe, "The Orders in Council of 7 January 1807 and 26 April 1809 cease to exist. . . . Under these circumstances I am commanded to propose to your government the immediate cessation of hostilities."

Given how vigorously the United States was prosecuting the war, Warren entertained little hope of success. His misgivings were confirmed when Monroe waited almost a month before writing back on October 27 that an armistice would only be possible if Britain gave up the practice of impressment. Warren had no power to negotiate this complicated issue, but it was obvious to him, and certainly to Monroe, that Liverpool would never agree to end impressment as a condition for opening talks. The prime minister and his colleagues believed impressment was essential to Britain's security; they would never give it up.

Warren now understood that he was going to be doing far more fighting than talking. Their lordships had come to the same conclusion. The two unexpected American naval victories had caused such an uproar in London that the Admiralty's first priority became destroying the U. S. fleet or blockading it. They expected Warren to seal enemy warships, privateers, and letters of marque in their ports. Their lordships never wanted another American man-of-war active on the high seas. Lord Melville wrote to Warren, emphasizing that he was to blockade all the principal ports south of Rhode Island, including the Mississippi, and put "a complete stop to all trade and intercourse by sea with those ports."

New England was to be treated differently. Melville wanted naval traffic stopped, but not commercial trade. He did not want to offend Federalist sympathizers in Rhode Island, Connecticut, Massachusetts, and New Hampshire, but he did want to stop enemy warships from using their harbors, particularly Boston.

Liverpool also wanted Warren to encourage New England separatism by the judicious issuing of trading licenses, which allowed an American ship to trade in Halifax or anywhere else. British newspapers like the *Times* of London had fed the public with such a steady diet of the antiwar diatribes printed in Boston's Federalist newspapers that it appeared to many in Britain that if given the proper incentives, New England would secede from the Union.

Unfortunately for Warren, while New England was a hotbed of anti-Madison sentiment, Massachusetts, New Hampshire, Connecticut, and Rhode Island were also producing half of America's privateers and letters of marque, and they were indistinguishable from unarmed traders. New England privateers had become so annoying that in Warren's first days at Halifax he ordered the 64-gun *Africa* and the 74-gun *San Domingo* (his flagship) to lead a squadron patrolling the Gulf of St. Lawrence to stop the murderous attacks of privateers on ships carrying supplies to Quebec. By the end of October, Yankee privateers had taken an astonishing one hundred and fifty British vessels.

Warren was also expected to guard all of Britain's extensive commercial traffic within his jurisdiction. The Convoy Act stipulated that every merchant vessel, without exception, was to sail as part of a convoy, but even when sailing together, protected by warships, traders were vulnerable to attack.

Initiating a tight blockade, guarding merchant convoys, and encouraging New England separatism were not Warren's only assignments; he was directed to conduct amphibious raids in the Chesapeake Bay area, to keep the population in a perpetual state of alarm, not knowing when or where mobile British forces would strike next. Warren was cautioned to conduct only raids. He did not have enough soldiers to penetrate inland or to hold territory after the raids. The Admiralty provided a small number of ground troops for these operations—two battalions of six hundred forty men each and an artillery company.

By the end of December, Warren still had not gotten his blockade or raids going to the satisfaction of London, and when it became clear that Napoleon had met with disaster in Russia, and Britain no longer needed to placate America, the Admiralty was far more forceful in pressing Warren to get on with his blockade and raids.

Early in his tenure Warren recognized, as Admiral Lord Richard Howe did during the Revolutionary War, that it was impossible to establish even the semblance of an effective blockade without a much larger fleet. But when Warren requested more ships, the Admiralty told him to make do with what he had—the same advice given to Admiral Howe. The United States, after all, was a secondary theater. The Admiralty was already stretched thin blockading Napoleonic Europe, convoying merchant vessels, and servicing a sprawling overseas empire.

The American navy became so annoying, however, that the Admiralty grudgingly dispatched additional ships, increasing Warren's sail of the line from six to ten, adding a 50-gun ship, bringing his frigate total up to thirty-four, and increasing the number of sloops of war to thirty-eight. With the various other smaller vessels at his command, Warren now had a total of ninety-seven warships. In addition, the Admiralty was cutting down four seventy-fours and converting them to razees (a sail of the line cut down and converted to a heavy frigate), and sending six to eight more war brigs.

The four additional sail of the line, along with a few frigates, came from the Cadiz station at the end of 1812, under the command of Rear Admiral George Cockburn, a fighter whom the Admiralty hoped would inject a more aggressive spirit into Warren's operation. And Captain Henry Hotham, a notably harsh disciplinarian, was sent to be Warren's captain of the fleet.

With the addition of all these warships, the Admiralty expected quick results, particularly when, as they never tired of telling Warren, the Americans had so few men-of-war. London continued to emphasize that the best way to deal with the American navy and privateers was to blockade them.

Even with an expanded fleet, however, blockading the vast American coast was exceptionally difficult. The Admiralty conceded that during the winter months of November through March weather conditions made northern ports tough to blockade. Contrary winds regularly blew ships off their stations, while the same winds were fair for swift-sailing privateers or warships to sortie. Recurring fog in all ports, north and south, blinded blockaders and allowed courageous American skippers to sneak past them.

Thus, no matter what Warren did, privateers were sure to roam in great numbers, as they did during the Revolutionary War, endangering, among other things, the shipment of vital supplies to the Duke of Wellington. It was all well and good to keep the duke supplied with American food through the issuing of licenses, but this could be negated by privateers capturing everything else coming from the British Isles, including even essential shoes for Wellington's army.

WHILE LONDON WAS trying to get its blockade up and running, Commodore Rodgers and his colleagues were preparing for extended cruises against Britain's navy and commerce. During the first week of October—long before Admiral Warren was settled in his new post—Rodgers had the *President* repaired, provisioned, and set to sail from Boston. The *Congress* was ready at the same time, but Jacob Jones and the *Wasp* were in Philadelphia. Jones would have to rendezvous with the *President* at sea. Rodgers ordered him to patrol in specific latitudes north of Bermuda, where they could meet later.

Rodgers and Decatur left Boston together on October 8 with the *President*, the *Congress*, the *United States*, and the *Argus*. They had no trouble getting to sea. Two days later, in the afternoon, Rodgers caught a fleeting glimpse of the British frigate *Nymphe*, but lack of wind and the approach of night prevented him from chasing her. The next day, October 11, Rodgers split off from Decatur, steering the *President* and the *Congress* in an easterly direction, while Decatur stood to the southeast with the *United States* and the *Argus*. The following day, the *Argus* separated from Decatur and shaped a course that would take her to the northeast coast of South America—a high-traffic area.

On October 15 lookouts aboard the *President* spied a strange ship, and Rodgers put on all sail in chase. Not long afterward, the *President*'s main topgallant carried away, but Rodgers persevered and caught his prey. She turned out to be the 10-gun British packet *Swallow*, traveling from Kingston, Jamaica, to Falmouth, England, and she was carrying an astounding eighty-one boxes of gold and silver specie (coins), weighing ten tons—nearly $200,000 dollars, a king's ransom. A few hours later, after Rodgers had taken all the money aboard the *President*, he happened on a pathetic-looking American schooner, the *Eleanor*. A storm had carried away both her masts. Only the captain's ingenuity and luck kept her afloat, but his chances of reaching port were next to nothing. To the captain's great surprise and joy, Rodgers gave him the *Swallow*.

The *President* then headed toward the Canary Islands, and on November 1, when she was four hundred miles southwest of the Azores, lookouts spied three sails to the southward. Rodgers, accompanied by the *Congress*, gave chase, and caught one, but the other two escaped. (One of the escapees was the 36-gun British frigate *Galatea*, a ship Rodgers would have given his right arm to fight.) The prize was the 10-gun *Argo*, a whaler stuffed with spermaceti oil, whalebone, and ebony, returning to England after a successful cruise in the Eastern Pacific. On the way home she had stopped at St. Helena, as many British ships did coming from the Pacific. When her captain reached St. Helena, he must have felt fortunate to have the *Galatea* to protect him on the way to England. Being captured by two American men-of-war must have astonished him.

Rodgers now shaped a course that took him down the trades west of the Cape Verde Islands, a Portuguese colony four hundred miles off the coast of Africa. When he reached the fiftieth meridian, he steered west toward the Bermudas, where he hoped to rendezvous with Jacob Jones and the *Wasp*. He cruised for four weeks north and west of the Bermudas but never saw Jones. With water and supplies running low, he reluctantly stood for Boston, putting in on the last day of 1812.

Rodgers had been cruising for eighty-five days, and he had covered 11,000 miles, but his accomplishments had been slight. "We chased everything we saw," he told Secretary Hamilton. Unfortunately, he saw very little. He did have the $200,000 taken from the *Swallow*, and that was considerable consolation. It not only meant prize money but was a serious blow to Britain's war effort. Gold and silver were of great importance to Wellington in the Iberian Peninsula. In order to win the support of the Spanish people, he paid for all the supplies he took in gold and silver. It was a practice that served him well but strained the British treasury—and made losses like that of the *Swallow* all the more devastating.

WHILE RODGERS WAS stalking British vessels in the mid-Atlantic, Jacob Jones, in obedience to his orders, had sailed the *Wasp* beyond the Delaware Capes on October 13 and set a course that would take him north of the Bermudas to rendezvous with the *President*. On the sixteenth a heavy gale struck, and Jones lost his jib boom and two men. Organizing a jury rig, he carried on, the sea running high after the storm. The following night at 11:30, in latitude 37° north and longitude 65° west, lookouts discovered several sails in the distance, two of them large. They looked to be part of a British convoy accompanied by an escort. Jones stood from them for a time and then, for the remainder of the night, steered a parallel course. At daylight on Sunday the eighteenth, he saw them ahead. They were six large, armed merchantmen, mounting sixteen to eighteen guns with a powerful British gun brig for an escort. Without hesitating, he went after them.

When he did, the 22-gun *Frolic*, under Captain Thomas Whinyates, dropped astern of the merchantmen and hoisted Spanish colors to decoy the *Wasp* and allow the convoy to escape. As Whinyates watched the *Wasp* bearing down, he must have been apprehensive. His brig was not in good shape. The same violent gale that had struck *Wasp* the night before had carried away the *Frolic's* main yard, ripped up her topsails, and sprang the main topmast. Whinyates was repairing damages when he saw the *Wasp*.

Jones closed with the enemy quickly, and at 11:30, when he was within sixty yards, Whinyates fired a broadside, which did little damage but initiated a fierce exchange. The *Frolic's* guns hit the *Wasp* hard, and it looked at first as if Whinyates would prevail. But Jones continued to close, and the two ships ran alongside each other, firing as they went. After several minutes, Jones shot away the *Frolic's* gaff and the head braces, and since there was no sail on the mainmast,

Figure 10.1: Irwin Bevan, Poictiers *Takes* Wasp, *19 October 1812* (courtesy of Mariner's Museum, Newport News, Virginia).

the brig was unmanageable. Jones was now able to rake her fore and aft. Within minutes, Jones could see that every brace and most of Whinyates's rigging had been shot away.

Jones continued to lessen the distance between the ships until they were almost touching. The unmanageable *Frolic*'s bowsprit fell between the *Wasp*'s main and mizzen rigging, at which point First Lieutenant James Biddle led a boarding party onto Whinyates's deck. He found every British officer injured and a sickening number of men killed or wounded. No more than twenty were left to fight. There was nothing Whinyates could do but surrender. In his report to the Admiralty he insisted that had the *Frolic* not been so beaten up in the gale he would have taken the *Wasp*. Jones, of course, would have disputed that. In the end, at least thirty of the *Frolic*'s crew were killed and about fifty wounded, among them Captain Whinyates. The *Wasp* had five killed and five wounded.

Jones's triumph was short-lived, however. A few hours later, H.M.S. *Poictiers*, a 74-gun ship-of-the-line, under Captain John Beresford, spotted him and made all sail in pursuit, clearing for action as she went. At four o'clock Beresford fired a few warning shots, and Jones struck his colors. The *Wasp* was too beat up from the fight to get away. Beresford took the *Frolic* in tow, and with the *Wasp* and one of the merchantmen in company, he steered for Bermuda.

ON DECEMBER 11, shortly after separating from Rodgers, Commodore Decatur encountered a merchantman who turned out to be an American, the *Mandarin*. She was bound for Philadelphia with a hold full of British goods and a packet of British licenses for use by American traders bringing Pennsylvania grain to Wellington's army. Decatur put a prize master on board and sent her into Norfolk with instructions to deliver the licenses to Secretary Hamilton. Like all American captains, Decatur found the licensing trade offensive and wished the government would put a stop to it, but for political reasons Madison and the Congress chose not to. By the end of 1812 American farmers were shipping an astonishing 900,000 barrels of grain per year to Wellington.

Two days later, after separating from Arthur Sinclair and the *Argus*, Decatur shaped a course that would take him to a watery highway midway between the Azores and the Cape Verde Islands. Northeast trade winds and ocean currents made this area ideal for stalking British ships traveling to the West Indies, South America, the Cape of Good Hope, the Indian Ocean, the Far East and around Cape Horn to the rich fishing grounds of the Eastern Pacific.

Decatur could not have been more pleased. He was right where he had hoped to be when the war started—in command of the *United States*, operating alone, hunting for British warships and for glory. He was the navy's premier officer, widely known and admired by the public and his peers for his heroic exploits during the war with Tripoli. He was following in the footsteps of his father, Stephen Decatur Sr., who was a naval hero during both the War of Independence and the Quasi-War with France. By coincidence, the *United States* was the first ship young Decatur had served on, coming aboard in 1798 as a nineteen-year-old midshipman during the Quasi-War with France. The Revolutionary War hero John Barry was her captain. Decatur would learn the arts of war and seamanship from Barry and from Lieutenant James Barron, who took a particular liking to him. Even back then, Decatur was a risk taker with an aggressive streak, yearning for adventure and combat. Six years later he would become a national hero when he led the *Intrepid* in her successful mission to destroy the captured American frigate *Philadelphia* in Tripoli harbor. For this amazing exploit President Jefferson promoted him to captain, the highest rank in the service. Decatur was only twenty-five at the time—the youngest man ever to hold the rank of captain in the history of the navy.

Crewmen respected Decatur as much as his superiors. One who served under him remembered Decatur giving his men advice on how to be successful. "The first quality of a good seaman is personal courage," he said. "The second [is] obedience to orders, the third, fortitude under sufferings; to these may be added, an ardent love of country. I need say no more—I am confident you posses them all."

WHILE DECATUR WAITED for his prey, Arthur Sinclair steered the *Argus* toward Cape St. Roque, at the eastern tip of Brazil. On the way he ran into a powerful six-ship British squadron. Two were battleships. He immediately threw on all sail and sped away, outdistancing their fastest ship. He continued on to the coast of Brazil and patrolled for a time before traveling to Surinam; finding nothing there, he cruised farther north in the Atlantic until his stores were so low he had to return home.

Sinclair was away for ninety-six days with little to show for his effort except the capture on November 15 of the *Ariadne*, an American ship out of Boston that had stopped in Alexandria, Virginia, and picked up a cargo of flour for Wellington's army, taking it under a British license to Cadiz, Spain's largest port. Sinclair seized the vessel and gave command of her to his purser, Henry Denison, with orders to sail to the first port he could make in the United States. As luck would have it, Denison—flying British colors—was stopped soon after by two British cruisers, the sloop of war *Tartarus* and the brig *Colibri*. Denison deftly used the license to convince his captors to set him free. They even gave him nine American prisoners to help work the ship.

Decatur, meanwhile, was having much better luck than Sinclair. The commodore spent nearly two weeks on his cruising grounds before lookouts at the fore and main mastheads spied what appeared to be a promising looking stranger two points on the weather bow. It was October 25, and the *United States* was in latitude 29° north, longitude 29° 30' west, midway between the Azores and the Cape Verde Islands.

At about the same time, lookouts aboard His Majesty's 38-gun frigate *Macedonian* saw the *United States*. They were twelve miles apart. It was Sunday morning, just after the crew had finished breakfast. The men were looking forward to a day of idleness. In response to cries from lookouts of "Sail ho," Captain John S. Carden shouted back, "Where away?" When one lookout shouted that she was a large frigate, Carden immediately cleared for action. A drum beat to quarters as the crew raced to their battle stations, and the ship, having the weather gauge, stood for what Carden hoped was an American man-of-war. He could not make out exactly who she was at this distance, but he had intelligence that the 32-gun *Essex* was in the vicinity. If that's who this was, she would have little chance against the *Macedonian*, unless Carden got too close. The *Essex*'s guns (actually

46 in number) were nearly all forty-two-pound carronades, very effective at short range (five hundred yards or less) but useless at longer distances.

Carden thought of running up and firing away with his long eighteens, just beyond the range of the *Essex*'s carronades. But as the two ships approached, it became obvious that the stranger was a much larger ship than the *Essex*. That didn't faze Carden; he still intended to attack. In one-on-one duels the British had, almost without exception, crushed the ships of every other navy, often against seemingly impossible odds.

As Carden examined the stranger, she appeared to be the *United States*, a ship he knew well. In February 1812, when he had sailed the *Macedonian* into Hampton Roads, Virginia, on a special mission, he met Decatur and had a good look at the *United States*. He was even invited to Decatur's home with his officers, where they discussed the relative merits of their two frigates. They got along well, and Carden developed a liking for the young American hero.

Despite his regard for Decatur, Carden was eager to do battle, and he had confidence in his ship, even though relations with the crew had been uneasy. The *Macedonian* was almost new, having been built at Woolwich and launched on June 2, 1810. And she had recently had a complete refit, so she was in excellent condition.

It wasn't long before John Card, an impressed American, came up to the captain and, acting as spokesman for the other Americans aboard, requested that they be excused from fighting their own countrymen. Carden glared menacingly at him and ordered him back to his station, threatening to shoot him and any others who didn't want to fight. That settled the matter quickly, and Card returned to his gun crew.

The *United States* was a notoriously slow sailer, which put her at a disadvantage, but she was far more powerful than her opponent. She carried 55 guns to the *Macedonian*'s 49. For a main battery the *United States* had thirty twenty-four-pounders on the main deck while the *Macedonian* had twenty-eight eighteen-pounders. The *United States* also carried twenty-two forty-two-pound carronades on her spar deck and two long twenty-four-pounders and an eighteen-pound carronade on her forecastle. The *Macedonian* had sixteen thirty-two-pound carronades on her spar deck and two long twelve-pounders, two long eight-pounders, and an eighteen-pound carronade on her forecastle. The *United States* had 478 hands to the *Macedonian*'s 306. Carden hoped his advantage in speed would offset Decatur's firepower.

The *Macedonian*'s main battery of eighteen-pounders was typical of British frigates. The Admiralty judged they were superior, all things considered, to the heavier twenty-fours on the big American frigates. This contest would test the Admiralty's theory once more, just as the battle between the *Constitution* and the *Guerriere* had.

Decatur now pulled to within three miles of the *Macedonian* and wore ship, trying to gain the weather gauge. But Carden was ready and foiled him by putting his helm to port and heading him off. Decatur then wore round again, and the two ships passed each other on opposite courses at about a mile's distance. As they did Decatur unleashed two broadsides with his twenty-fours. The first fell short, but the second hit home.

Judging the range to be too long for his eighteen-pounders, Carden held his fire and then wore round to keep the weather gauge, putting the *Macedonian* and *United States* on roughly parallel courses, where Decatur's long twenty-four-pounders could be employed to full advantage. Decatur had assiduously prepared his men for just such a battle. The first lieutenant, William Allen, had trained the gun crews to a point where they were probably the finest afloat. They would need to be to cope with the veteran Carden.

Lieutenant Allen had been with Decatur for five years and was considered by many to be the best first mate in the American fleet. Rodgers, Bainbridge, and Decatur had all vied for his services. Allen had worked under each of them at one time or another and knew them intimately. By choosing Decatur, and sticking with him, he indicated just how good Decatur was himself. But would their skill be enough?

As Carden attempted to close with the *United States*, Allen's gunners, even in the heavy swell that was running, found their mark. Their murderous broadsides kept smashing into the *Macedonian*, tearing her up, inflicting gruesome carnage on her decks, killing and wounding dozens of men. One of the dead was the American John Card.

Captain Carden reported later that he "soon found the enemy's force too superior to expect success." But he would not relent. Hoping for a miracle, believing it unthinkable for a British frigate to strike her colors to an American, he continued the action long after he realized that his situation was hopeless and he was needlessly prolonging a bloodbath.

Meanwhile, Decatur slowed the *United States* to allow the *Macedonian* to get closer, while Lieutenant Allen's gunners continued blasting away. By now the *Macedonian* was in bad shape. Her main topmast was shot away by the caps, the main yard was smashed to pieces, several shots had hit her below the water line, the lower masts were badly damaged, the lower rigging was cut up, and all the guns on the quarterdeck and the forecastle were disabled but two. While she lay helpless—filled with wreckage—her crew was being killed and wounded at a horrific rate.

Decatur now maneuvered the *United States*, which had suffered hardly at all, into a position from which she could rake the *Macedonian* and crush her completely. But Decatur held his fire, hoping Carden would see the hopelessness of his situation and not force him to completely destroy the *Macedonian*, for he wanted to take her home as a prize and be one up on Hull, who had been compelled to sink the *Guerriere*.

Carden had no idea why his ship was being granted a reprieve. For a moment he fancied that the *United States* was as wounded as the *Macedonian* and might even in the next instant flee. Within moments his entire mizzenmast went overboard, however, and as it did, he had another look at the *United States*. He could see that she had not left but was simply waiting and could renew her assault at any time. He finally grasped how desperate his situation was, and to prevent further killing, he called a council of officers, who agreed to surrender, except for the first lieutenant, David Hope—a savage, sadistic disciplinarian—who urged fighting to the death.

The battle had been a stunning victory for the United States. Out of a crew of 306, Carden had 36 killed and 68 wounded, 36 of them severely. The *United States* was barely touched. She had 12 casualties—5 killed and 7 wounded. Two of the wounded, Lieutenant John Mercer Funk of Philadelphia and John Archibald of New York, later died. Decatur reported that the ship was in condition to continue her cruise, but he wanted to get the *Macedonian* back to the United States and never considered sending her to America with a prize crew while he carried on. Not only was he anxious to display his personal prowess at home, but the effects of another victory at sea on American morale would be enormous, far more valuable than capturing more merchantmen unseen by the public.

Decatur sent a longboat to pick up Carden, who was waiting, having changed into his best uniform and sword. Crestfallen, he seated himself in the stern sheets for the melancholy ride over to the *United States*. He stepped through the entry port believing he was the first British captain to surrender a frigate to an American. The thought sickened him. When he offered his sword, Decatur, like Hull, refused to take it from so gallant and brave an opponent. Decatur informed Carden that he was not the first to surrender; that dubious honor had already gone to Dacres in the *Guerriere*. The miserable British skipper was somewhat mollified, but not much.

For a veteran, Carden's performance had been dismal. He never used the *Macedonian's* speed to good effect; his pedestrian tactics had consistently played into Decatur's hands. The poor relations he had with his crew were his own doing. He had not curbed his cruel first lieutenant. Carden's humiliation was as much his own fault as it was Decatur's. In more skillful hands the *Macedonian* could have put up a much better fight, even if she would have ultimately succumbed to an American ship that had one of the best fighting crews afloat.

When men from the *United States* arrived to take charge on the *Macedonian*, the British tars were so angry and depressed—and not a little drunk from having broken into the spirits—that they were in a mood to resume the fight hand to hand, even though their wounded mates were all around suffering indescribable pain. But when the tars observed how decently the Americans were treating them, they calmed down, and not very long afterward, the two crews melded together as if they were no longer enemies. "We ate together, drank together, joked, sung, laughed, [and] told yarns," one of the British seamen remembered. "In short, a perfect union of ideas, feelings, and purposes, seemed to exist among all hands."

Decatur spent two weeks preparing the battered *Macedonian* for the long voyage to the American coast. When he started the repairs, she had so many shot holes below the water line that she would have sunk had he not worked fast to fother them and stabilize her. He gave Lieutenant Allen the honor of sailing her home. Getting back to New York safely would be a tricky proposition, however. British cruisers could be anywhere, particularly around New York. But as luck would have it, the *United States* and the *Macedonian* sailed straight home without seeing a single enemy warship, although they did see many other ships and even had to fight a three-day storm, which seriously threatened the jury-rigged *Macedonian*. When they reached the American coast, Decatur put into New London, but a sudden shift in the wind made it impossible for the *Macedonian* to follow. She was forced to stand off and on for several hours before Lieutenant Allen managed to sail her into Newport, his hometown, on December 5.

Oliver Hazard Perry, the naval commander at Newport, was ecstatic—and more than a little jealous—when Allen sailed in unexpectedly with the first and only defeated British frigate ever to be brought into an American port. Even though Rhode Island was strongly Federalist and antiwar, Newport gave Allen a hero's welcome. So did Federalist New London when Decatur arrived.

People in Great Britain, of course, were crestfallen. The *Times* of London cried, "Oh! what a charm is thereby dissolved! What hopes will be excited in the breasts of our enemies! The land-spell of the French is broken and so is our sea-spell.

"We have sunk our own maritime character; for, with a navy that could admit of no competition, we have suffered ourselves to be beaten in detail, by a power that we should not have allowed to send a vessel to sea."

CHAPTER ELEVEN

The *Constitution* and the *Java*

O N OCTOBER 26, 1812, Commodore William Bainbridge and the *Constitution* sortied from Boston accompanied by the *Hornet*, under Master Commandant James Lawrence, to begin their cruise as Secretary Hamilton had ordered in September. The third member of Bainbridge's squadron, Captain Porter's *Essex*, was still in the Delaware River completing repairs and taking on supplies for a long voyage. Bainbridge did not wait for her. He sent Porter instructions to visit several rendezvous points where they might meet, and then set sail.

Bainbridge would have preferred leaving Boston when Rodgers and Decatur did, but the *Constitution* needed extensive repairs after her fight with the *Guerriere*. Her lower masts and several spars had to be replaced, and an entire new gang of standing rigging installed. In addition, patches were required for the hull. Bainbridge drove the navy yard hard, requiring men to work even on the Sabbath—no small demand in puritanical Boston. After the repairs were completed, Bainbridge loaded the *Constitution* with four to five months' provisions and one hundred days of water.

While repairing his ship, Bainbridge had to soothe the wounded feelings of Master Commandant Lawrence, who was threatening to resign from the navy. Lawrence was miffed that Charles Morris had been promoted from lieutenant to captain, skipping the grade of master commandant. Lawrence acknowledged that Morris was a fine officer and had performed brilliantly in the fight with the *Guerriere*, but he thought he had just as good a claim to promotion. Lawrence pointed out that he had been in the navy since the Quasi-War with France and had performed heroically as well, most notably during the burning of the *Philadelphia* in February 1804, when he was Stephen Decatur's first lieutenant aboard the *Intrepid*.

Bainbridge took Lawrence's side and protested to Hamilton. "I do not think that he [Morris] or any lieutenant ought to be promoted over all the master commandants to captain," he wrote. "We have some very valuable officers in the class of master commandants. No man can excel Captain [Master Commandant] Lawrence in the character of a brave and valuable officer." Since the days of Benjamin Stoddert during the Adams administration, merit and experience had been the navy's principal criteria for promotion above midshipman. But for the officers in this deeply conservative service, seniority weighed more heavily than it did for their civilian bosses. Giving a man—however meritorious—a double promotion over so many others went against the grain.

Master Commandant Arthur Sinclair also wrote to Hamilton, objecting to Morris's unusual promotion. The secretary would not change his mind, however, and when the high-strung, impulsive Lawrence threatened to resign, Hamilton was furious. "Your letter of the 10th . . . has reached me," he fired back on October 17. "The suggestion with which that letter concludes prevents an answer in detail, and confines me to the single observation, that [if] without cause you leave the service of our country, there will still remain heroes and patriots to support the honor of its flag."

The rebuke stung. Lawrence shot back, "After devoting near fifteen years of the prime of my life faithfully [in] the service of [my] country, I deserve a promotion to captain." Hamilton was unmoved. He dug in his heels and defended his decision, even though it was a bad one, made on the spur of the moment without a full awareness of its ramifications. Promoting Morris to master commandant, instead of to captain, would have been acceptable to all his colleagues and to him. He was well-liked, and he did perform magnificently in the fight with the *Guerriere*, but to jump him over others like Lawrence, who had also performed valiantly in the service of the country, was an unnecessary blow to their morale and to the entire officer corps. It was one more example of Hamilton's ineptness.

Although angry at Hamilton for his clumsy handling of the matter, Bainbridge urged Lawrence not to resign; he did not want to lose one of the navy's stellar fighters. Lawrence thought hard about what to do and in the end—still distraught—decided to stay. Bainbridge was relieved; he wanted Lawrence with him when he left Boston.

THE *CONSTITUTION* AND THE *JAVA*

Bainbridge planned to cruise off the coast of Brazil from Bahia to Rio and then off strategically important St. Helena in the South Atlantic. It was an inviting prospect. Following the prevailing winds and currents, nearly all British ships sailing from the Indian Ocean or from the Pacific stopped at St. Helena, or in South America. Bainbridge had previously consulted his friend William Jones, the future secretary of the navy, on where he ought to cruise, and the South Atlantic around St. Helena seemed ideal. British ships were sure to be there in abundance, and provisions to keep his squadron going would be easy to obtain along the South American coast.

Before Bainbridge left Boston, however, Secretary Hamilton attempted to change his orders. He wrote to him and to David Porter that they were to take the *Constitution*, *Hornet*, and *Essex* to Charleston and "clear the coast of the enemy's cruisers," before doing anything else.

What prompted the secretary's new instructions was the 32-gun frigate H.M.S. *Southampton*, under Captain James Yeo. The *Southampton*, traveling in company with two brigs, had been active along the South Carolina coast during the summer and fall, and Hamilton wanted to get rid of her. She was the oldest warship in the Royal Navy, having been launched in 1757. Operating out of Nassau in the Bahamas, she lurked off Charleston and had taken a few prizes, much to the annoyance of Captain John H. Dent, commander of the Charleston naval station.

Dent had tried to counteract the *Southampton* by purchasing and converting two small schooners, the *Viper* (previously the *Ferret*, with eight six-pounders and one long twelve in a circle) and the *Carolina* (fourteen guns). But these two vessels weren't enough to cope with the *Southampton* and her companions. On October 24, after receiving Dent's request for help, Hamilton ordered Bainbridge to the rescue. Dent watched impatiently for him to appear, but he never did. Hamilton's orders did not reach either Bainbridge or Porter before they departed for the South Atlantic.

AS THE *CONSTITUTION* drove beyond Boston Light and pushed out to sea, the atmosphere aboard was rife with tension. Bainbridge had inherited Isaac Hull's superb crew, which would have pleased any skipper, as, indeed, it did him, but the men who had served so cheerfully under Hull were not happy to be exchanging him for Bainbridge. Feeling had been so strong that when the "Constitutions" found out about the switch they were shocked and unable to understand why, after Hull's brilliant victory, the navy was replacing him. They were unaware that

Hull had asked to be relieved. When he returned to Boston after defeating the *Guerriere*, he learned of his brother's death, and in order to attend to his brother's affairs in New York, he asked Hamilton to replace him. The secretary agreed, directing Hull to turn over the ship to Bainbridge, who was senior to Hull and commandant of the Boston Navy Yard. In fact, Bainbridge had been given the ship back in July, but he could not take her, and Hull was given a temporary appointment. The July order had never been rescinded, so it was natural for Bainbridge to be appointed the new skipper.

Actually, as Bainbridge told his friend William Jones, he preferred to have command of the *President*, which he thought was "one of the finest ships in the world." He wanted command of her badly enough to offer Rodgers $5,000 to exchange ships. But Rodgers would not agree to the switch, and Bainbridge took command of "Old Ironsides" instead.

The Constitutions' unhappiness with Bainbridge was heightened by his reputation as a hard taskmaster. Unlike Hull, he had little regard for ordinary seamen. A tall, beefy, moody man, Bainbridge regularly addressed his men as "you damn rascals." He was quick to punish, often using his fists instead of waiting for a whipping to be organized. Having a crew protest his appointment was nothing new for him. When he was given command of the frigate *George Washington* back in 1800, nineteen sailors and four petty officers deserted rather than serve under him.

Not only did Bainbridge have a well-justified reputation for brutality, but he was known as a loser. With Hull in command, the crew could look forward to victories and prize money, but Bainbridge had been a notable failure his entire career. The crew considered him a Jonah.

Bainbridge's most egregious failure occurred in October 1803, when he surrendered the frigate *Philadelphia*. He ran her aground while engaged in a foolhardy chase off Tripoli, and despite frantic efforts, he could not free her. The Tripolitans came out in gunboats, seized the ship, and made prisoners of the 306-man crew. Two days later, they refloated the frigate and towed her into the nearby harbor, where she came under the protective guns of the batteries guarding the city of Tripoli. The Basha, Tripoli's ruler, now had himself a handsome prize and over 300 prisoners to ransom.

A depressed Bainbridge wrote to his commander, Commodore Edward Preble, "I have zealously served my country and strenuously endeavored to guard against accidents, but in spite of every effort, misfortune has attended me through my naval life—Guadeloupe and Algiers have witnessed part of them, but Tripoli strikes the death blow to my future prospects."

Although the *Philadelphia* debacle was not the first time, or even the second, that Bainbridge had been involved in humiliating incidents, his naval career had not been ruined. In each case he had been exonerated, but the cumulative effect had penetrated his psyche. He wrote to his wife, Susan, that he felt a terrible "apprehension which constantly haunts me, that I may be censured by my countrymen. These impressions, which are seldom absent from my mind, act as a corroding canker at my heart."

Bainbridge saw this voyage as an ideal opportunity to redeem himself and cover himself with glory, or die trying. All the navy's captains wanted to distinguish themselves, but Bainbridge had an added reason—his past humiliations—to crave a glorious battle with a British frigate. His fixation was likely to make conditions aboard ship even more difficult for the men, and they sensed it. Most of the Constitutions eventually came around and remained with the ship, but some, like Moses Smith, could not be pacified, and they left. Those who remained never liked Bainbridge. No crew ever did, for throughout his career he was a cruel martinet who showed contempt for the men working his ships.

AS THE CONSTITUTIONS anticipated, Bainbridge was an exacting skipper. He conducted drills continuously, exercising the great guns and practicing with small arms and muskets, preparing the men for battle, even though they were Isaac Hull's outstanding crew. This did not matter to Bainbridge; he was going to make certain the ship was ready when his chance came.

For the first leg of the voyage, he headed to Portugal's Cape Verde Islands. The initial point of rendezvous with Porter and the *Essex* was Porto Praya in St. Jago, the most important island in the archipelago. Britain was Portugal's closest ally, but since Napoleon's invasion of Portugal in 1807 and the flight of the royal family to Brazil in a British warship, Portuguese control of her empire was only nominal. St. Jago was a sadly neglected backwater. The slave trade and provisioning ships were its principal businesses. British warships traversing the Atlantic stopped there only occasionally.

When Bainbridge reached Porto Praya, the *Essex* wasn't there, and so he quickly took on supplies and left, steering southwest for Brazil. On December 2 he arrived off Fernando de Noronha, the wretched Portuguese penal colony two hundred twenty miles off the Brazilian coast. It was the second rendezvous point he had stipulated for the *Essex*. As the *Constitution* came into port, she was flying British colors.

Bainbridge posed as captain of the 44-gun British frigate *Acasta*, with Lawrence as skipper of the sloop of war *Morgiana*. Bainbridge left a coded message for Porter, addressed to Sir James Yeo of His Majesty's ship *Southampton*. "My dear Mediterranean friend: Probably you will stop here . . . I learned before I left England that you were bound off the Brazil coast; if so, perhaps we may meet and converse on our old affairs of captivity; recollect our secret in those times." Bainbridge signed it: "Your Friend, of H.M. ship *Acasta*, Kerr."

Porter arrived ten days later, posing as a British warship, as he and Bainbridge had previously arranged. A Portuguese official gave him Bainbridge's message, and after Porter heated the paper, the invisible ink revealed: "I am bound off St. Salvador, thence Cape Frio, to the northward of Rio Janeiro, and keep a look out for me. Your Friend."

ON DECEMBER 13 the *Constitution* and the *Hornet* arrived at St. Salvador in the Brazilian state of Bahia. Bainbridge's attention was immediately drawn to the *Bonne Citoyenne*, a powerful British sloop of war sitting in the harbor. He soon learned that she was carrying an astonishing 500,000 pounds in specie. Although he was sorely tempted to capture her, he decided to scrupulously observe Portuguese neutrality.

After anchoring off the city, Bainbridge sent Lawrence to confer with Henry Hill, the American consul, about a number of matters—the political situation in Brazil, the best places along the Brazilian coast to obtain provisions and water, where British men-of-war were operating, and where they were based. Hill submitted six detailed pages of information, explaining that although the Portuguese were allied with the British, they were neutrals in the war with the United States and would be hospitable to American warships. But to expect the governor of Bahia, Count dos Arcos, not to favor the British, which is what Bainbridge wanted, was asking too much. Portugal's life, after all, was in British hands. Hill went on to report that few British warships were operating along the Brazilian coast; the most important was the 74-gun *Montagu*, based at Rio de Janeiro. He estimated that forty to fifty British merchantmen stopped at Brazilian ports each year, and the best place to intercept them was probably farther south around Cape Frio.

Bainbridge decided to sail the *Constitution* out of the harbor but leave the *Hornet* to see if Lawrence could entice the *Bonne Citoyenne*'s skipper, Pitt Barnaby, out of the port for a fight. The *Hornet* and the *Bonne Citoyenne* appeared evenly matched. But when Lawrence challenged Barnaby to a one-on-one duel, Barnaby refused. He had no reason to risk his precious cargo, especially when he suspected that the *Constitution*, contrary to Bainbridge's promise, would be waiting out of sight to pounce on him.

Barnaby was wrong, however. Bainbridge had indeed left and was cruising south along the Brazilian coast, searching for prey. On December 29 at nine o'clock in the morning, he was thirty miles off the coast when lookouts spotted two strangers off the weather bow. An hour later Bainbridge saw the two ships split up, one heading toward land, away from the *Constitution*, and the other, a much larger ship, steering toward her.

Aboard His Majesty's 38-gun frigate *Java*, spyglasses had been trained on a strange sail to leeward, appraising her for almost an hour. Unlike Bainbridge, the *Java*'s veteran skipper Henry Lambert was not consumed with a desire to defeat an American frigate, but he was not reluctant to take one on either. He wasn't expecting to meet one, however. He was on his way to Bombay with the new governor, General Hislop, and his staff, a few supernumerary officers, one hundred extra seamen, and civilian passengers. He also had a load of copper for Indian shipyards. The *Java* was crowded, but that did not mean Lambert was reluctant to fight—far from it: He was delighted with the opportunity.

When Lambert spotted the *Constitution*, he was making for St. Salvador to resupply and give his passengers time ashore before resuming their journey. He might have kept right on sailing into St. Salvador, but he could not resist investigating who this stranger was. He had already captured the American merchantman *William*. She was the second ship Bainbridge had seen earlier. Lambert had a prize crew aboard her, and they made for St. Salvador, sailing right into the arms of Lawrence, who was just outside the port, blockading the *Bonne Citoyenne*.

Bainbridge, in the meantime, hoping the stranger was the British frigate of his dreams, stood for the *Java*. Although he still did not know for sure who she was, he hauled up his mainsail and took in his royals in preparation for battle. At 11:30 he made the private signal for the day, and when it went unanswered, he knew he was dealing with an enemy frigate of some size. When he was four miles from the *Java*, he felt he was too close to neutral territory, and setting back his mainsail and royals, he tacked and made all sail away upon the wind to get "off the neutral coast." Lambert chased him, and in doing so discovered he had a much faster ship. The *Java* was an excellent French-built frigate, only seven years old, captured by the British two and a half years before. The *Constitution* might be bigger, but Lambert expected his speed to give him a significant advantage.

Although not as fast as the *Java*, the *Constitution* was stronger—more guns, more men, a thicker hide, better gunnery, more experience, and better training.

She had thirty twenty-four-pound long guns for a main battery on the gun deck and sixteen thirty-two-pound carronades on the quarterdeck. On her forecastle she had one eighteen-pound carronade and eight thirty-two-pound carronades. The *Java* had twenty-eight eighteen-pound long guns for a main battery on her gun deck, sixteen thirty-two-pound carronades on her quarterdeck, and two nine-pounders and one eighteen-pound carronade on the forecastle. The *Constitution* had 475 men, the *Java* 426, 100 of them seamen she was carrying to other warships in the East Indies. Unlike other contests between American and British frigates, the *Java* was not undermanned, although the quality of her crew was not up to the *Constitution*'s. Lambert had an unusually large number of recently pressed men aboard, which made his fighters far less efficient. Lambert hoped to use the *Java*'s speed in the opening moments of battle, running up fast and raking the less maneuverable enemy, cutting her down to size and gaining a decisive edge.

At 1:30 P.M. "being sufficiently from the land . . . [Bainbridge] took in the mainsails and royals, tacked ship, and stood for the enemy." The two frigates came together fast, and when the *Java* was half a mile away, Bainbridge unleashed a full broadside with his larboard guns. Lambert did not immediately return fire. Trying to take advantage of his speed, he kept steering for the *Constitution*'s bow to rake her. Bainbridge countered by letting loose his main and fore course—an unusual and often fatal tactic—wearing ship and gaining speed, preventing Lambert from forereaching on him, thus neutralizing the *Java*'s main strength. General action now ensued with round and grape shot, each captain maneuvering to be in a position to rake the other, but neither succeeding.

At 2:30 Lambert shot away the *Constitution*'s wheel entirely. As the battle roared, her superb crew had relieving tackles rigged fast, allowing Bainbridge to continue steering by shouting orders down through a grating to the men working the ropes two decks below.

Early in the action, a musket ball struck Bainbridge in the left hip, but he carried on, and a little later, during the same broadside that destroyed the ship's wheel, a jagged slice of langrage tore into his upper leg and almost killed him. He refused to retire, however, and summoning all his strength, he continued to direct the battle.

The two ships slugged it out until three o'clock, when the *Constitution* shot away the head of *Java*'s bowsprit and with it her jib boom, making her headsails useless. With the rest of *Java*'s running rigging badly cut up, she could barely maneuver. Bainbridge was able to work the *Constitution* into a position to rake her by the stern with two devastating broadsides, which turned the tide of battle.

Feeling overwhelmed by the *Constitution*'s firepower, Lambert desperately sought to board her and fight it out hand to hand. It was his only chance. Just as he made the decision, however, his accomplished sailing master was struck down and had to be carried below. Lambert continued bringing his ship closer to the enemy, when his foremast was shot away. The remains of his bowsprit then passed over the *Constitution*'s taffrail, and at the same moment his main topmast toppled over, the wreckage sprawling over the starboard guns, rendering them useless. Lambert's attempt to board had failed. All the while, Bainbridge kept up a deadly fire.

At 3:30 a musket ball from a marksmen in one of the *Constitution*'s tops struck Lambert full in the breast, mortally wounding him. He was carried below, and the first lieutenant, Henry D. Chads, assumed command. The *Java* was shattered. Her crew was having to constantly extinguish fires that sprang up because of all the wreckage laying on the side engaged. Chads could not fire many guns, but he would not surrender. At 4:15 the *Java*'s mizzen mast was shot away, and the two combatants were once again brought broadside to broadside. They continued firing away for another twenty minutes, when the *Java*'s main yard went in the slings.

Chads still refused to surrender, but his guns were now completely silent, and his colors had gone down with the rigging. Since no ensigns were flying, the wounded Bainbridge assumed the *Java* had struck her colors, and at ten minutes to five he hauled about to shoot ahead and repair damages to the rigging, which was badly cut up. After an hour passed, Bainbridge realized the *Java* had not struck, and he returned to the fray, intent on raking her one more time, which would finish her.

She was lying helpless, floating like a log; only the mainmast was left, and it was tottering. In the hour's reprieve that Bainbridge had given them, Chads and his men had worked feverishly to repair their ship and get her ready to continue the fight, but her heavy rolling caused the mainmast to finally topple. Chads still intended to fight on, but when he saw that Bainbridge had maneuvered into a position from which he could rake the *Java* by the bow without her having any possibility of replying, he called his officers together, and as he reported to the Admiralty, "[with] a great part of our crew killed and wounded, our bowsprit and three masts gone, several guns useless, . . . our colors were lowered from the stump of the mizzen mast." It was 5:30. Bainbridge thought it a wise decision. Had he been forced to inflict the final blow, the "loss must have been extremely great," he wrote.

The butcher's bill was heartrending. The *Java* suffered 83 wounded and 57 killed—a staggering number out of a crew of 426. Lambert, of course, was among the seriously injured, and he would soon die. Lieutenant Chads was also hurt, but he recovered. The *Constitution* had 9 killed and 26 wounded, Bainbridge among them.

At 6:00 P.M. Bainbridge sent First Lieutenant George Parker in the *Constitution*'s last remaining boat (out of eight) to take possession of the *Java*. When he arrived, Parker discovered that in all the confusion Chads had forgotten to destroy his signal codes and dispatches. They were an unexpected gift. But the *Java* was too far gone for Bainbridge to take her home in triumph, as he dearly wanted to do. With great reluctance, he ordered Parker to remove the British prisoners, stuff all the supplies that could be retrieved into the *Constitution*, and burn the *Java*.

Bainbridge then returned to St. Salvador. On the way, he treated the *Java*'s officers, especially the dying Lambert, with the utmost civility, but he confined her crew below in cramped quarters under heavy guard. He did not want that many potential combatants left unrestrained. This was understandable, although extremely difficult for the British tars.

Bainbridge was taking a chance going back to San Salvadore; the 74-gun *Montagu* might have been there. He took the risk in order to relieve himself of the prisoners, whom he intended to put on parole. He also needed to repair the *Constitution* enough to get her home, and above all, he had to find out what happened to Lawrence, the *Hornet*, and the *Bonne Citoyenne*. Luckily, when Bainbridge arrived, the *Montagu* wasn't in the harbor, but she had been there recently, and he had narrowly missed her. He didn't see the *Hornet*, though, and he wondered if the *Montagu* had captured her. He soon found out that through some superb sailing at night, Lawrence had just managed to elude the battleship.

Bainbridge spent the next five days making temporary repairs to the *Constitution* and then set out for Boston on January 6, 1813. He must have been disappointed in not being able to continue his original plan to rendezvous with the *Essex*. The *Constitution* was too banged up, and so was Bainbridge. He later gave this description of the ship's condition:

> The *Constitution* was a good deal cut—some shot between wind and water—Her upper bulwarks considerably shot—foremast and mizzen mast shot through—main and mizzen stays shot through, eight lower shrouds cut off—foremast stays and every topmast shroud—all the braces standing and preventers and bowlines, were three times shot away during the action—but once again in the very heat of it—all but one of eight boats destroyed by shot—our sails extremely cut to pieces— the main topmast, main topsail yards, jib boom, spanker boom-gaff and

trysail mast were all so shot as to render them unserviceable. Yet this damage is incredibly inconceivable to the wreck we made the enemy.

Despite the *Constitution*'s injuries and his inability to bring the *Java* home, Bainbridge had finally achieved the victory he had always craved, making the burden of his previous disasters much lighter. He was now the hero he had always wanted to be, able to hold his head up among his peers. But he was not any easier on his crew, nor did his desire to seek more glory lessen. He was just as egotistical as he had always been and just as ambitious to outdo colleagues like Decatur and Hull.

WHILE BAINBRIDGE HAD been out looking for some action, Lawrence followed his instructions to the letter and remained just outside the harbor of St. Salvador, blockading the *Bonne Citoyenne*. During that time he captured the British schooner *Ellen*, and when he went on board and found she was quite valuable, he ordered his sailing master, Silvester Bill, to take charge of her and bring her to the United States. She was eventually sold in Newcastle, Delaware, for more than $32,000.

Lawrence's blockade came to a quick end on December 24—five days before the *Constitution*'s fight with the *Java*—when the 74-gun *Montagu* hove into sight, forcing him to run into port in a big hurry. Fortunately, night came on, and he was able to narrowly escape disaster by slipping unnoticed out of the harbor to the southward. When he was safely away, he turned eastward, and on the fourth of February came across the 10-gun English brig *Resolution*, which was carrying, along with coffee, jerked beef, flour, fustic, and butter, $23,000 in specie—a nice little bonus. Lawrence took out the money and set her on fire.

He then continued his cruise, sailing along the northeastern coast of Brazil, to Surinam, before reaching the Demerara River off Guyana. A former Dutch colony, Guyana was captured by the British in 1796. On February 24 at ten past four in the afternoon, Lawrence was sitting off the mouth of the Demerara when lookouts spotted a British man-of-war brig anchored outside the river's bar. Lawrence was beating up toward her when a much larger man-of-war brig appeared on his weather quarter, edging down for him. He immediately beat to quarters and cleared for action. The crew raced to its battle stations, while Lawrence steered for the enemy, keeping "close by the wind, in order if possible to get the weather gauge." Finding he could easily weather the enemy, he hoisted American colors and tacked.

At 5:25 the two ships passed each other, exchanging broadsides within half pistol shot. The American gunnery, as in the past, was faster and more accurate than the British. In fact, the *Hornet* was a stronger ship in every respect than the British brig, which turned out to be the *Peacock*, under Lieutenant William Peake. She carried sixteen twenty-four-pound carronades and two long six-pounders and had a crew of a hundred twenty men, while the *Hornet* had eighteen thirty-two-pound carronades, two long nine-pounders, and a crew of a hundred seventy men. The difference was significant. The damaged *Peacock* wore ship, and seeing this, Lawrence bore up, received an ineffective broadside, then ran close on board the *Peacock*'s starboard quarter, and kept up a devastating fire. Captain Peake was killed, and his first lieutenant, Frederick A. Wright, took command.

In fifteen minutes the *Peacock* struck her colors. Shortly afterward, however, her mainmast went by the board, and she started sinking. Lawrence got the wounded off as fast as he could, but she went down so quickly that nine of her crew and three of his own men, working to get everyone off, drowned. In addition to the nine men lost when the ship sank, four more of the *Peacock*'s crew had been killed during the fighting and thirty-two wounded, five of whom later died. The *Hornet* had two killed during the fighting, three more in the rescue operations, and three wounded.

Lawrence feared that the 16-gun British brig *Espiegle*, the ship he had first seen anchored off the Denerara's bar, might come to the *Peacock*'s aid. During the fight he had kept an eye on *Espiegle*, and after the *Peacock* sank, he rushed to get the *Hornet* prepared for another battle. But the *Espiegle* mysteriously remained anchored.

Lawrence decided he had enough to handle without going after her. With the *Peacock*'s crew and men from the other captures, he now had 277 men aboard. His first thought was getting them and his ship, which needed repairing, home safely. With a limited amount of water and no convenient place to parole his prisoners, he put everyone on a strict ration of two pints of water per day and sailed for home, arriving at Holmes Hole on the north side of Martha's Vineyard a little over three weeks later, on March 19, the crew and prisoners suffering badly from the severe rationing.

Shortly after arriving at Martha's Vineyard, Lawrence wrote to his wife, Julia, whom he was devoted to, "I have only time to inform you of my safe return and to tell you that I am in perfect health. . . . You were anxious I should have an action with John Bull, provided I would come off with a whole skin."

Julia knew Lawrence needed to distinguish himself, and now he had. She was also pleased that the disgruntled master commandant, who left Boston in a stew in October, had finally received the recognition he craved when he was promoted to captain on March 4.

A few days later, on March 25 President Madison said in his message to Congress, "In the continuation of the brilliant achievements of our infant navy, a signal triumph has been gained by Captain Lawrence and his companions in the *Hornet*."

MADISON'S PRIVATEERS WERE performing as well on the high seas as the blue-water fleet was. From the very start of the war—as the president had expected—privateers of every description suddenly appeared. Many of them had anticipated the declaration of war and had ships outfitted with captains and crews hired and ready. Madison intended to keep tight control of this quasi-public fleet. He viewed privateers' men and their vessels as part of an official naval force, not as licensed pirates. Unlike what happened during the Revolution, when privateer commissions were issued by the states as well as the national government and were loosely controlled, Madison insisted that only the federal government would issue commissions.

The declaration of war authorized the president to use the whole naval force of the United States, which meant privateers as well as the navy. And on July 4, 1812, Congress specifically authorized letters of marque and reprisal. The president himself signed each commission. Applications had to be made to the secretary of state, specifying the type of vessel and the number of crew and posting a bond of $5,000 or $10,000, depending on the size of the vessel. Every privateer was obliged to keep a journal. Prizes had to be adjudicated in the district courts of the United States and prisoners delivered to a U.S. marshall or other officer. The rights of neutrals were to be strictly observed, as were other usages of civilized nations. The secretary of state issued the commissions, and a federal marshal or customs official delivered them in the various ports. In Britain the Admiralty issued the commissions. If a privateer or letter of marque were caught by either side without a commission, they were considered pirates and subject to brutal penalties, including hanging.

One of the first commissions issued, if not the first, was to a group of eleven Baltimore businessmen. It was common throughout the war for a number of people to take shares in privateering enterprises. These Baltimore businessmen had a ninety-eight-foot schooner, the *Rossie*, armed with ten twelve-pound carronades and ready to sail. They convinced the legendary Revolutionary War hero Joshua Barney to be her skipper.

Barney was anxious to strike a blow against the British, and he sailed from Baltimore aboard the *Rossie* on July 11. He was ninety days at sea, not returning to Baltimore until October 22. During that time he captured eighteen British merchantmen, with a total value of a $1.5 million, and he acquired 217 prisoners. As with all privateers, the *Rossie* had as large a crew as the ship would hold so that Barney could man the many prizes he took.

Barney also got involved in two sharp fights, both of which he won handily. The first was on August 9 against a British letter of marque ship, the 12-gun (nines and sixes) *Jeannie*, and the second on the sixteenth of September against a British packet, the 8-gun *Princess Amelia*.

Barney sent most of his captures to ports along the coast, but the expenses for condemnation and the high taxes imposed on prizes by Congress cut substantially into his profit. Duties on prizes were so onerous that Congress had to reduce them in order to provide an incentive to go out on what was, after all, a dangerous and often unprofitable venture. After returning to Baltimore Barney retired to his farm. He did not consider his small profit worth the bother. But he was still interested in fighting the British, and later in the war, at the age of fifty-five, he would come back as a special naval officer, giving the enemy fits in Chesapeake Bay.

THE BRITISH NAVY managed some small victories during this time, but they in no way compared to American achievements. The frigate *Barbados* captured the small revenue schooner *James Madison*. On November 22 Captain James Yeo in the old frigate *Southampton* captured the 14-gun brig *Vixen*, under Master Commandant George Reed. Five days later, on the night of November 27, while on the way to Jamaica, both ships crashed into sunken rocks off the desolate islands of Conception and sank. Miraculously, all hands survived, including Sir James Yeo, but George Reed died in captivity in Spanish Town, Jamaica, on January 8, 1813.

On January 2, the British frigate *Narcissus* captured the much smaller 12-gun *Viper*, under Lieutenant John D. Henley. The *Viper* was based at the Balise on the Mississippi south of New Orleans and was in the Gulf of Mexico on a cruise. Henley had been out only ten days when he had to turn around and head back for repairs. He never made it. The *Narcissus* captured him fifty miles off the Balise.

THE VICTORIES OF the *Constitution*, and the *Hornet*, coming so soon after the triumphs of other American warships, not to mention the successes of her privateers, had a profound impact on British attitudes. The war was waged in part because Britain refused to accord America the respect she demanded. The naval victories were changing attitudes in London, laying the groundwork for a more equitable and peaceful relationship in the future.

CHAPTER TWELVE

A Sea Change

A S THE WAR progressed into the latter half of 1812, so did the presidential election campaign. Like his predecessors Adams and Jefferson, President Madison dearly wanted a second term. The wisdom of going to war and his management of it were the central issues before the country, and his leadership was found wanting by every Federalist and even by many Republicans. The navy that Madison had so lightly dismissed at the beginning of the war provided the only successes he could point to in his reelection bid. The army's stunning defeats were a political noose around his neck.

There was no question about his nomination. Republicans in Virginia's legislature began the process by nominating electors favorable to the president in February, followed by similar action by seven other states. The Republican congressional caucus met in Washington on May 18, and eighty-three members voted for Madison. Nine others added their votes later, giving him a comfortable two-thirds majority.

Still, nearly all of New York's Republican congressmen, as well as others from the north, refused to support him. When word reached Albany of Madison's nomination, disgruntled Republican members of the legislature refused to accept it. They held their own caucus on May 29 and nominated the popular forty-three-year-old Republican mayor of New York City, DeWitt Clinton, who quickly accepted. He was from a powerful political family, the nephew of Revolutionary War hero George Clinton, Madison's recently deceased vice president.

151

The Virginia dynasty rankled the New Yorkers enough that they simply could not support one more term for a tidewater aristocrat.

When Madison's blunders as commander in chief became more evident later in the year, Clinton's chances to defeat him improved dramatically. They rose further when many prominent Federalists decided the party should secretly support Clinton. Federalists were so weak nationally that nominating one of their own would guarantee defeat. The one Federalist who might have had enough national appeal was Chief Justice John Marshall, but he was a Virginian. Most Federalists thought a Virginian could never carry New York, a state that was considered essential. Others who were possibilities, such as Rufus King of New York and Charles Cotesworth Pinckney of South Carolina, garnered less support than Marshall.

The Federalist convention met in New York from September 15 to 17. Nearly all of the seventy delegates decided to secretly support Clinton. Rufus King of New York urged the members to reject secrecy and nominate a candidate of their own, even if it had to be Clinton, whom King called an opportunist, comparing him at one point to Caesar Borgia. But King failed to carry the day. Led by Harrison Gray Otis of Massachusetts, the party decided to secretly back Clinton. This is exactly what Clinton wanted. He felt that if the Federalist Party openly endorsed him, it would alienate enough Republicans to cost him the election. Federalists and antiwar Republicans now banded together in support of peace delegates in most states, which made Clinton a formidable national candidate.

Had he been able to articulate a plausible strategy to end the war honorably, Clinton might well have unseated Madison. Instead, he tried to be all things to all people, arguing in places where the war was popular that he would end it by winning and promising to people who did not support the war that he would simply end it. His duplicity did not escape notice, and it hurt him badly.

In spite of Clinton's campaign blunders, opposition to Madison was strong enough that by early fall his reelection was in doubt. To offset the devastating effects of the army's failures, the president ostentatiously embraced the navy's heroes, particularly Isaac Hull and Charles Morris of the *Constitution*. To what extent the naval victories improved his chances is impossible to tell, but Madison certainly felt they were a great political asset.

As the campaign progressed, Pennsylvania's twenty-five electoral votes appeared critical. Supporters of both Madison and Clinton pursued them vigorously. The candidates themselves did so through surrogates. In keeping with the custom followed by Adams and Jefferson, they affected to be above politics and did no campaigning directly. The president, however, continued to allow farmers to ship corn and flour on a massive scale to Wellington's army in Spain and Portugal under British licenses. This was an important source of his support in places like Pennsylvania and other mid-Atlantic and Southern states.

The grain shipments and the naval victories might have made the difference in the election. The results came in week by week and state by state. Except for Republican Vermont, New England went for Clinton. So did New York's twenty-nine electoral votes, thanks in part to the work of twenty-nine-year-old Martin Van Buren. Clinton also won New Jersey and Delaware, while Maryland divided five to six for Madison. On December 3 the electoral college cast 128 votes for James Madison and 89 for DeWitt Clinton. The president's margin was only twenty. Had Pennsylvania's electoral votes gone the other way, Madison would have lost the election.

The president's narrow victory underscored how disillusioned large segments of the country were with the war and his management of it. Even supporters like Henry Clay admitted in private that Madison was "wholly unfit for the storms of war. Nature has cast him in too benevolent a mould." In public, however, Clay and the War Hawks urged prosecuting the war with renewed vigor, as did the president. They had no other choice. The British were not in the mood to compromise on impressment. To the contrary, with rumors circulating in London of Napoleon's troubles in Russia, and unexpected victories at Detroit and Queenston, the Liverpool government was thinking more of revenge than of reconciliation.

So the president had to get on with the war as best he could, and the same went for the War Hawks and their followers in Congress. Madison's original strategic vision, with its heavy reliance on the Napoleonic menace in Europe, remained intact. The stories of Bonaparte's difficulties in Russia were at this point only rumors. As long as Napoleon remained master of France, the British would continue to be preoccupied with Europe. Madison thought that a renewed effort against Canada had good prospects for success, particularly with the Herculean efforts he was making to challenge British supremacy on lakes Ontario, Erie, and Champlain. Furthermore, American privateers were seriously disrupting British commerce. The naval victories on the high seas were an added bonus; they meant, among other things, that political support in Congress for strengthening the fleet would not be wanting.

On November 4, even before the electoral college confirmed his reelection, the president addressed the second session of the 12th Congress, urging members to strengthen the army and navy. He called for an increase in pay for army recruits and volunteers, more general officers, and a reorganization of the army's staff.

He also called for a dramatic increase in the navy. The president did not mention how all of this was to be paid for. The enthusiasm of his congressional supporters did not extend to raising internal taxes. Madison left that ticklish matter for another day.

When the president's program went to Congress, Republicans generally supported strengthening the army, but, in spite of the navy's splendid performance, many were skeptical of spending huge sums on naval expansion. Federalists, on the other hand, were strongly in favor of increasing the navy, as they had always been. On November 12, Secretary Hamilton summoned Isaac Hull and Charles Morris to Washington to celebrate their victory over the *Guerriere* and to help push through Congress a new approach to the navy. The chairman of the House Naval Committee, Burwell Bassett of Virginia, had written to Captain Hull that "we are determined to have a navy," by which he meant a much larger one. The president and Mrs. Madison warmly welcomed Hull and Morris to the White House. Madison expected to make good political use of the naval heroes.

Secretary Hamilton also employed Captain Charles Stewart, skipper of the newly refurbished frigate *Constellation*, moored at the Washington Navy Yard, to press the administration's case in Congress. Stewart wrote a letter, cosigned by Hull and Morris, urging the construction of large ships of war, seventy-fours, and heavy 44-gun frigates. He also advised the economy-minded congressmen to appropriate money for the best, most seasoned materials, "which will be by far the cheapest, and be longer in a state of active service. . . . Past experience [proves] that the best materials are always the cheapest and that a slow increase is better than a hasty and temporary one."

To aid the lobbying effort, Captain Stewart hosted a party aboard the *Constellation* on November 26. The president and his wife attended, along with Secretary Hamilton and key members of Congress. Twelve days later, Dolley Madison, the most renowned hostess of her day, followed with a ball of her own at Tomlinson's Hotel to honor Hull and Morris. The *Guerriere*'s huge, tattered flag was prominently displayed on a wall. The City of Washington sponsored the event. Captain Stewart attended, as did a significant number of the capital's most influential politicians.

In the middle of the festivities, Midshipman Archibald Hamilton, the secretary's son, appeared suddenly with the *Macedonian*'s flag. He had served aboard the *United States* during the battle, and he now proceeded to unroll the huge ensign at the feet of the First Lady, after which he read Decatur's dispatch describing the victory. Secretary Hamilton was in attendance, and he was delighted but no'ticeably unsteady from imbibing too much—a frequent occurrence that undermined respect for him.

Ironically, Decatur's triumph meant less money for Hull and his men. Since Decatur brought the *Macedonian* into port, and the navy eventually purchased her, the captain and crew received $200,000 to divide. Decatur's portion was $30,000. Congress had previously promised Hull $100,000 for the *Guerriere*. Hull thought the figure should be triple that amount. But because Congress appropriated so much for Decatur, it reduced the figure for Hull and his men to $50,000. Hull's share was $7,500. Needless to say, the *Constitution*'s crew were irate, and so was Hull. It was a bizarre, morale-destroying way for the country to reward its most successful fighters.

CHAIRMAN BASSETT OF the House Naval Committee welcomed help from Hull, Morris, and Stewart in his efforts to increase the navy's size and resources. From November 7 to 27 he held hearings before the Naval Committee on expanding the navy. Congress debated the resulting Naval Expansion Act for a month before both House and Senate agreed to Bassett's original proposal, which provided for building and fitting out four 74-gun battleships and six 44-gun frigates. Madison signed the bill into law on January 2, 1813. The support of antiwar but pro-navy Federalists was critical to its passage. A majority of Republicans in the House voted against the bill; it only passed because of Federalist support. Nonetheless, it represented a sea change in the president's—and the country's—commitment to a permanent navy. Six more sloops of war were authorized on March 3.

In due course, work was started on three ships of the line: the *Franklin* at Philadelphia, the *Washington* at Portsmouth, New Hampshire, and the *Independence* at the Boston Navy Yard in Charlestown, Massachusetts. Three frigates were begun in 1813: the *Columbia* at Washington, the *Guerriere* at Philadelphia, and the *Java* at Baltimore. Naming new warships after those defeated in battle was a British practice that the American navy copied. Because of wartime shortages, none of the ships were finished before the conflict ended. The nearly completed *Columbia* would eventually be burned to prevent her from falling into British hands.

Some of the Republicans who voted for a large increase in the navy did so only as a wartime necessity. They intended to cut the service drastically after the war, just as Congress did following the Quasi-War with France and the war with Tripoli. Jefferson, who had always opposed building both seventy-fours and frigates, told Monroe that, "Frigates and seventy-fours are a sacrifice we must make, heavy as it is, to the prejudices of a part of our citizens."

For a solid bloc of Republicans, however, including the president and all of the Federalists, deciding to build a strong navy was a decision to fashion a new defense policy for the United States. They wanted a fleet large enough to be a factor in the thinking of any European country, particularly Britain. They were determined to never again allow the United States to be defenseless on the high seas, dependent on the goodwill of the great powers, who still coveted American territory and had only ill will for the country's republican government. Thus the navy, despite some continuing Republican skepticism, found a permanent place in America's strategic thinking. For the first time in the young republic's history, the navy's existence was no longer in doubt. As time went by, most Republicans eventually accepted the idea that a strong navy was not a threat to the Constitution but an indispensable tool in protecting it, as, indeed, Washington and John Adams had always maintained. Even Albert Gallatin now believed the country needed a powerful navy.

The commitment to a stronger, permanent navy presaged a change of command at the Navy Department. Despite the stunning victories, political support for Secretary Hamilton had disappeared. He had long been criticized for his ineptitude. Rumors that he drank excessively and that little got done at the department after lunch were widespread. And, indeed, the secretary did imbibe too much too often, but the rumors were exaggerated. His major failings were a lack of administrative skill and an inability to form a strategic vision for the fleet. In addition, Hamilton suffered—as anyone would have—from having to serve under a chief executive who, for much of his tenure, thought and acted as though the navy were inconsequential. In fact, before the *Constitution*'s victory over the *Guerriere*, Madison showed less interest in the navy than any previous president, including Jefferson. No secretary of the navy, however able, could have performed well under such a chief. Now, with Madison having become a supporter of a strong navy, a new secretary had a chance to get the most out of the department.

Hamilton finally resigned, much against his will, on December 31, and Madison asked fifty-two-year-old William Jones of Philadelphia to replace him. Jones had strong credentials. He had fought as a youngster during the American Revolution at the battles of Trenton and Princeton, and later as a privateer under famed Captain Thomas Truxtun. After the war, Jones became a successful sea captain engaged in coastal trading from Charleston to Philadelphia and then a prominent Philadelphia merchant and banker. He had been a Republican congressman at the start of the Jefferson administration, and Jefferson had asked him to become secretary of the navy, but Jones turned him down. When Madison sought him out for the post, however, Jones felt that he could not decline again, since he had been a vocal advocate of the war.

Jones quickly proved himself to be a competent, energetic secretary. He did not have the gracious manners of Hamilton, or of Benjamin Stoddert, the first secretary of the navy, or of Robert Smith, the second secretary. But he was an able administrator and an experienced seaman who knew ships and the sea and had a clear idea of strategy and tactics. He was also a tireless worker, as he showed on January 23, 1813, the day he arrived in Washington. After a long, cold trip from Philadelphia, he rode into town at three o'clock in the afternoon, and instead of resting, immediately called on the president. After a long conversation with him, he went directly to the home of Secretary Gallatin for a lengthy meeting.

The following morning, Jones was hard at work at the department. One of his first acts was to hire Benjamin Homans as chief clerk, replacing Charles Golds-borough, the wealthy, articulate Marylander who had been in the department since its inception. Goldsborough began his service as confidential secretary to Benjamin Stoddert and then became chief clerk. Unfortunately, he had recently become involved in a nasty public dispute with a gunpowder manufacturer, Dr. Thomas Ewell, and the president wanted him replaced. Monroe pressured Jones to hire Homans, a well-connected Massachusetts man. Jones relented, but he never worked well with Homans; he relied instead on Edward W. Du Val, a former lawyer. Commenting on the place of Homans at the department, Samuel Hambleton wrote, "The first mate does not know much of what passes in the cabin."

Jones did not waste any time indicating his strong support for building the freshwater fleet. On January 27 he wrote to Commodore Chauncey, "It is impossible to attach too much importance to our naval operations on the lakes—the success of the ensuing campaign will depend absolutely upon our superiority on all the lakes—and every effort and resource must be directed to that object. . . . Whatever force the enemy may create, we must surpass." Giving priority to Chauncey and Macdonough included the politically unpopular decision to move men and supplies away from defending seaports and rushing them to the lakes.

On February 22 Jones outlined his strategic priorities for the blue-water fleet. He told the navy's leadership "to expect a very considerable augmentation of the naval force of the enemy on our coast [in] the . . . spring; . . . his policy will be to blockade our ships of war in our own harbors; intercepting our private cruisers, prizes, and trade, and harass the seaboard. Our great inferiority in naval strength, does not permit us to meet them on this ground without hazarding the precious germ of our national glory." Therefore, Jones wrote, the navy needed to create "a powerful diversion" by attacking British merchantmen in places like the West Indies, where their warships, although present, were not patrolling in overwhelming numbers. Jones's priority thus was commerce raiding. He told the captains that his intention was "to dispatch all our public ships, now in port, as soon as possible, in such positions as may be best adapted to destroy the commerce of the enemy." The secretary did not want to waste precious resources fighting spectacular individual ship battles; he stressed that the destruction of Britain's trade, not personal glory, should be the objective of every captain.

Jones thought sloops of war were better commerce raiders than frigates or battleships. They were faster, took less time to build, were much cheaper, and required smaller crews. Sloops could also beat the blockade more easily, and they could elude bigger warships in the open ocean. He supported building larger warships for the long term, but for an immediate impact he favored sloops of war. By the same token, Jones, the old privateer, had a high appreciation of the devastating effects a big privateer fleet could have on British commerce. He saw the navy and the privateers working in harness toward the same objective, not as competitors for men and supplies.

MADISON NEEDED NEW leadership for the army as much or more than for the navy. For weeks, supporters of the war had been calling for Secretary Eustis's resignation, and as defeat followed defeat, these calls grew deafening. As soon as Madison's reelection was official on December 3, Secretary Eustis resigned, and Monroe became acting secretary until Madison could choose a successor. The president considered appointing Monroe, who initially wanted to be either secretary of war or the commander of the army with the rank of lieutenant general— George Washington's title. Monroe undoubtedly thought a great military victory would open a clear path to the presidency, but when he realized that budget constraints would not allow him to raise the army he wanted, he decided to remain at the State Department. The president then, unaccountably, asked his friend General Dearborn and then Senator William Crawford, both of whom turned him down. Madison next considered two New Yorkers, Governor Tompkins and fifty-four-year-old Brigadier General John Armstrong. Removing Tompkins from the governorship of New York might have meant allowing Dewitt Clinton to obtain that sensitive position, so the president ultimately turned to Armstrong, the former ambassador to France who was now in charge of defending New York City. On January 8 Armstrong's name went to the Senate for confirmation.

The appointment was controversial. Among Armstrong's enemies was another former ambassador to France, James Monroe, who had a number of reservations. He distrusted Armstrong; the general had a reputation as an intriguer that went back to his close association with General Horatio Gates during and after the Revolutionary War. Armstrong's intrigues were so clumsy, and so fraught with peril for the Republic, they brought a resounding rebuke from General Washington. In 1783, when Armstrong was twenty-four years old, he wrote the infamous "Newburgh Addresses," urging army officers to be far more strident in their demands on Congress for back pay and, in fact, threatening a military coup. At the time, he was an aide to the ever-ambitious General Gates, Washington's persistent critic. At a tense meeting of officers on March 15, 1783, Washington, who still commanded the loyalty and affection of the army—apart from the Gates cabal—condemned the addresses as "unmilitary" and "subversive." Historian Thomas Fleming wrote that thanks to Washington, "the most perilous moment in the brief history of the United States of America ended peacefully."

Monroe felt that Armstrong had no loyalty to the president and would use his office to promote his own political ambitions. He believed Armstrong wanted to break Virginia's grip on the presidency by assuming the office himself. He thought Armstrong would blur the boundary between the secretary and his field commanders, and try to run the army in the field as well as in Washington for the purpose of acquiring enough military glory to propel him into the White House.

Others beside Monroe opposed Armstrong. The vote to confirm him was unusually close—18 for and 15 against, with Virginia's two senators not voting. It was an inauspicious beginning.

Like Jones, Armstrong went right to work the minute he arrived in Washington on February 4, 1813. Regardless of questions about his character, the new appointment seemed to portend better results from the War Department. But as time passed it would become painfully evident that Armstrong's reputation for duplicity was well deserved, and his abilities as a military leader greatly exaggerated.

———

BOTH ARMSTRONG AND Jones were constrained by the unwillingness of Congress to pay for the war through taxation. Internal taxes had been eliminated during the Jefferson administration, which left the Treasury dependent on tariffs for almost all its revenue. Since Britain was America's lead trading partner, wartime prohibitions drastically reduced the government's revenue. Loans were the only alternative, but Congress, under the influence of state-chartered banks, made securing them difficult by abolishing the United States Bank in 1811. A combination of Federalists and Republicans, by a single vote, declined to renew the bank's charter. Vice President George Clinton cast the deciding vote against, even though President Madison supported it. Congressmen who voted for the war but refused to provide for its funding hoped, like the president, that it would be of short duration, perhaps only a few months. When that proved not to be the case, Congress still refused to finance the war properly by enacting substantial internal taxes.

In his annual report in November, Secretary Gallatin announced that an additional $20 million was needed to fund the war. Republicans in Congress again refused to raise internal taxes, afraid the country would not support them, which it probably would not have. They remembered that when John Adams raised taxes to pay for the Quasi-War with France, he was defeated for a second term. On the other hand, when Jefferson did away with internal taxes, he was reelected overwhelmingly. That was not the only reason for his popularity, of course, but it certainly contributed to it.

Instead of internal taxes, Republican War Hawks like Calhoun, Lowndes, and Cheves proposed in December 1812 to renew trade with Britain. They claimed this would produce the desired revenue from customs duties. By some magic, taxes on imports were considered external, even though they led to higher prices internally. When Cheves and Lowndes introduced a bill to in effect allow free trade, they were voted down. Ironically, New England Federalists, who in other respects were strong advocates of rapprochement with Britain, did not support the legislation because their fledgling manufacturing plants were prospering under wartime restrictions against British imports.

Republicans preferred to borrow rather than tax, ignoring the fact that in doing so they were placing in the hands of the war's opponents—Federalist bankers in Boston and Philadelphia—the power to deny Madison the money he needed to carry on the war. Through privateering, smuggling, manufacturing, shipping, and banking, an inordinate amount of the country's specie was flowing into the coffers of Federalist banks in New England and Philadelphia, producing great wealth for those who opposed the war.

In February 1813, Gallatin told the House Ways and Means Committee that the Non-Importation Act would have to be modified and internal taxation increased to finance the war, particularly the expansion of the army and navy, which had just been voted on. As expected, the House of Representatives—firmly in control of the Republicans—resolutely refused to raise internal taxes or adjust the Non-Importation Act. Instead, it passed legislation authorizing Madison to borrow $16 million on the best terms he could obtain, as well as another bill, authorizing the president to issue five million one-year Treasury notes bearing 5.4 percent interest. These notes were only one step removed from bills printed by the Continental Congress during the Revolution.

Authorizing a loan and obtaining it were two very different things, as Gallatin could attest to. He was expected to find this massive amount for a government that had no national bank, and thus no national circulating medium, and that refused to raise taxes in one of the more prosperous countries in the world. The Congress adjourned on March 4, and by then the government was nearly out of cash. Federalist bankers in Boston and Philadelphia showed no interest in loaning the nearly bankrupt government any money. In fact, they hoped the administration would go broke. Gallatin narrowly averted catastrophe through the good offices of John Jacob Astor, who with Philadelphia bankers David Parish and Stephen Gerard loaned the government nearly $8.5 million at a whopping 7.5 percent.

The unwillingness of American politicians who had voted for the war to adequately fund it was noticed in London and substantially weakened the chances that President Madison could negotiate a satisfactory peace.

CHAPTER THIRTEEN

Napoleon
and Alexander

D URING THE SECOND week of November 1812, while Madison had been trying to stir a reluctant country to renew the war effort, incredible reports began circulating in London that Napoleon was suffering a catastrophic reversal in Russia. The British could scarcely believe the good news. Back on July 18, immediately after Napoleon's invasion, Liverpool had signed a treaty of peace and amity with Czar Alexander, and he had given him as much support as he could, shipping him, for instance, 100,000 muskets. The alliance had one object—destroying Bonaparte—but at the time few people in London believed the czar could. During the summer, the British watched with bated breath as the Grand Army drove into Russia against weak resistance. It looked as if the czar would soon be at the negotiating table—on his knees.

Napoleon knew the Russian climate necessitated that he not remain long. His army was forced to live off the countryside; it could not be supplied from France or its satellites. At all costs, he had to avoid being sucked into the Russian vastness during the brutally hot summer. He strove for an early climactic battle that would destroy the Russian army in a single engagement. Alexander's strategy was to deny him that opportunity. Once Napoleon crossed the Niemen River (the border between Poland and Russia) and marched into the Russian heartland, the die was cast; he had to defeat the czar or lose his aura of invincibility.

As the summer wore on, the British watched nervously as the czar's armies stayed just beyond Napoleon's grasp, luring him deeper into the country. Bonaparte pushed on, racing for Smolensk, where he hoped to induce his great battle, but again the czar's armies, although fighting briefly, escaped during the night of August 18–19 deeper into Russia, along the road to Moscow.

Napoleon might have stopped at Smolensk in August, consolidated his gains, and resumed the battle in the spring, but he never seriously considered that option. Instead, he marched on toward Moscow, something he knew was dangerous and had hoped to avoid. The heat was now unbearable and sustenance from the countryside nonexistent. As the Russian armies retreated, they carried out the czar's scorched-earth policy, burning village after village and field after field before the French reached them. The heat, impossible logistics, and scorched earth ate away huge chunks of the Grand Army. Men dropped by the thousands from lack of water and food, and so did Napoleon's irreplaceable horses. Nonetheless, he kept moving closer to Moscow, believing the Russians would not let their sacred city fall without a climactic fight. The alternative was to admit failure and retreat, and if he did that, he could no longer pretend to be master of Europe. Retreat meant the end of his regime, and perhaps his life. And so, the prisoner of his image, he pressed forward, marching on through Russia's poisonous countryside.

National honor finally forced the czar to fight the battle Napoleon craved. On August 29 Alexander gave overall command of his armies to sixty-five-year-old Mikhail Kutuzov, an immensely popular general with the troops, who were demoralized by the constant retreating and the destruction they were forced to inflict on their own people. They wanted to fight the French, and under Kutuzov they believed they had a chance to win. Influential members of the czar's court were also urging him to fight. They, too, were angry at what the French were doing to their country; they thought honor demanded that Russia defend herself. The czar finally agreed, but only after his scorched-earth policy had seriously weakened the Grand Army.

Kutuzov made his stand on September 7 at Borodino, seventy miles southwest of Moscow. The Russians arrived on the battlefield first, and they were prepared for the French when they attacked. A horrendous bloodbath followed. Perhaps 80,000 died—45,000 Russians and 35,000 of the Grand Army. At the end of the day, Napoleon controlled the battlefield, but his army was badly beaten up. More importantly, he failed to destroy the Russian army, and in that sense Borodino was anything but the decisive victory he needed.

Kutuzov, although staggered, was able to withdraw to Moscow. He thought about defending the city but then decided to evacuate. With much of the civilian population trailing behind, he marched out of the city and established himself southeast of Moscow, where he could rest and reconstitute his army.

On September 15 Napoleon entered Moscow and established himself in the Kremlin. The next day the city erupted in flames that destroyed three-quarters of the buildings, making life for the French army even more difficult than it already was. It became clearer by the hour that, even though Bonaparte was in Moscow, he had not captured Russia—Russia had captured him. Nonetheless, he continued acting as if he were a victor and demanded the czar's capitulation. Napoleon sent messages to St. Petersburg, urging Alexander to submit, but the czar refused. On the day the Grand Army crossed the Niemen, Alexander had pledged, "I will not sheathe my sword so long as there is an enemy within my imperial borders." He meant to keep that promise.

Convinced Alexander would soon relent, Napoleon wasted precious days waiting. And while he did, Kutuzov's army grew in numbers and strength, especially with the addition of thousands of Cossacks. All the while, French foraging parties, desperately seeking food, were meeting armed peasants willing to die in defense of their turf.

With his supplies running out, and the czar giving no indication he would surrender, Napoleon finally understood that he had to evacuate Moscow. He did not begin his retreat until October 19, however. By then, the start of the deadly Russian winter was only days away. His troubles were compounded by wasting nine more days fighting and maneuvering against Kutuzov south of Moscow before deciding that he had to retreat down the main road to Smolensk. Kutuzov forced him to travel along the same scorched earth he had come on.

As Napoleon sped toward Smolensk, Kutuzov harassed him constantly, but avoided a major battle. Cossack cavalry disrupted the frenzied attempts of the French to obtain food. With every mile, the Grand Army shrank. During the first week of November, heavy snow began falling. Instead of dying from heat, the French were succumbing to the cold. Bodies began appearing everywhere, thousands of them, partially covered with snow, looking like sheep huddled down in the middle of white fields. Horses in similar numbers were collapsing.

Napoleon took no notice of the sickening white lumps in the fields. He had only one thing on his mind—getting back to Paris fast. He reached Smolensk on November 9. Its supplies of food were quickly devoured. He left on the twelfth, heading for Krasnoye and then Orsha, where he crossed the Dnieper and continued west toward the river Berezina, a tributary of the Dnieper.

The czar hoped to cut Napoleon off and capture him at Borisov on the Berezina. Admiral Pavel Chichagov with 32,000 men, and a similar number under General Peter Wittgenstein, converged on Borisov. On November 26–29 the remnants of the French army—now amounting to perhaps 30,000 to 40,000—fought the Russians and suffered devastating losses but escaped destruction, crossed the river, and continued moving west. Napoleon himself crossed the Berezina at Studenkia, just north of Borisov, and avoided capture. He continued west to Smorgoni, midway between the Berezina and the Niemen. The Grand Army continued to dwindle.

On December 5, from Smorgoni, Bonaparte issued his famous Bulletin 29, admitting to the French people that there had been a dreadful calamity in Russia. At the same time he began calling up 300,000 men for a new army. He then completed conferences with his remaining generals and left secretly in the middle of the night, abandoning what was left of his army. He raced west to Vilna and then to Kovno, where he crossed the Niemen into Poland. From there he traveled by sleigh to Warsaw and then to Dresden, reaching it on December 13, accompanied only by his closest aide, Caulaincourt, Duc de Vicence.

Not wasting any time, Napoleon sped on to Paris, entering it the night of December 18, apprehensive about what awaited him. But Caulaincourt reported that "from the very first the complexion of Paris . . . looked cheering to him. His return had produced a tremendous effect. . . . and after the second day he felt reassured . . . 'The terrible bulletin [29] has had its effect,' he said to me, 'but I see that my presence is giving even more pleasure than our disasters give pain. There is more affliction than discouragement. This state of mind will communicate itself to Vienna; and all will be retrieved within three months.'"

Napoleon's luck was indeed holding out. He had arrived back in the nick of time; Paris had just found out about his disaster—too soon for a real opposition to form. Although he had issued Bulletin 29 on December 5, the news did not reach the capital until the day before his return. Ignoring his horrific Russian debacle as if it had never happened—claiming the weather caused it—he brazenly went to work raising another huge army, dreaming of being as powerful as ever.

The unreality of Napoleon's world and the pretense that his reign would continue as before could be seen in an announcement printed in the *Gazette de France* on December 7, when the emperor's Russian disaster was widely suspected. "We today celebrate that day which opens the 9th year of Napoleon's reign; a reign preceded by 8 years of immortal glory,—brilliant to himself by the most memorable exploits, and by the most elevated acts of policy and legislation,—a reign, the fruitful activity of which, insures to our country ages of grandeur, repose, and prosperity." The emperor's propaganda could not wipe away his appalling reversal in Russia, however. The world knew about it, and so did the French people, who had to send more of their sons to be sacrificed to his ambition.

DURING THE SECOND week of December in London, the earlier rumors of Napoleon's catastrophe were confirmed, and the British were exuberant. On December 11 the *Times* wrote, "Every day brings some fresh confirmation of the distress of the French armies, and some new instance of the disasters and defeats with which they are closing a campaign opened with so much ostentation and apparent success."

A week later, on December 17, the *Times* announced, "Bonaparte is wholly defeated in Russia: he is conquered, and a fugitive. And what can we say more?" The British prayed the Russians would capture him, but on Christmas Eve the *Times* had to concede that, "the wretched vagabond has returned home." The hope of ending the war with a new regime in Paris suddenly vanished. "We have scotched the snake, not killed it," the *Times* lamented.

Nevertheless, Napoleon's defeat was immensely satisfying to the British, and as his fortunes declined, their confidence grew. The distasteful necessity of making peace with America disappeared, replaced by a commitment to make her pay a steep price for her de facto alliance with Napoleon. With Bonaparte back in power in Paris, however, the Liverpool ministry would have to deal with him first before it settled scores with the United States. Although a hugely popular idea, humbling America would have to wait.

WHEN THE RUMORS of Napoleon's debacle were confirmed in Washington in January 1813, Madison was shocked, but he did not despair. Defeat in Russia did not mean the end of the Napoleonic regime in Europe. The dictator's fate depended on whether he reached Paris safely and could reestablish his authority, and on whether the great powers, Russia, Britain, Prussia, and Austria, allied with smaller states like Sweden and the German principalities, could form an effective alliance against him. Madison considered this unlikely. He thought chances were better that Napoleon would survive and regain his power. If that were the case, the foundation of the president's grand strategy would remain intact. He found himself hoping the dictator held on to power.

A titanic struggle over the fate of Europe was now in the offing. The British were focused on only one objective—annihilating Bonaparte. The czar was equally adamant. The invasion and the destruction of Moscow had outraged him, and he wanted revenge. On December 12 he proclaimed, "The arm of the giant is broken, but his destructive strength must be prevented from reviving; and his power over the nations, who served him out of terror, must be taken away."

Napoleon was rearming rapidly, however, and he still looked formidable. His enemies had a myriad of difficulties to surmount before they could hope to crush him. It was uncertain, for instance, what role Czar Alexander would play in Europe. Kutuzov, reflecting the views of many in the army, did not want to march beyond Russia's borders, at least not until the army had a chance to recover from what had been nearly as brutal a war for them as it had been for the French. Furthermore, Britain's small army, although doing well under Wellington, was totally occupied in Spain. And Austria was nominally a French ally and could not be counted on to join an alliance against him. Maria Teresa, the emperor's daughter, was married to Napoleon, and the powerful Austrian foreign minister Prince Metternich had no desire to have French power in Europe replaced by Russian, nor did he have any love for England. And he was leery of a resurgent Prussia. He expected Napoleon to remain on the French throne, less powerful but still potent.

Prussia, which Napoleon had reduced to a weak state of vassalage after Tilsit in 1807, was still nominally a French ally, although King Frederick William, who hated Napoleon, dearly wanted to change sides, as did a growing number of German patriots. Already, on December 20 the Prussian general von Yorck had deserted Napoleon and declared his Prussian Corps neutral. The czar had known for a long time of Frederick William's yearning to change sides, but the Prussian king could not make a move until Alexander decided to push beyond Russia's western border into Europe. The Prussians did not have to wait long. The Russian army crossed the Niemen on January 12 and marched into Prussia and the Grand Duchy of Warsaw. Frederick William felt liberated; he could now join Alexander. Still, Prussia at the moment was a small country. The king could produce only a limited number of soldiers.

In the midst of these epic events, Czar Alexander offered to mediate between the United States and his new ally, Britain. He had received news of the American declaration of war back in August 1812. Not wanting London's energies diverted by war with the United States, he proposed Russian mediation. And beyond the present conflict, the czar hoped to promote America as a counterweight to British sea power. He thought a check on Britain's uncontrolled dominance of the oceans was necessary.

The American ambassador in St. Petersburg, John Quincy Adams, reported the czar's offer in dispatches dated September 30 and October 17, 1812. John Levett Harris, nephew of the American consul general in St. Petersburg, brought them to Washington, arriving on February 24, 1813. The following day, the Russian chargé d'affaires, Andre Daschkoff, told Secretary Monroe that the czar was indeed anxious to act as a mediator.

On February 17, a week before he received word of the czar's offer, the president learned that Napoleon had, as Madison had hoped, eluded Russian troops, and in a daring, suspenseful journey across Europe, reached Paris in one piece and had taken up the reins of power once more. His regime and the French army were not about to disappear. The president, who had claimed not to be dependent on Bonaparte, was enormously relieved. At the White House during Dolley Madison's weekly levee, French ambassador Jean Serurier made an appearance, and the many Republican guests rushed to congratulate him on Napoleon's successful return to Paris.

Since Madison knew that Britain would continue to be preoccupied with Europe, it was not urgent for him to agree to Russian mediation until the British indicated they were receptive to the idea. He could afford to wait and see what Liverpool's reaction was. Instead, the president grasped the Russian offer as if it were a lifeline. He assumed that Liverpool and Castlereagh would have a hard time turning down Alexander, their new ally, when Napoleon was back in Paris raising another army with his usual electrifying energy.

To underscore America's desire to have a negotiated settlement as soon as possible, Congress, at Madison's urging, passed the Foreign Seamen's Act on March 3, 1813. The law stipulated that upon termination of the war, all foreigners would be prohibited from service in all American ships, public or private.

The president wrote to Count Nikolai Rumiantsev, the czar's anti-British chancellor and foreign minister, that out of his "high respect for the Emperor personally . . . [he was] not . . . waiting for the formal acceptance of the British government." He was accepting mediation immediately.

Madison's eagerness to negotiate was taken in London as a sign of weakness. The *Times* chortled, "the pressure of the war may have rendered Mr. Madison seriously anxious to extricate himself from the unpleasant situation in which he finds himself."

London's attitude would undoubtedly have been different had Madison done well on the battlefield, but the reverse was the case. With the commitment of only a few resources, the British were holding their own in Canada. The estrangement of His Majesty's Canadian subjects, which had worried the British so much, had not happened. Canadian militiamen had responded when called and had performed better than expected. French-Canadians had not shown any disaffection either. They viewed the Americans as the enemy and were willing to fight them. In marked contrast to the neutrality they exhibited in 1775, they were now decidedly in favor of the status quo in Canada. The Roman Catholic clergy, who exercised a powerful influence among the French-Canadians, strongly supported the English king's authority. Their antipathy to the atheistic French Revolution led them to support the Revolution's chief enemy, Britain, and that commitment continued into 1813.

Because British arms were holding their own in America, Liverpool had no incentive to negotiate. In the winter and spring of 1813, the prevailing mood in Britain was vengeance, not reconciliation. To reach out to Madison at this point would have run entirely against the political grain in London. Anger at the United States was never far from the surface in Britain, and now it surged. "The American President was the party that struck the first blow," the *Times* wrote on December 25, 1812. "It is a genuine British sentiment, to return a blow with interest." The belief that America had stabbed Britain in the back during her most vulnerable moment was widespread, and the British were demanding retribution.

On February 18, 1813, both houses of Parliament debated the American war. Even members formerly sympathetic to the United States competed in bitter attacks on Madison and his treacherous countrymen. Only Alexander Barring, America's London banker, and Samuel Whitbread, the brewer and longtime friend of the United States, expressed any sympathy for America. The Liverpool ministry made it clear they would never give in on impressment. Earl Bathurst, the secretary of state for war and the colonies, told the House of Lords that to abandon impressment would be "sapping the foundation of our maritime greatness." He declared that it was "essential to the interests of this country; and indirectly essential to the interests of Europe; and even to those of America herself."

Actually, Liverpool did not believe that impressment was the real cause of the war. "Who could believe," he asked the House of Lords, "that the right of impressment was the actual cause? . . . Amicable discussions might have reduced the whole controversy to nothing." Indeed they would have, and Madison had asked for them, but Liverpool and Castlereagh had turned him down. If Liverpool was willing to compromise on impressment and suspend the Orders in Council, what then was the reason for continuing the war? If the prime minister wanted to protect Canada, the easiest and least expensive way was to enter into a negotiation with Madison, who clearly wanted one. Accepting the czar's offer of mediation would have been a simple way to begin.

If the issues that started the war could be so easily settled, and with Napoleon building his strength, why would Liverpool refuse mediation? Beyond the fact that the British people were thirsting for revenge, and Russian interests as a small maritime power were more closely aligned with America than with Britain, Liverpool and his colleagues wanted to reduce the long-term threat they fancied America posed to their imperial ambitions. Liverpool contended that America's real reason for declaring war was not the Orders in Council or impressment but the desire to demolish Britain's power, particularly at sea.

When the Napoleonic menace was finally destroyed, which Liverpool was now confident would happen, he intended to dramatically limit the size and strength of Great Britain's only remaining rival on the high seas. In the course of the Napoleonic wars, the navies of France, Spain, Portugal, Denmark, Holland, Russia, and Sweden had been drastically reduced. The American marine was the only force that could possibly challenge the British colossus. The notion that the United States sought to destroy Britain's maritime power, although pure fantasy, was stated as a fact over and over again. "We ought to consider the United States as the wanton and bitter enemies of our existence, and treat them accordingly," the *Times* wrote, reflecting the views of a great many of Britain's leaders, including the Liverpool ministry.

Thus, despite the continuing threat from a resurgent Napoleon, and despite the fact that the issues that caused the American war could now be easily resolved, Liverpool decided to turn down the offer of mediation from his most important ally. Instead, he and Castlereagh intended to propose direct negotiations with Madison when circumstances in Europe and America were favorable for them to dictate a peace that would put the upstart republic in her place.

Liverpool's attitude came as no surprise to Republicans. Henry Clay had been convinced for years that Britain's fear of America's maritime potential underlay her policies. Madison and Jefferson thought the same. On December 11, 1811, Clay told the House, "you must look for an explanation of her conduct in the jealousies of a rival. She sickens at your prosperity, and beholds in your growth—your sails spread on every ocean, and your numerous seamen, the foundations of a power which, at no very distant day, is to make her tremble for naval superiority."

UNAWARE THAT LIVERPOOL had no intention of accepting Russian mediation, Madison appointed Treasury Secretary Albert Gallatin and Federalist senator James A. Bayard to join John Quincy Adams in Russia to conduct the negotiations.

Gallatin was anxious to get away from Washington. His major problem at the Treasury, funding the war for the rest of the year, had been solved for the moment by the loan he had negotiated with the bankers in Philadelphia. So he felt free to leave.

Anticipating Senate approval of their appointments, Gallatin and Bayard left for St. Petersburg on May 9, 1813, arriving on July 21. They sailed in the *Neptune*, a ship purchased by the navy from Philadelphia merchant Chandler Price, a friend of Secretary Jones. The British blockade of Delaware Bay had left Price with idle ships on his hands, and Secretary Jones wanted to buy a vessel instead of using one of the navy's scarce warships to convey Gallatin and Bayard to Europe. The *Neptune* could not proceed to sea, however, without permission from Admiral Warren. The Russian Chargé Daschkoff sent Counselor Svertchkoff to Norfolk to request a passport for the *Neptune* to pass through the blockade. Even though the British government had not yet agreed to the czar's mediation, Warren, an experienced diplomat, approved the arrangement.

On May 31 Madison submitted the names of Gallatin, Bayard, and Adams to the Senate to be the American commissioners in St. Petersburg and Jonathan Russell to be ambassador to Sweden. Adams and Bayard were approved with no trouble, but Gallatin and Russell ran into a political ambush, as Federalists, led by newly elected Congressman Daniel Webster, sought to embarrass the president over his handling of policy toward France and Britain in the months preceding the declaration of war. A fierce, often byzantine debate raged through the hot Washington summer over the nominations. In the end, the Senate rejected Russell because of supposed unhappiness over his actions in Paris as chargé d'affaires in 1811. The fact that he was entirely innocent did not matter. And in July, the Senate, moved by political animus, rejected Gallatin by a single vote, 17 yeas to 18 nays.

When the vote was taken, Gallatin and Bayard were at sea, unaware that the Senate had publicly humiliated the president by refusing to accept his envoy. Ambassador John Quincy Adams awaited their arrival in St. Petersburg to begin negotiations that the British had no intention of conducting. The peace talks that Madison had so eagerly sought appeared doomed from the start.

CHAPTER FOURTEEN

The Canadian Invasion Resumes

E VEN THOUGH MADISON was anxious to begin peace talks, he was also planning to attack Canada again as soon as the snow and ice melted. Success on the battlefield, he thought, was the key to a satisfactory settlement with Britain. Winning a few victories would give his envoys in St. Petersburg something to bargain with. He even entertained the idea that Britain might be persuaded to part with Upper Canada and perhaps Lower Canada as well.

Madison ruled out attacking either Quebec or Montreal for the moment. The American army was too weak to attempt either city. It still had not reached the level of 20,000 men. As an alternative, Secretary Armstrong proposed a move on Kingston, at the eastern end of Lake Ontario, followed by York in the center of the lake, and then the Niagara area to the west. That would give the United States control of Lake Ontario and, with it, Upper Canada. After that, a two-pronged drive on Montreal could be launched from Kingston and Plattsburg. The president accepted the plan, but ignoring the disasters of the previous year, he left his old friend General Dearborn in place to direct it.

On February 10 Armstrong ordered Dearborn to assemble 4,000 troops at Sackets Harbor and 3,000 at Buffalo. Working together with Commodore Chauncey, Dearborn was to use the troops at Sackets Harbor to attack Kingston, its garrison, and the British ships wintering in the harbor and those under construction. After that, he and Chauncey were to attack the capital of Upper Canada at York (now Toronto), capturing or destroying the stores and warships there.

After York, Dearborn's amphibious force was to combine with the troops sent to Buffalo and attack forts George and Erie and their dependencies in the Niagara region.

The timing of the operation depended on when the ice melted on Lake Ontario, which Armstrong thought would be around April 1. The St. Lawrence River would not be navigable until May 15. He hoped to attack Kingston, York, and the Niagara area while ice on the St. Lawrence made resupply and reinforcement from Montreal impossible.

While the administration was deliberating, General Prevost, in an uncharacteristically bold move, authorized Lieutenant Colonel George Macdonnell to attack Ogdensburg, New York, and put a stop to the harassment of British supply boats navigating the St. Lawrence. On February 22 Macdonald crossed the frozen St. Lawrence from Prescott and surprised the American post, under militia Captain Benjamin Forsyth, and captured it, thus gaining effective control of the St. Lawrence waterway. The attack on Ogdensburg added to fears that Chauncey and Dearborn had of Sackets Harbor being attacked over the ice from Kingston, only thirty-five miles away. They knew Prevost was strengthening the town's garrison, and they feared the reinforcement was just the start of what would become a much larger British contingent at Kingston, amounting to as many as 6,000 or 8,000 men.

Actually, only about 600 regulars and 1,400 militiamen were defending Kingston. Either Dearborn or Chauncey could have easily obtained intelligence of the actual number, but they did not. Judging their troops at Sackets Harbor to be far too few, and not wanting to risk another defeat, they persuaded secretaries Armstrong and Jones, as well as the president, to change plans and attack York and the Niagara area first, and then attempt Kingston. With only 700 inhabitants, York appeared to be an easy target. They planned to leave a sufficient force to protect Sackets Harbor while they conducted an amphibious operation against York. General Dearborn would lead the troops personally, seconded by the highly regarded Brigadier General Zebulon Pike. Chauncey would command the naval contingent.

Unaware of the faulty intelligence behind the change of plans, Madison approved them. He thought the psychological impact in London of an American victory was more important than anything else. Still convinced that Liverpool was going to accept mediation, the president wanted to give the negotiators in St. Petersburg a stronger hand. Armstrong and Jones both agreed.

Jones wrote to Chauncey that the change in strategy would have far-reaching consequences. It would determine not only "the fate of the campaign in that quarter; but the character and duration of the war, and the final object of that war, an honorable and secure peace." His words were prophetic. By not conducting a preemptive strike on Kingston—before the Royal Navy strengthened it—the president was losing an opportunity to secure control of both lakes Ontario and Erie with relative ease early in 1813. Based on faulty intelligence from two overly cautious commanders, the decision would be one of Madison's most important— and one of his worst.

THE BRITISH WERE also focusing their attention on Kingston and Lake Ontario. Since command of the lakes was looming ever larger in the war, the Admiralty on March 19, 1813, assigned thirty-year-old Sir James Yeo, former captain of the ill-fated *Southampton*, to command naval operations on the Great Lakes and on Lake Champlain under Warren and Prevost. The Admiralty directed Yeo to maintain a defensive posture on the lakes. "The first and paramount object for which this naval force is maintained [is] . . . the defense of His Majesty's Provinces of North America," Yeo's orders read. In other words, until the situation in Europe was clarified, Sir James was to avoid offensive operations—not a happy assignment for any commander.

Experienced seamen were the scarcest item on the lakes. Their lordships were concerned that the nearly five hundred seamen they were sending with Yeo might desert. "Their Lordships feel some anxiety on this subject . . . ," the secretary to the Admiralty, John Wilson Croker, wrote to Yeo, "[given] the efforts which the Americans have made on as many occasions to seduce His Majesty's subjects from their duty and allegiance." The Admiralty never looked to the horrid conditions aboard their ships as the real reason good sailors deserted whenever they could.

The British position on Lake Ontario markedly improved on April 28, when they launched the 22-gun *Wolfe* at Kingston. A few days later, Commander Robert Barclay of the Royal Navy reached the town and brought with him a number of lieutenants to take control of the lakes from the Provincial Marine. On May 15, Yeo sailed into Kingston with 465 officers and men to assume command from Barclay, who then traveled to Amherstburg to take charge on Lake Erie. The Royal Navy was now, for the first time, fully engaged on both lakes Ontario and Erie.

Before Barclay and Yeo arrived at Kingston, the ice had broken up on Lake Ontario sufficient to allow Chauncey's fleet of fourteen vessels to sail. He and Dearborn set out from Sackets Harbor on April 23, with General Pike and 1,700 troops to attack York. A ferocious storm temporarily forced them back into port, but two days later, they sailed again, arriving off York on the morning of the twenty-seventh. Chauncey's fleet included the new 24-gun *Madison* (his flagship), the 18-gun *Oneida*, the 9-gun *Hamilton*, the 8-gun *Scourge*, the 6-gun *Governor Tompkins*, the 5-gun *Growler*, and eight other small armed schooners.

At daybreak, while the *Madison* and the *Oneida* remained in deeper water offshore, Chauncey's schooners bombarded the beach west of town. Fire from a few shore batteries returned the complement but with little effect. Dearborn began debarkation at eight o'clock. General Pike led the landing. Supported by continuing fire from the schooners, and outnumbering the defenders by at least two to one, his men landed with little difficulty. It took only two hours to get them all ashore.

The British regulars in York were under the command of Major General Sir Roger Hale Sheaffe, the victor of Queenston, but they were no match for the Americans. After General Brock's death, Sheaffe had become temporary governor-general of Upper Canada. Seeing that the Americans had overwhelming superiority, Sheaffe decided to retreat without putting up a fight for the capital, something Brock would never have done. The cold-blooded Sheaffe thought it more important to save his troops than to lose them in a hopeless battle. He did not seem to care what happened to the town and its people.

Before leaving, he destroyed the *Sir Isaac Brock*, which was under construction, and all naval stores to prevent them from falling into Chauncey's hands. As a final measure, Sheaffe ordered the huge central magazine in the town's garrison blown up. The explosion did not occur until General Pike and a large party were close by, and it was devastating. Pike and two hundred men were killed. The Americans were momentarily stunned, but Sheaffe did not take advantage of the situation; he continued to retreat, much to the chagrin of York loyalists like Reverend John Stahan, who naturally expected their provincial governor to fight for them.

Chauncey was pleased that the *Sir Isaac Brock*, which was far from completion, had been destroyed, but he was disappointed that the 12-gun schooner *Prince Regent* (later renamed *General Beresford*) escaped. She had departed for Kingston a few days before. Chauncey did manage to capture the *Duke of Gloucester*, but she was in such terrible shape that when he got her back to Sackets Harbor, she could only be used for storage. Chauncey was also disappointed that the naval stores had been destroyed, but while he was deprived of them, so too was Commodore Barclay, and he needed them far more than Chauncey did. Barclay could not replace them at Amherstburg, and it made a big difference in the arms race he was already involved in with Oliver Hazard Perry for command of Lake Erie.

In the aftermath of the short battle, looting occurred in York, and a few buildings were burned, but it is not clear who the culprits were. Some of Dearborn's men were involved, but there may have been Canadians as well. It certainly was not the policy of either Dearborn or Chauncey to deliberately torch public, never mind private, buildings. And perhaps only three were actually destroyed. The damage in no way compared to what happened in Washington later in the war, when the British commanders ordered all public buildings in a much larger capital burned.

HAVING TAKEN YORK, the Americans now turned their attention to the Niagara region. A gale kept Chauncey's fleet trapped in York until May 9. The wind was strong enough for the *Madison* to have two anchors ahead and her lower yards and topgallant masts down. When the storm abated, Chauncey ferried Dearborn and his troops to Fort Niagara, where they prepared to assault Fort George, on the opposite side of the Niagara River. While the attack was being organized, Chauncey returned to Sackets Harbor to see to its defenses. He was concerned the British might attack there while he was occupied at Fort George. Admiral Yeo was anxious to destroy the 26-gun *General Pike*, which was nearing completion and would give Chauncey unquestioned command of the lake. The ship would carry twenty-six twenty-four-pound long guns and a complement of 432 men. After satisfying himself that the defenses at Sackets Harbor were adequate, Chauncey left on May 22 and stood west for the Niagara with 350 of Colonel Macomb's regiment to supplement Dearborn's force.

When Chauncey arrived off Fort George three days later, Dearborn's men at Fort Niagara were preparing for the attack. On the morning of May 27, Chauncey's schooners began firing at the British batteries covering the landing areas on the river and at the beach, putting them out of action, and driving back the few defenders. The armed schooners *Julie*, *Growler*, *Ontario*, *Governor Tompkins*, *Hamilton*, *Asp*, and *Scourge* all took part in the action. When they completed their initial bombardment, Colonel Winfield Scott, who had been recently exchanged as a prisoner of war and promoted, led the invasion force of 4,000, which outnumbered the British by more than two to one. Major General Dearborn gave Scott command because he considered him abler than brigadier generals Morgan Lewis, John P. Boyd, John Chandler, or William A. Winder. They led units behind Scott's assault troops.

Oliver Hazard Perry helped debark Scott's men. He had traveled all the way from Presque Isle to assist Chauncey, arriving on the twenty-fifth. Perry managed to get into the thick of things, coming under fire as he played a key role in the landing. Chauncey was favorably impressed, as he told Secretary Jones in a glowing report. With the schooners providing constant, well-directed fire, Scott was in possession of Fort George and the nearby town by noon.

WHILE SCOTT WAS taking Fort George, Prevost and Yeo were conducting a surprise attack on Sackets Harbor, hoping to destroy the entire base, particularly the *General Pike*, and to act as a diversion in favor of Fort George. They departed Kingston on May 27 with about 1,200 men, mostly regulars, and a fleet consisting of the *Wolfe*, the *Royal George*, the *General Beresford*, the *Earl of Moira*, two schooners, thirty large open boats, and a few gunboats. They arrived off Sackets Harbor the following afternoon, unaware that Fort George had already fallen.

Thirty-eight-year-old Major General Jacob Brown of the New York militia was in charge of the harbor's defense, along with Lieutenant Colonel Electus Backus of the regular army. Although Brown had little combat experience, he was a natural soldier. Back in October 1812, his men had repulsed an attack on Ogdensburg. As a young man, he had served as military secretary to Major General Alexander Hamilton during the Quasi-War with France.

Lieutenant Wolcott Chauncey (the commodore's younger brother) alerted Brown to Yeo's approach, ruining Prevost's surprise. Lieutenant Chauncey was scouting with two schooners, the *Fair American* and the *Pert*. His brother had wisely left them behind to serve as General Brown's eyes on the lake. After warning Brown, Lieutenant Chauncey sent an express to his brother, telling him the attack he most feared had begun.

Thanks to the younger Chauncey's warning, when Prevost and Yeo suddenly appeared, Brown and Backus were not taken by surprise. The British had more men, however, and a fleet whose heavy guns could make quick work of Brown and the entire complex at Sackets Harbor. Backus had only four hundred regulars; the rest were militiamen, who kept arriving, responding to Brown's call. By the time Prevost appeared, Brown had five hundred militiamen, and more were coming. Yeo wanted to attack immediately, and although Prevost thought it might be too late in the day to launch an assault, the landing went forward. By six o'clock in the evening, the landing parties were nearing shore, when Prevost changed his mind and decided a night attack would simply not succeed. He postponed the landing until the following morning, which infuriated Yeo and gave the defenders more time to prepare.

On the morning of the twenty-ninth, Prevost accompanied the troops ashore and remained the entire time, but Colonel Edward Baynes led the actual assault. His men landed on Horse Island, at the southern entrance to Sackets, where Brown's militiamen fired on them, wounding and killing quite a few, and then fell back, as Brown expected them to. They waded through shallow water to the mainland and positioned themselves in a wooded area behind a line of Backus's regulars. The British attackers pushed forward into the woods, where Backus and Brown put up a stout defense. They were so tenacious, the attackers had the impression they were outnumbered. Nonetheless, they kept pressing forward, and the Americans retreated to a blockhouse and four strategically located forts. Once there, only heavy guns from the fleet could dislodge them. But adverse winds made it impossible for Yeo to bring his ships into the fight to any great degree.

Seeing his ranks being decimated, the ever-cautious Prevost sounded retreat, which the beleaguered attackers instantly obeyed. Just at that moment, Colonel Backus was shot and killed. The British scrambled for their boats, and the fleet sailed back to Kingston without having attained any of its objectives. As the fleet disappeared, four hundred fifty more American regulars appeared to strengthen the harbor's defenses. Yeo blamed Prevost's timidity for the debacle. It created a permanent rift between them, which had important consequences for their future management of the war.

When Commodore Chauncey heard that Sackets Harbor had been struck, he raced back with his entire fleet. Even though General Brown had beaten off Prevost rather handily, Chauncey felt his fleet was necessary to protect the *General Pike*, which had been partially burned in the attack. To prevent her from falling into British hands, Lieutenant Chauncey, thinking the battle was lost, had started the fire. He quickly reversed himself, however, and no great damage had been done to the ship, but important naval supplies in nearby warehouses were lost. Commodore Chauncey's priority now became finishing the *General Pike*. From June 1 to July 21, Chauncey remained at Sackets Harbor, single-mindedly devoting his energies to completing her. While he did, Admiral Yeo had effective command of the lake.

ALTHOUGH COLONEL SCOTT had easily taken Fort George on May 27, he was not permitted to follow up his victory and crush the British. Brigadier General

John Vincent's small force escaped, withdrawing west in good order. Vincent instructed all his forces along the Niagara River—including the men stationed from Chippawa to Fort Erie—to abandon their fortifications and proceed with him to Burlington Heights at the head of Lake Ontario.

When the British troops withdrew, the five vessels at the American naval base at Black Rock could then be moved safely passed Fort Erie to Presque Isle and bolster the squadron Perry was building on Lake Erie. The schooners were: *Caledonia* (three guns), *Somers* (four guns), *Trippe* (one gun), *Ohio* (one gun), and *Amelia* (too far gone to be of use later). Chauncey had previously dispatched master shipbuilder Henry Eckford and thirty carpenters to prepare the schooners for moving, and when Perry arrived at Black Rock with fifty-five seamen to transport them, Eckford had the ships ready. It took a week for oxen to haul the schooners down the Niagara River against the strong current and contrary winds, past deserted Fort Erie to the lake. Once there, Perry sailed them to Presque Isle, hugging the shore as he went, narrowly missing a British squadron blinded by a lake fog.

Dearborn had now accomplished, rather easily, his initial objectives, but Vincent's force was still intact, and he was moving toward Burlington Heights to prepare for Dearborn's next attack. To support Vincent, Admiral Yeo left Kingston on June 3 with seven vessels, six gunboats, and a reinforcement of two hundred twenty regulars. He sailed west, planning to harass Dearborn's men wherever he could. Chauncey was alerted to Yeo's departure and considered going after him. But upon reflection, he decided it was more important to finish the *General Pike*, and he remained at Sackets Harbor. He told Secretary Jones that rather than engage Yeo's slightly more powerful squadron, he would be better off finishing the *General Pike* and gaining a distinct advantage when he met Yeo later.

During the first week of June, Dearborn dispatched 2,000 men with four field guns and 150 cavalry, under Brigadier General William H. Winder of Maryland, to pursue Vincent. On June 5 Brigadier General John Chandler joined Winder at Stoney Creek and assumed overall command, with Winder as his second. Both men had considerable political influence but little military acumen. The night that Chandler arrived at the front, before he even had time to get his bearings, Vincent attacked him with 700 men during the wee hours of a very dark morning. At first, utter confusion reigned in the surprised American camp, but the light troops gathered themselves and fought back heroically. Vincent suffered heavy casualties, and just before daylight, he pulled back. He took both

Chandler and Winder with him, however. They had been captured in the chaos and confusion of the early fighting.

Instead of going after Vincent's much smaller force, the confused Americans fell back. On June 7, Major General Morgan Lewis of the New York militia arrived to take command. He no sooner appeared on the scene, however, than Yeo's fleet and a contingent of Indians harassed him enough that Dearborn ordered him to return to Fort George. At the same time, Dearborn withdrew all his forces on the Canadian side of the Niagara to Fort George, allowing Vincent to return. When Lewis reached Fort George, he was ordered to Sackets Harbor, leaving Brigadier General John P. Boyd of the regular army in charge at the fort and the immediate vicinity. By then, the elderly Dearborn was too sick to lead.

To protect his position at the fort and to keep the British off balance, Boyd dispatched Lieutenant Colonel C. G. Boerstler to attack a British advanced post at Beaver Dam, seventeen miles south of Fort George. The hapless Boerstler wound up surrendering all five hundred forty of his men without a fight to a force that was a bit smaller than his own, composed mostly of Indians. Afterward, Dearborn, disheartened by one fiasco after another, asked to be relieved of command, which Secretary Armstrong and the president agreed to in July.

JUNE ALSO BROUGHT disaster for the Americans on Lake Champlain. Lieutenant Macdonough had moved his base from Burlington, Vermont, across the lake to Plattsburgh, New York, and while his flagship, the sloop *President*, was laid up for repairs, he sent Lieutenant Sidney Smith and Sailing Master Jairus Loomis out to patrol for enemy gunboats. They had Macdonough's other large vessels, the 11-gun sloop *Growler* (Smith's boat) and the 11-gun sloop *Eagle*, under Loomis. At daybreak on the third of June, Smith's lookout spotted some British gunboats on the lake, and he decided to go after them. He signaled Loomis, and they both tore after the enemy.

Smith knew that chasing fleeing gunboats back to their base at the Isle aux Noix could be tricky. His pilots had warned him, but even if they hadn't, he was experienced enough to appreciate that with the breeze from the south, if he stood down the lake and got too close to the Isle aux Noix, he would not be able to haul his wind and beat back, the width of the channel being only one hundred yards. For this reason, Macdonough had ordered him to stay on the American side of the international boundary and not cross over into Canada during his patrols.

Nonetheless, seeking to distinguish himself, Smith plunged ahead, chasing the gunboats across the Canadian boundary, until he was within two miles of the Isle of Noix. Suddenly realizing he was losing room to maneuver, he hauled his wind and tried to beat back, but he became trapped. Three gunboats from the British base, supported by three hundred men on shore, attacked him, and after a three-hour fight, Smith surrendered both the *Growler* and the *Eagle*. That was enough to give the British command of the lake. It was a crushing blow to Macdonough, who immediately afterward received orders from Secretary Jones to regain command of the lake as fast as possible. That would not be easy. The British would no doubt try to use their newfound superiority to destroy the fleet Macdonough was building. His first priority would be to protect it.

In the meantime, Smith was taken to Quebec as a prisoner and incarcerated in a bestial prison ship, where his health swiftly deteriorated. While there, he witnessed the British routinely taking Americans out of the ship, claiming they were British subjects, and sending them to England for employment in the Royal Navy. If they resisted, they could be hanged for treason.

During the course of the war the British captured around 14,000 American naval personnel—about 14 percent of the total number of seamen employed in the navy and private vessels combined. It was a very high percentage. How many of these men were forced into the Royal Navy is impossible to say, but it was probably a significant number.

MEANWHILE, COMMODORE CHAUNCEY continued his efforts to gain undisputed control of Lake Ontario. When the *General Pike* was completed on July 22, Chauncey made it his flagship and sailed out of Sackets Harbor with twelve other vessels in search of Yeo's fleet. He could not find it immediately and decided instead to destroy a large deposit of stores near Burlington Bay at the head of the lake. Brigadier General Boyd and Colonel Winfield Scott accompanied him with a detachment of two hundred fifty infantrymen.

When Chauncey discovered that the supplies he was after were heavily defended, he called off the attack and turned his attention to York again, arriving there the afternoon of July 31. Colonel Scott landed unopposed with a party of soldiers and marines and proceeded to destroy or carry away all the munitions, boats, and food he found, which were considerable. These supplies were destined for Commodore Barclay at Amherstburg on Lake Erie. He desperately needed them in his arms race with Oliver Hazard Perry. After Scott completed his work, Chauncey withdrew. Neither General Boyd nor Chauncey considered occupying York and cutting the line between Kingston and the British forces in the Niagara area.

After leaving York, Chauncey went to Fort Niagara and debarked eleven officers, including Lieutenants Jesse D. Elliott, Augustus H. M. Conkling, and Joseph E. Smith, along with one hundred sailors, sending them to Perry at Presque Isle, where they were critically needed. Afterward Chauncey returned to Sackets Harbor, planning to meet Yeo at the earliest opportunity.

Chauncey did not have to wait long. Yeo had already sailed from Kingston on July 31 to challenge Chauncey. A major battle was in the offing. Placid weather kept the fleets apart, until the seventh of August, when they met near the head of the lake, not far from Fort Niagara. Unfavorable winds separated them until the morning of the eighth, when a sudden squall overset Chauncey's *Hamilton* and *Scourge* and sank them. Chauncey judged that Yeo now had the stronger fleet. Continuing light wind made maneuvering impossible until the evening of the tenth, when Yeo bore down on Chauncey and captured the schooners *Julia* and *Growler*. Chauncey had now lost four schooners, and as he was low on provisions, he decided he was too weak to fight and returned to Sackets Harbor, "distressed and mortified," as he told Secretary Jones.

SOON AFTER SEIZING the sloops *Growler* and *Eagle* on Lake Champlain, the British used their newfound supremacy to unleash a series of attacks that became known as Murray's Raid. Governor General Prevost sent the crew of HM sloop of war *Wasp* (then at Quebec) to help man gunboats, and under the command of Lieutenant Colonel John Murray, Lieutenant Daniel Pring, and Commander Thomas Everard, an amphibious force of eight hundred men sailed south.

Macdonough knew they were coming, but he was powerless to stop them. He did move his base of operations back to Burlington, however, consolidating as much of his operation as possible. He had support from the new army commander in the region, Major General Wade Hampton.

Between July 29 and August 3 Murray attacked, without opposition, the military installations at Plattsburg, Champlain, and Swanton. He also appeared off Burlington on August 2 with two sloops and a row galley and began bombarding what was left of Macdonough's fleet. Macdonough fought back, keeping Murray at bay, using shore batteries and his ships, which were moored with springs on their cables so that they could fire their cannon from both sides without having to use their sails. The heavy fire eventually drove Murray off. Macdonough wanted to go after him, but he lacked the men and officers and had to just watch as the British disappeared. In spite of his troubles, Macdonough was promoted to master commandant on July 24, an honor that was long overdue but highly gratifying to the modest recipient.

IN THE NORTHWEST, meanwhile, General Harrison's operations continued to be stymied. Without command of Lake Erie, his army was forced to remain on the defensive. Back in April, Major General Henry Proctor, still commandant at Fort Malden and still hated by the Americans for the massacre of Kentucky militiamen at the River Raisin, sailed up the Maumee and laid siege to Fort Meigs with 500 regulars, an equal number of militiamen, and 1,200 of Tecumseh's warriors. Harrison's ranks had been seriously depleted when Virginia, Kentucky, and Pennsylvania militiamen had gone home earlier, after their six months of service were up.

Proctor dragged twenty-four-pounders and some smaller artillery to the heights overlooking the fort and opened fire on May 1. Harrison stoutly defended the fort, and he was heartened when on May 4 he saw 1,200 green Kentucky militiamen approaching. Half of them attacked the British batteries at great cost, while the rest scrambled into the fort with few casualties. With Harrison now strengthened, some Indians began drifting away, but many remained. Proctor, however, gave up the siege on May 9 and returned to Fort Malden, much to the disgust of Tecumseh. Harrison had lost far more men than Proctor, but he held the fort. The casualties he suffered made him less inclined to try retaking Detroit and capturing Fort Malden, unless the navy could establish supremacy on Lake Erie—at the moment an unlikely scenario.

Harrison would not have to worry about attacking the British, however, for he was soon on the defensive again. Proctor made another, halfhearted attempt on Fort Meigs two months later but failed again. He then decided to attack Harrison's supply depot at Fort Stephenson on the Sandusky River in Ohio—this time without Tecumseh's support. Twenty-one-year-old Major George Croghan was in command at Fort Stephenson with only a hundred sixty men and a single piece of artillery. The fort was decrepit, but Croghan intended to make the most of what he had.

Proctor sailed into Sandusky Bay and then up the river unopposed, landing eight hundred men on August 1, near what is today Fremont, Ohio. On the same day, Croghan received an unambiguous order from Harrison to evacuate. Harrison thought the fort was too vulnerable. Aware that Proctor had already landed, Croghan decided to stay put. He told Harrison that evacuating would be more dangerous than fighting. All the while, Croghan was preparing as strong a defense as he could. He had already evacuated the women, children, and sick, and he vowed to fight to the last man. "The example set me by my Revolutionary kindred is before me," he wrote to a friend. "Let me die rather than prove unworthy of their name." Croghan had inspired similar sentiments in the men who stood with him against seemingly impossible odds.

Proctor attacked Fort Stephenson on August 2 and unexpectedly ran into stiff opposition. Croghan's defenders put up such a ferocious fight that the British and Indians were forced back with heavy losses. Not wishing to endure more casualties, Proctor gave up and returned to his boats humiliated, sailing back to Fort Malden, where his supply problems were mounting. Harrison, who had been furious with Croghan for being insubordinate and had actually relieved him, was forced to restore him to command when the country hailed him as a great hero. Congress awarded Croghan a gold medal. He was the only bright spot in Harrison's dismal performance during the first seven months of 1813.

The failure to achieve any success against Canada during these months, except for the raids on York, shattered Madison's overall strategy. Accepting the advice of Dearborn and Chauncey to attack York and the Niagara region before moving on Kingston had proven a terrible mistake. It allowed Lord Liverpool to avoid negotiations while he and his allies dealt with Napoleon, who was still very much a threat.

CHAPTER FIFTEEN

The *Chesapeake* and the *Shannon*

W
HILE THE BRITISH were frustrating Madison along the Canadian frontier, the American blue-water fleet was running into difficulties its senior officers had long anticipated. Before the war began, Commodore Rodgers expressed a view generally held by his colleagues, that the navy would have the most success in the first months of the war. After that, the Royal Navy's overwhelming numbers would drastically curtail American naval operations. At the start of the war, the light regard in London for the naval prowess of the United States helped the navy achieve a series of remarkable victories, but they in turn caused the Admiralty to deploy additional resources to the American theater, which made life even more difficult for the navy than Rodgers had anticipated.

The British public clamored for the Royal Navy to destroy the maritime power of the United States, and the Admiralty kept pushing Admiral Warren to tighten his blockade along the coast. Their lordships pointed out to him that his failure to stop America's warships and privateers from putting to sea forced the Royal Navy in the first weeks of 1813 to deploy two line-of-battle ships, two frigates, and more sloops of war around St. Helena and a similar assortment of warships in the neighborhood of Madeira and the Western Islands. The Admiralty demanded to know why Warren, with all the ships he had, allowed the *Constitution*, the *President*, the *United States*, the *Congress*, the *Argus*, and the *Hornet* to come and go as they pleased from Boston Harbor. On March 20, 1813, Croker wrote to Warren emphasizing again that all the American warships must be blockaded. If they were allowed to roam, the problem of finding them would be nearly impossible, making the convoying of merchant fleets far more difficult. Furthermore, if privateers by the hundreds were allowed to prowl, they would add an even greater hazard. A tight blockade of the entire coast was the only remedy. The Admiralty insisted that Warren include a 74-gun battleship in every blockading squadron outside an American port.

Warren's strengthening blockade necessitated Commodore Broke's return from Halifax in late March to patrol off Boston in the 38-gun *Shannon*, accompanied by the 38-gun *Tenedos*, under Captain Sir Hyde Parker. They were part of a powerful squadron that was led by Captain Thomas Bladen in the 74-gun *La Hogue* and included the 38-gun *Nymphe*, under Captain Farmery P. Epworth.

Bladen was anxious to prevent John Rodgers and the *President* from leaving Boston Harbor, but recurring thick fog gave Rodgers an opening, and on April 23 he stole out to sea unmolested to begin his third cruise of the war, accompanied by the *Congress* (Captain John Smith). Contrary winds kept the two frigates confined to Boston Bay for a few days, but when the wind turned fair, they broke out on the afternoon of May 3. Near the shoal of George's Bank they passed to windward of the *La Hogue* and the *Nymphe*. Captain Bladen could not catch them, however, and they went on their way, splitting up and cruising singly after May 8.

Having failed to stop the *President* and the *Congress* from putting to sea, Commodore Broke set his sights on the *Chesapeake*, which was preparing to sortie from Boston. He yearned to fight her one-on-one. While he was watching for his chance, the Admiralty, dismayed by American naval victories, was contemplating issuing an order to forbid any frigate from engaging the 44-gun American frigates alone. The order was not issued until July 10, 1813, however, and in any event, it would not have applied to the *Chesapeake*, since she was not among the larger class of American frigates.

Broke was so anxious for a duel that during the last week of May he wrote a clever, insulting letter to Captain James Lawrence, the *Chesapeake*'s new skipper, challenging him to come out and fight, as if it were an affair of honor between the two men, rather than a battle that was sure to cause dozens of casualties. Broke sent a captured American prisoner to deliver his letter to Lawrence. The prisoner left it at the post office in Charlestown, but Lawrence never received it. The post office delivered it to Bainbridge by mistake, and he passed it on to Secretary Jones. Bainbridge was commandant of the Boston Navy Yard at the time, having turned command of the *Constitution* over to Charles Stewart.

To emphasize how urgently he wanted a single-ship duel, Broke sent the *Tenedoes* away and made the *Shannon* conspicuous by sailing her just outside the harbor in plain view. Captain Lawrence did not need an inducement to fight; he was anxious to have it out with the *Shannon*. When Broke sent his challenge, Lawrence had been in Boston only a few days. He had received orders from Secretary Jones on May 6, directing him to proceed to Boston and take command of the *Chesapeake*. Lawrence arrived in the city on May 18. His assignment was the most important the president had given to the seagoing navy. He was ordered to cruise in the Gulf of St. Lawrence, interdicting supply ships and troop transports making for Quebec, the principal port supplying British land forces in Canada. Madison's invasion plans for Canada in the spring of 1813 would be helped immeasurably if Lawrence could seriously limit enemy provisions getting through to Quebec.

It had taken Madison and Jones some time before they had settled on a new assignment for Lawrence. Since defeating the *Peacock* in February, he had become a national hero. To begin with, they appointed him commandant of the New York Navy Yard, which allowed him to be home with his wife and child. Jones then gave him command of the *Constitution*—as choice an assignment as the navy had to offer. But a short time later, Jones learned that the *Constitution* was not ready for sea and that the *Chesapeake*'s skipper, Samuel Evans, was seriously ill. Jones wanted the navy's few warships put into action as soon as possible, and he considered Lawrence an ideal replacement for Evans. On the first of May he ordered Lawrence to take command of the *Chesapeake*, which was in Boston along with the *Constitution*.

When he arrived in Boston, Lawrence went right to work, and two days later he reported to Jones that he found the *Chesapeake* "ready for sea." He also told him that he had tried unsuccessfully to exchange ships with Captain Stewart. Lawrence evidently felt that Jones would have no trouble approving the switch. Despite his preference for the *Constitution*, Lawrence was eager to get to sea and into action, which is exactly what Jones wanted. Lawrence's old ship, the *Hornet*, was to accompany him, but she was in New York, under James Biddle. Lawrence wrote to Biddle explaining his plans and places of rendezvous. The British were blockading New York, however, and getting to sea would be exceptionally difficult. Lawrence felt that if anyone could get the *Hornet* out, it was Biddle.

Lawrence was pleased with all of the *Chesapeake*'s young but experienced officers. His first lieutenant was twenty-one-year-old Augustus Ludlow, who had never been first officer on a ship before but was a veteran seaman, having been in the navy since 1804. He had served aboard the *President*, the *Constitution* (where he was promoted to lieutenant), and the *Hornet*, and more importantly, he had been on two cruises in the *Chesapeake*. Ludlow was a replacement for four older officers: Lieutenants Page, Thompson, and Nicholson were sick, and Acting Lieutenant Pierce was such a troublemaker that Lawrence got rid of him immediately, reporting to Jones that Pierce could not get along with anyone in the wardroom. The absence of all these officers required two midshipmen to be promoted to acting lieutenant, William Cox and Edward J. Ballard. Like Ludlow, they were young and new to their jobs, but both had been in the service a long time, had served on the *Chesapeake*, and were ready for their new duties. The second lieutenant was George Budd.

Lieutenant Ludlow wrote to his brother Charles that the *Chesapeake* was in better condition than he had ever seen her. Furthermore, her crew were all experienced seamen, except for the thirteen powder monkeys. Only 36 of the 379 men aboard were British seamen, and they appeared prepared to fight for their new country. Lawrence and Ludlow felt the crew was every bit as ready as the ship.

By the thirtieth of May the *Chesapeake* was ready for action, and Lawrence weighed anchor, leaving Boston's inner harbor and dropping down to President Roads off Long Island at the edge of the harbor, where he could spend a few days making final preparations for sea while keeping an eye out for the blockading squadron. Persistent fog and rain would likely give him enough cover to get to sea. The following morning, fog and rain, which had blanketed the area for the past few days, was still around. Instead of putting to sea, however, Lawrence left the ship and went into town for a luncheon. While he was there, he received word that a single British warship was off Boston Light. Deciding there was no immediate danger, he remained in town that night and rejoined his ship the following day.

When Lawrence came aboard first thing in the morning, Lieutenant Budd reported that the *Shannon* was visible, and, as far as he could tell, she was alone. Lawrence climbed the main rigging to have a look for himself. By then, the weather had cleared. He came back satisfied that she was the *Shannon*. He hailed a pilot boat and sent her out to see if there were other enemy warships about, and then mustered all hands to tell them that if the *Shannon* were alone, he meant to engage her and urged them to do their patriotic duty. Some hands took the occasion to protest that they had not received their prize money from the last cruise, whereupon Lawrence ordered the purser to pay them.

In deciding to fight the British ship, Lawrence was disregarding his orders to intercept supplies moving to Quebec. Lawrence's mission was important to the war effort; he was ignoring it for a chance at personal glory. Even if he succeeded against the *Shannon*, he would have to return to Boston for extensive repairs that might take months, making it impossible to pursue an assignment the president believed was vital. In addition, Lawrence was risking one of the few warships in the American arsenal for no good reason.

Going against the clear purport of his orders was not Lawrence's only problem. Unlike many frigates in His Majesty's service, the *Shannon* had a skipper who had been in command for seven years and a crew that had been with him for a long time. They were undoubtedly among the best in the Royal Navy. Lawrence would have his hands full.

On Tuesday, June 1, at eight o'clock in the morning, Lawrence ordered the *Chesapeake* unmoored and then went to his cabin and scratched out two letters. To Secretary Jones he wrote, "My crew appear to be in fine spirits, and I trust will do their duty." The second letter was to his wife's brother, James Montaudevert. "An English frigate is close in with the lighthouse, and we are now clearing for action. Should I be so unfortunate as to be taken off, I leave my wife and children to your care."

At noon Lawrence hove out to sea with a light seasonal wind from the southwest. The *Shannon* immediately came into view, looking a bit shabby from having been on blockade duty for weeks. The *Chesapeake*, on the other hand, having just been refurbished, looked brand new.

The two ships were evenly matched. The *Chesapeake* had fifty guns and 379 men. Her main battery was twenty-eight long eighteen-pounders on the gun deck, and on the spar deck above, she carried eighteen thirty-two-pound carronades, two long twelves, one long eighteen, and a twelve-pound carronade. The *Shannon* carried fifty-two guns and 330 men. Her main battery was twenty-eight long eighteen-pounders on the gun deck, and on the spar deck she carried sixteen thirty-two-pound carronades, four long nines, one long six, and three twelve-pound carronades. The officers and crews of both ships were experienced seamen, but Broke had a distinct advantage in that he had had command of his excellent crew for many years, while Lawrence was new to his men.

The instant the *Chesapeake* hove into sight off Boston Light, Broke and his officers had telescopes trained on her, and when they saw her coming toward them, it was obvious that Lawrence had taken up the challenge. Broke could not have been more pleased. He moved out to a position twelve miles south-southwest of Cape Ann under easy sail. He wanted to be offshore for maneuverability and sufficiently far from Boston that Lawrence would not be aided by other vessels, although, by the look of things, the American captain did not want any help. He was sailing directly at Broke. At 4:30 the *Shannon* lay to with her head to the southeast, having just steerage way, waiting for the *Chesapeake*. Broke was under topsails, topgallants, jib, spanker, and even royals, since he expected the wind to die away. He was taking a big chance, leaving it in Lawrence's power to begin the action in whatever way he chose.

At five o'clock Lawrence ordered royals and topgallants taken in, and half an hour later, he had the courses hauled up. Under topsails and jibs, he came down fast with the weather gauge. Broke had done nothing to deprive him of it. Lawrence could now sail straight for the *Shannon*'s stern, rake her with a deadly broadside or two, and gain a decisive advantage. Or, since he had more men than Broke, he could drive right up to the *Shannon*, firing as he went, and board. Instead, in what can only be described as a misguided act of chivalry, or a terrible mistake, Lawrence refused to exploit the opening Broke was giving him, and within forty-five minutes he rounded to within pistol shot (less than fifty yards), bringing the *Chesapeake* on a parallel course with the *Shannon*, setting up an artillery duel and playing to Broke's strength.

Because of the initial position Broke deliberately took, he was uncertain what direction Lawrence would take, until he saw the *Chesapeake* luffing up on the *Shannon*'s weather quarter and her foremast coming in a line with the *Shannon*'s mizzen. As she did, Broke fired his after guns and the others successively, until the *Chesapeake* came directly abreast. At that point, Lawrence unleashed his broadside. It was ten minutes to six. With the two ships continuing to run roughly parallel to each other, they unleashed terrifying broadsides, while from the tops their marksmen rained musket balls down on the enemy's deck. The first shots from the *Shannon* damaged the *Chesapeake*'s rigging, killed the sailing master Mr. White, and wounded Lawrence. Seconds later, full broadsides tore into the *Chesapeake* and cut her foresail tie and jib sheet, rendering her headsails useless. The *Chesapeake*'s broadsides did considerable damage to the *Shannon* as well, but the British ship did not have key officers killed and her captain wounded so early in the fighting, nor have her steering compromised.

The *Chesapeake* now shot up into the wind uncontrollably, presenting her stern and larboard quarter to the enemy, while making it impossible for Lawrence to bring more than one or two of his own guns to bear. Seeing the *Chesapeake*'s quarter presented to him, Broke unleashed devastating half-raking broadsides that tore into the quarterdeck, killing the men at the wheel and making the *Chesapeake* completely unmanageable. The wind now pushed her back toward the *Shannon*. Expecting the two ships to collide, Lawrence shouted, "Boarders away." A bugler sounded the call to assemble, and Lieutenant Ludlow took command of them. Just then, a hand-grenade thrown from the *Shannon* landed on one of the *Chesapeake*'s arms chests on the quarter deck, exploding the contents in a terrifying roar. In moments, the *Chesapeake*—in irons, unable to steer—backed into the *Shannon*, her mizzen channels locking in with the *Shannon*'s fore rigging.

When Broke saw Ludlow's men assembling, he called for his own boarders. As he did, Lawrence suddenly slumped to the deck, felled by a musket ball from a marksman in the *Shannon*'s tops. He cried out to be taken to his cabin. Lieutenant Ludlow was shot at the same time and severely wounded. At this point, Acting Third Lieutenant William Cox appeared from below. He had been in charge of the guns on the starboard side of the *Chesapeake*'s gun deck, the side that was not firing, and since he wasn't needed there, he climbed up to the quarterdeck. Hearing Lawrence's call to be taken below, he ordered a couple of men to help him carry the captain to his cabin. When he disappeared below, Cox did not realize he was the senior officer in command on the spar deck. After seeing to Lawrence, Cox attempted to return to the fight on the upper deck, but he ran into a flood of men retreating below and could not get past them.

Meanwhile, Broke had his boarders assembled and was leading them onto the *Chesapeake*'s quarterdeck. With Lawrence and Ludlow severely wounded and Cox having gone below, the *Chesapeake*'s boarders were leaderless and disoriented. Deadly musket balls continued raining down from the *Shannon*'s tops. Second Lieutenant George Budd, now the ship's senior officer, was below on the gun deck running operations there, unaware of the situation on the spar deck above.

Broke pressed his advantage, and as he led his boarders forward, a pistol shot fired by the *Chesapeake*'s chaplain hit him. It didn't stop him, though; he continued on against little organized opposition. Broke and his men quickly gained control of the quarterdeck and were fighting their way to the forecastle when Lieutenant Budd, having been alerted by one of Lawrence's aides, reached the spar deck with some men. He found that the *Shannon*'s boarders had already gained possession of the quarterdeck and were fighting their way forward. Budd ordered the fore tack hauled on board in hopes of shooting the *Chesapeake* clear of the *Shannon*. He then tried to regain control of the quarterdeck, but he was soon wounded himself and collapsed momentarily. Despite his injury, he rose and made another valiant effort to collect his men and resist the *Shannon*'s boarders, but many of the *Chesapeake* crew had fled below, desperate to get away from the slaughter.

In the course of the fighting, a cutlass had slashed Broke's hard hat and sliced through his skull, nearly killing him, but he retained command and now had control of the entire upper deck, which was a bloody mess. The dying Lawrence told his men in a whisper, "Don't give up the ship," and then repeated it. But with Broke in complete command of the upper deck, Lieutenant Budd was forced to surrender. After he did, Broke passed out.

The *Shannon*'s second lieutenant was now in command. Her first lieutenant, Mr. Watt, had been killed at the moment of victory. The entire battle lasted only fifteen minutes.

Totally dejected, Lieutenant Budd allowed himself to be taken down to the cockpit, where his wound could be treated. When he arrived, he found Lawrence and Ludlow mortally wounded; the sight badly shook him. Both the Fourth Lieutenant Edward J. Ballard and Marine Lieutenant James Broom were also wounded.

The butcher's bill was horrific on both ships. In addition to Lieutenant Watt, the *Shannon* lost her purser, the captain's clerk, and twenty-three seamen, while Captain Broke and a midshipman were wounded, along with fifty-six other men. As bad as these casualties were, the *Chesapeake* suffered much worse. She had forty-seven killed and ninety-eight wounded.

The high casualties and the damage done to the *Shannon* disprove the charge made later by historians that Lawrence and the *Chesapeake* were not ready to fight. They lost because of Lawrence's decision not to exploit the initial tactical advantage he had and because of bad luck, not because the *Chesapeake* was unprepared. Lawrence may have been guilty of not following orders; he undoubtedly should have avoided the *Shannon* and stuck to the mission the president had assigned him, but had he not given up his early tactical advantage, been mortally wounded, or lost his headsails, he might well have been the victor.

The baleful duty of reporting the defeat to Secretary Jones fell to George Budd. While he scratched out details of the fight, the *Shannon* and the *Chesapeake* sailed to Halifax with Captain Broke barely clinging to life, although eventually he recovered. Lawrence was not so lucky; he lay on the *Chesapeake*'s wardroom table in excruciating pain, unable to speak for four horrific days before mercifully succumbing. He and the other American officers who died were buried with full military honors in Halifax, the British paying solemn tribute to their bravery.

In all the confusion during the last moments of the fighting, George Budd had neglected to order the navy's signal book destroyed, and it was captured, which forced Secretary Jones to write a new one. The assignment went to Charles Morris, who was in Washington at the time waiting for his new command, the *Adams,* to be converted to a corvette.

When news of the *Shannon*'s victory reached London the first week of July, the reaction was initially subdued. The *Times* noted that "the heroism of British seamen prevailed" but refrained from its usual gloating. After giving the matter more thought, however, the *Times* wrote, "American vanity, raised to the most inordinate height by their former successes in three very unequal contests, has been . . . stung almost to madness, by this unequivocal proof of their inferiority to us in fair and equal combat."

The initial tepid response to the *Shannon's* victory was a result of rejoicing over Wellington's stunning triumph at Vittoria on June 21. After four years of vicious fighting, the French had suffered a crushing defeat and were retreating wholesale out of Spain back to the Pyrenees. No one doubted that Wellington would soon be on French soil. And Vittoria was only one indication that Napoleon's power was eroding. His spring and summer campaign in Saxony against Russia, Prussia, and their allies was sapping his strength, and he had agreed to an armistice. With these stupendous events to contemplate, the American war was far from British thoughts. But also far from their thoughts was a reconciliation with the United States. Liverpool was still intent on revenge; he was just biding his time.

Although Lawrence's heroic death and his dying admonition not to give up the ship were deeply inspirational, President Madison and Secretary Jones were angry that he had disregarded his important orders and by doing so had needlessly lost one of the navy's few frigates. Jones now issued explicit orders that captains avoid one-on-one battles. He wrote to Charles Stewart, who had assumed command of the *Constitution* in May, to put to sea when he saw an opening, but "should any attempt be made to allure you by a challenge to single combat, I am directed by the President to prohibit strictly acceptance either directly or indirectly."

In the aftermath of the battle, George Budd was mad enough with Lieutenant Cox to prefer charges against him, formally accusing him of cowardice. Budd claimed that Cox should have assumed command on the spar deck and not personally brought the captain below. A court-martial tried Cox almost a year later. Commodore Decatur was president of the court, serving with Captain Jacob Jones, Master Commandant James Biddle, and several lieutenants. Decatur convened the court in April 1814 and convicted Cox of neglect of duty and unofficer-like conduct, sentencing him to be cashiered from the navy. President Madison approved the verdict. Cox, who considered himself entirely innocent, responded by enlisting in the army and serving as a private until the end of the war. In 1952, 138 years later, after Cox's descendants had spent decades trying to clear his name, President Truman finally set aside the court's unwarranted verdict.

IN APRIL AND May 1813, the British blockade had tightened even more in New York than it had in Boston. The 74-gun *Valiant*, under Captain Robert Dudley

Oliver, and the 44-gun *Acasta* (the largest frigate in the British service), under Captain Alexander Kerr, patrolled off Sandy Hook, with other ships joining them periodically. The Royal Navy's most famous officer, Sir Thomas Masterman Hardy (Nelson's flag captain during the Battle of Trafalgar and his favorite) patrolled at the eastern end of Long Island in the 74-gun *Ramillies*, accompanied by the 36-gun *Orpheus*, under Captain Hugh Pigot. They were occupying Block Island and using it, among other things, to water their ships. From time to time additional men-of-war accompanied Hardy. Neither Oliver nor Hardy had any trouble obtaining food from farmers along the coasts of New Jersey, New York, and Connecticut.

Oliver was the senior officer in command of the blockading force. His first priority was keeping Stephen Decatur and the American warships confined in New York. Decatur's *United States* was being repaired, as were the *Macedonian*, under Jacob Jones, and the *Hornet*, under her new captain, Master Commandant James Biddle, who had joined her on May 22. The brig *Argus*, under Lieutenant William H. Allen, was also in New York, and she was ready for sea. As a reward for his brilliant work against the *Macedonian*, Secretary Jones gave Allen command of the *Argus*, but he did not promote him to master commandant, as Allen and every other officer in the navy expected.

During the first week of May, Jones ordered Decatur to cruise with the *Argus* off South Carolina and disrupt the British blockade there. Afterward, Decatur was to send the *Argus* to join the *Chesapeake* on patrol in the Gulf of St. Lawrence. Decatur worked hard to get the *United States* into shape, and on May 9 he sailed her, in company with the *Argus*, to Sandy Hook, planning to leave early the next morning. But at daybreak the *Valiant* and *Acasta* were in full view, and Decatur, ever conscious of the sluggish sailing of the *United States*, decided not to attempt a breakout until foul weather gave him more of an edge. The refurbished *Macedonian* soon joined him, and the three ships waited for dirty weather. Five uneventful days passed, and during that time revised orders arrived for the *Argus*, directing Allen to take Senator William Crawford, the new American ambassador to France, to L'Orient or any other place along the French coast where Allen could get in. After depositing Crawford, Allen was to cruise around the British Isles and take whatever ships came his way. Allen relished the assignment.

While Allen waited for the ambassador, Decatur, growing impatient, decided to exit the harbor by a different route. He withdrew to New York and then to Hell Gate, where he planned to pass into Long Island Sound and escape into the Atlantic between Montauk Point and Block Island at the eastern end of the island.

For six days an easterly breeze kept him in the East River, but on May 24 the wind hauled around to the west, fair for making the treacherous trip through Hell Gate, and Decatur sailed through easily with the *Macedonian* and *Hornet*. He then beat down the Sound against a persistent easterly and stormy weather. During the trip, lightning struck the mainmast of the *United States* and traveled through parts of the ship. Decatur made repairs as he went, and on the twenty-ninth he was off Fishers Island, near the mouth of the Thames River, waiting for an opportunity to break out into the Atlantic.

On the first of June, Decatur made his move, standing through the Race (a tidal rip west of Fishers Island at the eastern end of Long Island Sound that can run at four miles an hour), and steered for Block Island Sound. The *Valiant* and the *Acasta* were visible in the distance to the south and west. Captain Oliver had ordered Hardy to switch places with him so that he could capture Decatur, but he was too far away to even make an attempt. Decatur appeared to have a clear opening, but as he approached Block Island, he thought he saw two more warships of considerable size. At the same time, he spotted Oliver racing to cut him off from New London. Convinced that he would soon be trapped between two large British forces, Decatur hauled his wind and beat back through the Race, retreating to the safety of the Thames River and New London before Oliver could catch him. The *Acasta* got close enough to the slower *United States* to fire a few ineffectual shots, but that was all.

Since it was the renowned Decatur who failed to escape, no one questioned his account, but there were no British warships, large or small, off Block Island at the time he was trying to get to sea. He had a clear opening. The ships his lookouts saw were not British warships. Instead of being loose in the Atlantic, he was now trapped in the Thames River. Oliver stationed a large force at the mouth of the Thames to keep him bottled up.

After reaching New London, Decatur worked hard to protect himself. He wrote to Secretary Jones, "I immediately directed my attention and all my exertions to strengthening the defenses of the place." The Federalist government of Connecticut had left the seacoast defenseless. Decatur asked Jones to send him twenty pieces of heavy cannon.

WHILE ADMIRAL WARREN was making it difficult for the U. S. Navy to get to sea, American privateers were proving impossible to contain. Dozens were putting out, menacing British ships from the Gulf of St. Lawrence to the West Indies and any other place captains and their owners thought might be profitable, including around the British Isles. They seemed to be everywhere, even at the western end of the St. Lawrence River, operating out of Sackets Harbor. The *Neptune* and the *Fox* were two such. They performed a heroic action on July 19, 1813, capturing the British gunboat *Spitfire* and fifteen fully loaded bateaux she was escorting in the St. Lawrence.

Privateers were particularly effective in the West Indies, becoming bolder with time, even landing on Jamaica and raiding plantations for food. Cries for protection were heard in London from West Indian merchants and planters. Protests rained down on the Admiralty from every place the privateers swarmed. Especially vocal were British merchants trying to navigate in their home waters.

Taking advantage of dirty weather and adverse winds, privateers slipped out from their ports with relative ease. They became America's answer to Britain's blockade. Secretary Jones had always had a high appreciation of their value, unlike his captains, who scorned them. American naval officers felt that money alone motivated privateers. They could never be counted on to fight enemy warships unless they were forced to. And privateers drove up prices for everything naval vessels needed, often creating unnecessary shortages. In Jones's view, however, commerce raiding was so vitally important, and the navy's ships so few, that privateers, whatever their drawbacks, were necessary. In fact, they were the only possible response to Britain's blockade.

On March 3, 1813, a desperate Congress authorized any citizen to attack any British armed vessel of war without a privateer's commission. Few did. Preying on merchantmen was far easier. In the course of the war, Madison commissioned 526 privateers and letters of marque to operate on the high seas and on the Great Lakes. Most of them came from Massachusetts (150), Maryland (112), and New York (102). According to Lloyds of London's list, in the first seven months of the war, American privateers captured five hundred British merchantmen, and their success continued unabated, in spite of everything the Admiralty did to combat them.

Britain's privateering was on a much smaller scale. Unlike the United States, privateers were not a critical part of the Admiralty's naval strategy. Most British privateers were letters of marque, and Nova Scotia was their main base. In the opening months of the war, forty-four of them captured more than two hundred prizes.

CHAPTER SIXTEEN

Raids in
Chesapeake Bay

T HE ADMIRALTY PLACED even more emphasis on blockading Chesapeake Bay and the Delaware River than it did on Boston and New York. On December 26, 1812, Admiral Warren had received specific orders to establish "the most complete and vigorous blockade of the ports and harbors of the Bay of the Chesapeake and of the river Delaware."

Warren was acutely aware of the urgency felt in London, and he did his best to carry out his orders, but he continued feeling that he did not have enough resources. On December 29, from his winter headquarters in Bermuda, he again requested more ships and men. The extra ships that had been promised had yet to arrive. Warren also complained about the number of British seamen joining the American navy after they were captured and the devastating impact of enemy privateers pillaging with impunity in the Caribbean.

By January 1813, Warren had a battleship, two frigates, and a sloop of war blockading Chesapeake Bay, but they patrolled in the open ocean outside the Capes, and dozens of privateers out of Baltimore eluded them. During the first week of February, however, additional warships arrived—a sail of the line, a frigate, a brig, and a schooner. The entire squadron then moved just inside the Chesapeake Capes and anchored in Lynnhaven Bay, making it far more difficult for privateers to get to sea, although many still did.

The reinforced British squadron reached its new anchorage just hours after Captain Charles Stewart brought the refurbished *Constellation* to Hampton Roads.

After leaving Washington he had stopped at Annapolis and then, afraid ice might trap him there, proceeded to Hampton Roads, where he planned to stop briefly before slipping past the blockaders and driving out to sea for a lengthy cruise.

He was surprised on the morning of February 4 to find not only the British squadron inside the Chesapeake Capes, but a portion of it sailing after him. He immediately sought the protection of nearby Elizabeth River, hoving up "and kedging the ship up to the flats" where she grounded. Lacking detailed knowledge of the shallow Elizabeth, the British ships did not follow.

While waiting for high tide, Stewart lightened his ship—taking out stores and dumping water. At seven o'clock in the evening she floated free, and "by placing . . . boats along the narrows," he was able to work her up the Elizabeth to Norfolk, where the guns of Fort Nelson and Fort Norfolk, situated on opposite sides of the river, could protect her. Having survived this initial brush with the British fleet, Stewart erected strong defenses to protect the *Constellation* against an attack by land and sea. Secretary Jones ordered Captain John Cassin, commandant of nearby Gosport Navy Yard, to help him.

While Stewart was securing his frigate, Rear Admiral George Cockburn set out from Bermuda in the 74-gun *Marlborough* with a squadron to take command in the Chesapeake and in the Delaware. Fighting contrary winds in the Gulf Stream, he arrived at Lynnhaven Bay inside the Chesapeake Capes on the third of March. His fleet now consisted of three seventy-fours, *Poictiers*, *Victorious*, and *Dragon*; four frigates, *Maidstone*, *Junon*, *Belvidera* (Captain Richard Byron still in command), and *Statira*; along with assorted smaller vessels. Cockburn sent Captain Sir John Beresford in the 74-gun *Poictiers* with a few smaller vessels to secure Delaware Bay.

Cockburn's first objective was capturing the *Constellation*. Her defenses were now formidable. Craney Island, which guarded the mouth of the Elizabeth River, was heavily fortified. Even if Cockburn could drive the defenders off the island, his larger ships could not get up the Elizabeth River, nor could his smaller ones, since a flotilla of gunboats and shore batteries guarded Norfolk and Gosport. He did not have the resources to attack overland, so he reluctantly decided to wait for them. Once he had enough troops, he planned to attack the frigate "at the same time on both banks."

Nineteen days later, Admiral Warren himself arrived in the *San Domingo* with additional ships, increasing the British squadron to five 74-gun sails of the line (*Marlborough*, *San Domingo*, *Poictiers*, *Victorious*, and *Dragon*), five frigates, two sloops of war, three tenders, and assorted smaller vessels—by any measure, an immense fleet.

Captain Stewart expected an attack momentarily, but knowing the *Constellation* was trapped, Warren decided to wait for more ground troops before making a move on her. He turned instead to hit-and-run raids along the shores of the Chesapeake, up her great rivers—the James, York, Rappahannock, Potomac, Patuxent, Patapsco, and Susquehanna—and her innumerable creeks and inlets. He hoped to rattle Washington and bring home the war to the residents of the entire area, undermining support for the war. He also wanted to create a big enough diversion that Madison would be forced to pull resources from the Canadian theater to defend Chesapeake Bay. Governor-General Prevost had been urging Warren to help take the pressure off Canada.

Leaving a force to guard the Elizabeth River, Warren sailed the rest of his squadron up to Annapolis as a sort of demonstration, taking whatever prizes came his way and sending raiding parties up nearby rivers and creeks. He then dispatched Cockburn with an amphibious force of one frigate, two brigs, four schooners, and three hundred men to the head of the bay to conduct more raids. The aggressive Cockburn delighted in the assignment, but, as always, he and Warren had to be concerned with desertion. When their small boats rowed up the narrow creeks and rivers, men took whatever opportunity presented itself and ran away. The loss of men had to be balanced against sinking, capturing, or burning a few small vessels, plantations, villages, and towns. Seamen were not easily replaced.

On April 12 Cockburn landed on Sharpe's Island at the mouth of the Choptank River and made off with some cattle for the fleet, which he paid for because the residents offered no resistance. On April 18 he appeared off the mouth of the Patapsco River, alarming Baltimore, taking soundings, and assessing the city's defenses, particularly Fort McHenry.

Making charts wherever he went, Cockburn continued his rampage, dropping anchor on April 23 off Spesuite Island at the mouth of the Susquehanna River, where he obtained enough fresh food for Warren's entire fleet with no difficulty. Four days later his marines occupied Poplar Island, and the next day Tilghman Island. Cockburn then attacked tiny Frenchtown on the Elk River, burning the village's twelve buildings and destroying a few small vessels. On May 2 he attacked Harve de Grace, looting and burning forty of its sixty homes, Commodore John Rodgers's estate, Sion Hill, among them. As the British looted Rodgers's mansion, his mother, wife, and two sisters fled. They were allowed to depart before the invaders torched the building.

Cockburn then rowed four miles up the Susquehanna and destroyed—again without opposition—the Principio Iron Works, one of the country's largest cannon foundries, and took away all the cannon and small arms warehoused there. On May 6 he entered the Sassafras River and sailed to the Maryland towns of Fredericktown and Georgetown, where he finally met some resistance from Maryland militiamen. In the ensuing fight, five of his men were wounded before they swept away the militiamen and burned both towns.

In a month and a half, Warren and Cockburn, raiding at will, took forty prizes and created alarm throughout the bay area. Washington was certainly shaken. "I . . . keep the old Tunisian sabre within reach," Dolley Madison wrote to Edward Coles, the president's private secretary, on May 12. "One of our generals has discovered a plan of the British,—it is to land as many chosen rogues as they can about fourteen miles below Alexandria, in the night, so that they may be on hand to burn the President's house and offices. I do not tremble at this, but feel hurt that the admiral (of Havre de Grace memory) should send me word that he would make his bow at my drawing room very soon."

Cockburn was indeed interested in Washington. He had had such an easy time of it marauding in Chesapeake Bay that he yearned to do more, such as capturing the capital, along with Baltimore and Annapolis. He was convinced they would fall easily. But London was still occupied with Napoleon, and the British ministry was not ready for anything other than hit-and-run raids in the Chesapeake and a tight blockade.

This gave the federal and state governments time to prepare defenses. Only Baltimore woke up to its vulnerability, however. The city had a population of close to 50,000, and under the leadership of Senator Samuel Smith a stout defense was organized. Fort McHenry, which had become a pathetic wreck with only fifty regulars and a few pitiful guns, was transformed into a strongpoint. Situated on Whetstone Point, the fort guarded the approaches to the city by water. If large British warships were able to get past it, they could unleash a devastating bombardment on the city. Overcoming serious obstacles of every kind, Smith managed by the fall of 1813 to have sixty heavy naval guns mounted and ready at the fort. Fifty-six of the guns came from a French warship that sank in the Chesapeake. When the ship was salvaged, the French consul in Baltimore donated the guns. Ship hulks were readied to be sunk as well. They would help block any British attempt to rush by the fort into the inner harbor.

General Smith's experience with Baltimore's defenses went back to 1778, during the Revolution, when he prepared the city for a possible invasion. During the first months of the War of 1812, however, Smith could not rouse any interest in improving the city's defenses. The governor of Maryland, Levin Winder, ignored the danger. It took the outrage generated by Admiral Cockburn's raids to give Smith the political support he needed to dramatically improve Baltimore's security.

Smith thought North Point on Patapsco Neck was the logical place for the British to land an expeditionary force. Deep water there allowed large warships to come in close to shore and protect troop transports as they unloaded. Smith expected that a land attack would be combined with a sea bombardment of Fort McHenry. To give additional protection to the fort, he constructed two batteries on the Ferry Branch—Forts Covington and Babcock.

Unlike Smith, President Madison failed to improve Washington's defenses, even though he thought the city was bound to be an inviting target. It was the nation's capital, after all, and had a tiny population of only 8,200 (1,400 of whom were slaves). The difficulty vessels of any size would have in navigating the Potomac's shoals and sandbars was a natural defense, and Fort Washington, twelve miles below the city, could be an important obstacle as well, but the fort and its personnel were unaccountably not strengthened. All Secretary Jones did was organize an embarrassingly small Potomac flotilla, consisting of one schooner and three gunboats, under Master Commandant Arthur Sinclair, designed to counter small enemy vessels in the river.

A seaborne attack on Washington using the Potomac River was far less likely than an attack by land through the small town of Bladensburg, eight miles to the northeast. But Madison made no effort to erect defenses there either. Monroe wanted to prepare a vigorous defense of the capital, as Smith was doing in Baltimore, but Secretary Armstrong did not think Washington was in any immediate danger, and the president apparently accepted his appraisal.

ON MAY 17, 1813, Admiral Warren sailed to Bermuda with forty prizes, planning to return to the Chesapeake shortly. He was back in mid-June with 2,000 additional troops under General Sir Sydney Beckwith, a distinguished British officer. Warren now had the wherewithal to go after the *Constellation* in the Elizabeth River.

Before Warren could mount an assault, Captain Cassin ordered Master Commandant Joseph Tarbell to conduct a gunboat attack on three British frigates anchored off Newport News. On June 20 at four o'clock in the morning, Tarbell's fifteen boats went after the 38-gun *Junon*, under Captain James Sanders. The water was dead flat calm, and the *Junon* was sitting apart from her two companions. Tarbell opened fire at three-quarters of a mile, but as luck would have it, half an hour later, a fortuitous breeze sprang up, allowing the other two frigates, the *Narcissus* and the *Barossa*, to get under way and come to *Junon*'s rescue. Tarbell retreated, barely managing to escape. He wrote later that if the breeze had held off a while, he would have captured or destroyed the *Junon*.

Warren now proceeded against the *Constellation*. He first had to neutralize Craney Island. Captains Stewart and Cassin and Brigadier General Robert Taylor of the Virginia militia had made the island a tough obstacle, however, erecting a strong battery of seven guns, supported by seven hundred troops, sailors from the *Constellation*, and fifteen gunboats strung across the mouth of the river.

While Stewart had been in the midst of preparing to resist an attack, Secretary Jones, on May 7, ordered him unexpectedly to take command of the *Constitution* in Boston. It was a bizarre move. Stewart was one of the navy's stellar fighters, and he was getting ready for a showdown with the British commander in North America. To pull him away at this critical moment to command a frigate that would not be ready to sail for months was hard to believe. Instead of being at the center of the action, Stewart would be sitting idly in Boston. It was one of Jones's poorest decisions. Tarbell temporarily replaced Stewart.

Warren's attack came on June 22. Although outnumbering the defenders, and having vastly more firepower, the British were unable to even land on Craney Island, much less capture it. Beckwith's attack from the land failed to reach the island, as did Warren's men, when they attempted to land by boat. When Warren saw how difficult Craney was going to be—even before he got upriver to attack the defenses there—he called off the whole operation and reembarked the troops. He decided to leave the *Constellation* trapped for the rest of the war. The Admiralty was unimpressed with Warren's excuses. So far as London was concerned, his failure to capture the *Constellation* was more evidence of his ineffectiveness.

On June 25, to compensate for the Craney Island fiasco, Beckwith attacked the lightly defended village of Hampton, ten miles away on the north side of the James River. He captured it easily and let his men loose to rape and pillage, which they did with abandon. Their behavior was so gross that Warren and Beckwith were embarrassed, although no soldiers were punished for what they did. Beckwith blamed the atrocious behavior on French soldiers (convicts who preferred fighting for Britain to rotting in prison), but the damage was done. Accounts of the atrocity helped boost American support for the war.

Warren now turned his attention to destroying the 28-gun *Adams* in the Washington Navy Yard, hoping to gain some favor with the Admiralty, which still had destruction of the American fleet as its first priority. He arrived with his squadron at the mouth of the Potomac on the first of July, but the river's considerable impediments baffled him, and he withdrew. He then sailed toward Annapolis and Baltimore but attacked neither of them.

While Warren was sailing about rather aimlessly, Cockburn was active, leading a squadron of seven ships to Ocracoke Inlet, which connected Pamlico Sound with the Atlantic Ocean. He arrived on July 12. Goods from the Chesapeake area were getting to sea via the unguarded inlet. Warren ordered Cockburn to destroy all the vessels there, which he proceeded to do. Afterward, he replenished his ships, loaded all the food he could for Warren's fleet, and sailed back to Lynnhaven Bay.

On July 16, while Cockburn was at Ocracoke Inlet, an American inventor named Elijah Mix set out to sink the 74-gun *Plantagenet*, one of the battleships moored in Lynnhaven Bay, with a torpedo. Mix worked closely with Captain Charles Gordon, who had recently taken command of the *Constellation*, to fashion a weapon similar to one being experimented on by Robert Fulton. The "torpedo" was really a mine. Fulton had obtained his design from David Bushnell, who had developed an underwater explosive during the American Revolution. Fulton copied Bushnell's ideas without attribution until the publication of Bushnell's discoveries in Paris forced Fulton to admit his debt to the Revolutionary War hero.

Fulton's torpedo had been around since 1800, and he was still looking for a buyer. It had been taken seriously at one time by Napoleon and later by Prime Minister Pitt of Great Britain. But Fulton could never demonstrate that it was practical. Nonetheless, the idea continued to intrigue, and on March 3, 1813, the U.S. Congress passed a law to pay any person who sank a British ship, no matter how it was done, one half of the ship's value. That set scores of inventors to work, including Mix, who intended to transport his floating mine in a large open boat, row close to the target, drop the torpedo in the water, and let it drift into the warship's side, exploding on impact and making a hole large enough to sink it.

On the sixteenth of July, Mix's boat, *Chesapeake's Revenge*, approached to within two hundred forty feet of the *Plantagenet* before one of her guard boats ran him off. The setback did not deter Mix; he was determined to sink her. From the nineteenth to the twenty-third he made repeated attempts but failed each time. On the twenty-fourth, however, he crept to within a hundred yards of the target, dropped the torpedo in the water, and watched it drift toward the *Plantagenet*, closer and closer. Suddenly, just before reaching the ship, it exploded, sending a spectacular pyramid of water, fifty feet in circumference and fifty feet high, shooting into the air, close enough to spew water on the ship's deck and damage her side. The fireworks were inspiring, but the ship still rode at her anchor. Mix tried to improve his technique, but he could not get any more gun-powder from the navy and made no further attacks.

Meanwhile, Cockburn returned to the Chesapeake, and in August he re-sumed raiding, occupying Kent's Island in the upper bay and using it as a base. On August 10 he attacked the town of St. Michaels, but the Maryland militia, aroused by Cockburn's brutal tactics, put up a stout defense and drove him off. The massing of the militia led Cockburn to close down his operations and return to Lynnhaven Bay.

Warren now decided to withdraw most of his fleet from the Chesapeake during the first week of September. The success of the Maryland militia, losses from desertions and disease, as well as the need to refit and resupply his ships in a healthier climate caused him to leave temporarily. He sailed with some of his fleet to Halifax, and the rest he sent to Bermuda with Cockburn. Captain Robert Barrie stayed behind to continue the blockade with one sail of the line, two frigates, two brigs, and three schooners.

FURIOUS WITH THE lack of offense or defense against Cockburn on the water, fifty-four-year old Joshua Barney wrote to Secretary Jones on July 4, 1813, urging him to build a fleet of at least twenty row-galleys to combat the British ships when they returned in the spring of 1814, which Barney was confident they would do. Jones was as frustrated as Barney, and he immediately accepted the offer, appointing Barney to build and command a Chesapeake Bay flotilla. Barney would operate directly under Jones as a separate unit apart from the regular navy. The secretary did not want Barney and his officers complicating the navy's always delicate seniority system. Barney accepted the appointment and the rank of master commandant. He spent the next few months struggling to get his unique gunboats built and manned before spring.

CHAPTER SEVENTEEN

Oliver Hazard Perry

W HILE COCKBURN WAS marauding in Chesapeake Bay and the Outer Banks of North Carolina, the British and American navies were engaged in a fateful arms race on Lake Erie that would determine which country controlled the northwestern part of the United States and perhaps Upper Canada. The key figure on the American side was twenty-eight-year-old master commandant, Oliver Hazard Perry, from Newport, Rhode Island.

Back on January 20, 1813, Commodore Chauncey had written to Secretary Jones requesting that Perry be given command of the naval force building on Lake Erie. At the time, Perry was in charge of a small flotilla of gunboats at Newport, unhappy that he was not seeing any action. He came from a prominent navy family; his father, Christopher, had fought with distinction during the Revolution and had been captured twice. The first time, he was confined to the infamous prison ship *Jersey* in New York Harbor and the second time in a prison camp in Newry, Ireland. Captain Christopher Perry was also a hero of the Quasi-War with France and was taken back into the navy for a time in 1812 to serve as commandant of the Boston Navy Yard. He was at that post when Isaac Hull sailed the *Constitution* into Boston after his victory over the *Guerriere*.

Young Oliver had much to live up to, and he was ready for the challenge—in fact, desperate for it. Despite his age, he was an experienced, well-regarded officer. He had served with his father in the Quasi-War and later in the war against Tripoli, spending fifteen years in the service, rising to the rank of master commandant.

Perry did not want to spend the war stuck in Newport leading a few inactive gunboats. He had promised Chauncey he would bring a hundred scarce seamen to Lake Erie, and that was a powerful incentive for the commodore to request his appointment. The selection did not sit well with Lieutenant Jesse Elliott, who coveted the assignment for himself. Although junior in rank to Perry, Elliott was four years older, and after capturing the *Caledonia* and the *Detroit* off Fort Erie in 1812, he considered himself a hero, as did the country. Congress had presented him with a sword.

Perry arrived at Presque Isle with his Rhode Island seamen on March 27, 1813. Noah Brown, the master shipbuilder from New York, and his brother Adam were already there, along with their remarkable foreman, Sidney Wright, and a contingent of shipwrights. The Browns and their men had arrived on March 2 and immediately went to work building two identical 20-gun brigs, the *Lawrence* (named after the late Captain James Lawrence) and the *Niagara*. Both would displace four hundred eighty tons and mount two long twelve-pounders and eighteen thirty-two-pound carronades. The Browns were building four gunboats as well. Daniel Dobbins was also at Presque Isle. He had been in charge there during the winter and was staying on to help Perry.

Exquisite timber for the new ships abounded in the region—oak, poplar, ash, cedar, walnut, and pine. But nearly everything else—anchors, carronades, long guns, shot, powder, iron for making chain plates, and other items, such as canvas, rigging, fittings, tools, oakum, and cordage—had to be brought from Pittsburgh, which by then was the industrial center of the west. These supplies were conveyed up the Allegheny River and its tributary French Creek to Meadville, Pennsylvania, and then hauled north for forty-one miles over a primitive road to Presque Isle. If an item could not be procured in Pittsburgh, it had to come from Philadelphia or New York. Most of the carpenters, blacksmiths, and other skilled workmen came from eastern cities as well. In February Oliver Ormsby, a Pittsburgh merchant, became the naval agent in Pittsburgh. He facilitated the movement of supplies and workmen to Presque Isle. "Many are the difficulties we have to encounter," Perry wrote to Chauncey, "but we will surmount them all."

Perry was a natural leader: frank, friendly, courteous in his manners, and modest but at the same time strict and demanding. He never spared himself, working every day at an exhausting pace. He expected everyone else to do the same. From the start, he worried about being attacked before the brigs were finished. He had his men clear the hill in back of the ships and build a blockhouse. He then went to Pittsburgh and acquired four cannon. The governor of Pennsylvania helped by sending five hundred militiamen under Major General David Mead to defend Presque Isle.

As difficult as it was for Perry to accomplish his assignment, his British counterpart, twenty-eight-year-old Lieutenant Robert Heriot Barclay, had it much harder at Amherstburg. Barclay, although young like Perry, was also a seasoned, fifteen-year veteran, having fought at Trafalgar in 1805, when he lost an arm. He did not reach Amherstburg until June 5, two and a half months after Perry took charge at Presque Isle. Barclay's supply chain was infinitely more complicated than Perry's, running from England through Kingston, where his superior, Admiral Yeo, was engaged in his own arms race and was reluctant to part with the men and supplies Barclay needed. "There is a general want of stores of every description at this post," Barclay complained to Governor-General Proctor on June 29. Barclay desperately needed the naval stores and armament that Chauncey and Dearborn had destroyed when they attacked York back in April. Making matters worse for Barclay, London's first priority was defending Lower Canada. If absolutely necessary, Liverpool and his colleagues were prepared to let sparsely populated Upper Canada go.

Despite Barclay's supply and manpower problems, while Perry's 20-gun brigs were still on the stocks, the British had a significant advantage on Lake Erie. Barclay had the 18-gun *Queen Charlotte*, the 12-gun *Lady Prevost*, the 6-gun *Hunter*, the 2-gun *Erie*, the 2-gun *Little Belt*, and the 2-gun *Chippewa*, and he was constructing a 20-gun sloop of war, the *Detroit*. He also had Major General Henry Proctor's army at Fort Malden. With these forces and a bit of luck, he could squash Perry before he got started.

The first thing Barclay did when he arrived at Amherstburg was take his fleet up to Presque Isle and have a look. He then went back and planned an immediate land and sea attack. He would need help from Brigadier General Francis de Rottenburg, the new leader in Upper Canada, who had replaced General Roger Hale Sheaffe. De Rottenburg quickly informed Proctor, however, that he would not supply the troops and provisions they needed, and Barclay abandoned his plan.

Instead of attacking Presque Isle, he imposed a blockade on the port. Barclay thought that at some point Perry would have to float his two brigs over a formidable bar, and he did not think the Americans could manage it. Even if Perry did the impossible and got the brigs over the bar, he would have to remove their guns to do it, which would make them easy targets for Barclay's fleet. Whatever the difficulties, Barclay was certain that the Americans would try to move the brigs on to the lake. He hoped to have the *Detroit* finished in time to destroy them when Perry made his attempt.

Barclay was having problems completing the *Detroit*, however. He was also having difficulty obtaining enough men and supplies to keep the rest of his fleet going. He wrote to Prevost on July 16, pleading for more men, ammunition, guns, and stores. Prevost pressured Yeo to send what he could, but he also warned Barclay that the supplies would probably have to come from the enemy.

Perry was also woefully short of seamen. He sent urgent requests to Chauncey and to Jones for more. The secretary was now corresponding directly with Perry rather than going through Chauncey, thus setting up a separate command, which Chauncey objected to. Jones made the arrangement in order to hurry along the work at Presque Isle.

Perry became convinced that Chauncey was keeping the best seamen for his own fleet. Matters came to a head when Chauncey sent Perry sixty men from Sackets Harbor on July 16. Sailing Master Steven Champlain, Perry's nephew, who had served under him in the gunboat flotilla at Newport, led them. Perry was desperate for men, but when he saw what Champlain brought, he did not like their quality and sent a blistering letter to Chauncey, calling them "a motley set, blacks, soldiers, and boys." Chauncey shot back, "I have yet to learn that the color of the skin, or cut and trimmings of the coat, can effect a man's qualifications or usefulness. I have nearly 50 blacks on board of this ship [the *General Pike*] and many of them are amongst my best men." Chauncey insisted that the quality of the crews on both fleets was the same. Perry was unconvinced and annoyed. He got so angry he wrote to Secretary Jones requesting to be "removed from this station." But Jones refused, counseling Perry to carry on in his own interests and those of the country. After that, Perry calmed down and shouldered on, but his resentment continued to smolder.

DURING THE GREATER part of July, Barclay remained off Presque Isle blockading it with his squadron. He was unaware that the new brigs he was so concerned about were lightly guarded at night. General Meade's Pennsylvania militiamen refused to spend nights aboard the ships. Barclay could have sent in boats during the hours of darkness and destroyed both the *Lawrence* and the *Niagara*. He remained offshore, however, watching. Then suddenly, on July 31, he vanished. He was running low on supplies and had to travel to Port Dover in Upper Canada to replenish them. He thought if Perry tried to float the brigs over the bar in his absence, at least one of them—but more likely both—would get stuck fast aground.

Barclay's sudden departure was just what Perry had been hoping for. His two brigs had been completed by the fourth of July, and he was waiting for an opportunity to move them onto the lake. Barclay's blockade had stymied him until now. When Barclay's squadron suddenly disappeared, Perry made his move, even though Barclay's departure might have been a ruse and he could reappear at any moment.

The depth of water at the big sandbar blocking the entrance to the harbor was only four feet, but the 20-gun *Lawrence* and her twin, the *Niagara*, drew nine. Unknown to Barclay, Sidney Wright had solved the problem by devising giant "camels"—large, watertight containers attached to the ships' sides below the water. The camels were designed to be filled with water, which would be pumped out at the critical moment, raising the ships enough to slide them over the bar. On August 4 Perry was ready. He removed the armaments and ballast from the *Lawrence*, unmoored her at high tide, lifted her by means of the camels, and floated her over the bar with surprising ease. Barclay's squadron was nowhere in sight.

Perry was preparing the *Niagara* to be floated when Barclay suddenly reappeared.

A providential haze obscured his view, however, and Perry was able to glide the *Niagara* and his other vessels onto the lake without Barclay seeing them. When the haze cleared and Barclay saw the American fleet, he thought they were about to attack him. Believing he now had the weaker squadron, he exchanged a few shots and retreated. Perry then moved all his ships to the protection of the battery at the blockhouse, while Barclay sailed back to Amherstburg to work on getting the *Detroit* manned and equipped. Until he could, Perry would command the lake, and Barclay could no longer receive men and supplies by water. They would have to make the long trek overland through the wilderness—that is, if any were coming.

At nine o'clock that night, an exhausted but elated Perry wrote to Secretary Jones from the *Lawrence* at anchor outside the Erie bar: "I have great pleasure in informing you that I have succeeded after almost incredible labor and fatigue to the men, in getting all the vessels I have been able to man, over the bar, viz. *Lawrence, Niagara, Caledonia, Ariel, Scorpion, Somers, Tigress,* and *Porcupine.*"

Perry was still in dire need of men. On August 10 Commander Jesse D. Elliott arrived at Presque Isle with 102 sailors. Chauncey had sent them even though he badly needed them himself. Perry was happy to have the additional seamen, but he was annoyed that Chauncey had not sent more. Elliott became skipper of the *Niagara* and second in command of the Lake Erie squadron. Unfortunately, that was not good enough for him; he found it galling not to be the senior officer.

Perry lost no time putting his fleet to work. On August 12 he sailed to the western end of the lake and established a base at Put-in-Bay in the Bass Islands, thirty miles east of Fort Malden, where he could keep an eye on the British fleet while training his men. General William Henry Harrison was close by in Sandusky, Ohio, and Perry established a close working relationship with him. On September 2 he sailed the squadron to Sandusky Bay to confer with Harrison, who had a high appreciation of the importance of Perry's mission. Harrison was happy to give him a hundred thirty Kentucky riflemen for the fleet.

With Perry in control of the lake, the British supply problem at Amherstburg became acute. General Proctor had hundreds of Tecumseh's warriors and their families to feed, and with food running out, Proctor feared the Indians would turn on the British and massacre them all. "I do not hesitate to say," he wrote, "that if we do not receive a timely and adequate supply of Indian goods and ammunition we shall inevitably be subjected to ills of the greatest magnitude."

To regain control of the lake and acquire the desperately needed supplies, Barclay was compelled to engage Perry at least a month before he was ready. "So perfectly destitute of provisions was the post that there was not a day's flour in store," he wrote, "and the crews of the squadron . . . were on half allowance of many things, and when that was done there was no more."

Barclay continued to be woefully short of seamen. He was forced to rely on the army to man his vessels. Of the 364 crewmen in his fleet, not more than 50 were British sailors; the rest were either soldiers or Canadians, "totally unacquainted with such service," he wrote to Yeo. Many were French-speaking and could not understand English. Barclay also lacked naval guns; he was forced to use some of Proctor's artillery for the *Detroit*. Barclay blamed Yeo for not providing him the seamen and ordinance he needed.

At sunrise on September 9, Barclay stood out from his anchorage with the ships *Detroit* and *Queen Charlotte*; the brig *General Hunter*; two schooners, *Lady Prevost* and *Chippewa*; one small sloop, *Little Belt*; and two other light vessels. The following day, at seven o'clock in the morning, lookouts in Put-in-Bay spotted Barclay's fleet. In short order, Perry had his squadron under way and standing for the enemy. His flagship *Lawrence* was flying a banner emblazoned with the words, "Don't Give Up the Ship." Fully one-quarter of Perry's men were blacks, who were determined to give a good account of themselves.

Presently, Barclay's lookouts spotted Perry's fleet. The wind was from the southwest and light, giving Barclay the weather gauge and an edge. Perry was forced to beat to windward. Around ten o'clock, however, the breeze hauled around to the southeast, giving Perry the weather gauge and the advantage.

Miraculously, the wind remained light and steady for most of the next four hours. Because his crews were inexperienced, Barclay had planned to close quickly with Perry and board, but now, with the wind against him, he could not. Perry bore up for Barclay under easy sail in line abreast. Barclay formed a line of battle as well, so that each of his large ships, the *Detroit* and the *Queen Charlotte*, which would be in the center, could be supported by the smaller vessels, "against the superior force of the two brigs [*Lawrence* and *Niagara*] opposed to them."

The American fleet in general was stronger. Barclay's most powerful weapon, his flagship *Detroit*, had seventeen long guns (one eighteen; two twenty-fours; six twelves; eight nines) and two short guns, while Perry's lead ship, *Lawrence*, had eighteen thirty-two-pound carronades and two long twelve-pounders. Barclay's long guns were effective at a mile or less, while Perry's carronades were not effective beyond five hundred yards. The *Queen Charlotte* mounted sixteen twenty-four-pound carronades, but the *Niagara* had eighteen thirty-two-pound carronades and two long twelve-pounders. Perry expected to take a beating from the *Detroit*'s long guns before he could bring his carronades into play, but now that he had the weather gauge, he could close with Barclay much faster and negate to some extent his advantage in long guns. Furthermore, Barclay's long guns were not regular naval cannon but artillery from Fort Malden, whose effectiveness on the water at any range was uncertain.

Barclay arranged his ships from van to rear as follows: the *Chippewa, Detroit, Hunter, Queen Charlotte, Lady Prevost,* and *Little Belt.* On seeing this arrangement, Perry placed two schooners, the *Scorpion* (one long thirty-two and one short thirty-two) and the *Ariel* (four long twelves) in the lead, followed closely by the *Lawrence* to fight the *Detroit.* The *Caledonia* (two long twenty-fours and one short thirty-two) was behind *Lawrence,* followed by the *Niagara,* which was expected to engage the *Queen Charlotte.* The other schooners followed behind to support the *Niagara.*

Barclay opened fire at 11:45, directing his long guns at the *Lawrence,* hitting her hard and badly cutting her rigging, making her difficult to manage. Conscious of the limited range of his carronades, Perry continued straining to get within effective range, suffering for ten punishing minutes before he could bring his guns into play. Finally, at five minutes before noon, Perry, supported by the two schooners, unloaded on the *Detroit* at about two hundred and fifty yards— "canister range," Perry called it.

The *Niagara* and Jesse Elliott, for some unknown reason, remained far to windward and far from the action. Elliott's specific assignment was to take on the *Queen Charlotte,* and given the prevailing conditions, nothing prevented him from engaging her. Elliott's reluctance to get into the fray made it appear that Perry did not have command of his squadron. Before the action, Perry reminded his commanders of Nelson's famous admonition that "no captain could go far wrong who placed his vessel close alongside those of the enemy." Elliott was ignoring Perry's express order and endangering the fleet.

Seeing the *Niagara* hesitating, the *Queen Charlotte* moved up to support the *Detroit* in clobbering the *Lawrence*. Early in the action, the *Queen Charlotte's* captain, Lieutenant Robert A. Finnis, was killed, and his second, Acting Lieutenant Thomas Stokoe, was struck senseless by a splinter. Provincial Lieutenant Robert Irvine, an enthusiastic but inexperienced fighter, took command. Losing Finnis was a severe blow to Barclay, but Irvine continued to pummel the *Lawrence*. Perry was receiving fire from both of Barclay's large ships and the *Hunter* as well.

Whatever Elliott's motives in remaining apart from the fighting, the men aboard Perry's flagship were furious with him. The *Lawrence*, the *Caledonia*, and the two schooners ahead had to withstand the full fury of Barclay's heavy ships. For an excruciating two hours, Perry kept struggling against great odds, his ship being torn to pieces and his men being killed and wounded wholesale. Within two hours twenty-two men and officers lay dead on the *Lawrence's* decks, along with sixty-six wounded. Every gun was dismounted and their carriages knocked to pieces, every strand of rigging was cut off, and mast and spars were shot and tottering; the entire ship was a wreck. "Every brace and bowline being soon shot away, she became unmanageable, not withstanding the great exertions of the sailing master," Perry wrote. "In this situation, [we] sustained the action upwards of two hours, within canister distance, until every gun was rendered useless, and the greater part of *Lawrence's* crew either killed or wounded."

Miraculously, Perry himself was unscathed, and he refused to surrender. But he had nothing more to fight with; not another gun could be worked or manned. Instead of hauling down his colors, however, he had a brilliant inspiration—remove his flag to the untouched *Niagara*. He placed the crippled *Lawrence* in the capable hands of First Lieutenant John Yarnall and took his private flag displaying Captain Lawrence's inspirational words into the only small boat left on the *Lawrence*. With his younger brother, twelve-year-old Midshipman James Alexander Perry—also unscathed—Perry rowed toward the *Niagara*.

In a few minutes, Yarnall, in order to save what was left of the crew, struck his colors, while Perry rowed furiously to reach the *Niagara*, determined to fight on. When he arrived, Elliott—no doubt anxious to get away—volunteered to leave the ship and bring the schooners, which had been kept astern by the lightness of the wind, into closer action. Perry agreed. In the next instant he looked

Figure 17.1: Oliver Hazard Perry transfers from his flagship *Lawrence* to continue the Battle of Lake Erie aboard the *Niagara* (courtesy of Franklin D. Roosevelt Collection at Hyde Park, New York).

back and saw that Yarnall had lowered the *Lawrence*'s flag. But Barclay, whose ship had also suffered grievously, could not take possession of her, and circumstances soon permitted the *Lawrence*'s flag to again be hoisted. Barclay later described the *Detroit* as a "perfect wreck." His first lieutenant, Garland, was mortally wounded, and Barclay himself had been so severely injured just before Yarnall surrendered that he had to be carried below, leaving the *Detroit* in the hands of Provincial Lieutenant Francis Purvis.

At 2:45 Perry made the signal for "closer action" and immediately set after the British squadron in the undamaged *Niagara*. His luck continued to hold as the wind picked up, allowing him to reach his targets in fifteen minutes. "I determined to pass through the enemy's line; bore up, and passed ahead of their two ships and a brig," he wrote in his report, "giving a raking fire to them from the starboard guns, and to a large schooner and sloop from the larboard side, at half-pistol shot distance. The smaller vessels at this time, having got within grape and canister distance, under the direction of Captain Elliott, and keeping up a well-directed fire, the two ships, a brig, and schooner surrendered, a schooner and a sloop making a vain attempt to escape."

The victorious Perry now returned to the stricken *Lawrence.* "Every poor fellow raised himself from the decks to greet him with three hearty cheers," Sailing Master William Taylor reported. "I do not hesitate to say there was not a dry eye on the ship."

It was over. Perry's courage, and his incredible luck, had won the day—in spite of Elliott's treachery. "We have met the enemy and they are ours," Perry wrote to General Harrison. His words, like Captain Lawrence's "Don't give up the ship," would become immortal. To Secretary Jones he wrote, "It has pleased the Almighty to give to the arms of the United States a signal victory over their enemies on this Lake." Perry's triumph would have far-reaching consequences. It opened the way for the United States to regain the entire northwest territory lost by General Hull, and it effectively ended the alliance between the Indians and Great Britain. "[Perry] has immortalized himself," Commodore Chauncey wrote to Jones. Indeed he had.

Perry made certain that the severely wounded Barclay was well cared for, probably saving his life. In his report on the defeat, Barclay wrote that having the weather gauge gave Perry an edge by allowing him to choose his position and distance, which had an adverse effect on the ability of the *Queen Charlotte* and the *Lady Prevost* to make more effective use of their carronades. Barclay's greatest handicap, however, was manning. "The greatest cause of losing His Majesty's Squadron on Lake Erie," he wrote to Yeo, "was the want of a competent number of seamen." His criticism of Yeo's management could not have been plainer, and it was deeply felt. Prevost agreed with Barclay. He wrote to Earl Bathurst, the secretary of state for war and the colonies, that Yeo had appropriated for his own use on Lake Ontario all the officers and seamen sent from England, leaving Barclay to make do entirely with soldiers.

Perry's stunning, wholly unexpected triumph electrified the country. Elliott's duplicity was overlooked amid the celebrating. Lieutenant Yarnall, however, wrote a letter on September 15 to the Ohio newspapers condemning Elliott, but his complaints were drowned out by the widespread acclaim for Perry. He was the man of the hour, lionized everywhere, and no more so than in Washington, where President Madison desperately needed a victory.

AFTER BARCLAY'S DEFEAT, General Proctor knew he had to evacuate Fort Malden immediately and march east along the Thames River toward Burlington at the head of Lake Ontario, where he'd have protection not only from the Americans but from his Indian allies. Proctor's supplies had nearly run out, and most of his heavy guns had been on the *Detroit*, which Perry had captured, along with two hundred of Proctor's best soldiers.

Tecumseh strenuously objected to retreating. He wanted to remain at Fort Malden and have a showdown with General Harrison, his longtime foe. But Proctor was convinced that he had to escape as quickly as possible. Since he had no supplies, and none could reach him, he thought staying at Amherstburg was suicidal. For Tecumseh, however, abandoning Amherstburg and Detroit meant leaving all the Indians of the Northwest to the mercy of the voracious Americans. The British had deserted their Indian allies before—most notably after the American Revolution but also in the Jay Treaty—with disastrous consequences for all the tribes. To appease Tecumseh, Proctor made a promise (which he never meant to keep) to make a stand at the forks of the Thames. Having no alternative, Tecumseh was forced to go along.

Feeling more and more anxious as the days passed, Proctor retreated as fast as he could, worrying all the time that Harrison would be right on his heels. By September 23 Proctor had evacuated to Sandwich and burned Amherstburg and Detroit. Four days later, he began to panic when Harrison, working closely with Perry, started debarking thousands of troops at Amherstburg. Harrison's army included troops from Fort Meigs under General McArthur, and 3,000 Kentucky militiamen led by Governor Isaac Shelby, a hero of the Battle of King's Mountain during the War of Independence. At the same time, Kentucky congressman Richard M. Johnson, one of the War Hawks, was riding to Detroit at the head of 1,000 mounted infantrymen.

Harrison pursued the retreating Procter along the Thames River, and Perry, with a strong contingent of tough sailors, accompanied him. Tecumseh reluctantly stayed with Procter, but he was disgusted with him, as indeed were Proctor's own officers and men, who were unnerved by his panic. Many of Tecumseh's warriors had already melted away into the forest, along with British deserters.

On October 5 Harrison caught up with the enemy near Moravian Town on the Thames, fifty miles east of Detroit. By then Proctor's force had dwindled to 1,000, including 500 Indians. Harrison had 3,500 men, including Johnson's mounted infantry. Harrison had left most of his regulars to garrison Amherstburg and Detroit. What became known as the Battle of the Thames now ensued. It was over in half an hour. Given the disparity of forces and Proctor's poor leadership, a British defeat was inevitable. Tecumseh fought to the death. When he fell, any chance—admittedly slim to begin with—for the Indians to preserve their ancient way of life in the Northwest, or indeed east of the Mississippi, died with him.

Having always been most concerned with saving himself, Proctor managed to avoid surrender and, in unseemly haste, escaped from the battlefield with one quarter of his men to the safety of Burlington at the head of Lake Ontario. His performance did not go unnoticed by his superiors. A court-martial convicted him of misconduct and deprived him of his rank and pay for six months, after which the British army found no further use for him.

For Governor Shelby the victory was the realization of a dream that Kentucky and the entire Northwest had had since the days of Daniel Boone—the end of Indian and British power in those vast regions and the undisputed ascendancy of the United States. America was now free to exploit the entire territory unimpeded. Since Shelby had accomplished his great objective, he took his Kentuckians home. Harrison wanted to press on to Lake Ontario and play an important part in the general movement to wrest all of Upper Canada from the British. But most of his force was composed of Kentucky militiamen, and when they returned home, he had to fall back on Detroit and Amherstburg.

FOLLOWING THE BATTLE of the Thames, Perry, still angry with Chauncey, requested a transfer to Rhode Island. A grateful administration allowed him this indulgence. On September 29 Secretary Jones sent Perry a letter telling him he was promoted to captain and approving his transfer back to Newport. Chauncey was furious about the new assignment but not about the promotion, which he admitted was richly deserved. He wrote an angry letter to Jones, who understood Chauncey's objections but did not change his mind about moving Perry. Jesse Elliott became the new commandant on Lake Erie.

CHAPTER EIGHTEEN

Attack on Montreal

I N THE SUMMER of 1813, at the same time that Perry and Harrison were planning to secure the Northwest, Madison was preparing to attack Kingston and
Montreal, something he had intended to do back in the spring, before Dearborn
and Chauncey had talked him out of it. Even if he succeeded, the key British
strongholds at Quebec and Halifax would remain, but taking Upper Canada
would strengthen the president's diplomatic hand immeasurably. With Napoleon
in trouble, seizing Canada, or a substantial portion of it, was the only way Madison
could gain enough leverage to move Liverpool and his colleagues. Nothing had
been heard from the British about negotiations, although it was clear they were
not rushing to accept the czar's offer to mediate. The operations against Canada
were therefore critical. At the moment, all the president had to bargain with
was Amherstburg.

Unfortunately, Madison was sick for five weeks in June and July, suffering a
debilitating illness (similar to the one that had struck him the previous summer).
Dolley again feared for his life. Direction of the war fell to the president's department heads, and they were agreed that putting off the attacks on Kingston and
Montreal earlier in the year had been a huge mistake. Secretary Armstrong
wanted to make up for it now by striking both places during the late summer.
He hoped that by then Commodore Chauncey would have naval supremacy on
Lake Ontario. Secretary Jones, not a great admirer of Armstrong, nevertheless
agreed with the plan and did everything he could to support Chauncey. But time
was running out; winter in that part of Canada arrived in late October.

In preparation for the attacks, Armstrong appointed new leaders for the northern army. In May, he promoted fifty-six-year-old Brigadier General James Wilkinson to major general, and after accepting General Dearborn's resignation in July, Armstrong appointed Wilkinson to lead the assault on Kingston and Montreal. Wilkinson was given command of Military District 9, which included the Niagara region, Sackets Harbor, and Lake Champlain. His headquarters would be at Sackets Harbor. Armstrong had already appointed Major General Wade Hampton of South Carolina to lead the army gathering at Burlington, Vermont, on Lake Champlain. Hampton was expected to combine with Wilkinson in a joint attack on Montreal.

Choosing Wilkinson was, to say the least, baffling. What the inscrutable Armstrong was thinking is hard to imagine. Winfield Scott described Wilkinson as an "unprincipled imbecile," a characterization that most army officers would have agreed with. Wilkinson had been the most controversial and hated figure in the service for many years; Armstrong certainly knew this. Their relationship went back to the Revolutionary War, when both were ambitious young men working under the even more ambitious—and duplicitous—General Horatio Gates, notorious for his efforts to undermine General Washington.

A tireless self-promoter, Wilkinson was the darling of many uninformed Republicans. In March 1813 he had attained notoriety by leading the successful occupation of the rest of West Florida, which included the Mobile area and ran to the Perdido River. He was military commander of Louisiana at the time. Before then, his career had been marked by abject failure and well-founded charges of corruption. An inveterate intriguer, he had been closely associated with Aaron Burr, until he turned on him and became the prosecution's chief witness against him at Burr's trial for treason in 1807. Although Burr was acquitted, President Jefferson, who hated Burr, was grateful to Wilkinson. Earlier, the general had been secretly in the pay of the Spanish government while a senior American officer, and that treasonous relationship persisted. Spain even gave him a pension of $2,000. Prior to his elevation by Armstrong, Wilkinson's graft and incompetence in Louisiana had led to the unnecessary deaths of hundreds of his men. Both senators from Louisiana had demanded the secretary of war remove him.

The appointment of sixty-year-old Major General Wade Hampton was just as puzzling. In the later stages of the Revolutionary War, Hampton became a hero in South Carolina, serving under the famed guerrilla leaders Francis Marion and Thomas Sumter. Afterward, he became a rich plantation owner with thousands of slaves and a powerful Republican, serving in Congress for a time. His hatred for Wilkinson was no secret. He made it clear to Armstrong that he would follow Wilkinson's orders only if the forces at Sackets Harbor and those at Lake Champlain were joined in an attack on Montreal. Hampton's inability to work with his superior—indeed, his loathing of him—should have disqualified him. His lack of combat experience as a general officer and addiction to hard liquor were further reasons. But Hampton's shortcomings did not seem to matter to Armstrong.

The appointments of Wilkinson and Hampton were all the more mystifying when one considers the promising general officers that the army now had available who could have led the invasion, such as Brigadier Generals Jacob Brown and Ralph Izard or talented colonels like Winfield Scott, Alexander Macomb, Eleazer W. Ripley, Edmund P. Gaines, and Leonard Covington, whom Armstrong could have promoted. But once again Madison and his advisors, for reasons that remain obscure, selected elderly incompetents for vital positions.

Appearing in no hurry, Wilkinson reached Sackets Harbor on August 20 and held his first council of war six days later. Among those attending were General Jacob Brown, Wilkinson's second in command, and Commodore Chauncey. Wilkinson's orders were to attack Kingston and then Montreal, but he doubted that he could accomplish these objectives so late in the season. He preferred attacking in the Niagara area. Secretary Armstrong thought this was a sideshow, however, and quickly vetoed the idea. "You will make Kingston your primary object," he wrote to Wilkinson, "and you may choose (as circumstances warrant), between a direct and indirect attack upon that post." It was left to Wilkinson to construe what "direct" and "indirect" meant. He decided to interpret it as meaning a "strong feint" on Kingston before sending the army against Montreal, a city of 30,000.

General Brown was willing to do whatever Wilkinson wanted, but Chauncey was strongly in favor of attacking Kingston first. A mere feint would leave a substantial enemy force—including Yeo's fleet—in Wilkinson's rear when he attacked Montreal, placing Sackets Harbor in danger of assault from Kingston while the American forces were occupied in the St. Lawrence River. Nonetheless, even if his advice were ignored, Chauncey still intended to "afford the Army every facility of transport and protection" on its way to the St. Lawrence. But he refused to remain in the river and cooperate with Wilkinson. Chauncey felt that his primary duty was protecting Sackets Harbor, and he "deemed [it] unsafe to be in that river after the 1st of November, on account of the ice." After talking at greater length with Wilkinson, however, Chauncey became convinced that Armstrong's original plan was still intact and that Kingston was the general's first objective.

Of course, Kingston would be a much easier target if Chauncey first destroyed Yeo's warships. On August 29 he received word that Yeo's fleet had exited Kingston and was abroad on Lake Ontario. Chauncey went looking for him. His fleet of eleven vessels had been substantially strengthened by the 16-gun schooner *Sylph*, which Henry Eckford had built at Sackets Harbor in just twenty-three days.

On September 7 Chauncey discovered Yeo "close in with the Niagara River" and went after him with his heavy schooners in tow, which slowed him down considerably. Chauncey kept Yeo in sight, but he could not close with him. The British squadron remained just beyond his grasp. After days of fruitlessly chasing Yeo "round the lake day and night," Chauncey managed to engage him from a distance on the eleventh of September off the Genesee River near present-day Rochester, New York. Chauncey had an advantage in long guns; Yeo had mostly carronades. Chauncey also had the weather gauge, but he failed to deliver a decisive blow, claiming that Yeo ran away from him and escaped after a running fight of over three hours. Yeo in his report maintained that "it was impossible to bring them to close action." It seems that neither commodore wanted to hazard their precious fleets until they had an overwhelming advantage. Yeo escaped to the protection of Amherst Bay near Kingston, where the American fleet could not follow. Chauncey's pilots did not have detailed knowledge of the bay's deadly shoals.

On August 30, while Chauncey was chasing Yeo, Wilkinson left his command at Sackets Harbor in the hands of Jacob Brown and sailed to the Niagara area to acquire 3,500 additional troops from the army guarding Fort George and Fort Niagara. During the voyage Wilkinson became seriously ill, and he did not recover for a month. While he was away, Chauncey was again out after Yeo. They met on September 28 near Burlington Bay at the western end of Lake Ontario. After dueling at long range for three hours, Yeo broke off and raced for the protection of the batteries at Burlington Heights. Chauncey followed until gale force winds forced him to claw back to the protection of the Niagara River. Some vessels had been damaged on both sides, but there were few casualties. When the storm abated, Chauncey convoyed Wilkinson's troops from Niagara to Sackets Harbor. While he was doing so, Yeo returned unnoticed to Kingston. On the fourth of October Chauncey was out again looking for Yeo when he spotted four British troop transports making for Kingston and captured them. Two of the prizes were the schooners he had lost earlier, the *Growler* and the *Julia*.

When Wilkinson returned to Sackets Harbor the first week of October, he was still sick. To relieve his pain he took large doses of whiskey laced with laudanum.

During the third week of October, while he was trying to recover his health and get an attack organized, snow began falling. The dreaded winter had begun.

On October 29 Chauncey visited Wilkinson at his headquarters on Grenadier Island, midway between Sackets Harbor and Kingston, where 7,000 troops were gathering for the attempt on Montreal. Chauncey had protected all the movements of the troops from Sackets Harbor to Grenadier Island, often in severe weather. Chauncey was "mortified," as he told Secretary Jones, to hear for the first time that Wilkinson was not going to attack Kingston after all but would only make a feint and then proceed to Montreal.

Two days later, General Brown led an advance party to French Creek on the St. Lawrence, guarded by Chauncey's vessels. On November 2 sloops and gunboats of the Royal Navy, under Captain William Howe Mulcaster, slipped out of Kingston, past Chauncey's screen at the mouth of the St. Lawrence, and attacked Brown, but he was well prepared and beat them off, forcing Mulcaster to return to Kingston.

The following day, November 1, Chauncey convoyed the rest of Wilkinson's army to French Creek. Wilkinson, who was still sick, was the last to arrive.

On the fifth Brown led a flotilla of three hundred boats down the St. Lawrence toward Montreal. As he did, Yeo appeared with his fleet in the North Channel near the mouth of the river, while Chauncey and his fleet were in the South Channel. Wolfe Island separated them. Chauncey was anxious to engage the British fleet in a decisive action and made every effort to get at Yeo, who inexplicably retreated to Kingston.

Wilkinson now proceeded down the river, but Chauncey did not follow to protect his rear. Instead, he moved in stages back to Sackets Harbor. The commodore's first priority was still protecting his fleet and base, not taking Montreal. By November 11 he had all his vessels safely tucked in for the winter at Sackets Harbor. "It is now blowing a heavy gale from the westward with snow," he wrote to Secretary Jones, "and every appearance of the winter [has] set in."

Wilkinson landed his men just above Ogdensburg on November 6, and during the night he ran the empty boats that had transported his troops safely past the guns of Fort Wellington in Prescott. From the American camp seven miles above Ogdensburg he wrote to General Hampton, ordering him to move his army to St. Regis (opposite Cornwall) by the ninth or tenth, when they would join together for the attack on Montreal. Wilkinson added that Hampton was to bring two or three months' worth of supplies for the entire army. Wilkinson claimed his provisions would last only a few more weeks.

As far as Wilkinson knew, Hampton had a force of 4,000, whose principal object was to join him in attacking Montreal. He was aware that Hampton despised him and would not follow his orders if he could help it, which is why Wilkinson preferred to work through Armstrong, but the secretary, who was in upstate New York at the time, forced Wilkinson to communicate directly with Hampton. Armstrong's unwillingness to coordinate the movements of the two armies at this stage probably meant that he had lost faith in the enterprise and did not want to be blamed for its failure. People in Washington wondered where the elusive secretary was exactly, what he was doing, and why he was not at the War Department. He did not return to Washington until December 24.

Wilkinson's order surprised Hampton, who thought the attack on Montreal had been canceled because of the lateness of the season. Weeks earlier, a messenger from Sackets Harbor had arrived at Hampton's headquarters with instructions from Armstrong to build winter quarters for 10,000 men. Hampton assumed that Armstrong had given up the plan to attack Montreal. Thus, even before Wilkinson had embarked on the St. Lawrence, Hampton had put aside coordinating an attack on Montreal. Prevost knew of Hampton's withdrawal well before either Wilkinson or Armstrong did.

Wilkinson was unaware that back on October 26 Hampton had suffered a humiliating defeat at the hands of 1,300 French and English militiamen and a few Indians, commanded by Charles de Salaberry, a French-Canadian aristocrat of considerable experience, skill, and flair. At the time, Hampton had been trying to position himself for a junction with Wilkinson by traveling across the border toward Montreal via the Chateaguay River, which empties into the St. Lawrence just below the city. Secretary Armstrong knew of Hampton's movements and approved them, but Wilkinson did not.

On that day in October, Hampton ran into de Salaberry at Allan's Corners, near present-day Ormstown, Quebec, on the Chateaguay, fifty miles northeast of Cornwall and thirty-six miles southeast of Montreal. The subsequent fight became known as the Battle of Chateaguay, but it was hardly a battle. Hampton vastly overestimated the size of the enemy and withdrew before the fight was really joined. Embarrassed, discouraged, and confused, he retreated back across the border to Four Corners, New York, where he received Wilkinson's command to join him. By then, Hampton was totally demoralized and had no intention of carrying out the order.

In his reply to Wilkinson, Hampton wrote that his army was in terrible condition, that supplies were nonexistent, and that he could not possibly form a junction with him at St. Regis. Instead, he told Wilkinson he intended to retreat all the way back to Plattsburgh for the winter.

ON NOVEMBER 8, as of yet unaware of Hampton's situation, Wilkinson dispatched General Brown with 2,500 men to the Canadian side of the river with orders to clear enemy militia obstructing the road to Cornwall, seventy miles from Montreal. Brown met with weak resistance from Canadian militiamen and quickly dispatched them.

Meanwhile, a small force of about six hundred British regulars under Lieutenant Colonel Joseph Morrison left Kingston on November 6 to trail Wilkinson and hang on his rear. Commander William Howe Mulcaster of the Royal Navy transported them. Ice on the St. Lawrence did not encumber his squadron of two schooners, seven gunboats, and numerous bateaux. Since Commodore Chauncey's entire fleet was at Sackets Harbor, Mulcaster could traverse the St. Lawrence unimpeded. By the ninth Morrison was at Prescott, where two hundred fifty men from Fort Wellington reinforced him.

Bad weather on November 10 forced Wilkinson and the pursuing British to pause. Morrison established himself at John Crysler's farm and made preparations should Wilkinson detach a part of his force to get rid of the pesky enemy in his rear. This is exactly what Wilkinson did: He dispatched Brigadier General John Boyd with 2,000 men to attack Morrison.

The resulting Battle of Crysler's Farm began early in the afternoon of November 11, becoming heavy around two o'clock. Boyd's larger but poorly organized force attacked and was met by seasoned British regulars who stopped the ill-trained Americans and turned them back. Mulcaster's gunboats aided in the fight, pouring fire into the American lines. After two hours of close combat, Boyd's men went running back to their boats in a disorderly retreat. Most escaped to the American side of the river, but 100 were taken prisoner. In the fighting, 103 of Boyd's men were killed and 237 wounded, many of whom were left on the battlefield. The British had 22 killed, 148 wounded, and 9 missing and presumed dead.

The following day, Wilkinson, who had been sick during the battle and was still in poor condition, gathered what remained of his force and ran the Long Sault rapids, meeting up with General Brown and his men at Barnhart's Island above Cornwall. Wilkinson was still planning to attack Montreal, but his stores had nearly run out. He was counting on Hampton to bring supplies, as well as

4,000 reinforcements. But when Wilkinson arrived on Barnhart's Island, Colonel Henry Atkinson was waiting for him with a letter from Hampton, informing him that he was not coming to St. Regis for a rendezvous and that even if he did, he had no way of supplying the provisions Wilkinson requested. Hampton claimed that he had enough problems feeding his own men. Wilkinson was furious. He sent a blistering letter, telling Hampton that he could not find "language to express my sorrow" at Hampton's actions. Deprived of help, Wilkinson postponed the attack on Montreal and removed his army to winter quarters at nearby French Mills (Fort Covington), New York, just over the border.

Hampton's claim that he could not find sufficient supplies and Wilkinson's insistence that he was dependent on Hampton for provisions were curious, considering that New York farmers were then supplying all the food the British needed and would have done the same for the American armies if Wilkinson and Hampton could have somehow found the money. A month earlier Hampton had written that "we have and can have, an unlimited supply of good beef cattle." Wilkinson could have had plenty of food as well, but without Hampton's troops he had a perfect excuse for not attacking Montreal.

Wilkinson's decision was a relief to Governor-General Prevost, who had been working hard for weeks to improve Montreal's defense. When he first became aware that the Americans were going to attack Montreal and not Kingston, he rushed to Montreal to bolster its defenses, arriving on September 25. He brought marines from Quebec and called up a substantial number of militiamen, who looked formidable on paper but were untested. As Wilkinson approached, Prevost had mustered well over 10,000 militiamen, and he had 5,000 regulars under Major General Sheaffe. Prevost's sizable army would have, in all probability, administered a crushing defeat to Wilkinson.

WHILE ARMSTRONG AND Wilkinson were focused on attacking Montreal, Fort George and Fort Niagara were left with 850 regulars under Colonel Winfield Scott and 1,600 New York militiamen under Brigadier General George McClure. Believing the British had withdrawn from the Niagara region to defend Montreal, Wilkinson ordered Scott on October 13 to march most of his troops east to join the attack on Montreal, leaving McClure with only 324 regulars and the New York militiamen, whose six-month enlistments were about to expire. McClure was more of a politician than a soldier; he had no military credentials, and he could not inspire any loyalty in his troops. He watched nervously as almost all his militiamen—even with their pay in arrears—left forts George and Niagara and went home. By December 10 he was left with 150 militiamen and 300 plus regulars, who were guarding Fort Niagara.

Secretary Armstrong, hoping that Prevost had moved all the forces he could east, did not send reinforcements. McClure was already nervous and grew more so when he discovered that British brigadier general Vincent had moved men from Burlington closer to Fort George. McClure did not know how many.

On December 10 McClure learned that all his fears were confirmed—the British were advancing against Fort George. He evacuated the fort in a panic and ordered the nearby town of Newark, a thriving community with over one hundred buildings, including a library and a government center, burned. As many as four hundred innocent Canadians of all ages were driven from their homes with little notice during terrible weather. Snow and severe frost made finding shelter imperative, but none was available. Afterward, McClure led his men across the river to Fort Niagara. He claimed that he destroyed Newark in order to deprive the British of comfortable winter quarters and that Armstrong had given the order. But that simply was not the case. The administration denounced McClure for what he had done. Armstrong ordered Wilkinson, McClure's superior, to publicly repudiate the act. But that was not enough for Lieutenant General Gordon Drummond, who had just replaced Major General Francis de Rottenburg as the leader of Upper Canada. Drummond announced that "retributive justice demanded of me a speedy retaliation on the opposite shore of America." After his announcement, the British reoccupied Fort George.

On December 19, Drummond ordered a surprise attack on Fort Niagara. Lieutenant Colonel John Murray led the assault with six hundred men. Entering the fort at five o'clock in the morning, he caught the American regulars completely unawares. McClure wasn't even in the fort; he had gone to Buffalo. By 5:30, without firing a shot, using only bayonets, Murray captured all the men in the fort and their huge stock of cannon, muskets, ammunition, and supplies.

While Murray was taking Fort Niagara, Major General Phineas Riall, intent on avenging Newark, had crossed the Niagara River on December 18 with 1,000 British regulars and 400 Indians and marched down the New York side, ravaging Lewiston and the neighboring villages of Youngstown and Manchester, burning and pillaging without restraint. The *Albany Argus* reported that "bodies were lying dead in the fields and roads, some horribly cut and mangled with tomahawks, others eaten by hogs, which were probably left for the purpose."

Riall continued south, and on December 29, he overwhelmed weakly defended Black Rock, destroying four schooners that were part of the Lake Erie fleet wintering there, and threatening Buffalo. McClure was no longer in charge of the defense. Despised for burning Newark, even by his own people, and blamed for the Fort Niagara debacle and the massacre at Lewiston, he stole off to Batavia, lucky his own men had not killed him. Governor Tompkins appointed Major General Amos Hall to replace him.

Hall had 2,000 green militiamen to protect Buffalo, but at the first glimpse of British bayonets, panic seized them, and when they heard Indian cries, they broke and ran. "They gave way and fled on every side," Hall said. "Every attempt to rally them was ineffectual." Buffalo was left to face the enemy alone. Again, showing no mercy, Riall plundered and burned the town. Master Commandant Jesse Elliott feared he would attack the naval base at Presque Isle next, but the severity of the winter brought the British rampage to a halt.

Prevost justified Riall's butchery by pointing to Newark. But McClure never authorized the slaughter that Riall encouraged. Also, Prevost overlooked the ravaging of Hampton, Virginia, back in June, an atrocity that had all of Riall's savagery but no Indians to blame it on. When justifying their viciousness, the British liked to point to American violence, but it never remotely equaled the sadistic retaliation they practiced.

The armies now went into winter hibernation along the frozen border, each anticipating more ferocious fighting in the spring. The fort on Michilimackinac Island remained in British hands. After Harrison's victory over Procter and Tecumseh, severe weather prevented an attack on the fort, which was sure to be an objective come spring.

The defeats along the Canadian border delivered another devastating blow to the president's war plans and made getting Liverpool to the negotiating table all the more difficult. The British had been so successful not only against American arms but in garnering support from their Canadian subjects that their war aims, which initially had been purely defensive, now became far more expansive. Once the Napoleonic menace was destroyed, Liverpool and his colleagues could deal a crippling blow to the pretensions of the United States.

CHAPTER NINETEEN

The War
at Sea in 1813

IN THE LATTER part of 1813 the high seas were as much of a disappointment for the president as the disasters in Canada. Victories were hard to come by. One of the few occurred off the coast of Maine. On September 1, twenty-seven-year-old Lieutenant William Ward Burrows II, captain of the storied American warship *Enterprise*, weighed anchor and hove out of the Portsmouth Naval Shipyard into the fast-moving current of the Piscataqua River, which formed the boundary between the District of Maine and the state of New Hampshire. The commandant of the yard, Captain Isaac Hull, ordered Burrows "to proceed to sea on a cruise along the coast [of Maine] to the eastward as far as the Kennebec River" to protect the coasting trade, "interrupted by small cruisers of the enemy of late." The British were also using small craft to engage in unlawful trade with Mainers, who were ferrying goods out to them in defiance of the law. Hull wanted the *Enterprise* to put a stop to this traffic as well. He told Burrows to sail close to shore; British warships had grown in number, and Hull wanted the slow-sailing *Enterprise* to "have a port under your lee or near you, that you may run for." He ordered Burrows to return to Portsmouth in two weeks.

Three months earlier, Burrows had been a prisoner in a British jail in Barbados. He landed there after obtaining a furlough from the navy so that he could go on a voyage to Canton, China, in a merchantman to replenish his shrinking wallet. On the way home the British captured his ship and sent him to Barbados as a prisoner of war, but he was soon paroled, exchanged, and back on duty. The

Enterprise was his first assignment since rejoining the service. Burrows was a native of Philadelphia, active on the water his entire life. His father, William Ward Burrows I, was the first commandant of the Marine Corps when President Adams reestablished the Corps in 1798. Young Burrows was as committed to his country's service as his father had been, and like his peers Lieutenant Burrows was anxious to distinguish himself.

Isaac Hull was happy to have Burrows; he desperately needed more help. Hull was commanding officer of the navy's Eastern Station, in charge of building one of the 74-gun ships of the line (the *Washington*) approved by Congress in January 1813. He also had responsibility for protecting Portsmouth and the Maine coast, but he had practically no warships. When he asked for some, Secretary Jones assigned him the small brigs *Siren* and *Enterprise*. *Siren* was laid up for repairs in Charleston, South Carolina, and would never arrive. The *Enterprise* appeared in June, under Master Commandant Johnston Blakeley. The previous year, Blakeley had radically altered the classic schooner, converting her to a brig. He hoped to strengthen her as a gun platform without compromising her sailing qualities. Unfortunately, he transformed her from a fast schooner carrying twelve six-pounders into a stodgy brig. He was unhappy with the result, and when he handed her over to Burrows, whom he knew well and respected, it was with a sense of relief. Blakeley wanted a better fighting ship. He was grateful when Secretary Jones assigned him to superintend construction of one of the new sloops of war, the *Wasp*, then building in Newburyport, Massachusetts. Blakeley had just been promoted to master commandant, and the *Wasp* was more suited to his rank.

WHEN THE WEATHER was dirty, sailing the sixty miles from Portsmouth, New Hampshire, to Portland, Maine, could take a long time, but Burrows had a short, pleasant cruise. As Cape Elizabeth came into view at the southern entrance to Casco Bay on the third of September, a lookout spied a schooner off Wood Island near Biddeford Pool, and Burrows chased her into Portland, where he captured her and then anchored for the night. The following morning he received word of enemy privateers operating near Pemaquid Point, and he set out from Portland to find them. Steering east, he soon approached Sequin Island at the mouth of the Kennebec River and then decided to sail on to Monhegan Island, twenty miles farther east.

By passing beyond the Kennebec, Burrows was bending his orders a bit, but he was in luck. At nine o'clock on the morning of the fifth he saw a brig getting under way in Johns Bay west of the giant granite rocks at Pemaquid Point. She appeared to be a warship.

At about the same time, a lookout aboard the 14-gun British brig *Boxer* spied the *Enterprise*, and her captain, twenty-nine-year-old Commander Samuel Blyth, ordered his seventy-man crew to quarters and cleared for action. The *Enterprise* was obviously an American warship, and he went after her. Blyth's orders were to annoy American traders along the Maine coast, but of course he couldn't pass up an enemy warship.

The two ships looked evenly matched, with the *Enterprise* having a slight edge. She carried fourteen eighteen-pound carronades, two long nines, and a crew of 102, while the *Boxer* had twelve eighteen-pound carronades, two long sixes, and a crew of 76 officers and men plus 11 boys. The weather was clear and the wind light from the north-northwest. When the *Boxer* raced after the *Enterprise*, Burrows hauled upon a wind and stood to the west, keeping six miles away from the enemy. Blyth continued to chase him, firing his guns as he went, but with no impact at that distance. Burrows, who had the weather gauge, remained out of range until three o'clock, when he suddenly tacked and ran down directly at the *Boxer* "with an intention to bring her to close action."

In twenty minutes Burrows ran the *Enterprise* alongside the *Boxer* within half pistol shot (about ten yards). Each ship held its fire until the other was alongside, and then both broadsides erupted, initiating an intense, broadside-to-broadside gunfight. Both captains fell in the first exchange. An eighteen-pound ball struck Blyth, killing him instantly, and a musket ball hit Burrows, mortally wounding him. "Our brave commander fell," the officers aboard the *Enterprise* reported, "and while lying on deck, refusing to be carried below, raised his head and requested that the flag never be struck."

After fifteen minutes of a brutal exchange, the *Enterprise* pulled ahead and fired one of her nine-pounders with effect before rounding to on the starboard tack and raking the *Boxer*. The British ship soon ceased firing. All her braces and rigging were shot away, the main topmast and topgallant mast hung over the side, and the fore and mainmasts were nearly gone. Only the quarterdeck guns were manned. Three feet of water flooded the hold, and more was rushing in. Her deck was strewn with dead and wounded, and no surgeon was aboard to tend them. She was in desperate straits.

The *Enterprise* now pulled into a position from which to rake the *Boxer* again and completely destroy her but held her fire. While she did, British Lieutenant McCrery, who had assumed command when Blyth fell, consulted his officers and decided to give up. Since Blyth had nailed their ensigns to the masts, they could not be hauled down. McCrery had to hail the *Enterprise* in order to surrender. It was four o'clock.

Isaac Hull later described the *Boxer*'s condition. Her "masts, sails, and spars . . . [were] literally cut to pieces, several of her guns dismounted and unfit for service; her topgallant forecastle nearly taken off by the shot; her boats cut to pieces, and her quarters injured in proportion." The *Boxer* had four killed and eighteen wounded; the *Enterprise*, three killed and fourteen wounded.

Lieutenant Edward McCall, now in command of the *Enterprise*, sailed into Portland with the wounded *Boxer* in tow. The town gave the victorious Americans a rousing welcome. The bodies of the two captains were brought ashore and given an elaborate funeral. The crews of both ships attended, as did Portland's notables and Captain Isaac Hull, who came up from Portsmouth. "A great concourse of people assembled from town and country," the *Portland Gazette* reported. "The wharfs and streets were lined with people on both sides; tops of houses and windows were filled with men and women and children." The two young captains were buried side by side in Portland's Eastern Cemetery, where they rest today. The ceremony of their burials made a deep impression on all who witnessed it, including young Henry Wadsworth Longfellow.

The deaths of these two promising young men were a reminder of the terrible price being paid for the war. Deeply affected by the killing and wounding, Lieutenant McCall arrested Sailing Master William Harper, accusing him of cowardice. McCall charged that Harper had "endeavored to screen himself from the shot of the enemy behind the foremast and under the heel of the bowsprit while the enemy lay on our quarter by doing which he set an example to the crew of the *Enterprise* that might have led to her surrender and disgrace to the American character." McCall also charged that Harper "advised me to haul down the colors at a time when the firing from the enemy was much diminished and ours could be kept up with unabated effect."

A court-martial, held the following December and January, found Harper not guilty. Had the charge been substantiated, he could have been sentenced to death.

THE TRIUMPH OF the *Enterprise* came at the same time as Perry's far more important success on Lake Erie. They made up to a degree for the *Chesapeake*'s defeat back in June that year. President Madison, like most of the country, was profoundly disturbed by the *Chesapeake-Shannon* affair. He was anxious to celebrate any victory. Perry and the *Enterprise* were a welcome return to the path of glory.

Unfortunately, during the last six months of 1813, there were few other encouraging moments for the U.S. Navy. Even getting to sea was difficult for the American fleet. Two of the country's vaunted heavy frigates, the *Constitution* and the *United States*, were blockaded—"Old Ironsides" in Boston and the *United States* in the Thames River with the *Macedonian* and the *Hornet*. The other heavy frigate, John Rodgers's *President*, was out at sea on her third cruise. She had escaped from Boston earlier, but nothing had been heard from her or her companion, the *Congress* (John Smith). Charles Morris and the *Adams* were confined to Chesapeake Bay, and the *Constellation* was still trapped in Norfolk. What had happened to David Porter and the *Essex* was a mystery. He failed to rendezvous with Bainbridge as planned, but where he went and how well he was faring was unknown.

LIEUTENANT HENRY ALLEN'S *Argus* appeared, at first, to be a bright spot in this gloomy picture. On June 18 Allen stood out from New York, bound for France with Ambassador William Crawford aboard, eluding the blockade off Sandy Hook with no trouble. Allen was one of the navy's young stars. Decatur was loud in his praise, attributing their triumph over the *Macedonian* to Allen's masterful gunnery.

Allen's orders from Secretary Jones were to deliver Crawford to France and then undertake a commerce-destroying mission around the British Isles. Like Rodgers, Jones believed the British were vulnerable in their home waters. He also thought that a fleet of swift, powerful sloops of war attacking Britain's trade would create a huge problem for the Royal Navy and make a decisive contribution to ending the war. Allen's mission was something Jones would have liked to order on a large scale, but he did not have the ships or the men to do it.

The passage across the Atlantic was marked by heavy turbulence. Ambassador Crawford recounted a particularly uncomfortable day in his journal—Wednesday, June 30: "The wind increases to a storm. The *Argus* marches o'er the mountainous wave. The rain descends in torrents and drives me from the deck. The guns on the lee side are constantly underwater, and every heavy sea washes the deck with its mountainous billows. It is impossible to stand on the deck without clinging to a rope. It is extremely difficult to keep dry even in the cabin, unless I get into the berth, which I am the more inclined to do from the violent retching which the motion of the vessel communicates to my stomach."

The *Argus* arrived at L'Orient on July 11, having taken one prize en route. Allen immediately went to work preparing for his next mission, and on July 20 he set out for the mouth of the English Channel. During the next week the *Argus* took three small prizes between Ushant and the Scillies Islands. Allen's orders required him to burn all prizes. Jones did not want him weakening his crew by using men to sail captured vessels to friendly (French) ports.

Expecting the British to be out in force looking for him, Allen shaped a course for Cape Clear and the southwestern coast of Ireland. He disguised his ship by painting her black with a thick yellow stripe across her gun ports to make her look like a British man-of-war. On August 1, off the mouth of the River Shannon, Allen captured his fifth prize, the *Fowey*, and set her on fire. The next day he captured the *Lady Francis*, and in the following twelve days, sailing along the southern coast of Ireland and up St. George's Channel, he took fourteen more prizes—a spectacular performance, better than any ship on either side had managed.

The commander of Britain's Irish Station in Cork, Vice Admiral Edward Thornborough, was understandably embarrassed by the bold American raider operating in his backyard. The Royal Navy was spread so thin that Thornborough had few ships he could assign to chase Allen. That changed on August 12, however, when the brig *Pelican* put into Cork. Thornborough immediately dispatched her captain, Commander John F. Maples, to go after *Argus*. The *Pelican* was a new ship, having been launched in August 1812 and commissioned the following November. Her skipper was a veteran who knew his business. He had fought with Nelson at Copenhagen and Trafalgar, and also with Hyde Parker on the Jamaica Station in the frigate *Magicienne*.

Maples was in luck. The day after he left Cork, he was cruising in St. George's Channel when he spoke a brig whose captain told him he had seen a strange man-of-war steering to the northeast. Maples headed in that direction. The following morning, August 15, at four o'clock a lookout aboard the *Pelican* spotted a vessel on fire and a brig standing from her. The burning vessel was the large merchantman *Belford*, carrying, among other things, a large shipment of wine; the brig was the *Argus*. Maples immediately gave chase. In an hour and a half he pulled to within sight of St. David's Head off the coast of Wales. The *Argus* was only four hundred yards away.

Allen had been waiting for him. He had seen the *Pelican* as soon as Maples saw him, and there was no doubt in his mind that this was a British warship. At first, Allen attempted to gain the weather gauge, but failing that, he shortened sail and simply waited, determined to have it out toe-to-toe with the approaching enemy. When shortly it became clear that the *Pelican* was more powerful than the ten-year-old *Argus*, Allen stood his ground. He never gave a thought to running, as he undoubtedly should have, given his orders and the *Pelican's* strength. The *Argus* had eighteen twenty-four-pound carronades, two long twelve-pounders, and a crew of 104. The *Pelican* had sixteen thirty-two-pound carronades, two long twelve-pounders, two six-pound long guns, and a crew of 116.

Allen's primary mission was commerce destroying, and getting into a bloody fight with this larger British ship, even if Allen won, would make carrying out his orders impossible. He'd be lucky if he could limp into a French port afterward. While his orders did direct him to "capture and destroy" enemy warships as well as commercial vessels, Secretary Jones would have undoubtedly approved bypassing this engagement so that Allen could continue his remarkable reign of terror. Furthermore, Allen's crew was dead tired from their exertions of the last few days; his men needed a rest. But Allen could not pass up this opportunity for glory, and he had an important advantage. The *Argus* was faster and more maneuverable than the *Pelican*, and that could make all the difference. By the same token, *Argus's* speed would have allowed her to run away without much trouble. Allen chose not to because he had a good chance of winning, or so he thought.

When the two ships were two hundred yards apart, they opened fire. Oddly, the *Pelican's* broadsides were more effective. Allen was known as a superb gunner; it was hard to understand why his crew were not better marksmen—perhaps it was fatigue. In the opening rounds, a thirty-two-pound ball smashed Allen's left knee, and after gallantly trying to carry on, he fainted from loss of blood and had to be carried below. First Lieutenant William Watson was then hit in the head and knocked unconscious. Second Lieutenant Howard Allen (not related to the fallen captain) took command as Maples maneuvered to rake the *Argus* by the stern. Howard Allen responded by backing the main topsail, which slowed the *Argus* and put her into a position to cross the *Pelican's* bow and rake her. It was a critical moment in the battle. A well-directed broadside at that distance would have crippled the *Pelican* enough for Howard Allen to defeat her. But his broadside, inexplicably, did no damage. Maples took advantage of the reprieve and came up alongside the *Argus*, pummeling her with his heavy guns. He then raked her by the bow and the stern. The *Argus* was finished. Maples was preparing to board when Howard Allen struck his colors. The fighting had raged for forty-three minutes. The *Argus* had six killed and eighteen wounded, five of them mortally (Lieutenant Watson recovered). The *Pelican* had two killed and five wounded.

The battle was a stunning conclusion to the *Argus's* otherwise spectacularly successful cruise. Captain Henry Allen and the rest of the prisoners were taken to Dartmoor Prison in Plymouth, where four days later Allen died. The British gave him a hero's funeral and buried him in Plymouth's St. Andrews Churchyard, along with Midshipman Richard Delphey. Allen never found out that he had been promoted to master commandant in July. In London, the *Times* boasted, "The victory of the *Pelican* over *Argus* is another proof of British superiority on the ocean."

THE *ARGUS* WAS not the only American warship operating around the British Isles in the summer of 1813. Commodore Rodgers and the *President* were there as well. Rodgers had departed Boston on April 23 in company with Captain John Smith and the *Congress*. They split up on May 8. Rodgers hoped the *President* would see more action than she had on her first two voyages. His initial target was the homeward-bound Jamaica convoy. With this in mind, he cruised south of the Grand Banks. The only ships he saw, however, were Americans returning from Lisbon and Cadiz with British gold and silver in their coffers. Nothing annoyed him more than this blatant, legal trafficking with the enemy. The scandal of trading under British licenses would soon come to an end, however. In July 1813, Congress, with President Madison's strong support, finally passed a bill making the noxious practice illegal. A three- to five-month grace period was allowed for ships coming from the Far East, Africa, and—most importantly—Europe.

The first two months of Rodgers's cruise were frustrating. He missed the Jamaica convoy, and thick fog hindered him as he hunted along the eastern edge of the Grand Banks, looking for vessels bound for Canada. At the end of May he took up a position west of the Azores, but again with no results until the second week of June, when he captured two small merchantmen, a letter of marque, and a packet. He sent the merchantmen to France as prizes and the packet as a cartel ship to England with seventy-eight prisoners, hoping to annoy the Admiralty.

Rodgers then set sail for the northern area of the British Isles, something he had wanted to do since the war began. But as luck would have it, he did not see another ship until he was near the Shetland Islands off the northeast coast of Scotland. By then his provisions and water were running low, and he steered northeast for Bergen, Norway, to resupply.

Norway was part of Denmark—a bitter enemy of Britain. An American warship had never visited Bergen before, so when people found out who Rodgers was, they extended their warmest hospitality. Unfortunately it did not include the food he needed. Bread and other provisions were simply not available. All the Norwegians could give him were water and a tiny amount of cheese and rye meal.

When the Admiralty discovered the *President* had put into Bergen, it tried hard to catch her. On July 13 the *Times* reported that Rodgers was refitting and watering there, but by then he had already left. He stood out from Bergen on July 2 in search of a British convoy from the Russian port of Archangel. In the next two weeks he captured two small merchantmen, and on the eighteenth he met and joined forces with the American privateer *Scourge*, under Captain Samuel Nicoll, out of New York. Nicoll had been at work since June, along with another famous privateer, the *Rattlesnake* out of Philadelphia. During a busy month, the two raiders had captured twenty-two prizes. They did so well that the Admiralty thought they were part of an American squadron led by Rodgers. In fact, they were but a small part of an armada of American privateers swarming around the British Isles. The embarrassed Admiralty tried to get rid of them but never succeeded. The Royal Navy's hunters were too few and the American marauders too many.

Rodgers shaped a course for the North Cape off Norway's island of Mageroya. On the way he captured two more prizes, both brigs in ballast, which he burned after removing their crews and stores. He reported that "sun in that latitude, at that season, appeared at midnight several degrees above the horizon." On the nineteenth of July, with the *Scourge* in company, lookouts on the *President* spied two large British ships in the distance, and judging them to be a line-of-battle ship and a frigate, Rodgers put on all sail to avoid them. The *Scourge* did the same, parting company with the *President*. The British men-of-war ignored the smaller ship and concentrated on the *President*, a prize that, if caught, would have made their captains heroes in Britain. Capturing Rodgers was a high priority for the Admiralty.

Ironically, Rodgers was running from the very ships he had hoped to find. The men-of-war chasing him were the 38-gun frigate *Alexandria* and the 16-gun sloop of war *Spitfire*. Unfortunately, fog obscured his view, and he could not identify them. The *President* and the *Scourge* together could have easily beaten them; even the *President* alone could have.

After eluding his pursuers, Rodgers stood south, shaping a course to take him back to Scotland's northwestern coast, where he could watch for vessels at

Figure 19.1: Irwin Bevan, President *and* High Flyer, *23 September 1813* (courtesy of Mariner's Museum, Newport News, Virginia).

the northern end of the Irish Channel. He was there at the same time that Henry Allen and the *Argus* were patrolling at the southern end of the Channel. The tiny American navy, which was supposed to be blockaded in its home ports, was instead operating at both ends of a major British waterway. During the succeeding days, Rodgers captured three ships and sent them to England as cartels—more salt in the wound for the Admiralty.

He knew their lordships would be outraged and would intensify their hunt for him, which was gratifying, but at the same time he did not want to tempt fate any further. With provisions running low, he headed home, setting a course for the Grand Banks off Newfoundland, where he made two more captures and sent them as prizes to the United States.

He continued southwest, and near the southern shoal of Nantucket he spotted an armed schooner that looked interesting. When he saw her signaling, he looked at the Royal Navy's private signals he had acquired and answered appropriately. Whereupon, His Majesty's 5-gun schooner *High Flyer*, Admiral Warren's tender, sped toward the *President* with the British ensign flying and hove to under her stern. Lieutenant George Hutchinson, the schooner's dimwitted skipper, believed the *President* was His Majesty's frigate *Seahorse*. One of Rodgers's lieutenants, outfitted in a British uniform, went aboard the *High Flyer* and brought Hutchinson back to the *President* to meet Rodgers. Still believing he was on the *Seahorse* and that Rodgers was her captain, Hutchinson handed over Admiral Warren's instructions detailing the number of British squadrons along the American coast, their force, and their relative positions, along with pointed orders to capture the *President*. Hutchinson was unaware that he was talking to Rodgers until the commodore introduced himself.

Before the *High Flyer* became the Admiral's tender, she had been an American privateer out of Baltimore—and a famous one. British Captain John P. Beresford captured her in heavy seas on January 9, 1813, in the 74-gun *Poictiers*; he was very proud of his success and couldn't wait to tell Warren. Beresford reported that the schooner was "a particularly fine vessel, coppered and copper fastened, and sails remarkably fast." She was typical of the Baltimore schooners that were giving the Admiral so much trouble. Admiral Warren was delighted to have the *High Flyer* for a trophy. One can only imagine his reaction when she was so easily recaptured, and by his nemesis Rodgers.

After his conversation with the hapless Hutchinson, Rodgers sailed for Newport and slipped into port with his prize, dropping anchor on September 26, thwarting Britain's mighty effort to catch him. Warren wrote to the Admiralty, "I made the best disposition in my power to intercept his return to port," but that had not been enough. Warren had committed an unprecedented twenty-five warships to the effort. The frigates *Junon* and *Orpheus* and the sloop of war *Loup-Cervier* (the former American ship *Wasp*) were patrolling off Newport, but they never saw the *President* or the *High Flyer*.

In the end, Rodgers's cruise had not been spectacular, but he did capture twelve vessels and diverted a substantial number of enemy warships from other duties to hunt for him. Secretary Jones considered that worthwhile. Rodgers was not resting on his laurels, however. He moved the *President* to Providence for better protection and set to work getting her repaired and provisioned for another cruise. By the middle of November she was ready, but Rodgers did not attempt to sortie until the first week of December. Adverse weather and the British warships off Block Island kept him in port until December 4, when he sailed out, eluding the battleship *Ramillies* and the frigates *Loire* and *Orpheus*, as well as the smaller vessels cruising in shore.

Rodgers's departure was another blow to Warren. It reinforced the Admiralty's judgment that he was not up to the job and had to be replaced.

The British were interested as much in the *Constitution* as they were the *President*. After her return to Boston early in 1813, they kept a close eye on the harbor.

Charles Stewart had the big frigate ready for sea by the end of September, but adverse winds and the blockade kept him in port until the last day of the year, when he slipped out to sea. A determined skipper with a good ship could always break free in bad weather. No blockade could have stopped Stewart. Nonetheless, the Admiralty blamed Warren.

WHILE RODGERS AND Stewart were able to get to sea, Decatur remained trapped in the Thames River with the *United States*, *Macedonian*, and *Hornet*. When he fled there in June, he concentrated on escaping, looking for "the first good wind and a dark night" to break out and return to New York via Long Island Sound. But if that were impossible, he wrote Secretary Jones, he would take his ships six miles upriver, where "the channel is very narrow and intricate and not a sufficient depth of water to enable large ships to follow." The place he had in mind was Gales Ferry, six miles above New London. Decatur thought he'd be safe there if he had more twenty-four-pounders and some gunboats from the New York flotilla.

British Commodore Robert Oliver intended to keep Decatur bottled up. He ordered Captain Hardy in the 74-gun *Ramillies* and Captain Hugh Pigot in the 36-gun *Orpheus* to return to their station off the Thames, while he went back to patrolling off Sandy Hook in the 74-gun *Valiant*, accompanied by the 44-gun *Acasta*. Decatur was immediately aware of the switch. He was also painfully aware of the scandalous traffic in goods and intelligence between the British ships and traitors onshore. He was determined to interrupt that traffic and to harass, and even sink, the *Ramillies* and the *Orpheus*.

When Congress passed the so-called "Torpedo Act" in March 1813, all sorts of inventions appeared. On June 25 John Scutter Jr., using one of the more promising devices, made an attempt on the *Ramillies*. Scutter outfitted the schooner *Eagle* with food and a huge bomb that exploded when sufficient food was removed. He explained that the device contained "a quantity of powder with a great quantity of combustables . . . placed beneath the articles the enemy were to hoist out. The act of displacing these articles was to cause an explosion, by a cord fasten'd to the striker of a common gun lock, which ignited with a train of powder—the first or second hogshead moved the cord."

Scutter hoped the *Ramillies* would bring the *Eagle* alongside, and when she attempted to haul the food out, the explosion would blow a huge hole in her and sink her. Completely taken in by Scutter, Hardy sent barges to capture the *Eagle* and bring her to his battleship. Bad weather forced the barges to anchor the *Eagle*, however, and move the food themselves, causing a huge explosion that killed all aboard the boats but did not touch the *Ramillies*.

Another attempt was made using a submarine similar to David Bushnell's famous *Turtle*, which was deployed during the War of Independence and came very close to sinking Admiral Howe's flagship *Eagle* in New York Harbor in 1776. Unfortunately, the bomb the new submarine carried could not be fastened to the *Ramillies*'s hull, and the attempt failed, but it came close enough that afterward Hardy swept his hull every two hours.

Although these two attempts failed, Decatur was determined to try again, using one of Robert Fulton's inventions. When Decatur was in New York, he had been captivated by Fulton's active imagination, particularly his thoughts on torpedoes and submarines. Fulton visited New London and wanted to try out a new invention he called an underwater cannon. His torpedoes and mines had never proven practical. He thought he would overcome his difficulties with a cannon that could shoot underwater. Decatur was anxious for him to try, but the experiment never came off.

Captain Hardy and Admiral Warren were offended by Decatur's use of these "infernal machines," and Hardy threatened countermeasures. He announced that if any more attempts were made, he would retaliate against the coast, bombarding every place in range.

While Decatur was on the attack with unconventional means, he was also strengthening the defenses at Gales Ferry, where he had moved his three ships. Worried that Hardy would make a determined effort to recover the *Macedonian*, he built a fortification known as Fort Decatur, which protected approaches to Gales Ferry from the water. Decatur also received two companies of regulars to defend the fort from a land attack. He fashioned a huge chain that prevented warships from rushing up the Thames River. His defenses were solid—in fact, too solid for James Biddle, captain of the *Hornet*, who had his mind fixed on escaping. He thought Decatur should devote his energies to busting out rather than defending against an attack. "Decatur has lost very much of his reputation by his continuance in port," Biddle wrote to his brother. "Indeed he has certainly lost all his energy and enterprise."

Biddle was mistaken about his chief's character, however. When it appeared that Hardy's squadron offshore had shrunk and the danger of a British attack had lessened, Decatur moved his ships back downriver to Market Wharf in New London and prepared to escape on a dark night or in bad weather. By December 12, he was ready, but as his three ships were attempting to sortie in total darkness, he saw blue lights flashing from behind on both shores, and he interpreted them as signals to Hardy from Federalist traitors. He was forced to return to the protection of his fort.

Connecticut Federalists did indeed have a treasonous liaison with Captain Hardy. Many people in the New London area liked him. When Hardy first appeared as a blockader in April 1813, he did his best to get along with Connecticut's residents. New London historian Frances M. Caulkins wrote in 1852 that "Sir Thomas Hardy soon acquired among the inhabitants an enviable reputation for courtesy and humanity. He released some vessels, allowed others to be ransomed, paid kind attention to prisoners, and pledged his word that fishermen should not be disturbed. Liberal payment was made [in specie] for supplies taken from the coast or islands in the Sound, and parties landing for refreshment refrained entirely from plunder."

IN THE MIDDLE of December 1813, the *Congress* returned from her lengthy cruise in the South Atlantic and put into Portsmouth, New Hampshire. Captain John Smith was looking forward to being reunited with Isaac Hull, his old friend from Mediterranean days. The *Congress* had been eight months at sea, and during that time she had captured only four prizes, the most unproductive voyage of any frigate during the war. Secretary Jones wanted her repaired, refitted, and back out to sea as soon as possible. Her damage was not extensive, despite her long voyage, but her crew, their enlistments expiring, were leaving. Smith, who was seriously ill from consumption, found it impossible to enlist a new crew. Apparently, the deepwater navy could not compete with army enlistment bonuses, navy bounties for service on the lakes, or privateers. In May Secretary Jones decided to send what was left of the *Congress*'s crew to Sackets Harbor to help man Chauncey's *Mohawk*. Hull removed the *Congress*'s guns and sent her farther up the Piscataqua River for protection.

The *Congress* was the least of Hull's worries, however. Lack of money, men, and supplies continued to impede work on his major project, the 74-gun ship. As long as she was building, his navy yard was a prime target. The Admiralty was anxious to destroy the new American seventy-fours before they became active, and Hull's defenses were weak. He also had to deal with the rampant smuggling going on between Maine and Halifax, but he had almost no tools to do it with.

By the end of 1813, smuggling in Maine, Georgia, Vermont, and New York had reached such proportions that Madison and the Congress passed a far-reaching embargo on every type of shipping, including coastal shipping and fishing outside harbors. The law even prohibited inland waterways from being used for shipping without presidential permission. Massachusetts Federalists were indignant, viewing the act as aimed directly at their economy.

Despite the embargo, commerce across the Canadian border, by land and sea, flourished. Even more galling to Madison was the flow of supplies going to the British fleet off the American coast. Without this sustenance Warren's blockade would have been far less effective. By the end of 1813 the Admiral had a stranglehold on America's waterborne commerce. In New York Harbor, for instance, a hundred forty merchantmen were laid up, unable to sail. During 1813 shipping out of New York had dwindled to $60,000. In 1806 it had been nearly $16 million.

Yet, as difficult as it was for merchant shipping to continue trading, privateers came and went with relative ease. Even in Chesapeake Bay, the most closely guarded waterway, Baltimore privateers were able to get in and out. Warren wrote to the Admiralty on December 30 from Bermuda that "dark nights and strong winds" have allowed "several large clipper schooners, strongly manned and armed, [to] run through the blockade in the Chesapeake." Many of the merchants whose ships were sitting in port had invested in privateers. And they were often, but not always, richly rewarded for their enterprise, which made up for the losses inflicted by the blockade.

BEFORE THE YEAR was out, word finally came of David Porter and the *Essex* in the form of two letters from him dated July 2 and 22, 1813. Desperate for relief from the steady stream of bad news, the president was quick to tout Porter's accomplishments. The *National Intelligencer* published his letters on December 16. They revealed that before reaching the coast of Brazil, Porter captured the British brig *Nocton*, carrying $55,000 in specie. But he missed Bainbridge at their places of rendezvous, the penultimate being St. Catherine's Island off the southern coast of Brazil. Instead of proceeding to cruise in the vicinity of St. Helena, the last rendezvous point, Porter sailed south around treacherous Cape Horn into the eastern Pacific, the first American warship to do so. (The *Essex* had also been the first to round the Cape of Good Hope during the Quasi-War with France.)

After navigating the horrendous seas off Cape Horn, Porter reached Valparaiso, where he obtained provisions and then embarked on a remarkably successful career of attacking the substantial British whaling fleet in the eastern Pacific, particularly around the Galapagos Islands. His letters reported that he captured twelve British whalers, delivering a catastrophic blow to their sizable whaling industry in that part of the world. All told, the British had twenty whalers

in the eastern Pacific. Those that survived Porter's rampage had to confine themselves to port. Most of the enemy whalers carried letter of marque papers and
were a threat to American whalers. Porter was thus protecting the American
fleet while he was destroying Britain's.

Porter was also occupying a number of warships that the Admiralty had sent
to find him. Two of them searched the eastern Pacific, the 36-gun frigate *Phoebe*,
under Captain James Hillyar, and the 18-gun sloop of war *Cherub*, under Captain
Thomas Tucker. The 26-gun *Racoon*, under Commander William Black, accompanied them as far as South America and then headed north along the Pacific
coast. Black's mission was to sail to the mouth of the Columbia River, destroy
John Jacob Astor's settlement at Astoria, and take possession of the whole area
in the name of His Majesty. When the *Racoon* arrived, Black discovered that
the Canadian Northwest Fur Company—after threatening that the Royal Navy
was on the way—had already purchased Astor's American Pacific Fur Company,
which included Fort Astoria and the surrounding settlement. Dispatching the
Racoon was more evidence of the Liverpool ministry's imperial ambitions
in America.

President Madison knew the British would be after Porter, and he was anxious
for his return. Madison needed all the heroes he could get. The war was going
far worse than he had ever imagined, and the British were giving no indication
they were willing to negotiate an end to it.

CHAPTER TWENTY

The Allies
and Napoleon

D ESPITE AMERICA'S MYRIAD setbacks in 1813, the British were not in a position to capitalize on them. As much as they wanted to smite the United
States, they had to bide their time and deal first with a still dangerous Napoleon
Bonaparte. The battle to prevent him from again becoming master of Europe
occupied them throughout the year. Only after the dictator's defeat at the Battle
of Leipzig in October 1813, and his subsequent retreat to France, did it appear
that his ambitions would be curbed. And even then, his demise was uncertain.

Although Britain's life hung in the balance on the European continent, the
prime minister still refused to rid himself of the unnecessary war with America.
Madison had made it plain that he was desperate for a settlement. The only remaining issue was impressment, and the president had promised guarantees that
British seamen would not be permitted to serve on either American warships
or merchantmen. Liverpool, however, refused to listen.

The prime minister's intransigence came from an underlying confidence
that Napoleon would be beaten and from the success of British arms in North
America. With the expenditure of few resources, Britain had frustrated Madison's
attempts to acquire Upper Canada, and the Royal Navy had tightened its blockade
of the American coast. Instead of feeling pressure to make peace with Madison,
Liverpool and his colleagues saw an opportunity to deal a crippling blow to what
they thought were the republic's maritime ambitions and, at the same time, to
massively expand the British Empire on the North American continent.

Once Napoleon's power was smashed, Liverpool intended to treat the United States as if Madison had been a poor imitation of the French dictator. The *Times* proclaimed that, "Whilst Bonaparte was at once invading Russia and Spain, the President thought it not a shame to imitate him by overrunning the Canadas and Florida." As far as the British were concerned, there would be no compromise with Madison, as there would be none with Napoleon. Liverpool wanted a free hand in North America to make certain that neither Canada nor Florida was in American hands, nor even Louisiana. The ministry consistently maintained that Jefferson's Louisiana Purchase had been illegal.

British ambitions in North America had to be put on hold, however, while they dealt with Napoleon. When 1813 began, it was not at all clear that he could be swept away. He was back in Paris assembling an impressive new army. Britain controlled the sea, but only Russia, in alliance with Prussia and Austria, could destroy Bonaparte's army. The czar was committed to doing so, but his troops needed time to rest. They had suffered mightily in the struggle to expel the French from their country. Kutuzov, the commander in chief, insisted that his men needed to recuperate. He was not anxious to plunge into Central Europe. He was content with having thrown Bonaparte out of Russia. Alexander, on the other hand, wanted to push west across the Niemen into Prussia and the Duchy of Warsaw while Napoleon was on the run. He was determined to drive on to Paris and destroy the dictator's regime. What Russia chose to do would determine if a resurgent Bonaparte could be defeated.

The world did not have to wait long for an answer. Ignoring Kutuzov's doubts, Alexander drove his army into East Prussia in late December 1812 and early January 1813, proclaiming that he had come as a liberator. Immediately, the Prussian king, Frederick William, moved to ally Prussia with Russia, and after some negotiation he signed an alliance on February 28. It was a major step forward. Already, part of Frederick William's army under General Yorck had deserted Napoleon and changed sides.

The key to defeating Bonaparte was now Austria. If she joined Russia, Prussia, and Great Britain, Napoleon might be destroyed. But it was unlikely that Austria would join the alliance, and even if she did, it was by no means certain that the allies could achieved the degree of cooperation necessary to defeat the new army Napoleon was raising.

By the beginning of March the armies of Alexander and Frederick William had liberated all of Prussia. A lull followed, as the allies rested their soldiers and prepared for the inevitable showdown with Napoleon. Meanwhile, Bonaparte's new army had swollen to 120,000, and he marched east beyond the Rhine into

Saxony, intending to destroy the allies before they got stronger. It looked as if Napoleon would repeat the brilliant victories of the past. He met the allied armies at Lutzen, southwest of Leipzig, on May 2. The Russians and Prussians combined had around 85,000 men. Not only did they have fewer troops than the French, but they did not have a battlefield commander who could compare with Bonaparte.

Demonstrating his tactical genius once more, Napoleon defeated the allies decisively. They suffered 20,000 casualties and were barely able to escape total ruin. The French had an equal number of killed and wounded, however, and unlike previous victories, Napoleon failed to pursue and deliver a final blow. Even though his raw recruits had fought well, he did not have the cavalry he once had. If he had, the defeat might have been fatal to the allies.

The allied armies were able to retreat east and cross the Elbe to Bautzen, where Napoleon attacked them again on May 20–21. Once again, he had an advantage in numbers. The allies had around 100,000 troops, and Napoleon, having received reinforcements from France after Lutzen, now had nearly 200,000. Bautzen was almost another Austerlitz. The allies were nearly annihilated, but thanks to Marshall Ney's blunders, they were able to escape final destruction. As they retreated east, Bonaparte's star appeared on the rise again. When word of Lutzen and Bautzen reached Washington during the summer, Madison was relieved and encouraged. His gamble on Bonaparte was still viable.

Instead of pressing his advantage at this point, Napoleon sent Caulaincourt to seek an armistice with Alexander, which the czar eagerly accepted. It lasted from June 4 to August 10. Napoleon's casualties in the two great battles had been exceedingly high, and he needed to rejuvenate his army, particularly the cavalry. He later admitted that agreeing to the armistice was a major blunder. Alexander and the Prussians needed a respite more than the French did. They had been bloodied and were on the brink of disaster. They desperately needed to reconstitute their armies.

The armistice was supposedly for the purpose of arranging a peace settlement, but both sides used it to prepare for a fight to the death. Austria had still not committed to the allies. Napoleon's fate would hang on what she chose to do. Bonaparte saw with great clarity that he needed to placate Austria and to divide Prussia from Russia. Whether he could do so was another matter.

Shortly after the armistice began, news came of Wellington's stunning victory at Vittoria on June 21. The great British general had finally defeated Joseph Bonaparte and sent the French army reeling back to the Pyrenees. The victory influenced Austria's decision to enter the war on the side of the allies, something

Prince Metternich, the powerful Austrian foreign minister, had been considering for some time. Convinced that Austria could only achieve her goals if Napoleon were defeated, Metternich joined the allies on August 12. He did so only after trying to convince Napoleon to accept a modest diminution of his power. Bonaparte refused. He deluded himself into thinking he was as potent as ever and would overcome his adversaries, as he had before. Metternich concluded that Napoleon would never accept a balance of power in Europe compatible with Austria's interests. Helping Metternich decide was Britain formally joining the alliance on July 9 and committing large subsidies to her allies. Napoleon's intransigence created the grand coalition that alone could defeat him.

During the armistice, the Russian army was rejuvenated. By August the combined allied armies, including Austria, were now over 500,000. Napoleon had roughly 400,000. But the allies did not have a general who could match Bonaparte; he was still master of the battlefield. Numbers alone would not determine who won. When the armies took the field again, they met at Dresden on August 26–27, and once again Napoleon was the victor, sending the Austrian-Russian army retreating back to Bohemia.

Napoleon sent General Vandamme in pursuit. He caught up with the enemy just across the Austrian border at the Bohemian town of Kulm, where on August 29–30, he unexpectedly suffered a stunning defeat. The victory restored allied morale. Napoleon's generals suffered other losses in separate battles as well. On August 23, Marshall Oudinot was beaten at Grossbeeren by Bernadotte (Sweden's ruler, who was part of the alliance against Napoleon). Oudinot had been trying to attack Berlin. On August 26, Prussian General Blucher defeated Marshall Macdonald at Katzback; on August 27, General Major von Hirschfeld defeated General Girard at Hagelberg; and on September 6, General von Bulow defeated Marshall Ney at Dennewitz. Together these defeats administered a crushing blow to Napoleon. He had now lost over 100,000 men in the various battles, and he could not easily replace them. The allies, on the other hand, were having no trouble replenishing their ranks.

The armies rested during September and met again at Leipzig, where Napoleon had taken part of his army for tactical reasons but became trapped with an army half the size of the allies who closed in on him from the north and the south. The Battle of Leipzig took place October 16–18. The fighting was intense, and in the end Napoleon, with only 160,000 men, could not prevail against the allies, who had 320,000. During the night of October 18, his dispirited troops retreated out of Leipzig toward Mainz on the Rhine River, heading home to France. On the morning of October 19, when the bloodied allies discovered that the French had left the city, there was wild rejoicing, despite both sides having lost an astounding 120,000 men killed or wounded. The French may have sustained as many as 60,000 casualties.

Leipzig sounded the death knell for Napoleon, but he could not hear the sound. Unable to admit defeat, he intended to fight on, imagining he could still overcome his opponents. The allies were not able to cut him off before he reached the French border, condemning Europe to more weeks of suffering. On November 2 he crossed the Rhine at Mainz and rode into France. Europe east of the Rhine was now liberated, but no one doubted that when Bonaparte reached Paris, he would raise another army of conscripts and attempt another comeback.

ON DECEMBER 30, 1813, His Majesty's packet *Bramble*, under Lieutenant Pogson, arrived at Annapolis, Maryland, from Plymouth, England, with the momentous news: Napoleon had suffered a near fatal blow at Leipzig and had barely made it back to France. The *Bramble* also carried a letter from Castlereagh proposing direct negotiations between Britain and America without Russian mediation. The note was addressed to Secretary of State Monroe and dated November 4—after Castlereagh knew the outcome of Leipzig. Monroe immediately wrote back on January 5, 1814, accepting the offer.

Madison's swift approval of Castlereagh's proposal spoke loudly of how well the British were doing in America, and how desperate the president was to end the war. Liverpool and Castlereagh were confident that in any negotiation with Madison, they would dictate the terms. And although they had proposed talks, they were in no hurry to begin them until victories on the battlefield gave them the upper hand. The *Bramble* departed Annapolis on January 12 with Monroe's reply, arriving in London three weeks later. Liverpool and Castlereagh were pleased with Madison's acceptance and his unseemly haste.

The president moved quickly to augment his negotiating team. He added Jonathan Russell and Henry Clay to work with Bayard and Adams. Clay was particularly important as a symbol to the West and the South that their interests would be protected in the peace treaty. The president also reappointed Gallatin when he found out he intended to remain in Europe and not return to the Treasury. Admiral Cockburn issued a passport for Clay and Russell to travel to Europe, and on February 26, 1814, they sailed from New York on the *John Adams*.

At the beginning of 1814, things looked bleaker than ever for Madison. Repeated defeats along the Canadian border, except for Lake Erie, had undermined his hopes for a satisfactory peace. In addition, recruiting was going poorly. He had no hope of instituting conscription. Congress would never approve it. Militias from the New England states refused to march across the border into Canada, and money was hard to come by. Congress would not support a national bank or raise taxes enough to fund the war, and Federalist moneymen would not lend the president the money he needed to fight.

The British, on the other hand, were enormously gratified by their successes in Canada. They considered the defeat on Lake Erie an anomaly that would quickly be reversed. The future for Britain on the North American continent looked exceedingly bright.

Napoleon remained to be dealt with, of course, but optimism in London about finally destroying him was growing. He had returned to Paris in November 1813 and, as expected, immediately set about trying to raise another army of 300,000. At the same time, he held out to the allies the possibility of negotiations, and they responded on November 9 with a generous peace plan known as the Frankfurt Proposals. If accepted, they would allow Bonaparte to keep his throne, provided he evacuated the areas of Europe he still held, like Hamburg, and agreed to accept the "natural frontiers" of France, which meant withdrawing behind the Rhine, the Alps, and the Pyrenees. He would retain Belgium, the left bank of the Rhine, Savoy, and Nice. Napoleon rejected the offer out of hand.

Liverpool and Castlereagh were relieved. Their ambassador to Austria, the young Earl of Aberdeen, had approved the proposals, but the ministry was horrified by them. Liverpool and his colleagues wanted to get rid of Napoleon completely, and they wanted France's frontiers pushed back to what they were prior to 1792. In their view, Europe would never have peace as long as Napoleon was on the French throne. Aberdeen's misstep moved Castlereagh to take over British leadership on the continent personally, with important consequences not only for Britain but for Napoleon, the allies, the Bourbons, and America.

Before driving onto Paris and delivering the final blow to Bonaparte, the allies issued a declaration that the boundaries of France would be returned to those existing in 1792. It was not meant as an offer to Napoleon, but even if it had been, he would have scorned it. Returning to those boundaries would have meant that the size of France had been reduced while he was in power, a prospect that was anathema to him. Losing more contact with reality by the day, he fought on, believing he could still win. He was able to raise less than 100,000 men, however, while the allied armies gathering along the French border totaled over 400,000. The czar, who had never liked the Frankfurt Proposals either, wanted to get on with the march to Paris and dictate terms, as did some of the Prussians like General Blucher. By this time, Wellington was established in the south of France with an army of 80,000. He had consistently pursued a generous policy toward the French people and was warmly received in most places.

Napoleon tried to summon the patriotic spirit of the nation, hoping he could convince the French to fight a partisan war, as the Spanish had against him. "The whole nation will be under arms," he promised Caulaincourt. "We shall have to come to the enemy's rescue to stop the violence; they will slaughter everything that has a foreign look to it." But he was dreaming. The French people no longer supported him. They had had enough of heavy-handed government, excessive taxation, being deprived of free speech and political rights, and most of all, having their youths harvested three times a year to be consumed in endless war. Instead of support, Bonaparte found widespread hatred of him and his regime. Thousands of young men fled the country to avoid conscription.

It took some time for the allies to mount a successful drive on Paris, however. They had great difficulty working in harness. Their squabbling added considerably to Napoleon's chances for survival. Even with his small army of 70,000, he went on the attack and won a series of battles in February 1814 against the Prussians and the Austrians fighting separately. He did so well that Austria was on the verge of pulling her army back beyond the French border. Castlereagh's timely intervention kept them in the fight and prevented the alliance from splitting apart. In the end, Bonaparte's obstinate resistance forced the allies to bury their differences and continue working together. On March 9 they signed the Treaty of Chaumont, pledging to fight until France was reduced to her prerevolutionary boundaries.

As the allied armies closed in on Paris during the last two weeks of March, the French vigorously defended their capital, but they were overwhelmed and forced to surrender on March 30. Napoleon wasn't there; he had already left Paris to continue the fight.

The following day Alexander and Frederick William rode into the city in triumph. As they did, demonstrations in favor of Louis XVIII broke out. Talleyrand had organized them to show Alexander, who detested the Bourbons, that the people wanted the monarchy restored. Behind the scenes, Castlereagh gave tacit support to Talleyrand's efforts. The *Times* reported approvingly that "the cry of Vive Louis XVIII is heard everywhere." Meanwhile, Napoleon continued to believe that all was not lost. He tried to resume the struggle from Fontainebleau, but his marshals would have no more, and on April 11 he finally abdicated unconditionally.

In a few days, he began his journey from Fontainebleau to St. Raphael on the Mediterranean, where the British frigate *Undaunted* waited to take him to

Elba. The trip was one of the most dangerous of his life. Only the skill and bravery of his guards saved him from being torn to pieces by his own people. He managed to reach his destination, however, and Europeans, including the French, celebrated his departure. In London, the *Times* reported "heartfelt and universal joy." In America, however, the mood was more mixed. Thomas Jefferson wrote to John Adams, "I own that, while I rejoice, for the good of mankind, to the deliverance of Europe from the havoc which would have never ceased while Bonaparte should have lived in power, I see with anxiety the tyrant of the ocean remaining in vigor, and even participating in the merit of crushing his brother tyrant."

Britain's celebratory mood did not lessen her commitment to throttle the United States. "The reinforcements for North America all sailed last week," the *Times* noted with approval on April 11. The troops were expected to rendezvous at Bermuda and then sail to the St. Lawrence and Quebec. Four days later the *Times* wrote, "There is no public feeling in this country stronger than indignation against the Americans." It accused Madison of attempting "to consummate the ruin of Britain." "The American government," it cried, "is in point of fact as much of a tyranny . . . as that of Bonaparte. . . . It has already indulged in something more than dreams of the most unmeasured ambition. . . . [It seeks to] sap the foundations of our maritime greatness . . . seize our possessions on mainland America and later in the West Indies."

The *Morning Post* had been using even more extravagant language for months, calling the American government "unprincipled" and "contemptible." The *Courier* was equally vicious.

One would have thought that after more than twenty-two years of war, the British people, and especially their army and navy, were entitled to some relief. Instead, the Liverpool government intended to turn their war machine against the United States and cut her down to size. The *Times* wrote that substantial numbers of troops in France would be "immediately transferred to America."

In all the excitement over Napoleon's downfall, the Liverpool ministry— and indeed the country—were overly sanguine about how easily Europe's boundaries could be redrawn. Fundamental differences existed among the greater and lesser powers about what the new Europe should look like. Allied unity had been possible only because of a common enemy, and even then, getting the great powers to work together had been exceptionally difficult. Once Bonaparte was removed, ancient rivalries were bound to surface. Rearranging the European map might absorb as much of Britain's energy as Napoleon had. For the moment, however, intoxicated with success, the British minimized Europe's problems and fixated on curbing America's power.

MADISON RECEIVED WORD of Napoleon's demise in the middle of May and with it news that he had long feared—a huge British army was on the way to North America via Bermuda. The war that he had undertaken to insure free trade and sailors' rights was about to become one to save the United States, and in that sense it would be a second war of independence.

CHAPTER TWENTY-ONE

British and American War Plans

T HE LIVERPOOL MINISTRY'S plan of attack against the United States had been developing for weeks before Napoleon's abdication, but it could not be implemented until Bonaparte was packed off to Elba in April 1814. Once that event actually occurred, the prime minister and his colleagues intended to divert forces from Europe to smash the incipient power of the United States. They wanted to regain Britain's position as the dominant power on the North American continent and crush a bothersome maritime rival.

Their grandiose strategy included two major invasions of the United States—one from Canada and the other from New Orleans. Simultaneously, large-scale raids would be conducted along the Atlantic seaboard to act as diversions, and the blockade would be tightened from the Canadian border to Louisiana. The goal was to wrest the Louisiana Territory, including West Florida, from the United States and unite it with both Canada and the newly acquired base at Astoria on the Pacific coast. At the same time, Liverpool intended to further dismember the United States by encouraging New England to break away from the Union and either join Canada or become independent and by creating a huge Indian buffer state north and west of the Ohio River.

Liverpool's basic policy in America differed markedly from the one he and Castlereagh pursued in Europe, where they sought to restore a balance of power that would prevent a single country from gaining dominance, as Napoleon had, and directly threatening British security. In America their policy was to reassert dominance on the continent through the acquisition of territory. The central question, as Castlereagh put it later to Liverpool, was "Is it desirable to take the chance of the campaign, and then to be governed by circumstances? If the latter is advisable, we have the means of doing so." Being governed by circumstances meant taking advantage of opportunities presented by the military campaigns to be waged in North America during the spring, summer, and fall of 1814.

Although Liverpool's goals were extensive, they were also flexible. He could extend or contract them as the success of British arms warranted. Realities on the ground would ultimately determine the extent of his demands at the negotiating table. In the spring of 1814, with British hubris soaring after the great victory over Napoleon, the prime minister's expectations were high indeed.

On April 22, 1814, Albert Gallatin was in London witnessing the effect of Napoleon's abdication on Britain, and he was understandably concerned. He sent a letter to Henry Clay in Gothenburg, Sweden, analyzing why the British cabinet was adding substantially to its land and sea forces in North America instead of settling the war with the United States. "A well organized and large army is at once liberated from any European employment, and ready, together with a super abundant naval force to act immediately against us," he wrote. Gallatin was careful to point out that the Liverpool ministry "profess to be disposed to make an equitable peace." But the sheer weight of opinion in Britain, he thought, might move them in the opposite direction. "The hope not of ultimate conquest but of a dissolution of the union, the convenient pretense which the American war will afford to preserve large military establishments, and above all the force of popular feeling may all unite in inducing the Cabinet in throwing impediments in the way of peace. . . . That the war is popular, and that national pride inflated by the last unexpected success cannot be satisfied without what they call the chastisement of America, cannot be doubted."

Gallatin underestimated the extent of the cabinet's plans for North America. His portrayal of the ministers as reasonable men carried away by public opinion was inaccurate. Liverpool and his colleagues were as much caught up in the spirit of the moment as the rest of the country.

The euphoria of the spring and early summer led Liverpool to expect operations in America to be completed in a relatively short time. After fighting the French for twenty-two years, a long-term commitment of massive forces in North America would be too onerous for already overburdened British taxpayers. Liverpool expected that Madison would cave in quickly. British newspapers like the *Times* were constantly pointing out how weak American finances were, how difficult it was for Madison to increase the army and navy, and how divided the country was. Liverpool and Castlereagh also assumed that sufficient harmony existed among the European powers to make a peace settlement on the continent relatively easy to arrange, freeing their hand in North America.

Dispatching the land and sea forces necessary to carry out the ministry's ambitious strategy required time, however. Although plans for operations in America had been developing since November, nothing could be done until Napoleon actually abdicated, which did not occur until the second week of April. Assembling the troops necessary for the invasion of America and then transporting them would take weeks. The earliest the expeditionary forces would reach Bermuda and Canada was the summer.

Also, the number of troops that would be available was limited by conditions in Europe. Although Liverpool and Castlereagh were optimistic in the spring of 1814 about prospects of an early and satisfactory settlement in Europe, they still had to wait for it to happen before they diverted too many troops to North America. They were confident enough, however, to begin dispatching veterans from Wellington's army in France before a settlement in Europe was finalized. They were taking a big chance, but their confidence in the spring was so strong they were willing to assume the risk.

It is not surprising that the forces they actually dispatched were small, given their expectations. The hubris of the cabinet was so high the ministers vastly underestimated how many troops it would take to cow a nation of nearly eight million, divided though she might be. Only 13,000 were dispatched to Canada, bringing the total of British regulars there to 29,000. Of these, 3,000 were sent from Portsmouth and Cork in May, but the bulk of them, some 10,000, would come from Wellington's veterans in France. They would be sent later in June from Bordeaux and ports on the Mediterranean to Canada, traveling first to Bermuda and then to Quebec under their own generals. These troops and their officers were Wellington's best, but they had been fighting in the Iberian Peninsula and France for seven years without relief. By the time they reached Quebec they were not the crack troops they had once been.

To conduct raids along the American seacoast the ministry thought in terms of 4,000 to 5,000 men, and to invade New Orleans they planned to use the men conducting the seacoast raids and add enough troops to bring the total to 10,000. Thus, for the invasion of a country as large as the United States, they planned to use a tired army of fewer than 35,000. Of course, these forces could be augmented as the need arose, but London did not think that would be necessary.

The army Liverpool was sending was considerably smaller than George III had dispatched in 1775 and 1776 to subdue the colonies when their population was no more than two and a half million. In 1776 the number of British troops sent to occupy New York City alone had been over 30,000. An additional 8,000 had been in Canada, poised to invade, and 4,000 more had been on troop transports off the Carolinas preparing to subdue the South, bringing the total of the king's forces in America in 1776 to over 42,000.

Changing from defense to offense against America in 1814 required new leadership. On November 4, 1813, when the results of the Battle of Leipzig were first becoming known in London, and the British believed their long battle with Napoleon was finally coming to an end, the Admiralty decided to recall Admiral Sir John Borlase Warren and replace him with fifty-six-year-old Vice Admiral Alexander F. I. Cochrane. The son of a Scottish peer and a longtime navy veteran, Cochrane had plenty of experience during the American Revolutionary War and in the West Indies, where he was commander in chief on the Leeward Islands Station and governor of Guadeloupe. The Admiralty expected him to act far more aggressively along the Atlantic coast than Warren had and to invade New Orleans. Cochrane's fleet captain would be Trafalgar hero Edward Codrington.

Cochrane received his orders on January 25, 1814. After long discussions with Lord Melville (First Lord of the Admiralty) in London, Cochrane sailed for Bermuda, arriving on March 6 raring to go. His assumption of command was delayed for a month, however, until Admiral Warren finally departed on April 1. To make effective use of Cochrane, the Admiralty relieved him of some administrative responsibilities that had burdened Warren. Cochrane's new command was limited to the North American coast. The Jamaica and Leeward Islands Stations were once again separated, and Admiral Yeo was given an independent command on the lakes. To further support Cochrane, Rear Admiral Edward Griffith would direct the fleet from Nantucket to the St. Lawrence River. At the time the British were making these changes they were feeling an extravagant sense of their power, and they expected spectacular results. Cochrane understood the optimism in London. He wrote to Bathurst, "I have it much at heart to give them a complete drubbing before peace is made, when I trust their northern limits will be circumscribed and the command of the Mississippi wrested from them."

Cochrane was expected to work closely with Major General Robert Ross—one of Wellington's best generals—who would command the troops raiding the eastern seaboard as well as direct land operations against New Orleans. Ross departed Bordeaux with his soldiers on June 2, 1814, and reached Bermuda on July 25.

Governor General Prevost and Admiral Yeo were not replaced, however. They were expected to direct the land and naval offensives from Canada, even though they had shown no capacity for offensive operations in the preceding months nor even an ability to work together. Nonetheless, Prevost was expected to attack Sackets Harbor, the Champlain Valley, and possibly the Hudson Valley. Success, it was thought, would protect Canada from another American invasion, while encouraging New England to break away from the Union, and justify a radical adjustment of Canada's boundary southward.

WHILE LIVERPOOL AND his colleagues had a clear idea of the North American strategy they intended to pursue in the spring of 1814, President Madison, uncertain about British plans, was in a quandary. He hoped that faced with the monumental task of redrawing the map of Europe, Liverpool would end the war with America on reasonable terms. But that did not appear to be happening. Even though Castlereagh had proposed direct negotiations and Madison had accepted, the president was fearful that Liverpool was bent on achieving stunning military victories before undertaking any serious talks. Madison responded to the potential threat by continuing to attack Canada and hoping that meaningful negotiations would begin soon.

Thus, in the winter and spring of 1814, while London waited for Napoleon's final capitulation, Madison continued with his quixotic campaign against Canada. As had been the case during the previous two years, however, neither the army nor the navy was strong enough to accomplish the president's goals. In January, what remained of the army of the north was at Detroit and Amherstburg, under Lieutenant Colonel George Groghan, and at French Mills, New York, under General James Wilkinson. Bitter cold, poor food, inadequate clothing, filthy camps, and uncontrolled disease, especially dysentery, plagued Wilkinson soldiers. At the end of January, Secretary Armstrong ordered him to send Jacob Brown with 2,000 men to Sackets Harbor and march the rest of his army to Plattsburgh, where the troops could find some relief.

Wilkinson knew he was going to be cashiered for the disasters of the previous year. He spent the next few weeks recuperating and planning an action that might retrieve some of his lost reputation, perhaps even allow him to keep his job. On March 27, in what can only be described as a bizarre stunt, he marched 4,000 men and eleven pieces of artillery five miles across the Canadian border to attack a tiny British outpost at Lacolle Mill. It took three difficult days of plodding through deep snow and getting lost before he found his way to a giant, fortress-like millhouse made of thick stone and defended by 180 men. Wilkinson tried blasting them out with heavy guns, but the building remained intact. The British garrison at Isle aux Noix was ten miles away, and it attempted a rescue, but Brigadier General Alexander Macomb's brigade turned it back in some sharp fighting. Instead of then besieging the millhouse with his overwhelming numbers, Wilkinson called off the attack and marched back to Plattsburgh.

Eleven days later, he learned that Major General Ralph Izard would relieve him. Wilkinson claimed he was being persecuted. Actually, replacing him was part of a long overdue change in the army's leadership. The president and the secretary of war wanted generals who could perform better than relics like Wilkinson, Hampton, Hull, Dearborn, Boyd, and Morgan Lewis. Armstrong advised that the new leaders be appointed regardless of seniority. The president agreed, and he promoted two brigadier generals, Izard and Jacob Brown, to major general and six colonels to brigadier general: Winfield Scott, Alexander Macomb, Thomas Smith, Daniel Bissell, Edmund Gaines, and Eleazer E. Ripley. William Henry Harrison, pressured by Armstrong, resigned in May, opening up a slot for Brigadier General Andrew Jackson to become a major general. Peter B. Porter replaced Amos Hall as head of the New York militia. The average age for generals in the U. S. Army was now thirty-six instead of sixty. For the first time in the war, the army had leadership that was as good as the navy's. Madison and Armstrong also created a general staff for the army that markedly improved the efficiency of the War Department.

To further strengthen the army, Congress approved Madison's request to raise enlistment bounties to a whopping $124, plus 320 acres of land. As a result, the recruitment of regulars for five years or until the end of the war increased significantly. By the spring of 1814, the army had risen to 40,000 men, and by the end of the year to nearly 45,000. The president retained Armstrong, however, even though the secretary bore a major part of the responsibility for the failures of the previous year. Madison wasn't happy with him, but he evidently thought replacing him was more bother than it was worth.

GAINING NAVAL SUPREMACY on lakes Ontario and Champlain was as essential, in Madison's view, as reinvigorating the army. Secretary Jones spared no effort to carry out the president's policy, but he thought the forces building on the lakes should be part of a defensive, rather than an offensive, strategy. He did not think it wise, given the government's limited resources, to continue attacking Canada. He urged that emphasis be placed on the oceans, "where twenty of his ships cannot check the depredations of one of our ships or prevent the capture of his single ships." Secretary Armstrong disagreed; he wanted to move aggressively against

Canada. He continued to support attacking Kingston as a prelude to moving on Montreal, but if that failed, he was open to making an effort in the Niagara area and farther west with a view to acquiring all of Upper Canada. The administration gave little thought to defending the eastern seaboard against attacks.

Secretary Jones wrote to Commodore Chauncey on January 15, 1814, emphasizing again the president's urgent desire to obtain supremacy on Lake Ontario. "Every possible resource and effort must be directed to the creation of such a force at Sackets Harbor as will enable you to meet the enemy on the Lake the moment he may appear, and with means competent to ensure success."

Jones also urged Master Commandant Macdonough to do whatever was necessary to regain supremacy on Lake Champlain so that he "could meet the enemy on the first opening of navigation." Macdonough had a monumental task ahead of him. At the end of December 1813 he had only the 6-gun sloop *President*, the 7-gun sloop *Preble*, and the 7-gun sloop *Montgomery*, along with four gunboats carrying one long eighteen-pounder each. The British had four men-of-war at Isle aux Noix, including two captured the year before. The ships were small, the largest carried only 13 guns, but Commander Daniel Pring was building the 16-gun *Niagara* (renamed *Linnet*). Pring, who had been Yeo's flag captain in the *Wolfe*, was appointed commander of the Lake Champlain fleet in July 1813. He was one of the better officers in the Royal Navy.

To help Yeo win the arms races on both lakes, and to restore British supremacy on Lake Erie, the Admiralty sent him sailors, ships in frame, shipwrights, dockhands, guns, ammunition, and naval stores. The added resources were having an effect. During the winter of 1813–14, Chauncey fell seriously behind in the "war of the dockyards," as the great Canadian scholar Robert Malcomson called it. The energy and optimism that had marked Chauncey's work when he first arrived at Sackets Harbor in the fall of 1812 had considerably diminished. He estimated that it would not be until July that he had supremacy again on Lake Ontario.

During the winter, Yeo raced ahead at Kingston, building the 58-gun *Prince Regent*, the 40-gun *Princess Charlotte*, and three gunboats, *Crysler*, *Queenston*, and *Niagara*. Three more would come later. To help man them, the Admiralty sent seven hundred ten seamen and a battalion of marines—a considerable reinforcement. The ice broke on Lake Ontario the first of April, and two weeks later Yeo's ships and crews were ready to fight.

At Sackets Harbor, on the other hand, Henry Eckford and his men did not begin construction on new ships until January. He was building two brigs, the 20-gun *Jefferson*, under Master Commandant Melancthon Woolsey, and the 20-gun *Jones*, under Master Commandant Charles Ridgely. Both were launched the second week of April. Eckford was also building the 58-gun *Superior* and the 42-gun *Mohawk*. When completed, Chauncey would have unquestioned supremacy on Lake Ontario, but the *Superior* was not even launched until the first of May and the *Mohawk* not until the eleventh of June.

Obtaining enough men remained a problem for Chauncey. Madison tried to help by signing a law increasing wages for service on the lakes by 25 percent and increasing the bounty by a third. On March 7 the commodore wrote to Jones, "The increase pay and bounty I think will insure men for this service, and in fact they deserve it for they suffer much beyond what anyone can form an idea of unless they witness it—we seldom have less than 20 percent of our whole number sick and sometimes 30 percent—within three days we have buried seven marines out of a corps of 180 and have this day on the sick report of the same corps 40—and our seamen in nearly the same proportion." The commodore's own health was being compromised by long service on the lake, just as Oliver Hazard Perry's had been on Lake Erie.

IN PURSUANCE OF Secretary Armstrong's orders, General Brown split off from Wilkinson's army and marched west to Sackets Harbor with 2,000 men, arriving on February 16, 1814. In early March Brown received orders from Armstrong indicating he wanted to attack Kingston as soon as practicable. A direct attack on Montreal was ruled out because it was thought to be too strong. Moving on Kingston proved impossible, however. The mildness of the winter made traveling across the ice too hazardous, and Chauncey would not be ready with his fleet until July at the earliest.

Unable to attack Kingston, Brown marched west to Buffalo. He was under the impression that Armstrong wanted him to move to the Niagara area, but the secretary had intended only to make a feint in that direction. Nonetheless, when Armstrong discovered Brown had traveled west, he approved the move. General Brown waited at Buffalo for further orders, and his subordinate Winfield Scott trained the troops, something they badly needed.

At this point, the president still did not have a clear idea of how he was going to proceed. British forces in Canada were still relatively weak, and Madison continued to support an invasion, but without a definite plan. In the absence of a clear overall strategy, Armstrong, without the administration giving any thought to it, shifted the focus of the invasion west to the Niagara River, a peripheral area, when Kingston and Montreal were the original and more logical targets.

WHEN THE *Prince Regent* and *Princess Charlotte* were finished in Kingston the third week of April, Admiral Yeo and Lieutenant General Gordon Drummond prepared to attack Sackets Harbor, but Prevost, judging the defenses to be too strong, restrained them. Yeo and Drummond then looked for an easier target and decided to attack Oswego, through which Chauncey routed nearly all his supplies.

On May 5, the British fleet suddenly hove into view off the beach at Oswego, where U.S. Army Colonel George Mitchell prepared hurriedly to fight with only 290 men. Yeo opened fire on the American defenses a mile from shore. At the same time, he deployed fifteen boats loaded with troops. As they approached the beach, Mitchell's accurate artillery fire created so much havoc the boats turned around and went back to the ships. Undeterred, Yeo attacked again the next morning. His flagship *Wolfe* pounded Mitchell's batteries and the fort, while his huge landing force of as many as 1,000 rowed once more toward the beach.

After putting up what fight he could against overwhelming odds, Mitchell retreated in good order to Oswego Falls, twelve miles up the Oswego River, and prepared to defend the important supply depot there. For some unknown reason Yeo did not follow. Instead, he settled for capturing the schooner *Penelope*, a supply vessel that was sitting in the harbor with a cargo of three long thirty-two-pounders and two long twenty-four-pounders; two bateaux with a cargo of one thirty-two-pounder and one twenty-four-pounder; some ordinance; naval stores; a large quantity of rope; and 2,600 barrels of flour, pork, salt, and bread. Yeo overlooked the far more important heavy guns, cables, and other supplies at Oswego Falls. Had he captured those, Chauncey's shipbuilding would have been set back weeks. Secretary Jones wrote to the president that had the enemy destroyed what was at Oswego Falls, "the consequences would be disastrous indeed."

The following week Yeo began blockading Sackets Harbor. Chauncey was convinced that if the British had launched an attack right then, they would have taken the shipyard. "If Sir James had landed 3000 men when he first appeared off this harbor and made a simultaneous attack with the fleet," Chauncey wrote to Jones, "he must have carried the place, for our new vessels (with the exception of the *Jefferson*) at that time were without their armament and the military force had been considerably weakened by five hundred of the best troops being ordered from this place to Buffalo and a few days ago about seven hundred more marched in the same direction." General Brown, who was in charge of the army defending Sackets Harbor, strongly disagreed; he thought the defenses were more than adequate. He had placed General Gaines in command with 1,500 troops, and he thought Gaines had the matter well in hand. Yeo must have concluded the same thing, for he did not attack. Chauncey had a bad habit of overestimating the enemy's strength and underestimating his own.

Avoiding Yeo's blockade was a constant problem for Master Commandant Melancthon Woolsey, who was in charge of moving heavy guns and other essential equipment and provisions from Oswego to Sackets Harbor. Woolsey ran bateaux at night along the coast, hugging the shore. On May 28, nineteen bateaux, carrying twenty-one thirty-two-pounders, thirteen smaller guns, and ten heavy cables, silently moved out of the Oswego River for the trip. One of the bateaux lost its way, however, and fell into British hands. A captured sailor was forced to reveal details of the shipment. Yeo immediately dispatched Commander Stephen Popham with two hundred men to seize it. On May 30 Popham attacked Woolsey's remaining eighteen boats at Sandy Creek, twenty miles north of the Oswego and thirty miles south of Sackets Harbor.

Commander Popham was in for a surprise, however. Woolsey had laid a clever trap. Major Daniel Appling of the U.S. Army, with 120 men and an equal number of Oneida Indians, supported by cavalry and light artillery that Chauncey provided when he learned what was afoot, waited for Popham and attacked when he least expected it. In the ensuing melee, Popham lost 14 men and had 28 wounded before he surrendered. Appling captured 6 Royal Navy officers, 55 sailors and marines, and 106 soldiers. He also took two gunboats and five barges. The defeat induced more caution in Yeo; he could ill afford to lose either the men or the boats.

On June 6 Yeo returned to Kingston with his fleet. He was building the gargantuan 102-gun *St. Lawrence*, and he decided to wait for her to be completed and for more reinforcements from England before he attacked Chauncey. Drummond agreed that a delay was in order. Until Chauncey launched the *Mohawk* and the *Superior*, however, Yeo still had command of the lake. Drummond could move men and equipment wherever he pleased, and the Americans could not.

WHILE YEO WAS concentrating on Lake Ontario, he neglected Lake Champlain. He used the new powers the Admiralty had given him to command all the operations on the lakes to put the lion's share of his resources into building the *St. Lawrence*. His fixation with the giant ship drained men and materiel away from Commander Pring's operation on Lake Champlain. Yeo had done the same thing to Barclay on Lake Erie the previous year, depriving him of the resources needed to compete with Perry. Pring continued to build at Isle aux Noix but not with the speed that would have allowed him to keep ahead of Macdonough. Yeo's obsession also allowed Chauncey to regain superiority on Lake Ontario the first week of August, when the *Mohawk* and *Superior* were finally finished. Even by that time, the *St. Lawrence* was not yet launched. It would not be until September 10, and it would not be ready to sail until October 16, just as the season was ending.

Meanwhile, Master Commandant Macdonough was working hard preparing his fleet at Vergennes, Vermont, twenty-two miles south of Burlington and approximately fifty miles from Plattsburg. He had moved his squadron to Vergennes in December 1813 and had established a secure dockyard on Otter Creek, one of the state's largest rivers. The facility was situated at the head of navigation, seven miles from the mouth of the creek. Timber resources were plentiful, and Vergennes had a blast furnace, an air furnace, eight forges, a rolling mill, a wire factory, a grist mill, and a mill for fulling cloth.

Macdonough's biggest problem continued to be a lack of seamen. Even with added bonuses and more pay, finding sailors was difficult. Recruiting offices were opened in Boston and New York, but the bounties now being offered for service in the army, the attraction of privateers, the high price of clothing (which seamen had to pay for themselves), and little prospect of prize money on Lake Champlain continued to make recruiting slow. While Macdonough waited for sailors, he asked the army to fill the gap. General Izard loaned him 250 soldiers until more seamen arrived.

Macdonough was competing for resources with Chauncey, just as Pring was with Yeo. Fortunately, Secretary Jones had a higher appreciation of the critical needs on Lake Champlain than the Admiralty did. Jones induced Noah Brown and his brother Adam, the shipbuilders who had worked miracles for Perry on Lake Erie, to do the same at Vergennes. They arrived in February 1814 and went right to work. By March 2, two new gunboats were in the water, and a 26-gun ship, the *Saratoga*, was begun. By March 7 her keel had been laid, and on April 11 she was launched—a remarkable feat. The ship's timber had been standing in the forest less than six weeks before.

By April 2 Lake Champlain was free of ice, and Macdonough had to worry about Pring destroying his operation before the American force got too powerful. Macdonough erected strong defenses along Otter Creek and at its mouth. He received support from Brigadier General Macomb at Burlington and General Izard at Plattsburgh. Federalist governor Chittenden of Vermont also helped. Chittenden did not approve of the war, but he was willing to call out the Vermont militia to defend Vergennes. He sent 1,000 men to guard Otter Creek and another 500 to strengthen Macomb at Burlington.

On May 9 Commander Pring went after Macdonough, standing out from the Isle aux Noir with the new 16-gun *Linnet*, five sloops, thirteen galleys, and a bomb vessel. Five days later, he appeared off Otter Creek, where he planned to create an impassable obstruction by sinking two sloops in its mouth. Macdonough had been aware of Pring's movements for days, and he was waiting for him with seven long twelve-pounders and one fieldpiece posted on the high ground overlooking the entrance to the creek. He also had ten galleys strung across its mouth.

Pring's bomb vessel and eight galleys tested the creek's defenses, exchanging fire with the shore batteries for an hour and a half before it became obvious that Macdonough was too strong; Pring had no hope of putting obstructions at the mouth of the creek, so he withdrew. A short time later, observers at Burlington saw the British squadron sailing northward.

Thanks to the Browns, by May 30 Macdonough's fleet was superior to the British squadron. He assembled his ships at the mouth of Otter Creek—the 26-gun *Saratoga*, the 16-gun schooner *Ticonderoga*, the 10-gun sloop *President*, the 9-gun sloop *Preble*, the 6-gun sloop *Montgomery*, and six galleys with two guns each. The *Ticonderoga* was a former steamboat that the Browns had converted into a schooner, launching her on May 12, two days before Pring's attack. Two weeks later, Macdonough sailed north toward the Canadian border and the Richelieu River with his entire squadron, forcing Pring to move his vessels back to the safety of the Isle aux Noix.

Macdonough then moved his fleet to Plattsburg, anchoring in the bay on the twenty-ninth. Oliver Hazard Perry and Isaac Hull sent letters wishing him good luck with his mission. Macdonough was confident in his squadron. He wrote to Secretary Jones, "I find the *Saratoga* to be a fine ship." And he told Izard that his men-of-war were "remarkably fine vessels." He also informed the general that "the squadron is ready for service."

Pring was not sitting idle, however. Macdonough soon discovered the enterprising British commander had started a crash program to build the giant 37-gun frigate *Confiance*. In addition, eleven galleys had arrived at the Isle aux Noix from Quebec. With the new ship and boats the British would dominate the lake again. On June 11 Macdonough warned Jones of the imminent danger and requested funds to build another warship. Knowing how strapped the navy was for money, Jones hesitated. The president intervened, however, and ordered the ship built. Macdonough directed the Browns to start the 20-gun *Eagle* immediately, hoping it would be finished in time to help deal with the *Confiance*. Work went ahead at a furious pace, but the delay was potentially fatal.

Macdonough now returned to Pointe aux Fer just above Chazy, where he could watch the Richelieu River, remaining there until the end of August. His blockade materially slowed progress on the *Confiance*, when he captured three parties of Vermont traitors attempting to run a mainmast, three topmasts, and other spars to the Isle aux Noix, along with twenty-seven barrels of tar.

The Browns continued working hard on the *Eagle*. They did not begin until July 23, but they launched her in record time on August 11. And on August 27 she joined Macdonough, who by that time was back in Plattsburgh Bay.

Two days before the *Eagle* joined Macdonough, on August 25, Pring launched the *Confiance*. When she was in the water, Admiral Yeo decided that in spite of Commander Pring's excellent record, a higher ranking officer should be in charge at the Isle aux Noix, and he sent Captain Peter Fisher from Kingston. Pring remained as his second. The sudden, ill-thought-out change in command would have important consequences.

MEANWHILE, ON MAY 14–15 at Presque Isle on Lake Erie, Captain Arthur Sinclair—the new naval commander on the lake—and Colonel John B. Campbell, on their own initiative, led a raiding party of seven hundred across the lake to Port Dover on the Long Point peninsula to destroy the town and a large quantity of flour. Campbell landed his men on the fourteenth at the village of Dover, and in retaliation for General Riall's destruction of Buffalo, he burned all the private and public buildings in the defenseless town and three mills near Turkey Point. Campbell wrote to Armstrong, "I determined to make them feel the effects of that conduct they had pursued toward others." Madison, however, was chagrined. Colonel Campbell was court-martialed and censured. Unaware of the president's strong disapproval of Campbell's actions, five days after his raid, American troops from Amherstburg burned Port Talbot on the northern shore of Lake Erie, midway between Amherstburg and Buffalo. Pro-American Canadian volunteers participated in the raid.

When Lieutenant General Drummond informed Governor-General Prevost of Campbell's attack and the wanton destruction, Prevost was bitter. Ignoring the depraved acts of his own troops, as he always did, he sought retribution. On June 2 he wrote to Admiral Cochrane, the new commander of the North American station, demanding attacks on American coastal towns.

PRESIDENT MADISON SPENT the month of May 1814 at Montpelier. After he returned to Washington, he gathered the cabinet on June 7 to discuss strategy for the war. For weeks it had been obvious that the country faced a serious threat from Britain. Rear Admiral Cockburn was already sounding a loud alarm bell by ratcheting up his spring campaign in Chesapeake Bay. Madison recognized the danger. He warned Monroe that they had to be prepared for "the worst measures of the enemy and in their worst forms."

The major threat came from Canada, where troops from Wellington's army were gathering in large numbers. A force of that size could only have Montreal as its base, with Plattsburgh and Sackets Harbor the most obvious targets. Additional British forces at Bermuda threatened Washington and Baltimore, as well as Philadelphia, New York, Newport, Boston, and Portsmouth, New Hampshire—indeed, the entire eastern seaboard. The situation required the United States to adopt a defensive posture and immediately strengthen Plattsburgh and Washington, the two weakest areas.

Instead, Madison unaccountably decided to deploy a significant portion of his army west, away from the probable theaters of action. He ordered Captain Sinclair on Lake Erie to use four or five vessels from his small fleet to transport 800 to 1,000 men under Lieutenant Colonel Croghan and occupy the enemy's new base at Matchedash on Severn Sound in Georgian Bay, take Fort St. Joseph, and recapture Fort Michilimackinac.

The president also decided that when Chauncey acquired command of Lake Ontario, which the commodore predicted would be in mid-July, General Brown's army at Buffalo would cross the Niagara River and invade Canada with a view to "reducing the peninsula, and proceeding towards York." In addition, Madison approved building fourteen or fifteen armed boats at Sackets Harbor for use on the St. Lawrence after Chauncey had dominance on the lake. The boats were to interrupt water communication between Kingston and Montreal. The only role envisioned for Ralph Izard's force of 5,000 at Plattsburg was to create a diversion by making a demonstration against Montreal. Amazingly, the president continued in an offensive mode, placing large numbers of scarce troops in places least likely to be attacked.

THE EXPEDITION TO Lake Huron got under way from Erie, Pennsylvania, on June 19, at a time when the British were increasing their forces and activity in Chesapeake Bay. Arthur Sinclair sailed five vessels, *Lawrence*, *Niagara*, *Caledonia*, *Scorpion*, and *Tigress*, to Detroit, where for two weeks he loaded seven hundred of Colonel Croghan's troops. Sinclair departed Detroit on July 3, but delayed by contrary winds, he did not enter Lake Huron until July 12.

Sinclair's first priority was to take St. Joseph's and Michilimackinac. If possible, he was also to destroy the new enemy naval force building at Matchedash. Secretary Jones cautioned Sinclair to avoid burning private dwellings, as he and Campbell had done at Long Point in May. Jones emphasized that wanton destruction "excited much regret" on the president's part.

Sinclair first attempted to sail to Matchedash, but he found the fog, sunken rocks, and islands too difficult to navigate and turned away. He then sailed for St. Joseph's, which was abandoned. He destroyed the fort but not the town and then steered for Mackinac Island, arriving on July 26 to attack the fort.

Croghan debarked his men on August 4. He had scant intelligence about what awaited him, but looking at the terrain for the first time, he feared the worst. Captain Sinclair described Croghan's predicament: "Mackinac is by nature a perfect Gibraltar, being a high inaccessible rock on every side except the west, from which to the heights, you have near two miles to pass through a [thick] wood."

Lieutenant Colonel Robert McDouall directed the island's defense. Prevost had sent him out in the spring to take command. McDouall skillfully deployed two hundred British regulars and three hundred fifty Indians to stop Croghan, using the terrain to full advantage. "Our men were shot in every direction," Sinclair wrote, ". . . without being able to see the Indian who did it, and a height was scarcely gained, before there was another in 50 or 100 yards commanding it, where breastworks were erected, and cannon opened on them."

Seeing no way to attain his objective against a clever, hidden foe, Croghan soon ordered a retreat back to the boats. His losses were sixteen killed and sixty wounded. They might have been much worse had he not acted promptly. One of the dead was his second in command, Major A. H. Holmes. Croghan sent a flag of truce to the fort and asked McDouall for the body. The request was politely granted. McDouall also offered the fleet provisions and fruit, which were gratefully accepted. The body of Major Holmes was returned unharmed, but McDouall's Indian allies scalped and buried the other bodies.

When Sinclair departed, he sailed to the Nottawasaga River and destroyed the schooner *Nancy*. Her skipper, Lieutenant Miller Worsley, and his sparse crew escaped, however, and made their way to Michilimackinac in canoes. While they did, Captain Sinclair sailed for Detroit, leaving the small schooners *Tigress* (one gun, Sailing Master Stephen Champlin) and *Scorpion* (two guns, Lieutenant Daniel Turner) to maintain American naval supremacy on Lake Huron and make life difficult, if not impossible, for McDouall.

Lieutenant Worsley decided to turn the tables on the Americans, however, and McDouall supported him. On September 3, Worsley led a surprise night attack on the *Tigress*, using four small boats filled with armed men, including some Indians. They had rowed silently for six miles from a hiding place to within one hundred yards of the *Tigress* when her night watch spotted them and opened fire with muskets and a single twenty-four-pounder. Worsley was not deterred; he soon pulled up to the schooner's side and boarded. After a fierce hand-to-hand fight, his superior numbers told, and Sailing Master Champlin surrendered with thirty sailors.

The *Scorpion* had been fifteen miles away when the *Tigress* was captured, and Lieutenant Turner had no idea what had happened. Two days later, the *Scorpion* returned and anchored for the night two miles from the *Tigress*, where Worsley and his men were hiding. Worsley had the American flag flying conspicuously on the *Tigress*. Turner did not suspect a thing. At dawn, the *Tigress* crept toward the *Scorpion*. Worsley got to within ten yards before being discovered. As the *Scorpion*'s night watch fired at him, he ran up alongside, jumped aboard with his crew, and overpowered Turner and his thirty-two men.

Not long afterward, McDouall went on the offensive, sending a substantial force of over six hundred men to seize Prairie du Chien on the Upper Mississippi, in what is today southwestern Wisconsin but was then Illinois Territory. An American force of two hundred men had captured the area in May 1814 and built a fort. Prairie du Chien was strategically located at the terminus of the Fox-Wisconsin waterway that connected the Great Lakes with the Mississippi. It was an important fur trading center, where Jacob Astor had a large warehouse. McDouall's men easily captured the American fort, which surrendered on July 19. Major Zachary Taylor tried to regain control of the area later, marching three hundred thirty men in August to the mouth of the Rock River in Illinois, but he was checked on September 5 by Indians, supported by British regulars from Prairie du Chien, and he retreated to St. Louis. The British and their Indian allies held the area until the war was over.

The administration, meanwhile, went ahead with General Brown's invasion of Canada in the Niagara region, despite the threat to the eastern states from British forces gathering at Montreal, in Bermuda, and in Chesapeake Bay. It was decided that Brown would cross the Niagara and take Fort Erie, then proceed north and attack Fort George. After that, he would move on to Burlington. If all went well, he would combine with Chauncey and occupy York again and then Kingston. If that were accomplished, he was to push into the St. Lawrence with the armed galleys being made at Sackets Harbor and move on Montreal. It was a strategic vision divorced from reality, particularly with the thousands of re-inforcements Prevost was receiving at the port of Quebec from Wellington.

Brown's offensive depended on Chauncey regaining control of Lake Ontario. Without Chauncey's big guns, Brown could not hope to take even Fort George. He could subdue lightly defended Fort Erie, but that was about all. Since Chauncey would not be ready until mid-July at the earliest, Armstrong advised Brown: "To give . . . immediate occupation to your troops and to prevent their blood from stagnating—why not take Fort Erie and its garrison, stated at three or four hundred men. Land between point Albino and Erie in the night—assail the fort by land and water—push forward a corps to seize the bridge of Chippawa, and be governed by circumstances in either stopping there, or going further." Armstrong sent the necessary orders to Brown on June 10.

Brown decided to follow Armstrong's suggestion. He wrote to Chauncey asking when he'd be ready to stand out into Lake Ontario. Chauncey replied on June 25 that his movements would depend on Yeo. He would not move up the lake to Niagara unless Yeo led him. This amounted to no commitment at all. Brown conferred with his commanders, Generals Eleazer Ripley and Winfield Scott, who gave him conflicting advice. Ripley advised waiting for Chauncey, but Scott wanted to act now. He had been training his men for months, and he was anxious to lead them into battle. Brown decided that the United States needed a victory at this depressing time and planned to attack Fort Erie.

On July 2, in the dead of night, concealed by a heavy fog, Scott and Ripley led 3,500 men—Brown's entire army—across the Niagara River. Scott commanded the left division and Ripley the right. Scott was in the lead boat and nearly drowned when he stepped out too soon into deep water. Only 137 men were de-fending the fort, and their commander, Thomas Buck, immediately sent word of the invasion to the British commander at Chippawa. At eight o'clock Buck fired three small cannon, and four hours later he sent out a flag of truce and sur-rendered. When the residents of Chippawa heard what had happened, they evac-uated the town.

The following day, July 4, Brown sent Scott and his brigade north to Chippawa on what amounted to a recognizance in force. British lieutenant colonel Thomas Pearson, one of Wellington's veterans experienced in rearguard actions, harassed Scott the entire sixteen miles with a small detachment of light infantry and dra-goons, making Scott's march to Chippawa far more difficult than he had anticipated. Scott had to cross five creeks, and Pearson annoyed him at each one of them.

Major General Phineas Riall was in command on the Niagara peninsula, and he was at Fort George when he learned of the invasion. He immediately sent to General Drummond at York for reinforcements and then marched what troops he had to reinforce Chippawa. When Scott reached the south side of the Chippawa River, he found that Riall had taken up a strong defensive position on the north side. Deciding to wait for reinforcements, Scott withdrew south a short distance to Street's Creek, which he crossed, and settled down for the night. Brown and Ripley joined him later with additional troops. The former congressman, now militia general, Peter B. Porter arrived with New York volunteers and Indians early the next morning.

By July 5, Riall had 1,350 regulars, 200 militia, and 350 Indians led by John Norton. In spite of knowing he was greatly outnumbered, he crossed the Chippawa with 1,200 regulars and attacked, thinking the American militiamen would run. Scott reacted quickly, marching his brigade, 1,300 strong, over the single bridge at Street's Creek under heavy fire and deployed on the plain between the creek and the Chippawa River. Scott's soldiers were attired in grey uniforms, which Riall thought marked them as militiamen. He soon realized, however, that he was facing regular troops—militiamen would have run long before now. A vicious fight ensued for an hour, when Riall, much to his surprise, was forced to withdraw. He successfully retreated across the Chippawa, destroying the bridge as he went. Scott and Porter were close behind, but with little daylight left, Brown ordered them back to camp. Casualties on both sides were severe—485 British and 319 Americans.

"For completeness, Scott's victory at Chippawa could be compared with that of Isaac Hull over the *Guerriere*," Henry Adams wrote, "but in one respect Scott surpassed Hull. The *Constitution* was a much heavier ship than its enemy; but Scott's brigade was weaker, both in men and guns than Riall's force." Actually, Scott's force slightly outnumbered Riall's. Nonetheless, Chippawa was a source of immense pride to the fledgling U. S. Army. For the first time, American regulars defeated British regulars of nearly equal force in an engagement on an open plain. Instilling self-respect in the beleaguered American army was no mean achievement, but Scott paid a high price in lives for a victory that had only symbolic value.

Two days later, Brown crossed the Chippawa in force, and Riall retreated, falling back toward Burlington Bay to await reinforcements, leaving detachments at Fort George and Fort Niagara. Brown then moved his army up to Queenston, five miles from Fort George. He needed siege guns to attack the fort, however, and he did not have any. He also needed reinforcements and provisions, all of which he expected Chauncey to supply. But Chauncey, who was seriously ill at the time, still did not have command of the lake, despite his earlier promises. He could neither stop Drummond from moving troops and provisions across the lake to Riall nor help Brown. And even if he could, he had made it clear in his June 25 letter that his movements would be dictated by Yeo, not by Brown. In other words, Brown was not to count on him for either bombarding Fort George or for transporting men and supplies.

Anxious to counter Brown's movements, General Drummond took advantage of Yeo's dominance on the lake to ferry reinforcements from Kingston and York to the Niagara area. At the same time, sickness and desertion had reduced General Brown's army to 2,500 effectives. Chauncey's weakness put Brown in danger of being stranded on the west side of the Niagara, cut off from his bases at Buffalo, Black Rock, and Fort Schlosser on the east side of the river. All three places were weakly defended. If Drummond and Riall pushed down on both sides of the river, Brown would be trapped on the Canadian side.

Recognizing his exposed position, Brown withdrew south of Chippawa on July 24. Riall followed with 1,000 men, marching at night, stopping at Lundy's Lane, just north of town. On July 25 Brown dispatched Scott's brigade north toward Riall in the hope that Drummond, who was now at Fort Niagara, would notice and concentrate on coming to Riall's rescue, rather than marching down the east side of the river, taking the forts, and trapping the American army.

Drummond did exactly what Brown wanted. By late afternoon on the twenty-fifth, Drummond had crossed the river and was approaching Riall with a 2,000-man reinforcement. Before he arrived, Winfield Scott's brigade appeared and began attacking Riall, who ordered a retreat. But when Drummond arrived suddenly, Riall countermanded his order and turned on Scott. Riall's force was now three times larger than Scott's. It was 6 P.M.

Scott soon discovered he was badly outnumbered and sent for reinforcements while continuing to skirmish so fiercely that Drummond thought he was facing a much larger army than he was. In the initial fighting, Riall himself was captured. In the next couple of hours, Brown, Porter, and Ripley arrived with reinforcements and artillery. The American force now totaled 2,800 men.

A general battle developed that lasted from around 8:45 until midnight and was as fiercely fought as any in the war. The key was Drummond's artillery, which was posted on a small hill north of Lundy's Lane. Brown and his generals recognized that they had to seize the seven heavy guns there or lose the battle, and after heroic efforts they succeeded. They then beat off three of Drummond's counterattacks. The fighting went on hour after bloody hour, the armies often within half pistol shot of each other. "The slaughter had been prodigious," Brown reported, and as midnight approached, he decided to withdraw to Chippawa to regroup before returning to the fight. By that time, the battle had lasted for six ugly hours. It had been a ghastly bloodletting. Brown had 171 killed, 572 wounded, and 110 missing. Drummond had 84 killed, 559 wounded, 193 missing, and 42 prisoners. Brown was badly hurt, and so was General Scott. His wound was so severe he could no longer participate in the war.

Both sides claimed victory. Since the British remained on the battlefield, they maintained they had won. But Militia General Peter Porter wrote in his report to Governor Tompkins that "victory was complete, . . . but converted into a defeat by a precipitate retreat." In fact, Lundy's Lane was a bloody draw. If anything, it was an American victory. Brown held Drummond off with a decidedly weaker army. When Brown withdrew from the battlefield, Drummond, who had been shot in the neck himself, could not follow; his army was as totally exhausted as Brown's was.

The following morning, Ripley, under Brown's order, reluctantly led 1,200 exhausted men back to the battlefield. He soon found Drummond, who obviously had a larger force. Ripley did not attack as Brown had directed. Neither did Drummond. They simply watched each other warily from a distance. Believing the Americans outnumbered him, and knowing that the previous day's fighting had worn out his troops, Drummond let Ripley retire unmolested, which the American general chose to do.

Ripley's return to camp angered Brown, who was convinced that Ripley was robbing him of a chance for a clear-cut victory. Nonetheless, given the condition of his army, there was nothing Brown could do for the moment. He ordered Ripley to move the men sixteen miles back to Fort Erie; Ripley proceeded to do so that same day. Brown was taken to Buffalo to recuperate, and from there he sent to Sackets Harbor for General Gaines to assume command at Fort Erie. Brown did not trust Ripley to do the job.

COMMODORE CHAUNCEY, WHO had just regained command of Lake Ontario, finally appeared off Fort George on August 5 with a squadron, but it was much too late to coordinate an attack with Brown. Chauncey then returned to blockading Kingston, which prevented General Drummond from receiving supplies by water. Men marching overland reinforced Drummond, however, increasing his army to over 3,000.

With his new troops in camp, Drummond carefully planned an assault on Fort Erie. While waiting, he sent a detachment of six hundred exhausted regulars across the Niagara to attack Black Rock, but two hundred forty American riflemen beat them off, and the British returned to camp.

Before Drummond attacked Fort Erie, the Royal Navy pulled off a smart action on the Niagara River just outside the fort. On August 12 British commander Alexander Dobbs and seventy-five men surprised and captured the 3-gun schooner *Ohio*, under Lieutenant Augustus H. M. Conckling, and the 3-gun schooner *Somers*, under Sailing Master Gamliel Darling. The schooners were part of the American fleet on Lake Erie and had thirty-five men each. They had been anchored close to Fort Erie to assist the army. Dobbs narrowly missed capturing a third schooner, the *Porcupine*, under Acting Sailing Master Thomas Brownell, who heard the commotion, cut his cable, and, using the current in the Niagara, slipped away into the night.

The next day, August 13, Drummond began bombarding Fort Erie. His long delay had given generals Gaines and Ripley critical time to strengthen the dilapidated fort. On August 15, Drummond attacked in earnest, with 2,100 men in three columns rushing the fort. But they were beaten back with huge losses—57 killed, 309 wounded, and 539 missing. The Americans had 84 casualties. Drummond's repulse underscored the bloody stalemate that had developed on the Niagara frontier.

Despite Drummond's defeat, he remained outside the fort, rebuilding his force and planning another attack. Inside the fort, General Brown, although still recovering from the wounds he received at Lundy's Lane, had assumed command again. General Gaines had been wounded in the fighting. Brown was not content to remain on the defensive. On September 17 he launched a surprise attack on the enemy's three main batteries. The fighting was ferocious, and Drummond eventually drove Brown's men back with heavy losses on both sides. The Americans suffered 79 killed and 432 wounded, while Drummond had 115 killed, 176 wounded, and 315 missing. The butcher's bill was so excruciating it influenced Drummond to finally call off the siege on September 21 and retreat back to Chippawa. Brown could not follow; the casualties he had sustained made it impossible.

The standoff in the Niagara region continued. It demonstrated that Madison's dream of conquering Canada was dead, but also that the U. S. Army, with its new leadership, could stand up to British regulars, making the Liverpool ministry's plans for invading America look ill-advised. The strength shown by both sides in these bloody battles would have important consequences when the peace treaty was negotiated later in the year.

CHAPTER TWENTY-TWO

The British
Blockade

WHILE A STALEMATE had developed on Lake Ontario and along the Niagara River, Vice Admiral Cochrane was tightening his blockade along the American coast and conducting large scale raids to divert attention away from General Prevost's invasion of the Champlain Valley. As early as March 11, 1814, Cochrane wrote to Prevost, "I hope to be able to make a very considerable diversion in the Chesapeake Bay, to draw off in part the enemy's efforts against Canada." The decision about where to attack along the American seaboard was left to Cochrane, but clearly Washington and Baltimore were prime targets.

As Cochrane thought about the tasks assigned to him, he estimated that ninety-eight warships would be required—seven ships of the line, five razees, twenty-eight frigates, thirty-eight sloops, and twenty smaller vessels. When he arrived in Bermuda, Cochrane had a total of fifty-six warships under his command. By any measure, it was a large fleet, but not enough to tighten the blockade and conduct raids at the same time.

As one of his first acts, Cochrane extended the commercial blockade to include New England. The British blockade now ran from the Canadian border to Louisiana. Since General Ross and the additional troops needed to conduct substantial raids would not arrive until summer, Cochrane concentrated on the blockade. At the same time, he ordered his subordinates to carry out what raids they could. He wrote to Admiral Cockburn on April 24 that Americans in the seaports towns need to "be taught to know that they are now at the mercy of an invading foe."

Cochrane also planned to encourage slaves to leave their masters and join the British army. Luring slaves away from their masters was part of his attack on the American economy, just as the blockade was. He hoped to augment his strike force with ex-slaves and at the same time deprive the local economy of essential manpower. On April 2 Cochrane issued a proclamation urging slaves to join the British army or become "free settlers into some of His Majesty's colonies." He promised to receive them aboard the king's ships "or at the military posts that may be established upon or near the coast of the United States." He ordered Rear Admiral Cockburn to establish posts in Chesapeake Bay to receive the refugees. Bathurst prohibited Cochrane from encouraging slaves "to rise upon their masters." The admiral was expected to entice them into leaving peacefully, which in most cases they did.

Cochrane's blockade made getting in and out of port more difficult. Commerce was brought to a standstill. American exports fell to seven million from forty-five million in 1811, even with the trade restrictions in force during that year. The president's embargo, which was not repealed until April, had helped the British blockade. Not wanting to risk their ships, merchants kept them in port. International and coastal trade dwindled. At the same time, however, privateers were managing to get to sea—even those sailing from Baltimore—and they were harassing Britain's commerce everywhere, particularly in the West Indies and around the British Isles. Merchants, whose fleets were sitting idle in port, often invested in privateering enterprises, which sometimes were profitable, but sometimes not.

A FEW AMERICAN warships did manage to get to sea, and the successes they had enhanced the reputation of the American navy, which would be of signal importance during the peace talks and after the war. On December 4, 1813, in cold, dirty weather, Commodore Rodgers slipped out of Narragansett Bay in the *President*. Two days later he stopped the schooner *Comet*, and when he discovered she had been captured by the *Ramillies* and the *Loire* and had a British prize crew sailing her to Halifax, he took the British crew prisoner and set the *Comet* free. He then continued on to the Canaries and, afterward, ran down the fifteenth parallel to the West Indies, where he patrolled to windward of Barbados, and in January captured two armed merchantmen. Beginning on January 16, he cruised along the northern coast of South America. Finding nothing, he shaped a coarse for Puerto Rico and sailed through the Mona Passage. He then passed northeast of the Bahamas and steered toward the northern coast of Florida. Off St. Augustine he captured a British schooner and then continued north, running into the blockading squadron off Charleston, South Carolina. When he attempted to engage one of the warships, the whole fleet came after him, but he managed to escape and continued on northward. He happened on another blockading squadron off Delaware Bay in a heavy fog. The number of signal guns sounding around the *President* made him give up the idea of engaging one of the enemy ships, and he sailed on.

On February 18 Rodgers was off Sandy Hook when he saw two British warships approaching. One was a small schooner, but the other was a frigate. As he prepared for battle, the frigate unexpectedly fled. She was the 38-gun *Loire*. Her captain, Thomas Brown, was following Admiralty orders to avoid combat with the heavy American frigates. Rodgers went after her, but an American revenue cutter happened on the scene and told him he was chasing a seventy-four. Whether Rodgers believed that or not, other ships of the blockading squadron were approaching, and he decided to run for port, reaching the safety of New York Harbor, much to London's annoyance. The Admiralty wanted the *President* more than any other ship.

It was another disappointing cruise for Rodgers, but it was significant that Captain Brown decided not to challenge the *President*. When the war started, the captain of a 38-gun frigate who refused to engage even the largest American frigates would have been severely reprimanded. In fact, it is hard to imagine any British captain avoiding such an opportunity. Captain Brown's flight showed the respect the American navy had attained in the eyes of the Admiralty and the officers of the Royal Navy. The change in British attitudes would serve the U.S. Navy and the country well in the future.

Rodgers was anxious to return to sea as quickly as possible. Secretary Jones offered him a choice of assignments. One was to continue with the *President*; another was to become skipper of the new 44-gun frigate *Guerriere*, nearing completion at Philadelphia. Rodgers chose the new frigate. Before taking command, he traveled to Washington to confer with Jones. On the way, he visited his family at Havre de Grace. He had not seen them since the war began. Needless to say, the sight of his half-burned house did not make him enamored of the British.

The *Guerriere* was launched in Philadelphia on June 20, 1814, amid much ceremony. At the same time that Rodgers took command, he also assumed responsibility for the Delaware flotilla from Commodore Alexander Murray. Secretary Jones had ordered Rodgers to act against the British not only on the

Delaware but in Chesapeake Bay as well. Since the *Guerriere* was blockaded, Rodgers could potentially play an important part in defending Baltimore and perhaps Washington.

While Rodgers was at least able to get the *President* to sea, the *United States*, *Macedonian*, and *Hornet* remained trapped in the Thames River, much to Commodore Decatur's dismay. Traitors in New London County reported his every move to Captain Sir Thomas Masterman Hardy, making an escape impossible. Decatur had some hope for action, when in January 1814 the 44-gun heavy frigate *Endymion*, under Captain Henry Hope, joined Hardy's squadron. Hope and his colleague Captain Hazzard Stackpole, skipper of the 38-gun *Statira*, proposed single-ship duels—the *United States* against the *Endymion* and the *Statira* against the *Macedonian*. Hardy and Decatur liked the idea at first, and they exchanged messages, but in the end Hardy decided against the duel between the larger ships, and Decatur declined a fight between the smaller ones on the ground that he anticipated Hardy putting a crew of his best fighters aboard the *Statira*, and in order to do the same for the *Macedonian*, Decatur would have to weaken the crews of his other ships and make their later escapes more precarious. So the duels never came off.

During the winter Decatur remained alert for the possibility of escape, but the occasion never arose. Beginning on March 17 he tended to some unfinished— and especially unpleasant—business, presiding at the court-martial of Lieutenant William Cox of the *Chesapeake*, four midshipmen, and other men charged with various misdeeds during the fight with the *Shannon*. Master Commandant Biddle and ten lieutenants made up the rest of the court. The trial ended in May, and all were found guilty.

With the coming of warm spring weather in southern Connecticut, Secretary Jones saw no hope of the *United States* and *Macedonian* escaping. He ordered Decatur to secure both ships in the Thames River permanently and repair to New York with most of the crew of the *United States*. Decatur took the ships upriver fourteen miles, far beyond Gales Ferry, rearranged their guns for better protection, and stationed gunboats and shore batteries to support them. He then left skeleton crews aboard and proceeded to New York with the rest of his men. Captain Jacob Jones and the crew of the *Macedonian* went to Lake Ontario. Biddle and the *Hornet* remained to protect the frigates, a duty Biddle hated.

Biddle did not give up trying to escape, however, and on November 18, 1814, he slipped out of the Thames in bad weather and made his way to New York, where he would be serving again under Decatur. "It is a most infamous arrangement that the *Hornet* . . . should be placed under the orders of Commodore Decatur," Biddle complained to his brother.

In New York, Decatur had command of the *President*, which Rodgers had left when he became skipper of the new *Guerriere*. The *President* remained trapped by the blockade, but Decatur had plenty to do ashore. As the threat of an invasion increased, Secretary Jones ordered him to help with the city's defense and also be prepared to move his men to Philadelphia, should an attack come there. At one point in July, Jones ordered Decatur to take over for Chauncey at Sackets Harbor when Chauncey became ill, but he recovered, and Decatur remained in New York.

Captain Charles Gordon and the *Constellation* continued to be trapped by the blockade as well. He hoped to run the *Constellation* out to sea during a winter storm. Secretary Jones sent him sailing orders on January 5, cautioning him, as he did every captain, not to give or accept "a challenge ship to ship directly or indirectly." On February 11, during a stretch of particularly bad weather, Gordon saw his chance. He brought the *Constellation* from the safety of the Elizabeth River out to Hampton Roads in heavy rain. The wind was fair for running out to sea, and he sent a tender to scout the Chesapeake Capes. When the wind suddenly turned, however, the tender had to scurry back, and Gordon was forced to return to the protection of the river. He did not get another opportunity. Spring came all too soon, and he had to forget about racing out to sea and concentrate on defending Norfolk. In April, Jones directed him not to attempt an escape, for fear he'd lose the ship and endanger Norfolk and Gosport. It was a bitter pill for Gordon. He remained trapped for the rest of the war.

Secretary Jones expected more from the six sloops of war authorized by Congress on March 3, 1813, than he did from the *President*, the *Constitution*, or the *United States*. To be sure, the sloops were few in number, but Jones thought they would perform better as commerce raiders than either frigates or brigs, and certainly better than seventy-fours. Naval constructor William Doughty designed three of the sloops, *Argus*, *Ontario*, and *Erie*. *Argus* was built at the Washington Navy Yard under Doughty's supervision. *Ontario* and *Erie* were built in Baltimore under the supervision of Thomas Kemp.

When the *Erie* was ready for her first cruise, her skipper, Master Commandant Charles G. Ridgely, found that he could not get past the blockade. When spring came, Jones gave up on Ridgely ever getting to sea and on April 4 ordered him to lay up the ship in Baltimore and proceed with his officers and crew to reinforce Chauncey at Sackets Harbor.

The *Ontario* was ready to sail by the end of January, but Master Commandant Robert T. Spence could not get her past the blockade either. When spring came, Jones also ordered him to Sackets Harbor with his officers. The petty officers and the rest of the crew went to Joshua Barney's Flotilla Service in Baltimore. Spence became ill, however, and could not go to Lake Ontario. He remained in Baltimore and participated in its defense.

CHAPTER TWENTY-THREE

The *Essex*

O N JULY 6, 1814, at five o'clock in the afternoon, seamen from the 32-gun frigate *Essex* rowed Captain David Porter in a whaleboat onto the beach at Babylon, New York, looking as if they had been through a great ordeal. New York militiamen were soon on the scene, and alert to the possibility of an enemy invasion, they took all the strangers into custody, assuming they were British spies. When Porter convinced them who he actually was, they treated him like a hero, providing him with a wagon so that he could bring his boat and men to Brooklyn and from there cross the East River to New York City to tell his story to the world. It was an amazing one.

Porter's odyssey began on October 27, 1812, when he stood out beyond the Delaware Capes in the *Essex* with orders to rendezvous with Commodore Bainbridge in the *Constitution* and Master Commandant Lawrence in the *Hornet* for a commerce-destroying mission in the South Atlantic. Porter's first place of rendezvous was the Cape Verde Islands, off the west coast of Africa. He arrived at Porto Praya on November 27, but not finding Bainbridge, he quickly moved on, sailing for the northeast coast of Brazil. On the way, on December 11, he captured the British packet *Nocton*. She had £11,000 sterling in specie aboard (approximately $55,000). He took the money and sent the packet to the United States in charge of Lieutenant William B. Finch, but on January 5, 1813, the ubiquitous Captain Richard Byron in the *Belvidera* captured her.

Porter continued to the second place of rendezvous, the wretched Portuguese penal colony at Fernando de Noronha, three hundred miles off the Brazilian coast, reaching it on December 13. He just missed Bainbridge, who had been there and left a message written in invisible ink, advising Porter to meet him at the next place of rendezvous, Cape Frio off Rio de Janeiro. Porter dutifully traveled down the coast of Brazil to Cape Frio, arriving on Christmas day, but Bainbridge wasn't there either. Porter cruised off the coast until January 12, capturing only one small merchant schooner, the *Elizabeth*, before turning south for the penultimate rendezvous point, St. Catherine's Island off the coast of Brazil, five hundred miles south of Rio. Again, Bainbridge was nowhere to be found.

After taking on what supplies were available, Porter decided not to go to the last place of rendezvous—the waters around the important British base at St. Helena. Instead, he chose to fulfill a long-standing dream of sailing into the Pacific. He left St. Catherine's on January 26, 1813, and steered south, rounded hazardous Cape Horn, and, after nearly foundering, sailed up the coast of Chile to Valparaiso, standing into the harbor on March 15. The *Essex* was the first American warship to enter the Pacific.

When Porter set his hook in Valparaiso Harbor, he soon discovered that Spanish authority in Chile had collapsed. Instead of a frosty reception from Spanish officials, the revolutionary government of Jose Miguel Carrera greeted him warmly and gave him everything he needed to refurbish the *Essex* after her long voyage. Anxious to get on with his work, Porter remained in Valparaiso only a week. On March 22 he stood out from the half-moon-shaped harbor and steered north toward Peru, whose government was still loyal to the Spanish king, Ferdinand VII; even though he was Napoleon's prisoner in France. Peru's governor was pro-British and decidedly unfriendly. He was sending out privateers to attack the American whaling fleet in the eastern Pacific; British privateers and armed whalers were working with him.

Porter decided the best use of the *Essex* would be protecting American whalers by capturing or destroying the British whaling fleet and their privateers. Approximately twenty enemy whalers roamed the eastern Pacific, most of them well armed.

On the trip north, Porter captured the Peruvian privateer *Nereyda* and retook one of her prizes, the American whaler *Barclay*. The *Nereyda* had twenty-four American prisoners aboard from two captures. Porter liberated them, threw the *Nereyda*'s armament overboard, and sent the ship to Lima with a message for the governor of Peru, demanding the captain of the Nereyda be punished for his piratical conduct. Porter then headed for Lima himself, and after looking into the harbor and recapturing one of the American vessels as she was entering port, he put back to sea in search of Britain's whaling fleet.

Finding nothing along the Peruvian coast, he sailed five hundred miles west along the equator to the Galapagos Islands, the prime fishing grounds for all whalers. Porter described the islands as "perhaps the most barren and desolate of any known." He arrived on April 7 and remained, except for a brief trip back to the coast for water, until October 3. During those months he was remarkably successful, capturing twelve British whalers and disrupting their entire fleet. In the process, he acquired a large quantity of spermaceti oil, enough to fill three of the captured whalers. He sent them to the United States at various times. The prize money they would bring was potentially enormous. Unfortunately, enemy warships captured all three before they reached port. Captain Byron's *Belvidera* picked up one of them.

Porter turned his finest capture, the whaler *Atlantic*, into a warship and christened her *Essex Junior*. He ordered John Downes, the *Essex*'s first lieutenant, to take command. Needless to say, Downes was delighted. *Essex Junior*'s armament was ten long sixes and ten eighteen-pound carronades. During the entire time he was in the Pacific, Porter supplied most of his needs, including food, from captured ships—a remarkable feat. Even more amazing was the extraordinary good health of his crew. Thanks to his assiduous efforts, only one case of scurvy appeared aboard the *Essex* during her odyssey.

Porter's encounters with British captains and their crews in the desolate islands prompted him to contemplate the differences between the American and British navies. "It seems somewhat extraordinary," he wrote in his journal,

> that British seamen should carry with them this propensity to desert even into merchant vessels, sailing under the flag of their nation, and under circumstances so terrifying; but yet I am informed that their desertion while at Charles Island [in the Galapagos] has been very common, even when there was no prospect whatever of obtaining water but from the bowels of the tortoises. This can only be attributed to that tyranny, so prevalent on board their ships of war, which has crept into their merchant vessels, and is there aped by their commanders. Now mark the difference. While the *Essex* lay at Charles Island, one-fourth of her crew was every day on shore, and all the prisoners who chose to go; and even lent the latter boats, whenever they wished it, to go for their amusement to the other side of the island. No one attempted to desert or to make their escape; whenever a gun was fired, every man repaired to the beach, and no one was ever missing when the signal was made.

During the first week of October, Porter decided he needed a safe place not frequented by British men-of-war to overhaul his ship and refresh himself and his men. He sailed his fleet west for 2,500 miles to the isolated but thickly populated Marquesas Islands, 850 miles northeast of Tahiti. After so many months at sea the frigate needed her leaking seams caulked and her copper bottom repaired, and she was desperately in need of a thorough smoking to kill the army of rats who were eating the food and clothing, even chewing through the water casks. And the crew and officers were in need of the delightful diversions that Porter expected the Polynesians, particularly their young women, to provide.

On October 25, the *Essex* and her companions arrived off the island of Nuku Hiva, where the women and men greeted them warmly, Polynesian style. Porter remained on the island—the most important among twelve in the archipelago—until December 12, recuperating, enjoying the islanders' extraordinary hospitality, and refitting the *Essex*. Although he would have preferred not to, he could not help getting embroiled in the strange tribal wars on the divided island. With his overwhelming firepower, he was able to cow the tribes, and he completed work on his ships.

Despite these battles, during his weeks ashore, Porter formed a strong attachment to the island and its people, coming to regard Nuku Hiva as a paradise. He regretted that the islanders had come in contact with white men at all. Viewing the natives as people in a state of nature, he claimed to be saddened that they could not remain so. The next best thing, he thought, was making them Americans. And without any authorization whatever, he annexed Nuku Hiva in the name of the United States, renaming it Madison Island. When the president heard later of Porter's "conquest," however, he was not flattered and rejected the idea. The United States never annexed the South Pacific paradise. That was left for France to do many years later.

Before leaving Nuku Hiva, Porter ordered Marine Lieutenant John Gamble to continue America's presence on the island until he returned or until five months had elapsed. To support Gamble, Porter left three of the captured whalers and a surprisingly small number of men—Midshipman William Feltus, twenty-one volunteers, and six prisoners.

After easily thwarting a mutiny by a small number of men just before he was leaving, Porter set sail for Valparaiso in the refurbished *Essex*, intent on falling in with an enemy frigate. He knew British hunters were after him, and he meant to accommodate them. Lieutenant Downes and *Essex Junior* accompanied him. A stop at Valparaiso for supplies was unnecessary; Porter had enough to reach the South Atlantic safely or to sail west to East Asia, where he could have obtained provisions as well. He might also have been an important fighting force in either place. The need for supplies was not the reason he was going to Valparaiso. He was fixated on fighting a British frigate and achieving the glory that Isaac Hull had achieved—the very sort of wasteful dueling that Madison and Jones were dead set against.

After an uneventful voyage, Porter arrived at Valparaiso on February 3, 1814. He did not have to wait long for his fondest wish to be fulfilled. After midnight on February 8, lookouts spotted two enemy warships in the distance, and the following morning, the 36-gun *Phoebe*, under Captain James Hillyar, and the 28-gun *Cherub*, under Captain Thomas J. Tucker, sailed into the harbor prepared for battle. Porter was ready for them. But he did not know quite what to expect, since Valparaiso was a neutral harbor. The larger frigate sailed near enough to the *Essex* for her jib boom to sweep uncomfortably close to the *Essex*'s forecastle. But it did not touch any part of the ship. That was fortunate for Hillyar: Porter was ready to respond to any touching with a ferocious broadside of powerful carronades. Evidently Hillyar hoped to take Porter by surprise, but seeing that he had not, he backed off, pretending he was respecting the neutrality of the port. Porter held his fire and let Hillyar recover, something he deeply regretted later.

The *Phoebe* and the *Cherub* then took up stations outside the port to watch and perhaps to wait for more warships. Porter remained inside Valparaiso harbor. In the ensuing days and weeks he attempted to provoke Hillyar into a single-ship duel, but Hillyar would not accommodate him. Frustrated, Porter attempted a surprise night attack on the *Phoebe* using the *Essex*'s boats, but that too failed. During his attempts to lure Hillyar into battle, Porter discovered that the *Essex* was much faster than the *Phoebe*.

Porter now decided that since Hillyar was never going to fight him one-on-one, he would make a run for it, before more British warships arrived. An opportunity presented itself the afternoon of March 28, when a strong southerly wind parted the *Essex*'s port anchor cable, and the ship started dragging her starboard anchor out to sea. Porter reacted quickly, taking up the anchor and arranging his sails; he was convinced that this was his opportunity.

He took in the topgallants, which were set over single-reefed topsails, and braced up to pass to windward of the *Phoebe* and *Cherub*, who were in pursuit. Unfortunately, on rounding the western point of Valparaiso Bay, a sudden heavy squall carried away the *Essex*'s main topmast. Three men aloft fell into the sea and drowned. Porter decided to turn back and regain his original anchorage. But that proved impossible, and he was forced to put into the east side of the harbor within pistol shot of shore. Hillyar and the *Cherub* were right after him, and although Porter considered he was in neutral territory, Hillyar never hesitated, and a vicious battle developed.

The *Essex* had forty thirty-two-pound carronades and six long twelve-pounders. The *Phoebe* had twenty-six long eighteen-pounders, two long twelve-pounders, two long nine-pounders, fourteen thirty-two-pound carronades, and two eighteen-pound carronades. The *Cherub* had eighteen thirty-two-pound carronades, four eighteen-pound carronades, and four long nine-pounders.

The ever prudent Hillyar, who had obviously rehearsed for weeks how he was going to fight the *Essex*, used his big advantage in long guns to stay away from Porter's deadly carronades. In the initial exchanges, however, Porter managed to use three of his long twelve-pounders so well that the *Phoebe* and *Cherub* had to haul off after thirty minutes to repair damages. Porter insisted that all his men "appeared determined to defend their ship to the last extremity and to die in preference to a shameful surrender."

When Hillyar resumed the battle, he positioned the *Phoebe* out of range of *Essex*'s carronades, where Porter could not bring his long guns to bear either. Porter tried again and again to get springs on his cable, but he could not. The *Essex* was a sitting duck. Porter tried closing with Hillyar and boarding, but the *Essex* was so shot up he failed. Porter then tried to run the *Essex* on shore and destroy her, but when the wind would not cooperate, he had to give that up as well.

The grisly slaughter went on for two and a half hours before Porter finally surrendered at twenty minutes after six. His butcher's bill was appalling. Out of a crew of 255 he had 58 killed, 39 severely wounded, 26 slightly wounded, and 31 missing. Hillyar had 5 killed and 10 wounded. Porter himself was unscathed, although he had been in the thick of the fight the entire time.

Theodore Roosevelt wrote that "history does not afford a single instance of so determined a defense against such frightful odds." Porter said of his crew, "More bravery, skill, patriotism, and zeal were never displayed on any occasion."

"We have been unfortunate, but not disgraced," Porter wrote to the secretary of the navy. "The defense of the *Essex* has not been less honorable to her officers and crew, than the capture of an equal force; and I now consider my situation less unpleasant than that of Commodore Hillyar, who in violation of every principle of honor and generosity, and regardless of the rights of nations, attacked the *Essex* in her crippled state, within pistol shot of a neutral shore—when for six weeks I had daily offered him fair and honorable combat, on terms greatly to his advantage; the blood of the slain must be upon his head." Porter added that "I must in justification of myself observe that with our six twelve-pounders only we fought this action, our carronades being almost useless."

Looking back many years later, Midshipman David Farragut, who had fought alongside the captain, had these observations about Porter's tactics: "In the first place, I consider that our original and greatest mistake was in attempting to regain the anchorage; as, being greatly superior to the enemy in sailing qualities, I think we should have borne up and run before the wind. If the *Phoebe* caught the *Essex*, then Porter could have taken her by boarding. If Hillyar outmaneuvered the *Essex* and avoided her grasp, the *Essex* could have taken her fire and passed on, replacing her topmast as she went and sailing beyond Hillyar's reach." The slow-sailing *Cherub* would not have entered into the action and would have been left far behind, according to Farragut.

"Secondly," he wrote, "it was apparent to everyone that we had no chance of success, under the circumstances, the ship should have been run ashore, throwing her broadside to the beach, to prevent raking, [and] fought as long as was consistent with humanity, and then set fire to her."

The *Cherub* had been engaged in the battle only briefly, while *Essex Junior*, with her light armament and tiny crew of sixty, kept out of the fight entirely. Hillyar treated the survivors with great care, allowing Porter and his crew to return home on parole in the undamaged *Essex Junior*. One hundred and thirty men, including Porter, left Valparaiso on April 27. Two of the wounded were left behind.

Good weather accompanied Porter the entire way home. They rounded Cape Horn under topgallant studding sails and were off New York on July 5. Before they reached Sandy Hook, however, the British razee *Saturn*, under Captain James Nash, stopped them and, despite Hillyar's safe-conduct pass, detained them. Porter was furious. On the spur of the moment, he left Lieutenant Downes in charge and fled in a whaleboat with a few men, rowing sixty miles to Long Island. Nash later reconsidered and released *Essex Junior*. Downes, after some additional trouble, sailed her into New York, where he was reunited with Porter. The city gave them a stupendous reception.

Lieutenant Gamble, meanwhile, had as difficult a time on Nuku Hiva as Porter did in Valparaiso. In May, Gamble barely escaped from the island after some islanders—urged on by a man named Wilson, Porter's English interpreter, whom he found living on the island when he arrived—killed Midshipman Feltus and were about to do the same to the rest of them. Miraculously, Gamble managed to get away and sail all the way to Hawaii in the *Sir Andrew Hammond*, one of the captured whale ships, only to be caught by the *Cherub*, fresh from her triumph at Valparaiso. Gamble was eventually paroled. He finally reached the United States on August 27, 1815, long after the war was over.

Like the rest of the country, President Madison, although regretting the loss of the *Essex* and so many of her brave men, celebrated the heroism of Porter and the other survivors. Madison blamed the disaster on Captain Hillyar for attacking the *Essex* in neutral waters. Hillyar claimed that Porter violated Valparaiso's neutrality first, but the president was determined to make Porter a hero. On September 20, 1814, in his opening message to the third session of the 13th Congress, Madison acknowledged the capture of the *Essex*, but wrote that "the loss is hidden in the blaze of heroism with which she was defended . . . till humanity tore down the colors which valor had nailed to the mast. . . . [Captain Porter] and his brave comrades have added much to the rising glory of the American flag, and have merited all the effusions of gratitude which their country is ever ready to bestow on the champions of its rights and of its safety."

CHAPTER TWENTY-FOUR

Burning Washington

COMMODORES RODGERS AND Porter, as well as Oliver Hazard Perry, were available in the summer of 1814 to help defend against Vice Admiral Cochrane's east coast raids. It had been obvious for some time that Cochrane would concentrate on the Chesapeake Bay area, since it contained both the capital and Baltimore, the city with the largest and most bothersome privateer fleet. New York and Philadelphia were much harder to get at, and the ports of Federalist New England seemed even less likely targets. Secretary Jones positioned Rodgers, Porter, and Perry so that they could help defend whatever city Cochrane struck.

On April 4, Rear Admiral Cockburn began operations in Chesapeake Bay by establishing a forward base on Tangier Island, where he could receive escaped slaves and spread the news to others that a secure retreat awaited them. Alerted by friends, runaways watched for British barges rowing up rivers and creeks at night. Lighted candles signaled that boats were ready to take men, women, and children to safety. They came by the dozens and then the hundreds to an uncertain future. Anything was better than the hell they were experiencing, however. Cockburn's operation was so successful that as early as the middle of June he was employing former slaves as soldiers in the small-scale, hit-and-run raids he had resumed.

Situated ten miles southeast of the Potomac, Tangier Island was also an ideal base from which to attack Washington, Annapolis, and Baltimore. Cockburn could keep an eye on Joshua Barney's flotilla from there as well. Before attacking any of the major cities, Cockburn first had to deal with Barney. Small though they were, Barney's row galleys were the only naval force challenging the British in the bay.

On April 26 Barney was promoted to the rank of captain in the American Flotilla Service. He had been building his fleet in Baltimore all winter. It wasn't easy. Money was tight, as were men and resources, but by the third week in May, Barney had thirteen specially constructed galleys ready with one twelve-pounder in their bows and a single powerful carronade mounted in the stern. Each was powered primarily with oars. He also had a gunboat, a smaller galley, another smaller boat for surveillance, and the 5-gun cutter *Scorpion*, commanded by William Barney, his eldest son. The *Scorpion* was Barney's flagship. The schooner *Asp* joined him later.

On May 24, Barney set out with his fleet for a surprise attack on Tangier Island. A few courageous merchantmen, who wanted to get to the Atlantic, accompanied him. After leaving Baltimore, they stopped at the Patuxent River and then sailed south on June 1. At nine o'clock in the morning, they ran into a strong British squadron that included the 74-gun *Dragon*, under Captain Robert Barrie; the 13-gun armed schooner *St. Lawrence*, under Commander David Boyd; and a number of smaller boats. For a brief time the *Dragon* was separated from the others, which gave Barney an opportunity to attack the rest of the squadron, but he missed it, and when the *Dragon* reappeared he retreated in a big hurry to the Patuxent, twenty-five miles north of the Potomac and sixty miles south of Baltimore. Shots were exchanged at the mouth of the river near Cedar Point, but adverse weather and general fatigue made further fighting too difficult, and both sides pulled back. The Patuxent was a safe refuge for Barney's flotilla. His shallow draft vessels could travel forty miles upriver beyond Pig Point, where low water levels protected them from all British warships. Smaller enemy barges could get at the flotilla, but Barney was confident he could deal with them.

After the fight at Cedar Point, Cockburn went after Barney in earnest. He reinforced Barrie's *Dragon* and *St. Lawrence* with the 50-gun razee *Loire*, under Captain Thomas Brown; the 18-gun brig-sloop *Jaseur*, under Commander George E. Watts; and more barges. Barney responded by moving his flotilla farther up the Patuxent.

On June 8 and 9, all of Barrie's larger ships, except the *Dragon*, sailed up the Patuxent with fifteen barges. Barney drew back into St. Leonard's Creek for protection, where the barges attacked him. They began firing Congreve rockets at eight o'clock in the morning on June 9. The projectiles screeched as they flew at the Americans, but they all missed and did no damage. The small missiles were only good for frightening an opponent. Barney rowed his undamaged barges forward, firing twelve pounders, forcing the enemy barges to retreat back to the larger ships. When they did, he withdrew up the creek.

On June 10 Barrie made a more determined attack, but Barney stood firm, and the British retreated again. This time Barney pursued them down the creek, attacking fiercely, driving them back. The ferocity of his attack took the *St. Lawrence,* which was at the mouth of the creek, off guard, and in the ensuing melee she ran aground. Barney continued his assault, cutting up the stranded schooner and nearly capturing her before the larger ships, which were also taken by surprise, came to the rescue and forced Barney to retire. The battle lasted six grueling hours.

On June 26, after careful preparation, Barney attacked the larger warships blockading him in St. Leonard's Creek. He was supported this time by a battery firing from elevated ground at the mouth of the creek. His combined land and sea barrage forced Captain Brown to withdraw the *Loire* farther down the Patuxent. When he did, Barney escaped from the creek and rowed north up the Patuxent to safety above Pig Point.

BARNEY'S FLOTILLA WAS still secure in the Patuxent when, on July 24, forty-seven-year-old Major General Robert Ross arrived at Bermuda with 3,500 battle-tested veterans of Wellington's army in France, men who thought they'd be going home after defeating Napoleon. Instead, they were confined in the bowels of troop transports for a long, uncomfortable voyage. They were supplemented by 1,000 marines, bringing Ross's army to a total of 4,500 men.

Ross was expected to work closely with Admiral Cochrane to conduct large-scale raids along the American coast. Cochrane would decide where the raids were made, but Ross would command on the ground and have a veto if he disagreed about the places or timing of the raids. The Admiralty cautioned Cochrane not to advance his modest army "so far into the country as to risk its power of retreating to its embarkation."

According to Lord Bathurst the overall purpose of the raids was to "effect a diversion on the coast of the United States . . . in favor of the army employed in the defense of Upper and Lower Canada," but Cochrane intended to do more than simply create a diversion. He wanted to punish Americans for the atrocities they had committed along the Canadian frontier. Colonel Campbell's depredations at Long Point in May had so infuriated Governor-General Prevost that on June 2 he had asked Cochrane to "assist in inflicting that measure of retaliation which shall deter the enemy from a repetition of similar outrages." Cochrane was only too happy to comply. On July 18 he ordered his commanders "to destroy and lay waste such towns and districts upon the coast as you may find assailable. You will hold strictly in view the conduct of the American army towards His Majesty's unoffending Canadian subjects, and you will spare the lives merely of the unarmed inhabitants of the United States." Cochrane and Prevost ignored British massacres and depredations against American soldiers and civilians, acting as if only the United States savaged civilians.

Over a month later Cochrane sent a copy of his order to Secretary of State Monroe, who wrote back the first week of September, explaining that any acts of destruction or outrages committed by American troops were not sanctioned by the government, as Cochrane charged, and those responsible were disciplined. Cochrane was not interested in winning an argument, however; he intended to carry out a course of destruction no matter what, since it was what his government wanted and, indeed, what his countrymen wanted.

Although Cochrane told Prevost months before that he would be conducting raids in Chesapeake Bay, by August he had doubts about the timing. The heat, humidity, and generally unhealthy climate during the summer made it the worst time for an attack on Washington. Cochrane preferred October, when the weather was milder and the climate not so sickly. He also had to think about New Orleans. The battles in the Chesapeake, however important, were only diversions. New Orleans was a far more important objective, and it would take time to gather the forces for the invasion.

On the other hand, Cochrane yearned to hurl Mr. Madison "from his throne." He was also impressed with the psychological importance of taking the capital and of how easy it would be right then. Rear Admiral Cockburn had been urging Cochrane to attack right away. "It is quite impossible for any country to be in a more unfit state for war than this now is," he wrote to his chief, "and I much doubt if the American Government knew . . . every particular of the intended attack on them, whether it would be possible for them to . . . avert the blow." In another letter, written the same day, Cockburn boasted, "within forty-eight hours after the arrival in the Patuxent of such a force as you expect, the city of Washington might be possessed without difficulty or opposition of any kind."

In spite of Cockburn's assurances, Cochrane and Ross remained uncomfortable with the timing of an attack on Washington. They left Bermuda on August 1 in Cochrane's flagship, the 80-gun *Tonnant*, and sailed for Chesapeake Bay to confer with Cockburn. A flotilla of troop transports and warships, under Rear Admiral Pulteney Malcolm, left Bermuda two days later, arriving at the Virginia

Capes on the fourteenth, after six hundred often difficult miles, discomforting the long-suffering soldiers even more.

President Madison was convinced that Washington would be Admiral Cochrane's primary target. Secretary of State Monroe agreed with him. At one time Monroe entertained the idea that the British would be so tied down in Europe dealing with the aftermath of the war that they would not invade the United States at all, but when he saw them building up their forces in North America, he became convinced that Washington was in mortal danger. Secretary Jones thought that the British might attack Washington but that Baltimore or even Annapolis was a more likely target. Secretary Armstrong was fanatical in his belief that only Baltimore would be attacked.

Madison, however, was certain the British would aim at the seat of government. Attorney General Rush reported that the president thought Washington would be an inviting target because of "the éclat that would attend a successful inroad upon the capital." As apprehensive as the president undoubtedly was, it is difficult to explain why he hadn't strengthened the capital's defenses much earlier in the war. Madison thought a force of around 13,000, including 500 of Barney's sailors, would be sufficient to defend the capital, and he believed they could be obtained from the militias of the District of Columbia and the surrounding states of Virginia, Maryland, and Pennsylvania. Secretary Armstrong was in charge of the capital's defense, but he remained unshakable in his conviction that the British would not attack there, and he did nothing to prepare. Madison was well acquainted with the secretary's views and actions, but still he did not replace him.

To strengthen Washington's defense, Madison on July 1 created the tenth military district, which included the capital, Maryland, and parts of Virginia. And he put thirty-nine-year-old Brigadier General William Winder in command. It is difficult to explain why Winder was appointed. He had been one of the key figures responsible for the defeat at the important Battle of Stoney Creek on the Niagara Peninsula the previous year. That action stopped the progress Dearborn and Chauncey were making against Upper Canada.

Winder had been captured and removed to Quebec with the rest of the prisoners. He was then released to go to Washington and arrange a prisoner exchange, which he did, concluding a convention on April 16, 1814. He was the nephew of the antiwar Federalist governor of Maryland, Levin Winder, and that may be why the president appointed him.

Madison may have thought that having the governor's nephew in command would make calling out the Maryland militia easier. Whatever the president's reasoning, it was a baffling appointment. To make matters worse, the inscrutable Armstrong opposed Winder's selection and refused to work with him.

Winder's recruitment problems were daunting. Only 500 regulars were in the Tenth District. Primary reliance had to be on militiamen. Although 93,500 had been placed on alert, Winder had no authority to call them out until there was imminent danger. On July 12, he received permission to call up 6,000 from Maryland, but in the next six weeks his uncle managed to produce only 250. Even when called up, the militiamen were not under Winder's command until the War Department organized and equipped them and turned them over to him. On July 17 Winder was allowed to call up 7,000 more from Pennsylvania, 2,000 from Virginia, and 2,000 from the District of Columbia, but fewer than 1,000 appeared. It turned out that because of changes in state law, Pennsylvania could not send any.

Armstrong was indifferent to Winder's problems. The secretary was constantly complaining about the lack of money, absolving himself of any shortcomings, and placing the blame for whatever happened on the president and Congress. Avoiding responsibility was an old habit of Armstrong's.

The secretary's gross insubordination continued unabated throughout the crisis. He gave no direction to Winder, who had no idea how to proceed. The hapless general spent an inordinate amount of time simply reconnoitering the area under his supervision without doing anything to erect defenses along the major invasion routes to the capital. The first and most likely was through Bladensburg; another was through Old Fields to the Eastern Branch bridge, a mile from the Washington Navy Yard. Yet another was by way of the Potomac. That was the least likely: the river itself presented too many obstacles to navigation. And it was defended at a strategic point by Fort Washington on the Maryland side of the river, opposite Mount Vernon. Winder made no attempt to fortify Bladensburg or to strengthen Fort Washington.

ON AUGUST 14 General Ross and Admiral Cochrane arrived at the mouth of the Potomac in the *Tonnant* for talks with Rear Admiral Cockburn. They still entertained doubts about the wisdom of attacking Washington right then. The weather was a problem, as was the condition of the troops after their long voyages. Also, using 4,500 tired regulars to attack the capital of a nation of nearly 8 million would seem at first glance a harebrained scheme. Cockburn, however, was absolutely confident, as he always was, and he removed their doubts. They agreed to land the troops at Benedict, Maryland, on the Patuxent, and march them along

Figure 24.1: Irwin Bevan, *Attack on Fort Washington on Potomac, 17 August 1814* (courtesy of Mariner's Museum, Newport News, Virginia).

the west bank to Lower Marlboro and then Nottingham. At the same time, Cockburn would ascend the river with his squadron on Ross's flank, carrying supplies. Their immediate objective was the destruction of Barney's flotilla. Once that was accomplished, a final decision could be made about Washington.

On August 17, Cochrane ordered Captain James A. Gordon to sail up the Potomac with a powerful squadron, draw attention away from Ross's landing, and assist him as a rear guard. Beside his own 38-gun frigate *Seahorse*, Gordon had the 36-gun *Euryalus*, under Captain Charles Napier; the bomb vessels *Devastation* (Captain Alexander), *Aetna* (Captain Kenah), and *Meteor* (Captain Roberts); the rocket ship *Erebus* (Captain Bartholomew); the schooner *Anna Maria* (a tender); and a dispatch boat. The Potomac was extremely difficult for larger ships to ascend, which is one of the reasons Secretary Jones thought it unlikely the British would attempt it. Gordon, who had the temporary rank of commodore and was one of the senior—and most accomplished—captains in the Royal Navy, expected the river and Fort Washington to give him plenty of trouble.

As a further distraction in favor of Ross, Cochrane sent Captain Sir Peter Parker to create havoc farther up the Chesapeake above Baltimore with a squadron that included the 36-gun *Menelaus* and some smaller vessels. Cochrane then proceeded with the remainder of his naval force to the mouth of the Patuxent and landed Ross and his army on August 19 and 20 at Benedict, forty-five miles from Washington. The town was practically empty; the townspeople had fled. Ross had one six-pounder and two three-pounders. Attacking the American capital with only 4,500 troops might have seemed imprudent to Ross earlier, but now the utter lack of opposition impelled him forward.

WHEN GENERAL WINDER and President Madison heard about the landing at Benedict, they ordered obstructions put in the way of the invaders, but nothing happened. Winder also called out the militia. Armstrong had refused to let him call them out ahead of time, but now a crisis demanded it. The militiamen began gathering, and Winder soon had 2,000 camped ten miles southeast of the capital.

Unaware that Ross had actually landed, Secretary Jones wrote to Commodore Rodgers in Philadelphia on August 19: "The enemy has entered the Patuxent with a very large force, indicating a design upon this place, which may be real or it may serve to mask his design upon Baltimore." Since Jones thought Baltimore the more likely target, he ordered Rodgers to march there with three hundred men and combine them with the detachment of marines at nearby Cecil Furnace. Jones sent similar instructions to Commodore Porter in New York. Commodore Oliver Hazard Perry was already at Baltimore supervising construction of the new frigate *Java*.

HAVING DEBARKED HIS troops, Ross now marched—again unopposed—to Lower Marlboro and then to Nottingham on August 21, while the British squadron under Rear Admiral Cockburn made its way up the Patuxent on Ross's right flank toward Barney's flotilla. Barney knew they were coming. He had already put five heavy cannon (two eighteen-pounders and three twelve-pounders) on carriages and marched with them and four hundred men to Upper Marlboro and from there on the twenty-first to the Washington Navy Yard. A few of Barney's men remained with the flotilla, ready to set it on fire when Cockburn approached. The night of the twenty-second, when Cockburn's boats and marines appeared, Barney's men burned the flotilla and fled.

On the same day, August 22, Ross resumed his march and easily reached Upper Marlboro. No obstacles were in his path nor any resistance. He was now only fifteen miles from Washington, and being that close and having encountered no opposition, he decided—with Cockburn urging him on—to push on toward the capital.

Cockburn received a note from Cochrane congratulating him on the destruction of Barney's flotilla. Cochrane added, however, that "the sooner the army gets back the better." This was not an explicit order to return immediately, but it might have been read that way. The aggressive Cockburn chose to ignore its implications, however, and proceeded with the attack on Washington.

General Winder, in the meantime, had succeeded in gathering 2,000 militiamen at Battalion Old Fields, not far from Upper Marlboro and Ross's army. Barney and his men were with him. The president and his cabinet visited there on the twenty-second and conferred with Winder, stayed overnight, and returned to Washington the next day.

Ross put his troops back in motion the evening of the twenty-third. The heat and humidity, combined with the weak condition of the men, caused many to fall by the wayside from exhaustion and disease, forcing him to stop for the night after advancing only five miles.

For some unexplained reason, that same day, Winder, not knowing Ross's ultimate destination, marched his troops back to Washington, crossing the lower, or Eastern Branch bridge, into the city a mile from the navy yard. People were terrified. They thought the British had pushed Winder back. Barney and his men were still with him, and they remained through the night.

That same day, August 23, Baltimore militiamen, under Brigadier General Tobias Stansbury and Colonel Joseph Sterrett, numbering approximately 2,000, arrived at Bladensburg. The small town was at a crossing point on the Eastern Branch of the Potomac seven miles from Washington. Winder had ordered Stansbury to position his troops between Ross's army and the town. Stansbury wisely ignored the order, and on the morning of August 24 he marched his men through the town, crossed the wooden bridge (Stoddert's bridge) to the west side of the Eastern Branch, and took up a defensive position on the high ground overlooking the bridge and the shallow ford nearby. Stansbury ordered the bridge destroyed, but for some unknown reason it remained standing.

That same morning, Ross marched his army to Bladensburg, arriving at noon. Winder, meanwhile, having guessed wrong about what road Ross was taking to Washington, had his men guarding the Eastern Branch bridge six miles away. Incredibly, Winder at no time had intelligence of Ross's movements.

While Ross was marching to Bladensburg, the president and his advisors were conferring with Winder at the Washington Navy Yard. It was ten o'clock. Suddenly, word came that the British were on the road to Bladensburg. Monroe raced to the town, while Winder set his troops in motion and galloped off to Bladensburg himself, leaving Barney to defend the Eastern Branch bridge and to blow it up if necessary. The president followed Winder, but before he left, Barney asked him if he could march his flotilla men to the battlefield as well. Only a few were needed to blow up the Eastern Branch bridge, Barney argued. He was needed far more at Bladensburg. Madison agreed, and Barney set out for the battlefield, arriving with five heavy cannon and five hundred men. He was forced to set up a half mile from the bridge, well back of Stansbury's men. Barney arranged his big naval guns to cover the road to Washington.

WHEN ROSS REACHED Bladensburg, Winder's militiamen were well positioned on commanding heights on the other side of the river. Ross estimated there were between 8,000 and 9,000. Actually, there were fewer than 6,000. In spite of the enemy's numbers and the fatigue of his men, Ross attacked immediately. He began by firing Congreve rockets, and as they screamed overhead, the first of the British light infantry, led by Colonel William Thornton, rushed across the bridge under heavy fire. They were stymied by the heavy outpouring coming from cannon and muskets, however, and had to withdraw back across the bridge. But they attacked again, and the second wave, with Ross in their midst urging them on, managed to cross; more followed, and then even more.

President Madison was on the battlefield and withdrew with his party when the first rockets screeched overhead. There was a report that he was nearly captured, but this was not the case. As the president was leaving, disorder had already begun spreading among the inexperienced militiamen. A short while later, they began retreating in earnest, fleeing in all directions. But Barney and his five hundred sailors and marines with their heavy guns held firm, and militiamen from Maryland and Washington to Barney's left and right stood with them, halting the British advance.

Barney's guns and the militiamen beside him were the last line of defense— all that stood between Ross and Washington. The British continued their attack, with Barney's crew and the nearby militiamen desperately holding them off. The militiamen near Barney were under heavy fire when Winder rode up and inexplicably ordered them to fall back, which they did, and then fled like the others, leaving Barney and his seamen alone. They continued firing at the enemy. Barney's horse was shot out from under him, but he got up and continued to fight. A musket ball then struck him in the thigh, and he lay on the ground bleeding. With the British closing in, he ordered a retreat, which his men reluctantly carried out.

Barney could not go with them. He had collapsed in a pool of blood and was soon captured, as the British swarmed around. Admiral Cockburn and General Ross were directed to his side. When Barney saw them, he looked up with a grin, "Well admiral, you have got hold of me at last." Cockburn and Ross had an English surgeon tend to him right away and may have saved his life. They could not have been more solicitous. Ross promptly freed Barney and his officers on parole. He had Barney taken to Ross's Tavern in Bladensburg, where he'd be comfortable. Barney later said he was treated "as if I was a brother."

The one-sided battle was over by four o'clock. Of Ross's men, 64 were dead and 185 wounded. There were 71 American casualties, most of them Barney's flotilla men. During the entire crisis the enigmatic Armstrong had acted as if he were a spectator, offering no direction to Winder or advice to the president. He performed as he had the previous year during the abortive attack on Montreal, when, sensing disaster, he sought to place all the blame for it on Wilkinson and Hampton. Now he kept his head down, seeking to put all the onus for the debacle on Winder and Madison.

An hour earlier, just after three o'clock, Dolley Madison left the presidential mansion in a wagon with plates and portable articles, including George Washington's portrait. She crossed the Potomac on the Little Falls Bridge and made her way to Rokeby plantation in Loudoun County, Virginia, the home of Richard Love, where she would spend the night with her close friend Mrs. Love.

The day before, the president had warned her to be prepare to leave Washington at a moment's notice. He had told her to take care of herself and the papers, public and private, in the president's house. At the same time, he had ordered important papers from all government offices removed. Many of the documents dated back to the Revolution, including the Declaration of Independence and the papers and correspondence of George Washington.

Shortly after Dolley's departure, Madison himself reached the Potomac and crossed over to Virginia at Mason's Ferry. He would spend the night at Salona, the home of Reverend John Maffitt. The following day he and Dolley were reunited at Willey's Tavern, where she remained until the British left Washington.

AFTER THE BATTLE, Ross rested his men only two hours before marching them seven miles unopposed to the capital. Cockburn, who, as might be imagined, was exhilarated, went with them. He and Ross rode white horses, and even though it was eight o'clock and Washington was dark, they were conspicuous. As they entered the city, three hundred men from behind buildings next to Albert Gallatin's house opened fire, killing Ross's horse. The militiamen were quickly dispersed, however, and the British proceeded to burn the capital's public buildings and a few private ones.

Ross and Cockburn entered the White House, or President's House as it was then called, and found plenty of good wine to toast the Prince Regent before setting the place on fire. The Capitol and the Library of Congress were also burned, as was the building housing the *National Intelligencer*, which Cockburn personally attended to, since its editor, Joseph Gales Jr., was a persistent critic of his. Gales was surprised to learn that Cockburn was reading his newspaper. The August 24 edition had expressed complete confidence that Washington was safe.

The British later excused the wanton destruction of the capital by claiming it was done in retaliation for the burning and plundering that American troops did in Canada. Nothing the United States did in Canada, however, remotely justified the burning of Washington.

WHEN THE BRITISH entered the city, Commodore Tingey, under strict orders from Secretary Jones, destroyed the Washington Navy Yard. Tingey delegated the baleful task to Master Commandant John O. Creighton, and he carried out his duty with a heavy heart, burning the new frigate *Columbia* and the new sloop of war *Argus*. When Creighton and his crew were finished, the only building left standing was the marine commandant's red-brick house.

The British rampage through the city continued into the next day. It only came to an end when a severe hurricane struck, tearing off roofs, destroying buildings, and dousing fires. During the unexpected tempest, flying debris and collapsing houses killed thirty British soldiers. Ross and Cockburn had already decided to retreat to their ships. Since their attack was only a diversion, it seemed prudent to leave as quickly as possible.

When news of Washington's destruction reached London on September 27, Lord Bathurst, although delighted, was critical of how compassionately General Ross had treated the people of the city. "If . . . you should attack Baltimore, and could . . . make its inhabitants *feel* a little more of the effects of your visit than what has been experienced at Washington," he wrote, "you would make that portion of the American people experience the consequences of war who have most contributed to its existence."

On August 25, under cover of darkness, Ross and Cochrane pulled out of Washington and marched back to Benedict via Upper Marlboro and Nottingham.

Ross thought it possible that American militias might turn out in overpowering numbers, bent on revenge. He encountered no opposition, however, and on the evening of August 29 his weary men boarded their transports. Ross was immensely proud of their work. He was particularly delighted with the abundant cannon, powder, and musket cartridges they had hauled away.

General Winder, meanwhile, after the debacle at Bladensburg, gathered what men he could and retreated to Montgomery Court House (Rockville), sixteen miles from Washington, and then moved on to Baltimore, where he thought the next attack would occur.

THE PRESIDENT, AFTER fleeing the capital on August 24 and meeting Dolley the next day, turned around and returned to Washington with some cabinet members on August 27. General Ross had retreated much faster than Madison expected. The president stayed in Washington at the house of his brother-in-law Richard Cutts, which had once been his own home, and Dolley rejoined him there. She had shown remarkable courage throughout the crisis. Later, she and the president took up residence in Colonel John Tayloe's large residence, known as the Octagon House. (Tayloe was a wealthy Virginia planter, perhaps the richest in the state.)

Madison's character shone in the aftermath of the debacle. He remained steady and kept firm control of the government, providing essential leadership and demonstrating that Washington may have been burned but the United States was very much intact. And he finally rid himself of Armstrong, replacing him with Monroe for the time being. It was abundantly clear that Armstrong could no longer lead the army, having worn out his welcome with everyone. On September 1, wanting to demonstrate that he was in charge of a functioning government, Madison issued a proclamation urging Americans to expel the invader and accusing the British of "a deliberate disregard of the principles of humanity and the rules of civilized warfare."

CAPTAIN JAMES GORDON, meanwhile, continued to doggedly lead his squadron up the Potomac. Starting on August 17, he had pushed upriver, encountering no opposition. He kept at it for ten days, overcoming every natural obstacle, including a hurricane on the ninth day—the same storm that hit Washington. He warped his big ships over shallow waters, grounding continuously on shoals while fighting adverse winds. He reported that every one of his larger vessels had gone aground twenty times and were only gotten off by a prodigious effort. Nonetheless, he persevered. He did not reach Fort Washington until the evening of August 27, the same day that Madison returned to the capital.

The fort had a battery of twenty-seven guns, ranging in size from six to fifty-two pounders, and sixty men. Armstrong had not bothered to strengthen it, nor had the president. The pathetic number of men and guns could never withstand Gordon. When he commenced firing from the bomb vessels, he expected a fierce response, but to his utter amazement, none came. The bombardment went on for two hours, before Captain Samuel Dyson and his men fled from the fort and blew it up without firing a shot. Dyson was soon dismissed from the army. The entire blame for the fiasco was placed on him, not on the secretary of war and the president, where it belonged.

Alexandria now lay open to Gordon, and he stood off its wharves on the morning of August 29. The town was defenseless. Its militiamen, who had participated in the fiasco at Bladensburg, were nowhere to be found. Alexandria's leaders had pleaded with the administration to give them cannon and other munitions, and they were promised them, but none were delivered. There was nothing left to do now but throw themselves on Gordon's mercy. He made a deal to spare the town in return for supplies and prize ships—twenty-one of them, stuffed with tobacco, wine, sugar, and other goods. Alexandria agreed. It was an abject surrender. The leadership of the country in Washington watched, helpless, as Gordon exacted the humiliating ransom with impunity and then proceeded back down the Potomac on September 2 with his booty.

Secretary Jones tried to obstruct Gordon's descent. He had already ordered John Rodgers, Oliver Hazard Perry, and David Porter to help with Washington's defense, but they arrived too late. Jones now hoped that the trio could perform some miracle and stop Gordon as he struggled back to Chesapeake Bay. On August 28 Jones wrote to Rodgers, asking if he would "annoy or destroy the enemy on his return down the river." The next day, after Jones found out about Gordon's demands on Alexandria, he angrily ordered Rodgers to bring six hundred fifty men to Bladensburg and await further orders. Rodgers immediately dispatched Porter with a hundred men to march to Washington and then came along himself with additional men, but not the six hundred fifty Jones wanted.

Upon being informed of what Rodgers was doing, Jones wrote Porter on August 31, ordering him to take his detachment of seamen and marines, which had just arrived, and establish batteries with six eighteen-pounders "to effect the destruction of the enemy squadron on its passage down the Potomac."

On September 2 Acting Secretary of War Monroe, in desperation, suggested to Rodgers that he might reestablish the post at Fort Washington that night. At the time, Rodgers was busy organizing fire ships to attack Gordon as he came down the river, and he ignored Monroe.

The next day, September 3, Gordon's flagship *Seahorse*, the 50-gun *Euryalus*, and the bomb vessel *Devastation* were two and a half miles below Alexandria when Rodgers attacked them with three small fire vessels, conned by lieutenants Henry Newcomb and Dulany Forrest and Sailing Master James Ramage. Rodgers was in the river, directing them from his gig. The wind did not cooperate, however, and they failed to reach their targets. Gordon's boats towed the flaming fire ships away. At the same time, Gordon's men went after Rodgers, firing at him for thirty minutes as he raced away in his gig.

Rodgers tried again the next day, planning to send Lieutenant Newcomb back with a flaming cutter, but the wind again would not cooperate, and when a frigate came after Newcomb, he had to scurry away. That night, Gordon sent some barges to attack Rodgers's boats, but Rodgers beat them off. At seven o'clock the next morning, Rodgers assembled another fire ship. He hoped to coordinate with Porter, who had established himself farther downriver at the White House, a navigational landmark below Mount Vernon, thirty miles from Washington. But that did not work out either. Rodgers was forced to give up.

As Gordon continued down the Potomac, he encountered Porter with two hundred Virginia militiamen, under Brigadier General John P. Hungerford, at the White House (Belvoir plantation) on September 4. Master Commandant Creighton accompanied Porter. They had only three long eighteen-pounders, two twelve-pounders, and two four-pounders to begin with, but more came, and they put up a gallant fight. For the entire day on September 5, Gordon bombarded Porter's batteries, but with little effect. When Porter continued to fire back, Gordon committed more ships to the assault. As the hours passed, more cannon arrived for Porter. Army Captain Ambrose Spencer of the U. S. Artillery, who had been second in command at Fort Washington when it was blown up, fought alongside Porter with a small contingent. On the morning of September 6, Gordon brought up more of his big ships and commenced a terrific bombardment, which finally forced Porter and the Virginia militiamen to retire. Captain Spencer and his men convinced Porter by their bravery and sacrifice "that it was not want of courage on their part which caused the destruction of the fort."

Oliver Hazard Perry was the last obstacle Gordon had to face. Perry had hastily thrown up a battery at Indian Head, Maryland, with a single eighteen-pounder in it that arrived thirty minutes before Gordon appeared. Perry had little ammunition and started firing right away. Militiamen working with him had six-pounders, and they kept up a spirited fire. All the ammunition was quickly expended, however, and Perry and the militiamen were forced to retire under heavy fire from Gordon's ships. The exchange went on for an hour. Perry had one man wounded during the fight.

Before Gordon extricated himself from the Potomac completely, Admiral Cochrane received word that Gordon might be in trouble and began moving his big fleet toward the river on September 7. The next day the fleet was in the Potomac, making its way slowly upstream. Cochrane and his big ships were twenty miles from the mouth of the river on September 9, when Gordon suddenly appeared triumphantly with twenty-one prizes and the bomb ships and rocket vessel that were indispensable for an attack on Baltimore, or another place like Rhode Island, which Cochrane was considering.

In the end, Rodgers, Porter, and Perry put up as spirited a fight as they could with almost no resources, and they made an important contribution to the war by delaying Gordon and Cochrane, which gave other cities that were under the gun, like Baltimore, additional time to prepare their defenses.

Even Boston was finally realizing that the threat of a British invasion was real. Alexandria was known as a Federalist city with pro-English sympathies, but that had not saved it from a thorough looting by Gordon.

WHILE GORDON WAS on his diversionary raid up the Potomac, Captain Sir Peter Parker had been busy with his diversion as well. He wrote to Admiral Cochrane that he had "been continually employed in reconnoitering the harbors and coves and sounding the Bay and acting for the annoyance of the enemy." He found Annapolis practically defenseless and thought it could be taken easily. He also reconnoitered near Baltimore.

On August 30, after he had written to Cochrane, Parker became engaged in a sharp fight with Maryland militiamen near Chestertown, Maryland. He led a charge against what he thought were 500 militiamen, but were in fact fewer than 100. Whatever their number, he was confident they would run, as militiamen had several times before when he challenged them. This time, however, they stood their ground. Parker had 104 men armed with bayonets, pikes, and pistols. He attacked the militiamen at Caulk's Field near Chestertown around eleven o'clock during a dark night. Early in the action, Parker was shot and killed. His men fought on, uncertain how big a force they were fighting. Eventually, the Maryland militiamen ran out of ammunition and pulled back, but the British, believing they were up against a much larger force, did as well, retreating to their ship, the *Menelaus*. During the fracas, no Americans were killed; 3 were wounded. The British had 14 killed and 27 wounded.

AFTER THE WASHINGTON and Alexandria disasters, some Federalists felt vindicated. They had predicted blows of this kind, and they were not reluctant to say, "We told you so." "The Federalists now have great consolation that they always with all their might opposed this war," the *Salem Gazette* wrote. "They supplicated and entreated that it might not be declared, for they foresaw and foretold the ruin and misery and disgrace it would inevitably bring upon the nation."

Most of the country, however, was appalled and angry at the wanton destruction of the capital, as were Europeans. The French were loud in their condemnation of the desecration of Washington. Even some British newspapers were disgusted by what had happened.

WASHINGTON WASN'T THE only place Cochrane's squadrons were attacking. On April 7–8, 1814, the British sent a raiding party up the Connecticut River to Essex (then known as Pettipaug Point) and destroyed twenty-seven vessels without suffering any losses.

On May 22, Commodore Sir Thomas Masterman Hardy sailed his flagship *Ramillies* from its station off the eastern end of Long Island to Narragansett Bay near Boston. Seven days later, he transferred to the frigate *Nymph* and sailed up the coast to Portsmouth, New Hampshire, to ascertain if an attack on the battleship *Washington*, under construction there, was feasible. Hardy did not want to use the 74-gun *Ramillies* to reconnoiter for fear it would alarm the countryside and warn Isaac Hull.

On June 16, Hardy reported back to Cochrane that after a thorough reconnaissance, he believed the *Washington* could be easily destroyed. Hull had done everything he could to prepare a defense with extremely limited resources. He was getting little support from either the state government or the national government. Armstrong did not think Portsmouth needed help. Cochrane decided to postpone the project, however, even though he knew that destroying the battleship would be popular in England. The *Times* of London would certainly have loudly applauded.

Cochrane had a more important assignment for Hardy—seizing Moose Island in Passamaquoddy Bay. The important harbor of Eastport was on the island,

and Cochrane had orders from Bathurst to occupy it. Lieutenant Colonel Thomas Pilkington sailed from Halifax in the sloop *Martin*, and on July 7 he met Hardy in the *Ramillies*. Hardy was coming from Bermuda accompanied by two troop transports, which carried six hundred men, and the bomb vessel *Terror*. Pilkington landed at Eastport, in the Maine District of Massachusetts, and took over Moose Island. The eighty-six American defenders at Fort Sullivan, led by Major Perley Putnam, reluctantly surrendered on July 11 without a fight. Putnam had no other choice.

Raids were continuing in Boston Harbor. When the 38-gun *Nymph*, under Captain Famery P. Epworth, returned from her scouting trip to Portsmouth and was back at her station off Boston, she immediately went on the attack. "On the night of 20–21 June the *Nymphe*'s sailing master and a small party rowed from the frigate into Boston Harbor to burn a sloop 'within a mile' of the *Constitution*," Commodore Bainbridge reported. He was commandant of the Boston Navy Yard and had to worry about not only the *Constitution* but also the 74-gun *Independence*, which was under construction. The Admiralty wanted both destroyed. Bainbridge also had responsibility for protecting Boston Harbor and the city. He got no help from the ultrafederalists in Boston, but most ordinary people supported him. In another daring raid on July 7, armed barges from the *Nymphe* managed to cut out five more small sloops.

British raids in the summer and fall of 1814 in New England were extensive. They struck in the district of Maine and in Massachusetts, New Hampshire, Connecticut, and Rhode Island. Both Wareham and Situate in Massachusetts were attacked. No place was safe. The *Bulwark* raided Saco, Maine, on June 16. Bath and Wiscasset in Maine were attacked the day before, and Rye, New Hampshire, was threatened.

A particularly vicious raid was conducted against Stonington, Connecticut. Rear Admiral Henry Hotham, commander of the blockading squadron off Long Island, was obliged to carry out Cochrane's order to lay waste to towns, and he set his sights on Stonington. Hotham ordered Captain Hardy, who had just returned from Maine, to do the job. Hardy found the whole business distasteful: he thought that attacking defenseless towns was both cowardly and stupid. Nonetheless, he carried out his instructions and bombarded Stonington—an innocent place that had no strategic value—beginning on the evening of August 9. Hardy employed the 38-gun frigate *Pactolus*, the 20-gun brig *Dispatch*, the bomb vessel *Terror*, and barges from the *Ramillies*. The shelling went on for about four hours, ending at midnight. The townspeople bravely defended Stonington with three cannon. They were helped immeasurably when 3,000 Connecticut militiamen arrived to defend the fort that had been firing fruitlessly at the warships.

The bombardment resumed the next day for several hours. The British ships were joined by the *Ramillies* and the 18-gun *Nimrod*. Later, Hardy suspended the attack and did not resume until the afternoon of August 11, when the *Terror* threw shells into the town sporadically until evening. The following day, the *Terror* resumed her desultory shelling until noon, when Hardy called off the attack and left, greatly embarrassed.

Of far greater importance, the British initiated a large-scale invasion of eastern Maine. On August 26 Lieutenant General Sir John. C. Sherbrooke, the governor of Nova Scotia, and Rear Admiral Edward Griffith left Halifax with twenty-four ships and 2,500 men for the assault. Griffith's squadron included the 74-gun *Dragon*, under Captain Robert Barrie; the 74-gun *Bulwark*; the frigates *Endymion*, *Bacchante*, and *Tenedos*; the sloop *Sylph*; and two brigs, *Rifleman* and *Peruvian*. Sherbrooke's men landed unopposed at Castine in Penobscot Bay on September 1. Twelve thousand men suitable for military service were in the northeastern part of Maine, but Madison's war was not popular there, and the militias were poorly organized. Sherbrooke met no opposition. The tiny American garrison of regulars at Castine destroyed their small fort and withdrew up the Penobscot River. Sherbrooke then sent amphibious forces against Belfast, Hamden, Bangor, and Machias. Soon all of eastern Maine, from the Penobscot River to Passamaquoddy Bay, was in British hands. Federalists in Boston liked to think that the people of eastern Maine welcomed the British, but the general sentiment was more one of neutrality and a wish that the war would be over. Sherbrooke soon annexed the captured territory, and the *Times* was positively gleeful. "The district we speak of is the most valuable in the United States for fishing establishments," the editors wrote, "and has a coast of 60 leagues abounding in excellent harbors, from whence much lumber is sent to Europe and the West Indies."

By the end of August 1814 Admiral Cochrane's raids had been eminently successful. He had captured and burned the American capital and embarrassed Madison, and he had acquired a large chunk of Maine with no opposition. Smaller raids along the coast had also gone well. More importantly, his attacks did not unite Federalists and Republicans, as might have been expected; the country remained divided. The political parties were as bitterly opposed to one another as they had always been, perhaps even more so. Madison was desperately trying to hold the country together and continue the war. But his chances of withstanding the British invasions that were coming from the north and the south appeared extremely poor. Admiral Cochrane, on the other hand, as he prepared to tackle Baltimore and then New Orleans, was flush with victory, his confidence at a high level.

CHAPTER TWENTY-FIVE

The War at Sea
Continues in 1814

WHILE JOSHUA BARNEY, John Rodgers, David Porter, Oliver Hazard Perry, and their colleagues were engaged in fighting Cochrane's raids along the eastern seaboard, the blue-water fleet was still active, getting to sea and performing missions that would win it even more esteem from the Royal Navy. The growing respect commanded by the American fleet would be one of the more important outcomes of the war. The actions of single ships at sea might have appeared to have little relevance to the outcome of the war, but in fact they were of great consequence. Not every cruise was successful, but those that were had a decided impact on British views about the potency of American arms. London's newfound respect for the American navy would be an important factor in shaping the peace to come.

On the afternoon of December 31, 1813, during a wintry gale, Charles Stewart ran the *Constitution* out of Boston. The blockaders had been blown off their station. As Stewart raced out to sea, he shaped a course for the northern coast of South America, and on January 14 he encountered two strange sails. The first turned out to be an American schooner, and he never caught up with the second. The next day he encountered a warship that turned out to be Portuguese. The remainder of January was just as frustrating. On February 1 lookouts spied a sail off Georgetown, Guyana, and gave chase, but when she ran too close to shore, Stewart turned away. Two days later, he finally spied a British warship,

Figure 25.1: Irwin Bevan, *Escape of the* Constitution, *3 April 1814* (courtesy of Mariner's Museum, Newport News, Virginia).

the 18-gun *Mosquito*. Her captain threw on all sail and ran in close to shore, where the water was too shallow for the *Constitution* to follow. Stewart had to back off once more. On February 8 he chased the 18-gun brig HMS *Columbine*, but he could not catch her before dark, and she escaped.

Finally, on February 14 Stewart made his first captures—a merchantman in the morning and the 18-gun British schooner *Picton* in the afternoon. Two days later, he captured another small merchantman, and the next day he took one off Grenada. He then shaped a course for Puerto Rico. On February 23, after passing through the Mona Passage, he finally saw what he wanted, the 36-gun British frigate *Pique*. Both ships cleared for action, but the *Pique*, following the Admiralty's orders, ran away. Stewart went after her, but he was becalmed for a time, while the *Pique* had enough wind to stay ahead until darkness allowed her to escape.

Stewart then steered north, expecting to see some action. His bad luck continued, however. As he approached the New England coast, he had not seen either a convoy or another warship since passing the Bahamas. Then, on April 3, when he was approaching Boston, two frigates came into view, the 38-gun *Tenedos* and the 38-gun *Junon*, sailing in company. They immediately gave chase. What a prize the *Constitution* would be. Stewart threw on every sail, lightened his ship, and barely managed to reach Marblehead Harbor, where the British ships, respectful of the town's defenses, did not follow. When later bad weather gave Stewart an opening, he left Marblehead and sailed the fourteen miles back to Boston.

His frustrations from an unproductive voyage were exacerbated when Secretary Jones demanded to know why he had returned so soon. Commodore Bainbridge—no friend of Stewart's—was in charge in Boston, and he recommended a court of inquiry. It convened on May 2. Bainbridge and Oliver Hazard Perry, who had come up from Newport, were the only members of the court. Stewart explained that scurvy had broken out on board, he was low on water and food, and the mainmast was in such poor shape she might have given way at any time. Perry was uncomfortable during the proceedings, which he considered a needless waste of time. No court-martial was recommended. Bainbridge noted that he thought Stewart should not have returned so soon, and that was the end of the matter. Stewart immediately went back to work preparing the *Constitution* for her next cruise.

THE FIRST OF the new sloops of war to get to sea was the 22-gun *Frolic*, named after the ship taken by the *Wasp* in 1812. Master Commandant Joseph Bainbridge (the commodore's younger brother) was her skipper. She carried twenty thirty-two-pound carronades; two long eighteens; and a crew of a hundred and sixty. Bainbridge stood out from Boston in February, using a storm to avoid the blockade, and shaped a course for the Caribbean—Secretary Jones's preferred hunting grounds. Bainbridge captured two prizes before spotting a pair of strangers on April 20, sailing in company near Matanzas on Cuba's north coast. They were the British 36-gun frigate *Orpheus* (Captain Hugh Pigot) accompanied by the 12-gun schooner *Shelburne* (Lieutenant David Pope). Bainbridge identified them immediately and fled, while they threw on all sail and tore after him. The chase continued for sixty miles. Bainbridge lightened the *Frolic* in every way he could, including jettisoning her guns, but to no avail, and he was forced to surrender. Unexpectedly, Pigot allowed the *Orpheus*'s crew to pillage the captured ship and her crew, something Bainbridge never would have permitted. Hatred of the American navy ran high among some officers in the Royal Navy.

The *Peacock*, named for the ship that Lawrence sank in the *Hornet*, had a much different experience. Noah and Adam Brown built her in New York, launching her on September 19, 1813. She had a hundred forty men and carried twenty thirty-two-pound carronades and two long twelve-pounders. Her skipper, Master Commandant Lewis Warrington, was an ambitious fighter. He eluded the blockading squadron and slipped out of New York on March 12, 1814, sailing first to St. Mary's, Georgia. On the way, Warrington saw a number of larger British warships, but he successfully evaded them. He had orders to rendezvous with the *President*, but she remained trapped in New York.

While waiting for Decatur and the *President* to escape, Warrington cruised south to an area off Great Isaac, a Bahamian cay twenty miles north-northeast of Bimini—an excellent place to intercept a convoy coming from Jamaica or Cuba. When Warrington obtained intelligence that the Jamaica convoy he was expecting had powerful escorts, however, he changed his mind about attacking it and sailed north.

On April 29 a small convoy of three merchantmen out of Havana appeared off Cape Canaveral (now Cape Kennedy). The brig *Epervier*, under Commander Richard Wales, was guarding them. She carried eighteen thirty-two-pound carronades and 101 men. When the convoy spotted the *Peacock*, the merchantmen ran, while the *Epervier* steered toward the enemy and beat to quarters. Warrington, in turn, sailed to meet the *Epervier* and prepared for battle.

Approaching from opposite directions, the two ships closed quickly. The fight began at 10:20, with both ships sailing on opposite tacks, firing guns from their starboard sides. After *Epervier* raced past the *Peacock*, she turned downwind and sailed a parallel course to the *Peacock*'s, firing her port broadside, which disabled the *Peacock*'s foresail and foretopsail. But Warrington's jibs remained intact, and he kept his ship a little off the wind, which was blowing from the south, and delivered one devastating broadside after another, crushing the *Epervier*, whose gunnery, after the opening rounds, was remarkably poor.

In desperation, Wales tried to organize a boarding party, but his crew, thinking it would be suicide, refused. They appeared to be a disgruntled lot, and their marksmanship showed it. It was apparent that, as in most British cruisers, the crew had been given little or no practice at the guns. The battle lasted for forty-five minutes. At the end of it, the *Epervier* was a wreck, with forty-five shots in her hull and five feet of water in her hold and rising. She had eight killed and fifteen wounded, while the *Peacock* had two wounded and none killed.

The dissatisfaction of *Epervier*'s men had been in evidence long before she met the *Peacock*. Two months earlier, the *Epervier*, with the same crew, had captured the privateer *Alfred* out of Salem, Massachusetts. The privateer carried sixteen long nine-pounders and a crew of 108. While the *Epervier* sailed with her prize to Halifax, the prisoners conspired with *Epervier*'s prize crew to take over the *Alfred*—and possibly the *Epervier* herself—and run them into Salem. A sudden gale put the mutineers' scheme on hold while they fought the storm. Before the gale was over, Captain Wales reached Halifax with *Epervier* and the

Alfred, putting an end to the mutineers' plans. This same crew fought the *Peacock*. British Admiral Edward Codrington insisted (privately) that the disgruntlement among crews in the Royal Navy was caused by the hands being "tyrannically treated."

By nightfall, Warrington had the *Epervier* repaired and headed north for Savannah. On the way he examined the prize and found to his amazement that she was carrying $118,000 in specie. His joy was short-lived, however. During the night, he discovered two British frigates nearby and immediately sent the *Epervier* to sail close to shore, while he drove the *Peacock* south and escaped. The *Epervier* appeared at the mouth of the Savannah River on May 2 and the *Peacock* two days later.

After repairing his ship in Savannah, Warrington, having given up the idea of a rendezvous with the *President*, set out from Savannah on June 4 intent on pursuing an independent course. He sailed first to the Grand Banks and then to the Azores. From there he went to Ireland, traveling up the west coast, and then around the north of Ireland to the Shetland Islands off Scotland's northeast coast. From there, he turned northwest and sailed to the remote Faroe Islands, 62° north, halfway between Scotland's northern coast and Iceland. He then retraced his steps, sailing back down Ireland's west coast and from there to the Bay of Biscay and along the Spanish coast. He then headed for the West Indies and cruised there for a time before traveling north along the American coast and, on October 30, slipping into New York, where he became part of Decatur's squadron.

During this long voyage in the months of July and August, Warrington captured fourteen prizes. He burned twelve, as Jones had ordered, and two he used as cartels to ferry prisoners to England. It was one of the most successful voyages of the war, confirming Jones's belief in the sloops of war.

ON THE FIRST of May the *Peacock*'s sister ship *Wasp* departed Portsmouth, New Hampshire, on her first cruise. She had been built in nearby Newburyport, Massachusetts, and commissioned at Portsmouth; her skipper was Master Commandant Johnston Blakeley. She had a crew of 173 and carried twenty thirty-two-pound carronades and two long twelve-pounders—a fast, potent ship with an aggressive commander.

Blakeley shaped a course to take him one hundred to two hundred miles south of the Irish coast at the approaches to the English Channel—perfect hunting grounds for a commerce raider. On the way he captured a prize on June 2 and another on June 13, when he was on station. During the next fifteen days, Blakeley took seven additional merchantmen, burning all except one, which he used as a cartel ship to ferry prisoners to England.

On June 28, in latitude 48½° north and longitude 11° east, the *Wasp* spied the 18-gun *Reindeer*, under Captain William Manners, out of Plymouth, England. It was four o'clock in the morning. By ten the two ships were closing and signaling, and by one o'clock they both cleared for action. The *Reindeer* was much inferior to the *Wasp*. She had sixteen twenty-four-pound carronades, two long guns, and a crew of 118. Not only was Manners at a disadvantage in men and caliber of guns, but his ship was made of inferior Baltic fir. The *Reindeer* was well led, however, and had an excellent crew. She was as unlike the *Epervier* as two similar ships in the same service could be. She had the weather gauge, but the wind was unreliable. The gallant British captain pressed forward, intent on fighting an obviously stronger enemy. He approached on the *Wasp*'s weather quarter. His only chance was to use the weather gauge to cross the *Wasp*'s stern or bow, rake her, and then board. His first lieutenant, Thomas Chambers, had drilled the men hard in hand-to-hand combat.

Manners fired the first shot at 3:15. Blakely responded by putting his helm alee and turning the *Wasp* to the right. The *Reindeer* crossed the *Wasp*'s bows, however, and raked her, but her shots did not have the devastating effect that Manners, who was wounded in the early going, expected. The two ships then ran parallel to each other at close range, Blakeley firing his deadly thirty-two-pounders and crushing the weaker ship. The ships now came together, and Manners tried to board. As he was crossing over, however, he was killed and his first lieutenant severely wounded. Manners's well-trained men continued trying to board, but after savage hand-to-hand fighting, Blakeley's crew pushed them back before they ever reached the *Wasp*'s deck. Blakeley's men then boarded the *Reindeer*, and she quickly surrendered. The battle was over in nineteen minutes. The *Reindeer* was in terrible condition. She suffered twenty-three killed and forty-two wounded—over half her crew—while the *Wasp* had eleven killed and eighteen seriously injured.

The *Reindeer* was so badly torn up that Blakeley burned her and then proceeded to L'Orient, on France's west coast, to repair his ship. On the way he took two more prizes. The reception he got in the French port could not have been more hospitable. Even though France had a new monarch friendly to Britain, her people had not all of a sudden fallen in love with the English. "We have experienced every civility from the public authorities," Blakeley wrote to Jones. The British ambassador protested, but to no avail. The French allowed Blakeley to remain at L'Orient for seven weeks, restoring his ship and his crew.

On August 27 Blakeley sortied from L'Orient in his refurbished ship. In the next four days he took three British merchantmen and burned them. On September 1 he happened on an enemy convoy and managed to destroy the munitions transport *Mary*. One of the convoy's escorts, the 74-gun *Armada*, tore after him, but he raced away and easily eluded her.

Later in the afternoon of the same day, Blakeley spotted the 18-gun brig *Avon*, under Captain James Arbuthnot. She had been sailing in company with the 18-gun *Castillian*, under Captain David Braimer, and two other warships, but she got separated from them. The *Wasp* chased her, and by 8:45 in the evening, Blakeley was up with her. After some preliminary maneuvering and a broadside from each, the two ships closed to within half pistol shot of each other and blazed away. The smaller *Avon*, although well managed, could not stand the brutal fire, and when her mainmast fell at ten o'clock, she was in dire straits. It took ten more minutes and more punishment from the *Wasp*, however, before she finally submitted. The *Avon* had ten killed and thirty-two wounded. The *Wasp* had two killed and one wounded.

During the battle, the *Castillian* had seen the *Avon*'s distress signals and raced toward her. But by the time Braimer arrived, the *Avon* had surrendered, and she was sinking fast. Blakeley had already pulled away to force the *Castillian* to rescue the *Avon*'s crew and to gain some distance while he repaired his ship. The *Castillian* fired at the *Wasp* as she departed but did little additional damage, and then turned to help the doomed *Avon*. Working frantically, Braimer was able to get the *Avon*'s crew off just before she sank. While she did, Blakeley saw two additional warships steering toward the scene, whereupon he threw on all sail and disappeared into the night.

During the next three weeks, the *Wasp* sailed south, capturing three more merchantmen, the last being the *Atlanta*, on September 21, a hundred miles east of Madeira. Blakeley sent her to Savannah, where she arrived on November 4. Midshipman David Geisinger was in command, and he brought Blakeley's dispatches for Secretary Jones.

Three weeks later, on October 9, nine hundred miles farther south, the Swedish brig *Adonis*, bound for Falmouth, England, from Rio de Janeiro, encountered the *Wasp*. The brig had aboard two American officers who were anxious to transfer to the American warship—Lieutenant Stephen Decatur McKnight and Acting Midshipman James R. Lyman, both from the frigate *Essex*. They were on their way to England to testify in the condemnation proceedings for the *Essex*, which had been defeated in Valparaiso six months before. The chance meeting with the *Adonis* is the last that was ever heard of the *Wasp*; she never returned to port. Blakeley was probably on his way to the West Indies and met with a disaster of some sort, most likely a ferocious storm. It was hurricane season, and one of them probably sank the *Wasp*.

IN EARLY JANUARY 1814, Captain Charles Morris sailed the newly converted 28-gun corvette *Adams* to the mouth of the Potomac River and waited for an opportunity to run the blockade at the Chesapeake Capes. On January 18, he saw his chance. A strong northwest wind was blowing with occasional snow squalls. The *Adams* stood out from the river at five o'clock in the afternoon and made a run for it, moving fast with little visibility and poor pilots. As she plunged ahead in dim light, correct soundings were impossible. When the ship approached Middle Ground Shoals at the entrance to the bay, she struck ground once, then twice. The swell, however, pushed her into deeper water, and she was suddenly free. More importantly, she wasn't leaking. Morris did not know where she was exactly. The pilots disagreed. Unwilling to be imprisoned in the bay any longer, Morris sailed on. At midnight, when he was passing Lynnhaven Bay, he saw two enemy ships, and they could see the *Adams*. But she was traveling at twelve and a half knots and raced by them, passing Cape Henry without seeing the land. By daylight, Morris was well out to sea. He knew he had been lucky.

Morris was more than pleased with the *Adams*'s performance. She had been recently converted to a corvette at the Washington Navy Yard. The work began on August 12, 1813, and was completed on November 18. She had a crew of two hundred fifty and carried twenty-six eighteen-pounders and two twelve-pounders for bow chasers. Morris's first lieutenant was Alexander S. Wadsworth of Portland, Maine. Morris was from Maine himself, having been brought up in the little backwoods town of Woodstock. Wadsworth had been second lieutenant aboard the *Constitution* when she fought the *Guerriere*.

Morris headed for the Canaries and then the Cape Verde Islands. From there he sailed west to the northern end of the Caribbean. Along the way he captured two small merchant brigs. He then took the *Woodbridge*, a large East Indiaman, in thick weather. He had a crew aboard examining her cargo, when the visibility improved, revealing a twenty-five-ship convoy close by with two large warships for guards. They saw the *Adams* at the same time that she saw them, and they raced after her. Morris got his men off the rich prize quickly and fled, making good his escape, but he was very unhappy to be leaving all that booty behind.

On May 1 Morris was off the mouth of the Savannah River, desperate for food and water. The city was fifteen miles upriver, but the *Adams* drew too much water to get her there. Morris anchored off the lighthouse at the entrance to the river and sent boats to the city for provisions. The day after he arrived, the captured brig *Epervier* appeared, and Morris took whatever stores she could supply. Two days later the *Peacock* arrived, and Warrington, who was more than a little surprised to find Morris there, contributed more to the *Adams*.

By now the British at nearby Cumberland Island knew of the *Adams*. Aware of his exposure, Morris left on May 8, warping the ship out of the Savannah River in a light wind and beginning another cruise. He looked first for the Jamaica Convoy and found it on May 24, but two seventy-fours, two frigates, and three brigs were escorts, which made cutting out a merchantman nearly impossible. After hanging on the convoy for two days, Morris gave up and sailed to Ireland via the Newfoundland Grand Banks. On the way, he captured and destroyed two brigs. On July 4 he was off the mouth of the Shannon River. From there he sailed north along the Irish coast for five days but did not see a single ship. He then turned back south, and off the Irish Channel he ran into the 36-gun British frigate *Tigris*, under Captain Robert Henderson.

She chased him, and she was gaining in a light sea with a headwind as night came on. Morris "let the lower anchors drop from the bows," otherwise lightened the ship, and towed her during the night, as he had the *Constitution* in 1812, when she escaped from the Halifax squadron. In the morning, a providential breeze allowed him to leave the frigate. The *Adams* made "thirty-one miles in three hours, very close-hauled to the wind," he explained in his autobiography. He attributed the speed to the absence of the anchors.

On July 19 Morris met two more British frigates, which sped after him. He threw on all sail and managed to stay just beyond gunshot range of the fastest pursuer. The chase lasted for forty grueling hours, during which the *Adams* ran four hundred miles of latitude. A short squall in the middle of the night allowed Morris to change course unseen and finally escape.

Scurvy had now become a serious problem aboard the *Adams*. Several deaths had already occurred, and thirty men were unfit for duty. On July 25 Morris headed home. On the way he captured a ship, a brig, and a schooner. By August 16, his sick list had grown to fifty-eight, many of them serious cases of scurvy. It was urgent to get to port right away. Heavy fog enveloped the ship for three days, however, preventing accurate observations for latitude and longitude, but continual soundings made Morris confident he was on course for Portsmouth, New Hampshire. On August 17 the fog was still with them when, at four o'clock in the morning, a lookout suddenly shouted, "Breakers!" Before Morris could react, the forward part of the ship ran up on a slippery rock close to the Isle of

Haute off the coast of Maine. By a heroic effort, Morris and the remaining healthy men saved the crippled ship and then struggled to bring her to the mouth of the Penobscot River. Well before they reached it, however, the British brig-sloop *Rifleman* spotted them. Morris knew a frigate or two from Halifax would soon be after him.

Much worse was in store, however. In a few days General Sir John Sherbrooke's invasion of eastern Maine commenced, trapping Morris and the disabled *Adams* in the Penobscot. Learning that the British had attacked nearby Castine, Morris moved his ship father up the Penobscot to Hampden, just south of Bangor. He was certain the invaders would come after the *Adams*, and he prepared to defend her. He called for help from the Maine militia, and nearly four hundred unexpectedly appeared, along with thirty regulars under Lieutenant Lewis, who had escaped from Castine. Using the *Adams's* guns, Morris set up two batteries and made arrangements to destroy the ship, should it be necessary.

On the morning of September 2, Captain Robert Barrie of the Royal Navy and Lieutenant Colonel Henry John attacked Morris with three hundred fifty soldiers. They quickly dispersed the Maine militiamen, forcing Morris to burn the *Adams* to keep her out of Barrie's hands. Morris and his men fled into the Maine woods. He kept the crew together, and they made their way through difficult terrain to Canaan on the Kennebec River, where Morris borrowed money from the Bank of Waterville to feed his crew. He then made his way to Portsmouth, New Hampshire, and the welcoming arms of Commodore Isaac Hull at the navy yard. During the entire two-hundred-mile trek, not one man deserted, and none died.

In spite of all his efforts, Morris's cruise had been an abysmal failure. He did capture ten vessels, but they were of no importance. Of far greater consequence was the loss of one of the country's few warships and an inordinate number of men as a result of scurvy. Secretary Jones gave Morris a chance to redeem himself, however. Sitting idle near Portsmouth was the abandoned frigate *Congress*. Earlier, Jones had dispatched her crew to Lake Ontario. He now assigned Morris to restore her and be her new captain. Morris eagerly grasped the opportunity.

A HEAVY SNOW storm in January 1814 allowed the 14-gun *Enterprise* (restored after her battle with the *Boxer*), under Lieutenant James Renshaw, to break out from Portsmouth, New Hampshire, in company with the 16-gun *Rattlesnake*, under Master Commandant John O. Creighton. The brigs were on a commerce-destroying mission. They were warned to avoid single-ship duels. In his orders

Secretary Jones "strictly prohibited [them] from giving or receiving a challenge, to, or from an enemy vessel.—the character of the American Navy does not require those feats of chivalry. And your own reputation is too well established to need factitious support."

Sailing together, the brigs reached St. Thomas in the northeastern corner of the Caribbean. They then cruised west along the southern coast of Cuba, around Cape San Antonio at the island's western extremity, and ran east through the Florida Straits to the Atlantic coast.

While the brigs had been searching the northern Caribbean, Captain Stewart was cruising the southern part in the *Constitution*, neither having much luck. Off Florida, the *Enterprise* and the *Rattlesnake* were surprised when they chased a British privateer and saw more than two dozen of her crew suddenly making for shore in their boats. The privateer's men thought the brigs were British men-of-war who were going to impress them. They were more afraid of the Royal Navy than they were of the Americans.

The *Enterprise* and the *Rattlesnake* were then chased by a frigate, and on February 25 they had to separate. The frigate went after the *Enterprise*. At the end of a long chase, Renshaw slipped into the Cape Fear River and sailed up to Wilmington, North Carolina, where the frigate could not follow. The *Rattlesnake* reached the Cape Fear safely on March 9. The cruise had been a big disappointment for both ships.

In early May, Master Commandant Creighton was transferred from Wilmington, where he was refitting the two brigs, to the Washington Navy Yard to superintend construction of the new sloop of war *Argus*. He was Captain Thomas Tingey's chief lieutenant during the British attack on the capital in August. Creighton was thus spared the disaster that befell the *Rattlesnake* on her next cruise. On July 11, the 50-gun *Leander*, under Captain Sir George Collier, caught her near Cape Sable in a heavy sea and took her to nearby Halifax. The *Enterprise*, although a notoriously slow sailer, was never captured.

Another brig, the 16-gun *Siren*, under Master Commandant George Parker, slipped out of Boston during February. Parker steered to Madeira and then set his course southward. He passed the Canaries and planned to sail down the coast of Africa to the Cape of Good Hope. Parker had been first lieutenant aboard the *Constitution* when she defeated the *Java*. He was a much admired officer. During that battle, he had taken the place of Charles Morris, who was recuperating from injuries suffered in the fight with the *Guerriere*.

Before the *Siren* reached the Cape of Good Hope, however, Parker died, and Lieutenant Nathaniel D. Nicholson took command. On July 12, off the coast of

South Africa, a lookout spotted a large enemy ship. Nicholson did everything he could to get away, jettisoning carronades, anchors, boats, cables, and spare spars, but nothing helped. After a chase of eleven hours, the 74-gun *Medway*, under Captain Augustus Brine, captured the brig. Samuel Leech, a British deserter, was aboard the *Siren* when she surrendered, but his identity went undiscovered. The officers and men of the *Siren* were taken into the *Medway*, where Captain Brine, with a careless disregard for the rules of civilized warfare, allowed his men to plunder them. He also permitted the prize crew aboard the *Siren* to take whatever they pleased. No American captain ever allowed his crew to rob helpless prisoners.

WHILE THE SLOOPS and the *Adams* were engaged at sea, work on the 74-gun battleships continued at an excruciatingly slow pace—the *Washington* under Hull at Portsmouth, New Hampshire; the *Independence* under Bainbridge in Boston; and the *Franklin* in Philadelphia under Commodore Alexander Murray and Naval Agent George Harrison, superintendent of the Philadelphia Navy Yard.

Of the new 44-gun frigates, the *Guerriere* was in the Delaware River, ready for sea but blockaded. The *Java* was unfinished in Baltimore, being used as a receiving ship. Her captain, Oliver Hazard Perry, was overseeing construction, but he appeared bored with the assignment and spent a good deal of time in Newport, Rhode Island. While he was away, work slowed dramatically on the frigate. The *Columbia* was destroyed at the Washington Navy Yard in August to prevent her from falling into British hands when they burned the city.

Despite the myriad problems with the new American ships, the Admiralty continued to have them on its mind. The *Times* of London wrote that the new American navy being built "must be annihilated. . . . Let us never forget that the present war is an unprovoked attack on the very existence of Great Britain. . . . The United States is now persuaded that the sea is her element, and not ours. . . . Now America stands alone; hereafter she may have allies. Let us strike while the iron is hot."

The U.S. Navy was also trying to build Robert Fulton's steam frigate, designed to break the blockade of New York Harbor. Secretary Jones even considered a similar ship for Lake Ontario. David Porter was enthusiastic about her possibilities, and so was Stephen Decatur. While Decatur was in New York, he had become a strong supporter of Fulton's steam frigate and publicized its potential in an open letter on January 3, 1814.

The navy gave the inventor a substantial sum to build it, and *Fulton the First*, the world's first steam warship, was launched at New York on October 29, 1814.

Twenty thousand enthusiastic spectators witnessed her slide into the water. The giant ship was then towed to a New Jersey shipyard to have its 120-horsepower engine installed. *Fulton the First* was still there when the war ended. She was finally delivered to the navy in June 1816.

At year's end, the navy had 10,617 men in service. Of these, 3,250 were on the lakes—500 on Lake Champlain, 2,300 on Lake Ontario, and 450 on Lake Erie—while 405 were prisoners. The rest were in various ports around the country. Very few were at sea. The number of seamen in the service was entirely inadequate to compete with the British on the lakes and the oceans and to defend the coast. Secretary Jones was not reluctant to remind the president of this unpleasant fact, but there was little, apparently, they could do about it.

Privateers continued to be a bright spot for Madison. During the war 526 set out. Of these, 26 were ships, 67 brigs, 364 schooners, 35 sloops, and 34 miscellaneous small craft. By virtue of their exceptional speed and handling, especially when sailing close-hauled, schooners were the preferred model. The British managed to capture 148 of the privateers.

As had happened during the Revolution, the size of American privateers and their effectiveness improved as the war progressed. They often traveled in packs for protection and profit. Estimates of how many vessels they captured varied from 1,175 to 2,300. Lloyds of London claimed that during the war American privateers captured 1,175 British merchantmen and 373 had been recaptured or released. *Niles' Weekly Register* thought the number of captures was over 2,300. Other estimates were in between, but, by any measure, the number was high.

Privateers put out from ports all along the Atlantic coast, but New England, the bastion of Federalism, ironically sent out the largest number. Fifty-eight came from Baltimore; fifty-five from New York; forty-one from Salem, Massachusetts; thirty-one from Boston; and around fifteen from the smaller New England ports like Portland, Portsmouth, Marblehead, Beverly, Newburyport, Newport, and Providence. New Bedford, Massachusetts, had none: it was strongly Quaker and resolutely prohibited privateers from putting out or entering port.

Seamen consistently chose privateering over the navy or army. Marblehead, Massachusetts, for instance, had over 700 men in privateers and only 120 in the navy and 57 in the army, even though the town supported the war. *Niles' Weekly Register* estimated 100,000 seamen were ready to serve in privateers.

Britain's home islands were particularly lucrative hunting grounds. Many American privateers were large ships of twenty and even thirty guns with two-hundred-man crews. Powerful and fast, they wreaked havoc with shipping in the Irish Channel and the North Sea. British merchantmen found they could not sail safely around their own country without being attacked.

Britain's Convoy Act did not apply to vessels traveling around the British Isles. Traffic was so extensive it would have been impractical to force all vessels to travel in protected convoys. By the fall of 1814 insurance rates had climbed threefold—the highest they had been since the war with France began in 1793. The *Yankee* privateer out of Bristol, Rhode Island, alone made forty captures, which translated into $3 million for the investors. And there were many more privateers with almost as spectacular records.

Angry about losses at the hands of the privateers, shipowners, merchants, manufacturers, and underwriters of the City of Glasgow, Scotland, issued a strong statement on September 17, 1814, expressing outrage:

> That the number of American privateers with which our channels have been infested, the audacity with which they have approached our coasts, and the success with which their enterprise has been attended have proved injurious to our commerce, humbling to our pride, and discreditable to the directors of our naval power, whose flag till late waved over every sea and triumphed over every rival. . . . There is reason to believe that in the short space of less than twenty-four months above 800 vessels have been captured by that power whose maritime strength we have hitherto . . . held in scorn. . . . Our ships cannot with safety traverse our own channels, . . . insurance cannot be effected but at an excessive premium, and [it is shameful] that a horde of American cruisers should be allowed, unheeded, unresisted and unmolested to take, burn or sink our own vessels in our own inlets, and almost within sight of our own harbors.

The Scotsmen spoke for many other frustrated communities around the British Isles.

As frustrating as 1814 was for the American navy, the remarkable victories of individual warships contributed immeasurably to the respect the British ministry was developing for the capacity of the United States at sea. The success of American privateers reinforced this new attitude. The Liverpool government's altered view of the potential strength of America at sea would play a major role in fashioning a permanent peace, something that in August 1814 appeared unobtainable to President Madison and his supporters.

CHAPTER TWENTY-SIX

Negotiations
Begin at Ghent

T HE LONG DELAYED peace talks began the second week of August 1814, in the old Flemish city of Ghent. Since at least March 1813, President Madison had been eager for them. But Liverpool had been in no hurry. He was awaiting results from the battlefield that would support his demands at the negotiating table. By the time talks began at Ghent, however, the prime minister's delay was working against him. In the spring of 1814 Liverpool and his colleagues had assumed that European matters would no longer absorb their energies as they had during the Napoleonic Wars. But as spring became summer, this assumption proved incorrect. Dealing with the aftermath of the Napoleonic collapse proved far more difficult than Liverpool and Castlereagh had imagined. Napoleon had transformed the continent. The frontiers of nearly every European country needed to be redrawn, and there was no agreement among the great powers about how that should be done. In addition, Britain had conquered all the French, Dutch, and Danish overseas colonies, and they needed to be reallocated.

Liverpool and Castlereagh had hoped that agreement on new European boundaries and the overseas possessions in British hands would be made at the time the peace treaty was signed with Bourbon France on May 30, but the jealousies and rivalries among the powers made that impossible. Liverpool then hoped that a conference of the four great powers, scheduled in London for ten days in June, would accomplish the same result, but that too failed. Instead of being resolved, the differences among Russia, Prussia, Austria, and Britain widened.

None of the squabbling at the London conference reached the public. The *Times* was effusive in its praise of Czar Alexander and the king of Prussia (Metternich attended for Austria). Yet the real business of the conference remained unfinished, and as summer progressed, hopes for an early settlement evaporated. On August 1 the *Times* finally recognized that "much yet remains to be done in Europe." Indeed it did.

Of the many issues before the four powers, the most contentious was Russian dominion over Poland. Czar Alexander, by virtue of having an army in Poland, controlled its destiny, and he wanted not an independent country—none of the powers wanted that—but a state with a constitution that guaranteed Russian domination. Castlereagh regarded such an arrangement as a menace to the balance of power in Europe and a threat to British security. Austria also found Russian control of Poland unacceptable. Prussia, for her part, did not want Russian control of Poland either, but the Prussian king was weak and under Alexander's influence. Frederick William was unwilling to break with the czar unless compensated with all of Saxony. Austria, however, would not agree to Prussian absorption of Saxony. Thus, through the summer and fall of 1814, the four powers were hopelessly deadlocked.

Further complicating matters, the restored monarchy in France, which Castlereagh had helped engineer, was weak, unpopular, and in danger of being overthrown by a coup of disgruntled army officers or by Jacobins and their allies. If a coup succeeded, it would ignite another European war, which would require a substantial commitment of British troops and money, making Liverpool's diversion of resources to America look like a dreadful mistake.

Europe's tortured diplomacy and Louis XVIII's weakness had a decisive influence on the negotiations at Ghent. By the time talks finally began, Liverpool's thinking differed markedly from what it had been in the euphoric spring days immediately after Napoleon's abdication. Instead of being focused on redrawing the map of North America, Liverpool, Castlereagh, and Bathurst now had their attention on the European map and on Paris. Their expansive goals in America became much more elastic.

The American envoys at Ghent were unaware of the changing mood in London, and so, oddly, were the British negotiators—Vice Admiral James Gambier, Dr. William Adams, and Henry Goulburn. Liverpool, Castlereagh, and Bathurst did not keep their three representatives well informed of the ministry's thinking, nor did they allow them any independent judgments. London exercised tight control over the talks. As a result, when the British commissioners presented the cabinet's proposals, they made them appear as firm demands, when in fact they were tentative, designed to probe. If the Americans accepted them, fine, but if not, Liverpool was ready to soften his positions.

The three British envoys were neither powerful politicians nor distinguished diplomats. The titular head of the team, Vice Admiral Gambier, was a naval commander famous for leading the second Battle of Copenhagen in 1807, but he had no diplomatic experience. Adams was an Admiralty lawyer, a technician rather than a diplomat, and Goulburn was undersecretary of state for war and the colonies, a rigid, anti-American Tory—Bathurst's reliable instrument, almost unknown in Britain.

With the exception of Jonathan Russell, the American commissioners, by contrast, were accomplished and powerful. John Quincy Adams, Albert Gallatin, Henry Clay, and James Bayard were as fine a diplomatic team as ever represented the United States. Russell, for his part, had been minister to Sweden since January 18, 1814, and although not as celebrated as the others, he had extensive diplomatic experience.

The Americans had been waiting six weeks for their British counterparts to arrive in Ghent. Indeed, except for Clay and Russell, they had been waiting over a year for negotiations to start. Gambier and his colleagues finally got to Ghent on August 6, and their first meeting with the Americans took place two days later at the Hotel des Pays-Bas.

Although Gambier was the head of the mission, Goulburn took the lead when meeting with the Americans, and at the initial gathering he presented three subjects that London was prepared to discuss. The first was impressment, the second an Indian buffer state, and the third a revision of boundaries between the United States and adjacent British colonies. He also brought up the question of the Newfoundland fisheries and rights of navigation on the Mississippi. He said that Britain would no longer grant fishing rights without being given an equivalent, by which he meant rights to unlimited navigation on the Mississippi.

The Americans withdrew to their quarters to discuss a reply. That night, new instructions on impressment arrived from Secretary of State Monroe. "On mature consideration," he wrote, "it has been decided that, under all the circumstances alluded to, incident to a prosecution of the war, you may omit any stipulation on the subject of impressment, if found indispensably necessary to terminate it." Monroe sent the instructions on June 25 and 27.

Impressment was the issue that had sustained the war. The British considered it essential to their security and would never give it up, nor would they retreat on any other maritime question. The American delegation was presented with the choice of either accepting the British position on all maritime matters, including impressment, or ending the negotiations before they got started.

Monroe's latest dispatch permitted them to simply ignore the entire question of maritime rights. Free trade with liberated Europe had already been restored, and the Admiralty no longer needed impressment to man its warships. The president felt that with Europe at peace the issues of neutral trading rights and impressment could safely be set aside in the interests of obtaining peace. The British were also amenable to the idea of remaining silent on the maritime issues. Thus, from the start of the negotiations, the disagreements that started the war and sustained it were acknowledged by both parties to be no longer important. Neither country was giving up its positions; they were just not going to engage in a fruitless, abstract argument and ruin the talks before they began.

If the issues that caused the war could be so easily set aside, it would seem that a peace treaty could be just as easily arranged. But that was not the case. The British wished for far more than the recognition of their maritime rights. They wanted to extend their territory in North America and permanently weaken a potential rival. With this in mind, Liverpool intended to extend the talks until results from the battlefield arrived. He expected them soon. It's true that he had become less sanguine than he had been in the spring about what he could obtain in America, but having committed all the resources he had to that theater, he wanted to try for as much as he could get. He wrote to Castlereagh, "I think it not unlikely after our note has been delivered in, that the American commissioners will propose to refer the subject to their Government. In that case the negotiation may be adjourned till the answer is received, and we shall know the result of the campaign before it can be resumed. If our commander [Prevost] does his duty, I am persuaded that we shall have acquired by our arms every point on the Canadian frontier which we ought to insist on keeping."

In the course of the first few meetings, while London waited impatiently for news from the battlefield, Goulburn put forth demands reminiscent of what the *Times* proposed back in May when the editors and the country were intoxicated with Britain's power. The *Times* had expected the government to insist on the following: full security against renewal of attacks on Canada, undivided possession of the Great Lakes, abandonment of the Newfoundland fishery, restitution (to Spain) of Louisiana and the usurped territory of Florida, an amicable arrangement with the Eastern States (which meant secession of New England), a new boundary line restoring Nova Scotia and New Brunswick to their ancient limits, the exclusion of America from the St. Lawrence and its tributary waters, and providing Canada with access to the navigable part of the Mississippi. The *Courier*, Liverpool's mouth-piece, proposed similar terms on May 21. In addition, the cabinet wanted a huge Indian buffer state created out of American territory in the Northwest.

At the very first meeting with the American delegation, Goulburn had begun by putting forth the breathtaking proposal for an Indian buffer state to be carved out of existing American territory and set aside forever as Indian country under British guaranty. The proposed state would encompass the whole of the North-west, including one-third of Ohio, two-thirds of Indiana, and nearly the entire region from which the states of Illinois, Wisconsin, and Michigan were afterward created. It would be larger than England, Scotland, Wales, and Ireland combined. Such a state would blunt forever the westward expansion of the United States and incidentally guarantee British control of the all-important fur trade with the Indians. Goulburn presented the demand as a sine qua non, which meant that it must be in the treaty or the British would not sign it.

Liverpool's demand was obviously meant to cripple the United States. No American president could agree to it. Nor could he accept the further British demands as they were made in subsequent meetings. John Quincy Adams wrote to Ambassador William H. Crawford in Paris, "Great Britain has opened to us the alternative of a long, expensive, sanguinary war, or of submission to disgraceful conditions and sacrifices little short of independence itself."

Not surprisingly, when the American commissioners rejected the Indian state, the negotiations nearly broke down, but Adams and his colleagues had no intention of bearing the responsibility for breaking them off; they wanted the British to bear the onus for that. Liverpool was not about to end the talks, however. He was probing, seeing how far he could push.

On August 17 the Americans sent a dispatch to Washington specifying British demands. The *Chauncey* sailed with it on August 25. Adams and the others expected that when the extent of Liverpool's territorial demands were known, they would shock and outrage the entire country.

On August 18, the day after the Americans penned the dispatch, Lord and Lady Castlereagh arrived in Ghent. They were on their way to Paris and then Austria for the opening of the Congress of Vienna on October 1. Castlereagh remained at Ghent until the morning of August 20. He conferred with the British commissioners, but not with Adams or any of his colleagues. On August 19, the British envoys met with the Americans and again insisted on a permanent Indian state as a sine qua non. They also insisted that the United States have no naval force on the Great Lakes or any forts on their shores. And they demanded a revision of the boundary line west of Lake Superior down to the Mississippi, along with a treaty right of navigation on the Mississippi. In addition, they wanted a revision of the boundary line of Maine to permit a direct communication between Halifax, New Brunswick, and Quebec. These demands were immediately sent to Washington on the *John Adams*.

At this point the American commissioners were naturally pessimistic about the chances for an agreement. They did not intend to give up any territory. "The prospect of peace has disappeared," Henry Clay wrote to Ambassador Crawford on August 22. "Nothing remains for us but to formally close the abortive negotiations."

On August 25 the Americans sent a note to the British, dated the day before, formally rejecting Liverpool's proposals. On the Indian question they said, "To surrender both the rights of sovereignty and of soil over nearly one-third of the territorial dominions of the United States to a number of Indians, not probably exceeding twenty thousand" was beyond the powers of the commissioners. Gallatin asked what provision had been made for the 100,000 white settlers living in the proposed Indian territory, and the answer was: the settlers would have to shift for themselves as best they could. The American delegation made it plain that if the British insisted on this item, the negotiations were over. The Americans also rejected the demands concerning the Great Lakes and any boundary changes in Maine or anyplace else.

Ten days passed while the British delegates referred the matter to London. By that time Castlereagh had arrived in Vienna, and he was being kept informed, but he was fully occupied with the congress. Liverpool, and to a lesser extent Bathurst, had full responsibility for the negotiations. The prime minister did not want to break them off. He was expecting to hear soon of military victories, and he waited for them to move Adams and his colleagues.

On September 4 the British sent Adams another note insisting on the demands made previously. They were making no changes. The Americans replied on September 9, rejecting the proposals again but not breaking off negotiations. They still wanted to make Liverpool responsible for ending them. As usual, Goulburn sent the American refusal back to London.

Liverpool's answer arrived in Ghent on September 19. The demand for a permanent fixed boundary for an Indian buffer state and an end to the purchase of Indian lands was no longer included. Since the Americans were adamant on the question, and it was one that had the potential to unite the American people, the prime minister simply dropped it. But the rest of the note enunciated the other British terms more forcefully, leading the Americans to conclude that the talks were still going nowhere. Adams, Gallatin, and the others drew up a reply on September 25 and delivered it the following day. Once again, Goulburn forwarded the message to London.

Before Liverpool could reply, the good news from the battlefield that he had long expected arrived in London. The most exhilarating was the burning of Washington. He learned of it on September 27 and rejoiced, along with the rest of his country. Popular enthusiasm for the war surged in England. Liverpool now expected great things from General Prevost's invasion. He hoped it would move the negotiations along quickly. He needed to wrap them up, for conditions in France and among the great powers gathering at Vienna were deteriorating. The *Times* talked of time running out for the Americans; it was running out for Liverpool as well.

News of the burning of Washington reached Ghent on October 1. A gleeful Henry Goulburn, carrying out instructions from Bathurst, brought the newspapers to the Americans. Other bad news was reported as well: the capitulation of eastern Maine, the burning of the *Adams*, and the failure of Colonel Croghan at Michilimackinac. On October 8 the British presented a note that went beyond anything they had submitted before and questioned the legality of the Louisiana Purchase, while continuing all the demands made previously and doing it in an insulting tone. The U.S. commissioners answered with a note on October 18, rejecting the British proposals out of hand.

Gloom spread over the American delegation. The burning of Washington was a crushing blow. "What . . . wounds me to the very soul," Henry Clay wrote to Ambassador Crawford, "is that a set of pirates and incendiaries should have been permitted to pollute our soil, conflagrate our capital, and return unpunished to their ships. . . . I tremble indeed whenever I take up a late newspaper."

Adams wrote to his wife, "There can be no possible advantage to us in continuing [to negotiate] any longer."

ON OCTOBER 5, George M. Dallas arrived in New York aboard the *Chauncey* with dispatches from Ghent, recounting Liverpool's initial outrageous demands for an Indian buffer state. Three days later, Dallas presented them to the president, who was furious at British arrogance. Two days later, Madison transmitted the dispatches to Congress, which had been called into session early on September 20. The House was as angry as the president and immediately had 10,000 copies printed and widely distributed. The reaction around the country— especially, but not exclusively, in the regions that supported the war—was great indignation.

Madison had always expected British demands to range far beyond maritime issues, and he was determined to resist them. The Indian buffer state idea came as a surprise, but not the ministry's ambitions. On August 11, before the administration knew what the British were going to propose, Monroe gave the commissioners the president's estimate of Liverpool's objects in the war: "If Great Britain does not terminate the war on the conditions which you are authorized to adopt, she has other objects in it than those for which she has hitherto professed to contend. That such are entertained, there is much reason to presume. These, whatever they may be, must and will be resisted by the United States. The conflict may be severe, but it will be borne with firmness, and, as we confidently believe, be attended with success."

Adams and his colleagues, although unaware of a good deal of what was transpiring in Europe, and particularly in London, reflected the president's views and held firm, not giving in to any of Liverpool's territorial demands, even though it meant the war would continue.

On October 19 Monroe wrote to the commissioners, indicating that the *status quo ante bellum* would be a satisfactory basis for a settlement. Gallatin had already written to Secretary Monroe on June 13 suggesting the administration adopt this position. Indeed, the American team had been negotiating on this basis from the start. It meant that both sides would return to the borders that existed before the war.

After the success of British arms at Washington, Liverpool grew more confident about what could be obtained in America. He wrote to Castlereagh on September 27 that Cochrane and Ross "are very sanguine about . . . future operations. They intend, on account of the season, to proceed in the first instance to the northward, and to occupy Rhode Island, where they propose remaining and living upon the country until about the first of November. They will then proceed southward, destroy Baltimore, if they should find it practicable without too much risk, occupy several important points on the coast of Georgia and the Carolinas, take possession of Mobile in the Floridas, and close the campaign with an attack on New Orleans."

Liverpool and Bathurst were so confident about what was now obtainable that they dispatched Major General John Lambert with 2,200 additional troops for the campaign against New Orleans, bringing the total number for use there to 10,000.

CHAPTER TWENTY-SEVEN

〜〜〜〜〜〜〜〜〜

Baltimore

AFTER ADMIRAL COCHRANE'S successes at Washington and Alexandria, Baltimore appeared to be the next major target on his list in September. The city was in a panic. Philadelphia, New York, Norfolk, and Richmond felt threatened as well. Even Portsmouth, New Hampshire, and Newport, Rhode Island did. In fact, as Liverpool intimated, Cochrane preferred leaving the Chesapeake's sickly climate and invading Rhode Island.

Cochrane's reservations about Baltimore had to do with more than the climate. The city presented special difficulties for a waterborne assault, and it had a population of nearly 50,000, six times the size of Washington. Major General Ross, however, advocated attacking Baltimore, and he was supported by the ever aggressive Cockburn. Ross's experience in Washington had made him far more confident about what relatively small numbers of British regulars could accomplish when pitted against a much larger army of American militiamen.

Cochrane finally gave in to Ross. Severe tidal currents in the Chesapeake and storms in the Atlantic caused by the convergence of a new moon at equinox helped persuaded Cochrane to remain in the Chesapeake and concentrate on Baltimore.

Since the burning of Washington, Baltimore had been feverishly preparing for the worst. Some people thought the city should save itself by negotiating, as Alexandria did, but most, including Baltimore's leadership, were determined to prepare a defense and fight. On August 24 a Committee of Vigilance and Safety

333

was formed, with Mayor Edward Johnson as chairman. Baltimore's military leaders were all members—Militia Brigadier general John Stricker; Captain Oliver Hazard Perry, commander of the new frigate *Java*; Master Commandant Robert T. Spence, skipper of the sloop of war *Ontario*; and Lieutenant Colonel George Armistead, commander of Fort McHenry. They urged the committee to defend Baltimore and not imitate Alexandria. They recommended that Militia Major General Samuel Smith, the senator from Maryland, be placed in overall command. He was the logical choice.

The potential conflict between Smith and General Winder, the commander of District 10, was resolved when Governor Levin Winder of Maryland, the general's uncle, recognized Smith as the superior. To his credit General Winder, although he believed he should be in command, agreed to serve under Smith. Baltimore got precious little help from the federal government or from the Maryland state government. The city was thrown on its own resources. Smith had been responsible for organizing Baltimore's defenses the previous year, and he now augmented them. He put every able-bodied citizen to work building fortifications, digging trenches, setting up batteries, and obstructing the entrance to the harbor.

On August 25, Commodore John Rodgers marched into town with three hundred sailors and gave an enormous boost to Baltimore's worried citizens, showing them the city was not alone. Rodgers assumed command of all naval forces—Perry's, Spence's, David Porter's, and Barney's flotilla men, who had returned to the city after Bladensburg. Barney's flotilla was still a potent force. Lieutenant Solomon Rutter was now in command.

Barney was at his farm at Elkridge recovering from his wounds. He could not participate in the city's defense, although he dearly wanted to. After being wounded on August 24 and taken to the Ross Tavern in Bladensburg, he remained there, suffering until August 27, when his wife, son, and physician, Dr. Hamilton, arrived in a carriage and brought him home. Barney's son, Major William Barney, joined in the defense of Baltimore, and this was a source of great pride to his father.

Rodgers had 1,000 seamen, and he divided them into two divisions. Perry had command of one and Porter the other. Rodgers worked closely with General Smith in what was truly a joint command. The crusty old Smith admired Rodgers and his seamen. He relied on their professionalism to give his defenses, which depended on untested militiamen, backbone.

Smith worked at an exhausting pace, seeming to be everywhere at once. He was impatient for the troops to gather. Maryland's best militiamen had been at

Bladensburg, and it took a while for them to get back. He called for help from Virginia and Pennsylvania; Virginia militiamen were soon on the way, and so were volunteers from Pennsylvania. The burning of Washington had enraged so many people that they wanted to strike back. By September 4 Smith had 15,000 troops, mostly militiamen but some regulars. The moment the militiamen arrived, he organized and trained them.

In the middle of Smith's preparations, Secretary Jones ordered Rodgers, Perry, and Porter to hurry to Washington and attack Gordon's squadron in the Potomac. The trio left on August 30, much to Smith's dismay and the city's. "We deplore your absence," Master Commandant Spence wrote to Rodgers, "as you were looked upon [as] the bulwark of the city."

After doing his best to thwart Gordon, Rodgers returned to Baltimore. Secretary Jones had ordered him back. Rodgers arrived with his men on September 7 and threw himself into preparing the city's defense, certain that Cochrane's attack would come soon. Rodgers's return was an enormous morale booster, particularly for General Smith. Perry arrived later, but he was sick. He could no longer command his unit. His exertions on the Potomac had undermined his health, which already had been seriously compromised at Lake Erie. Perry remained on the scene, however. He may have been too sick to command, but he was prepared to fight if the British invaded. Porter, on the other hand, returned to New York to take command of Robert Fulton's new steam-powered frigate, leaving Baltimore's naval defense entirely to Rodgers. Actually, Rodgers had such a strong contingent of dependable lieutenants, Porter wasn't needed.

As the days passed, Baltimore's defense grew stronger. Cochrane could not attack without Captain Gordon's bomb and rocket vessels, which had been delayed on the Potomac by the attacks of Rodgers, Porter, and Perry. While Cochrane waited for them, Smith's force grew to over 16,000, including Rodgers's 1,000 seamen, and Lieutenant Colonel Armistead's 1,000 at Fort McHenry.

Cochrane's massive fleet did not arrive at the mouth of the Patapsco River until September 11. General Ross started debarking troops at three o'clock on the morning of the twelfth. By seven he had 4,700 men landed, just where General Smith thought he would, at North Point on Patapsco Neck, fourteen miles from Baltimore. Ross's army included 600 seamen and 300 Colonial Black Marines—ex-slaves. They had six cannon and two howitzers. Admiral Cockburn was with Ross.

After the troops were ashore, Cockburn joined them and marched with Ross and the army five miles along the North Point Road toward Baltimore. Cockburn predicted the city would fall just as easily as Washington had. Ross was also confident. He didn't care how many militiamen were defending Baltimore; he had lost all respect for them.

General Smith had excellent intelligence of Ross's movements, and he immediately dispatched Brigadier General Stricker with 3,200 men to take the measure of the enemy. Stricker marched down North Point Road toward the British and took up a position between Bear Creek and Back River with his main body and sent an advance party under Major Heath to scout ahead. Heath soon ran into Ross and his advance party of around sixty. A skirmish developed, and one of Heath's sharpshooters, noticing the splendidly attired general, took careful aim and fired, mortally wounding Ross. Heath withdrew back quickly to Stricker's position, while the British waited for the main body of their army to come up. They were stunned when Ross fell; they could scarcely believe what happened. One moment Ross appeared to be invincible, and the next he was down, fighting for his life.

Colonel Arthur Brooke, an experienced officer, assumed command, but the news of Ross's condition had a serious effect on morale. Ross was carried back to the landing area, his life slipping away, while Brooke resumed the march toward Baltimore along North Point Road. He progressed only two miles before running into what he thought were 6,000 to 7,000 militiamen. It was two o'clock in the afternoon. A major battle developed. Brooke used Congreve rockets to frighten the militiamen, as Ross had at Bladensburg. But the militiamen were not running. After an hour and twenty minutes, Stricker withdrew his smaller force in an orderly fashion. Brooke and Cockburn were under the impression they had dispatched twice their number and were encouraged to move forward. But given the time of day and all that had transpired, Brooke decided to rest his men and resume the attack on Baltimore the following day, September 13.

While Brooke rested, Admiral Cochrane began organizing a waterborne assault on the city to support Brooke's attack. He faced formidable obstacles. Star-shaped Fort McHenry was at Whetstone Point, guarding the water approaches to Baltimore. The Patapsco divided into two branches in front of the fort. The Northwest Branch forked to the right, running east of the fort, and led directly to the inner harbor and the city's waterfront. The Ferry Branch forked left, running west of the fort. At Ridgely's Cove the Ferry Branch came to within a mile of the city. Working closely with Rodgers, General Smith had erected strong batteries to protect the fort and both waterways. On the western shore of Ferry Branch he had built Fort Covington and a battery called Fort Babcock. Lieutenant Henry Newcomb, third of the *Guerriere*, was in command at Fort Covington. He had eighty seamen manning a battery of guns. Sailing Master John Webster of Barney's Flotilla was in command at Fort Babcock and had a six-gun battery.

On the Northwest Branch, directly across from Fort McHenry, was a projection called Lazaretto Point. Master Commandant Robert Spence was in command there. Lieutenant Solomon Frazier of the Flotilla Service worked with him, although, to begin with, the two had difficulty deciding who was in charge. After Commodore Rodgers straightened them out, they worked in harmony. They had the *Erie*'s guns at the Lazaretto, and forty-five seamen ready to defend the passageway. In the water between the fort and the Lazaretto, Smith blocked the entrance to the harbor with a boom, sunken ships, a string of barges, and the *Erie*. Lieutenant Rutter's barges were behind the barricade with eight- and twelve-pounders. Directly across the water from the Lazaretto, in the left wing of the water battery at Fort McHenry, Sailing Master Solomon Rodmond was in command with fifty flotilla men. Altogether, Fort McHenry and the supporting array of batteries, warships, and obstructions constituted an impassable barrier.

ON SEPTEMBER 13 Admiral Cochrane transferred to the frigate *Surprise* and led the attack on Fort McHenry with five bomb vessels—*Aetna, Devastation, Meteor, Terror,* and *Volcano*—and twelve additional ships, including the rocket ship *Erebus* and the frigates *Euryalus, Severn, Havannah,* and *Hebrus.* The hulks, booms, and batteries prevented him from making a dash past Fort McHenry into the inner harbor. He was forced to stand off and bombarded the fort from long distance. His ships took up a position in line abreast two miles from the fort and began shelling at first light on September 13 to coordinate with Brooke's attack by land. The fort returned fire, but the attack vessels were so far away that its guns could not reach them. Armistead soon ordered them to cease firing. Barney's flotilla men at the Lazaretto and on the barges blasted away ineffectually as well.

Despite the inability of Baltimore's batteries to reach the British ships, the overall strength of the defenses made a deep impression on Cochrane, and at 9:30 in the morning he wrote a cautionary note to Cockburn and Brooke: "It is impossible for the ships to render you any assistance—the town is so far retired within the forts." Cochrane estimated there were 20,000 defenders in the city. He told Brooke that he would have to decide if he could take the town with the forces he had—without naval support. If not, Cochrane told him, he "would be only throwing the men's lives away and prevent us from going upon other services."

Sending the warning to Brooke did not stop Cochrane from continuing the bombardment. Around two o'clock in the afternoon, he moved three bomb vessels closer to Fort McHenry. But Armistead's guns, and those on the barges and Lazaretto, drove them back in half an hour. At three o'clock, Armistead was able to elevate his guns and reach the bomb vessels to do some damage, but not enough to drive Cochrane away. The British bombardment continued through the night and did not stop until daylight on the fourteenth. For all its seeming ferocity, however, it did little damage.

Colonel Brooke was unaware of Cochrane's reservations when he marched his 5,000 regulars forward on the morning of the thirteenth. He was within two miles of Smith's lines when he paused to examine what was before him. He estimated that Smith had 20,000 militiamen with a hundred cannon, protected by strong barricades. He didn't like the odds, but he intended to probe, find any weakness, and attack that night.

Probing for soft spots in the defenses, Brooke maneuvered to Smith's left, but Generals Stricker and Winder adapted their movements to Brooke's and checked him. Smith had transferred Winder and his men from the defenses on the west side of Baltimore, where little was happening and Winder felt slighted, to the center of action on Baltimore's east side. Winder grasped his opportunity with enthusiasm and performed yeoman service for Smith, who much admired him for it. Colonel Brooke moved back to the center of Smith's lines between one and two o'clock, pushing to within a mile of the enemy's forward line. In response, Smith drew Stricker and Winder closer to him and looked for an attack in the early evening.

None came. Brooke later claimed that in spite of Baltimore's strong defense and larger army, he planned to attack that night. He had had a full view of Smith's forces and concluded he could defeat them but changed his mind only when he received Cochrane's cautionary message "during the evening," closing off naval cooperation. When the admiral's message arrived, Brooke held a council of officers, including Admiral Cockburn, and they decided to call off the planned attack. Brooke wrote to Bathurst, "the capture of the town would not have been a sufficient equivalent to the loss which might probably be sustained in storming the heights."

The heights he was referring to were Hampstead Hill and Rodgers's Bastion, where the commodore and his seamen manned the guns. The entire defense, as Brooke could plainly see when he approached it that morning, was impressive. His army stood little chance. Had Cochrane's message not given him a way out, he undoubtedly would have conducted a suicidal attack with Admiral Cockburn egging him on. Cochrane's communication gave Brooke a perfect excuse to re-treat, and he was quick to grasp it. Cockburn did not object. He knew that an early death awaited hundreds if they carried out Brooke's plan.

Between one and two o'clock that morning, while Cochrane's bombs con-tinued bursting over Fort McHenry and his rockets lit up the night sky, Brooke left his campfires burning brightly and quietly retreated three miles, where he waited to see if Smith reacted. Smith was considering an attack, but a heavy rain storm broke, and he decided, given the fatigue of his men, not to leave the safety of his entrenchments. Seeing that Smith was staying put, Brooke moved his army another three miles and camped for the night. The following morning, September 15, he marched the troops to their transports at North Point and reembarked them.

ON THE NIGHT of September 13–14, not knowing how Brooke was faring, Ad-miral Cochrane sent Captain Charles Napier, skipper of the frigate *Euryalus*, up the Ferry Branch for a previously planned attack. Napier led a party of barges carrying hundreds of men—far fewer than the 1,200 that *Niles' Weekly Register* later reported. Napier set out from the fleet at one o'clock in the morning—the same time that Brooke was preparing to retreat—and slipped past Fort McHenry with no trouble. The watch at Fort Covington, however, spotted his movements, and the batteries opened up on the barges. As soon as they did, the guns at Fort Babcock followed suit. The action alerted Fort McHenry, and Armistead started firing at the flashes from Napier's guns. The exchange lasted for two hours before Napier withdrew. He never attempted a landing. The bloodied remains of his party struggled back to their ships.

All the while, the bombardment of Fort McHenry continued mindlessly until seven o'clock that morning, long after the battle had been lost. For twenty-five hours the bombs fell. Cochrane's stubborn refusal to call off the shelling seemed purely vindictive. Lieutenant Colonel Armistead estimated that between 1,500 to 1,800 projectiles were thrown. Some fell short. A large proportion of them burst overhead, however, showering fragments inside the fort. About 400 fell within the fort. But the bombardment, while spectacular, was a total failure, just as the rest of Cochrane's operation was. The fort and the defenses outside held firm. Armistead had four men killed and twenty-four wounded. The injured all recovered.

The rockets' red glare illuminating the night sky and the bombs bursting in air inspired an American spectator aboard the 74-gun *Minden*, Francis Scott

Key, to begin a poem that later became the national anthem. Seeing the fort's immense flag still waving in the morning filled Key's sensitive heart with joy. He had been visiting the British fleet to obtain the release of a prisoner and was stranded when the action started. The inspiration he received that night still inspires.

Despite the later claims of Cochrane, Cockburn, and Brooke that they could have taken Baltimore, albeit with heavy losses, the strength of the defenses had in fact convinced them to withdraw. Had they persisted, they would have, in all probability, been badly beaten and never made it back to their ships. Brooke and Cockburn were lucky to escape while they could. Cochrane refused to consider his withdrawal a defeat. He termed it a "demonstration," which succeeded in frightening the public, undermining support for the war, and making the American government more amenable to British peace proposals. He thus attempted to turn a clear rebuff into a victory, but few in London were fooled.

On September 19 Cochrane sailed to Halifax and Cockburn to Bermuda to refurbish their ships and their men for the invasion of New Orleans, which was next on Cochrane's agenda. With the fleet went 2,400 ex-slaves—men, women, and children. The naval facilities at Bermuda could not accommodate all of Cochrane's ships, nor could the island house many former slaves. Cochrane had to take the bulk of his ships and nearly all his ex-slaves to Halifax. Rear Admiral Pulteney Malcolm remained with the loaded troopships and a few men-of-war to blockade Chesapeake Bay. On October 14 he sailed with the soldiers to Jamaica. On the same day, Admiral Cochrane stood out from Halifax with an impressive fleet bound for Jamaica and a grand rendezvous of the ships and men invading New Orleans.

CHAPTER TWENTY-EIGHT

Plattsburgh

THE BRITISH CROSSED the Canadian border and invaded northern New York at the same time they assaulted Baltimore. Plans for the attack had been finalized in London as soon as Napoleon abdicated in April. On June 3 Bathurst ordered Sir George Prevost to "commence offensive operations on the enemy's frontier." He had in mind "the entire destruction of Sackets Harbor and the naval establishments on Lake Erie and Lake Champlain," as well as capturing Plattsburgh and points farther south. He was leaving it up to Prevost to decide how far to penetrate into the American interior. But he cautioned him not to drive so far south "as might commit the safety of the force placed under your command."

Bathurst was covering himself in case things went wrong, as they had for General Burgoyne during the Revolutionary War. Actually, Liverpool expected great things from Prevost. Sackets Harbor and Lake Erie would obviously have to wait until Yeo regained supremacy on Lake Ontario, but marching down the Champlain Valley should not prove difficult.

Bathurst did not have to worry about Prevost marching too far. Offensive operations would be getting under way so late in the season that a man as cautious as Prevost, and as experienced as he was in the American theater, would not want to get caught in upstate New York in the middle of winter. The name of Commodore Macdonough's flagship, *Saratoga*, was a reminder of how dangerous that could be.

341

On September 1 Prevost marched across the border with an impressive army of 10,351, made up largely of Wellington's veterans. General Edward Pakenham, Wellington's adjutant general, had dispatched the troops directly from Bordeaux to Bermuda and thence to Canada. The men he sent had been fighting in Portugal, Spain, and France for seven years. They represented one-third of the total number of officers and men Prevost now had in Canada. Major General De Rottenburg was second in command, and under him were three of Wellington's best: major generals Manley Power, Thomas Brisbane, and Frederick Robinson.

Prevost's army was the largest on the continent, but at the same time, it was pathetically small for invading a country of nearly eight million. Liverpool and Bathurst blithely assumed the number was more than sufficient. And, if need be, Prevost could be reinforced after he took Plattsburg and gained control of Lake Champlain. Success might induce the British people to endure more sacrifice.

But that might not be necessary. The American commissioners at Ghent and their masters in Washington, disheartened by continual defeat, might give Liverpool what he wanted without Britain making any greater exertion. In any event, Liverpool expected Prevost to have immediate success, and when he did, the prime minister could judge how far south he would go from there. Reaction in Britain to the burning of Washington was so enthusiastic that Liverpool might be encouraged to push much farther. Or the army invading New Orleans might move north at a faster pace, in which case Prevost's army could tie down the Americans while the major thrust into the interior came from the south.

Prevost marched down the western, or New York, side of Lake Champlain rather than through Vermont. He did not want to stop the flow of Vermont food that was sustaining his army. "Vermont has shown a disinclination to the war," he wrote to Bathurst, "and, as it is sending in specie and provisions, I will confine offensive operations to the west side of Lake Champlain." He later told Bathurst that "two thirds of the army are supplied with beef by American contractors, principally of Vermont and New York."

Meeting scant resistance, Prevost entered Chazy on September 3 and marched unimpeded toward Plattsburgh. As he approached the northern part of the city on the morning of September 6, a few of Commodore Macdonough's gunboats attacked his left wing at Dead Creek, forcing him to stop and bring up heavy artillery. The British gunners fired on the spirited gunboats, but heavy seas prevented them from firing back, and they withdrew.

Prevost moved on, arriving that evening on the north side of the Saranac River. The American army was entrenched on the other side. Its commander, Brigadier General Alexander Macomb, had the planks already removed from the river's two bridges. Determined to fight no mater what the odds, he continued to prepare in the face of overwhelming numbers. He had only 1,500 regulars and an equal number of raw recruits and convalescents.

Up until August 29 there had been a strong American army of 5,500 regulars at Plattsburgh, under Major General Ralph Izard. They would have put up a stout defense against Prevost. Izard had been in command of Military District 9 since early May, when he took over from General Wilkinson. Izard had watched with growing anxiety as Prevost's huge army assembled on the other side of the border, only thirty miles away. By August, Izard expected an invasion at any time. With his well-trained regulars, and the addition of militiamen from New York and volunteers from Vermont, he expected to do well against whatever was thrown at him. He had already built two blockhouses and three redoubts in Plattsburgh south of the Saranac. Even with Wellington's veterans, Prevost was not going to have an easy time taking Plattsburgh, if he took it at all.

Izard was assiduously preparing for battle when Secretary Armstrong, in a letter dated July 27, ordered him to take 4,000 men and march west to the St. Lawrence River between Kingston and Montreal and threaten communications between the two towns. Izard received the order on August 10 and thought the secretary completely misunderstood the situation. He wrote to Armstrong that if he left Plattsburgh, Prevost would be in possession of the city within three days.

Armstrong wrote again on August 12, before he received Izard's protest, giving specific orders to "carry the war as far to the westward as possible, particularly while we have ascendancy on the lakes." On August 29, Izard reluctantly obeyed, and marched 4,000 regulars out of Plattsburgh, leaving Macomb and his troops to suffer the consequences.

Armstrong was more responsible than anyone else for the burning of Washington, and now he was handing Plattsburgh over to the British. If it wasn't well established that he was an incompetent, one would have thought he was in Liverpool's pay. Henry Adams wrote, "Armstrong's policy of meeting the enemy's main attack by annihilating the main defense never received explanation or excuse."

General Macomb was not giving up, however; he intended to fight. He called for militiamen from New York and Vermont, and he removed the garrison and heavy guns Izard had placed on Cumberland Head at Macdonough's suggestion and moved them to Plattsburgh. Patriotic volunteers from Vermont poured into the American camp. Federalist governor Martin Chittenden, son of Vermont's first governor, Thomas Chittenden, would not order the militia to march out of state, but they could volunteer, and they did. New York militiamen came as well, doubling the size of Macomb's force.

Originally, Prevost had planned to assault Plattsburgh first thing in the morning on September 7. But after the gunboat attack, he changed his mind and decided to wait for the British naval squadron to remove the threat from Macdonough's squadron before he moved on the city. Macdonough's ships were then in Plattsburgh Bay preparing for battle. Prevost expected the British lake fleet, under Captain George Downie—the second-ranking naval officer in Canada—to easily defeat Macdonough. Prevost planned to begin his attack on Macomb the moment Downie began his on Macdonough.

While waiting impatiently for the British squadron to arrive, Prevost sent Downie urgent, pointed messages to get his fleet under way. It wasn't clear why Prevost was in such a hurry. Taking Plattsburgh would consume only a few hours. It was true that winter was coming, but this was only the first part of September. If Prevost intended to march farther south, he could easily reach Ticonderoga before the end of the month.

The day Prevost crossed the border, Macdonough had moved his squadron back to Plattsburgh Bay and prepared for the expected British attack. He had his flagship, the 26-gun *Saratoga* (two hundred ten men), the 20-gun *Eagle* (one hundred twenty men), the 17-gun *Ticonderoga* (one hundred ten men), the 7-gun *Preble* (thirty men), and the galleys *Allen*, *Burrows*, *Borer*, *Nettle*, *Viper*, and *Centipede*, all of which had two heavy guns. In addition, he had the gunboats *Ludlow*, *Wilmer*, *Alwyn*, and *Ballard*, with one heavy gun each. Together, the galleys and gunboats had three hundred fifty men. The *President* was twenty miles south of Plattsburgh repairing damages, and the *Montgomery* was at Burlington ferrying Vermont volunteers to Macomb.

Macdonough's squadron appeared to be weaker than the enemy's because of the 37-gun frigate *Confiance*, Downie's flagship, which had a main battery of twenty-seven long twenty-four-pounders, one of which was on a pivot and could be fired from either side. In addition, she carried four thirty-two-pound carronades and six twenty-four-pound carronades. But the *Confiance* had problems. To begin with, Downie had just taken command. Since the abortive attack on Sackets Harbor in May 1813, Yeo and Prevost had difficulty working together, and Prevost's drive on Plattsburgh was no exception. Yeo decided at the last minute to remove the commander of the Lake Champlain fleet, Captain Peter Fisher, and replace him with Downie, who did not know the squadron or the men or even his own ship.

In June, Yeo had dispatched Fisher from Kingston to assume command on Lake Champlain from Commander Pring, who was to be his second. Then, a few weeks later, Yeo changed his mind and sent Downie to replace Fisher, who returned to Kingston. Although these sudden shifts would have a serious impact on Prevost's invasion plans, they were not coordinated with him. Downie did not appear at Isle aux Noix to replace Fisher until September 3—after Prevost began the invasion. Even worse, neither the crew nor the equipment for the *Confiance* was anywhere near ready. Commander Pring wrote later that "only sixteen days before [August 25], she had been on the stocks, with an unorganized crew, comprised of several drafts of men, who had recently arrived from different ships at Quebec, many of whom had joined the *Confiance* the day before, and were unknown to the officers or to each other, with the want of gun locks as well as other necessary appointments not found in this country." Apparently unaware of these naval problems, Prevost proceeded with the invasion.

After the battle, Admiral Yeo wanted to know what all the rush had been about. Why had Prevost pushed Downie to fight when he clearly wasn't ready? Macdonough's squadron was anchored in Plattsburgh Bay, midway between the city and Cumberland Head, a mile from shore. Admiral Yeo wanted to know why Prevost, instead of waiting for Downie to attack Macdonough, didn't take Plattsburgh and turn Macomb's batteries on Macdonough? Yeo maintained that Macdonough would have been forced to quit the bay and fight Downie in open water, which Downie much preferred and where he would have had a big advantage.

Yeo's argument was persuasive. By delaying the assault on Plattsburgh and prodding Downie to attack before his ship and crew were ready, Prevost was helping Macdonough immeasurably.

On September 7, the day after Prevost arrived at Plattsburgh, the *Confiance* left the dock at Isle aux Noix and was towed south, workmen still working furiously on her. They kept at it until two hours before the first shots were exchanged in Plattsburgh Bay, when they had to stop and get off. But the *Confiance* was still unfinished. Not only was the ship not ready, but the men had had almost no time to exercise at the guns. Prevost, who normally was ultracautious, blithely assumed the Royal Navy would prevail.

Even though the *Confiance* had problems, she was still powerful, and combined with the other vessels in the squadron, Downie's fleet was strong enough to destroy Macdonough. In addition to the *Confiance* (three hundred men), Downie had the 16-gun *Linnet* (one hundred men), under Captain Pring; the 11-gun sloops *Chub* and *Finch* (forty men each); five galleys with two guns each; and seven gunboats with one gun each. No accurate number of men from the British galleys and gunboats exists. Macdonough thought there were on average fifty to a boat, and that is probably the best estimate. The *Chub* and *Finch* were the former sloops *Growler* and *Eagle* captured from Macdonough's squadron on June 3, 1813.

While the British were scrambling to get the *Confiance* ready to fight, Macdonough was carefully positioning his squadron. He decided to anchor and wait for Downie to attack. The prevailing winds on Lake Champlain were from the north or the south. Lake ships were poor sailers close-hauled because of their flat bottoms and shallow draught. Macdonough reasoned that Downie would be forced to come down the lake with a northerly wind and then have to beat back against it in order to get into Plattsburgh Bay. When he did, he would be caught in the lee of Cumberland Head, where the wind would be light and erratic.

Macdonough situated his ships in a line north to south, one mile east of Plattsburgh's waterfront and parallel to it. The *Eagle*, under Master Commandant Robert Henley, was farthest north, followed by the *Saratoga*, the *Ticonderoga*, under Lieutenant Stephen Cassin, and the *Preble*, under Lieutenant Charles Budd. The *Eagle* was considerably south of the Saranac River, and the *Preble* was a mile and a half from Crab Island. The gunboats were in a line abreast, forty yards west of the four larger ships.

The *Saratoga* had eight long twenty-four-pounders, six forty-two-pound carronades, and twelve thirty-two-pound carronades. The *Eagle* had eight long eighteen-pounders and twelve thirty-two-pound carronades. The schooner *Ticonderoga* had four long eighteen-pounders, eight long twelve-pounders, and five thirty-two-pound carronades. The sloop *Preble* had seven long nine-pounders. The six galleys were seventy-five feet long with forty oars and had one long twenty-four-pounder and one eighteen-pound columbiad. The four gunboats had one long twelve-pounder each. The larger ships had springs on their cables that allowed them to turn without using their sails. They also had stern anchors. In addition, the *Saratoga* had a kedge anchor off each bow with a hawser attached to the quarter on that side, enabling Macdonough to turn the *Saratoga* and bring both the starboard and larboard batteries to bear. Being able to wind the ship in this fashion was an enormous advantage.

On September 10, the British fleet gathered at Isle la Motte, a tiny island at the mouth of the Chazy River, twelve miles north of Plattsburgh. At daylight on the eleventh Downie got under way with a northeast breeze. By five o'clock he was off Cumberland Head, where he signaled Prevost by scaling his guns (firing cartridges alone). Downie then stepped into his gig and slipped around Cumberland Head to get a look at Macdonough's arrangements. When he returned to the *Confiance*, he held a meeting of officers and presented his plan of attack. He decided to sail into the bay, run up north of Macdonough's line, then turn south and give the *Eagle* a broadside before laying across the bows of the *Saratoga* and raking her. Commander Pring in the *Linnet* would follow and engage the *Eagle*. Lieutenant James McGhie and the *Chub* would assist him. At the same time, Acting Lieutenant William Hicks would attack the *Preble* and the *Ticonderoga* with the brig *Finch* and the flotilla of gunboats. Downie expected the powerful *Confiance* to easily crush the *Saratoga*. Once that happened, he thought, the rest of the American squadron would quickly strike their colors.

At eight o'clock Macdonough's lookout boat signaled the approach of the British squadron, and when Downie hove into sight off Cumberland Head, Macdonough made the signal "Impressed seamen call on every man to do his duty." As the enemy approached, the deeply religious Macdonough knelt with his officers on the *Saratoga*'s deck and said a solemn prayer.

When the *Confiance*, the lead ship, came under the lee of Cumberland Head, the wind became light and fitful, just as Macdonough had predicted. As the *Confiance* pulled within range, Macdonough sighted and fired a long twenty-four-pounder himself, before ordering "close action." Fire from the American squadron concentrated on the *Confiance*, which was struggling to get into position. Her small bower anchor and the cable on her spare anchor were shot away, as well as the spring on her best bower.

At nine o'clock the contrary winds forced Downie to anchor two cable lengths from the American line and return fire—not where he had planned to be. But his ship was still potent. His first broadside from fourteen, double-shotted twenty-four-pound long guns smashed into the *Saratoga* and killed 20 percent of her crew. One of the dead was Macdonough's first officer, Lieutenant Peter Gamble, the brother of Marine Lieutenant John M. Gamble, who had served under Commodore David Porter on the *Essex*. Peter Gamble had taken over when Lieutenant Raymond Perry (Oliver's brother) fell sick just before the battle. Even though Perry wasn't there, Macdonough credited him with training the crew and had high praise for his efforts. Needless to say, Perry was depressed about not being aboard during the fight.

The first devastating broadside from the *Confiance* did not stop Macdonough or his men. They resumed firing, and a general battle raged. Fifteen minutes into the action, Captain Downie was standing in back of a gun when a ball from the *Saratoga* knocked the cannon off its carriage onto him, killing him instantly.

Losing a leader at such a critical moment was devastating. Lieutenant James Robertson assumed command.

Macdonough was in constant danger himself. He personally worked some of the guns and was in the act of sighting one when a ball struck the spanker boom and sent a piece of wood slicing into him. For a few moments he was unconscious. He recovered quickly, however, and resumed the fight. A while later, a head from a decapitated seaman smacked into his face and knocked him out again. When he regained his senses, he struggled to his feet and carried on.

The *Linnet* and the *Chub* had taken up stations near the *Eagle* and were firing at close range. The larger warships on both sides were now grouped together. The *Saratoga* and *Eagle*, supported by seven gunboats, were fighting the *Confiance*, *Linnet*, and *Chub*. The *Ticonderoga*, the *Preble*, and three gunboats engaged the *Finch* and four gunboats. The other seven British gunboats, under Lieutenant Rayot, stayed clear of the action and ran away. Shortly, Lieutenant McGhee in the *Chub* had his cables, bowsprit, and main boom shot away. He drifted within Macdonough's line and was forced to surrender. Midshipman Charles T. Platt, who had fought with David Porter on the Potomac River just days before, took possession and brought her inshore, where he anchored.

The *Ticonderoga* and the *Preble* pressed the *Finch* and four gunboats hard. Lieutenant Budd was forced to cut his cable and run the *Preble* inshore, firing his broadside to keep the *Finch* and the four gunboats at bay. While he did, Lieutenant Cassin in the *Ticonderoga* kept firing at the *Finch*. After being pounded for an hour, the *Finch* was pulverized. She drifted onto the rocks near Crab Island, where some of the men in the hospital there fired a six-pounder at her, and she struck her colors. The *Ticonderoga* continued battling the four active gunboats. Midshipman Hiram Paulding used his pistol to fire the guns when it was found that the slow match didn't work. Three of the gunboats were sunk and the other badly damaged.

By 10:30 Lieutenant Henley was having trouble aboard the *Eagle*. The *Linnet* and one-third of the *Confiance*'s guns had been pounding him for well over an hour, and he could no longer bring his guns to bear. In desperation, he cut the *Eagle*'s cable, sheeted home the topsails, and ran down and anchored by the stern between *Saratoga* and *Ticonderoga*, and a little inshore of them, which allowed him to fire his port guns at the *Confiance* without being hit by her. That was fine for the *Eagle*, but Henley left the *Saratoga* exposed to the deadly fire of both the *Confiance* and the *Linnet*, which Commander Pring was handling superbly.

Henley's ill-timed, unauthorized maneuver nearly caused Macdonough's defeat.

By this time, all thirteen of Macdonough's starboard guns were either dismounted or unmanageable. He had to bring his port guns to bear or strike his colors. Fortunately, he had planned for just such an event. He let go the stern anchor, cut the bow cable, and, using his kedges, wound the ship and brought his larboard guns to bear, firing a fresh broadside into the *Confiance*.

The big British frigate was in desperate condition from the pounding she had taken and from Macdonough's new assault. On the side facing the *Saratoga*, Lieutenant Robertson had nine long guns disabled. Only two carronades and the pivot gun were serviceable. Three long guns and two carronades were dismantled on the other side, but if he did not bring the rest of the guns on that side to bear, he would be forced to surrender. He managed to get a spring on the cable and tried to turn the ship as Macdonough had, but his battered crew "declared they would no longer stand to their quarters, nor could the officers with their utmost exertions rally them." With the ship making water fast, the rigging, spars, masts, and hull shattered, upwards of forty men killed, and the wind not admitting the slightest prospect of escaping, Robertson struck his colors. It was eleven o'clock.

The redoubtable Pring kept fighting for another twenty minutes. Macdonough had to wind his ship by hauling on the starboard kedge hawser. He brought his broadside to bear in this fashion, and around 11:20, Pring was forced to strike his colors as well. The battle lasted two hours and twenty minutes. Fifty-two Americans were killed and fifty-eight wounded, while the British had eighty-four killed and one hundred and ten wounded.

Macdonough wrote to Secretary Jones, "The Almighty has been pleased to grant us a signal victory on Lake Champlain." The surviving British officers came aboard the blood-soaked *Saratoga* and presented their swords to Macdonough, but he refused to take them, saying, "Gentlemen, return your swords into your scabbards and wear them. You are worthy of them."

Macdonough took special care of the British wounded, bringing them to Crab Island initially. He then put the more seriously injured on parole and sent them to their own hospital on Isle aux Noix. Pring reported to Yeo, "I have much satisfaction in making you acquainted with the humane treatment the wounded have received from Commodore Macdonough. They were immediately removed to his own hospital on Crab Island, and were furnished with every requisite. His generous and polite attention also to myself, the officers and men, will ever hereafter be gratefully remembered." The American and British seamen who died were buried side by side in unmarked graves on Crab Island, while the officers on both sides were buried with great ceremony in Plattsburgh.

THE *SARATOGA* HAD 55 round shot in her hull, the *Confiance* 105. "The enemy's shot passed principally over our heads," Macdonough recalled. The *Confiance's* poor shooting was a key factor in her defeat, and it was undoubtedly caused by Prevost rushing her into battle before she was ready.

Macdonough was particularly critical of Lieutenant Henley. He accused him of quitting his station when he did not have to. "He behaved like a brave man," Macdonough wrote, "[but] . . . he is a stranger; his disposition I take to be malicious." Macdonough was not the only superior who found Henley incompetent and hateful. In 1812 Captain John Cassin at the Gosport Navy Yard in Virginia had gotten so fed up with him he requested that Henley be transferred, which Secretary Hamilton did, moving him to Lake Champlain.

WHEN THE NAVAL action started, Prevost began attacking Macomb. Wellington's generals, Brisbane, Power, and Robinson, saw no difficulty securing victory within a few hours. But when Prevost saw the *Linnet* strike her colors, he called off the attack and initiated a precipitous retreat, leaving his wounded for Macomb to care for. Prevost wrote to Bathurst, "The disastrous and unlooked for result of the naval contest by depriving me of the only means by which I could avail myself of any advantage I might gain, rendered a perseverance in the attack of the enemy's position highly imprudent, as well as hazardous." General Robinson, who disagreed with Prevost in every particular, wrote that "the expectations of His Majesty's ministers and the people of England will be utterly destroyed in this quarter [unnecessarily]." On the hurried march back to Canada, 234 soldiers were reported as having deserted. The actual number was undoubtedly much higher.

The Battle of Plattsburgh, like the Battle of Saratoga during the Revolutionary War, was a turning point. Macdonough's wholly unexpected victory and Prevost's headlong retreat gave an immense boost to Madison's morale. After the humiliation of Washington, Macdonough's triumph was desperately needed to counteract the fast-growing defeatism that was spreading across the country. When combined with the successful defense of Baltimore and General Brown's repulse of the British at Fort Erie, the triumph on Plattsburgh Bay generated renewed hope in Madison and his depressed supporters. It now seemed possible that the British assault on America would be turned back. To be sure, there was still much to worry about. The British had a large army in Canada, a huge fleet offshore, and plans, which were widely suspected in Washington, to invade New Orleans.

And Madison had continuing problems raising money and men. Yet there were now solid grounds for believing the country would avert disaster.

In London, Prime Minister Liverpool and his colleagues would be thunderstruck when they heard the news from Plattsburgh. The British public would be as well. A major reappraisal of Britain's strategy in North America, however distasteful, would then be called for. Liverpool, the supreme pragmatist, would have to lead the way in what was sure to be a painful process of changing Britain's fundamental policy toward the United States.

CHAPTER TWENTY-NINE

A Peace Treaty

T HE NEWS OF Baltimore, Plattsburgh, and the successful defense of Fort Erie reached London the third week of October 1814 and Ghent shortly thereafter. Henry Clay wrote to Monroe that the victories were of great importance: "for in our own country, my dear sir, at last must we conquer the peace." Clay made sure that Goulburn received the newspapers giving accounts of the battles.

The British people were deeply shocked. The defeat of a Royal Navy squadron and the shameful retreat of Wellington's best troops were astonishing and impossible to believe. After the burning of Washington, the British had been expecting an uninterrupted string of victories. Suddenly, the war against America became hugely unpopular. The urge to punish the United States, while it hadn't entirely disappeared, was replaced by war fatigue. Liverpool was quick to note the new mood. Continuing to fight in the face of strong public disapproval would be extremely difficult. Asking for more sacrifice from an unwilling country that had been at war for as long as the British had was next to impossible.

At the same time that Liverpool was suffering setbacks in America, he was facing mounting problems in Europe. In France, Louis XVIII's government was weak, disunited, and despised. The French military was disaffected; a sudden coup was a constant threat. At the other end of the political spectrum, Jacobins, men out of work, and Republicans in general wanted to subvert the government as well. Paris, and indeed all of France, was ripe for an explosion. A single spark could ignite a crisis in which the royal family would be massacred. The Duke of Wellington, now the British ambassador in Paris, was himself in danger.

Liverpool had 40,000 troops in Belgium. If France changed regimes, Britain would inevitably be sucked into the maelstrom of another European war. The prime minister wrote to Castlereagh, "You will have heard from many quarters of the combustible state of the interior of France and the expectation of some explosion. . . . If the war . . . were to be renewed, there is no saying where it would end."

Nothing gratifying was happening in Vienna at the great congress to settle Europe's boundaries either. British and Austrian unwillingness to accept Russian dominion over Poland continued to be the main issue standing in the way of a settlement. Castlereagh's fundamental objective was to achieve a workable balance of power by creating a strong Prussia in Central Europe allied with a strong Austria to balance France in the west and Russia in the east. Allowing Russia to control all of Poland, Castlereagh believed, would upset the balance. He had already secured support from the powers on other issues Britain regarded as essential to her interests. In the peace treaty signed with Louis XVIII on May 30, the boundaries of France as they existed in 1792 were agreed to with minor modifications, along with an enlarged Holland that included Antwerp and the Scheldt estuary, which was deemed vital to Britain's security. Having the Prince of Orange as ruler of the new Holland was an added guarantee, as was the promise of marriage between his son and Princess Charlotte, the heir to the British throne. In addition, all maritime issues, such as the rights of neutral countries on the high seas, were excluded from discussion, which was a sine qua non for the British.

Castlereagh hoped that getting Prussia to side with Britain and Austria would move Czar Alexander to compromise and solve the Polish problem. Prussian minister Hardenberg, Metternich, and Castlereagh preferred dividing Poland between Russia, Austria, and Prussia to having Russia possess the entire country and bring Russian power into central Europe. In October, Hardenberg kept insisting that in order to break with the czar over Poland, Prussia would need all of Saxony and the fortress city of Mainz. Castlereagh was willing to accept this arrangement, and he succeeded in getting Metternich to grudgingly agree.

Castlereagh's hopes for a settlement were dashed, however, when King Frederick William of Prussia, who remained under Alexander's spell, told Castlereagh that he would not hear of breaking with the czar over the Polish question, even though he did not agree with Alexander on the issue. Thus, the negotiations broke down. By November matters appeared especially bleak. "Unless the Emperor of Russia can be brought to a more moderate and sound course of public conduct," Castlereagh wrote to Liverpool on November 11, "the peace which we have so dearly purchased will be of short duration."

While Liverpool worried about another war in Europe, he saw no hope for success at Ghent. "I see little prospect of our negotiations at Ghent ending in peace," he wrote to Castlereagh. And he warned about the horrendous expense of another year of fighting. "The continuance of the American war will entail upon us a prodigious expense, much more than we had any idea of."

The American conundrum was important enough for Liverpool to hold a full cabinet review on November 3, in preparation for the opening of Parliament. The prime minister pushed the idea of asking—not ordering—the Duke of Wellington to assume command in America. Doing so would solve a number of problems. It would get the duke out of France and out of immediate personal danger. More importantly, after the humiliations at Baltimore, Plattsburgh, and Fort Erie, the duke's prestige would reinvigorate the army and, indeed, the whole American enterprise. Wellington's standing with the public was so high that the country would go along with anything he suggested. The cabinet wholeheartedly supported the idea.

Liverpool wrote to Wellington telling him of the anxiety the cabinet felt for his safety and offering him a choice of either going to Vienna to assist Castlereagh or taking command in America with "full powers to make peace, or to continue the war." Of course, Liverpool hoped Wellington would choose America. There was nothing for him to do in Vienna. Castlereagh did not need him, and Wellington was well aware of that. He and Castlereagh kept in close touch.

Liverpool wrote to Castlereagh on November 4, explaining his reasoning: "The Duke of Wellington would restore confidence to the army, place the military operations upon a proper footing, and give us the best chance of peace. I know he is very anxious for the restoration of peace with America if it can be made upon terms at all honorable. It is a material consideration, likewise, that if we shall be disposed for the sake of peace to give up something of our just pretensions, we can do this more creditably through him than through any other person."

On November 7, Wellington wrote back to Liverpool that he had no "disinclination" about going to America, although that was hard to believe. But, he emphasized, "you cannot at this moment allow me to quit Europe. . . . You already know my opinion of the danger at Paris. There are so many discontented people, and there is so little to prevent mischief, that the event may occur on any night; and if it should occur, I don't think I should be allowed to depart."

The duke wrote to Liverpool again on November 9, emphasizing that he did not feel threatened in Paris and that if war broke out in Europe, he would be needed there far more than in America. He admitted that Paris continued to be unstable. He did "not see what means the King [had] of resisting the brisk attack of a few hundred officers, determined to risk everything. . . . It is impossible . . . to conceive of the distress in which individuals of all descriptions are."

Wellington then went on to give a frank appraisal of conditions in North America and how they related to the peace negotiations in Ghent. In the first place, he thought reinforcements already sent to Canada would assure its defense against another American invasion. He would not be needed to defend Canada. The only justification for sending him would be to invade the United States. He had unlimited confidence in his veterans from the Peninsula War; no American army could withstand them, he thought. There was one very large caveat, however. No invasion of America could succeed without command of the Great Lakes and Lake Champlain. "That which appears to me to be wanting in America," he wrote, "is not a general, or a general officer and troops, but a naval superiority on the Lakes: till that superiority is acquired, it is impossible, according to my notion, to maintain an army in such a situation as to keep the enemy out of the whole frontier, much less to make any conquest from the enemy. . . . The question is, whether we can obtain this naval superiority on the lakes. If we cannot, I shall do you but little good in America."

As to the current negotiations at Ghent, Wellington suggested that Liverpool settle for the *status quo ante bellum*: "I confess that I think you have no right, from the state of the war, to demand any concession of territory from America. . . . You have not been able to carry . . . [the war] into the enemy's territory, notwithstanding your military success and now undoubted military superiority, and have not even cleared your own territory on the point of attack. You cannot on any principle of equality in negotiation claim a cession of territory excepting in exchange for other advantages which you have in your power. . . . Why stipulate for *uti possidetis* [a peace treaty based on land the respective armies occupied]? You can get no territory; indeed, the state of your military operations, however credible, does not entitle you to demand any."

It was obvious the duke was not going to America unless formally ordered to, which Liverpool had no intention of doing. Given that fact, and all the pressures, both foreign and domestic, the prime minister was confronting, he decided to completely reverse his previous policy and end the war with America as quickly as possible. He wrote a letter to Wellington that must have surprised him. "I can assure you," the prime minister said, "that we shall be disposed to meet your views upon the points on which the negotiations appears to turn at present."

Liverpool then wrote to Castlereagh. "We have under our consideration at present the last American note of their projet of treaty [a proposed treaty], and

I think we have determined, if all other points can be satisfactorily settled, not to continue the war for the purpose of obtaining or securing any acquisition of territory.

"We have been led to this determination by the consideration of the unsatisfactory state of the negotiations at Vienna, and by that of the alarming situation of the interior of France. We have also been obliged to pay serious attention to the state of our finances, and to the difficulties we shall have in continuing the property tax."

Liverpool failed to mention the defeats at Baltimore, Plattsburgh, and Fort Erie and how they had turned the public decidedly against continuing the war. If he didn't know before, he got an earful when Parliament opened on November 8. British debt was the largest in history. Interest alone was now £30 million a year. "After such a contest for twenty years," he wrote to Wellington, "we must let people taste of the blessings of peace before we can fairly expect to screw them up to a war spirit, even in a just cause."

The British negotiators at Ghent had no idea Liverpool was liquidating the war. Goulburn wrote to Bathurst on November 14, "The American projet, I think, evidently shows that we shall have no peace with America unless we accede to their proposition of placing things upon the same footing, in point of privileges as well as rights, as they stood before the war was declared, to which I presume we are not ready to accede."

But this was precisely what Liverpool proposed to do. He would settle for the *status quo ante bellum*, just as the Americans had been proposing right along. Until this point, Liverpool had been insisting on the principle of *uti possidetis*. The American commissioners had resolutely rejected that idea, and now Liverpool was ready to accept an entirely different territorial arrangement.

The way now appeared open for a quick settlement, but two important issues remained. The British wanted the right to freely navigate the Mississippi, which Henry Clay was adamantly opposed to. Liverpool also wanted to end America's right—confirmed in the peace treaty of 1783—to fish within Newfoundland's territorial waters and to cure fish onshore. John Quincy Adams strongly opposed giving up a right his father had doggedly insisted be part of the Treaty of Paris. The American negotiators argued among themselves through several tense meetings until Albert Gallatin worked out an agreement that Clay and Adams could live with. Liverpool then accepted it, although not before proposing an alternative that might have wrecked the negotiations.

The American commissioners offered Liverpool the alternative of having rights to the Mississippi and the fisheries (as of 1783) confirmed or left out of the treaty. Liverpool responded by offering to include both matters in the treaty in return for a boundary concession. The Americans would under no circumstances agree to boundary concessions, but they did suggest omitting from the treaty altogether any boundary claims, rights to navigation on the Mississippi, and fishing rights. The cabinet unexpectedly agreed, which meant that both sides would settle these potentially explosive matters later.

The final treaty was silent not only on the Mississippi question and the Newfoundland fisheries but on all maritime issues. The territorial settlement was simply a return to the *status quo ante bellum*. The parties promised to have "restored without delay" the territory occupied by each, except for the disputed islands in Passamaquoddy Bay. Their fate was left to a commission composed of two representatives, one from each side. If they could not agree, the dispute would be submitted for final resolution to a friendly sovereign or state. As to the boundary between Canada and Maine, two commissioners would decide that as well, along with the boundary between Canada and the Connecticut River. If the commissioners could not agree, the dispute would again be settled by a friendly sovereign or state. Two more commissioners would decide the boundary running through the rivers, lakes, and land communications between Canada and the United States, and if no agreement was reached, the questions would be decided by a friendly sovereign or state. The same commissioners would determine who owned the many islands in the lakes and rivers. Prizes taken at sea after ratification were to be restored and all prisoners repatriated.

So far as the Indians were concerned, Article 9 put an end to hostilities between the United States and all the tribes, provided the Indians ceased fighting. The Indians had no representation at the negotiations, and, not surprisingly, their interests were ignored. The British pretended to act on their behalf, but in the end they deserted them, as they had after the Revolutionary War and in the Jay Treaty. Since the tribes had been unable to unite, as Tecumseh wanted, they lost the war and the peace. They were left to suffer the brutal policies sure to be followed by the United States.

In Article 10 the parties agreed to stop the slave trade, which both considered "irreconcilable with the principles of humanity and justice." In Article 1, however, the British acknowledged that slaves were private property and would be returned or compensation paid. London would never stoop to returning slaves, but after several years of wrangling, they did pay some compensation.

On December 22 Adams and his colleagues received confirmation that agreement had been reached on all matters, and the Treaty of Ghent was signed at the quarters of the British delegation on Christmas Eve. The diplomats from both countries celebrated the peace by having Christmas dinner together. Clay wrote to Monroe, "The terms of this instrument are undoubtedly not such as our country expected at the commencement of the war. Judged of however by the actual condition of things . . . they cannot be pronounced very unfavorable. We lose no territory, I think no honor." John Quincy Adams wrote in his diary a "fervent prayer" that the peace "may be propitious to the welfare, the best interests, and the union of my country."

WITHIN DAYS THE British public knew of the treaty, and there was widespread approval. The *Courier* reported, "Wherever . . . [the treaty] has been made known, it has produced great satisfaction, not merely because peace has been made, but because it has been made upon such terms."

Not everyone liked the treaty, however. The *Times* repudiated it. The editors declared that "we have attempted to force our principles on America and have failed. Nay . . . we have retired from the combat with the stripes still bleeding on our backs—with the recent defeats at Plattsburgh, and on Lake Champlain unavenged. To make peace at such a moment . . . betrays a deadness to the feelings of honor, and shows a timidity of disposition, inviting further insult. If we could have pointed to America overthrown, we should surely stood on much higher ground at Vienna." The following day, the *Times* contended that if the New Orleans invasion went badly for the British, Madison would "rejoice in adding to the indignities he has heaped upon us, that of refusing to ratify the treaty." The editors believed, in spite of everything Madison had done to demonstrate the opposite, that he wanted to continue the war.

The *Edinburgh Review*, after being silent about the war for two years, declared that the British government had embarked on a war of conquest, after the American government had dropped its maritime demands, and the British had lost. It was folly to attempt to invade and conquer the United States. To do so would result in the same tragedy as the first war against them, and with the same result.

CHAPTER THIRTY

The Hartford Convention

T
HE VICTORIES AT Baltimore, Plattsburgh, and Fort Erie were perceived differently in Britain and America. The British public united in opposition to the war, while in America the old political divisions widened. On the one hand, Madison was buoyed by the outcome of the battles, and so were most Republicans. They now had hope that the country could defend itself against British aggression, which they assumed would continue. Federalists, on the other hand, not knowing what the reaction in Britain would be to the victories, were pessimistic about defending the country. They did not think the battles were important. They continued to believe the war would end in catastrophe. They wanted to settle quickly with London on generous terms, including giving up substantial territory. Madison wrote to Wilson Cary Nicholas, the governor of Virginia, "You are not mistaken in viewing the conduct of the Eastern States as the source of our greatest difficulties in carrying on the war, as it certainly is the greatest, if not the sole inducement with the enemy to persevere in it."

The bitter disagreements between Republicans and Federalists that characterized the past were even more virulent when the president called the third and final session of the 13th Congress on September 19, 1814 (Congress normally convened in November or December). Madison wanted Congress back early to assure the country that the government was functioning and to secure more men and money for the war, which looked as if it would continue into 1815 and beyond. He expected Congress to find the resources to carry on when the war was more unpopular than ever and the government was essentially bankrupt. He was hoping Congress would change its ways. Its spineless members, after all, were responsible for the fiscal condition of the government. The Republican majority that consistently supported the war just as consistently refused to enact the tax legislation required to adequately fund it. The United States had more than enough resources, despite wartime disruptions, to support a much bigger war effort, but Congress refused to raise taxes in the amount required.

When members returned to Washington, the extent of the blackened ruins shocked them. The city had become even more dismal and depressing than it had been before. Reminders of Madison's gross mismanagement of the war were everywhere. Meetings had to be held in the only surviving public building— the Patent Office cum Post Office. Serious consideration was given to moving the capital back to Philadelphia.

The recent successes at Baltimore, Plattsburgh, and Fort Erie had offset, to some degree, the shock of defeat at Bladensburg and the burning of the capital, but few expected the victories would end Britain's savage attacks. In his opening message to Congress Madison wrote, "We are compelled . . . by the principles and manner in which the war is now avowedly carried on, to infer that a spirit of hostility is indulged more violent than ever against . . . this country." He accused the British of aiming "a deadly blow at our growing prosperity, perhaps at our national existence."

The president saw little prospect for peace. He had not heard how negotiations were progressing at Ghent, but he was not sanguine about their success. He had to prepare the nation for continued sacrifice. The burning of Washington and the invasion of New England and New York had not brought the country together, as he had hoped. Instead, calls were being made by Federalists for a convention of New England states to possibly make a separate peace. Trafficking with the enemy had gotten worse, and desertions from the army and navy, after men had received substantial bonuses, was widespread. In spite of these unmistakable signs of the war's growing unpopularity, Madison urged Congress to provide money and men for an extended conflict, something Congress had less stomach for than it had in the past.

As bleak as the situation appeared, it would have been far worse if the British had succeeded at Baltimore, Plattsburgh, and Fort Erie. The successes of American arms in these battles and General Jackson against the Creeks offset, in the president's mind, the galling defeat at Bladensburg and the failure to defend Washington. "On our side," he wrote, "we can appeal to a series of achievements which have given new luster to the American arms."

The recent success of American arms had led Madison and Monroe to believe they could successfully invade Canada again and end the war in 1815. The Republican Congress, however, reflecting the mood of the country, was aghast at the notion. Federalists had always been opposed to invading Canada, and Republican support for another attempt had drastically declined. The British now had 30,000 regulars in Canada, and, as far as anyone knew, more were coming. The Royal Navy completely dominated America's coast, and there was every reason to believe it would eventually take back Lake Erie and even Lake Champlain. Admiral Yeo's giant battleship would soon establish supremacy on Lake Ontario.

It was not surprising that when the administration proposed increasing the army to 100,000, Congress rebelled. Madison assured members that the citizenry would "cheerfully and proudly bear every burden of every kind which the safety and honor of the nation demand," but no one took him seriously. He proposed strengthening the regular army, rather than the militias, which had proven costly and ineffective. At the moment, the regular army had about 40,000 men; its authorized strength was 62,500. On October 17 Monroe requested that Congress raise the regular army to 100,000. Believing the army actually had 30,000, not 40,000, he requested 30,000 more regulars and 40,000 volunteers, bringing the effective total to 100,000. He also called for a conscription plan to obtain the additional regulars.

Given the government's fiscal condition, these numbers appeared wildly unrealistic. And when Congress realized that this massive new army was for another invasion of Canada, Monroe's requests found little support. As they had throughout the war, New England Federalists vehemently opposed invading Canada. They saw no reason to increase the army or to institute something as foreign to America as conscription. It was also hard for Republicans to see the urgency of a huge increase in spending to make another invasion of Canada. After haggling for weeks and then months, a divided Congress passed legislation late in January that authorized the president to accept 40,000 volunteers into the army and an additional 40,000 state militiamen to serve for twelve months. The militiamen, however, could be used only to defend their own state or an adjoining state. Approval of their governors was necessary before they could be used anywhere else. Madison reluctantly signed the bill on January 27, 1815. All the Federalists from New England voted against it. By this measure, Congress unmistakably vetoed any invasion of Canada. In spite of this clear signal, and Congress's strict guidelines, Monroe continued to plan to invade in the spring of 1815.

Raising more money proved to be as intractable a problem as obtaining more men for the army. "The Congress have met in a bad temper," Secretary Jones wrote to Madison, "grumbling at everything in order to avert the responsibility which they have incurred in refusing to provide the solid foundation for revenue and relying on loans. They have suffered the specie to go out of the country, adopted a halfway system of taxation, refused or omitted to establish in due time a national bank, and yet expect the war to be carried on with energy."

Madison hoped a new Treasury secretary could help solve the country's financial crisis. On September 26, just after Congress convened, the Senate approved the appointment of Philadelphia banker Alexander Dallas. He replaced George W. Campbell, the former senator from Tennessee, who was more than happy to be leaving. He had held office since February, but it seemed more like a lifetime. Trying to fund a war that Republicans voted for but would not finance wore him down. Campbell had replaced Secretary Jones, who held the position, along with his post at the Navy Department, on a temporary basis after Gallatin left.

Secretary Dallas lost no time in telling Congress what he thought about the country's desperate financial condition. He wrote a frank letter to Congressman John W. Eppes, the Republican chairman of the House Ways and Means Committee and Thomas Jefferson's son-in-law. Dallas told Eppes something Eppes already knew and approved of, namely, that the wealth of the nation was vast but remained "almost untouched by the hand of government." For small-government Republicans like Eppes and Jefferson, this was to be applauded, not condemned. In fact, they believed the country's prosperity was directly attributable to a dearth of taxation. For Dallas, however, the war, which the Republicans supported, necessitated extensive taxation to pay for it, something many Republicans found incompatible with their philosophy of government.

Dallas believed that borrowing to pay for the war had brought the country to the point of bankruptcy. "Contemplating the present state of the finances," he wrote, "it is obvious that a deficiency in the revenue and a deprecation in the public credit exist from causes which cannot in any degree be ascribed either to the want of resources or to the want of integrity in the nation. . . . The most operative [causes] have been the inadequacy of our system of taxation to form a foundation for public credit; and the absence even from that system of the means which are best adapted to anticipate, collect, and distribute public revenues."

To meet the immediate need for money, Dallas recommended raising taxes on duties, imposts, and excises, and the creation of a national bank, with capital of $50 million, 40 percent of which would come from the government and 60 percent from private sources. The bank would be authorized to loan the government up to $30 million. It would provide a circulating medium (national currency) for the country, whose commerce at the moment was threatened by lack of any adequate circulating medium as a result of the suspension of specie payment by state-chartered banks.

Eppes and many other Republicans opposed Dallas's request for more taxes and a national bank. Jefferson and his followers in Congress, like Eppes, believed Congress should pay for the war by issuing promissory notes—that is, paper money, not backed by specie. Monroe liked the idea, but Dallas was adamantly opposed, and so was Madison.

The off-and-on debate in Congress on how to fund the war went on for weeks. No happy solution appeared. As talk continued, the financial condition of the country deteriorated. The situation was so desperate that the navy was running months behind on its bills and could not even pay its seamen on time.

To meet urgent current expenses, Congress authorized Dallas to issue $10 million in Treasury notes and borrow $3 million. But Dallas could not raise the $3 million. He estimated that nearly $41 million would be necessary to fund the war through 1815. Weeks passed while Congress debated what to do. In the end it imposed some taxes, including $6 million in direct taxes. The total in taxes was almost $14 million—far less than what was required. At the same time, Congress refused to pass the president's national bank. After weeks of talk, it passed a bank bill so different from the one Dallas thought was needed that Madison vetoed it.

On October 8, while the president and Congress were wrestling with the problems of finance and defense, George Dallas (Alexander's son) arrived from Ghent with the first dispatches on the state of the negotiations. They shocked the president. British demands were arrogant and so outrageous that no hope existed for ending the war. Two days later, Madison sent the dispatches to Congress, and the Republican members were as incensed as the president. They distributed the dispatches throughout the country, which brought loud condemnation everywhere, except from hard-line New England Federalists. Even Federalists in the South and West were angry at British demands. Madison thought the dispatches made it more urgent than ever for Congress to act on his requests for a larger army and a sounder fiscal policy, but Congress continued to drag its feet. By then, it was widely known that the British were likely to invade New Orleans, yet Congress remained too deeply divided to act.

Not only did Madison need money to fund the army, but he wanted a major expansion of the navy as well. Secretary Jones was not adverse to strengthening the navy, but he thought that invading Canada again was a huge mistake. He carried out the president's orders, of course, but he thought it was wrongheaded for the United States to continue the arms race on Lake Ontario. Money was a problem, but lack of men and weapons was an even greater one. Jones warned that he would be forced to shift men and munitions from the seacoast to the lake. And even if he did, he did not believe they would be enough. He predicted the effort on the lake would "lock up all our disposable seamen, and thus free . . . [Britain's] commerce from depredation on the ocean, his flag from further humiliation, and expose our maritime frontier to incalculable vexation and pillage in consequence of the absence of our seamen on the lakes."

The president did not agree. He was determined to invade Canada, and he believed supremacy on Lake Ontario was necessary to do it. He ordered Commodore Chauncey to build two 94-gun battleships and an additional 44-gun heavy frigate during the winter to compete with Yeo's 104-gun ship of the line, which had seized control of Lake Ontario in the middle of October.

Madison was more likely to get support from Congress for strengthening the navy than he was for the army. Federalists consistently supported a strong fleet. On November 16, Congress gave the president a small amount for the navy, appropriating $600,000 to build twenty 16-gun sloops of war to be added to the seventy-fours and frigates already under construction.

The emphasis on the sloops was something Jones approved of. Even so, he unexpectedly resigned on December 1. He had submitted his resignation back in April but had stayed on at the president's request. Although it was a critical time in the war, and the country needed experienced leaders at the helm, Jones maintained that his personal finances forced him to retire. Madison was not happy with the secretary's decision. Despite Jones's denials, their fundamental disagreement over whether to invade Canada played a part in his resignation. And so too did the monumental annoyance Jones felt at not having funds even to pay ordinary bills such as salaries and wages at the department. Dealing with Congress had worn him down.

Madison found it difficult to replace Jones. His successor, Benjamin William Crowninshield, did not come aboard until January 16, 1815, and even he was not eager for the job. Crowninshield came from a prominent Salem merchant family. They were Republicans and had supported Jefferson's embargo, which nearly killed their business, but they had prospered as privateers during the war. When Jones left in December, Benjamin Homans, the chief clerk of the navy, ran the department until Crowninshield arrived. Homans and the new secretary, both Massachusetts Republicans, hit it off well.

Before leaving, Jones recommended an important naval reorganization. To help relieve the administrative burden on the secretary, he proposed the creation of a board of commissioners to consist of three post captains attached to the office of the secretary and under his supervision. The commissioners would superintend the procurement of naval stores and materials and the construction, armament, equipment, and employment of vessels of war, as well as all other matters connected with the naval establishment of the United States. The secretary of the navy would continue, as before, to direct and control the country's naval forces. On February 7, 1815, President Madison signed the legislation approving creation of the board of commissioners.

DISPATCHES FROM GHENT for the period August 19 to October 31, 1814, arrived in Washington in early December and were published. They indicated a softening of British demands when they proposed *uti possidetis* as the basis for an agreement. Federalists were eager to accept British terms. Many Republican congressmen thought peace was near, but Madison would never accept a treaty that conceded any American territory. So as far as the president was concerned, the dispatches offered no hope that the war would end soon.

New England Federalists were particularly upset that Madison planned to continue the war indefinitely. Grievances they had felt all during the war came to a head in the fall of 1814, when the British occupied northern Maine, tightened their blockade along the coast, burned Washington, and raided coastal towns with impunity. The Federalists were furious that while Madison had concentrated on invading Canada, he had left the coasts exposed and vulnerable. Instead of squandering money on invading Canada, they thought Madison should have spent it defending the coast and strengthening the navy. And Madison's embargoes, they contended, had annihilated the source of New England's prosperity, her commerce. The Federalists felt they were paying for a war they despised and that was bringing unnecessary ruin on them without any support from Washington. Extreme Federalists like Timothy Pickering wanted to secede and make a separate peace. Governor Strong of Massachusetts had gone so far as to send a representative to Nova Scotia to explore the possibility with Sir John Sherbrooke.

Pickering and Strong were in the minority, however. Most New England Federalists did not want to go so far as seceding from the Union, but they were unhappy enough to call, as they had in the past, for a convention of the New England states to articulate their grievances. Urged on by radicals all over the state, the Massachusetts legislature began the movement toward a convention in Hartford on October 1, 1814, to air their complaints and possibly to advocate a course of action. Some thought they might call for secession, others that they would simply talk and issue a meaningless statement. Speculation was rife. Madison and Secretary of War Monroe took the threat from the secessionists seriously, and they kept a close eye on developments.

On October 5, Governor Strong of Massachusetts convened a special session of the legislature for the purpose of considering what the Commonwealth should do in the face of the dire circumstances the country faced and the demonstrated inadequacy of the Madison administration to deal with it. Harrison Gray Otis became chairman of a joint committee to consider what was to be done. Gray reported in three days. He called for a New England convention to address a number of constitutional issues, particularly those related to defense.

To counteract the extreme Federalists, Massachusetts Republicans, led by former secretary of war William Eustis, met in Boston on October 19 to condemn British aggression and the Hartford Convention. Eustis called instead for unity. He pointed out that any move to separate states from the union would "inevitably" result in a civil war. He made it plain that there would be no separation of New England, or any part of it, from the United States that would not result in a bloody fight, in which the federal government would intervene on the side of Republicans. The calls for New England independence, thus, were calls for civil war. Eustis's blunt warning was heard by more sober Federalists like Otis and Cabot and undoubtedly influenced their thinking, whether they admitted it or not. They were aware that a large number of New England citizens were Republicans; Eustis was not making an idle threat.

Madison was concerned about how far the disgruntled Federalists might go and how many people would support them. The Federalists had done well in recent elections. He had no intention of letting New England secede without a fight, and despite the recent elections, he knew that New England had a strong contingent of Republicans who would support him. All of this meant that if the Federalists pressed the issue, they were inviting disaster. Governor Strong's notion of a separate peace was a pipe dream. Any move in that direction would ignite a tragic civil war.

Secretary of War Monroe prepared for the worst, as he had to. He was also preparing, as Madison wished, a plan to expel the British from Maine. Monroe ordered units of the army to Greenbush outside Albany and sent Colonel Thomas Jessup to Hartford to assess what was happening.

The Hartford Convention convened on December 15. Twenty-six delegates attended. They had been chosen by the legislatures of Massachusetts, Connecticut, and Rhode Island; by the New Hampshire counties of Grafton and Cheshire; and by the county of Windham in Vermont. George Cabot of Massachusetts was chosen president and Theodore Dwight of Connecticut secretary. Leaders like

Otis and Cabot excluded Federalist firebrands from the meeting. Otis and Cabot did not want to secede from the Union, nor did any other delegate. They wanted to express grievances and threaten future, more radical conventions, but they also wanted to preserve the Union.

The convention lasted three weeks, from December 15 to January 5. As befitted a group who fancied that because of their wealth, education, and virtue, they were wiser than other citizens, their meetings were held in secret. On January 6 the convention issued a report for the public. It announced that the delegates were commissioned to devise means for defense against "dangers" and to obtain relief from "oppressions proceeding from acts of their own government, without violating constitutional principles or disappointing the hopes of a suffering and injured people."

Theodore Dwight wrote many years later that "the expectation of those who apprehended the report would contain sentiments of a seditious, if not a treasonable character, were entirely disappointed. . . . Equally free was it from advancing doctrines which had a tendency to destroy the union of the states. On the contrary, it breathed an ardent attachment to the integrity of the republic. Its temper was mild, its tone moderate, and its sentiments were liberal and patriotic."

Looking at the report, it was hard to disagree with Dwight. Defense matters had occupied most of the convention's time. The report stressed that state militias could only be called into national service to execute laws, suppress insurrection, or repel foreign invasion, not to invade another country. In fact, the report contended that the whole notion of offensive war was unconstitutional. It went on to insist that states must control their militias and appoint their officers, not the federal government. It maintained that a forcible draft, or conscription, was unconstitutional, as was the impressment of seamen. And the enlistment of minors and apprentices without consent of parents or guardians (as Monroe had proposed) was likewise unconstitutional. The report maintained that a state must interpose its authority to protect its citizens. It must also defend itself if the federal government cannot or will not do so. If the states were forced to provide for their defense, Congress should agree to refund a portion of their taxes paid to the federal government to defray the costs.

The report then proposed seven amendments to the Constitution. The first would eliminate the provision that counted slaves as three-fifths of a person for purposes of determining the number of members of Congress from each state, direct taxes, and presidential electors. The second would require a two-thirds vote of Congress for the admittance of a new state into the Union. Third, embargoes would be limited to sixty days. Fourth, a two-thirds vote would be required to pass a non-intercourse law. Fifth, a two-thirds vote would be required to declare war. Sixth, a naturalized citizen would not be eligible for federal office, either elected or appointed. And seventh, the president would be limited to one term, and his successor could not be from the same state.

Before adjourning, the delegates empowered Cabot and two others to call the convention back into session. It was obvious that, for the moment, moderation had triumphed. If the hated war continued, however, more radical measures would undoubtedly be called for and another convention held.

CHAPTER THIRTY-ONE

New Orleans

I N THE WINTER and spring of 1814, when Liverpool and his colleagues were planning to invade New Orleans, they viewed it as a first step to acquiring the entire Louisiana Territory, including West Florida, and eventually linking up with Canada and the newly acquired base at Astoria on the Pacific coast. Admiral Cochrane and Major General Ross were to direct the invasion, using the same dual-command structure they employed in Chesapeake Bay. Operational details were left to them. As time passed and the exuberance in London following Napoleon's abdication faded, the planned invasion of New Orleans remained, but what Liverpool intended to do afterward, assuming his army was successful, became nebulous.

From the moment Admiral Cochrane arrived on the North American Station in March 1814, he worked on the plan for New Orleans. On June 20, he sent a proposal for the invasion to the Admiralty. He thought he would need a relatively small number of regulars to take the city, given the help he expected from Indians, escaped slaves, and perhaps John Lafitte's Baratarian pirates. Liverpool supported Cochrane's approach, although the prime minister planned to send far more troops than the 3,000 Cochrane requested.

Liverpool and Bathurst expected Cochrane's amphibious forces to assemble at Negril Bay on the west coast of Jamaica no later than November 20. Cochrane and Ross were to depart for the island as soon as operations in Chesapeake Bay were completed. Bathurst sent Ross orders on July 30 and August 10, and the Admiralty dispatched Cochrane's orders on August 10.

When General Ross was killed during the fighting at Baltimore in September, Bathurst—after rejecting the idea of replacing him with Lieutenant General Lord Hill, Wellington's second in command—ordered Sir Edward Pakenham, Wellington's adjutant general and his brother-in-law, to lead the land army at New Orleans. Until Pakenham arrived, however, Cochrane was in command of the entire operation, and he had high expectations for its success. The potential fortune he would derive from the city's overstuffed warehouses heightened his interest.

The first thing Cochrane attended to was organizing more Indian resistance in the south. On March 14, 1814, he ordered Captain Hugh Pigot to load the frigate *Orpheus* with arms for the Creeks and other tribes. Bathurst wrote to General Ross that by "supporting the Indian tribes situated on the confines of Florida, and in the back parts of Georgia, it would be easy to reduce New Orleans, and to distress the enemy very seriously in the neighboring provinces."

Pigot sailed south in company with the schooner *Shelburne*, a former American privateer. His first stop was Nassau on New Providence Island in the Bahamas, where he conferred with Governor Cameron about the Creeks. Pigot then sailed to the mouth of the Apalachicola River in Florida to consult with Creek and other Indian chiefs, arriving on May 10. He reported to Cochrane that the Indians gave him a warm reception.

Pigot thought that as many as 2,800 Creeks could be enlisted for an attack on New Orleans and an equal number of Choctaw, along with perhaps 1,000 other tribesmen. He suggested training them and then using them alongside regular troops. He recommended landing on the Florida coast at Mobile and from there pushing two hundred miles west to Baton Rouge on the Mississippi River, eighty miles from New Orleans. With Cochrane's fleet offshore and the British army at Baton Rouge, New Orleans would fall easily. Once the city was in British hands, a determined movement north along the Mississippi and eventually to the Canadian border could follow. Pigot left behind George Woodbine, a brevet captain of marines, with some aides to coordinate with the Indians.

Pigot's assessment was wildly optimistic. Major General Andrew Jackson, commander of Military District 7, had already crushed the Creeks in March 1814. Their destruction as a military force began months before, in August 1813, when some of their younger members, inspired by Tecumseh and by their experiences with white settlers, became embroiled in a war with the United States.

Armed conflict became inevitable when, following Tecumseh's vision, the younger Creeks refused to abandon their traditional way of life and become farmers. The American Indian agent Benjamin Hawkins had worked hard, and successfully, to convince many older Creeks to change their ways, but the younger warriors decided to fight for their land and their traditions. They became known as Red Sticks. Their leader was Red Eagle, also known as William Weatherford, a man at home with either whites or Indians.

At the time, there were perhaps 18,000 Creeks. Of these, only 4,000 or so were warriors. They relied principally on the bow and arrow, although reportedly they had 1,000 muskets. Their territory was around three hundred square miles in the southeastern part of the United States, extending from the middle of Georgia to the Mississippi Territory and from the Gulf of Mexico to Tennessee.

The war engendered by the Red Sticks began in earnest on August 30, 1813, when Red Eagle led an attack on Fort Mims, the fortified residence of merchant Samuel Mims, on the east bank of the Alabama River, forty miles north of Mobile. Red Eagle's 1,000 Red Sticks massacred 400 of the 500 people at the fort, including women and children. The stories of his atrocities were gruesome. The attack was in retaliation for the ambush of Creek leader Peter McQueen at Burnt Corn Creek in Alabama, sixty-five miles north of Pensacola on July 27, 1813.

The episode at Fort Mims signaled not a triumph for the Creeks, but the beginning of the end of their power. Shortly after the massacre, Oliver Hazard Perry won his great victory on faraway Lake Erie, which led to the collapse of British influence in the Northwest and the death of Tecumseh. The great Indian leader had hoped to unite all Indians north and south in a war against the United States, but with his passing, any hope for the Choctaws, Chickasaw, Creeks, and other tribes to resist American expansion died as well.

The massacre at Fort Mims outraged and frightened people in western Tennessee—indeed in the whole Southeast. Their anger would fuel reprisals that would eventually be fatal for the Red Sticks and all the Creeks. Combining forces against the Red Sticks in the various states and territories, however, proved impossible for many months. Small units from Georgia, the Mississippi Territory, and Tennessee fought a few inconclusive battles. Ultimately, the task of crushing the Red Sticks fell by default to an obscure, backwoods militia general from western Tennessee, Andrew Jackson. He took the field with a relatively small number of militiamen with limited terms of enlistment, and by the end of 1813, his force had reached a low ebb. It looked as if his entire army would desert him. The few men Jackson had left were in danger of being wiped out by Red Eagle.

For a brief time Jackson was almost alone, but on January 14, 1814, he acquired eight hundred raw militiamen, and he reconnoitered Red Eagle's stronghold at Horseshoe Bend on the Tallapoosa River in what was then the Mississippi Territory and is now Alabama. Red Eagle attacked him at Emuckfaw Creek with a much larger force, and Jackson prudently withdrew. As he retreated, he was attacked again at Enotachopco Creek but managed to fight and then withdraw without having to surrender.

Jackson was later able to reconstitute and expand his army. By the end of February, with help from his friend Willie Blount, the governor of Tennessee, Jackson built an army of 4,000 men, and he marched 3,000 of them back to Horseshoe Bend. At the time, Red Eagle was away, and only 1,200 Red Sticks were present. Jackson attacked on March 27, provoking a savage battle. The Red Sticks had a few rifles and muskets, but mostly they used more primitive weapons. They did not have a chance. Jackson overwhelmed them with numbers and superior weapons.

Jackson did not have the satisfaction of capturing Red Eagle, but Creek power was broken. Jackson moved on to the Creek camp at the junction of the Tallapoosa and Coosa rivers, known as the Holy Ground. Chiefs came and submitted to him, including Red Eagle. The great chief asked sustenance for his women and children, and Jackson, admiring the chief's courage, extended help. Red Eagle recognized sadly that his people were defeated and had to come to terms with the Americans. Jackson gained immense respect for the chief, who later became useful in subduing other Creeks. Red Eagle eventually became a farmer with a large plantation and a friend of Jackson's, even visiting him at the Hermitage from time to time.

Jackson still had unfinished business with the Creeks, however. He wanted to destroy their power forever. He was determined to prevent the British and Spanish from using them anymore, and on August 9, 1814, he forced the chiefs, even those who were friendly, to sign the suicidal Treaty of Fort Jackson, in which the Creeks ceded twenty-two million acres—half their territory—to the United States, destroying their nation forever. Many Red Sticks wanted to continue the fight, and they had already fled to Florida. They were the Creeks who met Captain Pigot in the spring of 1814, but by then they were too few in number to be of real help to Cochrane against Jackson.

ON JULY 23, 1814, Cochrane dispatched Major Edward Nicholls to Pensacola (in Spanish territory) with one hundred men to negotiate an understanding with the Red Stick Creeks and to facilitate slaves leaving their masters. Nicholls had arms for the Indians, but what Indians wanted most was evidence of British strength. Captain William Percy in the *Hermes* and the sloop *Carron* transported Nicholls and his munitions. Percy was directed to remain in the Gulf of Mexico and take command of the small squadron there. When Nicholls arrived on August 14, he established himself at Pensacola. The Spanish governor, fearing an attack from Jackson, had invited him.

Jackson was paying close attention to what the British and Spanish were doing. Expecting a British attack in the Gulf, he left Fort Jackson with his army and traveled four hundred miles south, down the Coosa and Alabama rivers to Mobile, arriving on August 22. He went immediately to work reconstituting Fort Bowyer, which sat on a spit of beach commanding the entrance to Mobile Bay. Jackson put Major William Lawrence of the Second Infantry in command at the fort with a hundred sixty regulars. In two weeks Lawrence had twenty guns mounted, mostly twelve- and nine-pounders, and two larger guns.

From his base in Pensacola, Major Nicholls planned an attack on Fort Bowyer with Captain Percy. On September 12 Percy approached Mobile Bay with four warships—the 20-gun sloop of war *Hermes*, his flagship; the 20-gun *Carron*, under Captain Robert Churchill Spencer; the 18-gun *Sophie*, under Captain Nicholas Lockyer; and the 18-gun brig-sloop *Childets*, under Captain John Umfreville. Major Nicholls was aboard the ships with sixty marines, twelve marine artillery pieces, and one hundred and thirty Indians.

Percy landed his troops nine miles from Fort Bowyer, but he could not get his ships over the bar at the entrance to Mobile Bay until September 15. When he did, he immediately brought the *Hermes* and *Sophie* in close to the fort and began bombarding it at four o'clock in the afternoon. Adverse winds made it impossible for the *Carron* and *Childets* to get into position.

Major Lawrence's guns fired back, and the battle raged for the next three hours, until the *Hermes*, badly shot up, went aground. Major Nicholls, who was ill, stayed aboard rather than accompany his men ashore. He was wounded in the leg and lost an eye when a splinter pierced it. Percy managed to refloat the *Hermes*, but when she grounded a second time, he order the crew to evacuate and set fire to her. In minutes, she blew up with an earsplitting roar. That ended the attack. Percy's squadron had thirty-two killed and thirty-seven wounded. Lawrence had four killed and five wounded. The defeat was a severe blow to Cochrane's plan to attack New Orleans by way of Mobile and Baton Rouge. And seeing the British so easily defeated undermined the confidence the Red Sticks had in them.

After the victory, Jackson strengthened the fort and the town, and then concentrated on the British base at Pensacola. While he did, he ignored the desperate need for building up the defenses of New Orleans. The city was so politically and ethnically divided it could not organize its own defense, and neither the state government nor the federal government was of any help. Jackson had to provide the leadership; he was the indispensable man.

But Jackson was not going to move until he dealt with the British at Pensacola. He was still convinced that their invasion of New Orleans would come through Pensacola or through Mobile. On the evening of November 6 he arrived before Pensacola with 3,000 troops, including Choctaw warriors. Jackson sent Major Pierre with a flag of truce to communicate with the Spanish governor at Fort St. George, but before Pierre could reach the fort, he was fired on and had to return. Jackson then went himself to reconnoiter and decided to storm Pensacola the following morning.

The British were in no position to help the Spanish governor; they were simply too far removed from the town. Seven men-of-war were anchored six miles distant in Pensacola Bay, and Major Nicholls had some regulars and Indians in Fort Barrancas, overlooking the entrance to the bay. He also had a contingent in the small fort at the tip of Santa Rosa Island, directly across the narrow entrance to the bay from Fort Barrancas.

Jackson attacked Pensacola on the seventh and won a quick victory, the governor surrendering the town and tiny Fort St. George without at fight. On the morning of the eighth Jackson prepared to storm Fort Barrancas, but before he could, Major Nicholls blew it up, along with the small fort on Santa Rosa Island. Nicholls then retreated to the men-of-war with Captain Woodbine and a few remaining Red Sticks. After Jackson's victory even more Indians deserted the British.

AS EARLY AS September 5, 1814, Secretary of War Monroe had warned Jackson that New Orleans was the probable British target, not Mobile or Pensacola. On October 10 Monroe sent another warning, telling Jackson that intelligence from the American ministers at Ghent indicated Cochrane would attack New Orleans directly. But other than warnings of an impending direct attack—which Jackson already knew was a good possibility, since he had strengthened Mobile and Pensacola—no help was forthcoming from Washington.

Jackson now returned to Mobile. He continued to worry that the British would strike there first, so he kept bolstering its defenses. He gave command to his old friend Brigadier General James Winchester, who had been taken prisoner by Proctor's troops at Frenchtown on the River Raison in January 1813 and then exchanged. Winchester was also in charge of making spoiling operations against both the Indians and the British, particularly Major Nicholls's new operation on the Apalachicola River.

On November 22, Jackson finally left for New Orleans. He stationed his old Tennessee comrade-in-arms General Coffee at Baton Rouge with 1,300 men.

From there, Coffee could travel quickly to either Mobile or New Orleans. It was late in the day for Jackson to be turning his attention to New Orleans. The city desperately needed a strong hand to organize it. Without Jackson, the British could have walked in unopposed. He rode in on December 1, and the city's notables, led by Governor William Claiborne, greeted him enthusiastically. Jackson looked haggard from his journey and the dysentery that was plaguing him, but his hawk-like eyes showed the fire within. He vowed to defend New Orleans or die in the attempt. Jackson's biographer Robert Remini writes, "Andrew absorbed a near-permanent hatred for the British not only because of his mother's instruction but as a result of his own revolutionary war experiences." Admiral Cochrane never had a more determined, resourceful enemy.

Jackson had already issued emergency calls for troops from Tennessee, Kentucky, and anywhere else he could get them, and he posted men at the probable invasion routes into the city to give him as much warning as possible of the British approach. He also needed supplies in great quantities, especially muskets, gunpowder, and ball. On December 11, to his amazement, the steamboat *Enterprize*, commanded by Henry Miller Shreve (Shreveport is named after him), arrived towing ammunition barges. Captain Shreve brought his precious cargo all the way from Pittsburgh. His munitions would be of critical importance.

Twenty-nine-year-old Commodore Daniel T. Patterson commanded the navy in New Orleans, having replaced Captain John Shaw on December 10, 1813. Since the navy viewed New Orleans as a secondary theater, Patterson had precious little to work with—six old gunboats; two small warships, the *Carolina* and the *Louisiana*; a tiny schooner; and an even smaller tender. With this pathetic squadron he was expected to defend a city of over 25,000, the second largest port in the United States. He was determined to make the most of what he had, however. He ordered twenty-four-year-old Lieutenant Thomas ap Catesby Jones to Lake Borgne—a likely invasion route—to watch for the enemy. Jones had the schooner *Seahorse*, the tender *Alligator*, and five gunboats, carrying twenty-three guns and manned by 182 officers and men.

The five gunboats had numbers but no names. Gunboat Number 5, under Sailing Master John D. Ferris, had one long twenty-four-pounder, four twelve-pound carronades, and a crew of thirty-six. Number 23, under Sailing Master Isaac McKeever, had one long thirty-two-pounder, four six-pounders, and a crew of thirty-nine. Number 156, Jones's flagship, had one long twenty-four-pounder, four twelve-pound carronades, and forty-one men. Number 162, under Sailing Master Pollock, had one long twenty-four-pounder, four six-pounders, and a crew of thirty-two. Number 163, under Sailing Master George Ulrick, had one long twenty-four-pounder, two twelve-pound carronades, and a crew of thirty-five. The *Alligator*, under Sailing Master Richard S. Sheppard, carried one four-pounder, and the *Seahorse*, under Sailing Master William Johnson, carried one six-pounder and a crew of fourteen.

Jones stationed his mosquito fleet at Pass Christiana, blocking the entrance to Lake Borgne. On December 8, lookouts saw Admiral Cochrane hove into view aboard his flagship, the 80-gun *Tonnant*, accompanied by four other ships, and anchor between Cat Island and a thin sliver of land called Ship Island, ninety miles east of New Orleans. Shallow waters and hidden shoals in Lake Borgne prevented Cochrane from getting any closer to the city. General Keane, temporarily in command of the army until General Pakenham arrived, was on the *Tonnant*. On December 11 and 12 the rest of Cochrane's huge armada of fifty ships arrived, carrying 7,800 soldiers. There were 2,200 more on the way from England, under Major General John Lambert. When Jones saw the *Tonnant*, he immediately sent the tender *Alligator* to warn Patterson of Cochrane's arrival. Patterson quickly passed the information on to Jackson.

Jones's initial orders were to position his boats across Pass Christiana at the mouth of Lake Borgne and then fall back west, across the lake to the Rigolets, the small passageway connecting Lake Borgne with Lake Pontchartrain. Patterson ordered Jones to make his stand at the Rigolets with help from the guns at Fort Petites Coquilles. Wind and tide could intervene, however, and make it impossible for Jones to get back to the Rigolets.

Since the bar at the entrance to Lake Borgne blocked access to all the British ships, once Cochrane and Keane chose a landing place from which they could march on the city, the troops would have to be ferried to it in small craft. Cochrane had requested large numbers of shallow draft boats for just this situation, but the Admiralty refused to send them, telling Cochrane he would have to make them in Jamaica. He needed too many for that to be practical, however.

The troops could not be debarked until Cochrane got rid of Lieutenant Jones and his gunboats. On December 12 he dispatched 1,200 men in forty-five open boats with carronades in many of their prows, under veteran Captain Nicholas Lockyer, to attack Jones. It was late in the afternoon, about 3:30, when Lockyer's odd squadron began rowing toward the American boats. Lockyer's rowers had to labor for many miles before they got near the enemy. They rowed all through a cold, damp night, and it was not until late in morning on the thirteenth that Lockyer got almost in range of his target. He then stopped to have breakfast and to rest.

At ten o'clock Jones spotted the enemy flotilla advancing toward Pass Christian and then stopping. He had already pulled his squadron back from the pass. At first he thought the British were going to land troops. At two o'clock, however, when the barges rowed beyond Pass Christian without stopping, it was clear they were after him. The wind was strong from the west, and the water in Lake Borgne was unusually low. Gunboat numbers 156, 162, and 163 got stuck in mud. At 3:30 the flood tide allowed them to break free, and Jones beat back west toward the Rigolets.

Fifteen minutes later, Lockyer sent three barges after the *Seahorse* in the Bay of St. Louis, where Jones had sent her that morning to help remove public stores to keep them out of British hands. As the barges approached, Sailing Master Johnson fired on them and checked their advance, but they were soon joined by four more. Johnson used two six-pounders on the bank and his own six-pounder to mount a sharp action on all seven for thirty minutes before the British retreated. At 7:30 Johnson, fearing more barges were coming, blew up the *Seahorse* and the stores.

Lockyer's rowers, in the meantime, continued straining to get within range of Jones, but the tide had turned, and they made little progress against it. At eight o'clock Lockyer rested them again.

At 1 A.M. on the fourteenth, the wind died away, forcing Jones to anchor in the west end of Malhereux Island's passage, long before he reached the Rigolets. No breeze came up during the night. At daylight, the water was flat. Lockyer's barges now pulled to within nine miles of Jones. At 9:30 the *Alligator*, which had been caught to the eastward of Jones, was captured trying to rejoin the squadron. A strong ebb tide was running, and with no wind, Jones still could not sail west to the Rigolets. Unable to withdraw, Jones prepared to fight, forming the five gunboats in a tight line abreast between Malhereux Island and the mainland. At 10 Lockyer's entire force was under way, forming a line abreast and rowing directly at Jones. The rowers were battling the strong current the entire way. As the enemy rowed toward him, Jones counted forty-two boats—heavy launches, gun barges, and light gigs.

The current pushed Jones's gunboat (number 156) and gunboat number 163 one hundred yards in front of the others. When Lockyer's barges were in range, Jones and gunboat number 163 fired on them as fast as they could. But the barges were small and hard to hit. At 10:50 Lockyer opened fire with all his guns, and the battle raged. At 11:50, three advanced barges reached Jones's boat and attempted to board, but he beat them off, killing or wounding every officer and

Figure 31.1: T. L. Hornbrook, *The Gallant Attack and Capture of the American Flotilla near New Orleans, December 1814* (courtesy of U.S. Naval Academy Museum).

sinking two of the barges. Four more barges made a second attempt, and Jones beat them off as well with a similar number of casualties. During the fracas, a musket ball hit Jones in the left shoulder, forcing him to quit the main deck and go below. Master's Mate George Parker took command and fought on. But he was soon severely wounded himself. By 12:10, Lockyer had enough men on Jones's boat to overwhelm the crew and take her. He then turned her guns on the other American boats, while the gunboat's American colors were still flying, taking the Americans by surprise. They thought Jones was firing on them.

By 12:40 it was all over. Gunboat number 23 was the last to surrender. The British had seventeen killed and seventy-seven wounded. Jones had ten killed and thirty-five wounded. Lockyer allowed his men to plunder Jones's boats and steal the personal belongings of his men, an indication of what was in store for New Orleans if the British were victorious. Jones survived, but it took a long time for him to heal. The musket ball remained in his shoulder for the rest of his life. Jones and his crews were eventually taken as prisoners to Bermuda, where they were released when the war ended.

Commodore Patterson could ill afford to lose Jones and his men. Nor could he afford to lose five of his six gunboats. Jones did not fight in vain, however; he gave Jackson precious time to prepare. Inexplicably, when Jones and his flotilla were crushed and removed, Jackson did not replace them with scouts. He was without effective intelligence on Lake Borgne for ten days, an egregious oversight that might have been fatal.

When the British questioned Jones and the other prisoners, they gave estimates of Jackson's strength at 20,000. Some American deserters made the numbers much smaller, however—as few as 5,000. Cochrane had estimates from a number of sources, and in the end he overestimated Jackson's strength, although not to the degree that Jones hoped. Regardless of what the British thought they were up against, they had scant regard for American militiamen, and this attitude would work decidedly in Jackson's favor.

With Lieutenant Jones and his boats out of the way, Cochrane moved his army thirty miles west to Pea Island at the mouth of the Pearl River, where he set up an advance base. With almost no trees, but a surfeit of alligators and snakes, Pea Island was a barren, wet, godforsaken place halfway across Lake Borgne. Getting men from the fleet to the island was itself a monumental, backbreaking chore. Cochrane did not have enough boats to take his men across all at once. Several round trips of sixty miles had to be made. Not until December 19 was General Keane's army finally on the island. With no tents or huts, the troops suffered in the cold rain that poured down on them nearly every afternoon.

Admiral Cochrane and Admiral Malcolm were on Pea Island with General Keane, making final decisions on how to proceed. Three possible invasion routes presented themselves east of the Mississippi. Cochrane had already ruled out the two routes to the west, as well as the Mississippi River itself. One possible route of attack was by way of the shallow, difficult Rigolets passage into Lake Pontchartrain and thence by boat to a point two miles north of the city. Cochrane did not have enough shallow draft vessels for this otherwise attractive course, and Fort Petites Coquilles, which guarded the Rigolets passage, presented an important obstacle. The second approach was to row to Bayou Chef Menteur and then to the Plain of Gentilly, where the Chef Menteur Road went from the Rigolets directly to the city. The road was narrow, however, and could be easily blocked. Jackson, aware of its attractiveness, had it well guarded.

The third potential route was by way of Bayou Bienvenue to a narrow branch, Bayou Mazant, and then to Villeré Canal, which would take the British to a point one mile from the Mississippi and seven miles south of the city. Cochrane chose this final route. Keane had little say in the matter. The entrance to Bayou Bienvenue was sixty miles west of Cochrane's fleet and thirty miles from Pea Island.

General Keane prepared to transport 1,600 men from Pea Island to the entrance to Bayou Bienvenue. He did not have enough boats to move them all at once, so the exhausting work had to be performed three times. At midnight on

December 22, eight days after the Battle of Lake Borgne, the first of Keane's troops arrived at Bayou Bienvenue. Colonel William Thornton, the same intrepid officer who led the charge for General Ross at the Battle of Bladensburg, was in command.

It had been fourteen days since Admiral Cochrane's flagship dropped anchor off Cat Island—precious time for Jackson to prepare. Colonel Thornton immediately captured Jackson's post at the fishing village beside the entrance to Bayou Bienvenue. Keane then led the army up Bayou Bienvenue (one hundred yards wide) to the much narrower Bayou Mazant, which ran to the Villeré plantation at the edge of the Mississippi. Keane arrived undetected on the morning of the twenty-third. No obstructions had been placed anywhere to delay them, although Jackson had ordered them. Obstacles blocked the other invasion routes, but not this one. Remarkably, Jackson had no idea the British had a large force only seven miles south of the city. Keane's advance party captured a small detachment of militia—thirty men led by Major Gabriel Villeré. Fortunately for Jackson, Major Villeré escaped and alerted him to Keane's presence.

WHILE KEANE WAS moving his army unseen to within easy striking distance of New Orleans, Jackson, unaware of the danger, continued preparing for some sort of attack. When word of Jones's defeat at the Battle of Lake Borgne reached the city on December 15, Jackson redoubled his efforts, and New Orleans panicked. Jackson called out the entire Louisiana militia and sent urgent calls to William Carroll, who had 2,500 Tennessee militiamen on the way, and to John Coffee with 1,300 men, and to Kentucky militiamen, hoping for a large contingent, perhaps 2,500 or more. He declared martial law in the city on December 16. He also did something he never thought he'd have to do—accept help from Jean Lafitte and his pirates. Jackson had some regulars, as well, from the Fourth and Forty-fourth U.S. regiments (about 600 men). He was woefully short of arms, however; Monroe had promised them but had not delivered any as yet.

Jackson had indispensable help from the redoubtable Commodore Daniel Patterson, who after Jones's defeat was left with only the 15-gun schooner *Carolina*, the 16-gun *Louisiana*, and a single gunboat. But he had a large supply of munitions captured during a successful raid on the Baratarian pirate base on September 16. Secretary Jones had ordered Patterson specifically to attack the pirates and had sent the *Carolina* from Charleston for that purpose. She arrived in New Orleans in August. But for the secretary's action, the *Carolina* would not have been available. She was a well-built schooner, made in Charleston and purchased by the navy in November 1812. She had five six-pounders a side and two twelve-pounders at the bow and stern on swivels that allowed them to be fired on either side. Her seventy-man crew were tough navy veterans, many of them from New England.

The *Louisiana* was a converted merchantman, purchased in New Orleans by the navy in 1812. She was not put to use, however, until August 1814. Until then, she sat idle with no crew. She carried four twenty-four-pounders, eight twelve-pounders, and four six-pounders. Unlike the *Carolina*'s crew, the *Louisiana*'s was gathered from the streets of New Orleans—men from all nations (except England). Two-thirds of them could not speak English. After Jackson declared martial law, Patterson could impress whomever he needed. The *Louisiana*'s skipper, Lieutenant Charles C. B. Thompson, used coercion to round out his crew.

Laffite's pirates did not serve in the *Carolina* or the *Louisiana*, as many historians have supposed. Patterson and the pirates hated each other. Jackson sent the Baratarians to man the guns at the forts guarding the city—Petites Coquilles, St. Philip, and Bayou St. Jean. A few of them later manned two batteries on Jackson's line and performed well, but that was all.

Admiral Cochrane made no attempt to get any warships, even small ones, up the Mississippi before the main battle. The mouth of the river was 105 miles south of New Orleans. The current and the bar at Balize made it impossible for large warships to ascend and difficult for smaller ones. Jackson had made it even more unattractive as an invasion route by reinforcing Fort St. Philip, situated fifty miles from the mouth of the river at a difficult turn in the river. The swamps around the fort made a land attack impossible. Cochrane thus conceded naval supremacy on the Mississippi to Commodore Patterson, who had only two small warships and the number 65 gunboat. Cochrane's decision was a great help to Jackson.

AT NOON ON December 23, Jackson finally was alerted to the threat from Keane's army. He had to act fast to prevent the British from overrunning the city. Fortunately, Keane's troops were in a weak condition, and reinforcements were not coming for a while. The normally aggressive Keane would have liked to strike unprepared New Orleans that day, but his troops were in no condition to attempt it.

Recovering quickly from his surprise, Jackson decided to attack the enemy that night. He worried that Keane's threat was only a feint, and that a second British force, perhaps the main one, would attack the city using the Chef Menteur

Road. To guard against that, he left General Carroll's force and the city's militia to protect the road. By a Herculean effort, Jackson mustered 1,500 troops of various kinds, and at five o'clock in the afternoon he marched to meet Keane, planning to attack with infantry (including 200 free men of color) and Major Thomas Hind's Mississippi dragoons. Jackson believed the British force to be 3,000, or twice his own. He arrived at Villeré's plantation around seven o'clock. Jackson's movements had gone entirely undetected by the British sentries.

Meanwhile, Commodore Patterson and Master Commandant John D. Henley had silently brought the *Carolina* downriver to the British flank, and at 7:30 began pouring deadly grape shot into their camp. Keane's surprised troops fired two ineffective three-pounders at her and then ran for cover. The ship's cannon going off was the signal for Jackson to attack. Coffee charged from the left along the cypress swamp, while Jackson moved along the Mississippi with the main force and struck from the right directly at the camp, which was close to the river. The *Carolina* ceased firing when Henley judged Jackson and Coffee's Tennessee riflemen were within range of her guns.

The two armies battled in the dark singly and in small groups hand to hand. Around eight o'clock, a fog descended over the battlefield, and around ten, Jackson withdrew. He wrote, "Fearing the consequence, under this circumstance, of the further prosecution of a night attack with troops, then acting together for the first time, I contented myself with lying on the field that night."

He rested less than a mile from the battlefield, remaining on the river road leading to the city. At four o'clock in the morning he withdrew two more miles to a stronger position in back of Rodriguez Canal. "As the safety of the city will depend on the fate of this army," Jackson wrote, "it must not be incautiously exposed."

Even though Keane had been reinforced during the fighting, he did not pursue the retreating Americans. Jackson had inflicted so much pain that Keane thought he was up against 5,000 militiamen. Keane lost 46 killed, 167 wounded, and 64 missing. Jackson had 24 killed, 115 wounded, and 74 missing.

As a result of Jackson's daring raid, Cochrane committed his entire army to the confined area south of Rodriguez Canal, which meant that Jackson did not have to divide his small force and defend the city against simultaneous attacks coming from two or more directions. Cochrane was making a major strategic blunder on the spur of the moment with little thought and no consultation.

After Jackson withdrew, the *Louisiana* joined the *Carolina*, and the two ships kept peppering Keane's camp. Their guns protected Jackson at the Rodriguez Canal and the road leading to New Orleans, although Keane was so shaken by Jackson's surprise night attack that there was no chance he'd move on the city immediately. He ordered heavy naval artillery brought up to counteract the deadly fire from the warships, but it would not arrive soon.

The following morning, December 24, Jackson began building a defense barrier at Rodriguez Canal that stretched from the Mississippi for nine hundred yards to a huge cypress swamp. The canal was twelve feet wide and four to eight feet deep. At the same time, Jackson cut a levee below the canal to swamp the British. He did not accomplish his objective, but the water was a problem for them, as were the two warships, which continued shelling Keane's camp from time to time, keeping him off balance and thus preventing a surprise attack on Jackson. Close collaboration between Patterson and Jackson characterized their operation throughout.

ON THE MORNING of December 24, the frigate *Statira* arrived off Cat Island with thirty-seven-year-old Lieutenant General Edward Pakenham, the new British commander. Later that night, Pakenham met Captain Sir Thomas Hardy on the brig *Anaconda*, and Hardy brought him up to date on the naval battle with Jones and Keane's fight with Jackson. On Christmas morning, Pakenham and his party were rowed to Fisherman's Village near the mouth of Bayou Bienvenue, where Cochrane had his headquarters. Over breakfast, the admiral gave Pakenham his version of what happened the previous night.

Later that day, Pakenham moved on to the base at Villeré's plantation. For the first time, he saw the terrible position Cochrane had placed him in, including the Americans having command of the water. In fact, a few more enemy warships would have made attacking New Orleans from Keane's camp unthinkable. Pakenham had to immediately decide if he was going to abandon the site and develop a new strategy or make the best of what he had. He chose to stay. His regard for American militiamen was so low that he decided to press on. By now the British force had dwindled to 5,500, what with losses in the battle, desertions, sickness, and the all-black West Indian regiments finding the weather intolerable. General Lambert's 2,200 reinforcements had not yet arrived.

Having made the critical decision to remain at Villeré's plantation, Pakenham now had to stop the enfilading fire from the *Carolina* and the *Louisiana*. He brought with him from Wellington's army in France one of the best artillery officers in the world, Alexander Dickson. A two-day delay followed while Dickson assembled a battery of nine field pieces. At eight o'clock on the morning of December 27, Dickson's guns opened up on the *Carolina* with red-hot shot. Master Commandant Henley could not get away. The current was running against him, and he was becalmed. In a little over two hours the *Carolina* blew up. Before she exploded, however, Henley and his crew took to the boats, narrowly escaping. Patterson was not on board at the time. One of Henley's men drowned, and six were wounded; the rest survived. Somehow they managed to rescue two heavy guns. While Dickson was directing his fire exclusively at the *Carolina*, Lieutenant Thompson got his boats out quickly and warped the *Louisiana* upriver, beyond the range of the deadly guns.

Jackson in the meantime continued strengthening the fortifications in back of Rodriguez Canal. While he did, many of New Orleans's prominent Creole citizens were getting nervous, wondering how Jackson was going to withstand the obviously superior numbers, training, and munitions of the British. Jackson had already announced that the enemy would never take the city. If he were defeated, he intended to destroy New Orleans before he left. No one doubted that he would. The concerned citizens did not want their great city ruined by Jackson or by Pakenham. To protect themselves and New Orleans, they were seriously considering surrendering.

Sinking the *Carolina* emboldened Pakenham. On the twenty-eighth, he decided to make a reconnaissance in force. If things went well, a full-fledged attack would immediately follow. At daylight, he moved his troops to within half a mile of Jackson's line and began firing bombs and Congreve rockets. Jackson responded with an unexpectedly strong, well-directed artillery barrage from behind the canal and from the *Louisiana*. A fierce battle ensued, with the *Louisiana*'s twelves and twenty-fours wreaking havoc on Pakenham's flank. The *Louisiana*'s fire and Jackson's were so accurate and powerful that Pakenham was forced to pull back and order more heavy artillery brought up from the fleet. Jackson could not counterattack. "I lament that I have not the means of carrying on more offensive operations," he wrote. "My effective force at this point, does not exceed 3000."

The following day, December 29, Commodore Patterson removed some of the guns from the *Louisiana* and placed them on the west bank of the Mississippi. He was afraid Dickson would sink the ship, as he had the *Carolina*, and they would lose the guns. Patterson thought the cannon could be put to better use and be better protected on the riverbank. The *Louisiana* was thus retired from further action. She had done great service, however, in two battles on December 23 and the 28. Jackson ordered Brigadier General David Morgan and five hundred sixty Louisiana militiamen to protect Patterson's new batteries.

Pakenham was confident that heavy naval artillery would blast Jackson out of his stronghold. More time was consumed as Pakenham brought four twenty-four-pound carronades and ten eighteen-pound long guns from the distant fleet.

While this arduous operation was in progress, Jackson continued strengthening his line, increasing his artillery platforms from five to twelve.

On the opposite side of the Mississippi, three-quarters of a mile from Pakenham's big guns, Commodore Patterson was busy installing a strong battery with some of the *Louisiana*'s cannon. He soon had one twenty-four-pounder and two twelve-pounders ready to enfilade Pakenham's line and blast his artillery. Master Commandant Henley had a battery of two twelve-pounders on the west bank of the river overlooking the city.

On January 1, 1815, Pakenham's artillery was ready to blow a big hole in Jackson's line through which the infantry could rush into the city. Thick fog covered the battlefield until about ten o'clock. When it lifted, Pakenham's guns blasted away at Jackson's headquarters (from which he barely escaped) and his fortifications. A ferocious artillery duel developed, as Jackson, with thirteen heavy guns, and Patterson with three, targeted Pakenham's artillery. On and on the big guns roared, until, after three hours, Dickson ran out of ammunition. His shooting was unexpectedly poor because of the inadequate gun platforms he had to contrive and also because of the unexpected, deadly accuracy of the American artillery. Jackson's gunners had serviceable platforms, and they had plenty of ammunition.

It galled Pakenham to have to stand down a second time. It was a blow to the morale of the troops, who had dreams of spending the night in New Orleans. In the artillery exchange, Pakenham had forty-four killed and fifty-five wounded. Jackson had eleven killed and twenty-three wounded. When Pakenham withdrew, Jackson did not pursue. He remained behind his barricade, as he had after the battle on the twenty-eighth.

Pakenham now decided to wait for Lambert's brigade to arrive. When it did, he planned to assault Jackson with everything he had. He intended to capture Patterson's battery and turn the guns on Jackson, while Dickson's artillery on the east bank blasted the American fortifications and the infantry stormed them.

Pakenham ordered Colonel Thornton to organize a surprise night attack on Patterson with 1,200 troops. To accomplish this, Cochrane widened and deepened Villeré's Canal, so that boats could carry a large raiding party to the other side of the river. This took more time, and while the British were doing it, Jackson extended his line well into the cypress swamp to protect his left flank. The previous battles had shown that area to be vulnerable. General Coffee was in charge of Jackson's left.

Patterson was also strengthening his position. He brought up four more twelve-pounders and two twenty-four-pounders from the *Louisiana* and erected another battery. And he added a twelve-pounder to General Morgan's force. Patterson now had ten big naval guns ready to use against Pakenham's left flank. The batteries themselves were weakly defended, however. Morgan had fewer than six hundred inexperienced, poorly trained Louisiana militiamen. Jackson was not giving Patterson and the west bank full support because he was convinced the main British thrust would come on the east side of the river.

General Lambert reached the fleet off Cat Island on January 1, but getting his troops to the battlefield consumed four days. By January 5 all the men were at the camp below Rodriguez Canal. Again, the delay helped Jackson. On January 3, more than 2,300 green Kentucky militiamen, under Major General John Thomas, arrived in New Orleans. They had only seven hundred guns, however. Jackson immediately ordered 500 of the troops to cross the river and reinforce Morgan.

Each night, a few of Jackson's sharpshooters stole up to the British outposts and picked off the sentries with deadly accurate rifle fire. The riflemen created such havoc that Pakenham actually protested this method of warfare to Jackson, who scoffed at him, reminding him that he was invading another country.

Finding the constant delays intolerable and knowing they were sapping the morale of his troops, Pakenham decided to assault Jackson's line on the morning of the eighth. Ladders and fascines were readied to fill the ditch in front of Jackson's great mud wall and scale it. Colonel Thornton prepared to cross the river on the evening of the seventh, seize Patterson's guns, and enfilade Jackson while Pakenham made a frontal attack with the main body of his troops.

Fifty boats assembled in Villeré's canal to move Thornton's men. The colonel planned to depart for the west bank at nine o'clock in the evening, but the extended canal collapsed, and few boats could be brought up to take him across. He did manage to embark six hundred men, but the current took them beyond their planned landing place, destroying Pakenham's timetable. Nonetheless, Thornton carried on, still determined to attack Morgan and then Patterson.

Behind Rodriguez Canal, Jackson had erected a strong fortification two to three feet thick. His 5,200 troops could wait there, protected behind a rampart, while the British advanced in the open, easy targets for his sharpshooters and especially for his heavy guns. Jackson had twelve artillery batteries on his line. Lieutenant Ortho Norris and seventeen seamen from the *Carolina* manned number two battery with one twenty-four-pounder. Lieutenant C. E. Crawley of the *Carolina* commanded battery number four with one thirty-two-pounder, also manned by seamen from the *Carolina*. Only battery number three, consisting of two twenty-four-pounders, was operated by Baratarian pirates.

ON THE MORNING of January 8 Pakenham arose at five o'clock to find that Thornton had failed to make it across the river in time to coordinate with him. He was not surprised. He had always been skeptical about Thornton's ability to get his men across the river in a timely fashion. Pakenham was prepared to go on without him. He was supremely confident in the superiority of his artillery and his regular infantry when pitted against American militiamen. He ordered Lieutenant John Craley to fire a rocket, signaling the attack to begin. Pakenham knew that without Thornton his casualties would be much higher, but he was willing to accept the losses rather than call off another action.

It was no mystery to Jackson that Pakenham was going to attack, and he was ready. Sailing Master Johnson of the American navy had captured a British sloop in Lake Borgne, and the crew gave details of Pakenham's plans. There were many British deserters reporting to Jackson as well. He knew what was coming and when.

At six o'clock a heavy mist covered the battlefield as Dickson got his twenty heavy guns ready. He was to commence firing only when he heard musketry fire. Major General Sir Samuel Gibbs led the main thrust with 2,300 regulars against Jackson's center left. Gibbs's column stepped forward, two hundred yards to the left of the cypress swamp. When they were five hundred yards from Rodriguez Canal, the fog suddenly lifted, and Jackson's men got a good view of what was coming at them. They waited with their loaded weapons for the enemy to get closer. Suddenly, American artillery opened fire. Dickson immediately replied, and the battle was on in earnest. When Gibbs was three hundred fifty yards from the canal, Jackson's sharpshooters opened fire with their deadly rifles.

General Keane, meanwhile, was advancing against Jackson's center right with 1,200 men. As Keane's column moved forward, Commodore Patterson kept up a heavy fire on it. Ahead of Keane was Brevet Lieutenant Colonel Robert Rennie with some light troops advancing to capture Jackson's forward redoubt near the river and render the guns useless so that they could not enfilade the area directly in front of Jackson's line.

If Gibbs made a breakthrough, Keane was to immediately move to the right and join him. Gibbs was experiencing severe problems, however. Jackson's number two and four batteries, those manned by seamen from the *Carolina*, were cutting a wide swath through Gibbs's advancing line with grapeshot. Jackson wrote, "Lieutenant Norris of the Navy, with Mr. Walker Martin, and a detachment of seamen, was stationed at the 2nd battery, and Lieutenant Crawley, with Mr. W. Livingston, master's mate, with a similar detachment, were stationed at number four with a 32-pounder, which was remarkably well directed." The Baratarians, led by captains Dominique and Belluche, manned battery number 3, and they were commended by Jackson as well for "the gallantry with which they have redeemed the pledge they gave at the opening of the campaign to defend the country."

The fascines and ladders that were supposed to be available to Gibbs in large quantities and that he was counting on were not on hand because of a mix-up. But it hardly mattered. His men were being mowed down by the incessant, accurate fire from rifles, muskets, and especially the naval guns. Through it all, however, the disciplined British regulars kept reforming and marching forward to be slaughtered. Jackson reported that "twice the column which approached me on my left, was repulsed by the troops of General Carroll, those of General Coffee, and a division of the Kentucky militia, and twice [the British] formed again and renewed their assault."

Eventually, Gibbs's troops broke and fled to the nearby swamp to get away from the grapeshot and rifles. The general tried to rally them, as did Pakenham, who road up on his horse and waved them forward. He was having some success when Gibbs suddenly fell, mortally wounded. Then Pakenham was hit in the knee by grapeshot, while a musket ball felled his horse. He was soon hit a second time, and a third struck him in the back, killing him. Utter confusion then reigned.

General Keane, meanwhile, having been ordered by Pakenham himself to turn his column right and join Gibbs, was trying to do so when the deadly fire from Jackson's line, and from Patterson across the river, forced Keane's regulars to hit the ground and seek cover. Soon a ball struck Keane in the groin and mortally wounded him.

Three of Britain's generals were now out of action; only Lambert remained. He was an experienced commander, but he had only arrived at the front on January 5. His men had been held in reserve, but when conditions deteriorated, Pakenham ordered them into the fray. Lambert was moving 1,400 of them forward, but all around was slaughter and chaos, and he called a halt to the advance. If his reserves were decimated as the rest of the army had been, he would be forced to surrender to Jackson, something he wanted to avoid at all costs.

Lambert sent Dickson across the river to see what Thornton's situation was, and he held a council of war with those officers who were still alive. By then, American fire had ceased. Jackson's artillery stopped around two o'clock, but his infantry had stopped five hours earlier for lack of targets. Lambert's situation was desperate. If he renewed the attack and it failed, which it almost surely would, he would have to surrender. He had no alternative but to retreat.

On the other side of the river, Dickson discovered that, although Thornton was severely wounded and reinforcements were needed, he had dispatched Morgan's militiamen easily and captured Patterson's battery. The commodore had fired at the British across the river with good effect and had turned a gun on Thornton as well, but as the British regulars closed in, Patterson spiked his guns in great haste and withdrew. Thornton easily cleaned them and carried them to a point where he could enfilade Jackson's line, which could have destroyed him. Before Thornton could execute, however, Lambert ordered him back. Jackson was very lucky, and he knew it. When Thornton withdrew, Patterson returned, fixed the guns, and used them again against Lambert, cannonading sporadically day and night. Jackson never considered going on the offensive for the same reasons he did not do so after the previous engagements. He feared the British regulars, even in their weakened condition, would destroy his militiamen.

The butcher's bill on the British side was horrendous—291 killed and 1,262 wounded on January 8. An additional 484 were listed as missing, but they were surely either prisoners or deserters. Jackson had 13 killed, 39 wounded, and 19 missing, probably Morgan's men. The numbers were so astounding that Jackson told Monroe they "may not everywhere be fully credited."

THE NEXT DAY, Cochrane attacked Fort St. Philip, which Jackson had strengthened long ago when he first came to New Orleans. The fort had a solid battery of twenty-nine twenty-four-pounders, two thirty-two-pounders, heavy mortars, and howitzers. Commodore Patterson's sole remaining gunboat, under Lieutenant Thomas Cunningham, was in the water outside. Four hundred regulars manned the fort under Major Walter Overton.

Cochrane sent five small ships to test the fort's defenses. They arrived on January 9 and shelled it from a distance of one mile. That night they tried running past the fort with a fair wind, but they could not make it and returned to their previous position. They resumed the bombardment and kept at it until January 18. During the nine days, a thousand shells fell into the fort but had little effect.

Cochrane's maneuver was a distraction designed to hold Jackson's attention while Lambert went about the difficult, time-consuming business of readying his army for a retreat back to their ships off Cat Island. Five hundred British soldiers had surrendered to Jackson, and many others had deserted, but Lambert still had a powerful force. He kept Jackson off balance by pretending he was going to attack again, and Jackson had to take the threat seriously, particularly with

Cochrane's bombardment going on. If Cochrane could get his warships up the Mississippi, he might turn the tables on the Americans.

On January 18 Lambert was ready, and he conducted a masterly, secret retreat, while Jackson waited for another onslaught. The sorely tried British troops made it back to their troop transports off Cat Island and climbed aboard, chilled to the bone. They were hoping to weigh anchor immediately, but bad weather delayed the fleet, and it did not sortie until January 25.

When Lambert was safely away, he decided to have another go at Fort Bowyer, and in this he easily succeeded. Major Lawrence surrendered with four hundred men on February 11. Lambert could now threaten Mobile and then possibly New Orleans itself again. But on February 14 he received word that the war was over, and he could relax. His men enjoyed Dauphin Island, which was something of a paradise.

Lambert still had to negotiate with Jackson about prisoners and former slaves, who left with the British. Jackson wanted all the slaves back, viewing them simply as property. Lambert considered them human beings, and he refused to return anyone who did not want to go, even though they were more mouths to feed and a burden on his resources. He stuck to his guns; he would not return anyone to slavery. The ex-slaves who wanted their freedom sailed away with him.

THE SUCCESSFUL DEFENSE of New Orleans had a decided impact on the attitude of Liverpool, Castlereagh, and their colleagues toward the United States. The military prowess of America now appeared far more substantial, and this new assessment would help alter relations between the two countries from then on. Britain and America, through two centuries, never fought each other again. The battle at New Orleans contributed to bringing about a remarkable new relationship. Thus, even though the battle occurred after the peace treaty was signed, it played a major role in winning the peace that followed.

CHAPTER THIRTY-TWO

An Amazing Change

W HEN THE NEW year of 1815 began, a pervasive gloom hung over Washington while the city waited anxiously for reports from New Orleans and Ghent. Prospects for an acceptable peace appeared remote, and the British invasion of New Orleans seemed certain to succeed. Madison thought it was a good possibility that Spain would secretly turn Florida over to Britain. If Cochrane then captured New Orleans, the British would control the southern extremity of the United States and threaten all of Louisiana. They would also have northern Maine. The outcome of the meeting of disgruntled Federalists at Hartford was unknown but troubling. The country appeared to be coming apart.

Even though the belief that the war would continue was widespread, the president could not get Congress to enact a system of taxation or a national bank to properly finance it. Nor would Congress approve the army Madison wanted. The United States seemed to be growing weaker, while Britain appeared stronger than ever. Thousands of veteran British troops and some of Wellington's best generals were in Canada. And Admiral Yeo was again dominant on Lake Ontario. How long would it be before he regained control of lakes Erie and Champlain? All of these problems would disappear if the war ended, but the president saw little chance of that. What seemed more likely was a continuation of the fighting with an inadequate army and navy, and a divided country whose government was essentially bankrupt.

The gloom in Washington was relieved somewhat by news the second week of January that the ultrasecret Hartford Convention had issued a moderate report that reflected the views of most Federalists, who, although unhappy with Madison, did not want to secede and ignite a civil war. "The proceedings are tempered with more moderation than was to have been expected," the *National Intelligencer* wrote. "A separation from the Union, so far from being openly recommended, is the subject only of remote illusion."

This relatively good news was more than offset by word that on January 15 a British squadron forced Stephen Decatur to surrender the 44-gun *President* off New York after a bloody fight in which Decatur lost one-fifth of his crew, including Lieutenant Paul Hamilton, the son of the former secretary of the navy, who was cut in half by a cannonball.

Decatur's depressing story began during the evening of January 14, when he saw an opening and stood out from New York. A snowstorm had blown the British blockaders out to sea. Decatur had pilots at the bar off Sandy Hook positioning boats with blazing lights to mark a safe passage. But "owing to some mistake of the pilots" (or treachery) the *President* ran aground, where she struck heavily for an hour and a half, breaking rudder braces, cracking masts, and making her hogged. The tide rose, and it was necessary to force her over the bar lest she get stuck again. By ten o'clock Decatur was finally off the treacherous sand. He needed to return to port for repairs, but a strong westerly forced him out to sea. He sailed along the shore of Long Island for fifty miles and then steered southeast by east, hoping to break free.

Decatur's hopes were dashed, however, when at five o'clock in the morning lookouts spied three ships ahead. He had run into the British squadron. He immediately hauled up and tried passing to the northward of them, but he soon discovered that four ships were chasing him. The lead one was a razee (the 56-gun *Majestic*), and she commenced firing, but with no effect. At noon the *President* was outdistancing the razee, but another large ship (the 50-gun *Endymion*) was gaining because of the injuries the *President* had sustained and the amount of water she was taking in. Decatur immediately started lightening the ship by starting the water, cutting the anchors, and throwing overboard provisions, cables, spare spars, boats, "and every article that could be got at," while keeping the sails wet from the royals down to coax every bit of speed out of her.

At three o'clock Decatur had a light wind, but the ship in chase had a strong breeze, and she was coming up fast. The *Endymion* began firing her bow chasers, and Decatur responded with stern guns. By five o'clock the *Endymion* was close on the *President*'s starboard quarter, where neither Decatur's stern guns nor his quarter guns would bear. He was steering east by north; the wind was from the northwest. Dusk was approaching, and the *President* was being cut up without

Figure 32.1: *President* versus *Endymion* (courtesy of Naval Historical Center).

being able to fight back. Decatur tried to close and board, but the *Endymion* was yawing from time to time to keep her distance and fire with impunity.

Desperate to get out of this deadly trap, Decatur abruptly turned south and brought the enemy abeam. A savage battle ensued broadside to broadside for the next two and a half hours, during which Decatur's superb gunnery dismantled the *Endymion*. For several minutes, the British ship was such a wreck she could not fire a gun.

By now, it was 8:30, and two more enemy ships were coming up, the 38-gun frigates *Pomone* and *Tenedos*. Decatur threw on every sail he could and tried to outrun them, but by eleven o'clock the *Pomone* had caught up with him. Visibility was poor enough that Decatur thought the *Tenedos* was close as well, but she was much farther back, perhaps two or three miles.

The *Pomone* fired two devastating broadsides into the struggling *President*, causing Decatur to examine his alternatives. With one-fifth of the crew killed or wounded, his ship badly damaged, and so many enemy ships opposed to him, with no chance of escaping, he decided to strike his colors. Twenty-five of his veteran crew were dead and sixty wounded. Many of the men had been with

Decatur when he fought the *Macedonian*. The British took the *President* and prisoners to Bermuda, where the big frigate, so long sought by the Admiralty, was repaired and taken to England.

The loss of the *President* dramatically increased the sense of doom in Washington—but that pervasive pessimism disappeared practically overnight as wonderful news began flooding into the capital. On February 4, incredible, scarcely believable reports arrived of victory at New Orleans. Everyone breathed a giant sigh of relief. Only seven days later, on February 11, the British sloop of war *Favorite*, after a tempestuous passage, sailed into New York with the peace treaty.

On the evening of February 13, the treaty was delivered to the secretary of state in Washington, and the following day the city erupted in a giant celebration. Torches and candles were everywhere. The charred reminders of the fires of August could not dampen the bliss. Overnight, the entire complexion of American politics changed, and everywhere a rebirth of national confidence was evident. Boston and all of New England were deliriously happy. The Senate ratified the treaty unanimously, and on February 17 an enormously relieved president declared the war was over.

The actual terms of the peace treaty seemed unimportant; the country had been saved from the abyss, and that was enough. People would have willingly paid a much higher price for peace. The terms turned out to be relatively benign. In fact, they were much better than expected. The commissioners' fear that the country would be unhappy with their compromises turned out to be unfounded.

In the midst of these momentous events, three delegates, Harrison Gray Otis, William Sullivan, and Thomas Perkins, arrived in Washington from Boston to press the Hartford Convention's demand that the states be allowed to use federal tax money to pay for their defense. Governor Strong had appointed them. They arrived on February 13, the day before news of peace became public. The delegates already knew about New Orleans and were anticipating a frosty reception, but the unexpected peace turned their mission into a pathetic joke. They called upon the secretaries of War and the Treasury and were introduced to the president, but Madison treated them coldly. Otis was greatly annoyed. He wrote to his wife, calling the president "a mean and contemptible little blackguard." After the way Massachusetts Federalists had treated Madison, it is hard to understand why Otis expected any other kind of reception.

FOR THE AMERICAN navy the war did not end with the signing of the treaty at Ghent. Warships were already at sea and did not receive word of peace, and neither did their British counterparts. While the celebration was going on in Washington, the *Constitution* was still at sea. Captain Charles Stewart had slipped out of Boston on December 17, 1814. The blockading squadron, composed of three frigates and a brig of war, were not on guard. The frigates had departed for repairs at the Royal Navy Dockyards at Halifax, and the brig was in Provincetown. Stewart had a clear field. When he was well out into the Atlantic, he painted the *Constitution*'s sides black with a distinctive thick yellow stripe across her gun ports, making her appear British, and he flew the Union Jack.

On Christmas Eve he captured the brig *Nelson*. Days and then weeks passed uneventfully, however. On February 10, he was ten miles off Cape Finisterre, on the northwest coast of Spain. By that time, he knew for certain that a peace treaty had been signed. He did not know if it had been ratified, but he could assume that it had. Nonetheless, he continued the hunt. On February 16, he captured a small British merchantman and sent her to New York as a prize.

Four days later, Stewart was sailing a hundred eighty miles west-southwest of Madeira when lookouts spotted a stranger two points off the larboard bow. Stewart immediately hauled up and gave chase. Forty-five minutes later, a second ship appeared ahead. It was soon apparent they were both enemy warships. In fact, they were the British men-of-war *Cyane* (Captain Gordon Falcon) and *Levant* (Captain George Douglas). The *Cyane* was a small frigate with a battery of thirty thirty-two-pound carronades, two eighteen-pound carronades, and two long nines. Her companion, the *Levant*, was a sloop of war carrying eighteen thirty-two-pound carronades and two long nines.

Signals from the British ships quickly identified the *Constitution* as an enemy. Falcon and Douglas were ten miles apart, and they closed ranks to fight the larger frigate together, rather than separating and trying to outrun her. By four o'clock the *Cyane* was ten miles to leeward of the *Constitution*. Stewart "bore up after her, and set lower topmast, topgallant, and royal studding sails."

In thirty minutes the *Constitution*'s main royal mast carried away, but Stewart had a crew clear the wreckage and prepare a replacement, while he kept on after the enemy. At five o'clock he opened fire with two larboard bow guns but with little effect. By 5:30 the two enemy ships had come together. They hauled up their courses and prepared for battle. At first they tried to obtain the weather gauge, but failing that, they formed a line a half cable's length from each other (a hundred yards).

At six o'clock all the ships raised their flags and commenced firing at about three hundred yards. Stewart concentrated on the *Cyane*. Both enemy ships fired on the *Constitution*. The exchange lasted for fifteen minutes, when the

Constitution's heavy twenty-four-pounders began to tell, and the *Cyane*'s fire slackened. Great columns of smoke now surrounded the *Constitution*, and Stewart ceased firing. In three minutes the smoke cleared, and he saw that the *Constitution* was abreast of the much smaller *Levant*. Stewart poured a punishing broadside into her, as the *Cyane* came up on the *Constitution*'s larboard quarter.

Stewart reacted quickly. He "braced aback . . . main and mizzen topsails, and backed astern under cover of the smoke" that had hung around. He pulled abreast of the *Cyane*, and both ships blazed away at each other for fifteen minutes, when the *Cyane*'s fire slackened once more. She had been badly cut up. Stewart then discovered the gallant *Levant* bearing up. He filled his topsails, shot ahead, and raked her by the stern twice with his larboard guns, severely damaging her. Meanwhile, the struggling *Cyane* had worn, and Stewart wore short round and raked her by the stern. The nearly crippled *Cyane* managed to then luff to on the *Constitution*'s starboard bow and fire a broadside into her from her larboard battery. But Stewart then ranged up on the *Cyane*'s larboard quarter within hail and was about to unleash a crushing broadside when she fired a gun to leeward, signaling surrender. It was ten minutes before seven o'clock. The action had lasted for fifty minutes.

An hour later, Stewart went after the *Levant*, which was not running, despite the *Constitution*'s overwhelming superiority. In fact, to Stewart's amazement, Captain Douglass was standing toward him. At ten minutes before nine the two ships ranged close alongside on opposite tacks and exchanged broadsides. Stewart wore immediately under *Levant*'s stern and raked her with a broadside. Only then did the plucky Douglass try to escape. Stewart chased him, firing his starboard bow chaser to good effect, cutting the *Levant*'s sails and rigging, which slowed her considerably. At ten o'clock Douglass fired a single gun to leeward indicating surrender. The *Constitution* had 3 killed and 12 wounded, while the two British ships had 35 killed and 42 wounded. Stewart took 313 prisoners.

He brought his prizes to Porto Praya in the Cape Verde Islands, arriving on March 10. The next day, lookouts spied three British frigates approaching the roadstead. Stewart tried to escape with his prizes, and the frigates chased him. The *Cyane*, the dullest sailer, fell behind and disappeared into a providential fog, but the enemy frigates kept after the *Constitution* and the *Levant*. The *Levant* soon lost ground, and she was recaptured. Oddly, all three frigates went after her and let the *Constitution* escape. The *Cyane* struggled into New York on April 9. On April 28 Stewart finally received confirmation that the war was indeed over, and he steered for Boston.

THE *CONSTITUTION* WAS not the only American fighting ship at large when the war ended. On January 23, 1815, five days after the *President* departed New York, the sloop of war *Peacock*, under Master Commandant Lewis Warrington, swept passed Sandy Hook in a strong northeasterly gale and sped out to sea in full view of the slower British sentinels. Right on Warrington's tail were the sloop of war *Hornet*, under Master Commandant James Biddle, the 12-gun store-brig *Tom Bowline*, under Lieutenant B. V. Hoffman, and the private armed merchant brig *Macedonian*. The *Peacock*, *Hornet*, and *Tom Bowline* were under orders to rendezvous with Decatur and the *President* at the island of Tristan da Cunha in the remote South Atlantic, 1,750 miles west of the Cape of Good Hope, 2,088 miles east of South America, and 1,510 miles south of St. Helena. Decatur had planned to use the prevailing westerlies in those latitudes to sail east beyond the Cape of Good Hope into the Indian Ocean, perhaps even visiting the East Indies. Warrington and Biddle had no idea the *President* had been captured.

In a few days, the *Hornet* separated from the others and made her way to the South Atlantic. During the trip a neutral vessel told her the war had ended, but Biddle chose not to believe it. He pressed on to the place of rendezvous, arriving at Tristan da Cunha on March 23. Biddle was about to drop anchor at 10:30 in the morning when he spied a British warship of his same size, the *Penguin*, under Commander James Dickinson. Biddle went after her.

When Dickinson saw the *Hornet*, he came up to her prepared for battle. The two ships were evenly matched. The *Penguin* carried eighteen thirty-two-pound carronades; one twelve-pound carronade; and two six-pound long guns. The *Hornet* had eighteen thirty-two-pound carronades and two twelve-pound long guns. A little over two hours later, the action commenced at around a hundred yards with murderous broadsides for about twenty-five minutes, during which Dickinson was cut in half by a ball. The superior gunnery of the *Hornet* devastated the *Penguin*.

Lieutenant McDonald, who had taken command on the *Penguin*, decided his only hope was to board. He bore up and ran his bowsprit into the *Hornet*'s mizzen shrouds on her starboard side, but when he tried to board, the *Hornet*'s marines and sailors fired their muskets with good effect and drove the boarders back to their crippled ship. A heavy sea was running, causing the *Penguin* to pull free of the *Hornet*, but when she did, her bowsprit tore away, carrying away the *Hornet*'s mizzen shrouds, stern davits, and spanker boom. It also brought down the *Penguin*'s foremast, and when McDonald saw Biddle preparing to fire another broadside, he surrendered. The fight lasted for twenty-two minutes.

The *Penguin* was so badly damaged she had to be scuttled. She had 14 killed and 28 wounded out of a crew of 132. The *Hornet* had 1 killed and 11 wounded, including Biddle, who was shot in the neck but soon recovered. The *Hornet* did not receive a single round shot in her hull or any material wound to her spars, and although her rigging and sails were cut up, Biddle quickly repaired them.

Immediately after the battle, the *Peacock* and *Tom Bowline* appeared. Biddle transferred 118 prisoners to the store ship and then waited with Warrington for three weeks for Decatur. When he failed to appear, they sailed east on April 12 for the second place of rendezvous, running before the westerlies beyond the Cape of Good Hope into the Indian Ocean, where on April 27 they sighted what they thought was a large East Indiaman. When they closed with her, however, they discovered she was a battleship, the 74-gun *Cornwallis*, and they fled, separating as they went. The *Peacock* was the fastest ship and soon disappeared, while the *Cornwallis* went after the slower *Hornet*. The big battleship turned out to be far more weatherly than Biddle had supposed, and she kept up with him, even gaining, as he sailed close-hauled trying to shake her. In desperation Biddle started lightening his ship, throwing overboard heavy spars, boats and ballast, anchors and cables, shot, and six guns. He thought when night came he'd sneak away, but the *Cornwallis* stayed right on his tail. At first light her big bow guns fired from long range and just missed touching the *Hornet*'s masts.

As tenacious as ever, Biddle threw more gear over the side, including small arms, all his remaining guns except for one, all his shot, the rest of his spare spars, and whatever else he could think of. He kept just ahead, while the *Cornwallis* fired and scored three hits, but nothing fatal. The ships were now less than a mile apart in a smooth sea. Fortunately for Biddle, in the afternoon the wind hauled to the westward, enabling him to lengthen his lead to four miles. During the night he manage to sail at nine knots with a fresh wind.

At daylight on April 30 he was twelve miles from the *Cornwallis*, and she gave up the chase. Her remarkably poor shooting saved the *Hornet*. Biddle now had to get his toothless ship home. On June 9 he reached the neutral port of San Salvador, where he finally allowed himself to be convinced that the war was over.

All the while, Captain Warrington and the *Peacock* kept sailing to the East Indies, capturing four large prizes as she went, before finding out on June 30 in the Straits of Sundra that the war was long over.

THE WAR DID not end immediately for American prisoners either. When the peace treaty was signed, 6,000 of them were still in Dartmoor Prison. The British and Americans had exchanged prisoners during the war, but Britain had accumulated far more than the United States, and these remained at Dartmoor. During the last year of the war the British had moved all their naval prisoners to Dartmoor. They were gathered from places like Chatham, Stapleton, Plymouth, and Portsmouth and from Halifax, Bermuda, the Cape of Good Hope, Jamaica, Barbados, New Providence, and Newfoundland. Many had been on Melville Island, a prison in Halifax Harbor that became known as Deadman's Island because 195 prisoners had died there, most of them Americans. Men had also been kept in prison hulks in various ports, including St. Helena. These decrepit ships were often death traps full of disease.

At the end of the war the colossally inefficient American government could not manage to bring the Dartmoor prisoners home. The prisoners were not fed or clothed properly, and the prison was rife with disease, particularly smallpox. In addition, there were 1,000 black prisoners who naturally refused to go to a port in the southern part of the United States.

On April, 6, 1815, the American prisoners complained more forcefully than usual about food and other poor conditions at Dartmoor, and the rattled commandant, naval captain Thomas G. Shortland, ordered his troops to fire on them, killing seven and wounding fifty-four. Not wanting this tragedy to upset relations with America while Napoleon remained to be dealt with, Castlereagh organized a commission to look into the matter. It was composed of one American (Charles King, the son of Rufus King) and one Briton (Mr. Seymour Larpent). They concluded that the troops were poorly disciplined but that the incident was an accident. Castlereagh wrote to Chargé Baker in Washington and to Gallatin and Clay in London expressing "sincere regret on this unfortunate affair, and of [the government's] . . . desire to make every suitable compensation to the families of the persons who suffered on this melancholy occasion."

Castlereagh's conciliatory tone was in keeping with his new policy of establishing friendly relations with the United States. The Admiralty soon made ships available to transport the prisoners home. Of course, the blacks had to be careful where they were taken; they did not want to exchange one hell for another. They were the last to leave.

CHAPTER THIRTY-THREE

A New Era

A S WITH ALL wars, the most important question at the end of the War of 1812 was: Could the gains possibly justify the deaths and disfiguring of so many young men, the disruption of lives, the tearing apart of families, the sorrow of parents, wives, children, and friends, the robbing and slaughter of innocent civilians? Could anything compensate for the sacrifice of the baby-faced soldiers, dead before their time, their decaying bodies rotting in common graves? What purpose did it serve to kill so many? Where was the honor, the glory, the victory?

When the terms of the peace treaty became known, it looked as if the young men and their families had sacrificed in vain. The combatants simply agreed to return to the status quo before the war started. The maritime disputes about free trade and sailors' rights were not even mentioned. The war seemed to have settled nothing. John Quincy Adams famously declared the Treaty of Ghent to be only "an unlimited Armistice [rather] than a peace, . . . hardly less difficult to preserve than . . . to obtain."

The maritime rivalry of Great Britain and the United States, and the uncertainty of their borders in North America, provided fertile grounds for continued conflict. If war resumed in Europe, as Liverpool, Castlereagh, Bathurst, and Wellington thought likely, the old problems of neutral rights and impressment would inevitably come to the fore again, as would competition over who controlled Canada, Florida, the Caribbean, the Mississippi, the Louisiana Territory, and the Pacific coast. The potential points of friction were so numerous that a new and more terrible conflict appeared inevitable.

Madison believed the danger would be significantly increased if the United States demobilized—as she had after the Revolution and the Quasi-War with France. Disarmament might tempt Britain to renew her aggressiveness on the high seas and expand her North American empire. Presidents Washington and Adams had also believed that military weakness invited European meddling. For years, Madison and his mentor Jefferson had rejected that view. Keeping the army and navy small and inexpensive was fundamental to their political philosophy. The war changed Madison's mind, however. He now thought Washington and Adams had been right. A politically united country with a respectable army and navy was the best safeguard against a renewal of war with Britain or any other imperialist country.

On February 18, 1815, Madison warned Congress not to dismantle the military establishment built up during the war. He wrote:

> The reduction of the public expenditures, the demands of a peace establishment will doubtless engage the immediate attention of Congress. There are, however, important considerations which forbid a sudden and general revocation of the measures that have been produced by the war. Experience has taught us that neither the pacific dispositions of the American people nor the pacific character of their political institutions can altogether exempt them from that strife which appears beyond the ordinary lot of nations to be incident to the actual period of the world, and the same faithful monitor demonstrates that a certain degree of preparation for war is not only indispensable to avert disasters at the outset, but affords also the best security for the continuance of peace. The wisdom of Congress will therefore, I am confident, provide for the maintenance of an adequate regular force; for the gradual advancement of the naval establishment; for improving all the means of harbor defense; for adding discipline to the distinguished bravery of the militia, and for cultivating the military art in its essential branches, under liberal patronage of the government.

Madison was addressing a receptive audience. A significant portion of the Republican Party, and all Federalists, were committed to a strong navy, an adequate professional army, and the financial reforms necessary to support them. Albert Gallatin wrote, "the war has laid the foundations of permanent taxes and military establishments, which the Republicans had [in the past] deemed unfavorable to the happiness and free institutions of the country."

The 14th Congress, which convened on March 4, 1815—heavily influenced by British aggressiveness the previous year—heeded Madison's advice. It approved a strong naval expansion program and a regular army of 10,000. The president had asked for a force twice that size, but he accepted the smaller one as adequate. Congress had no similar qualms about increasing the navy. It authorized an eight-year naval armament program that included nine 74-gun battleships, twelve 44-gun heavy frigates, three steam batteries, one smaller battleship, two smaller frigates, and two sloops of war to be built each year.

Not only did Congress approve a strong defense, but it also enacted the financial reforms to fund it, raising taxes and establishing a national bank. In doing so, it was enacting the program begun by Alexander Hamilton, George Washington, and John Adams and rejected by Jefferson when he took office in 1801. America had now come full circle; the war had crystallized political opinion in favor of a strong national defense as the best guarantee against more wars. The notion that a disarmed country could protect itself against imperialist Europe by using "peaceful coercion" and diplomacy was forever rejected.

THE NEWFOUND STRENGTH of the United States was put on display immediately after the treaty with Britain was ratified. On February 23, while the country was celebrating peace, Madison asked Congress to declare war on Algeria. The president wrote that the Dey of Algiers had been in "open and direct warfare" against the United States since 1812, and it was time to put a stop to his depredations. On March 3, after lopsided votes of approval in both the House and the Senate, Madison signed the declaration of war.

Spearheaded by the new secretary of the navy, Benjamin W. Crowninshield, and with an efficiency unknown during the war, the government prepared enough naval power to force Algeria to mend her ways. Madison was determined to use overwhelming force to bring about a quick settlement. He was doing the exact opposite of what Jefferson did in 1801, when he was confronted with a similar problem. Jefferson's war against the Barbary pirates dragged on for four years, from 1801 to 1805, because he would not apply sufficient force until the very end. Madison was not going to repeat that mistake. The American navy was now the strongest it had ever been, and he intended to use it.

The president decided to dispatch two powerful squadrons to the Mediterranean—and three if necessary. He appointed Decatur to lead the first and Bainbridge the second. At the moment, Decatur was occupied with a court of inquiry on the loss of the *President*, but that did not deter Madison, who assumed Decatur would be exonerated—and he was.

Bainbridge was senior to Decatur, and normally the president would have given the lead to him, but Madison much preferred Decatur and gave him the coveted assignment. Bainbridge was miffed, of course—not surprising to either Madison or Crowninshield—but that did not matter. Decatur would lead the way with the first squadron, and Bainbridge would follow with the second. When Bainbridge reached the Mediterranean, he would become overall commander, so Decatur rushed to get there first. In fact, he refused to serve under Bainbridge. Madison allowed Decatur the option of returning to the United States when Bainbridge arrived. The arrangement was, to say the least, extraordinary. Madison must have felt that Decatur needed special treatment after the loss of the *President*. It was also clear that the president wasn't enamored with Bainbridge.

Decatur received his orders on March 27 and went full speed ahead. By the third week in April his squadron was waiting off Staten Island ready to sail. It included his flagship, the new 44-gun *Guerriere*, with Master Commandant William Lewis as flag captain; the 38-gun *Macedonian*, under Captain Jacob Jones; the 38-gun *Constellation*, under Captain Charles Gordon; the 22-gun sloop of war *Ontario*, under Master Commandant Jesse Elliott; the 18-gun brig *Epervier* (captured by the *Peacock*) under Lieutenant John Downes, who unaccountably had not yet been promoted to master commandant; the 14-gun brig *Firefly*, under Lieutenant George W. Rodgers (the commodore's nephew); the 12-gun brig *Flambeau*, under Lieutenant J. B. Nicolson; the12-gun brig *Spark*, a former privateer, under Lieutenant Thomas Gamble (brother of Peter Gamble, who died at the Battle of Plattsburgh); the 11-gun schooner *Spitfire*, under Lieutenant A. J. Dallas; and the 10-gun schooner *Torch*, under Lieutenant Wolcott Chauncey. By any standard it was a strong squadron with outstanding leaders. In fact, it was the most powerful ever assembled under the American flag.

On April 29, Decatur, straining to get going, was put on hold. Word reached Washington that on February 26 Napoleon had slipped away from Elba with 1,100 troops and on March 1 landed at Golfe Juan near Cannes on the Riviera. Not unexpectedly, the French army rallied to him. With no support among the people, Louis XVIII secretly fled Paris on March 20 at two o'clock in the morning. Later that day, Bonaparte entered the capital. Wellington was in Vienna at the time, and the allies unanimously agreed not to recognize Napoleon. They vowed to get rid of him. With the advent of a new war, the same old maritime problems that had bedeviled British-American relations in the past could well rise again.

Nonetheless, after receiving assurances from the Liverpool ministry, Madison allowed Decatur to proceed. He stood out from New York on May 20 and shaped a course for Cadiz and Gibraltar. The squadron had just reached the outer edge of the Gulf Stream off the Atlantic coast when a severe three-day tempest struck and scattered the ships, damaging the *Firefly* so much that she had to return to New York for repairs. When the storm abated, Decatur gathered up the rest of his fleet and continued on to Cadiz, reaching it in three weeks. After taking on supplies there, he headed for Tangier in Morocco. The American consul told him that two days before, Admiral Rais, head of the Algerian navy, stopped in Tangier with his big 46-gun flagship, the *Mashuda*. The news whetted Decatur's appetite.

The American fleet pushed on to Gibraltar, with the commodore wondering how the British were going to treat him now that Napoleon was back in power. Despite Decatur's apprehension, he was received cordially. At Madison's request, the ministry agreed to allow American warships into British ports while engaged in the war with Algeria. Liverpool's policy was not to antagonize the United States. Bathurst sent orders that the American navy was to be accorded "all the privileges to which the vessels of a nation in amity with this country are entitled." Decatur was allowed to refit and resupply. Of course, the British officers who saw the name of his flagship *Guerriere*, and the names of his other ships like *Macedonian* and *Epervier*, were none too pleased.

Decatur did not remain long at Gibraltar. When he learned that Hammida and the *Mashuda* were off nearby Cape de Gatt, waiting to receive tribute from Spain, he raced out of port, and on June 17 he found the *Mashuda*. Hammida tried to get into Cartagena—a neutral port—but the American squadron blocked his way. Decatur brought the *Guerriere* close alongside the Algerian and unleashed two punishing broadsides, frightening the Algerian crew, who ran below. When he saw them disappearing, he ordered a cease-fire.

The lull allowed Decatur to deal with a terrible accident that had occurred when the *Guerriere* fired her first broadside. One of her double-shotted main deck guns burst, killing five men and badly wounding thirty others. Decatur blamed the tragedy on the lack of adequate inspection for new guns. His two broadsides appeared to have beaten the Algerians, however. Hammida had been killed, and his crew looked as if they were surrendering. They may have been initially, but they now tried to make a run for it. Lieutenant Downes in the *Epervier* alertly got on their starboard quarter, however, and unleashed nine broadsides, forcing them to surrender.

Decatur sent the *Mashuda* into Cartagena with a prize crew and 406 prisoners. Two days later, he captured another Algerian, the 22-gun brig *Estedio*, and also sent her into Cartagena. He then sailed for Algiers, arriving on June 28. Negotiations soon began on board the *Guerriere*. One of her passengers, William Shaler, the prospective American consul general at Algiers who had been appointed as a joint commissioner with Decatur and Bainbridge, carried on one-sided talks with the Algerians, who had a high appreciation of the power of the American squadron anchored in their harbor. Shaler and Decatur had no trouble dictating a peace. Within twenty-four hours the dey agreed to terms, which included the end of tribute, which had been paid by the United States since the treaty of 1796; the release of ten American prisoners; and the return to the dey of the two captured Algerine ships. Decatur wrote to Crowninshield that the treaty had "been dictated at the mouth of the cannon, has been conceded to the losses which Algiers has sustained, and to the dread of still greater evils apprehended; and I beg leave to express to you my opinion that the presence of a respectable naval force in this sea will be the only certain guarantee for its observance."

Wasting no time, Decatur prepared the treaty and dispatches and sent them to Washington in the *Epervier*, along with the ten freed prisoners. Before she left, he changed her officers, putting Lieutenant John Shubrick, first of the *Guerriere*, in command and transferring Lieutenant Downes to the *Guerriere*, making him the new flag captain. Downes was replacing William Lewis, who was returning to the United States. Decatur made these odd changes as a favor to Lewis, so that he could go home and be with his new wife. Lieutenant Neale was also permitted the same indulgence; he had married the sister of Lewis's wife. Sadly, the *Epervier* never made it back. She went down with all hands in a hurricane.

Scurvy had now begun to appear in the squadron, and Decatur stopped it by sailing to Cagliari on the southern coast of Sardinia for ten days of rest and recuperation. Afterward, he traveled to Tunis to settle matters with the bey, arriving in Tunis Bay on July 25, with a six-ship squadron—the *Guerriere*, *Macedonian*, *Constellation*, *Ontario*, *Flambeau*, and *Spitfire*. The bey had violated Tunis's treaty with the United States by allowing the British brig *Lyra* during the recent war to take two prizes belonging to the American privateer *Abellino* out of the Bay of Tunis to Malta and for allowing local merchants to obtain the contents of those ships much below their real value. Decatur demanded and immediately received 46,000 Spanish dollars in compensation for the two prizes. Seeing the power of Decatur's squadron, the bey decided not to fight, although he had a fleet and his capital was well protected.

Decatur sailed next to Tripoli on August 2 to make a similar impression on its ruler, arriving in the harbor on August 5. The bashaw had allowed a British warship, the *Pauline*, to seize two more prizes of the *Albellino*, in violation of Tripoli's neutrality, and take them to Malta, thus breaking the existing treaty with the United States. Decatur demanded 30,000 Spanish dollars. He and the bashaw finally settled on 25,000 and the release of ten Christian slaves. Two were Danes and eight Sicilians.

Again wasting no time, Decatur left Tripoli on August 9 and stopped in Messina to release eight prisoners and then sailed for the Bay of Naples, arriving on September 8, where he was greeted warmly and thanked by the foreign minister and the king of the two Sicilies for obtaining the release of the prisoners. By this time Decatur had accomplished everything Madison wanted and then some, and he prepared to go home. He sent his squadron on ahead to rendezvous with Bainbridge at either the Spanish port of Malaga or Gibraltar. He then stood out alone from Naples on September 13 in the *Guerriere* and shaped a course for Gibraltar, expecting to meet Bainbridge.

On the way he spotted the Algerian fleet—seven warships: four frigates, and three sloops—sailing toward him. He cleared for action. But he warned the crew that the menacing ships ahead would have to fire first; America was now at peace with Algeria. If the Algerians fired, however, Decatur meant to take the lot of them. Tension lessened considerably aboard the *Guerriere* when the Algerians ran to the leeward side of the frigate, indicating they were not interested in a fight. For amusement, the Algerian admiral shouted to Decatur through a speaking trumpet, asking in Italian where he was going, and Decatur shouted back, "Where I please." The Algerians sailed on, and Decatur maintained his course for Gibraltar.

MEANWHILE, COMMODORE BAINBRIDGE, full of ambition, stood out from Boston on July 2 and arrived off Cartagena on August 5, traveling in the brand-new 74-gun *Independence*, the first ship of its size to sail under the American flag. The sloop of war *Erie*, the brig *Chippewa*, and the schooner *Lynx* made up the rest of Bainbridge's squadron. The *Spark* and *Torch* from Decatur's fleet were in port, and they informed Bainbridge of Decatur's success against Algiers. None too pleased, Bainbridge changed his plans and decided to visit Tunis and Tripoli, only touching at Algiers on the way. He sailed from Cartagena on September 13 and visited Algiers, Tunis, and Tripoli, exhibiting his powerful squadron, reinforcing the impression Decatur had made on the dey, bey, and bashaw. Bainbridge was sorely disappointed that Decatur had settled with all three states before he arrived, but the American consuls assured him that his appearance

Figure 33.1: Michele Felice Cornè, *Triumphant Return of the American Squadron under Commodore Bainbridge from the Mediterranean, 1815* (courtesy of Naval Historical Center).

so soon after Decatur would have a lasting salutary effect on the rulers. Bainbridge wasn't appeased.

He set sail for Malaga, where the *United States, Enterprise, Boxer, Firefly,* and *Saranac* joined him. They had just arrived from the United States. Madison was making sure he had enough force in the Mediterranean to accomplish his goals. Secretary Crowninshield was even getting a third squadron ready to sail under Isaac Chauncey if good news did not come from either Decatur or Bainbridge.

In a few days Bainbridge sailed his entire fleet the short distance to Gibraltar to await Decatur's arrival. On October 3, Decatur's squadron arrived, except for the *Guerriere* and Decatur himself. Bainbridge had no way of knowing when Decatur would appear, so he made preparations to leave for the United States. On orders from Secretary Crowninshield, Bainbridge left a few ships in the Mediterranean to protect American interests. Captain John Shaw was in command of the new squadron with the *United States,* the *Constellation,* the *Ontario,* and the *Erie.* Bainbridge wrote to Shaw, "The object of leaving this force is to watch the conduct of the Barbary powers, particularly . . . Algiers." The United States has had a naval presence in the Mediterranean ever since.

Bainbridge stood out from Gibraltar on October 6, and as he was leaving the harbor, the *Guerriere* hove into view and saluted the *Independence.* Bainbridge returned the salute but kept right on going, apparently wishing to avoid meeting

Decatur face-to-face. Not understanding what was going on, Decatur jumped into his gig and chased the *Independence*, caught her, and climbed aboard for a talk. He knew something was wrong when the *Independence* did not even slow down so that he could board, but he wasn't quite prepared for the icily formal reception he got from Bainbridge, who apparently blamed Decatur personally for robbing him of his chance for glory. The meeting was short and awkward and irritated Decatur no end. There was nothing he could do about it, however. He returned to his frigate and sailed home alone, reaching New York on November 12 to receive a hero's welcome, as he deserved.

Decatur's success underscored the need for a strong navy and helped build support in the country for a long-term commitment to bear the burden of a respectable defense force, all of which Madison hoped the Mediterranean mission would accomplish, beside ridding him of the Barbary pirate nuisance.

By moving a divided nation to agree that a strong navy and army would protect rather than undermine the Constitution, the horrific burdens of those who fought the war could ultimately be justified. And this new consensus on defense policy would in turn lay the foundation for a profound change in Anglo-American relations, further justifying the great sacrifices of the young soldiers and sailors.

CHAPTER THIRTY-FOUR

From Temporary Armistice
to Lasting Peace:
The Importance of the War

AMERICANS WERE QUICK to forget the gross failures of their leaders during the war and the horror people felt in the fall of 1814, when it looked as if the fighting would continue. The country concentrated only on its successes. The amnesia served America well, as her people looked confidently to the future. A major component of this new confidence was the remarkable, totally unexpected political unity that arose immediately after the peace. Albert Gallatin wrote, "The war has renewed and reinstated the national feelings and character which the Revolution had given, and which were daily lessening. The people now have more general objects of attachment, with which their pride and political opinions are connected. They are more Americans; they feel and act more as a nation; and I hope that the permanency of the Union is thereby better secured."

America's newfound unity and her commitment to a strong military forced Europe to take her more seriously. Before the war, the United States was a big, prosperous country without military capacity. Now she was an incipient power that Britain and the other European imperialists could no longer treat lightly, as they had in the past. The Liverpool ministry's cynical perpetuation of the war to expand British territory and dismember a rival had unintentionally amplified America's maritime power. Instead of curbing a competitor, the British had markedly increased her strength.

413

As Castlereagh and his colleagues considered Britain's North American policy going forward, the central question was whether to concede the growing power of the United States and reach an accommodation with her or to treat her as a rival and potential enemy, contesting her expansion and inviting conflict at every turn. The combination of a strong army and navy, sound fiscal underpinnings, and political unity in America led the foreign minister to adopt a policy of accommodation rather than confrontation. Liverpool endorsed the new approach, initiating a fundamental change in British policy that became the most important outcome of the War of 1812. It more than compensated for all the horrors borne by ordinary people in America, Canada, and Great Britain.

The reactionary Castlereagh had no love for the American republic; he was simply recognizing that given the new strength of the United States, it was in British interests to prevent their inevitable disagreements from turning lethal. He did all he could to remove barriers to cooperation and promote the peaceful settlement of disputes. And he brought Liverpool and the rest of the cabinet along with him. The British historian Charles K. Webster wrote that Castlereagh "was the first British statesman to recognize that the friendship of the United States was a major asset . . . , and to use in his relations with her a language that was neither superior nor intimidating." An augury of things to come had been the Duke of Wellington (the new British ambassador in Paris) taking the unprecedented step of calling on American ambassador Crawford and congratulating him on the treaty of peace.

It took a considerable amount of time before the United States recognized the fundamental change in British policy. America's leaders remained leery of London's intentions. Madison, Monroe, Gallatin, Adams, Clay, and their colleagues would have to be shown by concrete action that a new relationship existed. They wanted one, of course—every administration since Washington had wanted it—but they were not expecting a basic change in British policy. For them, the most important question was: would Britain's leaders finally accept the independence of the United States and treat her with respect? They had not in the past, and their attitude had eventually led to war. A change of the magnitude that Castlereagh envisioned appeared unlikely to an American leadership that for years had dealt with British ministries with wholly different attitudes.

Napoleon's triumphal entry into Paris on March 20, 1815, so soon after the Treaty of Ghent, helped move Britain and America toward a new rapport. His appearance was not a surprise in London. For many weeks, Liverpool and his colleagues had worried about a military coup in Paris. Nonetheless, when the event happened, Liverpool had half his army in North America in the quixotic pursuit of more territory. That army was needed immediately in Flanders, but it would not be available for weeks. In that time Bonaparte could raise an immense army and become as big a menace as ever.

Immediately after seizing power, Napoleon tried to reassure the allies that he had changed, that his intentions were peaceful, but they were having none of it. When he entered Paris, the great powers unanimously committed themselves to destroying him before he got too strong. They were ready to bring their full weight to bear against him. Wellington was in Vienna at the time, and the powers looked to him to lead the coalition armies. He had to act fast, however. If Bonaparte were given sufficient time, he could raise an immense army and be hard to defeat. For Liverpool to have a large part of the British army in North America at this critical moment appeared the height of folly.

Fortunately, Napoleon's timing was not propitious for another grand attempt to rule Europe. The divisions that had plagued the allies since his demise were well on their way to resolution at Vienna. In January the czar had chosen to compromise on Poland, and Prussia and Austria had done the same on Saxony, paving the way for a general agreement.

President Madison was naturally concerned that a renewal of the old war in Europe might reignite the maritime issues that caused the War of 1812. The peace treaty was silent on them because the parties could not agree. Castlereagh was alive to the danger, and he moved quickly to prevent neutral trade and impressment from reemerging to disrupt his rapprochement with the United States. The British were careful not to interfere with American trade, and naval officers were given strict rules to prevent impressment from becoming a problem again. Instead of a callous disregard of American rights on the high seas, there came a sensitivity from London that avoided conflict. Madison, for his part, although unaware of London's new attitude, was slow to take offense at British actions. Thus, tentatively, the two old enemies took the first, halting steps toward a new relationship.

But would this new British policy continue after Napoleon was defeated and packed off to St. Helena? That critical question was answered quickly as well, when Castlereagh at every opportunity avoided serious controversy. His new policy did not turn out to be an expedient to get Britain through her trial with Napoleon. Castlereagh's strategy was based on the conviction that the long-term interests of Britain required friendship with America. Castlereagh and Madison thus laid the foundation of a peaceful relationship between the two great English-speaking countries that was to last more than two centuries and was to serve both them and the world extraordinarily well.

The U.S. Navy's role in bringing about Britain's newfound respect for the United States was critical. The part played at the battles of Lake Erie and at Plattsburgh Bay are obvious and have been celebrated by historians and the public alike. The role of the navy at Baltimore, although not as well-known, has been recognized. Less so the Battle of New Orleans, where the navy's part has remained hidden but was nonetheless a key factor in victory, as Jackson himself acknowledged. Even less appreciated is the importance of the great victories on the high seas. Historians, without exception, portray these episodes as spectacular but of no strategic significance. Yet when one considers that they played a major role in changing London's attitude toward America, they were of great strategic importance, as was the triumph at New Orleans. The battle may have come after the peace treaty, but in turning that document from a temporary armistice into a lasting peace, the victory at New Orleans was of fundamental value. The public was not wrong in celebrating it, for, in many ways, it was the greatest triumph of the war for America and had the most lasting impact.

Of equal significance was the way President Madison conducted the war. He did so within the confines of the Constitution. He managed the conflict in strict accordance with the republican principles he had always espoused. He did not aggregate great power to himself and build up a strong central government, nor did he try to crush his opponents by passing sedition laws. In conducting himself in this manner, he immeasurably strengthened the democratic forces that had been building in America since the start of the Revolution and that had accelerated under Jefferson.

The war strengthened these democratic forces even more by reducing the elitist Federalist Party to insignificance in national politics and by extending the franchise. During the war so much reliance was placed on militias that men who risked their lives demanded that the property qualifications to vote be relaxed so they could participate in elections. It seemed absurd to ask them to fight and die when they could not vote.

The War of 1812 was thus of great importance in the nation's history because it initiating a fundamental change in Britain's relationship with the United States while strengthening the nation's democratic principles. In that sense it was a second War of Independence. Of course, the actual independence of America was never an issue and never in doubt, but her experiment in republican government, which, when the conflict began, was not fully secure, became so as a result of military and political successes achieved during and immediately after the war. America proved that its republican form of government could deal with a crisis and deal with it successfully without discarding its constitution. In that way the War of 1812 completed the fight for independence begun in 1775. The new unity and strength of the republic freed her for a century from European entanglements and allowed her people to prosper in spite of the vicissitudes that would continually challenge them.

ACKNOWLEDGMENTS

I am deeply indebted to many people for their generous help in writing this book, beginning with my wife, Kay, who has provided consistent support and sage advice through the vicissitudes of what is an all-consuming task over a long period. My gifted agent, Rob McQuilkin of Lippincott Massie McQuilkin, provided astute guidance and much needed encouragement through the various stages of the project, from initial conception to final publication. Lara Heimert, executive editor at Basic Books, improved the manuscript immeasurably by her brilliant critiques offered at critical moments. Associate editor Alex Littlefield assisted her and made an enormous contribution to the quality of the final product. Vice Admiral George Emery, U.S. Navy (Retired), generously shared his incomparable knowledge of the naval aspects of the War of 1812, reading the entire manuscript with great care and providing detailed, thoughtful advice. My nephew, Michael Daughan, who has worked for the navy his entire career and has an avid interest and broad knowledge of the early history of the service, read and brilliantly criticized the entire manuscript twice, improving it significantly. My daughter, Mary Daughan Sheft, read and commented on the text with her usual skill and insight. Kay Mariea, Perseus's director of editorial services, oversaw editorial production with good humor and great expertise.

I also want to thank my friend Alexander (Sandy) Brook, Maine's legendary editor, publisher, and writer, for his consistent encouragement; my son-in-law, Mark Sheft; and my brother William (Jerry) Daughan for their unfailing support as well.

A work that encompasses the entire history of the War of 1812 must inevitably draw on the studies of innumerable scholars and writers; they are listed in the endnotes and bibliography. I was particularly blessed by the exceptional outpouring of thoughtful scholarship that has appeared in the last twenty-five years. I also want to thank my former students and colleagues at the Air Force Academy, Connecticut College, and the Coast Guard Academy and my teachers at the University of New Hampshire, Stanford, and Harvard who excited my long-standing interest in the great issues of war and peace that are at the heart of this book and my previous work, *If By Sea: The Forging of the American Navy— From the Revolution to the War of 1812.*

NOTES

INTRODUCTION

x   *Byron did not have to wait:* Charles O. Paullin, *Commodore John Rodgers: Captain, Commodore, and Senior Officer of the American Navy, 1773-1838* (1909; reprint, Annapolis, MD: United States Naval Institute, 1967), 252.

xi   *Midshipman John Taylor was:* Samuel Eliot Morison, *Old Bruin: Commodore Matthew Calbraith Perry, 1794–1858* (Boston: Little, Brown, 1967), 35.

xi   *"by altering [his] course":* Excerpt from *Commodore Rodger's Journal*, June 23, 1812, in *The Naval War of 1812: A Documentary History*, ed. William S. Dudley (Washington, DC: Naval Historical Center, 1985), 1:154–57.

xii   *"I acknowledge":* Byron to Vice Admiral Herbert Sawyer, June 27, 1812, in Dudley, ed., *Naval War of 1812*, 1:159.

xii   *"We have lost":* Leonard F. Guttridge, *Our Country, Right or Wrong: The Life of Stephen Decatur, The U.S. Navy's Most Illustrious Commander* (New York: Tom Doherty Associates, 2006), 133.

xiii   *"in furtherance of that spirit":* *Times* (London), Aug. 22, 1812.

CHAPTER 1

2   *the American ambassador to France:* In 1785 Jefferson succeeded Benjamin Franklin as the U.S. ambassador in Paris, where he remained until 1789. Dumas Malone, *Jefferson and the Rights of Man* (Boston: Little, Brown, 1951), 185.

3   *might not even survive:* Forest McDonald, *Alexander Hamilton* (New York: Norton, 1979), 147–49, 165–71.

4   *the culture in which they were raised:* Drew R. McCoy, *The Elusive Republic: Political Economy in Jeffersonian America* (New York: Norton, 1982), 91–92; Irving Brant, *James Madison*, vol. 3: *Father of the Constitution, 1787–1800* (Indianapolis: Bobbs-Merrill, 1950), 289.

5   *Washington issued his famous proclamation:* James Flexner, *George Washington: Anguish and Farewell (1793–1799)* (Boston: Little, Brown, 1972), 25–37.

6   *These six frigates:* Marshall Smelser, *The Congress Founds the Navy* (Notre Dame, IN: University of Notre Dame Press, 1959), 68.

6   *Washington was disappointed:* Stanley Elkins and Eric McKitrick, *The Age of Federalism* (New York: Oxford University Press, 1993), 388–96; Steven Kurtz, *The Presidency of John Adams: The Collapse of Federalism, 1795–1800* (Philadelphia: University of Pennsylvania Press, 1957), 19–77.

7   *to fight the Quasi-War:* Michael Palmer, *Stoddert's War: Naval Operations During the Quasi-War with France, 1798-1801* (Annapolis, MD: Naval Institute Press, 2000); Alexander Deconde, *The Quasi-War: The Politics and Diplomacy of the Undeclared War with France 1797–1801* (New York: Scribner's, 1966).

7   *"first mentor of the Federal Navy"*: Retired Vice Admiral George Emery, "Thomas Trux-
        tun: First Mentor of the Federal Navy," *Pull Together: Newsletter of the Naval Historical
        Foundation* (Fall/Winter 2010–11): 12–14.

8   *Federalists continued to believe*: Sean Wilentz, *The Rise of American Democracy: Jefferson
        to Lincoln* (New York: Norton, 2005), 162.

10   *The tiny navy that Jefferson*: Dumas Malone, *Jefferson the President: First Term, 1801–
        1805* (Boston: Little, Brown, 1971); George C. Daughan, *If By Sea: The Forging of the
        American Navy—From the Revolution to the War of 1812* (New York: Basic Books,
        2008), 346–74.

11   *Napoleon wanted to fight them*: Alan Schom, *Napoleon Bonaparte* (New York: Harper-
        Collins, 1997), 450–52.

11   *Nelson demonstrated at the Battle*: David Howarth, *Trafalgar: The Nelson Touch* (New
        York: Atheneum, 1969).

CHAPTER 2

13   *Ambassador James Monroe*: Monroe had replaced Rufus King in August 1803.

14   *Orders in Council*: Orders in Council were executive degrees.

15   *"strangling the maritime power"*: Madison to Jefferson, March 12, 1815, quoted in
        Irving Brant, *James Madison*, vol. 6: *Commander in Chief, 1812–1836* (Indianapolis:
        Bobbs-Merrill, 1961), 355.

15   *Harrison Gray Otis wrote*: Samuel E. Morison, *Harrison Gray Otis: The Urbane Federalist*
        (Boston: Houghton Mifflin, 1969), 327.

15   *"The general business of impressing"*: Morison, *Harrison Gray Otis*, 281.

15   *"This whole controversy"*: Morison, *Harrison Gray Otis*, 281.

15   *seizing ships at a faster rate*: By June 1812 France had seized 434 American vessels and
        Great Britain 389. Glenn Tucker, *Poltroons and Patriots: A Popular Account of the War
        of 1812* (Indianapolis: Bobbs-Merrill, 1954), 2:52.

16   *Humphreys was not about*: Spencer C. Tucker and Frank T. Reuter, *Injured Honor: The
        Chesapeake-Leopard Affair, June 22, 1807* (Annapolis, MD: Naval Institute Press, 1996),
        113–14; Alfred T. Mahan, *Sea Power in Its Relations to the War of 1812* (Boston: Little,
        Brown, 1905), 1:155.

17   *"the decayed and heartless"*: *Times* (London), July 5, 1813.

18   *"an American in England pines"*: Benjamin Waterhouse, *A Journal of a Young Man of
        Massachusetts* (Boston, 1816), reprinted as Extra No. 18 of the *Magazine of History*
        (New York, 1911).

18   *Alcohol was liberally*: James Tertius De Kay, *Chronicles of the Frigate Macedonian, 1809–
        1922* (New York: Norton, 1995), 37.

19   *"inhuman [resembling] roasted meat"*: Samuel Leech, *Thirty Years from Home: A Sea-
        man's View of the War of 1812* (1843; reprint, Tucson, AZ: Fireship Press, 2008), 20.

19   *In 1806 the Admiralty*: Dudley Pope, *The Black Ship* (Philadelphia: Lippincott, 1964),
        62–63 and Appendix A.

19   *"Fifty were laid"*: Leech, *Thirty Years from Home*, 41.

19   *"No plea of necessity"*: Leech, *Thirty Years from Home*, 26–27.

20   *"Hence, what with poor"*: Leech, *Thirty Years from Home*, 60.

20   *Worse, men wounded*: Pope, *The Black Ship*, 123–26.

20   *"Here was encouragement"*: William Richardson, *A Mariner of England: An Account
        of William Richardson from Cabin Boy in the Merchant Service to Warrant Officer in
        the Royal Navy, 1780–1819, as Told by Himself*, ed. Colonel Spencer Childers (London:
        John Murray, 1908), 100–11. For a different view of life in the Royal Navy, see N. A.
        M. Rodger, *The Command of the Ocean: A Naval History of Britain, 1649–1815* (New

York: Norton, 2004), 565–66, and Jon Latimer, *1812: War with America* (Cambridge, MA: Harvard University Press, 2007), 6.

20   *it is generally agreed:* Castlereagh speech in the House of Commons, reproduced in *Times* (London), Feb. 19, 1813; James F. Zimmerman, *Impressment of American Seamen* (New York: Columbia University, 1925), 27.

21   *"We must on no account":* *Times* (London), Jan. 11, July 3, and Aug. 2, 1813.

21   *offering five pounds for:* C. S. Forester, *The Age of Fighting Sail: The Story of the Naval War of 1812* (New York: Doubleday, 1956), 39.

22   *Deserters from the Royal Navy:* Rodger, *The Command of the Ocean*, 569.

22   *the British felt that the real reason:* *Times* (London), Dec. 25, 1812.

22   *The ministry wanted:* *Times* (London), Feb. 20, 1813.

CHAPTER 3

23   *At the end of 1807:* "Eighth Annual Message to Congress, November 8, 1808," in *Thomas Jefferson: Writings*, ed. Merrill D. Peterson (New York: Literary Classics of the United States, 1984), 544; Ralph Ketcham, *James Madison: A Biography* (Charlottesville: University Press of Virginia, 1971), 457.

23   *In December 1807:* Ketcham, *James Madison*, 456–57.

24   *By the end of 1807:* Dudley W. Knox, *A History of the United States Navy* (Annapolis, MD: Naval Institute Press, 1936), 96.

24   *"withdraw from the reach":* Leonard D. White, *The Jeffersonians: A Study in Administrative History, 1801–1829* (New York: Macmillan, 1956), 268.

24   *The British were indeed hampered:* George Dangerfield, *The Era of Good Feelings* (New York: Harcourt, Brace, 1952), 43.

26   *The stranger turned out to be:* Commander Arthur Bingham, R.N., to Vice Admiral Herbert Sawyer, R.N., May 21, 1811, and Commodore John Rodgers to Secretary of the Navy Paul Hamilton, May 23, 1811, in *The Naval War of 1812: A Documentary History*, ed. William S. Dudley (Washington, DC: Naval Historical Center, 1985), 1:40–50.

26   *During the summer he conferred:* Ketcham, *James Madison*, 508.

26   *"We have been so long":* Monroe to James Taylor, June 13, 1812, in Gordon Wood, *Empire of Liberty: A History of the Early Republic, 1789–1815*, Oxford History of the United States (New York: Oxford University Press, 2009), 670.

27   *"Perceval [and his colleagues]":* Irving Brant, *James Madison*, vol. 6: *Commander in Chief, 1812–1836* (Indianapolis: Bobbs-Merrill, 1961), 16.

27   *Republican malcontents:* Frank A. Cassell, *Merchant Congressman in the Young Republic: Samuel Smith of Maryland, 1752–1839* (Madison: University of Wisconsin Press, 1971), 144–70.

27   *Madison felt that he:* Richard Buel Jr., *America on the Brink: How the Political Struggle Over the War of 1812 Almost Destroyed the Young Republic* (New York: Palgrave Macmillan, 2005), 138.

27   *"commerce, character":* Quoted in David S. Heidler and Jeanne T. Heidler, *Henry Clay: The Essential American* (New York: Random House, 2010), 91.

27   *In April, with war:* J. C. A. Stagg, *Mr. Madison's War: Politics, Diplomacy, and Warfare in the Early American Republic, 1783–1830* (Princeton, NJ: Princeton University Press, 1983), 175.

28   *"was not more at a loss":* Quoted in Henry Adams, *History of the United States of America During the Administrations of James Madison* (New York: Library of America, 1986), 493.

28   *Macon's slur against Paul Hamilton:* Frank L. Owsley Jr., "Paul Hamilton," in *American Secretaries of the Navy*, ed. Paolo E. Coletta (Annapolis, MD: Naval Institute Press, 1980), 1:93–98.

29   *"a powerful engine"*: *Annals of Congress*, House of Representatives, 12th Congress, 1st
        Session, 825, 830.

30   *its small size:* For the debate on expanding the navy in early 1812, see *Annals of Congress*,
        12th Congress, 1st Session, 803ff. Congressman Cheves for the Naval Committee pro-
        posed building twelve 74-gun ships and twenty frigates at a cost of $7.5 million in Jan-
        uary 1812. Craig Symonds, *Navalists and Anti-Navalists: The Naval Policy Debate in
        the United States, 1785–1827* (Newark: University of Delaware Press, 1980).

CHAPTER 4

31   *"there is . . . nobody"*: George Dangerfield, *The Era of Good Feelings* (New York: Har-
        court, Brace, 1952), 49.

32   *War between Napoleon:* Dominic Lieven, *Russia Against Napoleon* (New York: Viking,
        2010), 92–96; Samuel Flagg Bemis, *John Quincy Adams and the Foundations of Amer-
        ican Foreign Policy* (New York: Knopf, 1950), 176–79.

32   *When the reluctant guests:* Harold Nicolson, *The Congress of Vienna: A Study in Allied
        Unity, 1812–1822* (1946; reprint, New York: Viking, 1961), 7–8.

33   *"Our government will not"*: *National Intelligencer*, Aug. 4, 1812.

34   *protected by British licenses:* For a copy of one of these licenses, see Alfred T. Mahan,
        Sea Power in Its Relations to the War of 1812 (Boston: Little, Brown, 1905), 1:410–11.

34   *"in the event of a pacification"*: Irving Brant, *James Madison*, vol. 6: *Commander in
        Chief, 1812–1836* (Indianapolis: Bobbs-Merrill, 1961), 63.

34   *"Had the French emperor"*: Madison to Henry Wheaton, Feb. 26, 1827, quoted in Henry
        Adams, *History of the United States of America During the Administrations of James
        Madison* (New York: Library of America, 1986), 476–77.

34   *Legislation in April 1808:* J. C. A. Stagg, *Mr. Madison's War: Politics, Diplomacy, and
        Warfare in the Early American Republic, 1783–1830* (Princeton, NJ: Princeton University
        Press, 1983), 164.

35   *The tiny War Department:* Stagg, *Mr. Madison's War*, 155.

35   *Even if the public were:* Donald R. Hickey, *The War of 1812: A Forgotten Conflict* (Ur-
        bana: University of Illinois Press, 1989), 80.

35   *The time to act:* For a different point of view, see Stagg, *Mr. Madison's War*, 3–47.

35   *"It had become impossible"*: Madison quoted in Stagg, *Mr. Madison's War*, 109.

36   *"The acquisition of Canada"*: Jefferson to William Duane, Aug. 1, 1812, quoted in
        Adams, *History of the United States*, 528; Mahan, *Sea Power*, 1:291.

36   *"The partisans of England"*: Jefferson to General Thaddeus Kosciusko, June 28, 1812,
        in *Thomas Jefferson: Writings*, ed. Merrill D. Peterson (New York: Library Classics of
        the United States, 1984), 1265.

36   *Imperialism was inherent:* Jefferson to Madame de Stael, May 24, 1813, in Peterson,
        ed., *Thomas Jefferson*, 1271–77.

36   *Conquering Canada would:* Stagg, *Mr. Madison's War*, 7–47.

37   *Tecumseh's power grew:* James H. Madison, *The Indiana Way: A State History* (Bloom-
        ington: Indiana University Press, 1986), 3–50; Frederick Merk, *History of the Westward
        Movement* (New York: Knopf, 1978), 153.

37   *"The Author of Nature marked"*: *Annals of Congress*, 12th Cong., 1st Sess., 657.

38   *"We must take"*: David S. Heidler and Jeanne T. Heidler, *Henry Clay: The Essential
        American* (New York: Random House, 2010), 88–89.

38   *Clay's enthusiasm was strengthened:* Mark Zuehlke, *For Honor's Sake: The War of 1812
        and the Brokering of an Uneasy Peace* (Toronto: Alfred A. Knopf Canada, 2006), 71.

38   *Four of the War Hawks:* Dangerfield, *The Era of Good Feelings*, 38. For a brief, solid
        description of the political makeup of the 12th Congress, see Hickey, *The War of 1812*,
        29–30.

38   *"In case of war"*: Mahan, *Sea Power*, 1:293.

39   *"difficult to relinquish"*: Stagg, *Mr. Madison's War*, 4; Gordon Wood, *Empire of Liberty: A History of the Early Republic, 1789-1815*, Oxford History of the United States (New York: Oxford University Press, 2009), 676.

39   *Southerners, including the president*: J. C. A. Stagg, *Borderlines in Borderlands: James Madison and the Spanish-American Frontier, 1776-1821* (New Haven, CT: Yale University Press, 2009), 122–24.

39   *Some thought*: Secretary Hamilton to Representative Langdon Cheves, Chairman of the House Naval Committee, Dec. 3, 1811, in *The Naval War of 1812: A Documentary History*, ed. William S. Dudley (Washington, DC: Naval Historical Center, 1985), 1:56

40   *He had heard a version*: Monroe to Jefferson, quoted in Mahan, *Sea Power*, 1:281.

40   *Instead of wasting*: Stagg, *Mr. Madison's War*, 145.

40   *Concerned about the president's*: David Long, *Ready to Hazard: A Biography of Commodore William Bainbridge, 1774-1833* (Hanover, NH: University Press of New England, 1981), 129–33; Mahan, *Sea Power*, 281.

CHAPTER 5

43   *Madison approached his call*: See Bradford Perkins, *Prologue to War: England and the United States, 1805-1812* (Berkeley: University of California Press, 1970).

43   *He tried to convince*: Ralph Ketcham, *James Madison: A Biography* (Charlottesville: University Press of Virginia, 1990), 530.

44   *It did not help matters*: Ambassador Foster to Wellesley, Jan. 31, 1812, quoted in Bradford Perkins, *Prologue to War: England and the United States, 1805–1812* (Berkeley: University of California Press, 1970), 372.

44   *The ambassador was encouraged*: Perkins, *Prologue to War*, 343–76.

44   *"British cruisers"*: "Madison's War Message, June 1, 1812," in *James Madison's Writings*, ed. Jack N. Rakove (New York: Library Classics of the United States, 1999), 685–92.

45   *Federalist strength*: Roger H. H. Brown, *The Republic in Peril, 1812* (New York: Norton, 1971), 193.

45   *"Go to war"*: Henry Adams, *History of the United States of America During the Administrations of James Madison* (New York: Library of America, 1986), 440.

45   *Randolph insisted that war*: Richard Buel Jr., *America on the Brink: How the Political Struggle Over the War of 1812 Almost Destroyed the Young Republic* (New York: Palgrave Macmillan, 2005), 130–31.

46   *"against the nation"*: Adams, *History of the United States*, 574.

46   *Governor Strong wanted*: Buel, *America On the Brink*, 160.

46   *"let the sound"*: Samuel Eliot Morison, *Harrison Gray Otis: The Urbane Federalist* (Boston: Houghton Mifflin, 1969), 326.

46   *"an event awful"*: Robert A. McCaughey, *Josiah Quincy, 1772–1864: The Last Federalist* (Cambridge, MA: Harvard University Press, 1974), 58.

46   *That night, a menacing crowd*: Donald R. Hickey, *The War of 1812: A Forgotten Conflict* (Urbana: University of Illinois Press, 1989), 52–71.

47   *The mob's violence upset*: Adams, *History of the United States*, 578–81.

47   *On May 11, a man*: Spencer Walpole, *The Life of the Right Honorable Spencer Perceval Including His Correspondence with Numerous Distinguished Persons* (London: Hurst and Blackett, 1874), 2:293–99.

47   *the veteran Lord Liverpool*: Charles D. Yonge, *The Life and Administration of Robert Banks, Second Earl of Liverpool* (London: Macmillan, 1868), 1:401.

48   *"Arguments and expostulations"*: "Second Inaugural Address," in Rakove, ed., *James Madison's Writings*, 693–96.

48   *"not independent people"*: Robert Rutland, *James Madison: The Founding Father* (New York: Macmillan, 1987), 225.

49   *"As our councils"*: Richard Beale Davis, ed., *Jeffersonian America: Notes by Sir Augustus John Foster* (San Marino, CA: Huntington Library, 1954), 99–103.

49   *Pinkney departed*: Ambassador Pinkney to Secretary of State Robert Smith, March 1, 1811, in *American State Papers: Foreign Relations* (Washington DC: Gales & Seaton, 1833–58), 3:415.

50   *"To render the justice"*: "Second Inaugural Address," in Rakove, ed., *James Madison's Writings*, 695.

50   *The president's terms*: Irving Brant, *James Madison*, vol. 6: *Commander in Chief, 1812–1836* (Indianapolis: Bobbs-Merrill, 1950), 34–5.

51   *The president did not want*: Brant, *James Madison*, vol. 6, 62.

51   *"consent to suspend"*: Castlereagh to Russell, Aug. 29, 1812, and Sept. 18, 1812, in *American State Papers: Foreign Relations*, 3:589–92; *Times* (London), Aug. 1812.

51   *"to give assurance"*: Russell to Castlereagh, Aug. 24, 1812, in *Times* (London), Dec. 26, 1812.

51   *"to give assurance*: Secretary of State Monroe to Ambassador Jonathan Russell, June 26, 1812, in *American State Papers: Foreign Relations*, 3:585.

51   *"demand of us"*: *Times* (London), Dec. 25, 1812.

51   *Castlereagh was willing*: Castlereagh to Russell, Aug. 29 and Sept. 18, 1812; Russell to Monroe, Sept. 17, 1812; and Castlereagh to Russell, Sept. 18, 1812, in *American State Papers: Foreign Relations*, 3:592–95.

51   *"Still more precise"*: *National Intelligencer*, Aug. 4, 1812.

CHAPTER 6

53   *"For God's sake"*: Charles O. Paullin, *Commodore John Rodgers: A Biography* (Cleveland: Arthur H. Clark, 1910), 247.

54   *"Now lads"*: Paullin, *Commodore John Rodgers*, 248.

54   *As on all American warships*: Christopher McKee, *A Gentleman and Honorable Profession: The Creation of the U.S. Naval Officer Corps, 1794–1815* (Annapolis, MD: Naval Institute Press, 1991), 219.

54   *After the Quasi-War*: Paullin, *Commodore John Rodgers*, 31–207.

55   *"out with as large"*: Captain Decatur to Secretary Hamilton, June 8, 1812, in *The Naval War of 1812: A Documentary History*, ed. William S. Dudley (Washington, DC: Naval Historical Center, 1985), 1:122–24.

56   *"menacing them in the very teeth"*: Commodore John Rodgers to Secretary Hamilton, June 3, 1812, in Dudley, ed., *Naval War of 1812*, 1:119–22.

56   *"I apprize you"*: Paullin, *Commodore John Rodgers*, 249–50.

57   *"We may be able"*: Commodore Rodgers to Secretary Hamilton, June 19, 1812, in Dudley, ed., *Naval War of 1812*, 1:138.

57   *Within ten minutes*: Spencer Tucker, *Stephen Decatur: A Life Most Bold and Daring* (Annapolis, MD: Naval Institute Press, 2005), 123.

57   *The Jamaica convoy*: Samuel Eliot Morison, *Old Bruin: Commodore Matthew Calbraith Perry, 1794–1858* (Boston: Little, Brown, 1967), 34.

58   *"arrivals from foreign"*: Irving Brant, *James Madison*, vol. 6: *Commander in Chief, 1812–1836* (Indianapolis: Bobbs-Merrill, 1961), 37; Henry Adams, *History of the United States of America During the Administrations of James Madison* (New York: Library of America, 1986), 553.

58   *Hamilton wrote to Rodgers*: Secretary Hamilton to John Rodgers, June 22, 1812, in Dudley, ed., *Naval War of 1812*, 1:148–49.

58   *The orders appeared:* Wade G. Dudley, *Splintering the Wooden Wall: The British Blockade of the United States, 1812–1815* (Annapolis, MD: Naval Institute Press, 2003), 65.

59   *The commandant of the New York Navy Yard:* Captain Isaac Chauncey to Secretary Hamilton, June 22, 1812, in Dudley, ed., *Naval War of 1812*, 1:144.

59   *As he passed Sandy Hook:* David Long, *Nothing Too Daring: A Biography of Commodore David Porter, 1780–1843* (Annapolis, MD: Naval Institute Press, 1970), 64–65.

60   *Porter decided it:* Captain Porter to Secretary Hamilton, Sept. 3, 1812, in Dudley, ed., *Naval War of 1812*, 1:446; Long, *Nothing Too Daring*, 65.

61   *In short order:* Lieutenant Crane to Secretary Hamilton, July 29, 1812, in Dudley, ed., *Naval War of 1812*, 1:209–11.

62   *"If . . . you fall in":* Secretary Hamilton to Captain Hull, July 3, 1812, quoted in Linda M. Maloney, *The Captain from Connecticut: The Life and Times of Isaac Hull* (Boston: Northeastern University Press, 1986), 170.

63   *Luckily, Nathaniel:* Captain Tingey to Secretary Hamilton, July 9, 1812 and July 15, 1812, in Dudley, ed., *Naval War of 1812*, 1:188–89.

64   *"The crew, you will":* Captain Hull to Secretary Hamilton, July 2, 1812, in Dudley, ed., *Naval War of 1812*, 1:160–61.

66   *"At midnight moderate breeze":* Quoted in Tyrone G. Martin, *A Most Fortunate Ship: A Narrative History of "Old Ironsides"* (Chester, CT: Globe Pequot, 1980), 9.

67   *Having won this:* Captain Hull to Secretary Hamilton, July 21, 1812, in Dudley, ed., *Naval War of 1812*, 1:161–65; Martin, *A Most Fortunate Ship*, 102–11; Maloney, *The Captain from Connecticut*, 168–210.

67   *Inevitably, details were:* Maloney, *The Captain from Connecticut*, 26–27, 178; Louis Arthur Norton, *Captains Contentious: The Dysfunctional Sons of the Brine* (Columbia: University of South Carolina Press, 2009), 61.

68   *When he met Admiral Duckworth:* Admiral Duckworth to Captain Porter, Aug. 5, 1812, and Admiral Duckworth to Secretary Hamilton, Aug. 21, 1812, quoted in David Dixon Porter, *Memoir of Commodore David Porter of the United States Navy* (Albany, NY: J. Munsell, 1875), 95–96.

69   *The Essex's larboard guns:* Captain Porter to Secretary Hamilton, Sept. 3, 1812, in Dudley, ed., *Naval War of 1812*, 1:443–44.

69   *"trifling":* Captain Porter to Secretary Hamilton, Sept. 3, 1812, in Dudley, ed., *Naval War of 1812*, 1:444.

70   *In a flash, the:* Charles Lee Lewis, *David Glasgow Farragut: Admiral in the Making* (Annapolis, MD: United States Naval Institute, 1941), 44–45; Long, *Nothing Too Daring*, 66–67; Loyall Farragut, *The Life of David Glasgow Farragut, First Admiral of the United States Navy, Embodying His Journal and Letters* (New York: D. Appleton, 1882), 16–17.

70   *Porter was unhappy:* Captain Porter to Secretary Hamilton, Sept. 5, 1812, in Dudley, ed., *Naval War of 1812*, 1:462–63.

70   *"At least 6 days":* Commodore Rodgers to Secretary Hamilton, Aug. 31, 1812, quoted in John H. Schroeder, *Commodore John Rodgers: Paragon of the Early American Navy* (Gainesville: University Press of Florida, 2006), 117.

CHAPTER 7

74   *Hull sent a letter:* Captain Hull to Secretary Hamilton, July 28, 1812, in *The Naval War of 1812: A Documentary History*, ed. William S. Dudley (Washington, DC: Naval Historical Center, 1985), 1:206–7.

74   *"remain at Boston":* Linda M. Maloney, *The Captain from Connecticut: The Life and Times of Isaac Hull* (Boston: Northeastern University Press, 1986), 180–82.

76   *In these waters:* Benjamin W. Labaree, *Patriots and Partisans: The Merchants of New-buryport, 1764–1815* (Cambridge, MA: Harvard University Press, 1962), 187–88.

77   *"Hull was now":* Moses Smith, *Naval Scenes in the Last War; or, Three Years on Board the Frigate* Constitution, *and the* Adams, *Including the Capture of the* Guerriere (Boston: Gleason's Publishing Hall, 1846), 30–31.

79   *"I feel it my duty":* Dacres to Sawyer, Sept. 7, 1812, in Dudley, ed., *Naval War of 1812,* 2:243–45.

80   *Lieutenant Morris:* Charles Morris, *The Autobiography of Commodore Charles Morris, U.S. Navy* (Annapolis, MD: Naval Institute Press, 2002), 61–63.

80   *his report to Secretary Hamilton:* Captain Hull to Secretary Hamilton, Aug. 28, 1812, and Captain Dacres to Vice Admiral Sawyer, Sept. 7, 1812, in Dudley, ed., *Naval War of 1812,* 1:238–45; Maloney, *Captain from Connecticut,* 184–94; and Charles Francis Adams, "Wednesday, August 19, 1812, 6:30 P.M.: The Birth of a World Power," *American Historical Review* (1918): 519–20.

80   *It was common:* Christopher McKee, *A Gentlemanly and Honorable Profession: The Creation of the U.S. Navy Officer Corps, 1794–1815* (Annapolis, MD: Naval Institute, 1991), 219.

81   *"At daylight discovered":* Charles O. Paullin, *Commodore John Rodgers: Captain, Commodore, and Senior Officer of the American Navy, 1773–1838* (1909; reprint, Annapolis, MD: United States Naval Institute, 1967), 257–58.

81   *because of scurvy:* Paullin, *Commodore John Rodgers,* 258. Paullin claims there were three hundred men on the two frigates suffering symptoms, but that figure seems too high; see John H. Schroeder, *Commodore John Rodgers: Paragon of the Early American Navy* (Gainesville: University Press of Florida, 2006), 117.

81   *"Even if I did":* Paullin, *Commodore John Rodgers,* 258–59.

82   *A remarkable 250:* Wade G. Dudley, *Splintering the Wooden Wall: The British Blockade of the United States, 1812–1815* (Annapolis, MD: Naval Institute Press, 2003), 76; George Coggeshall, *History of American Privateers and Letters of Marque During Our War with England, 1812, '13, '14* (New York, George Putnam, 1856), 81.

82   *"having been much favored":* Paullin, *Commodore John Rodgers,* 258.

82   *when news of the* Constitution's: *Times* (London), Oct. 7, 1812; Henry Adams, *History of the United States of America During the Administrations of James Madison* (New York: Library of America, 1986), 624.

82   *At his court-martial:* "Court Martial of Captain James R. Dacres, Formerly of HMS Guerriere," *Naval Chronicle* 28:422–24, quoted in *The Naval Chronicle: The Contemporary Record of the Royal Navy at War, 1811–1815,* ed. Nicholas Tracy (London: Chatham, 1999), 5:113–14.

CHAPTER 8

86   *Thanks to the wise:* John Sugden, *Tecumseh: A Life* (New York: Henry Holt, 1997), 310; Gerald M. Craig, *Upper Canada: The Formative Years, 1784–1841* (Toronto: McClelland and Stewart, 1963), 5.

86   *Brigadier General William Hull:* J. C. A. Stagg, *Mr. Madison's War: Politics, Diplomacy, and Warfare in the Early American Republic, 1783–1830* (Princeton, NJ: Princeton University Press, 1983), 177–88.

87   *Tecumseh was open to:* Sugden, *Tecumseh,* 271.

88   *Along with Hanks:* Pierre Berton, *The Invasion of Canada: 1812–1813* (Boston: Little, Brown: 1980), 103–13.

89   *Governor-General Sir George Prevost:* Kenneth McNaught, *The Penguin History of Canada* (London: Penguin, 1988), 60–75.

90   *Far more cautious:* Mark Zuehlke, *For Honor's Sake: The War of 1812 and the Brokering of an Uneasy Peace* (Toronto: Alfred A. Knopf Canada, 2006), 90-94.

90   *"the British cannot hold":* Hull to Eustis, March 6, 1812, quoted in Berton, *The Invasion of Canada*, 89.

91   *"My situation is most":* Quoted in Alfred L. Burt, *The United States, Great Britain and British North America from the Revolution to the Establishment of Peace After the War of 1812* (Toronto: Ryerson Press, 1940), 327-28.

91   *Given this political reality, Madison:* The Secretary of War to Major General Dearborn, June 26, 1812, in Ernest A. Cruikshank, ed., *Documents Relating to the Invasion of Canada and the Surrender of Detroit, 1812* (Ottawa, Canada: Government Printing Bureau, 1912), 33.

91   *"of the unanimity":* Quoted in Irving Brant, *James Madison*, vol. 6: *Commander in Chief, 1812-1836* (Indianapolis: Bobbs-Merrill, 1961), 6:53.

91   *"sacrificing the Western":* Madison to Jefferson, Aug. 17, 1812, quoted in Brant, *James Madison*, vol. 6: *Commander in Chief*, 53.

92   *The Canadian Provincial Marine:* Commodore Isaac Chauncey to Secretary Hamilton, Nov. 6, 1812, in *The Naval War of 1812: A Documentary History*, ed. William S. Dudley (Washington, DC: Naval Historical Center, 1985), 1:343-44; Robert Malcomson, *A Very Brilliant Affair: The Battle of Queenston Heights, 1812* (Annapolis, MD: Naval Institute Press, 2003), 53.

92   *"The decided superiority":* Prevost to Bathurst, Aug. 24, 1812, quoted in Henry Adams, *History of the United States of America During the Administrations of James Madison* (New York: Library of America, 1986), 529.

92   *Hull was compelled:* Berton, *The Invasion of Canada*, 89-90.

93   *From the rapids:* Stagg, *Mr. Madison's War*, 193, and Donald R. Hickey, *War of 1812: A Forgotten Conflict* (Urbana: University of Illinois Press, 1989), 81.

94   *"You will be emancipated":* Quoted in J. Mackay Hitsman, *The Incredible War of 1812: A Military History* (Montreal: Robin Brass Studio, 1999), 65.

94   *"The surrender opened":* Hull to Eustis, Aug. 26, 1812, in John Brannan, *Official Letters of the Military and Naval Officers of the United States During the War with Great Britain, in the Years 1812-1815* (Washington City: Way and Gideon, 1823), 45.

95   *Tecumseh was keeping:* Berton, *The Invasion of Canada*, 146-48.

95   *Ignoring instructions:* Eustis to Dearborn, June 4 and 26, 1812, quoted in Malcomson, *A Very Brilliant Affair*, 44-45.

96   *"I consider the agreement":* Quoted in Adams, *History of the United States*, 519.

96   *"you will inform":* Eustis to Dearborn, Aug. 15, 1812, quoted in Adams, *History of the United States*, 534-35.

96   *"which I had considered":* Dearborn to Madison, Aug. 15, 1812, quoted in Adams, *History of the United States*, 534.

97   *"If the troops":* Dearborn to Eustis, Aug. 15, 1812, quoted in Adams, *History of the United States*, 535.

97   *"secure Upper Canada":* Eustis to Dearborn, Aug. 15, 1812, quoted in Adams, *History of the United States*, 534-35.

98   *"It is far from":* Brock to Hull, Aug. 15, 1812, in Brannan, *Official Letters*, 41.

99   *Brock's unexpected triumph:* Brannan, *Official Letters*, 42; Malcomson, *A Very Brilliant Affair*, 78.

100   *Tecumseh's dream of expelling:* Sugden, *Tecumseh*, 310.

100   *"The treachery of Hull":* Jefferson to Thomas Duane, Oct. 1, 1812, quoted in Adams, *History of the United States*, 528.

100   *"weak, indecisive":* Monroe to Jefferson, Aug. 31, 1812, in Stagg, *Mr. Madison's War*, 207.

100   *Colonel Lewis Cass: National Intelligencer*, Sept. 15, 1812; Colonel Lewis Cass to the Secretary of War, Sept. 10, 1812, in Cruikshank, ed., *Documents Related to the Invasion of Canada*, 153-56.

101   *"was a glorious"*: *Times* (London), Oct. 7, 1812.

101   *"The disaster"*: *Times* (London), Oct. 7, 1812.

101   *"We would gladly"*: *Times* (London), Oct. 21, 1812.

101   *In the middle of September*: Brant, *James Madison*, vol. 6: *Commander in Chief*, 73–75.

CHAPTER 9

103   *"The President"*: Hamilton to Chauncey, Aug. 31, 1812, in *The Naval War of 1812: A Documentary History*, ed. William S. Dudley (Washington, DC: Naval Historical Center, 1985), 1:297–98.

103   *"the finest frigate"*: Eugene S. Ferguson, *Truxtun of the Constellation* (Baltimore: Johns Hopkins University Press, 1956), 217.

103   *Before joining the service*: Robert Malcomson, *Lords of the Lake: The Naval War on Lake Ontario, 1812–1814* (1998; reprint, Montreal: Robin Brass Studio, 2009), 38–42.

104   *Daniel Dobbins appeared*: Hamilton to Dobbins, Sept. 11, 1812, in Dudley, ed., *Naval War of 1812*, 1:307.

106   *"cut out [the] two British"*: Elliott to Hamilton, Oct. 9, 1812, in Dudley, ed., *Naval War of 1812*, 1:329–31.

107   *Despite the loss*: Brock to Prevost, Oct. 11, 1812, in Dudley, ed., *Naval War of 1812*, 1:331–33.

107   *On August 17*: Henry Adams, *History of the United States of America During the Administrations of James Madison* (New York: Library of America, 1986), 536.

107   *When Major General Van Rensselaer*: Solomon Van Rensselaer, *A Narrative of the Affair of Queenstown: In the War of 1812* (New York: Leavitt, Lord, 1836), 10–14.

107   *Van Rensselaer's position*: Van Rensselaer, *A Narrative of the Affair of Queenstown*, 15–16.

108   *He believed that Brock had 3,000*: Pierre Berton, *The Invasion of Canada: 1812–1813* (Boston: Little, Brown: 1980), 209.

108   *By the middle of October*: Robert Malcomson, *A Very Brilliant Affair: The Battle of Queenston Heights, 1812* (Annapolis, MD: Naval Institute Press, 2003), 117.

109   *Even with all his difficulties*: Malcomson, *A Very Brilliant Affair*, 107–20.

109   *"the partial success of Lieutenant*: Major General Van Rennsselaer to Dearborn in John Brannan, *Official Letters of the Military and Naval Officers of the United States During the War with Great Britain, in the Years 1812–1815* (Washington City: Way and Gideon, 1823), 74.

109   *Continuing to be overly cautious*: Malcomson, *A Very Brilliant Affair*, 150–51.

111   *George Jervis*: Malcomson, *A Very Brilliant Affair*, 155.

111   *If reinforcements arrived*: Malcomson, *A Very Brilliant Affair*, 153.

112   *In the meantime*: Malcomson, *A Very Brilliant Affair*, 121–92.

112   *"the victory was really"*: General Stephen Van Rensselaer to General Henry Dearborn, Oct. 14, 1812, in Brannan, *Official Letters*, 74–78.

113   *"showed fortitude equal"*: McFeeley to General Smythe, Nov. 25, 1812, in Brannon, *Official Letters*, 93–95, and John K. Mahon, *The War of 1812* (Gainesville: University Press of Florida, 1972; reprint, New York: DaCapo Press, 1991), 82–83.

114   *Many wanted to kill*: Smyth to a Citizens Committee of Buffalo, Dec. 3, 1812, in Brannon, *Official Letters*, 101–4.

114   *"showed no talent"*: Winfield Scott, *Memoirs of Lieutenant-General Scott, LLD: Written by Himself* (New York: Sheldon, 1964), 1:31.

114   *Having lost the confidence*: Lt. Samuel Angus to Secretary Hamilton, Dec. 1, 1812, in Dudley, ed., *Naval War of 1812*, 1:355–59; and Malcomson, *A Very Brilliant Affair*, 203–5.

115   *With good intelligence:* Pierre Berton, *Flames Across the Border: The Canadian-American Tragedy, 1813–1814* (Boston: Little, Brown, 1981), 22; Adams, *History of the United States,* 669–89.

116   *Before Chauncey arrived:* Woolsey to Hamilton, June 9, 1812, in Dudley, ed., *Naval War of 1812,* 1:274; Woolsey to Hamilton, July 21, 1812, in Dudley, ed., *Naval War of 1812,* 1:283–84.

117   *"rather a latish month":* James Fenimore Cooper, *Ned Myers; or Life Before the Mast* (1843; reprint, Annapolis, MD: Naval Institute Press, 1989), 56.

117   *Hard as it was for Chauncey:* Chauncey to Hamilton, Nov. 4, 1812, in Dudley, ed., *Naval War of 1812,* 341–42.

118   *Although he failed:* Chauncey to Hamilton, Nov. 13, 1812, in Dudley, ed., *Naval War of 1812,* 1:344–46; Robert Malcomson, *Capital in Flames: The American Attack on York, 1813* (Annapolis, MD: Naval Institute Press, 2008), 49–58.

118   *"nine weeks since":* Chauncey to Hamilton, Nov. 26, 1812, in Dudley, ed., *Naval War of 1812,* 1:353.

119   *Like Chauncey, Macdonough:* Sidney Smith to Hamilton, June 16, 1812, in Dudley, ed., *Naval War of 1812,* 1:275; and New York Navy Agent John Bullus to Hamilton, July 16, 1812, in Dudley, ed., *Naval War of 1812,* 1:281–83.

119   *By then, Macdonough had:* Macdonough to Hamilton, Dec. 20, 1812, in Dudley, ed., *Naval War of 1812,* 1:370.

CHAPTER 10

121   *Secretary Hamilton ordered:* Secretary of the Navy to Commodore John Rodgers, Sept. 9, 1812, in *The Naval War of 1812: A Documentary History,* ed. William S. Dudley (Washington, DC: Naval Historical Center, 1985), 1:471.

121   *"pursue that course":* Secretary Hamilton to Commodore John Rodgers, Sept. 9, 1812, in Dudley, ed., *Naval War of 1812,* 1:471.

123   *"seems to assume":* Admiral John Warren to Secretary of the Admiralty John W. Croker, Oct. 5, 1812, in Dudley, ed., *Naval War of 1812,* 1:508–9.

123   *"The Orders in Council":* *American State Papers: Foreign Relations* (Washington DC: Gales & Seaton, 1833–58), 3:495–96.

123   *Lord Melville wrote:* Lord Melville to Admiral John Warren, March 26, 1813, in Dudley, ed., *Naval War of 1812,* 2:78–79.

123   *Melville wanted naval traffic:* First Secretary of the Admiralty John W. Croker to Admiral John Warren, March 20, 1813, in Dudley, ed., *Naval War of 1812,* 2:75–78.

124   *the* Times *of London had fed:* *Times* (London), Aug. 1, 1812.

124   *the Admiralty was far more:* Lords Commissioners of the Admiralty to Admiral Sir John B. Warren, R.N., Dec. 26, 1812, in Dudley, ed., *Naval War of 1812,* 1:633–34.

124   *the Admiralty told him:* First Secretary of the Admiralty John W. Croker to Warren, Jan. 9, 1813, and Feb. 10, 1813, in Dudley, ed., *Naval War of 1812,* 2:14–19; *Times* (London), March 20 and 24, 1813.

125   *With the addition of all:* Admiral John Warren to Secretary Croker, Oct. 5 and Dec. 29, 1812, Jan. 25 and Feb. 26, 1813, in Dudley, ed., *Naval War of 1812,* 1:508–9.

126   *The* President *then headed:* Charles O. Paullin, *Commodore John Rodgers: Captain, Commodore, and Senior Officer of the American Navy, 1773-1838* (1909; reprint, Annapolis, MD: United States Naval Institute, 1967), 261.

127   *"We chased everything":* Commodore John Rodgers to Secretary Hamilton, Jan. 2, 1813, in Dudley, ed., *Naval War of 1812,* 2:5.

128   *Jones's triumph was short-lived:* Captain Whinyates to Admiral Sir John Warren, Oct. 23, 1812, in Dudley, ed., *Naval War of 1812,* 1:539–540; Captain Jones to Secretary

Hamilton, Nov. 24, 1812, in Dudley, ed., *Naval War of 1812*, 1:579–83; Captain John P. Beresford, *Journal of H.M.S. Poitiers*, in Dudley, ed., *Naval War of 1812*, 1:536–39.

129   *Decatur put a prize master*: Decatur to Hamilton, Oct. 12, 1812, in Dudley, ed., *Naval War of 1812*, 1:527.

129   *By the end of 1812*: Christopher Bell, *Wellington's Navy: Sea Power and the Peninsula War, 1807–14* (London: Chatham, 2004), 6.

129   *"The first quality"*: Leonard F. Guttridge, *Our Country, Right or Wrong: The Life of Stephen Decatur, The U.S. Navy's Most Illustrious Commander* (New York: Tom Doherty Associates, 2006), 46.

130   *Sinclair seized the vessel*: Henry Denison to Secretary Hamilton, Nov. 11, 1812, in Dudley, ed., *Naval War of 1812*, 1:566.

134   *When men from the* United States: Samuel Leech, *Thirty Years from Home: A Seaman's View of the War of 1812* (1843; reprint, Tucson, AZ: Fireship Press, 2008), 78–79; Captain John S. Carden to Secretary of the Admiralty John W. Croker, Oct. 28, 1812, and Decatur to Hamilton, Oct. 30, 1812, in Dudley, ed., *Naval War of 1812*, 1:548–53. Of the many accounts of this famous battle, the best are James Tertius de Kay, *Chronicles of the Frigate Macedonian, 1809–1922* (New York: Norton, 1995), 63–99; Ira Dye, *The Fatal Cruise of the Argus: Two Captains in the War of 1812* (Annapolis, MD: Naval Institute Press, 1994), 78–100; C. S. Forester, *The Age of Fighting Sail* (New York: Doubleday, 1956), 107–11; and Alfred T. Mahan, *Sea Power in Its Relations to the War of 1812* (Boston: Little, Brown, 1905), 1:415–23.

134   *"Oh! what a charm"*: *Times* (London), Dec. 29, 1812.

CHAPTER 11

135   *Bainbridge would have preferred*: Bainbridge to Jones, Oct. 5, 1812, in *The Naval War of 1812: A Documentary History*, ed. William S. Dudley (Washington, DC: Naval Historical Center, 1985), 1:510–12.

136   *"after devoting near fifteen"*: Lawrence to Hamilton, Oct. 10, 1812; Sinclair to Hamilton, Oct. 7, 1812; Bainbridge to Hamilton, Oct. 8, 1812; Hamilton to Lawrence, Oct. 17, 1812; Lawrence to Hamilton, Oct. 22, 1812, in Dudley, ed., *Naval War of 1812*, 1:516–23.

137   *"clear the coast"*: Hamilton to Captain John H. Dent, Oct. 24, 1812, in Dudley, ed., *Naval War of 1812*, 1:583–84.

137   *Dent had tried to counteract*: Hamilton to Dent Oct. 24, 1812, and Dent to Hamilton, Nov. 5, Nov. 14, Nov. 16, and Nov. 24, 1812, in Dudley, ed., *Naval War of 1812*, 1:583–87.

138   *"one of the finest"*: Bainbridge to William Jones, Oct. 5, 1812, in Dudley, ed., *Naval War of 1812*, 1:510–12.

138   *The Constitutions' unhappiness*: Ira Dye, *The Fatal Cruise of the Argus: Two Captains in the War of 1812* (Annapolis, MD: Naval Institute Press, 1994), 6.

138   *"I have zealously"*: Bainbridge to Preble, Nov. 12, 1803, *Naval Documents Related to the United States Wars with the Barbary Powers* (Washington, DC: U.S. Government Printing Office, 1939–44), 3:174.

139   *"apprehension which constantly"*: Commodore Bainbridge to Susan Bainbridge, Nov. 1, 1803, quoted in Thomas Harris, *The Life and Services of Commodore William Bainbridge, United States Navy* (Philadelphia: Carey Lea & Blanchard, 1837), 91–93.

139   *Bainbridge saw this voyage*: Linda M. Maloney, *The Captain from Connecticut: The Life and Times of Isaac Hull* (Boston: Northeastern University Press, 1986), 200; David F. Long, *Ready to Hazard: A Biography of Commodore William Bainbridge, 1774–1833* (Hanover, NH: University Press of New England, 1981), 138–39.

140   *"My dear Mediterranean"*: David Porter, *Journal of a Cruise* (1815; reprint, Annapolis, MD: Naval Institute Press, 1986), 52.

140   *After anchoring off:* Long, *Ready to Hazard*, 145–47.

142   *"being sufficiently from":* Tyrone G. Martin, *A Most Fortunate Ship: A Narrative History of "Old Ironsides"* (Chester, CT: Globe Pequot, 1980), 131–34; and Long, *Ready to Hazard*, 151.

143   *"[with] a great part of":* Lieutenant Henry D. Chads to Secretary of the Admiralty John W. Croker, Dec. 31, 1812, in Dudley, ed., *Naval War of 1812*, 1:639–49.

143   *"loss must have been": Journal of Commodore William Bainbridge,* Dec. 30, 1812, in Dudley, ed., *Naval War of 1812*, 1:639–49.

144   *The* Constitution *was a good deal:* Bainbridge to Dr. John Bullus, Jan. 23, 1813, quoted in Long, *Ready to Hazard*, 158–159.

145   *During that time:* Albert Gleaves, *James Lawrence, Captain, United States Navy, Commander of the Chesapeake* (New York: Putnam, 1904), 123.

146   *At 5:25 the two ships:* Lawrence to Secretary Jones, March 19, 1813, and Lieutenant Frederick A. Wright, R.N., to Lords Commissioners of the Admiralty, March 26, 1813, in Dudley, ed., *Naval War of 1812*, 2:70–75.

146   *"I have only time":* James Lawrence to Julia Lawrence, March 19, 1813, James Lawrence Papers, Misc. Mss., New York Historical Society.

147   *"In the continuation of":* Gleaves, *James Lawrence*, 138.

148   *The British navy managed:* Yeo to Vice Admiral Charles Stirling, Nov. 22 and Dec. 11, 1812, in Dudley, ed., *Naval War of 1812*, 1:594–95.

CHAPTER 12

152   *Had he been able:* Samuel E. Morison, *Harrison Gray Otis: The Urbane Federalist* (Boston: Houghton Mifflin, 1969), 257–63; James M. Banner Jr., *To the Hartford Convention: The Federalists and the Origins of Party Politics in Massachusetts, 1798–1815* (New York: Knopf, 1970), 294–312.

153   *The grain shipments:* Sean Wilentz, *The Rise of American Democracy: Jefferson to Lincoln* (New York: Norton, 2005), 158; Norman K. Risjord, "Election of 1812," in *History of American Presidential Elections, 1789–1968*, ed. Arthur M. Schlesinger Jr. et al. (New York: Chelsea House, 1985), 1:249–96.

153   *"wholly unfit for":* James F. Hopkins, ed., *The Papers of Henry Clay: Volume I, The Rising Statesman, 1797–1814* (Lexington: University Press of Kentucky, 1959), 750–51.

153   *On November 4:* "Madison's Annual Message to Congress, November 4, 1812," in *A Compilation of the Messages and Papers of the Presidents*, ed. James D. Richardson (Washington, DC: Bureau of National Literature and Art, 1904), 1:514–21; Ralph Ketcham, *James Madison: A Biography* (Charlottesville: University Press of Virginia, 1971), 547–48.

154   *"we are determined":* Linda M. Maloney, *The Captain from Connecticut: The Life and Times of Isaac Hull* (Boston: Northeastern University Press, 1986), 202.

154   *"which will be by far":* Hamilton to Congressman Burwell Bassett, Nov. 13, 1812, in *The Naval War of 1812: A Documentary History*, ed. William S. Dudley (Washington, DC: Naval Historical Center, 1985), 1:571–73; Charles Stewart to Hamilton, Nov. 12, 1812, in *American State Papers, Naval Affairs* (Washington, DC: Gales and Seaton, 1834), 1:278–79.

154   *To aid the lobbying effort: National Intelligencer,* Nov. 28, 1812.

154   *In the middle of the festivities:* Claude Berube and John Rodgaard, *A Call to the Sea: Captain Charles Stewart of the USS* Constitution (Washington, DC: Potomac Books, 2005), 65–67; Irving Brant, *James Madison*, vol. 6: *Commander in Chief, 1812–1836* (Indianapolis: Bobbs-Merrill, 1961), 122–25; Spencer Tucker, *Stephen Decatur: A Life Most Bold and Daring* (Annapolis, MD: Naval Institute Press, 2005), 121.

155   *Since Decatur brought:* Maloney, *Captain from Connecticut*, 204.

156   *"Frigates and seventy-fours":* Jefferson to Monroe, Jan. 1, 1815, in Henry Adams, *History of the United States of America During the Administrations of James Madison* (New York: Library of America, 1986), 598–99.

156   *For a solid bloc:* Craig Symonds, *Navalists and Anti-Navalists: The Naval Policy Debate in the United States, 1785–1827* (Newark: University of Delaware Press, 1980), 171–91.

156   *Despite the stunning victories:* Christopher McKee, *A Gentlemanly and Honorable Profession: The Creation of the U.S. Naval Officer Corps, 1794–1815* (Annapolis, MD: Naval Institute Press, 1991), 9–11.

157   *He did not have the gracious:* McKee, *A Gentlemanly and Honorable Profession*, 11–13.

157   *"The first mate does not know":* Quoted in McKee, *A Gentlemanly and Honorable Profession*, 15–19.

157   *Jones did not waste any time:* William Jones to Eleanor Jones, Jan. 23, 1813, in Dudley, ed., *Naval War of 1812*, 2:34–35.

157   *"It is impossible to attach":* Jones to Chauncey, Jan. 27, 1813, in Dudley, ed., *Naval War of 1812*, 2:419–20.

157   *"to expect a very considerable":* Circular from Secretary of the Navy Jones to Commanders of Ships Now in Port Refitting, Feb. 22, 1813, in Dudley, ed., *Naval War of 1812*, 2:48.

158   *Madison needed new leadership:* J. C. A. Stagg, *Mr. Madison's War: Politics, Diplomacy, and Warfare in the Early American Republic, 1783–1830* (Princeton, NJ: Princeton University Press, 1983), 276–84.

159   *The appointment was controversial:* Thomas Fleming, *The Perils of Peace: America's Struggle for Survival After Yorktown* (New York: HarperCollins, 2007), 268–72.

160   *Republican War Hawks like:* Adams, *History of the United States*, 601–2.

160   *When Cheves and Lowndes introduced:* Donald R. Hickey, *The War of 1812: A Forgotten Conflict* (Urbana: University of Illinois Press, 1989), 113–17; Adams, *History of the United States*, 606.

161   *it passed legislation authorizing:* Brant, *James Madison*, vol. 6: *Commander in Chief*, 135–36.

161   *Authorizing a loan and obtaining:* Henry Adams, *Albert Gallatin* (1879; reprint, New York: Chelsea House, 1983), 288–89; Brant, *James Madison*, vol. 6: *Commander in Chief*, 196–97; Donald R. Adams Jr., *Finance and Enterprise in Early America: A Study of Stephen Girard's Bank, 1812–1831* (Philadelphia: University of Pennsylvania Press, 1978), 30–34.

CHAPTER 13

163   *As the summer wore on:* Dominic Lieven, *Russia Against Napoleon: The True Story of the Campaigns of War and Peace* (New York: Viking, 2010), 138–70.

164   *As the Russian armies retreated:* Lieven, *Russia Against Napoleon*, 170–73.

165   *"I will not sheath":* *Times* (London), July 25, 1812.

166   *On December 5, from Smorgoni:* Alan Schom, *Napoleon Bonaparte: A Life* (New York: HarperCollins, 1997), 629–44.

166   *"From the very first":* Armand Louis Augustin de Caulaincourt, *Memoirs du General de Caulaincourt* (New York: Enigma Books reprint, 2003), 399.

166   *"We today celebrate":* *Gazette de France*, Dec. 7, 1812.

167   *"Every day brings some fresh":* *Times* (London), Dec. 11, 1812.

167   *"We have scotched":* *Times* (London), Dec. 14, 1812.

168   *"The arm of the giant":* Quoted in *Times* (London), Jan. 20, 1813.

169   *The American ambassador:* Irving Brant, *James Madison*, vol. 6: *Commander in Chief, 1812–1836* (Indianapolis: Bobbs-Merrill, 1961), 154.

169   *Andre Daschkoff:* Daschkoff confirmed this with a letter dated March 8, cited in Henry Adams, *History of the United States of America During the Administrations of James Madison* (New York: Library of America, 1986), 648.

169   *Since Madison knew that Britain;* Brant, *James Madison,* vol. 6: *Commander in Chief,* 154.

169   *"high respect for the Emperor":* Madison to Count Nikolai Rumiantsev, July 10, 1813, in Russell Papers, Ms Russell Codex 7, 16, John Hay Library, Brown University.

169   *"the pressure of the war":* Times (London), May 8, 1813.

169   *London's attitude would undoubtedly:* Fernand Ouellet, *Lower Canada: 1791–1840: Social Change and Nationalism,* trans. and adapted by Patricia Claxton (Toronto: McClelland and Stewart, 1980), 100–106.

170   *"The American President was":* Times (London), Dec. 25, 1812.

170   *"sapping the foundation":* Quoted in *Times* (London), Feb. 19, 1813.

170   *"Who could believe":* Quoted in *Times* (London), Feb. 19, 1813.

171   *"We ought to consider":* Times (London), March 20, 1813.

171   *he and Castlereagh intended to propose:* Times (London), May 17, 1813.

171   *"you must look for an explanation":* James F. Hopkins, ed., *The Papers of Henry Clay: Volume I, The Rising Statesman, 1797–1814* (Lexington: University Press of Kentucky, 1959), 609.

172   *a ship purchased by the navy:* Secretary Jones to George Harrison (navy agent in Philadelphia), April 3, 1813, in *The Naval War of 1812: A Documentary History,* ed. William S. Dudley (Washington, DC: Naval Historical Center, 1992), 2:87–92; Brant, *James Madison,* vol. 6: *Commander in Chief,* 161.

172   *On May 31 Madison submitted:* J. C. A. Stagg, *Mr. Madison's War: Politics, Diplomacy, and Warfare in the Early American Republic, 1783–1830* (Princeton, NJ: Princeton University Press, 1983), 234.

CHAPTER 14

174   *The timing of the operation:* Reginald Horsman, *The War of 1812* (New York: Knopf, 1969), 89.

174   *Judging their troops:* Chauncey to Jones, March 18, 1812, in *The Naval War of 1812: A Documentary History,* ed. William S. Dudley (Washington, DC: Naval Historical Center, 1992), 2:430–32.

174   *"the fate of the campaign":* Jones to Chauncey, April 8, 1813, in Dudley, ed., *Naval War of 1812,* 2:433–34.

175   *"The first and paramount":* Lords Commissioners of the Admiralty to Commodore Sir James Lucas Yeo, R.N., March 19, 1813, in Dudley, ed., *Naval War of 1812,* 2:435–36.

175   *"Their Lordships feel":* John Wilson Croker to Yeo, March 19, 1813, in Dudley, ed., *Naval War of 1812,* 2:436–37.

175   *He and Dearborn set out:* Robert Malcomson, *Warships of the Great Lakes, 1754–1834* (Edison, NJ: Knickerbocker Press, 2004), 74–75.

176   *Before leaving, he destroyed:* Chauncey to Secretary Jones, April 28 and May 7, 1813, in Dudley, ed., *Naval War of 1812,* 449–50, 452–53; Dearborn to Secretary of War Armstrong, April 28, 1813, in Dudley, ed., *Naval War of 1812,* 2:450–51.

176   *Chauncey was pleased that:* Robert Malcomson, *Capital in Flames: The American Attack on York, 1813* (Annapolis, MD: Naval Institute Press, 2008), 178–238.

177   *In the aftermath of the short battle:* W. B. Kerr, "The Occupation of York (Toronto) 1813," *Canadian Historical Review* 5 (1924), and Malcomson, *Capital in Flames,* 242–61.

177   *Having taken York:* Chauncey to Jones, May 28, 1813, in Dudley, ed., *Naval War of 1812,* 2:463–64.

178   *Oliver Hazard Perry helped:* Chauncey to Jones, May 28, 1813, in Dudley, ed., *Naval War of 1812*, 2: 63–64.

178   *Thanks to the younger Chauncey's:* David Ellison, "David Wingfield and Sackets Harbor," *Dalhousie Review* 52 (1972); Brigadier General Jacob Brown to Secretary of War Armstrong, June 1, 1813, in Dudley, ed., *Naval War of 1812*, 2: 73–77.

180   *When the British troops withdrew:* Malcomson, *Warships of the Great Lakes*, 87–96, Alfred T. Mahan, *Sea Power in Its Relations to the War of 1812* (Boston: Little, Brown, 1905), 2:41.

180   *He told Secretary Jones:* Chauncey to Jones, June 11, 1813, in Dudley, ed., *Naval War of 1812*, 2:493–94.

181   *Instead of going after Vincent's:* James E. Elliot, *Strange Fatality: The Battle of Stoney Creek, 1813* (Montreal: Robin Brass Studio, 2009), 104–45; John R. Elting, *Amateurs to Arms: A Military History of the War of 1812* (Cambridge, MA: DaCapo Press, 1995), 131–32.

182   *In the meantime, Smith:* Lieutenant Thomas Macdonough to Secretary Jones, July 11, 1813, in Dudley, ed., *Naval War of 1812*, 2:514–15; Deposition of Abraham Walter before Court of Common Pleas, County of Clinton, NY, Nov. 23, 1813, in Dudley, ed., *Naval War of 1812*, 2:601–2.

182   *During the course of the war:* Ira Dye, "American Maritime Prisoners of War, 1812–1815," in *Ships, Seafaring and Society: Essays in Maritime History*, ed. Timothy J. Runyan (Detroit: Wayne State University Press, 1987), 293.

182   *When Chauncey discovered:* Pierre Berton, *Flames Across the Border: The Canadian-American Tragedy, 1813–1814* (Boston: Little, Brown, 1981), 98.

183   *Chauncey did not have to wait:* Chauncey to Jones, Aug. 13, 1813, in Dudley, ed., *Naval War of 1812*, 2:537–41; James Fenimore Cooper, *Ned Myers; or Life Before the Mast* (1843; reprint, Annapolis, MD: Naval Institute Press, 1989), 77–100.

183   *Macdonough knew they were:* David C. Skaggs, *Thomas Macdonough: Master of Command in the Early U.S. Navy* (Annapolis, MD: Naval Institute Press, 2003), 68–74.

183   *Macdonough wanted to go:* Macdonough to Jones, Aug. 3, 1813, in Dudley, ed., *Naval War of 1812*, 2:518.

184   *In spite of his troubles:* Macdonough to Jones, Aug. 14, 1813, in Dudley, ed., *Naval War of 1812*, 2:520.

185   *"The example set me by":* Harrison to Secretary of War, Aug. 4, 1813, in John Brannan, *Official Letters of the Military and Naval Officers of the United States During the War with Great Britain, in the Years 1812–1815* (Washington City: Way and Gideon, 1823), 181–84.

185   *Congress awarded Croghan:* Berton, *Flames Across the Border*, 142.

CHAPTER 15

187   *The British public clamored:* Croker to Warren, March 20, 1813, in *The Naval War of 1812: A Documentary History*, ed. William S. Dudley (Washington, DC: Naval Historical Center, 1992), 2:75–78; First Lord of the Admiralty Lord Melville to Warren, March 26, 1813, in Dudley, ed., *Naval War of 1812*, 2:78–79; First Secretary of the Admiralty John W. Croker to Warren, Jan. 9 and Feb. 10, 1813, in Dudley, ed., *Naval War of 1812*, 2:14–19; *Times* (London), March 20, 24, 1813.

188   *Bladen was anxious to prevent:* Commodore Rodgers to Secretary of the Navy Jones, Sept. 27, 1813, in Dudley, ed., *Naval War of 1812*, 2:251.

188   *the Admiralty, dismayed:* First Secretary of the Admiralty John W. Croker to Station Commanders in Chief, July 10, 1813, in Dudley, ed., *Naval War of 1812*, 2:183–84.

188   *he wrote a clever, insulting letter:* Broke to Lawrence, n.d., in Dudley, ed., *Naval War of 1812*, 2:126–29.

189   *"ready for sea"*: Lawrence to Jones, May 20, 1813, in Albert Gleaves, *James Lawrence, Captain, United States Navy, Commander of the Chesapeake* (New York: Putnam, 1904), 167.

189   *Lawrence wrote to Biddle*: Lawrence to Biddle, May 27, 1813, in Gleaves, *James Lawrence*, 171.

190   *Lieutenant Ludlow wrote*: Augustus Ludlow to Charles Ludlow, May 28, 1813, in Gleaves, *James Lawrence*, 168.

190   *her crew were all experienced*: Writing almost a century later, Admiral Alfred Thayer Mahan claimed that the crew had so many new "untrained men" that it amounted to a "reconstitution of the ship's company." He also emphasized that Lieutenant Ludlow was "extremely young," without explaining his long service in both the navy and the *Chesapeake*. And he claimed that the midshipmen promoted to acting lieutenants were "new to their duties and unknown to their men"; to the contrary, they were experienced officers and, in fact, knew their men well. So although Admiral Mahan was not satisfied with either officers or crew, Lawrence and Ludlow clearly were. Alfred T. Mahan, *Sea Power in Its Relations to the War of 1812* (Boston: Little, Brown, 1905), 2:132.

191   *"My crew appear"*: Lawrence to Jones, June 1, 1813, in Gleaves, *James Lawrence*, 175.

191   *"An English frigate is"*: *"Don't Give Up the Ship": A Catalogue of the Eugene H. Pool Collection of Captain James Lawrence* (Salem, ME: Peabody Museum, 1942), 29.

193   *When Broke saw Ludlow's men*: James Tertius de Kay, *A Rage for Glory: The Life of Commodore Stephen Decatur, USN* (New York: Free Press, 2004), 139–41.

194   *The high casualties*: Lieutenant Budd to Secretary of the Navy William Jones (from Halifax) June 15, 1813, in John Brannan, *Official Letters of the Military and Naval Officers of the United States During the War with Great Britain, in the Years 1812–1815* (Washington City: Way and Gideon, 1823), 167–68; Captain Chapel's account of the *Chesapeake-Shannon* duel, June 6, 1813, in Dudley, ed., *Naval War of 1812*, 2:129–33; C. S. Forester, *The Age of Fighting Sail: The Story of the Naval War of 1812* (New York: Doubleday, 1956), 160–65; Mahan, *Sea Power*, 2:131–48; and Theodore Roosevelt, *The Naval War of 1812* (New York: Modern Library, 1999), 100–109.

194   *In all the confusion*: Charles Morris, *The Autobiography of Commodore Charles Morris USN*, ed. Frederick C. Leiner (Annapolis, MD: Naval Institute Press, 2002), 70.

194   *"the heroism of British"*: *Times* (London), July 9, 1813.

195   *"American vanity"*: *Times* (London), Aug. 16, 1813.

195   *"should any attempt be made"*: Jones's orders to Stewart in June 1813, in Claude Berube and John Rodgaard, *A Call to the Sea: Captain Charles Stewart of the USS Constitution* (Washington, DC: Potomac Books, 2005), 74.

195   *Cox, who considered himself*: *Niles Weekly Register*, July 9, 1814.

195   *In April and May 1813*: Ira Dye, *The Fatal Cruise of the Argus: Two Captains in the War of 1812* (Annapolis, MD: Naval Institute Press, 1994), 144.

197   *Since it was the renowned Decatur*: W. M. P. Dunne, "Inglorious First of June," *Long Island Historical Journal* 2 (Spring, 1990): 214–16.

197   *"I immediately directed"*: Decatur to Jones, June 1813, in Dudley, ed., *Naval War of 1812*, 2:133–34.

198   *They performed a heroic action*: Chauncey to Jones, July 21, 1813, in Dudley, ed., *Naval War of 1812*, 2:523–25.

198   *they were the only possible response*: Alfred Thayer Mahan wrote, "In 1812 and the two years following, the United States flooded the seas with privateers, producing an effect upon British commerce which, though inconclusive singly, doubtless co-operated powerfully with other motives to dispose the enemy to liberal terms of peace. It was . . . the only possible reply to the commercial blockade." Mahan, *Sea Power*, 2:288.

198   *a desperate Congress authorized*: *National Intelligencer*, March 11, 1813; Donald G. Shomette, *Flotilla: The Patuxent Naval Campaign in the War of 1812* (Baltimore: Johns Hopkins University Press, 2009), 5.

198   *Madison commissioned 526 privateers*: David Long, *Ready to Hazard: A Biography of Commodore William Bainbridge, 1774–1833* (Hanover, NH: University Press of New England, 1981), 186–87; Edgar S. Maclay, *A History of American Privateers* (New York: D. Appleton, 1924), viii.

198   *According to Lloyds of London's*: *Times* (London), March 22, 1813.

198   *Britain's privateering*: Alfred L. Burt, *The United States, Great Britain and British North America from the Revolution to the Establishment of Peace After the War of 1812* (Toronto: Ryerson Press, 1940), 318.

CHAPTER 16

199   *"the most complete and vigorous"*: Lords Commissioners of the Admiralty to Admiral Sir John B. Warren, Dec. 26, 1812, in *The Naval War of 1812: A Documentary History*, ed. William S. Dudley (Washington, DC: Naval Historical Center, 1985), 1:633–34.

199   *On December 29*: Warren to Secretary of the Admiralty, John W. Croker, Dec. 29, 1812, in Dudley, ed., *Naval War of 1812*, 1:649–51.

200   *"and kedging the ship"*: Stewart to Jones, Feb. 5, 1813, in Dudley, ed., *Naval War of 1812*, 2:311–12; Claude Berube and John Rodgaard, *A Call to the Sea: Captain Charles Stewart of the USS* Constitution (Washington, DC: Potomac Books, 2005), 66–71.

200   *"by placing . . . boats:"* Stewart to Jones, Feb. 5, 1813, in Dudley, ed., *Naval War of 1812*, 2:312.

200   *Rear Admiral George Cockburn set out*: Cockburn to Warren, March 13, 1813, in Dudley, ed., *Naval War of 1812*, 2:320–24.

200   *"at the same time"*: Cockburn to Warren, March 23, 1813, in Dudley, ed., *Naval War of 1812*, 2:326–29.

201   *On May 2 he attacked*: Charles O. Paullin, *Commodore John Rodgers: A Biography* (Cleveland: Arthur H. Clark, 1910), 279.

202   *"I . . . keep the old Tunisian"*: Dolley Madison to Edward Coles, May 12, 1813, in Dolley Madison, *Memoirs and Letters of Dolly Madison*, edited by her grandniece (Boston: Houghton, Mifflin, 1886; reprint, Port Washington, NY: Kennikat Press, 1971), 89–92; Irving Brant, *James Madison*, vol. 6: *Commander in Chief, 1812–1836* (Indianapolis: Bobbs-Merrill, 1961), 169; Donald G. Shomette, *Flotilla: The Patuxent Naval Campaign in the War of 1812* (Baltimore: Johns Hopkins University Press, 2009), 9.

203   *Smith thought North Point*: Frank A. Cassell, *Merchant Congressman in the Young Republic: Samuel Smith of Maryland, 1752–1839* (Madison: University of Wisconsin Press, 1971), 186–92.

203   *All Secretary Jones did*: Jones to Sinclair, Feb. 17, 1813, in Dudley, ed., *Naval War of 1812*, 2:333.

204   *He wrote later*: Cassin to Jones, June 21, 1813, in Dudley, ed., *Naval War of 1812*, 2:358–59.

204   *He decided to leave*: Jones to Cassin, Feb. 16, 1813, in Dudley, ed., *Naval War of 1812*, 2:313–14.

204   *On June 25, to compensate*: Beckwith to Warren, July 5, 1813, in Dudley, ed., *Naval War of 1812*, 2:364–65.

205   *Warren ordered Cockburn*: Cockburn to Warren, July 12, 1813, in Dudley, ed., *Naval War of 1812*, 2:184–85.

205   *Fulton had obtained his design*: George C. Daughan, *If By Sea: The Forging of the American Navy—From the Revolution to the War of 1812* (New York: Basic Books, 2008), 102–3.

205   *Fulton copied Bushnell's:* James T. Flexner, *Steamboats Come True: American Inventors in Action* (Boston: Little, Brown, 1978), 248–61.

205   *On the sixteenth of July:* Cockburn to Warren, July 16, 1813, in Dudley, ed., *Naval War of 1812*, 2:355–56; *Times* (London), Sept. 8, 1813; Flexner, *Steamboats Come True*, 244–61.

206   *Warren now decided:* Shomette, *Flotilla*, 19.

206   *Joshua Barney wrote:* "Barney's Defense Proposal," in Dudley, ed., *Naval War of 1812*, 2:373–81.

CHAPTER 17

207   *Back on January 20, 1813:* Samuel E. Morison, *Old Bruin: Commodore Matthew Calbraith Perry, 1794–1858* (Boston: Little, Brown, 1967), 8–11.

208   *"Many are the difficulties":* Perry to Commodore Chauncey, April 10, 1813, in *The Naval War of 1812: A Documentary History*, ed. William S. Dudley (Washington, DC: Naval Historical Center, 1992), 2:440–41.

209   *"There is a general want":* Barclay to Proctor, June 29, 1813, in Dudley, ed., *Naval War of 1812*, 2:483.

210   *Barclay was having problems:* Barclay to Prevost, July 16, 1813, and Prevost to Barclay, July 21, 1813, in Dudley, ed., *Naval War of 1812*, 2:544–45.

210   *"a motley set":* Perry to Chauncey, July 27, 1813, and Chauncey to Perry, July 30, 1813, in Dudley, ed., *Naval War of 1812*, 2:529–31.

210   *"removed from this":* Perry to Chauncey, July 27, 1813; Chauncey to Perry, July 30, 1813; Perry to Jones, Aug. 10, 1813; and Jones to Perry, Aug. 18, 1813, in Dudley, ed., *Naval War of 1812*, 2:529–33.

210   *During the greater part:* David Curtis Skaggs and Gerald T. Altoff, *A Signal Victory: The Lake Erie Campaign, 1812–1813* (Annapolis, MD: Naval Institute Press, 1997), 84.

211   *When the haze cleared:* Pierre Berton, *Flames Across the Border: The Canadian-American Tragedy, 1813–1814* (Boston: Little, Brown, 1981), 149–51.

211   *Barclay sailed back to Amherstburg:* Barclay to Yeo, Aug. 5, 1813, in Dudley, ed., *Naval War of 1812*, 2:546–47.

211   *"I have great pleasure":* Perry to Jones, Aug. 4, 1813, in Dudley, ed., *Naval War of 1812*, 2:546.

212   *Harrison was happy to give:* Harrison to Secretary of the Army Armstrong, Sept. 15, 1813, in Dudley, ed., *Naval War of 1812*, 2:565–66.

212   *"I do not hesitate":* Proctor to Noah Freer, British Military Secretary, Sept. 6, 1813, in Dudley, ed., *Naval War of 1812*, 2:552.

212   *"So perfectly destitute":* Barclay to Yeo, Sept. 12, 1813, in Dudley, ed., *Naval War of 1812*, 2:555.

212   *"totally unacquainted":* Barclay to Yeo, Sept. 12, 1813, in Dudley, ed., *Naval War of 1812*, 2:555–57.

212   *In short order, Perry:* Morison, *Old Bruin*, 42.

213   *"against the superior force":* Barclay's report of the battle to Yeo, Sept. 12, 1813, in Dudley, ed., *Naval War of 1812*, 2:555–557.

213   *The* Niagara *and Jesse Elliott:* Alfred T. Mahan, *Sea Power in Its Relations to the War of 1812* (Boston: Little, Brown, 1905), 2:80–89.

214   *"Every brace and bowline":* Perry to Jones, Sept. 13, 1813, in Dudley, ed., *Naval War of 1812*, 2:557.

215   *"I determined to pass":* Perry to Jones, Sept. 13 1813, in Dudley, ed., *Naval War of 1812*, 2:557–59.

216   *"Every poor fellow":* Taylor to his wife, Abby Taylor, Sept. 15, 1813, in Dudley, ed., *Naval War of 1812*, 2:559–60.

216 *"We have met the enemy"*: Perry to Harrison, Sept. 10, 1813, in Dudley, ed., *Naval War of 1812*, 2:553.

216 *"It has pleased the Almighty"*: Perry to Jones, Sept. 10, 1813, in Dudley, ed., *Naval War of 1812*, 2:554.

216 *"[Perry] has immortalized"*: Chauncey to Jones, Sept. 25, 1813, quoted in Robert Malcomson, *Lords of the Lake: The Naval War on Lake Ontario, 1812–1814* (1998; reprint, Montreal: Robin Brass Studio, 2009), 197.

216 *"The greatest cause"*: Barclay to Yeo, Sept. 12, 1813, in Dudley, ed., *Naval War of 1812*, 2:555–56.

216 *He wrote to Earl Bathurst*: Prevost to Bathurst, Sept. 22, 1813, quoted in Malcomson, *Lords of the Lake*, 199.

217 *Perry, with a strong*: Perry to Jones, Sept. n.d., 1813, in Dudley, ed., *Naval War of 1812*, 2:569.

218 *Having always been most*: John R. Elting, *Amateurs to Arms: A Military History of the War of 1812* (Cambridge, MA: DaCapo Press, 1995), 110–15.

218 *For Governor Shelby*: Berton, *Flames Across the Border*, 208; Reginald Horsman, *The War of 1812* (New York: Knopf, 1969), 107–15.

218 *On September 29*: Jones to Perry, Sept. 29, 1813, and Chauncey to Jones, Oct. 13, 1813, in Dudley, ed., *Naval War of 1812*, 2:577–79.

CHAPTER 18

220 *"unprincipled imbecile"*: Winfield Scott, *Memoirs of Lieutenant-General Scott, LLD: Written by Himself* (New York: Sheldon, 1964), 1:37; Timothy D. Johnson, *Winfield Scott: The Quest for Military Glory* (Lawrence: University Press of Kansas, 1998), 10, 34–40.

220 *A tireless self-promoter*: James Ripley Jacobs, *Tarnished Warrior: Major-General James Wilkinson* (New York: Macmillan, 1938), 284–85; Andro Linklater, *An Artist in Treason: The Extraordinary Double Life of General James Wilkinson* (New York: Walker, 2009), 284–88.

220 *He was military commander*: Linklater, *An Artist in Treason*, 299–300.

221 *"You will make Kingston"*: Armstrong to Wilkinson, *American State Papers: Military Affairs* (Washington, DC: Gales & Seaton, 1832–61), 1:464.

221 *"afford the Army"*: Chauncey to Jones, Oct. 30, 1813, in *The Naval War of 1812: A Documentary History*, ed. William S. Dudley (Washington, DC: Naval Historical Center, 1992), 2:594–96.

222 *On September 7 Chauncey*: Chauncey to Jones, Sept. 13, 1813; Yeo to Admiral Warren, Sept. 12, 1813, in Dudley, ed., *Naval War of 1812*, 2:579–81.

222 *During the voyage Wilkinson*: Wilkinson to Brown, Sept. 20, 1813, Jacob Brown Papers, Reel 1, Massachusetts Historical Society.

222 *To relieve his pain*: John D. Morris, *Sword of the Border: Major-General Jacob Jennings Brown, 1775–1828* (Kent, OH: Kent State University Press, 2000), 63.

223 *Chauncey was "mortified"*: Chauncey to Jones, Oct. 30, 1813, in Dudley, ed., *Naval War of 1812*, 2:594–96.

223 *General Brown led*: Wilkinson to Brown, Oct. 28, 1813, Jacob Brown Papers, Reel 1.

223 *On November 2 sloops*: Mulcaster to Yeo, Nov. 2, 1813, in Dudley, ed., *Naval War of 1812*, 2:596–97.

223 *"It is now blowing"*: Chauncey to Jones, Nov. 11, 1813, in Dudley, ed., *Naval War of 1812*, 2:597–98.

223 *he wrote to General Hampton*: Wilkinson to Hampton, Nov. 6, 1813, in John Brannan, *Official Letters of the Military and Naval Officers of the United States During the War*

with Great Britain, in the Years 1812–1815 (Washington City: Way and Gideon, 1823), 258.

224   *People in Washington wondered:* J. C. A. Stagg, *Mr. Madison's War: Politics, Diplomacy, and Warfare in the Early American Republic, 1783–1830* (Princeton, NJ: Princeton University Press, 1983), 363.

224   *Weeks earlier:* Hampton to Armstrong, Nov. 1, 1813, *American State Papers: Military Affairs,* 1:462.

224   *Hampton assumed that Armstrong:* Henry Adams, *History of the United States of America During the Administrations of James Madison* (New York: Library of America, 1986), 759.

224   *Secretary Armstrong knew:* Armstrong to Hampton, Sept. 28, 1813, *American State Papers: Military Affairs,* 1:459.

224   *On that day in October, Hampton:* J. Mackay Hitsman, *The Incredible War of 1812: A Military History* (Montreal: Robin Brass Studio, 1999), 181–87.

224   *In his reply to Wilkinson:* Hampton to Wilkinson, Nov. 8, 1813, Brannan, *Official Letters,* 259–60.

225   *The resulting Battle of Crysler's Farm:* Donald E. Graves, *Field of Glory: The Battle of Crysler's Farm, 1813* (Montreal: Robin Brass Studio, 2000), 185–264.

225   *The following day, Wilkinson:* Graves, *Field of Glory,* 279.

226   *"language to express":* Wilkinson to Hampton, Nov. 12, 1813, in Brannan, *Official Letters,* 268–69; Wilkinson to Brown, Nov. 24 and 26, 1813, Jacob Brown Papers, Reel 1.

226   *"we have and can have":* Alfred T. Mahan, *Sea Power in Its Relations to the War of 1812* (Boston: Little, Brown, 1905), 2:116.

226   *Prevost had mustered well over:* Graves, *Field of Glory,* 83.

226   *Prevost's sizable army:* Reginald Horsman, *The War of 1812* (New York: Knopf, 1969), 126.

226   *Fort George and Fort Niagara were:* Scott to Wilkinson, Oct. 11, 1813, in Brannan, *Official Letters,* 241–44.

227   *On December 19, Drummond:* Drummond to Prevost, Dec. 20, 1813, in Dudley, ed., *Naval War of 1812,* 2:624–25.

227   *"bodies were lying":* *Albany Argus* (New York), Dec. 26, 1813; McClure to Armstrong, Dec. 12, 1813, in Brannan, *Official Letters,* 288–89.

228   *"They gave way and":* Amos Hall to Governor Hopkins, Dec. 30, 1813, in Brannan, *Official Letters,* 289–90.

228   *The armies now went:* Pierre Berton, *Flames Across the Border: The Canadian-American Tragedy, 1813–1814* (Boston: Little, Brown, 1981), 303–14.

CHAPTER 19

229   *"to proceed to sea":* Hull to Burrows, Aug. 28, 1813, in *The Naval War of 1812: A Documentary History,* ed. William S. Dudley (Washington, DC: Naval Historical Center, 1992), 2:233.

230   *The previous year, Blakeley:* Stephen W. H. Duffy, *Captain Blakeley and the Wasp: The Cruise of 1814* (Annapolis, MD: Naval Institute Press, 2001), 95–98.

231   *"with an intention":* Lieutenant Edward R. McCall to Captain Isaac Hull, Sept. 7, 1813, in Dudley, ed., *Naval War of 1812,* 2:235.

231   *"Our brave commander":* *Eastern Argus,* Sept. 8, 1813.

232   *"masts, sails, and spars":* Hull to Bainbridge, quoted in *Eastern Argus,* Sept. 10, 1813.

232   *The* Boxer *had four killed:* Lieutenant David McCrery, R.N., to Commander Alexander Gordon, R.N., Sept. 6, 1813, and Lieutenant Edward R. McCall to Captain Isaac Hull, Sept. 7, 1813, in Dudley, ed., *Naval War of 1812,* 2:235–38.

232   *"A great concourse of people":* *Portland Gazette,* Sept. 13, 1813.

232   *The two young captains:* George C. Daughan, *If By Sea: The Forging of the American Navy—From the Revolution to the War of 1812* (New York: Basic Books, 2008), 442; C. S. Forester, *The Age of Fighting Sail: The Story of the Naval War of 1812* (New York: Doubleday, 1956), 193; Henry Adams, *History of the United States of America During the Administrations of James Madison* (New York: Library of America, 1986), 816.

232   *"endeavored to screen himself":* McCall's charge in Dudley, ed., *Naval War of 1812,* 2:289–92; Sailing Master William Harper to Secretary Jones, Dec. 5, 1813, and Jones to Hull, Dec. 13, 1813, in Dudley, ed., *Naval War of 1812,* 2:289–92.

232   *The triumph of the* Enterprise: Irving Brant, *James Madison,* vol. 6: *Commander in Chief, 1812–1836* (Indianapolis: Bobbs-Merrill, 1961), 20; Linda M. Maloney, *The Captain from Connecticut: The Life and Times of Isaac Hull* (Boston: Northeastern University Press, 1986), 232–34.

233   *Unfortunately, during the last six:* Brant, *James Madison,* vol. 6: *Commander in Chief,* 201–2.

233   *"The wind increases to":* Journal of William Crawford, in Dudley, ed., *Naval War of 1812,* 2:217.

234   *He disguised his ship:* Ira Dye, *The Fatal Cruise of the Argus: Two Captains in the War of 1812* (Annapolis, MD: Naval Institute Press, 1994), 267.

235   *Allen's primary mission:* Dye, *The Fatal Cruise,* 254–55.

236   *Captain Henry Allen and:* Commander Maples to Admiral Thornborough, Aug. 12, 1813, in Dudley, ed., *Naval War of 1812,* 2:223; Dye, *The Fatal Cruise,* 276–79.

236   *"The victory of the* Pelican": *Times* (London), Aug. 24, 1813.

236   *The scandal of trading:* Annals of Congress, 13th Cong., 1st Session, 55, 485; Donald R. Hickey, *The War of 1812: A Forgotten Conflict* (Urbana: University of Illinois Press, 1989), 123, 373.

236   *The first two months of Rodgers's:* Charles O. Paullin, *Commodore John Rodgers: Captain, Commodore, and Senior Officer of the American Navy, 1773-1838* (1909; reprint, Annapolis, MD: United States Naval Institute, 1967), 265–66.

237   *All the Norwegians could:* Paullin, *Commodore John Rodgers,* 265–66.

237   *They did so well:* Alfred T. Mahan, *Sea Power in Its Relations to the War of 1812* (Boston: Little, Brown, 1905), 2:223.

237   *Ironically, Rodgers was:* Paullin, *Commodore John Rodgers,* 268–69.

238   *One of Rodgers's lieutenants:* Paullin, *Commodore John Rodgers,* 270; *Times* (London), Nov. 13, 1813.

239   *"a particularly fine vessel":* Beresford to Warren, Jan. 9, 1813, in Dudley, ed., *Naval War of 1812,* 2:27.

239   *"I made the best disposition":* Warren to Croker, Oct. 16, 1813 in Dudley, ed., *Naval War of 1812,* 2:261.

239   *In the end, Rodgers's cruise:* Rodgers to Secretary Jones, Sept. 27, 1813, in Dudley, ed., *Naval War of 1812,* 2:250–55.

240   *"the channel is very narrow":* Decatur to Jones, June 6, 1813, in Dudley, ed., *Naval War of 1812,* 2:136–37.

240   *"a quantity of powder":* Master Commandant Jacob Lewis to Secretary Jones, June 28, 1813, and Hardy to Warren, June 26, 1813, in Dudley, ed., *Naval War of 1812,* 2:161–62.

241   *David Bushnell's famous* Turtle: Daughan, *If By Sea,* 102–3.

241   *the bomb the new submarine:* Jacob Lewis to Secretary Jones, June 28, 1813, in Dudley, ed., *Naval War of 1812,* 2:161; Spencer Tucker, *Stephen Decatur: A Life Most Bold and Daring* (Annapolis, MD: Naval Institute Press, 2005), 129.

241   *"Decatur has lost very":* Quoted in David Long, *Sailor-Diplomat: A Biography of Commodore James Biddle, 1783-1848* (Boston: Northeastern University Press, 1983), 48.

241   *By December 12, he was ready:* Decatur to Secretary Jones, Dec. 20, 1813, in James Tertius de Kay, *The Battle of Stonington: Torpedoes, Submarines, and Rockets in the*

War of 1812 (Annapolis, MD: Naval Institute Press, 1990), 86–87; Robert J. Allison, *Stephen Decatur: American Naval Hero, 1779–1820* (Amherst: University of Massachusetts Press, 2005), 135.

242   *Connecticut Federalists did indeed:* Brant, *James Madison*, vol. 6: *Commander in Chief*, 233.

242   *"Sir Thomas Hardy soon acquired":* Frances M. Caulkins, *History of New London, Connecticut, from the First Survey of the Coast in 1612 to 1852* (Hartford, CT: Case, Tiffany, 1852), 631.

242   *In the middle of December 1813:* Maloney, *Captain from Connecticut*, 235–36.

242   *The Congress was the least:* Adams, *History of the United States*, 816–17.

243   *"dark nights and":* Warren to Croker, Dec. 30, 1813, in Dudley, ed., *Naval War of 1812*, 2:307–8.

244   *Porter was also occupying:* George F. G. Stanley, *The War of 1812: Land Operations* (Toronto: Macmillan of Canada, 1983), 163–65; Mark Zuehlke, *For Honor's Sake: The War of 1812 and the Brokering of an Uneasy Peace* (Toronto: Alfred A. Knopf Canada, 2006), 211.

244   *The war was going far worse:* In another disappointment for the navy in 1813, the schooner *Vixen*, under Sailing Master Thomas Hall, had been captured by an old nemesis, Captain Richard Byron and the *Belvidera*, on Christmas Day, off the Delaware Capes. Byron brought her to Bermuda as a prize.

CHAPTER 20

246   *"Whilst Bonaparte was":* *Times* (London), Feb. 3, 1814.

246   *part of Frederick William's army:* Alan Schom, *Napoleon Bonaparte: A Life* (New York: HarperCollins, 1997), 655.

247   *The allied armies were able:* Schom, *Napoleon*, 658–65.

247   *Instead of pressing his advantage:* Georges Lefebvre, *Napoleon: From Tilsit to Waterloo, 1807–1815*, trans. J. E. Anderson (Paris, 1936; reprint, New York: Columbia University Press, 1990), 330–31.

247   *Bonaparte saw with great:* Schom, *Napoleon*, 665.

247   *Shortly after the armistice began:* Lefebvre, *Napoleon*, 331–32.

248   *When the armies took:* Dominic Lieven, *Russia Against Napoleon: The True Story of the Campaigns of War and Peace* (New York: Viking, 2010), 362–363.

248   *The Battle of Leipzig took place:* Lieven, *Russia Against Napoleon*, 458.

249   *The Bramble also carried:* Castlereagh to Monroe, Nov. 4, 1813, and Monroe to Castlereagh, Jan. 5, 1814, in *American State Papers: Foreign Relations* (Washington, DC: Gales & Seaton, 1833–58), 3:621–29; Harry Ammon, *James Monroe: The Quest for National Identity* (Charlottesville: University Press of Virginia, 1990), 325.

249   *At the beginning of 1814:* Irving Brant, *James Madison*, vol. 6: *Commander in Chief, 1812–1836* (Indianapolis: Bobbs-Merrill, 1961), 238–39.

250   *Losing more contact:* Schom, *Napoleon*, 683.

251   *"The whole nation will":* Quoted in Charles Esdaile, *Napoleon's Wars: An International History, 1803–1815* (New York: Viking, 2008), 525.

251   *"the cry of Vive Louis":* *Times* (London), April 8, 1914.

252   *"heartfelt and universal joy.":* *Times* (London), April 11, 1814.

252   *"I own that, while I rejoice":* Jefferson to John Adams, July 15, 1814, in *The Adams-Jefferson Letters: The Complete Correspondence Between Thomas Jefferson and Abigail and John Adams*, ed. Lester J. Cappon (Chapel Hill: University of North Carolina Press, 1988), 430–34.

252   *"The reinforcements for":* *Times* (London), April 11, 1814.

252   *"There is no public feeling"*: *Times* (London), April 15, 1814.

252   *"unprincipled"* and *"contemptible"*: *Morning Post* (London), Jan. 27, 1814, quoted in Adams, *History of the United States*, 1187.

252   The *Courier* *was equally vicious*: *Courier* (London), Jan. 27, 1814, quoted in Adams, *History of the United States*, 1187–8.

252   *"immediately transferred to America"*: *Times* (London), April 15, 1814.

CHAPTER 21

255   *Their grandiose strategy included*: Samuel Flagg Bemis, *John Quincy Adams and the Foundations of American Foreign Policy* (New York: Knopf, 1950), 198–99.

256   *"Is it desirable to take"*: Viscount Castlereagh to Lord Liverpool, Aug. 28, 1814, in Robert Stewart Castlereagh, *Correspondence, Despatches, and Other Papers of Viscount Castlereagh, Second Marquess of Londonderry* (London: H. Colburn, 1848–53), 10:62–63.

256   *"A well organized and large army"*: *The Papers of Henry Clay*, ed. James F. Hopkins (Lexington: University Press of Kentucky, 1959), 1:883–85.

257   *Only 13,000 were dispatched*: J. Mackay Hitsman, *The Incredible War of 1812: A Military History* (Montreal: Robin Brass Studio, 1999), 232; Jon Latimer, *1812: War with America* (Cambridge, MA: Harvard University Press, 2007), 339.

258   *"I have it much at heart"*: Cochrane to Bathurst, July 14, 1812, in *The Naval War of 1812: A Documentary History*, ed. Michael Crawford (Washington, DC: Naval Historical Center, 2002), 3:131.

259   *Nonetheless, Prevost was expected*: Bathurst to Prevost, June 3, 1814, quoted in Hitsman, *The Incredible War of 1812*, 287–88.

259   *Bitter cold, poor food*: Wilkinson to Brown, Dec. 18, 1813, Jacob Brown Papers, Reel 1, Massachusetts Historical Society.

260   *the army had leadership*: The new leaders would guide the army until the Civil War. Russell F. Weigley, *History of the United States Army* (New York: Macmillan, 1967), 123; Irving Brant, *James Madison*, vol. 6: *Commander in Chief, 1812–1836* (Indianapolis: Bobbs-Merrill, 1961), 252–53; John R. Elting, *Amateurs to Arms: A Military History of the War of 1812* (Cambridge, MA: DaCapo Press, 1995), 177.

260   *Congress approved Madison's request*: Brant, *James Madison*, vol. 6: *Commander in Chief*, 252.

260   *By the spring of 1814*: Donald R. Hickey, *The War of 1812: A Forgotten Conflict* (Urbana: University of Illinois Press, 1989), 183.

260   *"where twenty of his ships"*: Jones to Madison, May 25, 1814, in Crawford, ed., *Naval War of 1812*, 3:495–96.

261   *"Every possible resource"*: Jones to Chauncey, Jan. 15, 1814, in Crawford, ed., *Naval War of 1812*, 3:386.

261   *he "could meet the enemy"*: Jones to Macdonough, Dec. 7, 1813, in *The Naval War of 1812: A Documentary History*, ed. William S. Dudley (Washington, DC: Naval Historical Center, 1992), 2:605.

261   *At the end of December 1813*: Macdonough to Jones, Dec. 28, 1813, in Dudley, ed., *Naval War of 1812*, 2:606.

261   *To help Yeo win*: Reginald Horsman, *The War of 1812* (New York: Knopf, 1969), 139.

261   *the "war of the dockyards"*: Robert Malcomson, *Lords of the Lake: The Naval War on Lake Ontario, 1812–1814* (1998; reprint, Montreal: Robin Brass Studio, 2009), 225.

261   *During the winter, Yeo*: Robert Malcomson, *Warships of the Great Lakes, 1754–1834* (Edison, NJ: Knickerbocker Press, 2004), 102; Malcomson, *Lords of the Lake*: 225.

262   *"The increase pay and bounty"*: Chauncey to Jones, March 7, 1813, in Crawford, ed., *Naval War of 1812*, 3:401.

262   *In early March Brown:* Armstrong to Brown, Feb. 24, 1814, Jacob Brown Papers, Reel 1.

262   *He was under the impression:* Brown to Chauncey, March 24, 1814, and Armstrong to Brown, Feb. 28, 1814, in Jacob Brown Papers, Reel 1.

262   *Nonetheless, when Armstrong discovered:* Armstrong to Brown, March 20, 1814, and April 7, 1814, in Jacob Brown Papers, Reel 1.

262   *Armstrong, without the administration:* C. Edward Skeen, *John Armstrong, Jr., 1758–1843: A Biography* (Syracuse, NY: Syracuse University Press, 1981), 177–78; John D. Morris, *Sword of the Border: Major-General Jacob Jennings Brown, 1775–1828* (Kent, OH: Kent State University Press, 2000), 77.

263   *Admiral Yeo and Lieutenant General:* Drummond to Prevost, April 28, 1814, and Prevost to Drummond, April 30, 1814, in *The Documentary History of the Campaign upon the Niagara Frontier, 1812–1814*, ed. E. A. Cruikshank (Welland, Ontario: Lundy's Lane Historical Society, 1908), 9:313–14, 318–19.

263   *After putting up what fight:* Lieutenant-Colonel Mitchell to General Brown, May 6, 1814, in Jacob Brown Papers, Reel 1; Jones to Madison, May 25, 1814, in Crawford, ed., *Naval War of 1812*, 3:495; Yeo to Croker, May 9, 1813, in Crawford, ed., *Naval War of 1812*, 3:477–79; Lieutenant-Colonel George Mitchell to Major-General Jacob Brown, May 8, 1814, in Crawford, ed., *Naval War of 1812*, 3:474–76; Horsman, *The War of 1812*, 173–74.

263   *"If Sir James had landed":* Chauncey to Jones, June 15, 1815, in Crawford, ed., *Naval War of 1812*, 3:522.

263   *He had placed General Gaines:* Morris, *Sword of the Border*, 80.

264   *Woolsey had laid a clever:* Major Daniel Appling to Brown, May 30, 1814, in Jacob Brown Papers, Reel 1.

264   *On June 6 Yeo returned:* Major Daniel Appling to Brigadier-General Edmund P. Gaines, May 30, 1814, and Woolsey to Chauncey, June 1, 1814, in Crawford, ed., *Naval War of 1812*, 3:508–12; Malcomson, *Warships of the Great Lakes*, 108–9, 295–96.

265   *It would not be until:* Malcomson, *Lords of the Lake*, 307–8.

265   *Recruiting offices were:* Rodney Macdonough, *The Life of Commodore Thomas Macdonough, U.S. Navy* (Boston: Fort Hill Press, 1909), 145.

266   *Pring's bomb vessel:* Macdonough to Jones, May 14, 1814, in Macdonough, *Life of Commodore Thomas Macdonough*, 142.

266   *Macdonough then moved his fleet:* Macdonough, *Life of Commodore Thomas Macdonough*, 146.

266   *"I find the* Saratoga *to be":* Macdonough to Jones, May 29, 1814, quoted in Macdonough, *Life of Commodore Thomas Macdonough*, 147.

267   *"I determined to make them":* Campbell to Armstrong, May 18, 1814, in Crawford, ed., *The Naval War of 1812*, 3:486–87.

267   *When Lieutenant General Drummond:* Colonel John B. Campbell to Armstrong, May 18, 1814, in Crawford, ed., *Naval War of 1812*, 3:486–87; Captain Arthur Sinclair to Jones, May 19, 1814, in Crawford, ed., *Naval War of 1812*, 3:487–89; Drummond to Prevost, May 27, 1814, in Crawford, ed., *Naval War of 1812*, 3:141, 489–90; Hitsman, *The Incredible War of 1812*, 219.

268   *he gathered the cabinet:* Brant, *James Madison*, vol. 6: *Commander in Chief*, 259, 263.

268   *The president also decided:* Notes on Cabinet Meeting, June 7, 1814, in Crawford, ed., *Naval War of 1812*, 3:497–98.

269   *"excited much regret":* Jones to Sinclair, June 1, 1814, in Crawford, ed., *Naval War of 1812*, 3:513–14. A court of inquiry with General Scott as president also condemned the destruction of private property.

269   *"Mackinac is by nature":* Sinclair to Jones, Aug. 9, 1814, in Crawford, ed., *Naval War of 1812*, 3:568–70.

269   *"Our men were shot"*: Sinclair to Jones, Aug. 9, 1814, in Crawford, ed., *Naval War of 1812*, 3:568–70.

269   *Seeing no way to attain*: Diary of Surgeon Usher Parsons on the Brig Lawrence, in Crawford, ed., *Naval War of 1812*, 3:558–62.

270   *The Scorpion had been fifteen*: Lieutenant Andrew H. Bulger, Royal Newfoundland Fensible Infantry, to Lieutenant Colonel Robert McDouall, British Army, Sept. 7,1814, in Crawford, ed., *Naval War of 1812*, 3:605; Hitsman, *The Incredible War of 1812*, 236; Elting, *Amateurs to Arms*, 274–80; Barry Gough, *Fighting Sail on Lake Huron and Georgian Bay: The War of 1812 and Its Aftermath* (Annapolis, MD: Naval Institute Press, 2002), 103–12.

270   *Not long afterward, McDouall*: Horsman, *The War of 1812*, 169–72.

270   *The administration, meanwhile*: Brown to Peter B. Porter, May 19, 1814, in Jacob Brown Papers, Reel 1; Armstrong to Brown, May 25, 1814, in Jacob Brown Papers, Reel 1; Armstrong to Izard, June 10, 1814, in Crawford, ed., *Naval War of 1812*, 3:498–99.

271   *"To give . . . immediate occupation"*: Armstrong to Brown, June 2, 1814, in Jacob Brown Papers, Reel 1; Armstrong to Brown, June 10, 1814, in Crawford, ed., *Naval War of 1812*, 3:500.

271   *At eight o'clock Buck fired*: Donald E. Graves, *Where Right and Glory Lead! The Battle of Lundy's Lane, 1814* (Montreal: Robin Brass Studio, 1999), 75–76.

272   *"For completeness, Scott's victory"*: Henry Adams, *History of the United States of America During the Administrations of James Madison* (New York: Library of America, 1986), 937–38.

272   *Chippawa was a source of immense pride*: The best account of the battle is in Donald E. Graves, *Red Coats & Grey Jackets: The Battle of Chippawa, 5 July 1814* (Toronto: Dundurn Press, 1994), 79–135; see also Graves, *Where Right and Glory Lead*, 75–92; Elting, *Amateurs to Arms*, 187. The grey uniforms of the cadets at West Point were not chosen in 1816 to commemorate Scott's grey uniforms, but the legend that they were has persisted.

273   *he had made it clear*: Chauncey to Brown, June 25, 1814, in Crawford, ed., *Naval War of 1812*, 3:527.

273   *"The slaughter had"*: General Brown to Major Samuel Brown, July 30, 1814, in Jacob Brown Papers, Reel 1.

274   *"victory was complete"*: Porter to Tompkins, July 29, 1814, quoted in Graves, *Where Right and Glory Lead*, 208.

CHAPTER 22

277   *"I hope to be able"*: Cochrane to Prevost, March 11, 1814, in *The Naval War of 1812: A Documentary History*, ed. Michael Crawford (Washington, DC: Naval Historical Center, 2002), 3:38–39.

277   *As Cochrane thought about*: Cochrane to Croker, March 8, 1814, in Wade G. Dudley, *Splintering the Wooden Wall: The British Blockade of the United States, 1812–1815* (Annapolis, MD: Naval Institute Press, 2003), 116.

277   *The British blockade now ran*: Cochrane to Bathurst, July 14, 1814, in Alfred T. Mahan, *Sea Power in Its Relations to the War of 1812* (Boston: Little, Brown, 1905), 2:330–31.

278   *"be taught to know"*: James A. Pack, *The Man Who Burned the White House: Admiral Sir George Cockburn, 1772–1853* (Annapolis, MD: Naval Institute Press, 1987), 166–67.

278   *"free settlers into some"*: Quoted in J. Mackay Hitsman, *The Incredible War of 1812: A Military History* (Montreal: Robin Brass Studio, 1999), 238.

278   *Bathurst prohibited Cochrane*: Bathurst to Major General Edward Barnes, May 20, 1814, in Crawford, ed., *Naval War of 1812*, 3:72–74.

280   *Decatur had some hope:* Spencer Tucker, *Stephen Decatur: A Life Most Bold and Daring* (Annapolis, MD: Naval Institute Press, 2005), 133–34.

280   *Beginning on March 17:* Tucker, *Stephen Decatur,* 137; Robert J. Allison, *Stephen Decatur: American Naval Hero, 1779–1820* (Amherst: University of Massachusetts Press, 2005), 136–37.

280   *With the coming of warm spring:* Tucker, *Stephen Decatur,* 137; and David Long, *Sailor-Diplomat: A Biography of Commodore James Biddle, 1783–1848* (Boston: Northeastern University Press, 1983), 48–49.

280   *"It is a most infamous arrangement":* Long, *Sailor-Diplomat,* 50.

281   *At one point in July:* Tucker, *Stephen Decatur,* 139.

281   *"a challenge ship":* Jones to Gordon, Jan. 5, 1814, in Crawford, ed., *Naval War of 1812,* 3:6–7.

281   *In April, Jones directed:* Jones to Gordon, April 15, 1814, in Crawford, ed., *Naval War of 1812,* 3:13.

281   *Jones gave up on Ridgely:* Jones to Ridgely, April 4, 1814, in Crawford, ed., *Naval War of 1812,* 3:31–32.

282   *The* Ontario *was ready:* Jones to Spence, April 4, 1814; Spence to Jones, April 9, 1814; Jones to Spence, April 18, 1814, in Crawford, ed., *Naval War of 1812,* 3:23–24.

CHAPTER 23

283   *On July 6, 1814, at five:* Porter to Jones, July 9, 1814, in *The Naval War of 1812: A Documentary History,* ed. Michael Crawford (Washington, DC: Naval Historical Center, 2002), 3:764–65.

283   *on January 5, 1813, the ubiquitous:* Lieutenant William B. Finch to Secretary Jones, Feb. 13, 1813, in *The Naval War of 1812: A Documentary History,* ed. William S. Dudley (Washington, DC: Naval Historical Center, 1992), 2:684–85.

283   *Porter continued to the second:* Porter to Bainbridge, March 23, 1813, in Dudley, ed., *Naval War of 1812,* 2:688–89.

285   *"perhaps the most barren":* Porter to Jones, July 3, 1814, in Crawford, ed., *Naval War of 1812,* 3:730–33.

285   *Porter turned his finest:* Porter to Secretary of the Navy Hamilton, July 2, 1813, in Dudley, ed., *Naval War of 1812,* 2:697–99.

285   *"It seems somewhat":* David Porter, *Journal of a Cruise* (1815; reprint, Annapolis, MD: Naval Institute Press, 1986), 204.

286   *Viewing the natives:* Porter, *Journal of a Cruise,* 355.

286   *To support Gamble:* John M. Gamble to Secretary of the Navy, Aug. 28, 1815, in John Brannan, *Official Letters of the Military and Naval Officers of the United States During the War with Great Britain, in the Years 1812–1815* (Washington City: Way and Gideon, 1823), 362.

287   *Porter held his fire:* Porter, *Journal of a Cruise,* 476.

288   *The* Essex *had forty:* Theodore Roosevelt, *The Naval War of 1812* (New York: Modern Library, 1999), 170; Alfred T. Mahan, *Sea Power in Its Relations to the War of 1812* (Boston: Little, Brown, 1905), 2:248.

288   *"appeared determined to defend":* Porter to Jones, July 3, 1814, in Crawford, ed., *Naval War of 1812,* 3:734.

288   *The grisly slaughter went on:* Porter to Jones, July 3, 1814, in Crawford, ed., *Naval War of 1812,* 3:733–37; Porter, *Journal of a Cruise,* 452–60.

288   *"history does not afford":* Roosevelt, *The Naval War of 1812,* 171.

288   *"More bravery, skill, patriotism"*: Porter, *Journal of a Cruise*, 458.

288   *"We have been unfortunate"*: Porter, *Journal of a Cruise*, 459.

289   *"I must in justification of myself"*: Porter, *Journal of a Cruise*, 460.

289   *"In the first place, I consider that"*: David G. Farragut, "Some Reminiscences of Early Life," in Crawford, ed., *Naval War of 1812*, 3:751–52.

289   *Good weather accompanied*: David Long, *Nothing Too Daring: A Biography of Commodore David Porter, 1780–1843* (Annapolis, MD: Naval Institute Press, 1970), 165.

289   *Lieutenant Gamble, meanwhile*: Gamble to Secretary of the Navy, Aug. 28, 1815, in Brannan, *Official Letters*, 362–66; Long, *Nothing Too Daring*, 135–41.

290   *"the loss is hidden"*: President's Message to Congress, Sept. 20, 1814, in Brannan, *Official Letters*, 431–35. The *Essex*, despite her injuries, was repaired and brought to England, where she was taken into the Royal Navy and served until 1837.

CHAPTER 24

291   *On April 4, Rear Admiral Cockburn*: Roger Morriss, *Cockburn and the British Navy in Transition: Admiral Sir George Cockburn, 1772–1853* (Columbia: University of South Carolina Press, 1997), 99; Donald G. Shomette, *Flotilla: The Patuxent Naval Campaign in the War of 1812* (Baltimore: Johns Hopkins University Press, 2009), 74.

293   *On June 10 Barrie made*: Shomette, *Flotilla*, 92–101; Louis Arthur Norton, *Joshua Barney: Hero of the Revolution and 1812*, Library of Naval Biography (Annapolis, MD: Naval Institute Press, 2000), 168–77.

293   *"so far into the country"*: Croker to Cochrane, April 4, 1814, and Crocker to Cochrane, May 19, 1814, in *The Naval War of 1812: A Documentary History*, ed. Michael Crawford (Washington, DC: Naval Historical Center, 2002), 3:70–72.

293   *"effect a diversion"*: Secretary of State for War and the Colonies Earl Bathurst to Major General Edward Barnes, British Army, May 20, 1814, in Crawford, ed., *Naval War of 1812*, 3:72–74.

293   *"assist in inflicting"*: Quoted in Henry Adams, *History of the United States of America During the Administrations of James Madison* (New York: Library of America, 1986), 998.

294   *"to destroy and lay waste"*: Orders of Vice Admiral Cochrane, July 18, 1814, in Bryan Perrett, *The Real Hornblower: The Life of Admiral Sir James Gordon, GCB* (Annapolis, MD: Naval Institute Press, 1997), 106.

294   *Over a month later Cochrane*: Cochrane to Monroe, Aug. 13, 1814, and Monroe to Cochrane, Sept. 6, 1814, reprinted in *Salem Gazette*, Sept. 16, 1814, 6.

294   *"from his throne"*: Cochrane to Cockburn, July 1, 1814, in Crawford ed., *Naval War of 1812*, 3:129–30.

294   *He was also impressed*: Anthony S. Pitch, *The Burning of Washington: The British Invasion of 1814* (Annapolis, MD: Naval Institute Press, 1998), 19; Cochrane to Croker, July 23, 1814, in Crawford, ed., *Naval War of 1812*, 3:135–36.

294   *"It is quite impossible"*: Cockburn to Cochrane, July 17, 1814, in Crawford, ed., *Naval War of 1812*, 3:136–37.

294   *"within forty-eight hours"*: Cockburn to Cochrane, July 17, 1814, in Crawford, ed., *Naval War of 1812*, 3:137–39; Irving Brant, *James Madison*, vol. 6: *Commander in Chief, 1812–1836* (Indianapolis: Bobbs-Merrill, 1961), 285; Shomette, *Flotilla*, 253.

295   *At one time Monroe*: Harry Ammon, *James Monroe: The Quest for National Identity* (Charlottesville: University Press of Virginia, 1990), 328–29.

295   *"the éclat that would"*: Rush report in Brant, *James Madison*, vol. 6: *Commander in Chief*, 270–71.

295   *Madison thought a force*: Brant, *James Madison*, vol. 6: *Commander in Chief*, 271–72.

295   *Secretary Armstrong was in charge:* C. Edward Skeen, *John Armstrong, Jr.: A Biography 1758–1843* (Syracuse, NY: Syracuse University Press, 1981), 189.

295   *He had been one of the key:* James E. Elliott, *Strange Fatality: The Battle of Stoney Creek, 1813* (Montreal: Robin Brass Studio, 2009).

296   *Armstrong was indifferent:* John K. Mahon, *The War of 1812* (1972; reprint, New York: DaCapo Press, 1991), 292; Skeen, *John Armstrong, Jr.,* 187–93.

297   *Gordon, who had the temporary rank:* Perrett, *The Real Hornblower,* 111.

298   *"The enemy has entered":* Charles O. Paullin, *Commodore John Rodgers A Biography* (Cleveland: Arthur H. Clark, 1910), 284.

298   *Barney knew they were:* Norton, *Joshua Barney,* 178–79.

298   *The night of the twenty-second:* Cockburn to Cochrane, Aug. 22, 1814, in Crawford, ed., *Naval War of 1812,* 3:195–96.

299   *"the sooner the army":* Morriss, *Cockburn and the British Navy in Transition,* 106.

299   *Incredibly, Winder at no time:* Court of Inquiry on Winder, in *Niles' Weekly Register,* Feb. 25, 1815. General Winfield Scott presided. The court exonerated Winder.

300   *President Madison was on:* Mahon, *War of 1812,* 295–300; Shomette, *Flotilla,* 306–27; Brant, *James Madison,* vol. 6: *Commander in Chief,* 301–3.

301   *Barney could not go:* Shomette, *Flotilla,* 326–27; James A. Pack, *The Man Who Burned the White House: Admiral Sir George Cockburn, 1772–1853* (Annapolis, MD: Naval Institute Press, 1987), 15.

301   *There were 71 American:* Shomette, *Flotilla,* 329.

301   *An hour earlier:* Brant, *James Madison,* vol. 6: *Commander in Chief,* 306–7.

301   *The day before:* Brant, *James Madison,* vol. 6: *Commander in Chief,* 295.

301   *Many of the documents dated:* Brant, *James Madison,* vol. 6: *Commander in Chief,* 292; Edward D. Ingraham, *Sketches of the Events Which Preceded the Capture of Washington* (Philadelphia: Carey and Hart, 1849), 48.

301   *Shortly after Dolley's:* Brant, *James Madison,* vol. 6: *Commander in Chief,* 306–8.

302   *Ross and Cockburn entered:* Pack, *The Man Who Burned the White House,* 187–90; *National Intelligencer,* Aug. 24, 1814.

302   *The British rampage through the city:* Ross's account of the entire battle and the burning of Washington is given in his letter, Ross to Bathurst, Aug. 30, 1814, in Crawford, ed., *Naval War of 1812,* 3:223–26.

302   *"If . . . you should attack":* Quoted in Robin Reilly, *The British at the Gates: The New Orleans Campaign in the War of 1812* (Montreal: Robin Brass Studio, 2002), 167–68.

303   *"a deliberate disregard":* *National Intelligencer,* Sept. 1.

304   *The fort had a battery:* Gordon to Cochrane, Sept. 9, 1814, in Crawford, ed., *Naval War of 1812,* 3:238; Walter Lord, *The Dawn's Early Light* (New York: Norton, 1972), 197.

304   *"annoy or destroy the enemy":* Jones to Rodgers, Aug. 28, 1814, in Crawford, ed., *Naval War of 1812,* 3:242–43.

304   *he angrily ordered Rodgers:* Jones to Rodgers, Aug. 29, 1814, in Crawford, ed., *Naval War of 1812,* 3:243.

304   *Rodgers immediately dispatched:* Rodgers to Jones, Aug. 29, 1814 in Crawford, ed., *Naval War of 1812,* 3:244.

304   *"to effect the destruction":* Jones to Porter, Aug. 31, 1814, in Crawford, ed., *Naval War of 1812,* 3:245.

304   *Monroe, in desperation, suggested:* Monroe to Rodgers, Sept. 2, 1814, in Crawford, ed., *Naval War of 1812,* 3:245.

305   *Rodgers tried again:* Rodgers to Jones, Sept. 9, 1814, in Crawford, ed., *Naval War of 1812,* 3:256–58.

305   *"that it was not want":* Porter to Jones, Sept. 7, 1814, in Crawford, ed., *Naval War of 1812,* 3:251–55; Hungerford to Monroe, Sept. 9, 1814, in John Brannan, *Official Letters*

of the Military and Naval Officers of the United States During the War with Great Britain, in the Years 1812-1815 (Washington City: Way and Gideon, 1823), 409–10.

305 *Oliver Hazard Perry was the last:* Perry to Jones, Sept. 9, 1814, in Crawford, ed., *Naval War of 1812*, 3:256.

306 *Before Gordon extricated:* Gordon to Cochrane, Sept. 9, 1814, in Crawford, ed., *Naval War of 1812*, 3:242; Lord, *The Dawn's Early Light*, 245–46.

306 *Even Boston was finally:* David Long, *Ready to Hazard: A Biography of Commodore William Bainbridge, 1774-1833* (Hanover, NH: University Press of New England, 1981), 184.

306 *"been continually employed":* Captain Sir Peter Parker to Cochrane, Aug. 30, 1814, in Crawford, ed., *Naval War of 1812*, 3:232–33.

306 *On August 30, after:* Lieutenant Colonel Philip Reid, Maryland Militia, to Brigadier General Benjamin Chambers, Maryland Militia, Sept. 3, 1814, in Crawford, ed., *Naval War of 1812*, 3:235–36; Lieutenant Henry Crease, R.N., to Cochrane, Sept. 1, 1814, in Crawford, ed., *Naval War of 1812*, 3:234–35.

307 *"The Federalists now have":* *Salem Gazette*, Sept. 9, 1814, 7.

307 *On April 7-8, 1814:* Richard Buel Jr., *America on the Brink: How the Political Struggle Over the War of 1812 Almost Destroyed the Young Republic* (New York: Palgrave Macmillan, 2005), 212.

307 *On June 16, Hardy reported:* Linda M. Maloney, *The Captain from Connecticut: The Life and Times of Isaac Hull* (Boston: Northeastern University Press, 1986), 248–49; Hardy to Cochrane, June 16, 1814, in James Tertius de Kay, *The Battle of Stonington: Torpedoes, Submarines, and Rockets in the War of 1812* (Annapolis, MD: Naval Institute Press, 1990), 111–12.

307 *The* Times *of London would certainly:* *Times* (London), July 2, 1814.

308 *The eighty-six American defenders:* De Kay, *The Battle of Stonington*, 114–19.

308 *"On the night of 20-21 June":* Long, *Ready to Hazard*, 180.

309 *The bombardment resumed:* De Kay, *The Battle of Stonington*, 146–87; Hardy to Hotham, Aug. 12, 1814, in De Kay, *The Battle of Stonington*, 187.

309 *The tiny American garrison:* Adams, *History of the United States*, 974–75.

309 *"The district we speak of":* Quoted in De Kay, *The Battle of Stonington*, 120.

CHAPTER 25

313 *a court of inquiry:* Charles Berube and John Rodgaard, *A Call to the Sea: Captain Charles Stewart and the USS* Constitution (Washington, DC: Potomac Books, 2005), 76–83.

313 *Bainbridge stood out from Boston:* William James, *The Naval History of Great Britain from the Declaration of War Against France in 1793 to the Accession of George IV* (London: Richard Bentley, 1847), 6:290–91; Henry Adams, *History of the United States of America During the Administrations of James Madison* (New York: Library of America, 1986), 1037–38.

314 *In desperation, Wales:* James, *The Naval History of Great Britain*, 6:291–94; Adams, *History of the United States*, 1038–39; Warrington to Jones, April 29, 1814, in Letters Received by the Secretary of the Navy from Commanders, National Archives, Washington, DC.

315 *British Admiral Edward Codrington insisted:* Lady Bourchier, ed., *Memoir of the Life of Admiral Sir Edward Codrington* (London: Longsman, Green, 1873), 1:310.

315 *By nightfall, Warrington had:* Alfred T. Mahan, *Sea Power in Its Relations to the War of 1812* (Boston: Little, Brown, 1905), 2:261.

315 *During this long voyage:* Warrington's report of this cruise in *Niles' Weekly Register*, Nov. 11, 1814.

316 *"We have experienced":* Blakely to Jones, July 10, 1814, in Stephen W. H. Duffy, *Captain Blakeley and the* Wasp: *The Cruise of 1814* (Annapolis, MD: Naval Institute Press, 2001), 224.

317   *In the next four days:* Duffy, *Captain Blakeley and the* Wasp, 202–14; Mahan, *Sea Power*, 2:253–55.

317   *Three weeks later:* Mahan, *Sea Power*, 2:252–53.

318   *By daylight, Morris was:* Charles Morris, *The Autobiography of Commodore Charles Morris, USN* (Annapolis, MD: Naval Institute Press, 2002), 72.

319   *"let the lower anchors":* Morris, *Autobiography*, 74.

319   *On July 19 Morris met:* Morris, *Autobiography*, 74; Theodore Roosevelt, *The Naval War of 1812* (New York: Random House, 1996), 185–86.

319   *On August 17 the fog was:* Morris, *Autobiography*, 75.

320   *On the morning of September 2:* Morris, *Autobiography*, 82.

320   *Secretary Jones gave Morris:* Morris, *Autobiography*, 83.

321   *"strictly prohibited [them] from":* Jones to George Parker, Dec. 8, 1813. Jones issued identical commands to the *Siren*, under George Parker; see *The Naval War of 1812: A Documentary History*, ed. William S. Dudley (Washington, DC: Naval Historical Center, 1992), 2:296.

321   *The* Enterprise *and the* Rattlesnake *were:* Mahan, *Sea Power*, 2:232; Adams, *History of the United States*, 836; *Niles' Weekly Register*, July 11, 1814, 391.

321   *On July 11, the 50-gun* Leander, *under:* *The Naval War of 1812: A Documentary History*, ed. Michael Crawford (Washington, DC: Naval Historical Center, 2002), 3:200.

321   *Before the* Siren *reached:* Nathaniel D. Nicholson to Captain Samuel Evans, Aug. 24, 1815, in John Brannan, *Official Letters of the Military and Naval Officers of the United States During the War with Great Britain, in the Years 1812–1815* (Washington City: Way and Gideon, 1823), 498–99.

322   *While he was away:* David Curtis Skaggs, *Oliver Hazard Perry: Honor, Courage, and Patriotism in the Early Navy* (Annapolis, MD: Naval Institute Press, 2006), 164.

322   *"must be annihilated":* *Times* (London), July 2, 1814.

322   *Secretary Jones even considered:* Jones to Decatur, Nov. 8, 1814, in Crawford, ed., *Naval War of 1812*, 3:640–41.

322   *David Porter was enthusiastic:* James Tertius de Kay, *The Battle of Stonington: Torpedoes, Submarines, and Rockets in the War of 1812* (Annapolis, MD: Naval Institute Press, 1990), 89–90.

322   *The navy gave the inventor:* Kirkpatrick Sale, *The Fire of His Genius: Robert Fulton and the American Dream* (New York: Free Press, 2001) 159–60.

323   *Secretary Jones was not reluctant:* Jones to Madison, Oct. 26, 1814, in Crawford, ed., *Naval War of 1812*, 3:631–36.

323   *Privateers continued to be:* George F. Emmons, *Navy of the United States from the Commencement, in 1775, Through 1853* (Washington, DC: Gideon, 1853), 170–97; Mahan, *Sea Power*, 2:233–44; Adams, *History of the United States*, 834–53.

323   *Marblehead, Massachusetts, for instance:* Samuel E. Morison, *The Maritime History of Massachusetts* (Boston: Houghton Mifflin, 1921), 199.

323   *estimated 100,000 seamen:* William M. Marine, *The British Invasion of Maryland* (1913; reprint, Hatboro, PA: Tradition Press, 1965), 13.

323   *Britain's home islands were:* C. S. Forester, *The Age of Fighting Sail: The Story of the Naval War of 1812* (New York: Doubleday, 1956), 218–19; Mahan, *Sea Power*, 2:262–63.

324   *Britain's Convoy Act did not apply:* Mahan, *Sea Power*, 2:226.

324   *That the number of American privateers:* Marine, *The British Invasion of Maryland*, 16–17.

CHAPTER 26

325   *Dealing with the aftermath:* Charles K. Webster, *The Congress of Vienna, 1814–1815* (London: G. Bell & Sons, 1934), 1.

326   *"much yet remains"*: *Times* (London), Aug. 1, 1814.

326   *the most contentious was*: Webster, *The Congress of Vienna*, 99.

327   *"On mature consideration"*: Monroe to the Joint Commissioners of the United States for Treating of Peace with Great Britain, June 27, 1814, in *American State Papers: Foreign Relations* (Washington, DC: Gales & Seaton, 1833–58), 3:700–704.

328   *"I think it not unlikely"*: Liverpool to Castlereagh, Sept. 2, 1814, in *Supplementary Despatches, Correspondence, and Memoranda of Field Marshall Arthur, Duke of Wellington, K. G.*, ed. Arthur R. Wellesley (London: John Murray, 1862), 9:245.

328   *The* Times *had expected the government*: *Times* (London), May 20 and 24, 1814.

329   *The Courier, Liverpool's mouthpiece*: *Courier* (London), May 21, 1814, in Bradford Perkins, *Castlereagh and Adams* (Berkeley: University of California Press, 1964), 64.

329   *Liverpool's demand was obviously*: George Dangerfield, *The Era of Good Feelings* (New York: Harcourt, Brace, 1952), 67–69.

329   *"Great Britain has opened"*: Adams to Crawford, Aug. 29, 1814, in *Writings of John Quincy Adams*, ed. Worthington Chauncey Ford (New York: Macmillan, 1915), 5:105.

329   *On August 19, the British envoys*: American ministers to Monroe, Aug. 19, 1814, in *American State Papers: Foreign Relations*, 3:708–9.

330   *These demands were immediately*: Journal of Ghent Negotiations, Aug. 19, 1814, in *The Papers of Henry Clay*, ed. James F. Hopkins (Lexington: University Press of Kentucky, 1959), 1:968–71.

330   *"The prospect of peace"*: Clay to Crawford, Aug. 22, 1814, in Hopkins, ed., *Papers of Henry Clay*, 1:971–72.

330   *"To surrender both the rights"*: Dangerfield, *The Era of Good Feelings*, 69.

330   *The demand for a permanent*: Frank A. Updyke, *The Diplomacy of the War of 1812* (Baltimore: Johns Hopkins University Press, 1915), 250–53.

330   *But the rest of the note*: Updyke, *Diplomacy of the War of 1812*, 256.

331   *Popular enthusiasm for the war*: *Times* (London), Sept. 16, 1814.

331   *A gleeful Henry Goulburn*: Fred L. Engelman, *The Peace of Christmas Eve* (New York: Harcourt Brace, 1962), 197.

331   *On October 8 the British presented*: *American State Papers: Foreign Relations*, 3:724–25; David S. Heidler and Jeane T. Heidler, *Henry Clay: The Essential American* (New York: Random House, 2010), 114.

331   *"What . . . wounds me"*: Clay to Crawford, Oct. 17, 1814, in Hopkins, ed., *Papers of Henry Clay*, 1:989.

331   *"There can be no possible"*: Adams to Louisa Adams, Oct. 4, 1814, in Ford, ed., *Writings of John Quincy Adams*, 5:151.

331   *10,000 copies printed and widely distributed*: *American State Papers: Foreign Relations*, 3:695–703, gives the documents released.

332   *"If Great Britain does not"*: Monroe to Commissioners, Aug. 11, 1814, *American State Papers: Foreign Relations*, 3:705.

332   *Adams and his colleagues*: Commissioners to Monroe, Aug. 12, 1814, *American State Papers: Foreign Relations*, 3:705–7.

332   *Gallatin had already written to Secretary Monroe*: Gallatin to Monroe, June 13, 1814, in Updyke, *The Diplomacy of the War of 1812*, 282.

332   *"are very sanguine about"*: Liverpool to Castlereagh, Sept. 27, 1814, in Mahan, *Sea Power*, 2:424–25.

CHAPTER 27

333   *Cochrane finally gave in*: Cochrane to First Lord of the Admiralty Viscount Melville, Sept. 17, 1814, in *The Naval War of 1812: A Documentary History*, ed. Michael Crawford (Washington, DC: Naval Historical Center, 2002), 3:289.

334   *After being wounded*: Mary Barney, *A Biographical Memoir of the Late Commodore Joshua Barney* (Boston: Gray and Bowen, 1832), 269.

334   *Rodgers had 1,000*: Porter to Jones, Aug. 27, 1814, in Walter Lord, *The Dawn's Early Light* (New York: Norton, 1972), 232.

335   *"We deplore your"*: Spence to Rogers, Aug. 31, 1814, in Crawford, ed., *Naval War of 1812*, 3:261.

335   *Actually, Rodgers had such*: Charles O. Paullin, *Commodore John Rodgers: A Biography* (Cleveland: Arthur H. Clark, 1910), 289–90.

336   *Colonel Arthur Brooke, an experienced*: Lord, *Dawn's Early Light*, 259–62.

337   *After Commodore Rodgers straightened*: Rodgers to Spence, Sept. 8, 1814, in Crawford, ed., *Naval War of 1812*, 3:263.

337   *"It is impossible for"*: Cochrane to Cockburn, Sept. 13, 1814; Brooke to Cochrane, Sept. 13, 1814, in Crawford, ed., *Naval War of 1812*, 3:277–79.

338   *"the capture of the town"*: Brooke to Bathurst, Sept. 17, 1814, in Crawford, ed., *Naval War of 1812*, 3:282–85.

339   *Between one and two o'clock*: Cockburn to Cochrane, Sept. 15, 1814; Brooke to Bathurst, Sept. 17, 1814; Brooke to Cochrane, Sept. 14, 1814, in Crawford, ed., *Naval War of 1812*, 3:279–85; Roger Morriss, *Cockburn and the British Navy in Transition: Admiral Sir George Cockburn, 1772–1853* (Columbia: University of South Carolina Press, 1997), 113.

339   *On the night of September 13–14*: Cochrane to Napier, Sept. 13, 1814, in Crawford, ed., *Naval War of 1812*, 3:278; Irving Brant, *James Madison*, vol. 6: *Commander in Chief, 1812–1836* (Indianapolis: Bobbs-Merrill, 1961), 324.

339   *Lieutenant Colonel Armistead estimated*: Armistead to Monroe, Sept. 24, 1814, in Crawford, ed., *Naval War of 1812*, 3:302–4.

339   *inspired an American spectator*: Lord, *Dawn's Early Light*, 240–45, 293–97.

340   *With the fleet went 2,400 ex-slaves*: Robin W. Winks, *The Blacks in Canada*, 2nd ed. (Montreal: McGill-Queens University Press, 1997), 114–27.

CHAPTER 28

341   *"commence offensive operations"*: Bathurst to Prevost, June 3, 1814, in J. Mackay Hitsman, *The Incredible War of 1812: A Military History* (Montreal: Robin Brass Studio, 1999), 289–90.

342   *On September 1 Prevost marched*: Hitsman, *The Incredible War of 1812*, 254.

342   *"Vermont has shown"*: Prevost to Bathurst, Aug. 5 and 27, 1814, in Alfred T. Mahan, *Sea Power in Its Relations to the War of 1812* (Boston: Little, Brown, 1905), 2:363.

342   *a few of Commodore Macdonough's*: Rodney Macdonough, *The Life of Commodore Thomas Macdonough, U.S. Navy* (Boston: Fort Hill Press, 1909), 160–61.

343   *Armstrong wrote again*: Armstrong to Izard, July 27, 1814, and Izard to Armstrong Aug. 11, 1814, in Henry Adams, *History of the United States of America During the Administrations of James Madison* (New York: Library of America, 1986), 976–77; Hitsman, *The Incredible War of 1812*, 253; C. Edward Skeen, *John Armstrong, Jr., 1758–1843: A Biography* (Syracuse, NY: Syracuse University Press, 1981), 184–86.

343   *"Armstrong's policy of meeting"*: Adams, *History of the United States*, 976–78.

345   *"Only sixteen days before"*: Pring to Yeo, Sept. 12, 1814, in *The Naval War of 1812: A Documentary History*, ed. Michael Crawford (Washington, DC: Naval Historical Center, 2002), 3:609–12.

345   *Yeo's argument was*: Macdonough, *Commodore Thomas Macdonough*, 174–75; Mahan, *Sea Power*, 2:370–71.

345   *Downie had the 16-gun* Linnet: The *Linnet* had sixteen long twelve-pounders. The *Chub* had ten eighteen-pound carronades and one long six-pounder. The *Finch* had

four long six-pounders, six eighteen-pound carronades, and one eighteen-pound columbiad. The six galleys had one long twenty-four-pounder and one thirty-two-pound carronade. Two galleys had one long eighteen-pounder and one thirty-two-pounder. Two other galleys had one long eighteen-pounder and one eighteen-pound carronade. Four gunboats had one thirty-two-pound carronade, and three others had one long eighteen-pounder.

346   *Macdonough thought there were*: Macdonough, *Commodore Thomas Macdonough*, 161.

346   *The* Saratoga *had eight long*: Macdonough, *Commodore Thomas Macdonough*, 165.

347   *At eight o'clock Macdonough's*: Macdonough, *Commodore Thomas Macdonough*, 176.

347   *Macdonough credited him with*: Macdonough to Jones, Sept. 13, 1814, in Crawford, ed., *Naval War of 1812*, 3:614–15. Perry had been ordered to Lake Champlain on April 22, 1814.

348   *Macdonough was in constant*: Macdonough, *Commodore Thomas Macdonough*, 182.

349   *his battered crew "declared"*: Robertson's statement written from the *Saratoga*, Sept. 12, 1814, in *Select British Documents of the Canadian War of 1812*, ed. William Charles Henry (Toronto: Publications of the Champlain Society, 1920–23), 3:373–77.

349   *around 11:20, Pring was forced*: Pring to Yeo, Sept. 12, 1814, in Crawford, ed., *Naval War of 1812*, 3:609–12.

349   *"The Almighty has been pleased"*: Macdonough to Jones, Sept. 11, 1814, in Macdonough, *Commodore Thomas Macdonough*, 185.

349   *"Gentlemen, return your swords"*: Macdonough, *Commodore Thomas Macdonough*, 185.

349   *"I have much satisfaction"*: Pring to Yeo, Sept. 12, 1814, in Crawford, ed., *Naval War of 1812*, 3:612.

349   *The American and British seamen*: Macdonough, *Commodore Thomas Macdonough*, 188–89.

350   *"The enemy's shot"*: Macdonough to Jones, Sept. 13, 1814, in Crawford, ed., *Naval War of 1812*, 3:614–15.

350   *Macdonough was particularly critical*: Christopher McKee, *A Gentlemanly and Honorable Profession: The Creation of the U.S. Naval Officer Corps, 1794–1815* (Annapolis, MD: Naval Institute Press, 1991), 294; Macdonough, *Commodore Thomas Macdonough*, 191–92.

350   *"The disastrous and unlooked for"*: Prevost to Bathurst, Sept. 22, 1814, in Hitsman, *The Incredible War of 1812*, 264.

350   *"the expectations of His Majesty's"*: Pierre Berton, *Flames Across the Border: The Canadian-American Tragedy, 1813–1814* (Boston: Little, Brown, 1981), 399.

CHAPTER 29

353   *"for in our own country*: Clay to Monroe, Oct. 26, 1814, in *The Papers of Henry Clay*, ed. James F. Hopkins (Lexington: University Press of Kentucky, 1959), 1:995–96.

353   *Clay made sure that Goulburn*: David S. Heidler and Jeane T. Heidler, *Henry Clay: The Essential American* (New York: Random House, 2010), 113.

353   *The Duke of Wellington, now*: Major General C. Macaulay to Liverpool, Oct. 31, 1814, in *Supplementary Despatches, Correspondence, and Memoranda of Field Marshall Arthur, Duke of Wellington, K. G.*, ed. Arthur R. Wellesley (London: John Murray, 1862), 9:407.

354   *"You will have heard from"*: Liverpool to Castlereagh, Nov. 2, 1814, in Wellesley, ed., *Supplementary Despatches*, 9:401–2; Major General C. Macaulay to Liverpool, Oct. 31, 1814, in Wellesley, ed., *Supplementary Despatches*, 9:487.

354   *Castlereagh hoped that getting:* Charles K. Webster, *The Foreign Policy of Castlereagh, 1812-1815* (London: G. Bell and Sons, 1931), 10:342-61.

354   *"Unless the Emperor of Russia":* Castlereagh to Liverpool, Nov. 11, 1814, in Charles K. Webster, *The Congress of Vienna, 1814-1815* (London: G. Bell & Sons, 1934), 104.

355   *"I see little prospect":* Liverpool to Castlereagh, Nov. 2, 1814, in Wellesley, ed., *Supplementary Despatches,* 9:401-2.

355   *Liverpool wrote to Wellington:* Liverpool to Wellington, Nov. 4, 1814, in Wellesley, ed., *Supplementary Despatches,* 9:405-7; Frank A. Updyke, *The Diplomacy of the War of 1812* (Baltimore: Johns Hopkins University Press, 1915), 303-6.

355   *"The Duke of Wellington would restore":* Liverpool to Castlereagh, Nov. 4, 1814, in Wellesley, ed., *Supplementary Despatches,* 9:405.

355   *"you cannot at this moment":* Wellington to Liverpool, Nov. 7, 1814, in Wellesley, ed., *Supplementary Despatches,* 9:422.

355   *The duke wrote to Liverpool again:* Wellington to Liverpool, Nov. 9, 1814, in Robert Stewart Castlereagh, *Correspondence, Despatches, and Other Papers of Viscount Castlereagh, Second Marquess of Londonderry* (London: H. Colburn, 1848-53), 10:118-19.

356   *"I confess that I think":* Wellington to Liverpool, Nov. 9, 1814, in Wellesley, ed., *Supplementary Despatches,* 9:422, 424-26, 435-37; Updyke, *The Diplomacy of the War of 1812,* 306-7.

356   *"I can assure you":* Liverpool to Wellington, Nov. 13, 1814, in Wellesley, ed., *Supplementary Despatches,* 430.

356   *Liverpool then wrote:* Liverpool to Castlereagh, Nov. 18, 1814, in Wellesley, ed., *Supplementary Despatches,* 9:438.

357   *"After such a contest":* Updyke, *The Diplomacy of the War of 1812,* 302.

357   *"The American projet, I think":* Goulburn to Bathurst, Nov. 14, 1814, in Wellesley, ed., *Supplementary Despatches,* 9:432.

357   *the principle of* uti possidetis: The clearest expression of the cabinet's view of *uti possidetis* was given by Bathurst in his notes of Oct. 18 and 20, 1814, in Castlereagh, *Correspondence, Despatches, and Other Papers,* 9:168-69.

357   *The American commissioners offered:* Irving Brant, *James Madison,* vol. 6: *Commander in Chief, 1812-1836* (Indianapolis: Bobbs-Merrill, 1961), 368; *American State Papers: Foreign Relations* (Washington, DC: Gales & Seaton, 1833-58), 3:732-44.

358   *The final treaty:* A copy of the complete peace treaty is conveniently in John Brannan, *Official Letters of the Military and Naval Officers of the United States During the War with Great Britain, in the Years 1812-1815* (Washington City: Way and Gideon, 1823), 504-10.

359   *"The terms of this instrument":* Hopkins, ed., *Papers of Henry Clay,* 1:1007.

359   *Adams wrote in his diary:* Quoted in Samuel Flagg Bemis, *John Quincy Adams and the Foundations of American Foreign Policy* (New York: Knopf, 1950), 218.

359   *"Wherever . . . [the treaty] has been":* Courier (London), Dec. 30, 1814.

359   *"we have attempted to force":* Times (London), Dec. 30, 1814.

359   *"rejoice in adding":* Times (London), Dec. 31, 1814.

359   *The* Edinburgh Review, *after being:* Brant, *James Madison,* vol. 6: *Commander in Chief,* 372.

CHAPTER 30

361   *"You are not mistaken":* Madison to Wilson Cary Nicholas, Nov. 25, 1814, in Irving Brant, *James Madison,* vol. 6: *Commander in Chief, 1812-1836* (Indianapolis: Bobbs-Merrill, 1961), 343.

362   *"We are compelled":* President's Message to Congress, Sept. 20, 1814, in John Brannan, *Official Letters of the Military and Naval Officers of the United States During the War*

with Great Britain, in the Years 1812–1815 (Washington City: Way and Gideon, 1823), 431–35.

362   *"On our side," he wrote*: President's Message to Congress, Sept. 20, 1814, in Brannan, *Official Letters*, 432.

363   *"cheerfully and proudly bear"*: Brannan, *Official Letters*, 435.

363   *On October 17 Monroe requested*: Donald R. Hickey, *The War of 1812: A Forgotten Conflict* (Urbana: University of Illinois Press, 1989), 240.

363   *All the Federalists from New England*: *Annals of Congress* (Washington, DC: Gales & Seaton, 1834–1856), 13–3:162, 1895–1899.

363   *"The Congress have met"*: Jones to Madison, Oct. 4, 1814, in Brant, *James Madison*, vol. 6: *Commander in Chief*, 327.

364   *"almost untouched by the hand"*: Dallas to House Committee of Ways and Means, Oct. 14, 1814, in George M. Dallas, *Life and Writings of Alexander James Dallas* (Philadelphia: Lippincott, 1871), 234.

365   *The situation was so desperate*: Brant, *James Madison*, vol. 6: *Commander in Chief*, 345.

365   *To meet urgent current expenses*: Hickey, *The War of 1812*, 246–51.

366   *"lock up all our disposable"*: Jones to Madison, Oct. 26, 1814, in *The Naval War of 1812: A Documentary History*, ed. Michael Crawford (Washington, DC: Naval Historical Center, 2002), 3:632.

366   *The president did not*: Brant, *James Madison*, vol. 6, 345–46; Jones to Madison, Oct. 26, 1814, in Crawford, ed., *Naval War of 1812*, 3:631–36.

366   *His successor, Benjamin*: Christopher McKee, *A Gentlemanly and Honorable Profession: The Creation of the U.S. Naval Officer Corps, 1794–1815* (Annapolis, MD: Naval Institute Press, 1991), 17–18.

366   *Before leaving, Jones recommended*: Brant, *James Madison*, vol. 6: *Commander in Chief*, 346, 388.

368   *On October 5, Governor Strong*: Samuel Eliot Morison, *Harrison Gray Otis: The Urbane Federalist* (Boston: Houghton Mifflin, 1969), 356–57.

368   *Eustis called instead*: *National Intelligencer*, Nov. 15, 1814.

368   *Madison was deeply concerned*: Brant, *James Madison*, vol. 6: *Commander in Chief*, 360.

368   *Secretary of War Monroe prepared*: J. C. A. Stagg, *Mr. Madison's War: Politics, Diplomacy, and Warfare in the Early American Republic, 1783–1830* (Princeton, NJ: Princeton University Press, 1983), 477–83.

369   *"The expectation of those"*: "Report of the Hartford Convention," in Theodore Dwight, *History of the Hartford Convention* (New York: N & J White, 1833), 352, 380.

369   *The report then proposed*: Dwight, *History of the Hartford Convention*, 370.

CHAPTER 31

371   *On June 20, he sent a proposed plan*: Cochrane to Croker, June 20, 1814, in Alfred T. Mahan, *Sea Power in Its Relations to the War of 1812* (Boston: Little, Brown, 1905), 2:384.

371   *Liverpool and Bathurst expected*: Bathurst to Ross, July 10, 1814, in Henry Adams, *History of the United States of America During the Administrations of James Madison* (New York: Library of America, 1986), 1126; Croker to Cochrane, Aug. 10, 1814, in Mahan, *Sea Power*, 2:384.

372   *"supporting the Indian tribes"*: Bathurst to Ross, Sept. 6, 1814, in Mahan, *Sea Power*, 2:383.

373   *there were perhaps 18,000 Creeks*: John K. Mahon, *The War of 1812* (1972; reprint, New York: DaCapo Press, 1991), 231.

373   *The episode at Fort Mims signaled*: Adams, *The History of the United States*, 782.

373   *Ultimately, the task of crushing*: Robert V. Remini, *Andrew Jackson and the Course of American Empire* (New York: Harper & Row, 1977), 187–205.

374   *Captain William Percy*: Reginald Horsman, *The War of 1812* (New York: Knopf, 1969), 228.

375   *Jackson was paying close*: Remini, *Andrew Jackson*, 236.

375   *Major Lawrence's guns fired*: Jackson to Secretary of War, Sept. 17, 1814, in John Brannan, *Official Letters of the Military and Naval Officers of the United States During the War with Great Britain, in the Years 1812–1815* (Washington City: Way and Gideon, 1823), 426–27; William M. James, *The Naval History of Great Britain* (Mechanicsburg, PA: Stackpole Books, 2002), 6:356–57; Robin Reilly, *The British at the Gates: The New Orleans Campaign in the War of 1812* (Montreal: Robin Brass Studio, 2002), 176–77.

375   *While he did, he ignored*: Remini, *Andrew Jackson*, 238–39.

376   *Jackson attacked Pensacola*: Jackson to Secretary of War Monroe, Nov. 14, 1814, in Brannan, *Official Letters*, 451–53.

376   *As early as September 5*: Harry Ammon, *James Monroe: The Quest for National Identity* (Charlottesville: University Press of Virginia, 1990), 342; Monroe to Jackson, Oct. 10, 1814, in Remini, *Andrew Jackson*, 239.

376   *Jackson now returned*: Remini, *Andrew Jackson*, 244; Adams, *History of the United States*, 1139–40.

377   *"Andrew absorbed a near-permanent"*: Remini, *Andrew Jackson*, 15.

377   *Captain Shreve brought*: Reilly, *The British at the Gates*, 223.

378   *Jones stationed his mosquito*: Cochrane to Croker, Dec. 7, 1814, in Mahon, *The War of 1812*, 353; Wilburt S. Brown, *The Amphibious Campaign for West Florida and Louisiana, 1814–15: A Critical Review of Strategy and Tactics at New Orleans* (Tuscaloosa: University of Alabama Press, 1969), 93.

380   *By 12:40 it was all over*: Thomas ap Catesby Jones to Daniel Patterson, March 12, 1815, in Brannan, *Official Letters*, 487–89; Gene A. Smith, *Thomas ap Catesby Jones: Commodore of Manifest Destiny* (Annapolis, MD: Naval Institute Press, 2000), 26–29.

380   *Commodore Patterson could ill*: Reilly, *The British at the Gates*, 233–35.

381   *Cochrane moved his army*: George Robert Gleig, *The Campaigns of the British Army at Washington and New Orleans . . . in the Years 1814–15* (London: J. Murray, 1847), 141–42.

381   *Three possible invasion routes presented*: The routes are explained in Brown, *The Amphibious Campaigns*, 66.

381   *The third potential route was*: Smith, *Thomas ap Catesby Jones*, 27.

381   *He did not have enough*: Reilly, *The British at the Gates*, 248–49.

382   *Obstacles blocked the other*: Reilly, *The British at the Gates*, 251.

382   *Jackson called out the entire*: Horsman, *The War of 1812*, 239.

382   *She was a well-built schooner*: Patterson to Secretary Jones, Oct. 10, 1814, in *National Intelligencer*, Nov. 14, 1814.

383   *The* Louisiana *was a converted*: Patterson to the Secretary of the Navy, Jan. 27, 1815, in Brannan, *Official Letters*, 461–63.

383   *Laffite's pirates did not serve*: Brown, *The Amphibious Campaign*, 39–43.

383   *Admiral Cochrane made no attempt*: Reilly, *The British at the Gates*, 253.

384   *"Fearing the consequence"*: Jackson to Monroe, Dec. 27, 1814, in Brannan, *Official Letters*, 453–54.

384   *Jackson had inflicted so much*: Remini, *Andrew Jackson*, 264.

384   *Cochrane committed his entire*: Brown, *Amphibious Campaign*, 105.

386   *many of New Orleans's prominent*: Reilly, *The British at the Gates*, 287.

386   *"I lament that I have not"*: Jackson to Monroe, Dec. 29, 1814 in Brannan, *Official Letters*, 455.

387   *Patterson was also strengthening*: Brown, *Amphibious Campaign*, 121–42.

388   *Jackson had erected*: Brown, *Amphibious Campaign*, 137; Mahon, *Sea Power*, 2:362.

389   *"Lieutenant Norris of the Navy"*: Jackson's General Orders from Headquarters, Seventh Military District, Jan. 21, 1815, in Brannan, *Official Letters*, 478.

390   *"twice the column"*: Jackson to Secretary of War Monroe, Jan. 9, 1815, in *National Intelligencer*, Feb. 6, 1815.

391   *On the other side of the river*: Reilly, *The British at the Gates*, 330.

391   *"may not everywhere"*: Jackson to Monroe, Jan. 13, 1815, in Ralph Ketcham, *James Madison: A Biography* (Charlottesville: University Press of Virginia, 1971), 596.

391   *Cochrane sent five small ships*: Reilly, *The British at the Gates*, 334–35.

392   *The successful defense of New Orleans*: Admiral Cockburn was supposed to create a diversion in favor of Cochrane when he attacked New Orleans, but Cockburn was late beginning an attack on Georgia. He did not commence his assault on Georgia's coast until January 13. After bombarding a fort guarding the St. Mary's River, he sailed up to the town of St. Mary's and captured it on January 14. He then took Cumberland Island and established his headquarters there on January 22. He was waiting for ground troops to attack Savannah when word of peace came with an order to cease all military operations.

CHAPTER 32

393   *Prospects for an acceptable peace*: *National Intelligencer*, Jan. 20, 1815.

394   *"The proceedings are tempered"*: Quoted in Samuel Eliot Morison, *Harrison Gray Otis: The Urbane Federalist* (Boston: Houghton Mifflin, 1969), 381.

394   *"owing to some mistake"*: Decatur to Secretary of the Navy Crowninshield, Jan. 18, 1815, in John Brannan, *Official Letters of the Military and Naval Officers of the United States During the War with Great Britain, in the Years 1812–1815* (Washington City: Way and Gideon, 1823).

394   *"and every article that"*: Decatur to Crowninshield, Jan. 18, 1815, in Brannan, *Official Letters*, 481–83.

395   *The Pomone fired two devastating*: Decatur to Crowninshield, Jan. 18, 1815, in Brannan, *Official Letters*, 481–83.

396   *On the evening of February 13*: Irving Brant, *James Madison*, vol. 6: *Commander in Chief, 1812–1836* (Indianapolis: Bobbs-Merrill, 1961), 366–67.

396   *The actual terms of the peace*: Henry Adams, *History of the United States of America During the Administrations of James Madison* (New York: Library of America, 1986), 1222–23.

396   *In the midst of these momentous events*: Morison, *Harrison Gray Otis*, 385–95.

397   *"bore up after her"*: *Constitution's* log, Feb. 20, 1815, in Brannan, *Official Letters*, 493.

398   *"braced aback . . . main"*: *Constitution's* log, in Brannan, *Official Letters*, 494.

398   *At ten o'clock Douglass*: *Constitution's* log, in Brannan, *Official Letters*, 494.

398   *He brought his prizes to Porto Praya*: Tyrone G. Martin, ed., *The USS* Constitution's *Finest Fight, 1815: The Journal of Acting Chaplain Assheton Humphreys, US Navy* (Mount Pleasant, SC: Nautical and Aviation Publishing, 2000), 5–53; Claude Berube and John Rodgaard, *A Call to the Sea: Captain Charles Stewart of the USS* Constitution (Washington, DC: Potomac Books, 2005), 86–93.

399   *Right on Warrington's tail*: *Niles' Weekly Register*, July 8, 1815.

399   *During the trip a neutral vessel*: David Long, *Sailor-Diplomat: A Biography of Commodore James Biddle, 1783–1848* (Boston: Northeastern University Press, 1983), 50.

400   *The Penguin was so badly damaged*: Biddle to the Secretary of the Navy, March 25, 1815, in Brannan, *Official Letters*, 490–92; Long, *Sailor-Diplomat*, 50–55.

400   *At daylight on April 30:* Biddle to Decatur, June 10, 1815, in Brannan, *Official Letters*, 494–96; C. S. Forester, *The Age of Fighting Sail: The Story of the Naval War of 1812* (New York: Doubleday, 1956), 276–78.

400   *All the while, Captain Warrington:* Theodore Roosevelt, *The Naval War of 1812* (New York: Random House, 1996), 169–70.

400   *The war did not end:* Reginald Horsman, *The War of 1812* (New York: Knopf, 1969), 263–64.

401   *At the end of the war the American:* Horsman, *The War of 1812*, 263.

401   *"sincere regret on this":* Castlereagh to Baker, May 23, 1815, in Castlereagh, *Memoirs*, 232.

401   *Castlereagh's conciliatory tone:* Lord Bathurst to Baker, April 11, 1815, in Robert Stewart Castlereagh, *Correspondence, Despatches, and Other Papers of Viscount Castlereagh, Second Marquess of Londonderry* (London: H. Colburn, 1848–53), 10:198; Bathurst to Baker, April 21, 1815, in Castlereagh, *Correspondence, Despatches, and Other Papers*, 10:205; Horsman, *The War of 1812*, 264; Charles Andrews, *The Prisoners' Memoirs or Dartmoor Prison . . .* (New York: Printed for the Author, 1815), 144–51, 167–206, 222–35; Bradford Perkins, *Castlereagh and Adams* (Berkeley: University of California Press, 1964), 165.

CHAPTER 33

403   *"an unlimited Armistice":* Bradford Perkins, *Castlereagh and Adams* (Berkeley: University of California Press, 1964), 130.

404   *The reduction of the public expenditures:* Jack N. Rakove, *James Madison's Writings* (New York: Library Classics of the United States, 1999), 708; George C. Daughan, *If By Sea: The Forging of the American Navy—From the Revolution to the War of 1812* (New York: Basic Books, 2008), 466–67.

404   *"the war has laid":* Albert Gallatin, May 7, 1816, in Alfred T. Mahan, *Sea Power in Its Relations to the War of 1812* (Boston: Little, Brown, 1905), 2:436.

405   *"open and direct warfare":* Irving Brant, *James Madison*, vol. 6: *Commander in Chief, 1812–1836* (Indianapolis: Bobbs-Merrill, 1961), 381.

407   *after receiving assurances:* Perkins, *Castlereagh and Adams*, 162–63.

407   *The American consul told:* Frederick C. Leiner, *The End of Barbary Terror: America's 1815 War Against the Pirates of North Africa* (New York: Oxford University Press, 2006), 91–92.

407   *"all the privileges:* Bathurst to Baker, July 10, 1815, in Robert Stewart Castlereagh, *Correspondence, Despatches, and Other Papers of Viscount Castlereagh, Second Marquess of Londonderry* (London: H. Colburn, 1848–53), 10:268.

407   *Of course, the British:* Perkins, *Castlereagh and Adams*, 165.

407   *The lull allowed:* Decatur to Crowninshield, June 19, 1815, in *American State Papers: Naval Affairs* (Washington, DC: Gales and Seaton, 1834), 1:396; Spencer Tucker, *Stephen Decatur: A Life Most Bold and Daring* (Annapolis, MD: Naval Institute Press, 2005), 158.

408   *"been dictated at the mouth":* Decatur to Crowninshield, July 5, 1815, in *American State Papers: Naval Affairs*, 1:396.

408   *Decatur made these odd changes:* *American States Papers: Naval Affairs*, 1:396.

408   *Sadly, the* Epervier *never:* Tucker, *Stephen Decatur*, 163.

408   *Scurvy had now begun:* Decatur to Crowninshield, July 31, 1815, in *American State Papers: Naval Affairs*, 1:397; Tucker, *Stephen Decatur*, 164.

409   *Decatur left Tripoli:* Decatur to Crowninshield, Aug. 31, 1815, in *American State Papers: Naval Affairs*, 1:398.

409 *On the way he spotted:* Leiner, *The End of Barbary Terror*, 123–39; Robert J. Allison, *Stephen Decatur: American Naval Hero, 1779–1820* (Amherst: University of Massachusetts Press, 2005), 173–74.

409 *they informed Bainbridge of Decatur's:* Leiner, *The End of Barbary Terror*, 143.

410 *Secretary Crowninshield was even getting:* Leiner, *The End of Barbary Terror*, 145.

410 *"The object of leaving this":* Bainbridge to Shaw, Oct. 1815, in Thomas Harris, *The Life and Services of Commodore William Bainbridge, United States Navy* (Philadelphia, 1837; reprint, Whitefish, MT: Kessinger, 2007), 203.

410 *Bainbridge stood out:* Tucker, *Stephen Decatur*, 168. In 1816 the British sent twenty warships under Admiral Lord Exmouth to Algiers and mercilessly bombarded the place, ending the Barbary menace once and for all.

CHAPTER 34

413 *"The war has renewed":* Gallatin, May 7, 1816, in Alfred T. Mahan, *Sea Power in Its Relations to the War of 1812* (Boston: Little, Brown, 1905), 2:436.

414 *"was the first British statesman":* Charles K. Webster, ed., *Britain and the Independence of Latin America* (London: G. Bell & Sons, 1938), 1:42.

414 *An augury of things to come:* Irving Brant, *James Madison*, vol. 6: *Commander in Chief, 1812–1836* (Indianapolis: Bobbs-Merrill, 1961), 376.

415 *the great powers unanimously:* Wellington to Castlereagh, March 25, 1815, in *British Diplomacy, 1813–1815: Select Documents Dealing with the Reconstruction of Europe*, ed. Charles K. Webster (London: G. Bell & Sons, 1921), 316–17.

415 *In January the czar:* Wellington to Castlereagh, March 12, 1815, in Webster, ed., *British Diplomacy*, 312–13.

GLOSSARY

Abaft: to the rear of.

Aft: toward, or in, the stern of a vessel.

Astern: behind a vessel.

Ballast: any heavy substance used to maintain a vessel at its proper draft or trim, or its stability.

Beam: the breadth of a ship at its widest part.

Beam ends: a ship lying so far over on its side that the ends of her beams are touching the water and she is in danger of capsizing.

Beat to quarters: a marine drummer calling a crew to its battle stations.

Beat up: to sail in the direction from which the wind is coming.

Bilge: the lowest point of the hull, usually containing foul water.

Binnacle: box on the quarterdeck near the helm that houses the compass and has drawers where telescopes are kept.

Boom: a long spar used to extend the foot (or bottom) of a specific sail.

Bomb vessel: a small ketch used to hold mortars for hurling bombs.

Bow: the forward part of a ship.

Bow chasers: long guns placed on both sides of the bow to allow firing ahead.

Bower: large anchor placed at the bows of a ship.

Bowsprit: a spar extending forward from the bow or stem of a ship to carry a sail forward and to support the masts by stays.

Braces: ropes attached to the end of yards that allow them to be turned.

Brig: a two-masted, square-rigged vessel.

Broach to: to veer a ship's stern suddenly to windward so that her broadside is exposed to the wind and sea, putting her in danger of capsizing.

Bulkhead: a partition separating compartments on a vessel.

Cable's length: six hundred feet.

Capstan: a vertical, cleated drum used for moving heavy weights powered by capstan bars pushed by hand.

Carronade: form of cannon used to throw heavy shot at close quarters.

Chasers: a chase gun.

Chevaux-de-frise: a piece of timber or an iron barrel traversed with iron-pointed spikes or spears or pointed poles, five or six feet long, hidden under water, and used to defend a passage.

Clew: a lower corner of a square sail or after lower corner of a fore-and-aft sail.

Clew garnets: one of the ropes by which the clews of the courses of a square-rigged ship are hauled up to the lower yards.

Clew lines: a rope by which the clew of an upper square sail is hauled up to its yard.

Clew up: to haul a sail by means of the clew garnets, clew lines, etc., up to a yard or mast.

Close-hauled: sails pulled tight to allow a ship to sail close to the wind.

Collier: ship carrying coal.

Columbiad: a large, muzzle-loading gun for shooting at a high angle of elevation.

Con: steer.

Consolato del mare: the right to take enemy goods from neutral ships.

Coppering a warship: sheathing with rolled copper.

Corvette: warship with flush deck, slightly smaller than a frigate.

Courses: the lowest sails on any square-rigged mast.

Cutter: a broad, square-sterned boat for carrying stores and passengers and either rowed or sailed.

Fall off: to steer to leeward, or away from the direction of the wind.

Fascines: a long bundle of wooden sticks bound together.

Fire Ship: a vessel carrying combustibles sent among enemy ships to set them on fire.

Fleches: a salient outwork of two faces with an open gorge.

Fore-and-aft rig: having, instead of square sails attached to yards, sails bent to gaffs or set on the masts or on stays in the midship line of the vessel.

Forecastle: that part of the upper deck of a ship forward of the foremast.

Foremast: the mast closest to the bow.

Forereach: to gain upon.

Frigate: a three-masted, square-rigged warship carrying a full battery of from twenty to fifty guns on the main deck and having a raised quarterdeck and forecastle.

Gaff: the spar upon which the head, or upper edge, of a fore-and-aft sail is extended.

Gallant: third highest sail on a square-rigged ship above the top sail and course.

Grapeshot: small iron balls held together by a canvas bag that act like shotgun pellets.

Halyards: a rope or tackle for hoisting and lowering sails, yards, flags, etc.

Hawse: the bows of a ship.

Hawser: a large rope for towing, mooring, or securing a ship.

Headsails: sails situated forward of the foremast.

Heel: (noun) the lower end of a mast, a boom, the bowsprit, etc.

Heel: (verb) to tilt or incline to one side.

Inshore: near the shore or moving toward it.

Jib boom: a spar that serves as an extension of the bowsprit.

Jibe: to shift a fore-and-aft sail or its boom suddenly and with force from one side of a ship to the other until the sails fill on the opposite side. A maneuver done when a vessel is running with the wind and changes direction.

Kedge anchor: a small iron anchor used to hold a ship fast during changes of tide and to tow a ship forward during a calm by dropping the anchor forward and pulling the ship toward it.

Knot: a unit of speed equivalent to 1 nautical mile or 6,080.2 feet an hour.

Larboard: the left-hand side of a ship when facing toward the bow. The opposite of starboard. Also called "port."

Lateen sail: a triangular sail, extended by a long yard slung to the mast and usually low.

Lee: the quarter toward which the wind blows.

Lee shore: a shore on the lee side of a vessel, potentially dangerous in a storm.

Letter of marque: a license granted by a government to a private person to fit out an armed vessel to cruise as a privateer.

Lifts: chains or ropes used to hold yards to masts.

Line-of-battle ship: see "sail of the line."

Luff: to turn the head of a vessel toward the wind.

Mainmast: the large center mast of a three-masted ship.

Maintop: the platform above the head of the mainmast in a square-rigged ship.

Main topmast: a mast next above the mainmast.

Merlon: one of the solid intervals between embrasures or openings of a battlement or parapet.

Mizzenmast: the aftermost mast, usually the smallest, in a two-masted or three-masted ship. The mast closest to the stern.

Play upon: fire at.

Port: the left-hand side of a ship when facing toward the bow. The opposite of starboard. Also called "larboard."

Privateer: an armed private vessel operating under the commission of a government.

Prow: the bow of a vessel.

Pounders: refers to the weight of a cannonball.

Quarter deck: that part of the upper deck abaft the mainmast reserved for officers.

Ratlines: one of the small traverse ropes attached to the shrouds and forming the steps of a rope ladder.

Razee: a sail of the line that has had one of its decks removed to transform it into a heavy frigate.

Redoubt: small enclosed work of varying size used to fortify hills and passes.

Reef: that part of a sail which is taken in or let out by means of the reef points, in order to regulate the size of a sail.

Reef point: one of the pieces of small rope used in reefing a sail.

Royal: a small sail immediately above the topgallant sail.

Sail of the line: largest of the warships, carrying from 50 to 120 guns, large enough to have a place in the line of battle. Most often a 74-gun ship with three decks. Also called ship of the line.

Scow: a large, flat-bottomed boat, having broad, square ends.

Sheet: a rope that regulates the angle at which a sail is set in relation to the wind.

Ship of the line: see "sail of the line."

Slow-match: a slow-burning fuse used to ignite the powder charge in a cannon.

Spring on her cable: a line leading from a vessel's quarter to her cable so that by hauling in or slackening it she can be made to lie in any position.

Spring tide: a tide greater than usual, occurring at full moon and new moon.

Stand: depart, or head toward.

Starboard: the right-hand side of a ship when facing toward the bow. The opposite of larboard (or port).

Starboard tack: the course of a ship when the wind is coming over the starboard side.

Steam anchor: a small spare anchor.

Stern: the rear end of a vessel.

Stern Sheets: the space at the stern not occupied by the thwarts of an open boat.

Studding sail: used in a fair wind to extend the sails on a square-rigged ship.

Swivel: a small gun fixed on a swivel on a stanchion so that it can be rotated. Usually shoots a one-pound ball.

Tack: to change direction by bringing the head of a vessel into the wind and then shifting the sails so that she comes up into the wind and then falls off on the other side until she is sailing at about the same angle, with the wind coming from the opposite side of the ship.

Taffrail: the rail around a ship's stern.

Tender: a vessel employed to attend larger ships, to supply them with provisions, etc.

Topgallant: a mast or sail situated above the topmast and below the royal mast.

Topmast: The second mast from the deck, between the lower mast and the topgallant. On large ships the masts were organized in sections.

Topsail: the sail above the course.

Trim: to adjust sails and yards to get the best effect from the wind. Also, to arrange ballast, cargo, or passengers so that the ship will sail well.

Veer: to alter the course of ship by turning away from the direction of the wind.

Warp: to move a ship by hauling on a line, or warp.

Wear: to go about or change direction by turning the head of a vessel away from the wind.

Weather gauge: the position of a ship to the windward of another, giving an advantage in maneuvering.

Wherry: a long light rowboat, sharp at both ends.

Windward: the point or side from which the wind blows.

Yard: a long, narrow, cylindrical, tapered, wooden spar that supports and extends a sail.

Author's Note: The majority of the above definitions are based on *Webster's New International Dictionary of the English Language*, edited by William Allan Neilson, 2nd ed. (Springfield, MA: Merriam, 1938).

SELECT BIBLIOGRAPHY

DOCUMENTS

Adams, Charles Francis. *The Memoirs of John Quincy Adams*. 12 vols. Philadelphia: Lippincott, 1874–77.

Adams, John. *The Adams-Jefferson Letters: The Complete Correspondence Between Thomas Jefferson and Abigail and John Adams*. Edited by Lester J. Cappon. Chapel Hill: University of North Carolina Press, 1988.

Andrews, Charles. *The Prisoners' Memoirs or Dartmoor Prison. . . .* New York: Printed for the Author, 1815.

Bourchier, Lady, ed. *Memoir of the Life of Admiral Sir Edward Codrington*. 2 vols. London: Longmans, Green, 1873.

Brannan, John. *Official Letters of the Military and Naval Officers of the United States During the War with Great Britain, in the Years 1812–1815*. Washington City: Way and Gideon, 1823.

Carden, John Surman. *A Curtail'd Memoir of Incidents and Occurrences in the Life of John Surman Carden*. 1850. Reprint, Oxford: Clarendon Press, 1912.

Castlereagh, Robert Stewart. *Correspondence, Despatches, and Other Papers of Viscount Castlereagh, Second Marquess of Londonderry*. 12 vols. London: H. Colburn, 1848–53.

Cooper, James Fenimore. *Ned Myers; or Life Before the Mast*. 1843. Reprint, Annapolis, MD: Naval Institute Press, 1989.

Crawford, Michael, ed. *The Naval War of 1812: A Documentary History*. Vol. 3. Washington, DC: Naval Historical Center, 2002.

Cruikshank, Ernest A. *The Documentary History of the Campaign Upon the Niagara Frontier, 1812–1814*. 9 vols. Welland, Ontario: Lundy's Lane Historical Society, 1896–1908.

———. *Documents Relating to the Invasion of Canada and the Surrender of Detroit, 1812*. Ottawa: Government Printing Bureau, 1912.

Cutts, Lucia Beverly. *Memoirs and Letters of Dolly Madison*. Boston: Houghton Mifflin, 1896.

Dudley, William S. *The Naval War of 1812: A Documentary History*. Vol. 1. Washington, DC: Naval Historical Center, 1985.

———. *The Naval War of 1812: A Documentary History*. Vol. 2. Washington, DC: Naval Historical Center, 1992.

Evan, Amos A. "Journal Kept on Board the United States Frigate Constitution, 1812. . . ." *Pennsylvania Magazine of History and Biography* 19, no. 1 (1895).

Ford, Worthington Chauncey, ed. *Writings of John Quincy Adams*. Vol. 5. New York: Macmillan Co., 1915.

Foster, Augustus John. *Jeffersonian America: Notes on the United States of America, Collected in the Years 1805–6–7 and 11–12*. Edited by Richard Beale Davis. Westport CT: Greenwood Press, 1980.

Gallatin, Albert. *Writings of Albert Gallatin*. Edited by Henry Adams. 3 vols. Philadelphia: J. B. Lippincott, 1879.

Gallatin, Count, ed. *The Diary of James Gallatin: Secretary to Albert Gallatin—A Great Peacemaker, 1813–1827*. New York: Scribner's, 1920.

Gleig, George R. *The Campaigns of the British Army at Washington and New Orleans.* . . . 1821. Reprint, London: J. Murray, 1847.

Graves, Donald E., ed. *Soldiers of 1814: American Enlisted Men's Memoirs of the Niagara Campaign.* Youngstown, OH: Old Fort Niagara Press, 1995.

Hamton, Stanislaus Murray, ed. *The Writings of James Monroe.* . . . 7 vols. New York: Putnam, 1901–2.

Hawthorne, Nathaniel, ed. *The Yarn of a Yankee Privateer.* New York: Funk and Wagnalls, 1926.

Historical Statistics of the United States, Colonial Times to 1957. Washington, DC: Bureau of the Census, 1960.

Hopkins, James F., ed. *The Papers of Henry Clay: Volume I, The Rising Statesman, 1797–1814.* Lexington: University Press of Kentucky, 1959.

King, Dean, and John B. Hattendorf. *Every Man Will Do His Duty: An Anthology of Firsthand Accounts from the Age of Nelson, 1793–1815.* New York: Henry Holt, 1997.

Knox, Dudley W., ed. *Naval Documents Related to the United States Wars with the Barbary Powers.* Vol. 3. Washington, DC: U.S. Government Printing Office, 1941.

Leech, Samuel. *Thirty Years from Home: A Seaman's View of the War of 1812.* Boston: Tappan & Dennet, 1843. Reprint, Tucson, AZ: Fireship Press, 2008.

Madison, Dolley. *Memoirs and Letters of Dolly Madison.* Edited by her grandniece. Boston: Houghton Mifflin, 1886. Reprint, Port Washington, NY: Kennikat Press, 1971.

Martin, Tyrone G., ed. *The USS* Constitution's *Finest Fight, 1815: The Journal of Acting Chaplain Assheton Humphreys, US Navy.* Mount Pleasant, SC: Nautical and Aviation Publishing, 2000.

Morris, Charles. *The Autobiography of Commodore Charles Morris, USN.* Annapolis, MD: Naval Institute Press, 2002.

Perry, Matthew Calbraith. *Documents in Relation to the Differences Which Subsisted Between the Late Commodore O. H. Perry and Captain J. D. Elliot.* Washington, 1821.

Peterson, Merrill D., ed. *Thomas Jefferson, Writings.* New York: Literary Classics of the United States, 1984.

Porter, David. *Journal of a Cruise.* Philadelphia: Bradford and Inskeep, 1815. Reprint, Annapolis, MD: Naval Institute Press, 1986.

Scott, Winfield. *Memoirs of Lieutenant-General Scott, LLD: Written by Himself.* 2 vols. New York: Sheldon, 1964.

Smith, James Morton. *The Republic of Letters: The Correspondence Between Thomas Jefferson and James Madison.* 3 vols. New York: Norton, 1995.

Smith, Moses. *Naval Scenes in the Last War; or, Three Years on Board the Frigate* Constitution, *and the* Adams; *Including Capture of the* Guerriere. Boston: Gleason's Publishing Hall, 1846.

Tracy, Nicholas. *The Naval Chronicle: The Contemporary Record of the Royal Navy at War.* Vol. 5, 1811–1815. Consolidated ed. London: Chatham, 1999.

United States Bureau of the Census. *Historical Statistics of the United States, Colonial Times to 1970 Bicentennial.* 2 vols. Washington, DC: US Government Printing Office, 1975.

Van Rensselaer, Solomon. *A Narrative of the Affair of Queenston: In the War of 1812.* New York: Leavitt, Lord, 1836.

Webster, Charles. K., ed. *Britain and the Independence of Latin America.* 2 vols. London: G. Bell & Sons, 1938.

———, ed. *British Diplomacy, 1813–1815: Select Documents Dealing with the Reconstruction of Europe.* London: G. Bell & Sons, 1921.

Wellesley, Arthur R., ed. *Supplementary Despatches, Correspondence, and Memoranda of Field Marshall Arthur, Duke of Wellington, K. G.* London: John Murray, 1862.

White, Samuel. *History of the American Troops in the Late War, Under the Commands of Cols. Fenton and Campbell.* 1829. Reprint, Whitefish, MT: Kessinger Publishing, 2008.

Wood, William Charles Henry, ed. *Select British Documents of the Canadian War of 1812*. 3 vols. Toronto: Publications of the Champlain Society, 1920–23.

SECONDARY WORKS

Abernethy, Thomas Perkins. *The South in the New Nation, 1789–1918*. Baton Rouge: Louisiana State University Press, 1961.

Adams, Henry. *History of the United States of America During the Administrations of James Madison*. New York: Library of America, 1986.

Allgor, Catharine. *A Perfect Union: Dolley Madison and the Creation of the American Nation*. New York: Henry Holt, 2006.

Allison, Robert J. *Stephen Decatur: American Naval Hero, 1779–1820*. Amherst: University of Massachusetts Press, 2005.

Altoff, Gerard T. *Oliver Hazard Perry and the Battle of Lake Erie*. Rev. ed. Put-in-Bay, OH: Perry Group, 1999.

Ammon, Harry. *James Monroe: The Quest for National Identity*. Charlottesville: University Press of Virginia, 1990.

Anthony, Katharine. *Dolly Madison, Her Life and Times*. Garden City, NY: Doubleday, 1949.

Asprey, Robert B. *The Reign of Napoleon Bonaparte*. New York: Basic Books, 2001.

Banner, James M., Jr. *To the Hartford Convention: The Federalists and the Origin of Party Politics in Massachusetts, 1789–1815*. New York: Knopf, 1970.

Barney, Mary. *A Biographical Memoir of the Late Commodore Joshua Barney*. Boston: Gray and Bowen, 1832.

Bemis, Samuel Flagg. *John Quincy Adams and the Foundations of American Foreign Policy*. New York: Alfred A. Knopf, 1950.

Berton, Pierre. *Flames Across the Border: The Canadian-American Tragedy, 1813–1814*. Boston: Little, Brown, 1981.

———. *The Invasion of Canada, 1812–1813*. Boston: Little, Brown, 1980.

Berube, Claude, and John Rodgaard. *A Call to the Sea: Captain Charles Stewart of the USS Constitution*. Washington, DC: Potomac Books, 2005.

Bothwell, Robert. *The Penguin History of Canada*. Toronto: Penguin Canada, 2008.

Bradford, James C., ed. *Command Under Sail: Makers of the American Naval Tradition, 1775–1850*. Annapolis, MD: Naval Institute Press, 1985.

Brant, Irving. *James Madison*. Vol. 3: *Father of the Constitution, 1787–1800*. Indianapolis: Bobbs-Merrill, 1950.

———. *James Madison*. Vol. 5: *The President, 1809–1812*. Indianapolis: Bobbs-Merrill, 1950.

———. *James Madison*. Vol. 6: *Commander in Chief, 1812–1836*. Indianapolis: Bobbs-Merrill, 1961.

Broussard, James H. *The Southern Federalists, 1800–1816*. Baton Rouge: Louisiana State University Press, 1976.

Brown, Roger H. H. *The Republic in Peril, 1812*. New York: Norton, 1971.

Brown, Wilburt S. *The Amphibious Campaign for West Florida and Louisiana, 1814–15: A Critical Review of Strategy and Tactics at New Orleans*. Tuscaloosa: University of Alabama Press, 1969.

Buel, Richard, Jr. *America on the Brink: How the Political Struggle over the War of 1812 Almost Destroyed the Young Republic*. New York: Palgrave Macmillan, 2005.

Burt, Alfred L. *The United States, Great Britain and British North America from the Revolution to the Establishment of Peace after the War of 1812*. Toronto: Ryerson Press, 1940.

Cassell, Frank A. *Merchant Congressman in the Young Republic: Samuel Smith of Maryland, 1752–1839*. Madison: University of Wisconsin Press, 1971.

Caulkins, Frances M. *History of New London, Connecticut, from the First Survey of the Coast in 1612 to 1852*. Hartford, CT: Case, Tiffany, 1852.

Cooper, James Fenimore. *The History of the Navy of the United States of America*. 2 vols. 2nd ed. Philadelphia: Lea & Blanchard, 1840.

——. *Lives of Distinguished American Naval Officers*. 2 vols. Philadelphia: Carey and Hart, 1846.

Craig, Gerald M. *Upper Canada: The Formative Years, 1784–1841*. Toronto: McClelland and Stewart, 1963.

Dallas, George M. *Life and Writings of Alexander James Dallas*. Philadelphia: Lippincott, 1871.

Dangerfield, George. *The Era of Good Feelings*. New York: Harcourt, Brace, 1952.

Daughan, George C. *If By Sea: The Forging of the American Navy—From the Revolution to the War of 1812*. New York: Basic Books, 2008.

Dearborn, H. A. S. *The Life of William Bainbridge, Esq.* 1816. Reprint, Princeton, NJ: Princeton University Press, 1931.

Deconde, Alexander. *The Quasi-War: The Politics and Diplomacy of the Undeclared War with France 1797–1801*. New York: Scribner's, 1966.

de Kay, James Tertius. *The Battle of Stonington: Torpedoes, Submarines, and Rockets in the War of 1812*. Annapolis, MD: Naval Institute Press, 1990.

——. *Chronicles of the Frigate Macedonian, 1809–1922*. New York: Norton, 1995.

——. *A Rage for Glory: The Life of Commodore Stephen Decatur, USN*. New York: Free Press, 2004.

Delderfield, R. F. *Imperial Sunset: The Fall of Napoleon, 1813–14*. New York: Stein & Day, 1980.

Dewey, Davis R. *Financial History of the United States*. 12th ed. New York: A. M. Kelley, 1968.

Dudley, Wade G. *Splintering the Wooden Wall: The British Blockade of the United States, 1812–1815*. Annapolis, MD: Naval Institute Press, 2003.

Duffy, Stephen W. H. *Captain Blakeley and the Wasp: The Cruise of 1814*. Annapolis, MD: Naval Institute Press, 2001.

Dwight, Theodore. *History of the Hartford Convention*. New York: N & J White, 1833.

Dye, Ira. *The Fatal Cruise of the Argus: Two Captains in the War of 1812*. Annapolis, MD: Naval Institute Press, 1994.

Eckert, Edward K. *The Navy Department in the War of 1812*. Gainesville: University Press of Florida, 1973.

Elkins, Stanley, and Eric McKitrick. *The Age of Federalism*. New York: Oxford University Press, 1993.

Elliott, James E. *Strange Fatality: The Battle of Stoney Creek, 1813*. Montreal: Robin Brass Studio, 2009.

Elting, John R. *Amateurs to Arms: A Military History of the War of 1812*. Cambridge, MA: Da-Capo Press, 1995.

Emmons, George F. *Navy of the United States from the Commencement, in 1775, Through 1853*. Washington, DC: Gideon, 1853.

Engleman, Fred L. *The Peace of Christmas Eve*. New York: Harcourt Brace, 1962.

Esdaile, Charles. *Napoleon's Wars: An International History, 1803–1815*. New York: Viking, 2008.

Eshelman, Ralph E., Scott S. Sheads, and Donald R. Hickey. *The War of 1812 in the Chesapeake: A Reference Guide to Historic Sites in Maryland, Virginia, and the District of Columbia*. Baltimore: Johns Hopkins University Press, 2010.

Everest, Allan S. *War of 1812 in the Champlain Valley*. Syracuse, NY: Syracuse University Press, 1981.

Farragut, Loyall. *The Life of David Glasgow Farragut, First Admiral of the United States Navy, Embodying His Journal and Letters*. New York: D. Appleton and Co., 1882.

Ferguson, Eugene S. *Truxtun of the Constellation: The Life of Commodore Thomas Truxton, U.S. Navy, 1755–1822*. Baltimore: Johns Hopkins University Press, 1956.

Fleming, Thomas. *The Perils of Peace: America's Struggle for Survival After Yorktown*. New York: HarperCollins, 2007.

Flexner, James T. *Steamboats Come True: American Inventors in Action*. Boston: Little, Brown, 1978.

Ford, Worthington Chauncey, ed. *Writings of John Quincy Adams*. New York: Macmillan, 1915.

Forester, C. S. *The Age of Fighting Sail: The Story of the Naval War of 1812*. New York: Doubleday, 1956.

Gash, Norman. *Lord Liverpool: The Life and Political Career of Robert Banks Jenkinson Second Earl of Liverpool, 1770–1828*. Cambridge, MA: Harvard University Press, 1984.

Gleaves, Albert. *James Lawrence, Captain, United States Navy, Commander of the* Chesapeake. New York: Putnam, 1904.

Goldsborough, Charles W. *The United States Naval Chronicle*. Washington: James Wilson, 1824.

Gough, Barry. *Fighting Sail on Lake Huron and Georgian Bay: The War of 1812 and Its Aftermath*. Annapolis, MD: Naval Institute Press, 2002.

Graves, Donald E. *Field of Glory: The Battle of Crysler's Farm, 1813*. Montreal: Robin Brass Studio, 2000.

———. *Red Coats and Grey Jackets: The Battle of Chippawa, 5 July 1814*. Toronto: Dundurn Press, 1994.

———. *Where Right and Glory Lead! The Battle of Lundy's Lane, 1814*. Montreal: Robin Brass Studio, 1999.

Guttridge, Leonard F. *Our Country, Right or Wrong: The Life of Stephen Decatur, The U.S. Navy's Most Illustrious Commander*. New York: Tom Doherty Associates, 2006.

Guttridge, Leonard F., and J. D. Smith. *The Commodores*. New York: Harper & Row, 1969.

Hammond, Bray. *Banks and Politics in America from the Revolution to the Civil War*. Princeton, NJ: Princeton University Press, 1991.

Harris, Thomas. *The Life and Services of Commodore William Bainbridge, United States Navy*. Philadelphia, 1837. Reprint, Whitefish, MT: Kessinger, 2007.

Heidler, David S., and Jeane T. Heidler, eds. *Encyclopedia of the War of 1812*. Annapolis, MD: Naval Institute Press, 2004.

———. *Henry Clay: The Essential American*. New York: Random House, 2010.

Hickey, Donald R. *Don't Give Up The Ship! Myths of the War of 1812*. Urbana: University of Illinois Press, 2006.

———. *The War of 1812: A Forgotten Conflict*. Urbana: University of Illinois Press, 1989.

Hitsman, J. Mackay. *The Incredible War of 1812: A Military History*. Montreal: Robin Brass Studio, 1999.

Horsman, Reginald. *Expansion and American Indian Policy, 1783–1812*. Norman: University of Oklahoma Press, 1992.

———. *The Frontier in the Formative Years, 1783–1815*. Albuquerque: University of New Mexico Press, 1979.

———. *The War of 1812*. New York: Knopf, 1969.

Ingersoll, Charles J. *History of the Second War Between the United States of America and Great Britain*. 2 vols. Philadelphia: Lippincott, Grambo, 1852.

Ingraham, Edward D. *Sketch of the Events Which Preceded the Capture of Washington*. Philadelphia: Carey & Hart, 1849.

Jacobs, James Ripley. *Tarnished Warrior: Major-General James Wilkinson*. New York: Macmillan, 1938.

James, William. *The Naval History of Great Britain from the Declaration of War Against France in 1793 to the Accession of George IV*. 6 vols. London: Richard Bentley, 1847.

Johnson, Timothy D. *Winfield Scott: The Quest For Military Glory*. Lawrence: University Press of Kansas, 1998.

Knox, Dudley W. *A History of the United States Navy*. Annapolis, MD: Naval Institute Press, 1936.

Kurtz, Steven. *The Presidency of John Adams: The Collapse of Federalism, 1795–1800*. Philadelphia: University of Pennsylvania Press, 1957.

Labaree, Benjamin W. *Patriots and Partisans: The Merchants of Newburyport, 1764–1815*. Cambridge, MA: Harvard University Press, 1962.

Langley, Harold D. *Social Reform in the United States Navy, 1798–1862*. Urbana: University of Illinois Press, 1967.

Latimer, Jon. *1812: War with America*. Cambridge, MA: Harvard University Press, 2007.

Lavery, Brian. *Building the Wooden Walls: The Design and Construction of the 74-Gun Ship Valiant*. Annapolis, MD: Naval Institute Press, 1991.

———. *Nelson's Navy: The Ships, Men and Organization 1793–1815*. Annapolis, MD: Naval Institute Press, 1989.

Lefebvre, Georges. *Napoleon: From Tilsit to Waterloo, 1807-1815*. Translated by J. E. Anderson. Paris, 1936. Reprint, New York: Columbia University Press, 1990.

Leiner, Frederick C. *The End of Barbary Terror: America's 1815 War Against the Pirates of North Africa*. New York: Oxford University Press, 2006.

Lewis, Charles L. *David Glasgow Farragut: Our First Admiral*. Annapolis, MD: Naval Institute Press, 1943.

———. *The Romantic Decatur*. Philadelphia: University of Pennsylvania Press, 1937.

Lieven, Dominic. *Russia Against Napoleon: The True Story of the Campaigns of War and Peace*. New York: Viking, 2010.

Linklater, Andro. *An Artist in Treason: The Extraordinary Double Life of General James Wilkinson*. New York: Walker, 2009.

Long, David. *Nothing Too Daring: A Biography of Commodore David Porter, 1780–1843*. Annapolis, MD: Naval Institute Press, 1970.

———. *Ready to Hazard: A Biography of Commodore William Bainbridge, 1774–1833*. Hanover, NH: University Press of New England, 1981.

———. *Sailor-Diplomat: A Biography of Commodore James Biddle, 1783–1848*. Boston: Northeastern University Press, 1983.

Lord, Walter. *The Dawn's Early Light*. New York: Norton, 1972.

Lossing, Benson J. *The Pictorial Field-Book of the War of 1812*. New York: Harper & Bros., 1867.

Macdonough, Rodney. *The Life of Commodore Thomas Macdonough, U.S. Navy*. Boston: Fort Hill Press, 1909.

Mackenzie, Alexander Slidell. *Life of Decatur: A Commodore in the Navy of the United States*. Boston: Little, Brown, 1846.

Mahan, Alfred T. *Sea Power in Its Relations to the War of 1812*. 2 vols. Boston: Little, Brown, 1905.

Mahon, John K. *The War of 1812*. Gainesville: University Press of Florida, 1972. Reprint, New York: DaCapo Press, 1991.

Malcomson, Robert. *Capital in Flames: The American Attack on York, 1813*. Annapolis, MD: Naval Institute Press, 2008.

———. *Historical Dictionary of the War of 1812*. Lanham, MD: Scarecrow Press, 2006.

———. *H.M.S. Detroit: The Battle for Lake Erie*. Saint Catharines, Ontario: Vanwell Publishing, 1990.

———. *Lords of the Lake: The Naval War on Lake Ontario, 1812–1814*. 1998. Reprint, Montreal: Robin Brass Studio, 2009.

———. *A Very Brilliant Affair: The Battle of Queenston Heights, 1812*. Annapolis, MD: Naval Institute Press, 2003.

———. *Warships of the Great Lakes, 1754–1834*. Edison, NJ: Knickerbocker Press, 2004.

Malone, Dumas. *Jefferson and the Rights of Man*. Boston: Little, Brown, 1951.

Marine, William M. *The British Invasion of Maryland*. 1913. Reprint, Hatboro, PA: Tradition Press, 1965.

Martin, Tyrone G. *A Most Fortunate Ship: A Narrative History of "Old Ironsides."* Chester, CT: Globe Pequot, 1980.

Masefield, John. *Sea Life in Nelson's Time.* Annapolis, MD: Naval Institute Press, 1971.

McCaughey, Robert A. *Josiah Quincy, 1772–1864: The Last Federalist.* Cambridge, MA: Harvard University Press, 1974.

McCormick, Richard P. *The Presidential Game: The Origins of American Presidential Politics.* New York: Oxford University Press, 1982.

McCoy, Drew R. *The Elusive Republic: Political Economy in Jeffersonian America.* New York: Norton, 1982.

McDonald, Forest. *Alexander Hamilton.* New York: Norton, 1979.

McKee, Christopher. *A Gentlemanly and Honorable Profession: The Creation of the U.S. Naval Officer Corps, 1794–1815.* Annapolis, MD: Naval Institute Press, 1991.

McNaught, Kenneth. *The Penguin History of Canada.* London: Penguin, 1988.

Miller, John C. *The Federalist Era, 1789–1801.* New York: Harper, 1960.

Millet, Allan R. *Semper Fidelis: The History of the United States Marine Corps.* New York: Macmillan, 1980.

Morison, Samuel Eliot *Harrison Gray Otis: The Urbane Federalist.* Boston: Houghton Mifflin, 1969.

———. *The Life and Letters of Harrison Gray Otis.* 2 vols. Boston: Houghton Mifflin, 1913.

———. *The Maritime History of Massachusetts.* Boston: Houghton Mifflin, 1921.

———. *Old Bruin: Commodore Matthew Calbraith Perry, 1794–1858.* Boston: Little, Brown, 1967.

Morison, Samuel E., Frederick Merk, and Frank Freidel. *Dissent in Three American Wars.* Cambridge, MA: Harvard University Press, 1970.

Morris, John D. *Sword of the Border: Major-General Jacob Jennings Brown, 1775–1828.* Kent, OH: Kent State University Press, 2000.

Morriss, Roger. *Cockburn and the British Navy in Transition: Admiral Sir George Cockburn 1772–1853.* Studies in Maritime History. Columbia: University of South Carolina Press, 1997.

Muller, Charles G. *The Darkest Day: 1814; The Washington-Baltimore Campaign.* Philadelphia: Lippincott, 1963.

———. *The Proudest Day: Macdonough on Lake Champlain.* New York: John Day, 1960.

Nicolson, Harold. *The Congress of Vienna: A Study in Allied Unity, 1812–1822.* 1946. Reprint, New York: Viking, 1961.

Norton, Louis Arthur. *Joshua Barney: Hero of the Revolution and 1812.* Library of Naval Biography. Annapolis, MD: Naval Institute Press, 2000.

Ouellet, Fernand. *Lower Canada, 1791–1840: Social Change and Nationalism.* Translated and adapted by Patricia Claxton. Toronto: McClelland and Stewart, 1980.

Owsley, Frank L., Jr. *Struggle for the Gulf Borderlands: The Creek War and the Battle of New Orleans, 1812–1815.* Gainesville: University Press of Florida, 1981.

Pack, A. James. *The Man Who Burned the White House: Admiral Sir George Cockburn, 1772–1853.* Annapolis, MD: Naval Institute Press, 1987.

Palmer, Michael A. *Stoddert's War: Naval Operations During the Quasi-War with France, 1798–1801.* Annapolis, MD: Naval Institute Press, 2000.

Paullin, Charles O. *Commodore John Rodgers: A Biography.* Cleveland: Arthur H. Clark, 1910.

———. *Paullin's History of Naval Administration.* Annapolis, MD: Naval Institute Press, 1968.

Perkins, Bradford. *Castlereagh and Adams.* Berkeley: University of California Press, 1964.

———. *The Causes of the War of 1812.* New York: Holt, Rinehart and Winston, 1962.

———. *Prologue to War: England and the United States, 1805–1812.* Berkeley: University of California Press, 1970.

Perrett, Bryan. *The Real Hornblower: The Life of Admiral Sir James Gordon, GCB.* Annapolis, MD: Naval Institute Press, 1997.

Petrie, Donald A. *The Prize Game: Lawful Looting on the High Seas During the Age of Sail.* Annapolis, MD: Naval Institute Press, 1999.

Picking, Sherwood. *Sea Fight Off Monhegan: Enterprise and Boxer.* Portland, ME: Machigonne Press, 1941.

Pitch, Anthony S. *The Burning of Washington: The British Invasion of 1814.* Annapolis, MD: Naval Institute Press, 1998.

Pope, Dudley. *The Black Ship.* Philadelphia: Lippincott, 1964.

Pratt, Julius W. *Expansionists of 1812.* New York: Macmillan, 1925.

Prett, Bryan. *The Real Hornblower: The Life of Admiral Sir James Gordon.* London: Weidenfeld and Nicolson, 1998.

Reilly, Robin. *The British at the Gates: The New Orleans Campaign in the War of 1812.* Montreal: Robin Brass Studio, 2002.

Remini, Robert V. *Andrew Jackson and the Course of American Empire, 1767–1821.* New York: Harper and Row, 1977.

Rodger, N. A. M. *The Command of the Ocean: A Naval History of Britain, 1649–1815.* New York: Norton, 2004.

——. *Press Gang: Naval Impressment and Its Opponents in Georgian Britain.* London: Continuum, 2007.

——. *The Wooden World: An Anatomy of the Georgian Navy.* New York: Norton, 1986.

Roosevelt, Theodore. *The Naval War of 1812.* New York: Modern Library, 1999.

Rosenberg, Max. *The Building of Perry's Fleet on Lake Erie, 1812–13.* Harrisburg: Pennsylvania Historical and Museum Commission, 1987.

Schom, Alan. *Napoleon Bonaparte: A Life.* New York: HarperCollins, 1997.

Schroeder, John H. *Commodore John Rodgers: Paragon of the Early American Navy.* Gainesville: University Press of Florida, 2006.

Shomette, Donald G. *Flotilla: The Patuxent Naval Campaign in the War of 1812.* Baltimore: Johns Hopkins University Press, 2009.

Skaggs, David Curtis. *Oliver Hazard Perry: Honor, Courage, and Patriotism in the Early Navy.* Annapolis, MD: Naval Institute Press, 2006.

——. *Thomas Macdonough: Master of Command in the Early U.S. Navy.* Annapolis, MD: Naval Institute Press, 2003.

Skaggs, David Curtis, and Gerard T. Altoff. *A Signal Victory: The Lake Erie Campaign, 1812–1813.* Annapolis, MD: Naval Institute Press, 1997.

Skeen, C. Edward. *Citizen Soldiers in the War of 1812.* Lexington: University Press of Kentucky, 1999.

——. *John Armstrong, Jr., 1758–1843: A Biography.* Syracuse, NY: Syracuse University Press, 1981.

Smelser, Marshall. *The Democratic Republic, 1801–1805.* New York: HarperCollins, 1968.

Smith, Gene A. *Thomas ap Catesby Jones: Commodore of Manifest Destiny.* Annapolis, MD: Naval Institute Press, 2000.

Smith, Page. *John Adams.* 2 vols. New York: Doubleday, 1962.

Stabile, Donald R. *The Origin of American Public Finance: Debates over Money, Debt, and Taxes in the Constitutional Era, 1776–1836.* New York: Praeger, 1998.

Stagg, J. C. A. *Borderlines in Borderlands: James Madison and the Spanish-American Frontier, 1776–1821.* New Haven, CT: Yale University Press, 2009.

——. *Mr. Madison's War: Politics, Diplomacy, and Warfare in the Early American Republic, 1783–1830.* Princeton, NJ: Princeton University Press, 1983.

Stivers, Reuben Elmore. *Privateers & Volunteers: The Men and Women of Our Reserve Naval Forces, 1766–1866.* Annapolis, MD: Naval Institute Press, 1975.

Sugden, John. *Tecumseh: A Life.* New York: Henry Holt, 1997.

Symonds, Craig. *Navalists and Anti-Navalists: The Naval Policy Debate in the United States, 1785–1827.* Newark: University of Delaware Press, 1980.

Taylor, Alan. *The Civil War of 1812: American Citizens, British Subjects, Irish Rebels, & Indian Allies*. New York: Knopf, 2010.

Tucker, Glenn. *Poltroons and Patriots: A Popular Account of the War of 1812*. 2 vols. Indianapolis: Bobbs-Merrill, 1954.

Tucker, Spencer. *Stephen Decatur: A Life Most Bold and Daring*. Annapolis, MD: Naval Institute Press, 2005.

Tucker, Spencer C., and Frank T. Reuter. *Injured Honor: The Chesapeake-Leopard Affair, June 22, 1807*. Annapolis, MD: Naval Institute Press, 1996.

Updyke, Frank A. *The Diplomacy of the War of 1812*. Baltimore: Johns Hopkins University Press, 1915.

Valley, James E. *Rocks and Shoals: Naval Discipline in the Age of Fighting Sail*. Annapolis, MD: Naval Institute Press, 1996.

Walpole, Spencer. *The Life of the Right Honorable Spencer Perceval Including His Correspondence with Numerous Distinguished Persons*. 2 vols. London: Hurst and Blackett, 1874.

Walters, Raymond. *Albert Gallatin*. New York: Macmillan, 1957.

Webster, Charles K. *The Congress of Vienna, 1814–1815*. London: G. Bell & Sons, 1934.

——. *The Foreign Policy of Castlereagh, 1812–1815: Britain and the Reconstruction of Europe*. London: G. Bell & Sons, 1931.

——. *The Foreign Policy of Castlereagh, 1815–1822: Britain and the European Alliance*. London: G. Bell & Sons, 1925.

Weigley, Russell F. *History of the United States Army*. New York: Macmillan, 1967.

White, Leonard D. *The Jeffersonians: A Study in Administrative History, 1801–1829*. New York: Macmillan, 1956.

White, Patrick C. T. *While Washington Burned: The Battle of Fort Erie*. Baltimore: Nautical and Aviation Publishing, 1992.

Wilentz, Sean. *The Rise of American Democracy: Jefferson to Lincoln*. New York: Norton, 2005.

Winks, Robin W. *The Blacks in Canada*. 2nd ed. Montreal: McGill-Queens University Press, 1997.

Wood, Gordon. *Empire of Liberty: A History of the Early Republic, 1789-1815*. Oxford History of the United States. New York: Oxford University Press, 2009.

Yonge, Charles D. *The Life and Administration of Robert Banks, Second Earl of Liverpool*. 3 vols. London: Macmillan, 1868.

Zaslow, Morris. *The Defended Border: Upper Canada in the War of 1812*. Toronto: Macmillan of Canada, 1964.

Zimmerman, James F. *Impressment of American Seamen*. New York: Columbia University, 1925.

Zuehlke, Mark. *For Honor's Sake: The War of 1812 and the Brokering of an Uneasy Peace*. Toronto: Alfred A. Knopf Canada, 2006.

PERIODICAL ARTICLES AND BOOK CHAPTERS

Bolster, W. Jeffrey. "'To Feel Like a Man': Black Seamen in the Northern States, 1800–1860." *Journal of American History* 76 (1989–90).

Bond, Beverly W., Jr. "William Henry Harrison in the War of 1813." *Mississippi Valley Historical Review* 13 (1927).

Brown, Kenneth L. "Mr. Madison's Secretary of the Navy." *U.S. Naval Institute Proceedings* 73 (1947).

Calderhead, William L. "Naval Innovation in Crisis: War in the Chesapeake, 1813." *American Neptune* 36 (July 1976).

Carr, James A. "The Battle of New Orleans and the Treaty of Ghent." *Diplomatic History* 3 (1979).

Cray, Robert E., Jr. "Explaining Defeat: The Loss of the USS *Chesapeake*." *Naval History* (August 2007).

Dangerfield, George. "Lord Liverpool and the United States." *American Heritage* 6 (1955).

Dudley, William S. "Naval Historians and the War of 1812." *Naval History* 4 (Spring 1990).

Dye, Ira. "American Maritime Prisoners of War, 1812–15." In *Ships, Seafaring, and Society: Essays in Maritime History*, edited by Timothy J. Runyan. Detroit: Wayne State University Press, 1987.

Eckert, Edward K. "Early Reform in the Navy Department." *American Neptune* 33 (1973).

——. "William Jones: Mr. Madison's Secretary of the Navy." *Pennsylvania Magazine of History and Biography* 96 (1972).

Emery, George, Vice Admiral, U.S. Navy (Retired). "The Battle of Lake Erie." In *U.S. Navy: A Complete History*, edited by M. Hill Goodspeed. Westport, CT: Hugh Lauter Associates, 2003.

——. "Thomas Truxtun: First Mentor of the Federal Navy." *Pull Together: Newsletter of the Naval Historical Foundation* (Fall/Winter 2010–11).

Galpin, W. Freeman. "The American Grain Trade to the Spanish Peninsula, 1810–1814." *American Historical Review* (October 1922).

Gates, Charles M. "The West in American Diplomacy, 1812–1815." *Mississippi Valley Historical Review* 26, no. 4 (March 1940).

Goodman, W. H. "The Origins of the War of 1812: A Survey of Changing Interpretations." *Mississippi Valley Historical Review* 28 (1941).

Golder, Frank A. "The Russian Offer of Mediation in the War of 1812." *Political Science Quarterly* (1916).

Hadel, Albert K. "The Battle of Bladensburg." *Maryland History Magazine* 1 (1806).

Hatzenbuehler, Ronald L. "Party Unity and the Decision for War in the House of Representatives, 1812." *William and Mary Quarterly*, 3rd ser., 29 (1972).

——. "The War Hawks and the Question of Congressional Leadership in 1812." *Pacific Historical Review* 45 (1976).

Hickey, Donald R. "American Trade Restrictions During the War of 1812." *Journal of American History* 68 (1981).

——. "New England's Defense Problem and the Genesis of the Hartford Convention." *New England Quarterly* 50 (1977).

——. "The War of 1812: Still a Forgotten Conflict?" *Journal of Military History* 65 (July 2001).

Hitsman, J. Mackay. "Sir George Prevost's Conduct of the Canadian War of 1812." *Canadian Historical Association* (1962).

Jones, Wilbur D. "A British View of the War of 1812 and the Peace Negotiations." *Mississippi Valley Historical Review* 45 (1958).

Kaplan, Lawrence S. "France and Madison's Decision for War, 1812." *Mississippi Valley Historical Review* (March 1964).

Langley, Harold D. "The Negro in the Navy and Merchant Service—1798–1860." *Journal of Negro History* 52 (1967).

Lohnes, Barry J. "A New Look at the British Invasion of Eastern Maine, 1814." *Maine Historical Society* 15 (1975).

Mahon, John K. "British Command Decisions Relative to the Battle of New Orleans." *Louisiana History* 6 (1965).

——. "British Strategy and Southern Indians, War of 1812." *Florida Historical Quarterly* 44 (1966).

McClellan, Edwin N. "The Navy at the Battle of New Orleans." *U.S. Naval Institute Proceedings* 50 (December 1924).

McDaniel, Mary Jane. "Tecumseh's Visits to the Creeks." *Alabama Review* 33 (1980).

McKee, Marguerite M. "Service of Supply in the War of 1812." *Quartermaster Review* 6 (1927).

Merk, Frederick. "The Genesis of the Oregon Question." *Mississippi Valley Historical Review* 36 (1949–1950).

Mills, Dudley. "The Duke of Wellington and the Peace Negotiations at Ghent." *Canadian Historical Review* 2, no. 1 (March 1921).

Muller, H. N. "A Traitorous and Diabolic Traffic: The Commerce of the Champlain-Richelieu Corridor During the War of 1812." *Vermont History* 44 (1976).

Paullin, Charles Oscar. "Naval Administration Under Secretaries of the Navy Smith, Hamilton, and Jones, 1801–1814." *Proceedings of the U.S. Naval Institute* 32 (1906).

Pratt, Julius W. "Fur Trade Strategy and the American Left Flank in the War of 1812." *American Historical Review* 40 (1934–35).

Risjord, Norman K. "1812: Conservatives, War Hawks, and the Nation's Honor." *William and Mary Quarterly* 18 (April 1961).

——. "The Election of 1812." In *History of American Presidential Elections, 1789–1968*, vol. 1, edited by Arthur M. Schlesinger and Fred L. Israel. New York: Chelsea House, 1985.

Skelton, William B. "High Army Leadership in the Era of the War of 1812: The Making and Remaking of the Officer Corps." *William and Mary Quarterly* 3rd ser., 51 (April 1994).

Smelser, Marshall. "Tecumseh, Harrison and the War of 1812." *Indiana Magazine of History* 65 (1969).

Stacey, Charles Perry. "An American Plan for a Canadian Campaign." *American Historical Review* 46 (1941).

——. "The War of 1812 in Canadian History." *Ontario History* 50 (1958).

Stagg, J. C. A. "Between Black Rock and a Hard Place: Peter B. Porter's Plan for an Invasion of Canada in 1812." *Journal of the American Republic* 19 (1999).

——. "Enlisted Men in the United States Army, 1812–1815: A Preliminary Survey." *William and Mary Quarterly* 57 (2000).

——. "James Madison and the Malcontents: The Political Origins of the War of 1812." *William and Mary Quarterly*, 3rd ser., 33 (1976).

Stanley, George F. G. "The Indians in the War of 1812." *Canadian Historical Review* 31 (1950).

Steely, Anthony. "Jonathan Russell, Castlereagh and Impressment." *American Historical Review* (January 1952).

Taylor, G. R. "Agrarian Discontent in the Mississippi Valley Preceding the War of 1812." *Journal of Political Economy* 39 (1931).

Tiegle, Joseph G., Jr. "Andrew Jackson and the Continuing Battle of New Orleans." *Journal of the Early Republic* (1981).

Tyler, B. B. "Fulton's Steam Frigate." *American Neptune* (October 1946).

Valle, James E. "The Navy's Battle Doctrine in the War of 1812." *American Neptune* 44 (Summer 1984).

INDEX